Origins and Traditions of Organizational Communication

Origins and Traditions of Organizational Communication provides a sophisticated overview of the fundamentals of organizational communication as a field of study, examining the field's foundations and providing an assessment of the field to date, explaining and demonstrating a communicational approach to the study of organization.

It provides a set of literature reviews on focused topics written by experts in each area, and links organizational communication theory and research to practice. In reviewing foundational management theory, the book analyzes how early to mid-20th-century management theories shaped contemporary organizations, providing students both with background knowledge of these foundational theories and an understanding of their influence on our thinking and our organizational world. It also includes pedagogical features appropriate for graduate-level students including:

- Chapter bibliographies
- Annotated supplementary readings lists
- Concepts lists
- Discussion questions
- A "Practitioners' Corner" for every chapter translating the material to practice
- Glossaries (available online)
- PowerPoint presentations for every chapter (available online)

Written at an accessible level for early graduate students, yet still sophisticated enough for doctoral students, the book is ideal for students and teachers of organizational communication and communication history.

Anne M. Nicotera is Professor and Chair in the Department of Communication at George Mason University and an organizational communication consultant. Her research is grounded in a constitutive perspective. She has published six books and numerous articles in outlets such as *Management Communication Quarterly, Journal of Applied Communication Research*, and *Health Communication*.

Origins and Traditions of Organizational Communication

A Comprehensive Introduction to the Field

Edited by Anne M. Nicotera

NEW YORK AND LONDON

First edition published 2020
by Routledge
52 Vanderbilt Avenue, New York, NY 10017

and by Routledge
2 Park Square, Milton Park, Abingdon, Oxon, OX14 4RN

Routledge is an imprint of the Taylor & Francis Group, an informa business

Library of Congress Cataloging-in-Publication Data
Names: Nicotera, Anne Maydan, 1963- editor.
Title: Origins and traditions of organizational communication : a comprehensive introduction to the field / edited by Anne M. Nicotera.
Description: First edition. | New York, NY : Routledge, 2020. |
Includes bibliographical references and index. | ion record and CIP data provided by publisher; resource not viewed.
Identifiers: LCCN 2019005767 (print) | LCCN 2019008966 (ebook) |
ISBN 9780203703625 () | ISBN 9781138570306 (hbk) |
ISBN 9781138570313 (pbk)
Subjects: LCSH: Communication in organizations.
Classification: LCC HD30.3 (ebook) | LCC HD30.3 .O736 2019 (print) |
DDC 658.4/501--dc23
LC record available at https://lccn.loc.gov/2019005767

ISBN: 978-1-138-57030-6 (hbk)
ISBN: 978-1-138-57031-3 (pbk)
ISBN: 978-0-203-70362-5 (ebk)

Typeset in Sabon
by Integra Software Services Pvt. Ltd.

Visit the eResources: www.routledge.com/9781138570313

For my students—past, present, and future

Contents

Foreword

This book is a culmination of 30 years of teaching and studying organizational communication. Over the many years of being responsible for the instruction of organizational communication at the introductory graduate level, and with my own development as a theorist, I had developed an approach to teaching the course and a deep dissatisfaction with accessible texts available to help my students understand and become excited by the field. The book itself is a decade in the making, as I worked toward generating and trying out diagrams and explanations that I had confidence would work beyond my own classroom. I have been honored to work with students who engaged with me as I did so, providing incredibly helpful feedback to assist in the refinement of materials for future generations of my (and now your) students. The result is now in your hands.

My vision was to provide a single volume that explains organizational communication both as a set of human social phenomena and a field of study, to educate students about a communicational approach to studying organization and get them excited about its insights, and to do so at an accessible level for early-graduate-career students without sacrificing the requisite sophistication needed for graduate-level study. If the night-class discussions that had to be cut off at 10:00pm are any indication, I succeeded on at least a few occasions. I am grateful that the 19 other people who embarked on this project with me shared that vision. I am humbled by the caliber of scholars who worked with me on this project and am eternally grateful to all of them for their dedication to the project and careful attention to the details of its mission.

It has been ten years since I decided to do this book; five years since the actual writing began; two years since 19 other scholars agreed to join. It is my fervent hope that instructors find this volume, and the ancillary materials available online, helpful in making our fascinating and rich field accessible to students. I hope that students reading this book use it as a foundation to pursue further academic study in the area and to carry on with a communicational approach to understanding the fascinating everyday of organizational life.

Anne M. Nicotera

Introduction

The goals of this volume are to provide knowledge of the history of theorizing about communication and about organizations that led to the establishment of the field of organizational communication, an understanding of the ensuing paradigmatic advancements in that field, awareness of the field's place among other organizational studies disciplines, and surveys of the literature on a variety of specific organizational communication phenomena. The book provides a set of conceptual templates by which to understand the literatures on various topics according to the fundamental tension in all organizational communication theory between action and structure. As such, this is more than a set of literature reviews. It provides a framework for understanding organizational communication both as a set of phenomena and as a field of study.

The specific objectives are to educate the reader on the disciplinary definition and history of organizational communication as a field; to provide a perspective that situates the field of organizational communication in the broader multidisciplinary field of organizational studies; to critique foundational organizational theory from a contemporary framework; to provide a set of literature reviews on focused topics written by experts in each area following a common template for explanation and critique; and to link organizational communication theory and research to practice.

Each chapter will be accompanied by an annotated list of recommended supplementary readings; a set of key concepts and questions for discussion; and a "Practitioners' Corner" that provides concrete implications for application and practice. These pedagogical materials (with the concepts list expanded to provide definitions) are compiled in a single document downloadable from the Routledge website. PowerPoint presentations for each chapter are also provided there.

Organization of the Book

The book is divided into three parts. Part I summarizes the origins and history of the field of communication, providing a comprehensive overview of the field from its inception to the present. Chapter 1 defines the field and its fundamental concepts and explains the emergence of the field, in the context of the emergence of communication studies in general. A set of conceptual models (applied throughout the book) are presented that frame an understanding of conceptual approaches to organization and the reciprocally enabling and constraining relationship between organization and communication. Chapters 2 and 3 present the theoretical and conceptual developments in the 20th and 21st centuries, respectively. Finally, Chapter 4 explains the metatheoretical paradigms that drive ways of knowing in the field, providing overviews of each and analyses of how they approach organizational communication.

Part II reviews the traditional/historical organizational theories treated in previous generations as foundations of organizational communication—not just as conceptual foundations for the field, but also as societal forces that shaped (and continue to shape) organizational forms, practices, and management. One cannot adequately understand contemporary organizations as communicatively constructed and constituted without appreciation of the constitutive power of these foundational bodies of theory. As prescriptions, these theories quite literally wrote the scripts that contemporary organizations follow.

Part III provides comprehensive literature reviews of 14 areas of theory and research, each of which explains the trends over time in the area, major traditions, and contributions of organizational communication scholars. Chapters are authored by established scholars with specialized expertise. While it is not possible to cover every possible topic in the field, literatures that comprise the core knowledge base in the field are provided here. Each chapter applies the general conceptual models provided in Chapter 1 to explore the conceptual approaches of scholars in the area and to illustrate the reciprocally enabling and constraining relationship between organization and communication. These chapters can be read in any order.

Contributors

Dawna I. Ballard (Ph.D., University of California at Santa Barbara) is Associate Professor in the Department of Communication Studies at the University of Texas at Austin. Her research interests center on what drives our pace of life and its impact on the communication practices and long-term vitality of organizations, communities, and individuals. A member of INGRoup (Interdisciplinary Network for Group Research) and former Chairperson of the Group Communication Division of National Communication Association, she teaches and supervises courses in group and team communication.

Zhuo Ban (Ph.D., Purdue University) is an assistant professor in the Department of Communication at the University of Cincinnati. Broadly, her research explores globalization and labor activism from critical public relations/critical organizational communication perspectives. Specifically, she is interested in how industrial workers in offshore manufacturing units in Southern China construct their identities as marginalized publics in the global diffusion of production. She is also interested in the study of global-local dialectics of sweatshop activism, from consumer-based activism in the U.S. to grassroots organizing in sweatshop sites in China. Her research has been published in several of the field's top international journals—such as *Journal of Applied Communication Research, Management Research Quarterly, Public Relations Inquiry*, and the *Journal of International and Intercultural Communication*—in addition to presenting more than a dozen refereed papers and national and international conferences.

J. Kevin Barge (Ph.D., University of Kansas) is Professor and Head of Communication at Texas A&M University and is also a member of the planning team for the Aspen Conference, a community of engaged organizational communication scholars focused on developing practical theory and collaborative research that bridge academic–practitioner interests. Kevin's major research interests center on developing a social constructionist approach to leadership, articulating the connections between reflexive appreciative practice and organizational change, and examining ways to develop effective academic–practitioner collaborations. He has published articles on leadership, dialogue, and organizational change in *The Academy of Management Review, Management Communication Quarterly, Human Relations, Communication Theory, Journal of Applied Communication Research*, and *Communication Monographs*. He has been awarded the Gerald M. Phillips Award for Distinguished Applied Communication Research by the National Communication Association and is the recipient of the Central States Communication Hall of Fame Award.

Patrice M. Buzzanell (Ph.D., Purdue University) is Chair and Professor of the Department of Communication at the University of South Florida and Endowed Professor at Shanghai Jiaotong University. Fellow and Past President of the International Communication Association, she is a National Communication Association Distinguished Scholar and Past President of the Council of Communication Associations and Organization for the Study of Communication, Language and Gender. Her scholarship focuses on gendered career, resilience, and engineering design. She received ICA's Fisher Mentorship Award and Provost Outstanding Mentor Award from Purdue, where she was University Distinguished Professor and Endowed Chair/Director of the Butler Center for Leadership Excellence.

Lisa V. Chewning (Ph.D., Rutgers University) is Associate Professor of Corporate Communication at Penn State University–Abington. Research interests include social networks, crisis communication, public relations, and information and communication technology (ICT). Her research has been published in outlets such as *Management Communication Quarterly, Communication Monographs, Public Relations Review, Journal of Communication, Computers in Human Behavior*, and *Human Communication Research*.

Shiv Ganesh (Ph.D., Purdue University), is a professor in the Department of Communication Studies at the University of Texas in Austin. He studies communication and collective organizing in the context of globalization and digital technologies. His work spans critical-institutional and poststructural approaches to communication, and he has done fieldwork in a number of countries, including India, Aotearoa New Zealand, the United States, and Sweden. His research appears in journals including *Communication Monographs, Communication Theory, Human Relations, International Journal of Communication, Journal of Applied Communication Research, Management Communication Quarterly, Media, Culture & Society*, and *Organization Studies*. His research has won several awards from both the International Communication Association and the National Communication Association.

Jennifer L. Gibbs (Ph.D., University of Southern California) is Professor of Communication at the University of California, Santa Barbara. She is also editor of *Communication Research*. Her research focuses on collaboration in global teams and other distributed work arrangements, as well as the affordances of new technologies such as social media for strategic communication practices. She has published more than 50 peer-reviewed journal articles and book chapters, as well as a recent book entitled *Distracted: Staying Connected without Losing Focus*. Her work has been published in leading journals from a variety of disciplines including *Administrative Science Quarterly, American Behavioral Scientist, Communication Research, Computers in Human Behavior, Human Relations, The Information Society, Journal of Computer-Mediated Communication, Journal of Social & Personal Relationships, Management Communication Quarterly*, and *Organization Science*.

Jessica Katz Jameson (Ph.D., Temple University) is Professor of Communication at North Carolina State University. Her research and teaching are focused on organizational communication and conflict management, with special attention to third-party intervention, the roles of identity and emotion in conflict, and interorganizational and interdisciplinary collaboration. Jessica is affiliated faculty with NC State's Institute for Nonprofit Research, Education, and Engagement, and she is a Community Engaged Faculty Fellow. Her work appears in outlets such as *Conflict Resolution Quarterly, Harvard International Journal of Press/Politics, Journal of Health Communication, Negotiation and Conflict Management Research, Negotiation Journal*, and *Western Journal of Communication*.

Kerk F. Kee (Ph.D., The University of Texas at Austin) is an associate professor in the College of Media & Communication at Texas Tech University. His research primarily investigates the development, adoption, implementation, and the ultimate diffusion of workplace technologies in scientific organizations. He also studies the dissemination of health information in cultural communities and the spread of pro-environmental attitudes in modern societies. His diffusion research has been funded by the National Science Foundation, the Bill & Melinda Gates Foundation, and the Robert Wood Johnson Foundation. His work has appeared in international journals such as the *Journal of Computer-Mediated Communication, New Media & Society, Computers in Human Behavior*, and *CyberPsychology, Behavior, & Social Networking*.

Laurie Lewis (Ph.D., University of California at Santa Barbara) is Professor of Communication at Rutgers University. She is author of *Organizational Change: Creating Change Through Strategic Communication*, and co-editor of the *International Encyclopedia of Organizational Communication* as well as numerous academic publications on topics related to organizational change and stakeholder communication. Her research investigates how organizations work most effectively through collaboration, stakeholder engagement, input solicitation, and high-quality participative processes. She has provided consulting and training for dozens of organizations from a wide range of sectors. She is a Fellow at the Rutgers Center for Organizational Leadership.

Shawna Malvini Redden (Ph.D., Arizona State University) is Assistant Professor of Organizational Communication at California State University Sacramento. She uses qualitative, critical, and discursive methods to explore organizing processes involving emotion, identity, sensemaking, and social media. Her award-winning scholarship has appeared in publications including *Management Communication Quarterly, Communication Monographs, Journal of Applied Communication Research*, and *Qualitative Health Research*. She is currently writing a creative nonfiction book about communicating emotion and identity in airport security. To learn more about her scholarship, teaching, and writing, visit http://www.drmalviniredden.com.

Dron M. Mandhana (Ph.D., University of Texas at Austin) is an assistant professor in the Department of Communication at Villanova University. His research considers how effective organizing is an enacted capability that is constituted in everyday communication practices bound by time and space—from communication overload and media choice to messy talk in project teams. He currently teaches service-based learning courses in teambuilding and small group communication.

Jamie McDonald (Ph.D., University of Colorado Boulder) is an associate professor in the Department of Communication at the University of Texas at San Antonio in the United States. His research interests include identity and difference at work, occupational segregation, and feminist and queer approaches to organizing. His work has appeared in peer-reviewed journals such as *Communication Theory, Management Communication Quarterly*, the *Journal of Applied Communication Research*, and *Gender, Work, and Organization*. He also serves as an associate editor for *Management Learning*.

Anne M. Nicotera (Ph.D., Ohio University) is Professor and Chair in the Department of Communication at George Mason University. Her research is grounded in a constitutive perspective and focuses on management/leadership communication, culture and conflict, diversity, race and gender, and aggressive communication, with a particular interest in healthcare organizations. Her research has been published in *Management Communication Quarterly, Journal of Applied Communication Research, Health Communication, Nursing Administration Quarterly*, and other outlets. She has also published five books and numerous chapters. She is active as a consultant, designing and delivering organizational communication-based management and leadership training, with a special interest in serving professionals in the developing world.

Craig R. Scott (Ph.D. Arizona State University) is Professor in the Department of Communication at Rutgers University (U.S.). His research and teaching are primarily focused on organizational communication, where he examines issues of anonymity and identity/identification in various organizational settings. His research on issues of organizational identity and identification has been published in *Communication Theory, Management Communication Quarterly, IEEE Transactions on Professional Communication, Western Journal of Communication, Communication Studies*, and other outlets. His current interests center on "hidden organizations," which are found when an organization and/or its members conceal key parts of their identity from various audiences. He is co-editor of the *International Encyclopedia of Organizational Communication* and serves on editorial boards for multiple journals in Communication.

Yejin Shin is a Ph.D. student in the Department of Communication at University of Arizona. Her research interests include socialization, workplace relationships, and minorities in organizations. She is currently working on research regarding first-generation college students' socialization to college and interns' identity/identification development in an organization.

Patricia M. Sias (Ph.D., University of Texas at Austin) is a professor in the Department of Communication at the University of Arizona. She holds a doctoral degree in Organizational Communication, with a cognate area in Management. She specializes in organizational communication and conducts research on workplace relationships, uncertainty, and leadership. She has published articles in *Communication Monographs, Human Communication Research, Communication Research, Management Communication Quarterly, Journal of Social and Personal Relationships*, and many others. She also authored the book *Organizing Relationships: Traditional and Emerging Perspectives on Workplace Relationships*, published by SAGE Publications in 2010. She has served on the editorial boards of several academic journals and was Editor-in-Chief of *Management Communication Quarterly* from 2015–2018.

Keri K. Stephens (Ph.D., The University of Texas at Austin) is an associate professor in the Moody College of Communication, a Distinguished Teaching Professor, a Faculty Affiliate with the Center for Health Communication, and a Faculty Fellow with the Center for Health and Social Policy at the LBJ School of Public Affairs at The University of Texas at Austin. Her research and teaching interests bring an organizational perspective to understanding how people interact with communication technologies. She focuses on contexts of crisis, emergency, disaster, and healthcare. She has over 60 peer-reviewed publications, is an associate editor with *Management*

Communication Quarterly, and her most recent book is *Negotiating Control: Organizations and Mobile Communication* (Oxford University Press). Her research has been funded by organizations like the NSF and TxDOT, and she is a member of the Department of Homeland Security's Social Media Working Group.

Sarah J. Tracy (Ph.D., University of Colorado) is Herberger Professor of Organizational Communication and Qualitative Methodology and Co-Director of the Transformation Project in the Hugh Downs School of Human Communication at Arizona State University-Tempe. She is an expert in qualitative methodology, and her organizational communication scholarship examines compassion, identity, emotional labor, bullying, burnout, wellbeing, and leadership. Her research has resulted in two books including *Qualitative Research Methods: Collecting Evidence, Crafting Analysis, Communicating Impact* and more than 70 monographs appearing in outlets such as *Management Communication Quarterly, Communication Monographs, Qualitative Inquiry, Communication Theory*, and *Journal of Applied Communication Research*. She maintains a website and YouTube channel (see http://www.sarahjtracy.com) and approaches scholarship from a use-inspired standpoint that aims to leave people interacting in ways that create individual, group, and organizational wellbeing.

Heather M. Zoller (Ph.D., Purdue University) is a professor at the University of Cincinnati. Her research in health and organizational communication focuses on organizing and the politics of public health. She is a former associate editor at *Management Communication Quarterly* and *Human Relations*. Her work appears in outlets such as *Management Communication Quarterly, Communication Monographs, Communication Theory*, and *Health Communication*.

Acknowledgments

As with any project of this magnitude, the list of people I couldn't have done without cannot be generated. Those who worked with me, for me, around me; those who waited patiently for me to respond when I was drowning; those who depended on me for anything in the last five years of this writing and gave me room to be busy with something other than your needs—thank you. The number of people in my life who support what I do and help me do it is humbling.

Heartfelt thanks to Felisa Salvago-Keyes and Christina Kowalski at Routledge, both of whom inherited this project from predecessors. While it was disconcerting to be without editor or editorial assistant during a brief period of turnover (which any good organizational scholar understands), the fast response and attention to detail provided by both was refreshing and much appreciated.

Thank you to a long list of graduate students who didn't know when they enrolled in my class that they would be depended upon to critique chapters, make suggestions for improving explanations, and generate discussion questions (several of which were used in Parts I and II)—thank you: Landry Ayres, Elizaveta Bunina, Bridget Bush, Katrina Cheesman, Theresa Coco, Jennifer Collard, Victoria Cordova, Nicole Droney, Nicole Eller, Erin Harpine, Jacqueline Heller, Henri Huber, Nicole Kratzer, George Kueppers, Brynn Lampert, Scott May, Scott McLaughlin, Michelle McNealkidd, Grayson Moore, Kelly Morrison, Joshua Murphy, Lisa Ngenye, Phuong Nguyen, Sarah Pangle, Kelsey Parrish, Aliesha Pulliam, Sidra Sajid, Mary Tran, and Abigail Weiss.

Special thanks to Andrew Caulk for pushing me on the needs of practitioners (and for suggesting the "Practitioners' Corner"), to Kristin Timm and Andrea Malterud for another read and critique, and to Julia Hathaway for a thorough editing of my seven chapters with the combined eye of graduate student, scholar, communication practitioner, and professional writer.

Thanks to my colleague and friend Dr. Megan Tucker for preparing the indexes and ancillaries and to the magnificent Maria Carabelli for being my right hand in the office and keeping me afloat with my administrative duties—and my sanity—during this writing in the midst of our own organizational crises.

And I thank the most important people—my family: Gregory Maydan who never wondered where I disappeared to for long hours but simply made me dinner; and my sons Dan and Teddy Maydan who fed the dog, picked up the groceries, and unassumingly went on about their business of becoming adults.

Part I

Organizational Communication History

In this section, the origins and history of the field of communication are summarized, providing a comprehensive overview of the field from its inception to the present. Chapter 1 defines the field and its fundamental concepts and explains the emergence of the field in the context of the emergence of communication studies in general. A set of conceptual models (applied throughout the book) are presented that frame an understanding of conceptual approaches to organization and the reciprocally enabling and constraining relationship between organization and communication. Chapters 2 and 3 present the theoretical and conceptual developments in the 20th and 21st centuries, respectively. Finally, Chapter 4 explains the metatheoretical paradigms that drive ways of knowing in the field, providing overviews of each and analyses of how they approach organizational communication.

1 Organizing the Study of Organizational Communication

Anne M. Nicotera

Organizing and Communicating

Organizing, as a set of human social processes, is as old as human society. *Organizing* can be defined most simply as *the coordination of individual activities for the purposes of achieving the accomplishment of collective tasks*—whether the task at hand is warding off an approaching predator, cultivating crops, building a pyramid, leading an army to battle, managing a corporate budget, implementing grand-scale emergency response to a natural disaster, or planning a family holiday gathering. Organizing is natural to human social collectives and is accomplished through communication. It must be noted, however, that while organizations are social collectives, not all social collectives are organizations. *Organizational communication* refers to both the nature of the collective and the nature of its activity. An organization emerges from human interaction. Once it exists, the organization provides a context for communication—which it both drives and is driven by. And thus *organization* and *communication* are forever intertwined—continually enabling and constraining one another. Our organizing communication creates *organizations*—entities to whose authority we then surrender.

Organizations permeate all aspects of human life. Society is defined by organizations—from the manufacturers of our clothing and distributors of our food to the contracting companies that build our houses, the banks that hold our mortgages, and the governments that regulate them. The contemporary human being is an organizational being. *Organizational communication theory* is a body of scholarly work that seeks to untangle these fundamental processes of human social life—how do humans coordinate individual activities in the context of communicatively structured social collectives to get things done, to be who we are, and to create new realities and structured collectives? This book will help you to understand the field of organizational communication and provide a disciplinary base for your study of organizational communication phenomena. First, we need to define both *communication* and *organization*.

Defining "Communication"

We start by defining communication because it is more fundamental. Organization, whether as a process or a thing, is created only from communication. So, while communication and organization mutually drive one another, communication is more primary. The discipline of Communication is complex, with a vast literature representing over a century of theory and research from numerous scholarly traditions—all working toward an understanding of human communication processes. At its simplest core, *communication* can be defined as *a symbolic process of creating and sharing meaning*. Even after decades of wrestling with definitions, this is the field's fundamental cornerstone. The simplicity of this definition can be misleading, however, because it underlies a huge, complex, and increasingly specialized array of theories and abstract conceptual constructions. This elegant definition unifies the field. Communication theorists and researchers of all stripes, when they agree on nothing else, can still be recognized as members of the same field by their consensus on this fundamental definition.

Communication as human action. As a set of human phenomena, communication is contextual and transactional, the parties simultaneously and continually influencing one another as their interaction constitutes meaning. The conceptualization of humans as actors is crucial. We are defined by our actions, which are in turn defined by communicatively constructed social, organizational, and institutional structures, which are in turn defined by our actions, which define us—in full reflexivity. Human action is deeply embedded in a complex of social constructions that define our humanity. Following the tradition of communication rules theory (Cushman, Valentinson, & Dietrich, 1982), the human self is threefold: the identity self, the evaluative self, and the behavioral self—the last being the crucial agentic aspect of rules theory. We know who we are (identity) and how good we are (evaluative) only through what we do (behavioral). Cushman and his associates (Cushman & Cahn, 1985; Cushman & Craig, 1976; Cushman & Florence, 1974; Cushman et al., 1982) identify self-concept as a cybernetic control system for human action in coordination situations:

> Human actions that take place within a standardized communication situation require common intentions, an established set of rules for the cooperative achievement of those intentions, and a procedure for manifesting the variable practical force the actors feel for participating in the coordination task.
>
> (Cushman et al., 1982, pp. 96–97)

The primary assumption in the rules perspective is the action principle: Social behavior is structured and organized; action within and between human beings is governed by implicit and explicit rules. According to Cushman and Pearce (1977), rules take the form of practical syllogism:

A intends to bring about C;
A considers that to bring about C s/he must do B;
therefore, A sets her/himself to do B.

The possible range of actions (B) is delimited by enduring structures that underlie human interaction. Owing to the fundamental nature of humanity as defined by social action, human action is inherently communicative.

The first communication theories. Early communication theory took the form of models. In a classic communication theory textbook, Mortensen (1972) defined a *model* as a *systematic representation of an object or event in idealized and abstract form*. Models are helpful as metaphors that guide our ability to visualize concepts of interest in terms of one another as they help us to clarify complex processes, but they are also oversimplified and mask complex processes that cannot be modeled, often leading to premature conclusions. Models are very limited, and thus are best thought of as only a most rudimentary form of theory. The earliest known models of communication were developed by Aristotle in his theories of rhetoric and proof. Much like early organizational theory, as you shall see, Aristotle's purpose was *prescriptive* (in his case to provide instructions for persuasive speech).

Linear models. Early 20th-century views of communication treated communication as a machine-like process wherein information or messages are depicted as traveling through channels. These mechanistic models are also known as *linear models* because the communication process is depicted as a line. These models (in Figures 1.1 and 1.2) seem very rudimentary and unsophisticated by today's standards, and do not come close to capturing the complexity and nuanced understanding we have of communication processes today. However, they are an important piece of our theoretic history and continue to implicitly influence our thinking. It is important, therefore, to examine them explicitly. The most influential early linear model is Shannon and Weaver's mathematical model, developed to help telephone engineers design efficient ways to transmit electrical signals from place to place. The Shannon-Weaver mathematical model was essentially a line from left to right that traveled through boxes, depicting an *information source* sending a *message* through a *transmitter* (encoder), which transforms the message to a *signal* sending it through a *channel* that is affected by *noise*. The *signal* then passes through a *receiver* (decoder), which transforms the signal back to a *message* that finally reaches its *destination*. The Shannon-Weaver model was not meant to describe face-to-face human communication, but it provided a baseline from which to do so. Numerous linear models of face-to-face human communication were based on the Shannon-Weaver linear model.

By 1960, scholars of human communication had widely adopted a message-centered linear approach to modeling communication. The most basic form of linear communication models is often called a model of *communication-as-action*, depicting a *sender* (or a source or a speaker) transmitting a message through some *channel* to a *receiver*—still a line drawn from left to right (see Figure 1.1). Berlo (1960) coined the term "SMCR" to describe this type of linear model, denoting the model components Sender (or Speaker or Source), Message, Channel, and Receiver. Models that depicted communication-as-action were dissatisfactory because they were too heavily focused on the sender or source of the originating message.

Schramm (1954) created one of the first models of face-to-face human communication, which is particularly noteworthy because it focused more on the *interaction* of a dyad than the *action* of a sender/source. Rather than a sender and a receiver, Schramm's model depicted *interpreters* who were simultaneously *encoders* and *decoders*. Although messages were still depicted as traveling along a line, the line was circular, linking one first interpreter as an encoder, traveling to the another interpreter as a decoder, and then returning from the second interpreter as an encoder back to the original interpreter as a decoder. Schramm was thus the first scholar to model

Figure 1.1 Linear model: Communication as action

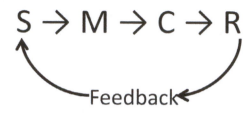

Figure 1.2 Circular model: Communication as interaction

communication as an interactive process. This form, the *circular model*, is also called a model of *communication-as-interaction*. Schramm's inclusion of the notion of *interpretation* is the conceptual basis for the meaning-centered approach we now widely embrace.

Early models of communication (linear/action and circular/interaction) are often referred to as a *transmissive view of communication* because they depict communication as a process by which something (a message, information, etc.) is *transmitted* from person to person. But even models of communication-as-interaction quickly became dissatisfactory, as our thinking became more sophisticated and our focus shifted from *messages* to *meaning*. Communication scholars began to focus on the communication process not solely as the *exchange* of messages or *transmission* of meaning, but as the *creation* of meaning as well.

Nonlinear models. The third generation of communication models were thus *nonlinear* models, also called models of *communication-as-transaction*. Transactional models focus on communication's functions (both including and moving beyond message-exchange), and represent the origins of the *constitutive view of communication* upon which a large body of organizational communication scholarship rests. The most famous of these transactional communication models was developed by Barnlund (1970), who used a complex diagram of spirals and curved arrows to represent the continuous, unrepeatable, irreversible nature of communication. Meaning was seen as assigned or attributed rather than received. Along with *interactants, decoding, encoding*, and *messages*, Barnlund's model included a set of valenced cues: *public cues* (in the environment), *private cues* (in or on the persons), and *deliberate behavioral cues* (nonverbal and verbal). All of these components were depicted as interrelated and constantly evolving. Transactional modeling proved to be far too complex to depict satisfactorily in a picture, although many scholars tried (e.g., Barnlund, 1970; Dance, 1967; Ruesch & Bateson, 1951; Westley & MacLean, 1957).

The idea of communication as a transaction through which communicators create meaning had a profound effect on the field. Scholars quickly moved beyond creating additional graphic representations of communication processes in the form of pictorial models. The rudimentary nature of pictorial representation can only roughly approximate the process of meaning-creation. This shift from linear to nonlinear modeling represents a shift in thinking from a transmissive to a constitutive view of communication that typifies the growing sophistication of communication theory in the 1960s. It was during this same time period that the field of organizational communication was being formed. To this day, organizational communication scholars presume that communication is constitutive—it creates things (organizations and their internal parts, documents, policies, procedures, events, relationships, etc.). But that does not mean we have abandoned our interest in individuals as sources and receivers of information, in messages and their channels for dissemination, in meaning-creation, and in human relationships.

Defining "Organizational"

The word *organizational* in the label *organizational communication* may refer to one of three basic types of enduring social constructions. First, O_1, *organizing* (v.), is a *process* of coordinating/ordering among members of a social collective. In this sense, organizational communication theory and research examines interaction processes by which members arrange themselves and manage their joint activities (e.g., decision-making, group formation). Alternatively, we could mean O_2, *organized* (n.), the *state* of a social collective's coordination/order. Organizational communication theory and research might explicate the structuring of said coordination (e.g., networks, organizational formation). Yet a third possibility is O_3, *organizations* (n.), coordinated/ordered *entities* arising from both O_1 and O_2. Organizational communication theory and research that examines formalization, institutions, boundaries, organizations as social actors (e.g., corporate social responsibility, branding) and the like is focused here. In another essay (Nicotera, 2013), I refer to O_3 as *entitative being*. Figure 1.3 depicts the conceptual relationship among these three expressions of organization.

O_3 lurks as a presumption under O_1 and O_2—only certain forms of social collective are studied in the field of organizational communication. *Organization* has often been erroneously equated with formalization or boundary recognition, but while both of these are properties of organization, neither is a defining feature. Moreover, regardless of implicit (or occasionally explicit) presumptions in the literature, *workplace* is not synonymous with *organization* as the site for organizational communication theory and research.

Rather an *organization*, as it is treated in the field of organizational communication, has three fundamental characteristics. First, the collective must be socially signified—named and referred to as a recognizable entity, but this alone does not make the collective an *organization*. For example, these are socially signified collectives: that family, the neighbors, American voters, this committee, that department. Clearly, these are not organizations, no matter how highly organized they may be at any given time. Second, the authority ascribed to the collective in its social signification must

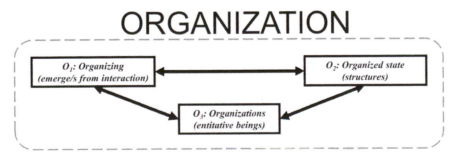

Figure 1.3 Three types of social construction for "organizational"

allow it to authorize individuals to *represent* its interests and act on its behalf. "An organization does not act *primarily* on behalf of and in the name of another entity (collective or not), but is attributed the authority to compel others (individual and collective actors and actants) to act on *its* behalf" (Nicotera, 2013, p. 68). Finally, to be an organization, the collective must also have *entitative being*. "A socially signified entity can be said to have *entitative being* (or to *be* an entitative being) when, by virtue of authority attributed to it, its identity *transcends and eclipses any human individual or human collective*" (Nicotera, 2013, p. 68, emphasis in original). So, the "organization" presumed in the label *organizational communication* is a particular form of socially signified social collective that, first, is granted authority to give individuals and groups permission to act on its behalf, and, second, has an identity that transcends its human membership as an entity unto itself. In this definition, an organization has three defining characteristics: social signification of the collective as an authority; authorization of representative agents; and entitative being.

The Communication-Organization Dynamic

Conrad and Haynes (2001) insightfully identify the action-structure pair as the central tension in organizational communication research and theory. *Action* is goal-oriented human behavior. *Structure* is the underlying social order that both enables and constrains action. For our purposes, however, it is more productive to see them not tensioned, but mutually constitutive. Action constitutes structure while structure constitutes action; each generates the other. A rudimentary definition of organizational communication aligns with this basic theoretic claim. If communication is defined as a symbolic process of meaning-creation (through which information is shared and interpreted and through which relationships are created and maintained); and organization is defined as a communicatively constructed socially collective entity to which authority and agency are attributed; then organizational communication is the set of symbolic processes that occur in the context of social collectives that have attained entity status and to which authority and agency are attributed.

This definition reconciles the tension between action and structure, relieving the pressure to privilege one over the other. Communication practices create and perpetuate enduring organizing structures. Those structures then enable and constrain communication practices. In perpetual spiraling fashion, communication is visible at the surface-level but cycles to create/perpetuate structural processes upon which we draw for communication. This basic dynamic permeates the organizational communication literature, often implicitly (see Figure 1.4).

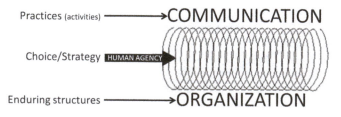

Figure 1.4 The communication-organization interplay in organizational communication theorizing

The spiral is driven by *agency*. *Agency* is a central construct in contemporary organizational communication theory (Brummans, 2018). "To be an agent means to be capable of exerting some degree of control over the social relations in which one is enmeshed, which in turn implies the ability to transform those social relations" (Sewell, 1992, p. 20). *Doing* anything rests on agency. Agency, or self-efficacy, is the human capacity to exercise control over one's life (Bandura, 2001). Agency depends on knowledge of the underlying structure (Sewell, 1992), which enables us to choose courses of action to accomplish our goals, corresponding to Cushman's practical syllogism. These actions then create new structures and transform old structures, in spiraling fashion (Figure 1.4), and human activity (inherently communicative) becomes increasingly self-reflexive through structure. In Figure 1.5, the definition of human action as communication and the threefold expression of organization are imposed on the communication-organization dynamic. As actors, our knowledge of the structure enables us to choose courses of action to accomplish our goals (agency). These actions then create new structures and transform old structures, in spiraling fashion as depicted in Figures 1.4 and 1.5.

Culture as an indispensable assumption. Most contemporary organizational communication scholars presume that organizations and organizational communication cannot be adequately described or understood in the absence of attention to *culture*. Organizations emerge from and exist in cultural contexts. Organizations are themselves cultural contexts. Culture suffuses organizations and organizational communication processes. Communication and culture are inextricably linked. Culture is "a negotiated set of shared symbolic systems that guide individuals' behaviors and incline them to function as a group" (Chen & Starosta, 1998, p. 26). At its deepest level, culture embodies the very way that an individual apprehends the world (through the learned symbolic system). Culture is not just the way a person perceives things differently than another might, but

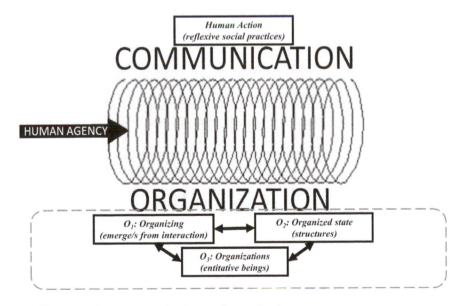

Figure 1.5 Human action, communication, and organization

is the very *way a person perceives*. Culture underlies norms, mores, values, beliefs, customs, rituals, ceremonies, morals, attitudes, practices, and other such concepts used by scholars in a variety of social disciplines to define culture. Such constructs are but manifestations of culture (Nicotera & Clinkscales, 2003). The conceptualization of *organization* in this text encompasses this understanding of culture. *Culture* is the essence of every societal and organizational structure that manifests in social practice (communication). Culture is the very way that individuals apprehend the world through their learned symbolic systems that are rooted in the structures depicted as *organization* in Figures 1.4 and 1.5.

> We are programmed by our culture to do what we do and to be what we are. In other words, culture is the software of the human mind that provides an operating environment for human behaviors. Although individual behaviors may be varied, all members within the same operating environment share important characteristics of the culture.
>
> (Chen & Starosta, 1998, p. 25)

Culture develops as a shared symbolic meaning system rooted in repeated interactions of a group (manifesting in norms, values, etc.). The implication of this view is that culture can be seen as driving and driven by all organizing activities. Culture is thus reflected not simply in organizational behavior but in organizational forms because culture drives the ways in which individuals interact to coordinate their actions. Culture drives the ways in which human beings arrange themselves structurally to accomplish the coordination necessary for organizing. In sum, this approach to culture allows a number of fundamental assumptions to enrich our understanding of organizational communication.

Defining Organization

With these presumptions about culture in mind, we can define organization as a process of ongoing interaction. Communication is the essence of organization. Organizations are constructed from communication processes, with interaction among individuals and groups as a primary characteristic of organizing. Further, organizations are created, maintained, changed, disintegrated, and dissolved only from communication. Organizations, as identifiable entities, are comprised of communicative relationships among individuals and groups oriented toward a common set of general goals, with diverse specific goals, and dependent on shared resources to accomplish them. A complex and thorough description of an organization needs to include all of these things: *An organization is a culturally suffused, living system of interconnected communicative relationships among a conglomerate of interdependent coalitions, composed themselves of interconnected communicative relationships and bound together by their homage to a common mission and dependence on a common resource base, with multiple and often incompatible instrumental and interactive goals and objectives.*

Assumptions about culture, in combination with the defining characteristics of an organization (social signification of authorized collective, authorization of representative agents, and entitative being), minimizes the risk of unintentionally treating organizations as merely containers for communication (Smith, 1993). The *container metaphor* is the implicit treatment of organizations as containing communication, usually with the phrase *communication in organizations*. Neither *communication* nor *organization* can be adequately understood with an implicit container metaphor because both organization and communication are dynamic and socially constructed—neither simply *contains* the other. The organizational communication literature continues to implicitly treat organizational boundaries as fixed, ignoring their fundamental socially constructed nature. To resist this tendency, this text consciously uses phrasing such as *in an organizational context* or *in organizational life*.

Pre-history of the Field

This section provides you with an overview of the pre-history of the field of Organizational Communication in the context of the field of Communication's history in general. From here on, these terms will be capitalized when referring to a field or discipline. Communication, as a discipline, is a 20th-century development. Communication emerged as a unique field from previously existing fields, developing independence in the early 1960s, moving out of departments of Psychology, Sociology, English, and Political Science. It was common in these early days to hear commentary about how we "borrowed" from other disciplines or how "fragmented" we were. Neither of these condemnations is now commonly heard because the field has matured to the point where our theoretic base has a strong disciplinary identity, which is distinct from that of other fields even as it maintains our multidisciplinary influences. Even so, Communication is a highly diverse discipline that studies everything from cognitive processes to texts and broad societal phenomena.

At its core, Communication is centered on the study of interaction among humans— from dyadic relationships to mass messaging. In so doing, we remain tightly connected to the literatures of other disciplines. Given that communication is the essence of social process, no social discipline can ignore communication phenomena. The field of Communication does not have territorial rights over the study of communication processes, but unlike other social science and humanities disciplines, our central focus is on explicating the communication process itself. In Organizational Communication, this is centered on communication processes that occur in the context of organizations, as defined above. Like the field as a whole, Organizational Communication seeks to explicate communication processes.

Organizational Communication is also an important contributor to the multidisciplinary area Organizational Studies, which also includes Management, Business, Organizational Psychology/Industrial Psychology, Human Relations, and a number of other disciplines interested in understanding organizational life. Sometimes, scholars from these other organizational disciplines do not recognize our field as a distinct scholarly discipline; sometimes they use the term *organizational communication* very differently than we would prefer. As multidisciplinarity grows, these issues will likely diminish. To accomplish this, it is extremely important for a scholar of Organizational Communication to have a good understanding of the intellectual history of the field, as well as a firm grasp on how Organizational Communication fits with Communication as a whole. This history is written here by juxtaposing important developments in the emergence of Communication (based on the comprehensive history provided by Delia, 1987) with important developments in the emergence of Organizational Communication (based on Redding, 1985, and Redding & Tompkins, 1988).

Birth of Communication: 1900–1930s

Communication has two fundamental roots, both heavily influenced by theories of persuasion: speech and media. Public speaking and rhetoric were originally taught in departments of English. In the early 20th century, a group of a group of public speaking teachers who were members of the National Council of Teachers of English (NCTE) voted to create the National Association of Academic Teachers of Public Speaking (NAATPS), which was established in 1914—about the same time that the first Eastern Public Speaking Conference was held. (This conference eventually developed into the Eastern Communication Association, which still meets annually.) The NAATPS went through several name changes as the field matured and is currently the National Communication Association—with a far broader mission and membership than its founders could have possibly envisioned.

During WWI, studies of propaganda formed the first body of research on media (Delia, 1987). In the 1920s, there emerged in Sociology a focused study of human interaction at the same time that public opinion research became an important area of study. In the 1930s, the advent of moving pictures and concerns about their impact on youth spurred the first research activities on "new media." By this time, public opinion research had become well-established as its own field of study and Social Psychology had emerged to become the central discipline for the study of human interaction. In addition during this period, the study of speech began to employ a scientific approach to persuasion, attitude change, decision-making and the sending and receiving of messages.

Organizational Communication. The origins of Organizational Communication can be traced to European industrialization in the 1750s. With industrialization came the advent of large organizational systems that forever changed the face of business (and eventually society itself). The scholarship of business began a century later, with the first academic unit devoted to its study established at Harvard. Redding and Tompkins (1988) refer to 1900–1940 as the *Era of Preparation*, a period during which the groundwork was laid for Organizational Communication. From the beginning, Business and Management scholarship emphasized the importance of communication for the effective management of organizations. Early management theory had a profound effect on both organizational practice and organizational theory. Early 19th- and 20th-century management theory has been traditionally taught as conceptually foundational to Organizational Communication theory, but this text takes the view that this foundational influence is far more profound. These early management theories, because they were overtly prescriptive, are not simply conceptual foundations for the field, but were powerful historic societal forces that shaped (and continue to shape) organizational forms, practices, and management. One cannot adequately understand contemporary organizations as communicatively constructed and constituted without appreciation of the constitutive power of these foundational bodies of theory. As prescriptions, these theories quite literally wrote the scripts that contemporary organizations follow. These theories and their influence will be covered in Part II of this text.

Public address was an already-established discipline, and this era saw a growing interest in applications to business, as well as increasing attention to business writing, managerial communication, and persuasion. By 1930, the importance of effective speaking and writing for business executives was widely recognized by both academics and practitioners. The study of effective message construction/delivery, including examinations of channels/media, forms the core of Organizational Communication's origins. Given its business-oriented foundations, such research was managerially biased, focusing solely on downward communication (from management to labor). Thus, Organizational Communication was formed with a managerial bias, as well. Although this bias is now overtly recognized and problematized, the very fabric of organizations themselves are constituted by the teachings of these early management theories—from the arrangement of authority hierarchies to conventions and sanctions for communication channels.

The World War II Era Through the 1950s

The WWII era provided an important historical context for Communication generally and Organizational Communication specifically. In general, applied research in the war effort brought increased attention to communication problems, which contributed to professional legitimacy and attracted prominent researchers. In this way, communication research entered the mainstream of American Sociology and Social Psychology. Interactions among scholars interested in communication problems created an interest area that would become the field of Communication as the postwar expansion of higher education made room for new disciplines (Delia, 1987). By 1950, university programs in Speech—both public address and human interaction—were well underway. Redding (1985) identifies during the war period a "triple alliance" (p. 24) of effort among the military, academia, and training-within-industry as the primary force that spawned the field of Organizational Communication, which emerged under the label *Business and Industrial Communication*. This early grounding in business and industry is a chief explanation for Organizational Communication's continuing orientation to the workplace. In the 1940s, business/industrial communication theory and research expanded beyond information-dissemination and managerial messaging to include studies of communication networks and employees' informal communication.

According to Delia (1987) during this period, at the same time that the field of Speech was beginning to attract and absorb research on human interaction, the terms *communication research* and *mass communication research* emerged as umbrella terms to replace more specialized labels such as *propaganda, persuasion, radio,* and *print*. This shift in labeling conventions created the unity and coherence necessary for the crystallization of a field. Communication saw the development of a disciplinary center emerge with emphasis on scientific analysis of public communication. Communication processes were seen as central to democratic life and the public good and best understood through scientific analysis. This development highlights an inherent axiological conflict between the value-free practice of science and the value-laden phenomena it strives to understand. Communication researchers quickly adopted Psychology's commitment to experimental methods and hypothesis-testing. The center of the Communication discipline was thus solidified partly as a rejection of atheoretical, politically driven work (Delia, 1987). Postwar, then, communication research became committed to social scientific theory development—as compared to the stronger focus on applied research in the emerging field of Business and Industrial Communication. Delia (1987) points to three factors that facilitated the development of a core of this new field of Communication: An organizing vocabulary, a core subject matter, and a standard conception of communication processes seen in models of flow (SMCR): Who says what through what channels to whom; what will be the results; and how can we measure what is said and its results?

During this same postwar period, four university campuses (Northwestern, Ohio State, Purdue, and Southern California) saw speech professors extending undergraduate work into doctoral-level research, resulting in "a small number of Ph.D. dissertations in 'industrial communication'" (Redding & Tompkins, 1988, p. 16) produced from Speech programs. In addition, Speech departments also began hosting annual conferences devoted to industrial communication, and the field's research literature proliferated from a number of disciplines.

In 1950, the National Society for the Study of Communication (NSSC) was founded, now the International Communication Association (ICA). In the 1950s, the label *communication research* became theoretically focused on media effects research (e.g., Berelson, Lazarsfeld & McPhee's, 1954 work on public opinion and Hovland's, 1954 work on media effects). There was a focus on attitude change as a communication effect, with two major continuing influences: Experimental methodology and social psychology. Work such as that by Katz and Lazarsfeld (1955) was highly influential, making theoretical connections between social organization and mass communication effects through the mechanism of a two-step flow model to describe social mediation of media effects.

At this time, two splits in the field were beginning to take shape—one between the study of mass communication and interpersonal communication and the other between communication theory/research and communication practice (Delia, 1987), with mass communication practical work branching off into Journalism. Redding and Tompkins (1988) note similar splits in the early Organizational Communication literature at the same time between internal communication and communication to external audiences and between theory/research and practice, with external/practice work evolving into the field of Public Relations. (Note here, the container presumption of the organizational boundary as a defining mechanism for organizing the field into specialties.)

For Organizational Communication at large, however, the importance of communication practice remained central. By the late 1950s, according to Redding and Tompkins (1988, p. 16), "the field—almost always referred to as 'business' or 'industrial' communication, it must be remembered—had crystallized to the point where at least those who were studying it could identify what they were studying." Redding's conclusions about the field (Redding, 1985; Redding & Tompkins, 1988) were based in part on a detailed cataloguing of publications in the field:

> In 1959, two publications appeared upon the scene, symbolizing the fact that (at least in the eyes of a cadre of social scientists) industrial communication was finally being identified as a recognizable entity: (a) a monograph published by the Foundation for Research on Human Behavior (loosely affiliated with the Institute for Social Research at the University of Michigan), *Communication in Organizations—Some New Research Findings*; and (b) the first literature review to appear in an academic journal under the label "business communication" (Sexton & Staudt, 1959).
>
> (Redding & Tompkins, 1988, pp. 16–17)

Redding's (1985) conclusions regarding the development of Organizational Communication are also based on examination of labels in the study of communication and organization and the awarding of graduate degrees, with 1953 noted as the first year Speech departments (at Northwestern and Ohio State) awarded doctoral degrees for work done specifically under the label *industrial communication*.

Arrival: The 1960s

By 1960, the field of Communication existed in Speech departments that housed faculty spanning the areas of speech and rhetoric, interpersonal interaction, and mass communication. Inherent to the field are philosophical conflicts between scientific and humanistic/rhetorical research, with the two sides united by their convergence on persuasion as a central interest. However, by 1970, the widely accepted notion that the study of communication was synonymous with the study of persuasion began to be questioned in a search for a broader perspective (Delia, 1987). Thanks to Berlo (1960) and like-minded others, the idea of communication-as-process emerged as the field's central focus.

The study of organizational communication expanded greatly in the 1960s to incorporate more relationally oriented research. The shift away from persuasion brought attention to the *receiver* of information. The change from a sender- to a receiver-orientation in organizational communication research at the time led to an increasingly popular presumption that the message received was the only one that mattered (Putnam & Cheney, 1985). The study of relationships in organizational contexts also increased, with particular attention to superior–subordinate communication and communication climate. In the context of the splintering of Mass Communication and Interpersonal Communication into separate disciplinary areas during this time period, it is easy to see how the reification of organizational boundary was perpetuated, and why Public Relations—with its focus on effective messaging to broad external audiences—remained associated with Mass Communication, whereas Organizational Communication became united with Interpersonal.

Organizational Communication, under that label, emerged in 1967, with three fundamental markers (Redding & Tompkins, 1988). First, Lee Thayer (1967) produced the monograph, "Communication and Organizational Theory," followed quickly by the book *Communication and Communication Systems* (Thayer, 1968). Second, and perhaps most influentially, the Conference on Organizational Communication was held in 1967 at NASA's Marshall Space Flight Center (MSFC).

> The four-day conference brought together management representatives from government agencies and MSFC contractors, as well as academic specialists from four universities, the major address, delivered by Phillip K, Tompkins (then of Wayne State University and a consultant to the Center) consisted of a comprehensive review of *empirical research* that had been completed in the field up to that time.
>
> (Redding, 1985, p. 22, emphasis in original)

Tompkins' address and accompanying paper represents the earliest work summarizing the field's research under the label *organizational communication*. The NASA conference was, likewise, the first-ever conference focused on theory and research to be held under that label. The following year, the International Communication Association (then the NSSC) established the Organizational Communication Division, firmly solidifying the label and firmly grounding Organizational Communication as a sub-discipline of Communication.

Organization of This Text

Part I of this book provides an overview of the history of organizational communication. Chapter 1, which you have just finished, has offered a set of foundational concepts from which to understand the field, as well as the pre-history of the field—discussing the socio-historical foundations of the field's emergence. Chapters 2 and 3 will provide overviews of the development of the field from its formation in the late 1960s to the present, including both theoretical shifts and trends in research topics. Chapter 4 will explain the dominant paradigms that guide theory and research in the field.

Part II of this book is comprised of chapters that explain the development of early 20th-century management theory that take us to about the same point (late 1960s) as the pre-history you have just read. Simultaneous with the socio-historical events and circumstances that came together to form the emergence of Organizational Communication, management theorists were developing foundational organizational theories for their field (which also profoundly influenced other organizational studies disciplines, including our own). In management theory, the three foundational schools of thought are *classical management*, which focused on formal communication processes and emphasized prescriptions to improve productivity (Chapter 5); *human relations* (HR), which focused on informal communication processes and emphasized prescriptions to improve worker satisfaction as a path to productivity (Chapter 6); and *human resources management* (HRM), which focused on participative management processes and emphasized prescriptions to maximize the potential of workers' intelligence for organizational gain (Chapter 7).

These bodies of early management theory are particularly important to organizational communication for two fundamental reasons. First, this body of work represents the first systematic thinking about communication and organization, influencing our ways of thinking about these phenomena (e.g., how we identify, define, and prioritize basic concepts). Second, as a prescriptive discipline, this early management theory profoundly shaped practice, in essence *creating* the organizational communication phenomena we study today (e.g., authority, hierarchy, and organizational form).

Finally, Part III offers reviews of numerous important specialized areas of research and theory, all written by subject matter experts. Every chapter will apply a template of understanding that will help you synthesize what you are learning about the field and its literature by providing answers to three central questions:

- What is the approach in this area taken to communication (message, meaning, constitutive)?
- What is the approach taken to organization (as process, as structured, as entity)?
- How can we see the communication/organization spiral in this body of literature (Figures 1.4 and 1.5)?

Recommended Supplementary Readings

Brummans, B. H. J. M. (Ed.). (2018). *The agency of organizing: Perspectives and case studies.* New York: Routledge.
Chapters from this book might be read by more advanced students to engage in study of the conceptual operation of agency as an important concept in organizational communication theory.

Buzzanell, P. M., & Stohl, C. (1999). The Redding tradition of organizational communication scholarship: W. Charles Redding and his legacy. *Communication Studies, 50*(4), 324–336.
Provides a critical appreciation of the influential work of Charles Redding, widely regarded as the "founding father" of organizational communication.

Craig, R. T. (1999). Communication theory as a field. *Communication Theory, 9*(2), 119–161.
The late 1990s brought a series of conversations and debates regarding the definition of the field and its theoretical contributions. This was an influential essay of the time.

Delia, J. G. (1987). Communication research: A history. In C. R. Berger & S. H. Chaffee (Eds.), *Handbook of communication science* (pp. 20–98). Newbury Park, CA: SAGE.
Provides a comprehensive history of the field of Communication from its inception to the 1980s.

Hawes, L. C. (1974). Social collectivities as communication. *Quarterly Journal of Speech, 60*(4), 497–502.
An in-depth conceptual treatment of social collectivity and how it can be conceptualized as communication.

Putnam, L. L., & Cheney, G. (1985). Organizational communication: Historical development and future directions. In T. Benson (Ed.), *Speech communication in the 20th century* (pp. 130–156). Carbondale: Southern Illinois University Press.
Provides a comprehensive history of the field of organizational communication up to the early 1980s.

Redding, W. C. (1985). Stumbling toward identity: The emergence of organizational communication as a field of study. In R. D. McPhee & P. K. Tompkins (Eds.), *Organizational communication: Traditional themes and new directions* (pp. 15–54). Beverly Hills, CA: SAGE.

Redding, W. C., & Tompkins, P. K. (1988). Organizational communication: Past and present tenses. In G. Goldhaber & G. Burnett (Eds.), *Handbook of organizational communication* (pp. 5–34). Norwood, NJ: Ablex.
These two chapters can be read as companion pieces. In the 1980s, these essays were regarded as the official history of the field.

Redding, W. C. (1992). Response to Professor Berger's essay: Its meaning for organizational communication. *Communication Monographs, 59*(1), 87–93.

Berger, C. R. (1991). Communication theories and other curios. *Communication Monographs, 58*(1), 101–113.
These two essays should be read as companion pieces. Like Craig (1999) listed above, this set of essays is a good representation of the 1990s debates about our field's contributions.

Tompkins, P.K. (1993). *Organizational communication imperatives: Lessons of the space program.* Los Angeles: Roxbury.
This book is an excellent historical accounts of Tompkins' work with NASA, how he came to develop theories of effective organizing based on NASA's Apollo-era organizational practices and principles, and how this applied work contributed to the birth of the field of organizational communication.

Tompkins, P.K. (2005). *Apollo, Challenger, Columbia: The decline of the space program.* Los Angeles: Roxbury.
Tompkins' second NASA book chronicles the changes in organizational communication practices at NASA in the shuttle era, providing an organizational communication analysis of the US space program's decline. These are excellent books to demonstrate the practical applications of organizational communication theory and are highly recommended reading for practitioners.

Important Concepts: Define and Discuss

Agency
Communication as human action
Culture
Organization
Redding's triple alliance
Reflexivity
Social collective
Social construction

Discussion Questions

1. Using concrete examples, explain how *organization* and *communication* are related.
2. Using an organization with which you are very familiar, illustrate O_1, O_2, and O_3. Explain how this organization possesses all three of the fundamental characteristics of entitative being. Then trace how the three expressions (organizing, organized, and organization) are interrelated in actual occurrences.
3. How do we continue to see Redding's *triple alliance* in the field today?
4. How might the conceptualization presented here of organization and organizational communication be applied to social networks? Are social networks examples of organizational communication in action? Why or why not?

Practitioners' Corner

Communication practitioners and their work vary considerably. Communication practitioners may serve any combination of a number of functions: Information dissemination, education, training, development, promotion, marketing, customer relations, and so on. These various functions are served across a wide variety of contexts, including corporate, government, nonprofit, and educational settings. Each chapter of this book will include a "Practitioner's Corner." Some of these will be suggestions for application of the material; some will be case studies illustrating application. Some chapters will provide more concrete applications than others, depending on the subject matter. This first chapter is necessarily abstract, but it provides a uniquely insightful vocabulary for communication practitioners to think through important issues.

All communication professionals have at least two fundamental things in common: They must act as agents of someone/something other than themselves and they must bridge the socially constructed organizational boundary that divides their audiences into *internal* and *external* publics. The abstract definitional material in this chapter can be helpful to the practitioner in several ways across these two commonalities. Underlying these implications are important questions of agency.

- *First, the communication practitioner is an agent who is professionally obligated to represent the interests of some entity.* Conceptualizing who/what constitutes that entity brings an important set of ethical considerations. Every communication professional must wrestle with the question of whose interests are primary to the task at hand. The practitioner must ask herself: Whose interests do I represent? The organization (O_3)? The stockholders? The public? Which public? What are the limits on that representation? The theoretic constructions of O_1, O_2, and O_3 provide a language to assist the practitioner in thinking through these questions to both devise strategy and create a code of ethics.

  o Representing *the organization* to a set of "external" publics is a very different task than representing one "internal" group to another, or representing *the organization* to its internal audiences. Who is accountable for actions attributed to O_3? Should that information be revealed to message recipients? How? When representing the entitative being, it is crucial to remember that the organization has no conscience of its own. Moreover, when the corporate body is the entity represented, the identities of those humans who are actually responsible and accountable for organizational actions are obfuscated. These implications of the construct O_3 have profound impact on considerations for ethical communication.

○ Strategic messaging can be very nuanced. For example, in public health communication, when is it best to attribute a message to *the CDC* or *the Department of Health and Human Services*, or *the Surgeon General's Office* rather than to the individual persons in charge of the project or announcement at hand? Thinking through the meaning and persuasive power of attributions using the theoretic considerations offered here can be helpful in the design of effective messages that accomplish ethical purposes.

- *Second, the line that divides "external" and "internal" publics is fluid and socially constructed.* In practice, organizational boundary is enforced, with audiences (or publics) divided into internal and external groups. Construction of strategic messaging is enhanced when the practitioner remembers that the boundaries are a human construction.

  ○ "Outsiders" can become "insiders"—carrying with them the memory of previous messaging. Are there inconsistencies between internal and external messaging? How might these inconsistencies be best addressed to successfully transition newcomers into "insider" roles?

  ○ "Insiders" simultaneously occupy "outsider" roles. Corporate employees are members of the public with families. Military officers and soldiers are consumers of goods. Public health officers drink from municipal water sources and breathe air from the same atmosphere as everyone else. Any construction of messages designed for internal audiences must be mindful of these blurs in the organizational boundary. Is it important for internal messaging to remain internal? How is "internal" defined, and how is this best communicated to the recipients? Given the ubiquity of social media, are leaks possible? How damaging might such leaks be? To whom? Is any training necessary to prevent them? Harkening back to the first point—whose interests does the practitioner serve in these matters?

While all of these questions can be thoughtfully considered without the organizational communication theoretical framework presented in this chapter, the framework does provide a useful language for the practitioner to think through these issues. The framework provides both the genesis of important questions and a language with which to formulate answers. Who am I? Where do I sit in the organizational construction? Whose interests do I represent? How can we best organize (O_1) to create organized structures (O_2) to achieve the goals of the organization (O_3)? A communication professional in any context will be better prepared to more effectively strategize and implement communication plans having thought through these kinds of questions.

References

Bandura, A. (2001). Social cognitive theory: An agentive perspective. *Annual Review of Psychology, 52*(1), 1–26. doi:10.1146/annurev.psych.52.1.1.

Barnlund, D. C. (1970). A transactional model of communication. In K. K. Sereno & C. D. Mortenson (Eds.), *Foundations of communication theory* (pp. 83–92). New York, NY: Harper and Row.

Berelson, B., Lazarsfeld, P. F., & McPhee, W. (1954). *Voting*. Chicago: University of Chicago Press.

Berlo, D. K. (1960). *The process of communication.* New York: Holt, Rinehart, & Winston.

Brummans, B. H. J. M. (Ed.). (2018). *The agency of organizing: Perspectives and case studies.* New York: Routledge.

Chen, G., & Starosta, W. J. (1998). *Foundations of intercultural communication.* Boston: Allyn and Bacon.

Conrad, C., & Haynes, J. (2001) Development of key constructs. In F. M. Jablin & L. L. Putnam (Eds.), *The new handbook of organizational communication* (pp. 47–77). Thousand Oaks: SAGE.

Cushman, D. P., & Cahn, D. D. (1985). *Communication in interpersonal relationships.* Albany, NY: SUNY Press.

Cushman, D. P. & Craig, R. T. (1976). Communication systems: Interpersonal implications. In G. Miller (Ed.), *Explorations in interpersonal communication* (pp. 37–58). Beverly Hills: SAGE.

Cushman, D. P. & Florence, B. T. (1974). The development of interpersonal communication theory. *Today's Speech, 22*(4), 11–15. doi:10.1080/01463377409369156.

Cushman, D. P., & Pearce, W. B. (1977). Generality and necessity in three types of communication theory, with special attention to rules theory. *Human Communication Research, 3*(4), 341–353. doi:10.1111/j.1468-2958.1977.tb00537.x.

Cushman, D. P., Valentinsen, B., & Dietrich, D. (1982). A rules theory of interpersonal relationships. In F. Dance (Ed.), *Human communication theory* (pp. 90–119). New York: Harper and Row.

Dance, F. (1967). Toward a theory of human communication. In F. Dance (Ed.). *Human communication theory* (pp. 288–309). New York: Holt.

Delia, J. G. (1987). Communication research: A history. In C. R. Berger & S. H. Chaffee (Eds.), *Handbook of communication science* (pp. 20–98). Newbury Park, CA: SAGE.

Hovland, C. I. (1954). Effects of mass media of communication. In G. Kindsey (Ed.), *Handbook of social psychology II* (pp. 1062–1103). Cambridge, MA: Addison-Wesley.

Katz, E., & Lazarsfeld, P. F. (1955). *Personal influence.* New York: Free Press.

Mortensen, C. D. (1972). *Communication: The study of human interaction.* New York: McGraw-Hill.

Nicotera, A. M. (2013). Organizations as entitative beings: Some ontological implications of communicative constitution. In F. Cooren & D. Robichaud (Eds.), *Organization and organizing: Materiality, agency, and discourse* (pp. 66–89). New York, NY: Routledge.

Nicotera, A. M., & Clinkscales, M. J. (2003). *Understanding organization through culture and structure: Relational and other lessons from the African-American organization.* Mahwah, NJ: Erlbaum.

Putnam, L. L., & Cheney, G. (1985). Organizational communication: Historical development and future directions. In T. Benson (Ed.), *Speech communication in the 20th century* (pp. 130–156). Carbondale: Southern Illinois University Press.

Redding, W. C. (1985). Stumbling toward identity: The emergence of organizational communication as a field of study. In R. D. McPhee & P. K. Tompkins (Eds.), *Organizational communication: Traditional themes and new directions* (pp. 15–54). Beverly Hills, CA: SAGE.

Redding, W. C., & Tompkins, P. K. (1988). Organizational communication: Past and present tenses. In G. Goldhaber & G. Burnett (Eds.), *Handbook of organizational communication* (pp. 5–34). Norwood, NJ: Ablex.

Ruesch, J., & Bateson, G. (1951). *Communication: The social matrix of psychiatry.* New York: Norton.

Schramm, W. (1954). How communication works. In W. Schramm (Ed.), *The process and effects of communication* (pp. 3–26). Urbana, IL: University of Illinois Press.

Sewell, W. H. (1992). A theory of structure: Duality, agency, and transformation. *The American Journal of Sociology, 98*(1),1–29. doi:10.1086/229967.

Sexton, R. & Staudt, V. (1959). Business communication: A survey of the literature. *Journal of Social Psychology, 50*(1), 101–118. doi:10.1080/00224545.1959.9921982.

Smith, R. C. (1993). *Images of organizational communication: Root-metaphors of the organization-communication relation*. Paper presented to the Organizational Communication Division at the International Communication Association Convention, Washington, D.C.

Thayer, L. (1967). Communication and organizational theory. In F. Dance (Ed.), *Human communication theory* (pp. 70–115). New York: Holt, Rinehart and Winston.

Thayer, L. (1968). *Communication and communication systems*. Homewood, IL: Irwin.

Westley, B., & MacLean, M. S., Jr. (1955). A conceptual model for communication research. *Audio-Visual Communication Review*, 3(1), 3–12. doi:10.1177/107769905703400103.

2 Developments in the 20th Century

Anne M. Nicotera

This chapter provides an overview of developments in the field from its formation in the late 1960s to the turn of the 21st century, including both theoretical shifts and trends in research topics. According to Krone (2005), trends in organizational communication theory and research are flexible, enduring, diverse, and problem-centered. Our *flexibility* reveals a field that is sensitive and responsive to our socio-historical context as we adapt to the changing landscape of organizational forms, processes, and problems. (See Conrad & Sollitto, 2017, for a thorough history of the field grounded in socio-historical contexts.) The field is *enduring* because it continually revisits and develops established lines of theory and research. Yet, our *diversity* of paradigms and methods may be our greatest strength. "Perhaps this is because some of the most consequential problems in and around organizations today are complex and intractable enough to require study using a variety of methodological approaches" (Krone, 2005, p. 100). Finally, organizational communication theory and research are *problem-centered*. The field maintains a sense of ethical obligation that our work be translational and applicable to solve practical problems and improve the quality of organizational life.

In the 1970s organizational communication theory and research were focused on understanding organizational communication processes scientifically, with variable-analytic research examining the links between effective performance and such things as communication networks, superior–subordinate communication, and communication climate. This era was heavily influenced by social psychology (scholars such as Kurt Lewin and Karl Weick). The 1980s brought an interpretive turn, accompanied by an enduring attention to culture and the mutual influence between self and society (anthropologist Clifford Geertz, sociologist George Herbert Mead). The 1990s saw a groundswell of critical theory, heavily influenced by Karl Marx and the Frankfort School of Critical Theory, as well as by Foucault and other continental theorists. During this period, our critical eye fell upon ourselves as well. Smith (1993), in one of the most influential and widely cited conference papers in our history, pointed out that the language in organizational communication literature encouraged an implicit container metaphor—the phrase *communication in organizations* perpetuating a counterproductive mechanical approach to organizations as static containers in which communication processes occur, rather than a socially constructed context that continually co-creates communication.

Late 1960s and 1970s

In its early years, the field of organizational communication had a decidedly business-focused orientation with a managerial bias toward effective communication—that which improved employee performance and other outcomes, such as job satisfaction. In the early part of this period, research followed a linear and deductive variable-analytic tradition in a structural-functionalist approach. Later, broader applications of systems theory emerged as a more dominant perspective. During this time period, popular research topics included message contents, channels, flows, barriers, and interpretations; rumors/grapevine; communication networks (formal and informal); nonverbal communication; communication load; methodologies for auditing communication effectiveness; symbolism and shared meaning systems; superior–subordinate communication and leadership; socialization; climate; productivity; participative decision-making; effectiveness and efficiency; rationality; control and coordination; innovation; and (toward the end of the period) gender. During this time, the ICA Communication Audit was developed by members of the Organizational Communication Division of the International Communication Association to provide the advantages of externally valid findings derived from a commonly employed methodology. The ICA Audit is a standard set of comprehensive instruments to measure organizational communication using a variety of respondents (supervisors, subordinates and peers) and data collection measures (open- and closed-ended surveys, network measures, and interviews) to assess numerous communication variables, including need, load, network, and effectiveness. As was typical of the time, communication was treated as nearly synonymous with information, albeit with an implicit assumption of the importance of relationship. The ICA Audit sought to integrate theory and practice by allowing organizational communication scholars/consultants to both improve organizational functioning and have access to a normed data bank for comparisons across organizations and for testing theories. The audit was developed in three phases (development of procedures and instruments; pilot testing, structuring, and forming dissemination plans; and implementation), with hundreds of researchers and practitioners in several countries. (For a history of the ICA Audit and its impact, see Goldhaber, 2002.)

Structural-functionalism. Structural-functionalism, a form of systems theory, was dominant across the social sciences at the time (see Katz & Kahn, 1978). *Functionalism* assumes that reality is external to human interaction and perceptions, and that human beings encounter the social world as receivers of that reality. Hence, the perspective is often called *the received view*. Functionalists assume organizations are unified in the pursuit of common goals through a cooperative system (Conrad & Sollitto, 2017). Functionalism is consistent with the positivist paradigm. *Positivism* relies heavily on deductive reasoning and seeks to apply the philosophy and techniques of scientific method (from physical science) to the social sciences. Conclusions are drawn from existing knowledge, reducing concepts to variables and providing the basis for objective hypotheses of relationships among those variables. These hypotheses are then tested by developing objective quantitative measures for those variables, applying those measurements in observation, and implementing statistical techniques to determine whether the hypothesized relationships can be confirmed or must be rejected. (See Chapter 4 for a fuller explanation of positivism.) The linear, reductionist, and variable-analytic tradition that prevailed until the late 1970s was challenged by systems theory and then, in the 1980s, by interpretive and qualitative approaches. Today, the field enjoys a healthy pluralism of perspectives and methodologies in a mutually respectful scholarly community.

Systems theory. Toward the end of the 1970s, the received view of structural-functionalism began to give way to less deductive applications of the systems perspective. Organizations were seen as less mechanical and more fluid as, in the latter 1970s, social scientists increasingly embraced von Bertalanffy's (1968) general systems theory, proposed first as a useful philosophy of science for biologists and then established as a multidisciplinary field. As more interpretive forms of the systems perspective supplanted the deductive approach of structural-functionalism, conceptions of both *communication* and *organization* evolved. As the meaning-centered approach described in Chapter 1 took hold, conceptualizations of communicators as *receivers* gave way to a social constructivist view of communicators as *interpreters*. Systems theory allowed us to explore the ways in which human interpretation is a social process.

In organizational communication, systems theorists relied on a number of assumptions, the most fundamental of which is the *organismic principle*. Organizations were seen as living organisms, rather than machines or mechanical constructions. A *system* is a set of interconnected components. Organizational communication scholars concentrate on three characteristics of systems: hierarchical ordering, interdependence, and permeability. The principle of *hierarchical ordering* establishes that systems are organized in nested fashion, so that systems exist inside and around other systems. First, the system of interest is seen to contain sub-systems, each of which contains sub-sub-systems of its own, in continual fashion. Likewise, a system exists within a larger supra-system, which itself is only one component of an even larger supra-supra-system, and so on. Second, the component parts of the system are *interdependent*, the function of each component relying upon the functions of others. Third, systems can be described according to their *permeability* or openness to their environment. Organizational scholars define organizations as open systems, dependent on context and intersecting with multiple other systems.

Open systems are, in part, analyzed according to their exchanges with their environment in an *input-throughput-output* process. Information is introduced to a system as *input* from the environment. *Throughput* can be defined as actions taken with and upon that input. *Output* is the end result placed back into the environment by the system. Output then becomes input for another system. For example, let's imagine that a patient in the U.S. checks in to a hospital emergency department complaining of chest pains. This patient and his symptoms are the inputs. The complex system of an emergency department then acts on these inputs. Throughput is accomplished by the rules established for that system and its sub-systems. Among other aspects of the throughput, a registration clerk records the patient's information and places the patient in queue in a waiting area. Triage nurses then assess the patient's condition with various screening tests and assign the patient a priority for care, with the patient then put into another queue. The rules of the system dictate that the patient's waiting period be determined by priority relative to other patients' needs and the availability of care providers. The patient is then moved to a treatment room where care is provided. Note that in each of these stages an input-throughput-output process occurs among the sub-systems (registration, triage, care), with the output of each becoming the input for the next. Once the patient is placed into care, the system's standard procedures for monitoring and treatment are performed. In the end, it is determined that this lucky patient has not experienced a heart attack, and he is transformed into *output* as he is discharged with a referral to a cardiologist. As he carries his emergency room records to a follow-up appointment with a private practitioner, he and these records become input for that private practice system.

In this process, *feedback* is crucial to the successful operation of the system in meeting its goals. Negative feedback is corrective, reducing deviance from rules. If the private practitioner sees something the hospital missed, she can provide feedback to that system, perhaps resulting in an investigation that uncovers error(s), deviation from procedures, or even faulty procedures. Positive feedback, on the other hand, is progressive, amplifying deviation from established rules to create new ones. This allows innovation and improvements to be made if someone discovers a better way to do something that results in improved outcomes. In this way, the quality of outputs reflects back on throughput processes.

Four other properties of systems are important to understand. First, the principle of *nonsummativity* (or holism) establishes that the system is not simply the sum of its component parts. Rather, the essence of the system emerges from interaction among those parts. For organizational communication scholars, this is particularly important because interaction is our focus. Nonsummativity can be illustrated in a simple exercise. Imagine, if you will, two people yearning to eat a delicious piece of chocolate cake. They assemble identical sets of ingredients. The first person stirs together the ingredients in a bowl, pours the batter into a pan, sets the pan in a hot oven for 30 minutes, allows it to cool, and then enjoys a perfect slice. The second simply eats each ingredient separately in sequence, choking down flour, unsweetened cocoa powder, baking powder, sugar, and salt, then washing it down with vegetable oil, raw eggs, and milk. What happened here? While each consumed precisely the same ingredients, only one ate cake. The other merely consumed the parts of the cake. Herein lies the principle of nonsummativity. What makes a cake a cake? Not the ingredients themselves; rather, a cake is a cake because of the way the ingredients interact with one another and are transformed together by environmental factors (the bowl, the mixer, the pan, and the heat of the oven). The cake is a system; the sum of its ingredients is not.

The second principle is *equifinality*; multiple processes can result in the same output. For example, one manufacturing organization may have very different processes than another, yet both might yield identical competitive products. The third principle is *negative entropy*. Closed systems decay; whereas, because of their exchanges with the environment, open systems counteract such decay. The human body is an excellent example. Our bodies are open to exchanges with the environment, through both inputs (nutrients, water, oxygen) and outputs (excretions of various sorts). Without this ability to interact with our environment, life would be impossible to sustain.

One last important principle is *requisite variety*. A system evolves internal complexities to match the complexity of its environment. Processes of throughput develop to deal with the complexity of inputs the system encounters. As environments, and thus inputs, grow more complex, organizations evolve internal complexities required to process those inputs successfully. For example, a store in a sparsely populated area with a culturally homogenous customer base must maintain a narrower variety of products and services than a store in a large metropolitan area with a dense and culturally diverse population. A successful system matches the variety demanded by its environment.

Cybernetic systems theory. Growing out of Shannon and Weaver's information theory (see Chapter 1), cybernetic approaches within systems theory focus on the function of control, using feedback loops, to improve efficiency. In organizational studies, cybernetic systems theory examines the ways in which communication controls a system's processes to achieve its goals. In organizational communication, cybernetics most popularly applies to improving human performance at the individual and group level through information/feedback (provided by managers, customers, etc.).

Cybernetics rests on four fundamental concepts. *Circularity* refers to feedback and mutual causality of system properties. *Variety* refers directly to communication; the use of multiple channels, networks, and intelligence to exchange information and provide control. *Process* provides a focus on adaptation, evolution, and growth. The system organizes through feedback loops that achieve goals by enabling equilibrium and change. *Observation* is a process of self-reference underlying crucial organizational functions such as decision-making and other applications of intelligence. For example, at the micro-level, a manager gives performance feedback to an individual employee, providing her with a review of her sales record, a critique of practices she employs, and information about the practices of coworkers with better records. As a result, she changes her activities and improves her record, causing better organizational goal-attainment. You can see here how information/communication about past group performance causes individual performance to improve, which in turn causes better group performance. At the macro-level, the organization's marketing strategy may fail to increase sales records. In that case, consumer and market feedback may

> force the organization to change its strategy in order to survive and maintain its desired goal of keeping up its sales performance. The disruptions or variations in the environment will thus force the system to respond and adjust in order to maintain this state of equilibrium.
>
> (Lai & Lin, 2017, p. 1)

Self-organizing systems theory. Linked to chaos and complexity theories, and also known as *new science systems theory*, self-organizing systems theory examines the ways that system functions emerge naturally to meet equilibrium. The key concept is *autopoiesis*—a process whereby a system produces its own organization to maintain and constitute itself. Quite literally, self-organizing systems theory examines the processes whereby an organization produces itself. An autopoietic organization is an autonomous and self-maintaining unity that contains component-producing processes. Components interact to recursively generate the same network of processes that produced them. Important concepts include the mutual causality between components, the self-generative properties of those components, a variable equilibrium state, and openness to the environment (Contractor, 1994; Contractor & Seibold, 1993).

For example, in a small group, communication is driven by, but also shapes, group norms (mutual causality). "Members' engagement in group tasks is influenced by and reflects their prior training and accumulated experience in the organization, which corresponds with the process of autopoiesis" (Lai & Lin, 2017, p. 8). Loss and gain of members, new work assignments, and changes to environmental conditions will cause communication behavior and norms to evolve accordingly. You can see here how changes in components of and inputs to the system bring the system to equilibrium. Social systems theory (Luhmann, 1995) extends self-organizing systems theory, examining communication as the mechanism of self-organizing. As communication processes are mutually influential and mutually recursive, the system's boundaries are created and maintained by communicative patterns. (See Chapter 3.)

The 1980s and the Interpretive Turn

The 1980s saw great theoretical advancement in organizational communication. First, systems theory continued to flourish (producing a multitude of textbooks promoting a systems approach). This is, in part, due to the unparalleled influence of Karl Weick.

A social psychologist working in the field of management, the second edition of his book *The Social Psychology of Organizing* (1979) revolutionized the field of organizational communication. Weick made a compelling argument that *organization* was more verb than noun. His *organizational information theory*, grounded in general systems theory, focuses on information management and complexity, addressing how organizations reduce uncertainty through information collection, use, and management. Weick proposed that organizing is accomplished collectively through processes of communication. For scholars seeking to explicate organizational communication processes, these ideas were electrifying.

Second, with the introduction of interpretive and critical approaches (described below), scholars began to question structural-functionalist presumptions about communication practices and processes, such as the primacy of top-down communication and the importance of authority hierarchies. One exemplar of such questioning was the introduction of the concept *strategic ambiguity*. Prior to this time, organizational communication scholars, teachers, and practitioners had adhered to an assumption that clarity in communication was both desired and practiced by effective organizational leaders and members. Eisenberg (1984), however, pointed out that ambiguity in communication is often deliberate and commonly used both strategically and effectively to accomplish a number of organizational and individual goals—only some of which are noble or for the common good. He advocated the intensive study of strategic ambiguity employing naturalistic and critical methods to examine its purposes and effects, such as promoting unified diversity, facilitating change, and preserving positions of power. This set of ideas was revolutionary, and would not have been possible without the field's interpretive turn.

Hence, the most important development of the 1980s was the first major paradigm shift in the field—from functionalism to interpretivism. Interpretivism rejected the objectivity of functionalism, arguing that disciplined subjectivity is an important source of knowledge and understanding. As such, interpretivism relies heavily on inductive reasoning, grounded in observation as a starting point for extracting theory, and on qualitative methods allowing rich description of lived experience (see Chapter 4 for a fuller explanation). While the systems perspective can support research consistent with functional or positivist research approaches, its social-constructivist assumptions also invite more interpretive and qualitative analyses aimed at explicating meaning-creation. In important ways, the introduction of systems theory to the field of Organizational Communication in the late 1970s, especially Weick's emphasis on *organizing* as a central focus of study, set the tone for the paradigm shift from positivism to interpretivism that took place in the early 1980s.

In the summer of 1981, the International Communication Association and the Speech Communication Association (now the National Communication Association), together with the communication departments of the University of Utah and Purdue University, co-sponsored the first Summer Conference on Interpretive Approaches to the Study of Organizational Communication. There, dozens of communication and organizational behavior scholars began a debate on the utility of interpretive approaches in studying organizational communication. This conference (held in Alta, UT, and thus often referred to as *the Alta conference*—not to be confused with the Alta conference series on argumentation) launched what came to be known as *the interpretive turn* in organizational communication. The following year, these debates were publicized in a special issue of the *Western Journal of Speech Communication* (Pacanowsky & Putnam, 1982) with a number of essays, including one on the critical-interpretive approach (Deetz, 1982) and a taxonomy of paradigms (Putnam, 1982). (See Chapter 4 for explanations of these paradigms in organizational communication.) Perhaps the most comprehensive, and thus important, publication during this time was a collection of essays, entitled *Communication and Organizations: An Interpretive Approach*, edited by Putnam and Pacanowsky (1983), with chapters written by leading scholars. Their interpretivist critique of positivism included, among other things, the mechanistic approach of functionalism and its inability to account for social process, meaning, and other nonlinear phenomena (Putnam, 1983).

Historical roots of interpretivism. Interpretivism is rooted in at least four important historical movements: German Idealism, hermeneutics, phenomenology, and symbolic interactionism. In the 1600s, Enlightenment philosophers established the foundational approach to knowledge that favored rationality and empirical data that led to logical positivism. Later, *German Idealists* (particularly Immanuel Kant writing in the 1700s) reacted to this approach by privileging subjectivity, rejecting René Descartes' widely accepted focus on rationality that underlies positivism. Kantian philosophy experienced a re-emergence in the mid-19th century, with a renewed emphasis on understanding the subjective, or the life world.

The discipline of *hermeneutics* had emerged earlier, with humanism, in the 15th century. Originally focused on the study of sacred texts, modern hermeneutics embraced the study of both literal and cultural texts. Any human action, product, or expression can be treated as text, and must be understood only through consideration of that text's author, context, and situation, as well as through the researcher's theoretical knowledge. The goal of hermeneutic analysis is *embedded understanding* or subjective significance. Through the *hermeneutic circle*, interpretivists reject any distinction between the knower and the known—such distinction being the hallmark of positivist approaches (see Chapter 4). The hermeneutic circle is the development of understanding through a constant interchange among frames of reference (of both the observer and the observed): Theory and scholarly knowledge; tacit knowledge (the taken-for-granted); actual textual data; and contextual/situational features.

Phenomenology is a complex theoretic discipline developed in the early 20th century and rooted in the core assumption that knowledge exists only in individual consciousness. Thus, the study of external experience cannot generate knowledge and any meaning ascribed to an object or experience must depend on the individual's consciousness of his/her background and current life. Phenomenologists also assume that experience of the world, and thus the development of meaning, is accomplished through language. In a method referred to as *époche*, Husserl's classical phenomenology posited that subjective understanding can be gained by transcendence—bracketing out attitudes of the taken-for-granted life world. Thus, understanding can be achieved only by transcending all personal biases, histories, values and interests. Later, Alfred Schutz developed *social phenomenology*, emphasizing the examination of *typifications* in social interaction. For the purpose of simplicity here, you can think of typifications as similar to social rules. We organize these typifications into complex bodies of cultural knowledge, and the central task of social researchers is to describe and understand them.

Finally, *symbolic interactionism* underlies interpretivism. Mead's 1930s treatise, *Mind, Self, and Society* (published from his papers after his death as Mead & Morris, 1934) delineates the central concepts. *Mind*, developed only by interaction with others, is the human ability to use symbols with common social meanings. Without social interaction we cannot think, and thought allows role-taking (seeing others' perspectives). *Self* is developed from that role-taking and is defined as the ability to see ourselves as others see us. We change our selves based on the feedback received from others (reflected appraisal or looking-glass self), and we change so as to match the expectations of others (Pygmalion self). The self is divided into the *I* and the *me*. The *I* is spontaneous and impulsive; whereas the *me* is reflective, evaluative, and socially aware. Finally, *society* is our web of social relationships. Society is comprised of *particular others* (people we know personally) and *generalized others* (the composite mental image of the community and its expectations). Symbolic interactionism assumes that humans are active agents who respond to one another based on meanings created in interaction and modified through interpretive processes. Further, self-concept is developed through interaction and provides motives for behavior. Finally, individuals and groups are influenced by cultural and social processes, which are created by social interaction.

Impact on organizational communication. These and other historical traditions of thought influenced the interpretive turn in organizational communication and other disciplines. The advent of the interpretivist perspective opened organizational communication to applications of qualitative and ethnographic research methods, inviting scholars to explore meaning-creation and other phenomena that emerge from interaction. The rise of interpretivism allowed increased attention to processes of social construction and identity formation. The field thus began to expand beyond its managerial, production, and business biases. Organizations began to be seen *as* cultures rather than *having* cultures (Pacanowsky & O'Donnell-Trujillo, 1982, 1983), and as communicative constructions rather than mere containers in which communication occurs (Smith, 1993). Applications of structuration theory (see Chapter 3) entered the communication literature, initially in the study of group interaction. Earlier ideas about organizations as social collectives (e.g., Hawes, 1974) were expanded. Alternative kinds of organizations began to be studied (e.g., religious, social, and community organizations). Interest in supervisor–subordinate communication and communication skills continued, with more emphasis on relational aspects. Likewise, the study of communication networks continued to grow (see Chapter 9). Interest developed in examining intercultural communication (but not diversity, which would come later; see Chapter 14 in this volume). Studies of power took on a social-constructionist nature, while interest in nonverbal communication and structure declined (Allen, Gotcher & Seibert, 1993). Examinations of gender increased, as did studies of organizational culture, organizing processes, systems, conflict, strategic ambiguity, technology, satisfaction, organizational rhetoric, and identification.

Weickian theory. Karl Weick is commonly credited with making *organization* a verb in the minds of communication scholars. His body of theory focuses on the intersection of organizing and communicating through processes of *collective sensemaking*. First, *sensemaking* is defined as both equivocality reduction and reality construction. Sensemaking is, most simply, the application of socially shared cognitive structures that transforms the incomprehensible into the comprehensible. Together, active agents communicate to structure the unknown, making events *sensable* (able to be sensed/perceived) and *sensible* (able to be understood). Sensemaking is both the social construction of cognitive frameworks and the application of those frameworks to equivocal stimuli. Sensemaking is driven by discrepancies between what we expect (based on assumptions and anticipations driven by cognitive frameworks) and what we encounter. Sensemaking processes involve discovery, interpretation, and creation. "To engage in sensemaking is to construct, filter, frame, create facticity, and render the subjective into something more tangible" (Weick, 1995, p. 14). According to Weick, sensemaking is retrospective: We make sense of our actions and situations after they occur. Weick (1995) defines *reality* as "an ongoing accomplishment that takes form when people make retrospective sense of the situations in which they find themselves and their creations" (p. 15).

Properties of sensemaking. Weick (1995) outlines seven fundamental properties of sensemaking. First, *sensemaking is grounded in identity construction.* Identities are constituted in interaction (see Chapter 11). We discover aspects of ourselves by observing ourselves in interaction, and we shift among definitions of self as we shift among interactants. Thus, we have multiple selves, and self and situation are mutually defining. Weick identifies three self needs: Self-enhancement (positive affect about the self); self-efficacy (perception of self as competent); and self-consistency (coherence and continuity). These needs impact individual sensemaking in organizational contexts. We know which self to enact by observing the behavior of others. The self that feels appropriate tells us what the situation means.

Second, *sensemaking is retrospective.* We attend to a stimulus to sensemaking after its occurrence. We act, then we reflect. Our current decision-making is impeded by unclear meaning of past events, and we make judgments based on outcomes. Third, *sensemaking is enactive of sensible environments.* Quite literally, we *make* that which is then *sensed.* Our individual and social actions create a large part of our environment. As we act, we create the material environments that become the constraints and opportunities we face. Thus, the organizational environment is created from interaction, to which each interactant has contributed. That environment then gets bracketed and punctuated, thus animated (made sensible). This socially created world then constrains our actions and orientations. Sensemaking can thus be seen as leading to institutionalization. (See Chapter 3 for an overview of institutional theory.)

Fourth, *sensemaking is social.* It occurs not just through subjectivity, but through intersubjectivity; not just through action, but through interaction. (Even our solitary actions are contingent upon the actions of others.) Thus, the meaning-making that is important is shared, rather than individual, and the cognition we must attend to is *social cognition.* Collective and coordinated action are key. Fifth, *sensemaking is ongoing.* It has no beginning or end, but rather is an ontological presumption. (See Chapter 7 for a discussion of ontology.) Intuition, or the *feel* of things guides our constructions of these ongoing flows

Sixth, *sensemaking is focused on and by extracted cues.* It is far easier to see sense that has been made than to see sensemaking in action. An extracted cue is that which is noticed, paid attention to, and embellished (interpreted). Like a seed, extracted cues are simple familiar structures from which we develop a larger sense of what is happening. These cues are intertwined with context. Context drives what is noticed and how it is then interpreted (embellished); this interpretation then, in turn, becomes context. These are tied together cognitively and become substantial (acted upon as real). Weick calls this process *bracketing.* Extracted cues evoke action, which then creates a material order in place of a presumed order. Weick (1995) cites a historical example of a military unit lost in a snowstorm in the Swiss Alps who maneuvered their way back to camp using a map of the Pyrenees that they mistakenly thought was of the Alps. Weick then explains: "Once people begin to act (enactment), they generate tangible outcomes (cues) in some context (social), and this helps them discover (retrospect) what is occurring (ongoing), what needs to be explained (plausibility) and what should be done next (identity enhancement)" (1995, p. 55). Finally, then, *sensemaking is driven by plausibility rather than accuracy*. Once the feeling of order, clarity, or rationality is achieved, retrospective sensemaking stops. Cues will continue to be extracted to enact a sensible/sensable environment and create the material reality that allows coordinated and collective action. Sensemaking is thus about coherence and reasonableness; it is about creating accounts that are socially acceptable and credible.

Weick's model of the process of organizing. Weick explains the process of organizing as a self-reflexive sequence of enactment, selection, and retention. In *enactment* processes, organizational members constitute their social environment through a process of bracketing (acting on interpretations). In *selection* processes, organizational members make sense of this enacted environment. In unequivocal information environments, sensemaking is accomplished through the application of assembly rules/recipes (pre-existing interpretive schemes). For equivocal information environments, they must employ communication cycles to discover plausible understandings of the environment. In *retention* processes, successful interpretive schemes are stored for future use. These interpretive schemes are stored in the form of *causal maps* that provide a link back to earlier phases of the model.

Applying Weick to the three-part model of organization in Chapter 1, *organizing* (O_1) can be seen as an ongoing process directed toward reducing the equivocality perceived in important enactments. *Organization* (O_2) results from natural selection —what works is retained. Change is constant and *organizations* (O_3) are never permanently organized ($O_{1\&2}$). Two Weickian concepts are of utmost importance for organizational communication. First, organizations are characterized by *loose coupling*: segmented sub-units (sub-assemblies or sub-systems) provide stability. These smaller units are linked together, but each has its own identity and autonomy and maintains its own adaptations. Second, organizing is accomplished by *social cognition*. Complex tasks are accomplished by *heedful interrelating*. Rather than merely repeating behaviors from previous experience, individuals link their actions together heedfully (carefully, critically, consistently, purposefully, attentively, studiously, vigilantly, conscientiously, pertinaciously) (Weick & Roberts, 1993). Thus, organizational intelligence is a set of complex patterns encoded by patterns of activation and inhibition among richly interpretively connected simple units, and is a process of collective mind. "This pattern of distributed representation explains the transindividual quality of collective mind. Portions of the envisaged system are known to all, but all of it is known to none" (Weick & Roberts, 1993, p. 365). Weick and Roberts (1993) provide copious examples of collective mind accomplished through heedful interrelating by examining the complex set of organizational tasks that operate a military aircraft carrier.

> The men in the tower (Air Department) monitor and give instructions to incoming and departing aircraft. Simultaneously, the men on the landing signal officers' platform do the same thing. They are backed up by the men in Air Operations who monitor and instruct aircraft at some distance from the ship. From the aviator's viewpoint, he receives integrated information about his current status and future behavior from an integrated source when, in reality, the several sources are relatively independent of one another and located in different parts of the ship.
>
> (Weick & Roberts, 1993, p. 362)

Weickian theory continues to have profound influence on organizational communication. In the 1980s, Weick's theories of organizing and sensemaking illustrated both the theoretic and practical value of an interpretive approach. Weick's theoretic constructions also enabled the field to conceptualize and explore connections among individual-, group-, and organizational-level processes.

Organizational communication as cultural performance. Pacanowsky and O'Donnell-Trujillo (1982, 1983) provided yet another important contribution at this time that united micro- and macro-processes and illustrated the value of an interpretive approach. Earlier approaches to organizational culture (from management studies) were prescriptive, focused in teaching executives and managers to impose strong, effective cultures. These top-down models were not widely embraced by communication scholars because of their values-engineering perspective. The three most commonly cited models were Deal and Kennedy's (1982) theory of cultural types, Peters and Waterman's (1982) treatise on excellence, and Schein's (1985) onion model. All models examined cultural features of financially successful organizations with high morale, advising how to impose such cultures to foster the development of organizationally desirable values and norms.

Pacanowsky and O'Donnell-Trujillo, on the other hand, focused on how the communication of organizational members both reflects and generates organizational culture, focusing not on how to impose or encourage cultural values and norms that foster task performance, but rather on the ways in which organizational culture *is performed* in interaction. They defined culture as an emergent, communication-centered, and naturally occurring interaction process. Cultural performances have four important features: *interactional* dialogues with multiple participants; *contextual*—situationally embedded in the very reality they bring to completion; *episodic*—nameable as distinct events (e.g., a budget meeting); and *improvisational*—loosely scripted. Through extensive field observations in a variety of organizations (including a car dealership and a police precinct), Pacanowsky and O'Donnell-Trujillo (1982, 1983) identified five types of cultural performance: ritual, passion, sociality, politics, and enculturation.

Rituals. Four types of rituals bring regularity into the culture. The car dealer's owner and general manager's *personal ritual* of delivering all the mail conveys to his employees that he is in touch with their activities. A patrol officer's *task ritual* of the standard question-answer sequence with a driver who has been pulled over (May I see your driver's license; do you know why I pulled you over; etc.) both establishes the exchange as polite and professional and allows the officer the opportunity to draw conclusions about the driver and make judgments about whether to issue a citation and what to issue. A weekly happy hour among factory supervisors is a *social ritual* that enhances their personal relationships and solidifies their cohesiveness. Finally, company picnics are examples of *organizational rituals* that establish and maintain norms, such as those of collegiality and friendly competition (e.g., manager vs. staff volleyball).

Passion. A second type of performance is *passion*, displaying metaphorical language. *Passionate repartee* is comprised of vocabularies, jargons, and other particular ways of speaking unique to the organization that signify salient features of organizational experience and enliven them. For example, in Pacanowsky and O'Donnell-Trujillo's (1983) study, "the Valley View Police do not deal with 'civilians,' but rather with … 'dirtbags, creeps, and maggots'—labels which serve as reminders that the 'negative element' is so much a part of the everyday experience of being a police officer" (p. 139).

From the managers who consider themselves "jungle fighters" or "coaches" or "nerve centers" to the secretaries who consider themselves "caged animals" or "team players" or "the *real* bosses," members of most organizational cultures frequently talk about their work in a way that transmutes the commonplace into passion. Thus, passions are not so much constituted in the organizational activities themselves but in the heightened descriptions of these activities.

(Pacanowsky & O'Donnell-Trujillo, 1983, p. 138)

Storytelling is a second form of passionate performance. *Personal stories* are those individuals tell about themselves, often accompanied by an underlying tone of one-upmanship, which embellish organizational entities. *Collegial stories* are narratives about other organizational members. These are not typically sanctioned by management, and they present the passions underlying the way the organization really works. *Corporate stories* represent the management ideology and are used to substantiate organizational procedures or pass on the unrecorded-but-managerial-favored customs of organizational life. Storytelling is important because it presents past events as being worthy of emulation (success stories) or deserving of caution (failure stories). Stories thus both constitute organizational passions and map future scenarios.

Sociality. Third, performances of *sociality* define social aspects of organizational life and establish smoothness in personal interaction. *Courtesies* set the politeness tone. *Pleasantries* (small talk) provide clues to others' working styles. *Sociabilities* (joking, gossiping) establish and maintain communicative norms. Finally, *privacies* establish relationships and cement norms of respect.

Politics. Fourth, *political* performances create systems of power, control, and influence, allowing people to show personal strength and cement allies. Organizational cultures are multidimensional, with numerous sub-cultures of self-interest. Political performances are aimed at influencing others. This can be done openly or surreptitiously—in private or public interaction—with forceful displays, favors, courtesies, or bargaining.

Enculturation. This fifth form of performance drives the process of becoming an organizational insider. Pacanowsky and O'Donnell-Trujillo (1983) distinguish *roles* and *ropes* learning through both formal and informal performances. Orientations, meetings, information sessions, and other such formal performances teach newcomers how to perform their roles. Informal performances, such as initiation rituals, also teach roles. *Ropes* knowledge is gained through commentary/meta-communication about other performances. For example, Pacanowsky and O'Donnell-Trujillo (1983) describe two senior police officers, in earshot of a rookie, engaged in "tough" talk about the possibility of engaging in physical altercation with a citizen during a call they had made the night before. When the rookie commented about one of the officers acting on the talk, the other officer quickly explained that neither of the seasoned officers would have actually let it come to that because they had the situation under control.

We take [the senior officer's] interaction with [the rookie] as a unique enculturation performance, a metacommunicative commentary that instructs [the rookie] in how he should interpret the prior performance … not as an endorsement of fighting but [as] backstage "play."

(Pacanowsky & O'Donnell-Trujillo, 1983, p. 145)

The Late 1980s to 1990s: Critical and Naturalistic Turns

The field's interpretive turn ushered in the *postmodern era*. Postmodernity is a term used broadly to describe cultural developments after the 1960s. In its application to organizational communication, the term refers to a rejection of the received view, which saw organizational phenomena as natural entities waiting for our discovery. Postmodern theory focuses on the ways in which organizational realities are constituted by interaction, and are thus multiple truths "competing for legitimacy" (Mease, 2017, p. 5). Postmodernists reject the idea that any explanation of human social life can be universally applied. Two major scholars had the most profound influence on postmodern thought in organizational communication: Jacques Derrida and Michel Foucault. (See Mease, 2017, for a full treatment of the historical influences on postmodernism in organizational communication.)

From Derrida, we gain *deconstruction*, a method of analyzing text by examining meaning as it emerges between words and signs rather than in them. The meaning of a word or sign is neither static nor fully apprehended, as it is found only in an infinite chain of reference to other words and signs. Words only gain meaning through *différance*, or juxtaposition. Further, no pair of words is free of a hierarchy of dominance. Inverting the hierarchy of a pair (e.g., rationality/emotion to emotion/rationality) reveals the power structure. From Lyotard, we gain the concept of *master narratives*—broad social structures of meaning that drive the sensemaking in local communities. Mutual understanding of local communities according to their own, and not a foreign, narrative is the foundation of ethical interpretation.

Foucault is arguably the most influential figure in organizational communication critical theory. His *history of the present* explores the relations between the present and the past. *Historical moments* are examined for their potential to create alternative, and more desirable, futures. Organizational communication scholars most commonly apply his ideas about discourse and power. First, discourse, which is inherently characterized by tension and contradiction, constrains and enables sensemaking in ways that perpetuate power structures. Second, power is defined as knowledge because a society's powerful create its knowledge (which reinforces their power). Further, power is a group phenomenon—it functions when the knowledge created is accepted by a group as truth. Yet, that knowledge generally serves the interests of the powerful.

Hence, the concept of *power* became increasingly important to organizational communication scholars throughout the 1980s as interpretivist examinations of organizational culture and identification made clear the struggle over meaning-creation between dominant and non-dominant groups. While rhetorical and critical-interpretivist theory and research was ongoing in organizational communication from its inception, and significant contributions were made throughout the 1980s, it was not until the early 1990s that the field experienced another paradigmatic turn, as critical approaches began to populate the literature more intensely. Critical theory in organizational communication grew from interpretivism. Broadly, the term *critical approach* refers to an "interdisciplinary body of theory and research that conceives of organizations as dynamic sites of control and resistance" (Mumby, 2008, p. 1). Critical theorists focus on day-to-day interaction, particularly language use and micro-practices, to examine the processes of power and resistance (see Chapter 12) in organizing. Organizations are viewed as political sites that are socially constructed and communicatively accomplished, with deep societal structures of dominance reproduced in daily interaction.

Like interpretivists, critical-interpretivists assume that reality is socially co-created and use methods of disciplined subjectivity to conduct research. Further, however, critical theorists examine the ways in which dominant societal groups create realities that subjugate the realities of other groups. The most prominent organizational communication scholars in the early days of the critical theory movement were Deetz (1982, 1987, 1988) and Mumby (1987, 1988; Deetz & Mumby, 1990). Feminist theory was also influential in furthering the development of critical theory in organizational communication (see Buzzanell, 1994, and Chapter 13 in this volume). Critical approaches to the democratization of work also took center stage; for example, Cheney's (1999) analyses of worker cooperatives that construct cooperative economies by reifying ideologies of participation to accomplish democratic organizing and subvert the hegemony of traditional bureaucracy. (See Chapter 7 for a review of organizational communication approaches to worker participation in this same era.)

Fundamentals of critical organizational communication theory. Critical theories of organizational communication center on four concepts: ideology, hegemony, naturalization, and praxis. First, *ideology* structures and controls thoughts and interpretations of reality, so that assumptions are controlled by a dominant class without question. Second, *hegemony* captures the processes by which dominated group members consent to their domination by their own complicit engagement in political, cultural, and economic ideologies that enforce the class structure. Third, examining processes of *naturalization* reveals how these hierarchical power relationships are reified—made concrete through action and social practices and then accepted as normal and natural. Finally, *praxis* requires some action be taken to resist or reverse the hegemonic system and emancipate the dominated class, or at least some members of it, from its hold.

> Organizations, bureaucratic or otherwise, are (arbitrary) sociohistorical creations made to *seem* natural and normal through discourse; are the products of political actions that privilege some interests and sacrifice others; are a key resource for perpetuating sociopolitical power inequalities; and are replete with tensions and contradictions that create a potential for transformation, democratization, and emancipation.
>
> (Conrad & Sollitto, 2017, pp. 11–12, emphasis in original)

Although previous approaches to organizational communication held the general goal of representing aspects of the social world, critical theorists sought to move beyond representation to be active agents of reform and change.

Historical roots. One of the strongest influences on critical theory in organizational communication is the work of Karl Marx, particularly his early work as it was influenced by Georg Hegel and Immanuel Kant. Marx saw the world as humanly created, then reified and seen as objective. Further, he maintained that this process of objectification and reification serves as a source of alienation for the individual. His later works developed a more realist view and materialist view of the social world. Marx argued that the mode and means of production (society's economic substructure) profoundly influences culture and politics (superstructure factors). While the *bourgeoisie* control the modes and means of production; the *proletariat* merely engage in production for wages. According to Marx, these substructure and superstructure processes create alienation and thus require critique.

Another influence on critical theory in organizational communication is the work generated by the *Frankfurt School*, a community of social theorists and philosophers loosely associated with the Institute for Social Research at the Goethe University Frankfurt. The group drew together between WWI and WWII and consisted largely of neo-Marxists who concentrated on critiquing existing oppressive political systems (capitalist, fascist, or communist), developing theory to explain the proliferation of postindustrial capitalist societies and critique Soviet socialism in an effort to develop alternative systems. They shared their commitment to Hegelian Marxism and the pursuit of similar questions. Frankfurt scholars may be thought of more as a professional association than a school of thought or political group. In addition to Hegel and Marx, they drew upon Kant, Freud, and Weber, among others. Frankfurt scholars were concerned with social change. They rejected positivism and determinism, emphasizing dialectic and contradiction as endemic to social reality. Critical theorists in the Frankfurt School also emphasized what they called *revolutionary praxis* that included the central concepts of totality, consciousness, alienation, and critique.

Mumby on narrative and ideology. Mumby (1987) reveals narrative as a meaning formation carrying dominant ideology and reproducing organizational power structures in everyday practice. A political treatment of narrative focuses on the complex and independent relationships among narrative, power, and ideology.

> Because of their embeddedness in the everyday practices of organizations, narratives are not easily perceived as legitimating devices—they often articulate an organizational reality that is accepted as "the natural order of things." By adopting a political reading of narrative, however, it is possible to demonstrate that story-telling is not a simple representing of a pre-existing reality, but is rather a politically motivated production of a certain way of perceiving the world which privileges certain interests over others.
>
> (Mumby, 1987, p. 114)

A political treatment of narrative draws attention to the relationship between narrative structure and processes of interpretation to focus on the process by which dominant meaning systems arise. Narratives work in this way by creating a *fit* between the narrative and the individual's world-as-experienced (i.e., naturalization). Yet, narratives can also delegitimize dominant meaning systems. Critical-interpretive theory focuses not only on dominance but on the dialectic of dominance and resistance (see Chapter 12).

In a critical analysis, power is not conceived of as possessed by individuals nor as a relation among individuals; power is both a medium and product of organizational structuring—a means of control. This depends on the concept of duality of structure (see Chapter 3): structure as both the medium and outcome of social practice. "At the heart of both domination and power lies the transformative capacity of human action" (Mumby, 1987, p. 117). Some organizational members are privileged with access to resources necessary to produce and reproduce certain relations of power. To understand this dynamic, the operation of ideology must be explored.

Ideology constructs consciousness (subjectivity) to articulate and legitimate certain forms of social reality. According to Mumby (1987), ideology is the legitimized dominant system of reality that directs our recognition of what exists (reality), what is good (values), and what is possible (agency). "Ideology is materially grounded in the organized practices of social actors" (p. 119).

Narrative, then, is a material social practice that produces, maintains, and reproduces ideological meaning formations. Narrative is a signifying system that functions to articulate a social reality acceptable by all organizational groups regardless of their position in the hierarchy. Mumby rests on Giddens' three principal ideological functions: Representation of sectional interests as universal; denial (or transmutation) of contradictions; and naturalization of the present through reification (e.g., corner offices).

Mumby (1987) adds a fourth function of ideology. Ideology is a means of control, expressed through hegemony. Hegemony is the ability of one class to articulate the interests of other social groups to its own, producing a *collective will* of self-identification with hegemonic forms. With hegemony, ideology functions as control through active consent, and the dominated are complicit in their own domination.

Mumby demonstrates his approach with an analysis of a famous organizational story that had been previously analyzed in a descriptive study of the common functions of and themes in organizational stories. The story, used repeatedly in orientation and training sessions at IBM, is of a young, petite woman working at the booth checking identification credentials of all who enter. IBM CEO Watson attempts to enter without his ID badge. Although she knows who he is, she refuses his entry. His response is to commend her for following the rules. Mumby's critical analysis examines all four functions of ideology. We will take each in turn.

Function 1: Representing the corporate interest. The story makes *adherence to rules* a corporate structure that applies to all groups. However, a more critical analysis shows that the story functions to further the interests of the corporate elite. The formal system of rules is created by that elite for the benefit of that elite.

Function 2: Denying/transmuting contradictions. Watson is depicted as subject to corporate rules just the same as any other employee. Again, the moral of the story is that everyone should follow the rules, regardless of rank. Yet, a critical analysis notes that Watson is not an ordinary human being. What makes this story powerful is that he is depicted as such. Watson actually is not subject to the corporate rules the same way as other employees—his being so in the story thus denies/transmutes the divide between the elite group and the groups they dominate. Hence, the story actually underscores Watson as dominant by making him submissive.

Function 3: Reification. Because it is dramatic and easy to recall, a story exemplifies and animates some aspect of the culture in which the story is set. The ongoing process of retelling it makes the events of the story taken-for-granted. Using sex-role stereotypes to sharpen the status difference between the two characters, the story caricaturizes both of those characters. The story is then able to demonstrate rules as having an importance all their own. Rules are enforced, and followed, because they exist. The rule itself is never questioned, but is taken as the natural order.

Function 4: Control. The story then functions to control organizational members by dramatizing hegemony: The worldview articulated by the ruling elite has been actively taken up and pursued by a subordinate group member. The impact in the story is that the rules are enforced from the bottom up, rather than from the top down—conveying the legitimacy and appropriateness of IBM's organizational structure and suggesting that employees are prepared to go to extreme lengths to protect that structure. The hegemonic process is revealed in the subordinate group's internalization of the elites' rules.

Mumby's conclusions. "The power structure in an organization is by no means unitary, and its ongoing structuring is dependent on this complex system of discursive formations that continually creates and re-creates the interdependent and interlocked ideological meaning formations in an organization" (Mumby, 1987, p. 125). Organizational narrative can be viewed politically because it can both sustain and subvert the underlying logic of an organization's power structure. Organizational narratives instantiate and are instantiated by deep structure power relations—they help to determine the way organizational practices are interpreted. Narratives do not simply inform organizational members, they constitute the organizational consciousness (create organizational rationality). Organizational narratives are produced by and reproduce ideological meaning formations and power relations—positioning subjects in the historical/institutional contexts of the material conditions of their existence. Narratives are an expression of the material conditions of the socio-economic context and reproduce these material conditions.

The influence of the naturalistic paradigm. In the 1990s, organizational communication scholars continued to be heavily influenced by advancements from other disciplines, most notably the naturalistic paradigm (e.g., Lincoln & Guba, 1985) and grounded theory (Glaser & Strauss, 1967). The *naturalistic paradigm* requires that we study things in their natural settings, interpreting phenomena according to the meanings people bring to them. *Grounded theory* is an intensive process of building theory inductively from naturalistic data. For example, the concept of *concertive control* (see Barker, 1993) was developed to explain how, through the process of identification, organizational members, especially those in self-managed teams, internalize organizational values and norms to self-discipline their actions in increasingly oppressive ways (see Chapters 7, 11, and 12). The first theories of the communicative constitution of organization (see Chapter 3) began to appear. Other trends in research topics included teamwork, globalization, leadership, self-organizing systems, organizational democracy, stories, metaphors, gender, feminist theory, conflict, technology, identity, race, diversity, work–life balance, and ethics.

The influence of naturalistic theory and methods (e.g., Lincoln & Guba, 1985) was seen most visibly in the development of the *bona fide groups* perspective (Putnam & Stohl, 1990). While group communication is itself a sub-discipline of Communication, it has significant overlap with organizational communication (see Chapter 15). The conceptual progress made by interpretive approaches in the 1980s made it increasingly apparent that contextual factors influence group and organizational communication functions far more profoundly than previous perspectives had accounted for. Hence, the bona fide groups (groups in context) model argued that the study of naturally occurring (or naturalistic) groups should replace the study of laboratory or classroom groups assembled solely for the purpose of research. Putnam and Stohl (1990) argued that bona fide groups have several characteristics that laboratory groups do not, and that these features are essential to the study of their communication: shifting memberships, permeable boundaries, multiple group memberships, and high interdependence with these and other features of their context. This is but one example of the shift in the 1990s to naturalistic research settings across the field of organizational communication.

Approaches to Communication and Organization

The period from organizational communication's birth in the late 1960s to the turn of the 21st century saw tremendous shifts in paradigm, with concomitant changes in how scholars approach communication and organization. While messages and meanings continued to be important to organizational communication scholars, a more consistent underlying presumption of communication as constitutive was well-developed by 2000. Early structural-functionalist theorizing cast organizations (O_3) as containers in which communication occurred, without much attention to the interplay between those processes (O_1) and the structuring of organization (O_2, O_3). With the advent of Weickian and interpretivist theory in the early 1980s, a process (O_1) orientation became dominant. Critical theory then brought an era that examined organizational structures (O_2) of domination, as well as illustrating the ways that communication practices perpetuate those structures—revealing the communication-organization dynamic in mutually reflexive form. By 2000, the idea that communication and organization constitute one another was a fairly uncontroversial idea—for many an unquestioned assumption.

Recommended Supplementary Readings

Barker, J. R. (1993). Tightening the iron cage: Concertive control in self-managing teams. *Administrative Science Quarterly, 38*(3), 408–437.

Analysis of this case study evolved to create concertive control theory. The study is good example of how critical-interpretive research can bring unique insight to organizational communication in situ.

Dailey, S. L., & Browning, L. (2014). Retelling stories in organizations: Understanding the functions of narrative repetition. *Academy of Management Review, 39*(1), 22–43.

This article is an exemplary illustration of the continuing influence of the organizational culture foundations laid in the 1980s.

Krone, K. (2005). Trends in organizational communication research: Sustaining the discipline, sustaining ourselves. *Communication Studies, 56*(1), 95–105.

This article is the text of a speech, which provides a first-person account of the field.

Martin, J., Feldman, M. S., Hatch, M. J., & Sitkin, S. B. (1983). The uniqueness paradox in organizational stories. *Administrative Science Quarterly, 28*(3), 438–453.

Mumby, D. K. (1987). The political function of narrative in organizations. *Communication Monographs, 54*(2), 113–127.

These articles can be read as companion pieces. Martin et al. is an interpretation of the IBM story, and Mumby re-examines the analysis with critical theory. Reading them together reveals the power of a critical lens.

Pacanowsky, M. E., & O'Donnell-Trujillo, N. (1983). Organizational communication as cultural performance. *Communication Monographs, 50*(1), 126–147.

Representing one of the earliest programs of interpretive research in organizational communication, this article is a perfect example of using data to derive theory. The excerpts of data provided are compelling and interesting.

Putnam, L. L. (1982). Paradigms for organizational communication research: An overview and synthesis. *Western Journal of Speech Communication, 46*(2), 192–206.

In this early explanation of the distinctions among theoretical paradigms, Putnam clearly explains the underlying dimensions differentiating positivism/functionalism, interpretivism, and critical-interpretivism.

Putnam, L. L. (1983). The interpretive perspective: An alternative to functionalism. In L. L. Putnam & M. Pacanowsky (Eds.), *Communication and organizations: An interpretive approach* (pp. 31–54). Newbury Park, CA: SAGE.

Traditionally used as a first reading on interpretivism, this chapter clearly lays out the problems posed by functionalism and the ways an interpretive approach provides conceptual advantages.

Weick, K. E. (1993). The collapse of sensemaking in organizations: The Mann Gulch disaster. *Administrative Science Quarterly*, 38(4), 628–652.
One of many case studies written by Weick, this analyzes sensemaking and organizational decision-making during the Mann Gulch fire disaster, resulting in wide-scale loss of life among the firefighters. Weick examines disintegration of role structure and sensemaking and discusses resilience that makes groups less vulnerable.

Important Concepts: Define and Discuss

Variable-analytic research
Structural functionalism
Positivism
Systems theory principles
Interpretivism and its roots
Organizational communication as cultural performance
Postmodernism
Ideology
Hegemony
Naturalization
Praxis
The naturalistic paradigm

Discussion Questions

1. Consider the paradigmatic shifts in the field from 1970 to 2000. Can you identify shifts in society and organizational phenomena that may be connected?
2. Identify an organizational system and give examples of its properties (nonsummativity, equifinality, openness, etc.).
3. Think of a time when you and coworkers were faced with a new or confusing situation. Apply Weick's theory of sensemaking to your subsequent interactions. Can you identify the enactment-selection-retention cycle?
4. How is critical theory in organizational communication an expansion of interpretivism?

Practitioners' Corner

It falls to a communication professional to figure out how to strategically communicate within and among groups, and how to guide that group in its communication strategy to external stakeholders. Perhaps the most important body of theory in this chapter for the communication practitioner is Weick's theory of organization. Communication professionals are often tasked with designing strategies that meet the need for stakeholders to act in concert in a context of equivocal environments and diverse views of the problems at hand.

All organizational action depends on processes of social sensemaking. Communication professionals are positioned to facilitate processes of problem analysis and solution-creation engaging Weickian concepts. Through a purposeful process explicitly guiding a group through dialogue that explicates the seven properties of sensemaking, a skilled facilitator can provide opportunities for mutual understanding. As you will learn in Chapter 15, thorough problem analysis is a crucial function for group problem-solving. Working relationships and organizational resilience improve when mutual understandings are achieved. A good understanding of Weickian theory and how to apply it is of great utility for a communication practitioner. Reading Weickian case studies (e.g., the 1993 Mann Gulch article in the Recommended Supplementary Readings list) is highly recommended. While sensemaking is retrospective, a purposeful sensemaking process that actively engages Weickian concepts provides organizational learning to prevent repetition of mistakes and improve organizational resilience.

For example, imagine you work as a communication director for a financial services organization. You are tasked with leading both internal and external communication. The company is about to launch a new online dashboard for its clients that will allow easier access to account information and more immediate customer-initiated changes to accounts. Just as the product is to be launched, a new federal regulation for data security is announced that will fundamentally alter the product and inevitably delay the rollout, as a redesign would be necessary to make the product compliant with the new law. No one expected the bill to be passed. The teaser advertising has already been made public, and customer service representatives have promised the opportunity to existing customers. The product is particularly attractive to high-balance account-holders, some of whom have previously expressed frustration about the existing online portal. Your management team fears they will lose their most valuable customers as a result of any delay. The team responsible for regulatory compliance are scratching their heads about how to provide the ease offered the clients while maintaining compliance with the new regulation. You have been tasked to assign people on your team to bring internal stakeholders to the table to discuss the problem and assign others to design an external communication strategy.

Let's examine the external communication problem first. Like all organizational crises, the stakes are high for the organization's PR team. Yet, from a Weickian perspective, the external communication demands are unequivocal. While the situation itself is fraught with ambiguity, how to communicate about it to clients is not. First, the communication problem is straightforward: Customers will be disappointed in the delay and potential cancellation of the product. Potential customers may be scared away. Second, the consequences are clear: A good strategy will keep customers and attract new ones. Third, and most importantly, sound principles for such communication are standard in the field—this is not a new kind of problem. These principles, embedded in PR practice, exist as Weickian causal maps. Knowing this, you assign people from your team who are well-versed in communicating unexpected and unwanted change to clients and who are well-versed in marketing to attract new business. Employing assembly rules, you select individuals who have performed well on such tasks in the past. These individuals will follow proven principles, informing customers of a delay, communicating the situation as it evolves, and delivering advertising sensitive to this crisis. Depending on the outcome, your strategy will either perpetuate those causal maps or create new ones through naturally occurring processes of retrospective sensemaking.

The internal problem-solving here is another story. This is an equivocal information environment. Do the new requirements actually protect data security? Is it possible to alter the product to be compliant, or is there too much contradiction between customer freedom and data control? Will the new law be enforced or challenged? Should we just cancel the project? Should we delay to see how things play out? Should we work on alteration of the product?

The various internal stakeholder groups will naturally employ communication cycles to discover plausible understandings of the environment. Data security programmers are immobile—caught up in complaining to one another about the stupidity of the regulations, enacted by "dinosaurs who don't know how the Internet actually works." The client relations team is divided—some want something to deliver to clients to keep them, while others point out that the company's competitors whose existing online portals are suddenly noncompliant have much larger problems and won't attract customers away. The legal team is convinced the law will be challenged successfully by competitors whose online portals were used as benchmarks in the design process. The web designers have jumped the gun and are already working on changing the dashboard's access protocols to get ahead of the competition—poorly, because they are not communicating with the data security programmers.

Your task is to get these groups communicating thoughtfully with one another in a purposeful process of sensemaking to arrive at the most plausible understanding of the current status and where to go from there. Let's examine the seven properties of sensemaking and how they are playing out here.

- *Sensemaking is grounded in identity construction.* Note how each of these groups is engaging in identity-based sensemaking, rooted in their self-preservation and revealing the cultures of their various professions.
- *Sensemaking is retrospective.* All are trying to get their heads around, in different ways, the unexpected turn of events.
- *Sensemaking is enactive of sensible environments.* All are trying to make sense of what comes next.
- *Sensemaking is social.* All of this is taking place through conversations within the groups. Your challenge is to create an opportunity for dialogue among the groups.
- *Sensemaking is ongoing.* No matter what you do, people will continue in their own sensemaking processes. A facilitated dialogue with a focus on mutual goals can provide far better decision-making capability.
- *Sensemaking is focused on and by extracted cues.* Note how each group is focusing on different cues unique to their interests and expertise. A dialogue among them brings information about cues they hadn't extracted, changing their overall understanding.
- *Sensemaking is driven by plausibility rather than accuracy.* In the end, the strategy enacted will be that which makes the most sense to the decision-makers at the executive level—regardless of what any individual stakeholder group feels is best. Your challenge is to unearth all the potentially plausible solutions from an open dialogue.

Such a process of Weickian *enactment* fills in information gaps, provides opportunities for learning, and improves organizational resilience. When a decision is made based on the *selection* of the most plausible sense made, whatever happens will be preserved in the organizational causal map (*retention*), to provide interpretive schemes and assembly rules evoked by similar occurrences in the future.

References

Allen, M. W., Gotcher, J. M., & Seibert, J. H. (1993). A decade of organizational communication research: Journal articles 1980–1991. *Annals of the International Communication Association,* 16(1), 252–330. doi:10.1080/23808985.1993.11678856.

Barker, J. R. (1993). Tightening the iron cage: Concertive control in self-managing teams. *Administrative Science Quarterly, 38*(3), 408–437. doi:10.2307/2393374.

Buzzanell, P. M. (1994). Gaining a voice: Feminist organizational communication theorizing. *Management Communication Quarterly, 7*(4), 339–383. doi:10.1177/0893318994007004001.

Cheney, G. (1999). *Values at work: Employee participation meets market pressure at Mondragón.* Ithaca, NY: Cornell University Press.

Conrad, C., & Sollitto, M. (2017). History of organizational communication. In C. R. Scott & L. Lewis (Eds.), *The international encyclopedia of organizational communication* (online edition). Hoboken, NJ: Wiley-Blackwell. doi:10.1002/9781118955567.wbieoc097.

Contractor, N. S. (1994). Self-organizing systems perspective in the study of organizational communication. In B. Kovacic (Ed.), *New approaches to organizational communication* (pp. 39–66). Albany, NY: State University of New York Press.

Contractor, N. S., & Seibold, D. R. (1993). Theoretical frameworks for the study of structuring processes in group decision support systems. *Human Communication Research, 19*(4), 528–563. doi:10.1111/j.1468-2958.1993.tb00312.x.

Deal, T. E. and Kennedy, A. A. (1982). *Corporate cultures: The rites and rituals of corporate life.* Reading, MA: Addison Wesley.

Deetz, S. (1982). Critical interpretive research in organizational communication. *Western Journal of Speech Communication, 46*(2), 131–149. doi:10.1080/10570318209374073.

Deetz, S. (1987). Stories, accounts, and organizational power. *Association of Communication Administration Bulletin, 61*(1), 36–41.

Deetz, S. (1988). Cultural studies: Studying meaning and action in organizations. In J. Anderson (Ed.), *Communication yearbook 11* (pp. 335–345). Thousand Oaks, CA: SAGE.

Deetz, S., & Mumby, D. K. (1990). Power, discourse, & the workplace: Reclaiming the critical tradition. In James Anderson (Ed.), *Communication yearbook 13* (pp. 18–47). Newbury Park, CA: SAGE.

Eisenberg, E. M. (1984). Ambiguity as strategy in organizational communication. *Communication Monographs, 51*(3), 227–242. doi:10.1080/03637758409390197.

Glaser, B. G., & Strauss, A. L. (1967). *The discovery of grounded theory: Strategies for qualitative research.* Chicago, IL: Aldine.

Goldhaber, G. M. (2002). Communication audits in the age of the internet. *Management Communication Quarterly, 15*(3), 451–457. doi:10.1177/0893318902153007.

Hawes, L. C. (1974). Social collectivities as communication: Perspective on organizational behavior. *Quarterly Journal of Speech, 60,* 497–502. doi:10.1080/00335637409383259.

Katz, D., & Kahn, R. (1978). *The social psychology of organizations* (2nd ed.). New York: John Wiley.

Krone, K. (2005). Trends in organizational communication research: Sustaining the discipline, sustaining ourselves. *Communication Studies, 56*(1), 95–105. doi:10.1080/0008957042000332269.

Lai, C., & Lin, S. H. (2017). Systems theory. In C. R. Scott & L. Lewis (Eds.), *The international encyclopedia of organizational communication* (online edition). Hoboken, NJ: Wiley-Blackwell. doi:10.1002/9781118955567.wbieoc203.

Lincoln, Y. S., & Guba, E. G. (1985). *Naturalistic inquiry.* Beverly Hills, CA: SAGE.

Luhmann, N. (1995). *Social systems.* Stanford, CA: Stanford University Press.

Mead, G. H., & Morris, C. W. (1934). *Mind, self & society from the standpoint of a social behaviorist.* Chicago, IL: University of Chicago Press.

Mease, J. J. (2017). Postmodern/poststructural approaches. In C. R. Scott & L. Lewis (Eds.), *The international encyclopedia of organizational communication* (online edition). Hoboken, NJ: Wiley-Blackwell. doi:10.1002/9781118955567.wbieoc167.

Mumby, D. K. (1987). The political function of narrative in organizations. *Communication Monographs, 54*(2), 113–127. doi:10.1080/03637758709390221.

Mumby, D. K. (1988). *Communication and power in organizations: Discourse, ideology, and domination.* Norwood, NJ: Ablex.

Mumby, D. K. (2008). Organizational communication: Critical approaches. In W. Donsbach (Ed.), *International encyclopedia of communication* (online edition). Hoboken, NJ: Wiley-Blackwell. doi:10.1002/9781405186407.wbieco019.

Pacanowsky, M. E., & O'Donnell-Trujillo, N. (1982). Communication and organizational cultures. *Western Journal of Speech Communication, 46*(1), 115–130. doi:10.1080/10570318209374072.

Pacanowsky, M. E., & O'Donnell-Trujillo, N. (1983). Organizational communication as cultural performance. *Communication Monographs, 50*(1), 126–147. doi:10.1080/03637758309390158.

Pacanowsky, M. E., & Putnam, L. L. (Eds.). (1982). Interpretive approaches to the study of organizational communication. *Western Journal of Speech Communication, 46*(2), 114–207. doi:10.1080/10570318209374071.

Peters, T. J., & Waterman, R. H. (1982). *In search of excellence: Lessons from America's best-run companies*. New York, NY: Harper & Row.

Putnam, L. L. (1982). Paradigms for organizational communication research: An overview and synthesis. *Western Journal of Speech Communication, 46*(2), 192–206. doi:10.1080/10570318209374077.

Putnam, L. L. (1983). The interpretive perspective: An alternative to functionalism. In L. L. Putnam & M. E. Pacanowsky (Eds.), *Communication and organizations: An interpretive approach* (pp. 31–54). Newbury Park, CA: SAGE.

Putnam, L. L., & M. Pacanowsky, M. E. (Eds.). (1983). *Communication and organizations: An interpretive approach*. Newbury Park, CA: SAGE.

Putnam, L. L., & Stohl, C. (1990). Bona fide groups: A reconceptualization of groups in context, *Communication Studies, 41*(3), 248–265. doi:10.1080/10510979009368307.

Schein, E. H. (1985). *Organizational culture and leadership*. San Francisco, CA: Jossey-Bass

Smith, R. C. (1993, May). *Images of organizational communication: Root-metaphors of the organization-communication relation*. Paper presented to the Organizational Communication Division at the International Communication Association Convention, Washington, D.C.

von Bertalanffy, L. (1968). *General system theory: Foundations, development, applications*. New York, NY: George Braziller.

Weick, K. E. (1979). *The social psychology of organizing* (2nd ed.). Redding, MA: Addison-Wesley.

Weick, K. E. (1995). *Sensemaking in organizations*. Thousand Oaks, CA: SAGE.

Weick, K. E., & Roberts, K.H. (1993). Collective mind in organizations: Heedful interrelating on flight decks. *Administrative Science Quarterly, 38*(3), 357–381. doi:10.2307/2393372.

3 Developments in the 21st Century

Anne M. Nicotera

This chapter provides an overview of developments in the field from the late 1990s to the present, including both theoretical shifts and trends in research topics. It is difficult to draw distinct demarcations for when particular threads of theory and research begin, as current theoretic developments will have roots that are decades, if not centuries, old. Recall Krone's (2005) observation that our field continually revisits and develops established lines of theory and research. The 21st century is clearly marked, however, by the increasing interdisciplinarity; the discursive turn; the maturation of structurational approaches; the development of theory in a genre that has come to be known as communicative constitution of organization (CCO); and increased attention to institutional theory. In this contemporary period, all three conceptual expressions of organization (O_1, O_2, O_3) are explicitly present in organizational communication theorizing.

At the turn of the century, organizational communication scholars engaged in self-reflection. Three major developments characterize this period. First, positivist, interpretivist, and critical approaches had been pursued in separate domains, with a great deal of debate and cross-critique. Now, scholars from across the paradigms (positivism/functionalism, interpretivism, and critical) began discussions in earnest to find common ground (e.g., Corman & Poole, 2000). Debates about the relative merits of one perspective over the others were put aside in favor of celebrating the advantages of their diversity. Rather than dispute whose philosophy was superior, the field settled into a healthy pluralism that recognizes each for its own merits—without demanding that any paradigm meet the philosophical demands of the others (see Chapter 4). The literature became more integrated, as scholars increasingly relied on research generated by paradigms other than their own. Further, rather than being pressured to adhere to a paradigm as a career choice, selection of perspective became more project-based. Scholars began to appropriate concepts and techniques from one perspective to another, as well as to integrate the perspectives in their research programs and in multi-methodological projects.

Second, the multidisciplinary and international network known as *organizational studies* expanded. Organizational communication scholars have become increasingly more involved with scholars from other disciplines, such as management, sociology, organizational behavior, organizational theory, and industrial psychology, through participation in conferences, professional associations (e.g., the European Group on Organizational Studies), and multidisciplinary journals (e.g., *Organization Studies*). Due to this interdisciplinary growth, structuration and CCO flourished during this period. (See below for details on each of these traditions.) Adding to an already rich and diverse set of phenomena studied in the field, this era saw growing interest in research and theoretical development in the following topics and concepts: Paradox, restructuring, institutions, terrorism, virtual organizing, framing, alternative organizations, diversity, corporate social responsibility, wellness, work–life balance, and spirituality. Studies of leadership, feminist organizing, ecological perspectives, participation, and democracy also saw surges in development, with particularly strong interest in agency and materiality.

Perhaps the most important development of this period was the dawn of discourse studies in the field, owing to a linguistic turn across the social sciences. *Discourse* is difficult to define, but scholars are consistent in their assumptions that discourse involves the production, use, processes, and consequences of language from the situated context of interaction to the broader and enduring level of social thought and ideology. Organizational communication scholars with a discourse approach can focus on language itself, examining meaning-making as a linguistic process with contradictions and hidden implications (O_1). Alternatively, they may examine language-in-use, studying language in everyday interactions to examine meaning-creation and the reproduction of cultural structures (O_2). A third approach is to examine the production of texts (O_3), with particular attention to research itself (Connaughton, Linabary & Yakova, 2017). Across approaches, discourse is assumed to produce reality, social structures, and collectives (organizations).

The 2000s: The Discursive Turn

Fairhurst and Putnam (2004) explain that the framing of organizations as discursive constructions operates as three particular orientations: organizations as objects reflected in discourse; organizations in perpetual states of becoming; or organizations as grounded in action. (These might be argued to correspond to O_3, O_1, and O_2, respectively.) First, it is important to note Fairhurst and Putnam's (2004) contention that communication and discourse are different things. Discourse, as a medium for social interaction, maintains a particular language emphasis distinguishing it from *communication*. *Discourse* refers not only to talk and social texts but also to enduring systems of thought. For the sake of this distinction here, with a lower-case "d," *discourse* is activity; whereas with an upper-case "D," *Discourse(s)* is an enduring set of broad social structures and processes.

An *organization as object* orientation to the study of organizations as discursive constructions casts the organization as stable and pre-existing, with discursive features or outcomes (artifacts). D/discourse, then, is produced by and reflective of organization. The implications include an implicit container metaphor, a focus on product rather than process of social construction, and a materialist reification of the organization (Fairhurst & Putnam, 2004). With the object orientation, "neither discourse (the microactivity of actors), nor organization (the macro) are problematized in terms of each other" (Fairhurst & Putnam, 2004, p. 12). Here, we clearly see a treatment of organization as entity (O_3).

In contrast, the *organization as becoming* orientation foregrounds agency and in so doing loses a clear understanding of structure. This orientation explicitly focuses on discourse as constitutive of organizing. "The becoming perspective not only treats discourse as language in use but it also focuses on Discourses that reside in power/ knowledge systems" (Fairhurst & Putnam, 2004, p. 14). Even so, this orientation fragments and obscures the whole. Enduring structures are underemphasized, and a clear view of them is lost. With the emphasis on human action and processes of agency, an O_1 orientation is clear.

The third orientation sees *organization as grounded in action*. Whereas an *object* perspective foregrounds structure at the expense of human agency and a *becoming* perspective foregrounds agency at the expense of structure, an *action* perspective "treats action and structure as mutually constitutive" (Fairhurst & Putnam, 2004, p. 16). In so doing, the operation of language-in-use is privileged as the most powerful explanation of the relationship between discourse and Discourse(s). Here, "the 'organization' emerges from associations among human actors and objects whose institutional origins carry the traces of past organizing" (p. 18). With the grounded orientation, human agency is conceived "from within … an active component of structure" (p. 19). Here, the emergence of structure is an obvious O_2 orientation. Even so, according to Fairhurst and Putnam (2004), many scholars observe a bias privileging action over structure in the focus on social practice and language-in-use. A chief concern is that the episodic view of social practice may lead researchers to overlook patterns across episodes (Fairhurst and Putnam, 2004). These do, however, seem to be language games that seek to differentiate the operation of society from the operation of our research of it. Given the reality that our research is part and parcel of the society it purports to study, such differentiation is itself a discursive creation. See also Putnam and Fairhurst (2015) for a discussion of subsequent implications of these three orientations and their connections with CCO schools of thought.

Organizational Contradictions

Traditionally, organizational communication researchers approached the study of contradictions and tensions in organizational life as anomalies in need of correction. The advent of critical and discursive approaches created a different approach. Rather than destabilizing irregularities, contradictions and paradoxes are seen as normal organizational conditions providing opportunities for growth and progress (Stohl & Cheney, 2001). Rather than examining contradictions as disruptions to be solved, scholars began examining the discursive processes through which contradictions are constructed and managed (Ballard-Reisch & Turner, 2017). Three broad areas of study have emerged: Sensemaking, power relations, and change/disruption (Putnam, 2013). While this literature varies conceptually, three common assumptions prevail: An organization-as-becoming orientation, the existence of paradox at multiple levels, and an overall aim for equilibrium. Putnam, Fairhurst, and Banghart's (2016) meta-analysis of dialectics and paradox identifies five metatheoretical traditions (process-based systems, structuration, critical, postmodern, and relational dialectics) and emphasizes the roles of discourse, developmental actions, socio-historical conditions, occurrence in multiples, and praxis. They conclude by recommending that researchers sharpen their focus on time in process studies, privilege emotion over rationality, and more closely examine the order/disorder dialectic.

A *dialectic* is generally defined as a unity of opposites—seemingly contradictory forces (needs, goals, drives, etc.) that naturally and necessarily coexist (e.g., connection/autonomy; openness/closedness). Dialectic theory was introduced to the communication discipline through applications to personal relationships (Baxter, 1988; Montgomery, 1988). Dialectical theory has been applied in organizational communication to work–life balance; power and resistance; intercultural competence; identity negotiation; image management; conflict management; occupational tensions; and community development. (See Ballard-Reisch & Turner, 2017, for a review. See Chapter 20 for a discussion of dialectical tensions in globalization.) The broader concept *paradox* gained far more traction among organizational communication scholars, spawning a large interdisciplinary literature. (In addition to Putnam et al., 2016, see the special issue edited by Trethewey & Ashcraft, 2004, for reviews and examples from organizational communication.)

Seminal Organizational Communication Theory: Participation as Paradox

Employee participation and workplace democracy initiatives attempt to involve employees at all levels in organizational decision-making. Participation programs were implemented in mid-20th-century organizations to increase employee involvement in organizational decision-making. Such programs began with gathering workers' input on task-related decision-making, with the goal being to improve their satisfaction. In the 1960s, participation programs progressed to an interest in engaging all employees' intellect to improve organizational processes. By the end of the 20th century, employee involvement in decision-making had progressed to an emphasis on policy-level strategic decisions and the introduction of self-managed team structures. (See Chapter 7 for an overview of employee participation programs; see Cheney et al., 1998, for a multidisciplinary literature review.)

One of the most influential critiques of employee participation programs was Cynthia Stohl's identification of communication paradoxes created by such programs (Stohl, 1995; Stohl & Cheney, 2001). Through systematic examination of tensions and contradictions in communication activities associated with worker participation groups, Stohl and Cheney (2001) derive four categories of paradox (Structure, Agency, Identity, and Power) within which 14 specific types of paradox reside.

Paradoxes of Structure. This category concerns the architecture of the participation program. Specifically, these include the paradoxes of *design, adaptation, punctuation,* and *formalization* (Stohl & Cheney, 2001). The *paradox of design* addresses imposed participation. Employee participation mandated by upper management becomes *what the top tells the middle to do to the bottom* (Frey, 1995), thereby placing in paradox participants at the bottom because the form and function of their input is driven from above rather than from within. Any empowerment gained from their participation is constrained (if not controlled) by the participation program designed, of course, by those at the top. Stohl (1995, p. 204) describes the paradox of design as an "incompatibility between the goals of participation interventions and the processes by which the interventions are initiated (the design)."

> The design process may create a system which workers perceive is dominated by the top and simultaneously feared by the middle to be dominated by the bottom. Input by employees is a fundamental value of all participation programs, yet often the implementation communicates that input is not valued. It is not surprising then that participatory groups often reproduce the very bureaucratic and inefficient structures they were designed to eliminate—as people struggle to find their place in a paradoxical system they tend to reproduce patterns of communication with which they are already familiar.
>
> (Stohl, 1995, p. 205)

Furthermore, in the paradox of design, middle managers "are required to give up traditional forms of control and feel forced to introduce the very schemes that threaten their grip on the work process" (Stohl, 1995, p. 204). Middle managers feel threatened by the participation program because they believe workers are given too much control; workers are distrustful of the program because they perceive it to be controlled by management. Participation programs are intended to increase worker involvement, but a hierarchical implementation functions to alienate workers as they receive contradictory messages about the value of their participation.

The *paradox of adaptation* reflects a "tension between the desire to keep structure going (by those who support it) and continuous adherence to participatory principles" (Stohl & Cheney, 2001, p. 363). The adaptation paradox occurs when restrictive rules are imposed to dictate the nature of democracy. Organizational members experience oppressive, rigid, restrictive policies paradoxically intended to enforce the democratic, fluid, liberating process of participation.

The *paradox of punctuation* is based on Watzlawick, Beavin, and Jackson's (1967) definition of punctuation as "the process of perceiving causal patterns and sequencing of events" (Stohl, 1995, p. 206). The processes involved in teaching workers to follow specific participatory processes designed to improve efficiency and quality (problem-solving agendas, discussion techniques, conflict management approaches, and so on) are perceived by workers to make them less efficient, and so they resist.

> This punctuation of events (i.e. viewing the group meetings and process dynamics that are essential to instantiate participation as a waste of time) makes groups resistant to the group dynamics training that is designed to enhance the quality of participation of all group members. Ironically, the resistance often contributes to the group's sense of powerlessness and dependence upon the external authority; as group members fight against or oppose facilitating efforts the group becomes less organized, less efficient, and positive contributions to the task decrease. Resistance thereby increases the time it takes to master the "tools" of participation, inadvertently separating participation from the real work of the worker, and thereby making the group less efficient.
>
> (Stohl, 1995, p. 207)

To explain the *paradox of formalization*, Stohl and Cheney (2001) cite Burke's (1954/1965) *bureaucratization of the imaginative* and Weber's (1978) *routinization of charisma*. "Actors try to formalize a process that at its very heart needs to be informal and adaptive to changing situations" (Stohl & Cheney, 2001, p. 368). In an attempt to preserve them, organizational members formalize participatory and democratic processes into institutional structures (decision-making rules, procedural formulas, codes of conduct, conflict-management regulations, etc.). The rigid rules imposed attempt to create a standard by which to measure the success of the participatory process, which, of course, negates the flexibility intended.

Paradoxes of Agency. This category of paradox concerns the individual's sense of efficacy: paradoxes of *responsibility, cooperation, sociality,* and *autonomy* (Stohl & Cheney, 2001). The paradox of *responsibility* addresses reward and compensation schemes. "Organizations that implement new team structures often continue to appraise and reward behavior at the individual level" (Stohl, 1995, pp. 208–209). When incentive systems are individually based, as is commonly the case, there is no motivation for the cooperative behavior required for effective team performance. Instead, the system rewards those who act autonomously.

In the *paradox of cooperation*, Stohl (1995; Stohl & Cheney, 2001) identifies an interesting interactive dynamic: "participate by not participating" (Stohl, 1995, p. 209). She illustrates this cyclical process with excerpts from a quality circle at a large manufacturing plant. As the leader plays the role of delegating tasks and giving pep talks about the value of the participation program, the workers increasingly play their roles of accepting, but not completing, assignments—acquiescence without compliance. "The interaction produces and reproduces a cooperative paradox, insofar as in order for the workers to cooperate with the manager they must not participate and let the manager do the participating" (Stohl, 1995, p. 209).

The *paradox of sociality* arises when organizational members are highly motivated by and committed to participatory processes. Individuals become so involved in so many activities, they lose focus and performance suffers. Moreover, the social aspect of participatory work overwhelms organizational members so much that the social aspects of their personal lives also suffer (Stohl & Cheney, 2001).

Similarly, the *paradox of autonomy* is the sacrifice of individual agency to the collective:

> Whether through a clearly defined contract or by evolving practice, individuals in democratic organizations may find themselves largely absorbed by the organization, thus experiencing a violation of the principal of 'partial inclusion.' This principal suggests that in all cases except for total institutions, it is an individual's role rather than the individual as a whole is contained within the social boundaries of the organization. … such absorption of the self may infringe on individual efficacy—especially the possibility for the member to alter the very organizational structure to which he or she adheres. This is a tremendous irony in many democratic organizations.
>
> (Stohl & Cheney, 2001, pp. 377–378)

Paradoxes of Identity. This category concerns issues of membership, inclusion, and boundaries: the paradoxes of *commitment, representation,* and *compatibility* (Stohl & Cheney, 2001). Stohl (1995; Stohl & Cheney, 2001) identifies the *paradox of commitment* of "whenever compelled conformity becomes the sign of commitment" (Stohl, 1995, p. 206). Evidence rests on a case study by O'Connor (1993), who found that organizational members voicing disagreement with or reservations about participatory design efforts were viewed by management as ignorant and uncommitted. The managerial solution to this perceived problem was to design persuasive campaigns—with those who remained unconvinced labeled as saboteurs. The paradox is that only an employee who is committed to organizational outcomes will voice dissent. "By voicing an alternative position employees are often demonstrating (rather than negating) their commitment to the process" (Stohl, 1995, p. 206).

The *paradox of representation* arises when the redesign of organizational communication practices involve participatory groups that include worker representatives. As the representatives meet with different levels of management,

> new communication patterns and networks that develop … have the paradoxical effect of making the workers no longer think like workers. … [W]orkers who have the most access to the participatory system, which is explicitly designed to increase workers' voice, become the very people who are least likely to represent the workers' voice.
>
> (Stohl, 1995, p. 208)

Individuals in such positions become detached from the very group they ostensibly represent. Their organizational identification becomes dialectical; they are workers, yet they have access to information and communicative networks that ordinary workers are not afforded. The resulting representation becomes even narrower than what had previously existed, as the worker representatives progressively provide input inconsistent with workers' experiences. Worker representatives become detached from other workers as their identification with management grows (Stohl & Cheney, 2001). Note here the clear interplay between *communication* and *organization* as mutually enabling and constraining processes—the C-O dynamic (see Figure 1.4, Chapter 1) is clearly in play as communication patterns become entrenched in ways that constrain the communication of any worker who enters the interaction system.

Finally, the last in this category is particularly problematic in international settings: The *paradox of compatibility*.

> Variations in national culture affect beliefs about the way work should be organized, the manner in which authority should be exercised, the ways in which organizational members should be controlled and rewarded, the career aspirations of organizational members, and so on. When participation programs are implemented in national cultures where the central values contrast greatly with the fundamental premises of participation, workers are put in the paradoxical position of being required to act in ways that are incompatible with their "natural inclinations" (i.e. the normative view of their culture). ... The paradox of incompatibility ... arises whenever the processes of participating do not match the prevailing organizational cultural milieu while simultaneously reflecting the organization's desires.
>
> (Stohl, 1995, p. 210–211)

Successful participation alters the organizational culture (everyday practices, communicative expectations, and central organizational values) to the degree that hierarchical patterns are eliminated. Often, the very objective of a participatory program is to change an organization's culture, but naturally, "participation works best in those organizations where the culture is already compatible with participatory goals" (Stohl, 1995, p. 211).

Paradoxes of Power. This final category of paradox concerns the locus, nature, and specific exercise of power to the organization: the paradoxes of *control, leadership*, and *homogeneity*. The paradox of *control* is centered on how workers' internalize and intensify organizational control mechanisms. In a case study highlighting absenteeism, Stohl and Sotirin (1989) document increasing worker resentment of the inflexibility and pressure interactively produced by the team design in an organization where teams were authorized to demand and evaluate absence accounts. Absenteeism was virtually eliminated in the short term; however, the intensity of the intra-team control mechanisms had quite negative long-term effects. Participation programs are explicitly intended to empower workers, but

> as controls become even more rigid and inflexible than they were in traditional bureaucracies, the innovative flexibility and responsiveness that are foundational to participation are lost. Second, workers may begin to withdraw from the participatory mechanisms as they experience the loss of control rather than the empowered position that was promised at the outset.
>
> (Stohl, 1995, p. 212)

In team-based structures, high employee identification, high consensus on values, and personal connections "create a powerful system of 'concertive control' in which workers control and monitor themselves to an even greater extent that found a typical bureaucratic organization" (Stohl, 1995, p. 212). *Concertive control* can be thought of as a form of internalized oppression. It occurs when organizational members internalize organizational control to the extent that their self-discipline becomes a damaging force.

Barker's (1993) case study, the basis of concertive control theory (see Chapters 11 and 12), likewise dramatically illustrates the result of team members replicating traditional management control practices. Although the outcome was positive at first, it soon deteriorated to an oppressive environment that tightened the iron cage of rationality and concertive control. Team members more rigidly controlled and more closely monitored each other than their traditional managers had prior to the restructuring. Barker (1993) documents the ways in which "the teams concertively reached a value consensus that, in turn, controlled their individual and collective work" (p. 422); discursively turned "their value consensus into normative rules that the new workers could readily understand and to which they could subject themselves" (p. 424); and then stabilized and formalized these emerging rules into a tight and rigid form of concertive control.

The *paradox of leadership* expresses the challenge of facilitating, fostering, and leading participation efforts without controlling them. Stohl and Cheney (2001) cite copious research documenting the importance of such strong leadership in the participatory process. Finally, the *paradox of homogeneity*: "the very unity that helps to maintain a democratic organization or give life to democratic practices also may be its limiting factor" (Stohl & Cheney, 2001, p. 389). Stohl and Cheney liken this paradox to Janis' (1982) groupthink, where consensus-seeking displaces fruitful disagreement (see Chapter 15). The very homogeneity that provides efficacy blinds the group to alternative viewpoints. The group's homogeneity provides a sense of comfort with agreement that makes disagreement difficult to appreciate. In addition, heterogeneity becomes discouraged. When this occurs, the group seeks to *control* heterogeneity and loses the advantage of fruitful disagreement.

Stohl and Cheney's taxonomy of paradox illustrates several hallmarks of 21st-century organizational communication theory. First, it relies on a discursive understanding of organization. Second, it derives theory inductively and critically (see Chapter 4). Third, it rests on an implicitly constitutive understanding of the mutually enabling and constraining relationship between communication and organization (see Figure 1.4, Chapter 1). Finally, it illustrates the field's evolution of a new approach to contradiction as normal and natural.

Structuration Theory

Structuration theory is a sociological explanation for the ways that daily social practices produce and reproduce deep structures of meaning (societal, institutional, and organizational). Meaning structures provide knowledge so that we know how to make sense of our daily interaction and act appropriately in social settings. Our social actions are thus constrained and to some extent dictated by these structures, but our actions can also change structures and create new ones. Structuration theory appeared in sociology in the mid-1970s to solve the conceptual dilemma posed by the incompatible notions of human choice and social constraint (Giddens, 1979, 1984). The first communication scholars to work with structuration theory were studying group decision-making (Poole, Seibold, & McPhee, 1985, 1986). Scholars in organizational communication continued to develop applications of structuration theory, with its most fertile development occurring in the past 15 years.

Structuration is the process by which social structures are produced and reproduced in social practice, structure being both the *medium* and *outcome* of social interaction, which Giddens (1984) referred to as *the duality of structure*. Social structures are conceptualized as culturally based repositories of meaning. Structures are unobservable rules and resources that generate *systems*, which are defined as observable patterns of behavior (Giddens, 1979, 1984; Poole et al., 1985, 1986). Structuration theory posits that people act and interact coherently based on meaning provided by institutionalized structures, and that in turn, those interactions produce and reproduce structures. The communication-organization dynamic guiding this text (see Figure 1.4, Chapter 1) is entirely consistent with structuration theory.

Rules and resources. *Structure* consists of "rules and resources, recursively implicated in the reproduction of social systems" (Giddens, 1984, p. 377). *Rules* are schemas that tell us what things mean and how to act (Sewell, 1992), just as in Chapter 1's explanation of communication rules theory. According to Giddens (1979), *resources* are authoritative and allocative (they provide command over persons and objects); human (intelligence, strength, knowledge) and non-human (tools, documents); material (buildings, land, supplies, equipment) and non-material (regulations, tax codes, influential relationships). All humans have the capacity to act, but it is both knowledge of rules and access to resources that empower individuals differentially. *Agency*—the human capacity to act on the world—is a central concept. Rules tell us how to act, and resources allow us to do so. Access to resources empowers: "To be an agent means to be capable of exerting some degree of control over the social relations in which one is enmeshed, which in turn implies the ability to transform those social relations" (Sewell, 1992, p. 20). *Doing* anything rests on agency provided by rules/resources. Agency is not power over others, but empowerment to act meaningfully. Power is the transformative capacity to change the social and material world (Giddens, 1987). Agency arises from knowledge of structure; recursively, structures arise from agency (ability to act and to apply knowledge to new contexts) (Sewell, 1992).

Systems are the recurrent social practices that result from the application of rules and resources to a given situation. This *duality of structure* means that structures shape the social practices that then recursively constitute those structures. The production and reproduction of structures in social practice is the heart of structuration. *Structure* thus also refers to "properties allowing the 'binding' of time-space in social systems, the properties which make it possible for discernibly similar social practices to exist across varying spans of time and space and which lend them 'systemic' form" (Giddens, 1984, p. 17). Rules, intertwined with resources, are "the modes whereby transformative relations are actually incorporated into the production and reproduction of social practices" (Giddens, 1984, p. 18). Rules both constitute meaning and sanction modes of social conduct. Action produces, reproduces, and transforms structures in a continuous cycle. The interplay of O_1, O_2, and O_3 are quite clear in this set of theoretical constructs.

Modalities of Meaning. Giddens (1984) also identifies three structural modalities: *signification, legitimation*, and *domination*. These modalities allow us to act via the assignment of three different kinds of meaning to every act/utterance. We assign denotative meaning to the act (signification), judge its appropriateness (legitimation), and ascertain our places in a hierarchy of power (dominance). In structuration theory, meaning is always plural; the three modalities function simultaneously. For example, recalling that agency is defined as the ability to act meaningfully, the behavioral convention of raising a hand in a classroom means the student is asking permission to speak, reproducing a signification recognized by most members of a particular culture. It also reproduces rules of legitimation, dictating for whom it is appropriate to speak and how they should do so. The reactions of others will inform whether audience interaction is appropriate and whether permission to speak will be granted. Finally, this action reproduces rules of dominance—who may speak without such permission.

If we invoke a structure that is not presumed by the culture to be applied to that context, we quickly learn that our actions are inappropriate and must be adjusted to achieve meaningful interaction. For example, one could be in a cultural context where hand-raising has no common signification, where students do not speak in class, or where attempting to do so is considered insubordinate. Moreover, a group may rebel against such conventions and create their own rules—such as in a small seminar where the instructor invites students to speak up in an egalitarian discussion, rather than wait to be called upon. New students joining the group quickly learn the structure by observing the social practice of speaking up as it reproduces the egalitarian rule for interaction. This example also illustrates the reproduction of dominance in the transformation of structure—the instructor retains the power to reinforce the existing structure or allow the new one. The dominance hierarchy remains undisturbed in this situation even as a specific structure for that specific setting is produced. Also, note that rules for legitimation remain in place in the form of politeness norms for discussion, such as turn-taking. Giddens' three modalities thus provide agency, as the group can smoothly interact to reproduce old structures, transform structures, and produce new ones, meeting their shared and individual goals and objectives. Structure is thus the socially shared or common meanings in these modalities that allow the exercise of agency to re/produce and transform structure. Structure is comprised of the common understandings of signification, legitimation, and dominance that provide coherence to interaction and power to produce, reproduce, and transform those very structures. The exercise of agency relies on knowledge of structure.

Structurational organizational communication theories. The fundamental principles of structuration theory are widely accepted in the field of organizational communication. The basic idea that our daily actions and interactions are enabled and constrained by social structures, and that those daily practices enable and constrain structures as they emerge and transform, is uncontroversial. Several scholars have developed organizational communication theories based on and extending structuration theory. Three stand out as most prominent: adaptive structuration theory; structurating activity theory; and structurational divergence theory.

Adaptive structuration theory (AST). AST is a theory of group communication that applies structuration theory to explain the use of technology in decision-making (DeSanctis & Poole, 1994; Poole & DeSanctis, 1990). The theory posits that group members intentionally adapt rules and resources as they interact through and with technology in ways that transform and create structures. AST challenged technological determinism—the presumption that technology itself is the root cause of organizational change. While technological systems have structures of their own, and are embedded in institutional structures, AST explains that human interaction with and through technology drives organizational change through the process of social construction. Technologies and institutions provide structures (rule and resources) that provide capabilities. These structures are accompanied with an underlying intent for their use, which DeSanctis and Poole (1994) call *spirit*, grounded in general values and goals. DeSanctis and Poole (1994) offer describe seven propositions in regard to advanced information technologies (AITs):

- AITs provide social structures that can be described in terms of their features and spirit. To the extent that AITs vary in their spirit and structural features sets, different forms of social interaction are encouraged by the technology (p. 128).
- Use of AIT structures may vary depending on the task, the environment, and other contingencies that offer alternative sources of social structures (p. 128).
- New sources of structure emerge as the technology, task, and environmental structures are applied during the course of social interaction (p. 128).
- New social structures emerge in group interaction as the rules and resources of an AIT are appropriated in a given context and then reproduced in group interaction over time (p. 129).
- Group decision processes will vary depending on the nature of AIT appropriations (p. 130).
- The nature of AIT appropriations will vary depending on the group's internal system (p. 131).
- Given AIT and other sources of social structure, ideal appropriation processes, and decision processes that fit the task at hand, then desired outcomes of AIT use will result (p. 131).

AST was important because it emphasized the importance of social interaction in the application of technology, providing empirical evidence to challenge the techno-centric view of technology use. The empirical research on group decision-making that resulted in the formulation of AST clearly illustrated that the impact of technology on group outcomes is heavily mediated by social practices and human interactions that draw from a number of other social and institutional structures.

Structurating activity theory (SAT). SAT is an extension of structuration theory applied to the construction of policy knowledge. SAT combines structuration theory with cultural-historical activity theory (CHAT). CHAT is grounded in three fundamental ideas: action is collective; interaction uses tools, which it also creates and adapts; and meaning-making is community-based (Vygotsky, 1978). Activity systems constantly evolve through responses to structural contradictions (Foot, 2001). Situated actions and interactions are mediated by elements of intersecting systems. "CHAT focuses on the mediation of activity, connections between systems in the policy process, and the transformation of systems as knowledge is constructed" (Canary, 2010, p. 28). Structuration theory can examine how system elements (i.e., rules and resources), reproduce and transform structures. CHAT can examine ongoing activity occurring through the mediation of system elements and how changes in these elements transform systems. SAT addresses these processes together through the application of four theoretic constructs: structuration through activity; mediation of social activity; contradictions; and intersections of systems to analyze and explain the process of constructing policy knowledge. These four constructs are combined in six propositions (Canary, 2010):

- Knowledge construction is situated within particular social contexts, with social structure enabling and constraining the knowledge construction process (p. 31).
- Elements of systems of ongoing activity mediate situated action and interaction, such that system elements shape how and what policy knowledge is constructed within and between activity systems (p. 34).
- Mediated activity draws on social structure as it also reproduces and transforms structure over time through system transformations (p. 34).
- Contradictions are generative mechanisms for the communicative construction of policy knowledge as individuals interact to resolve contradictions in the policy process (p. 36).
- Policy knowledge constructed between systems is mediated by elements of intersecting activity systems (p. 37).
- The construction of policy knowledge between intersecting activity systems is constrained and enabled by structural features, while at the same time constructed knowledge produces, reproduces, or transforms social structure (p. 37).

Policy knowledge and knowledge construction are very complex processes that transcend both human interaction and organizational boundaries. SAT provides a communication-centered approach to organizational knowledge construction with adequate complexity to examine these complicated processes.

Structurational divergence theory (SDT). SDT is an extension of structuration theory, with elements of institutional theory and CCO theory. While Giddens and others (e.g., Sewell, 1992) discuss the interpenetration of multiple structures and potential contradictions, and both AST and SAT include the role of contradictions as part of the structuration process, no previous structuration theory addresses the paradox of intractable contradictions. Previous applications of structuration theory assume that contradictions result in the transformation of structures or the evolution of new structures that provide rules and resources for managing the contradictions. However, SDT extends structuration theory by considering those contradictory interpenetrations of multiple structures that remain unresolved, resulting in recurrent conflict cycles. Further, SDT reveals that in such conditions the structures produced and then reproduced are unproductive or oppressive. SDT was developed in the healthcare context, specifically nursing communication. Yet, it is an institutional phenomenon. Like structuration, SDT is applicable to all human social systems.

There are two essential components of structurational divergence (SD): the SD-nexus and the SD-cycle (Nicotera, Mahon, & Zhao, 2010). The SD-nexus is an institutional positioning at the intersection of structures characterized by simultaneous and equally compelling contradictory obligations. SD-nexuses are conceptualized as the result of institutional positioning. SDT explicates the function and dysfunction of human interaction under conditions of intractable paradox. Rooted in structuration theory's fundamental assumptions about the recursive and mutually constitutive processes of everyday communication and enduring social structures, SDT provides a framework to examine the intersection of incompatible social structures that simultaneously drive oppositional actions, resulting in recurrent negative spirals of conflict.

The SD-cycle is that negative spiral of communication resulting from an SD-nexus: unresolvable conflict, immobilization, and the erosion of development (individual, group, organizational, and/or institutional) that exacerbates unresolved conflicts. The hallmark symptom of SD is immobilization—not lack of activity but a frustrating lack of progress, feeling stuck in the same place, repeatedly facing the same problems, with no end to the impasse. The individual feels futility and hopelessness. SD is measured with a diagnostic self-report scale that identifies the three components of the cycle, as well as the cyclic connections among them (Nicotera et al., 2010). Training interventions are in development to educate those in susceptible positions (e.g., those at intersections of organizational, cultural, and institutional boundaries) to recognize its signs and create dialogues to transcend the oppositional nature of SD communication (Nicotera, Mahon, & Wright, 2014).

SD has been conceptualized as agency loss (Nicotera & Mahon, 2013). Because incompatible meaning structures are not apparent, the underlying source of conflict is unclear, making efforts to resolve it ineffective. Because actions cannot reproduce a comprehensible structure, the resulting communication difficulties become entrenched. Agency can be defined as efficacy. Numerous studies illustrated that those entrenched in an SD-nexus lose their ability to act meaningfully, illustrating inefficacy in SD (e.g., Nicotera & Clinkscales, 2003, 2010). Those entrenched cannot make sense of interaction, cannot coherently use resources, and cannot apply rules smoothly. Because simultaneous oppositional structures are equally forceful and because the re/production of one violates another, the interaction system at the nexus is incoherent. In a structurationally divergent interaction system, social practice does not coherently re/produce or transform structure because the actor does not have adequate knowledge of resources. Action is thus impotent—without the force of agency.

> Agency is never zero; doing nothing is a choice. However, individual efficacy at the SD-nexus is so compromised that agency is nonfunctional. Without control over structures, we cannot transform them. An SD system is self-perpetuating; its contradictions re/produce contradictory actions. We always have action choices, but in SD none satisfy all structurational constraints in place. This positioning is mystifying because the opposition is invisible or stultifying because the opposition is unsolvable. If to avoid a kick from the mule, I must choose being run over by the cart, I may just not move. I have agency to decide not to act but no efficacy to impact either structure transformatively. Acting on one structure subverts another, negating agency for the whole.
>
> (Nicotera & Mahon, 2013, p. 94)

SDT posits that the interpenetration of equally compelling oppositional structures (SD-nexus) creates unknowable structures negating agency and giving rise to the self-perpetuating SD-cycle. In SD, we cannot assign meaning in a comprehensible socially sanctioned way, so interaction cannot (re)produce comprehensible structures. SDT provides a set of conceptual mechanisms to understand intractable conflict cycles at the intersection of incompatible and equally compelling structures.

Communicative Constitution of Organization

CCO examines the mutually constitutive relationship between communication and organization. CCO theory has grown exponentially since its inception at the turn of the century. Currently, this genre of theory is most often described as occupying three distinct branches: McPhee's four flows; the Montreal School; and Luhmann's social systems theory.

Four flows model. The term CCO was first used by McPhee and Zaug (2000) in a description of their four flows model of organizational communication. The model identifies four distinct communicative flows through which interaction generates organizational structuring: Organizational self-structuring, membership negotiation, activity coordination, and institutional positioning. Heavily influenced by structuration theory, McPhee and Zaug identify the ways these flows mutually influence one another through the structuring of the organization, both reproducing and resisting its rules/resources. Like most other contemporary organizational communication theories, and all CCO theories, the four flows model integrates all three conceptual treatments of organization (O_1, O_2, O_3).

Organizational self-structuring. People organize deliberately, and these activities comprise this flow. Individuals and groups occupying organizational roles communicate dialogically and recursively to create and maintain organizational structures. The organization's practices, procedures, norms, and relations are designed, documented, and controlled by communication in this flow. In these ways, an organization is distinguished from other forms of social collective. The process is both subjective and political, often ambiguous, and never error-free. Communication in this flow constitutes the organization by explicitly defining it as a distinct entity and by imposing governance on that entity through self-reflexive internal mechanisms and rule-governed cycles of response (e.g., manuals, formal reporting structures, organizational charts, etc.).

Membership negotiation. Organizations cannot exist without human membership, which is necessarily a communicatively negotiated process. These processes establish and maintain mutually agreed-upon relationships that link the organization to its members (through such practices as recruiting, orientations, socialization, promotions, etc.). Membership negotiation takes place in the context of pre-existing structures (including informal power structures) and expectations, to which all members must adapt. Membership negotiation is ongoing and includes constant renegotiating of roles as both the organization and its members develop.

Activity coordination. Self-structuring and membership negotiation define workflows, policies, roles, and other structures that provide purpose to human activities. To meet the demands of organizational structuring, those activities need to be coordinated. That coordination, in turn, restructures the organization as members adjust processes to accomplish tasks. Structuring is constant, and activity coordination presumes the interdependence of individual activities with each other, with social units, and with the organization as a whole. Even activities that resist organizational goals and structures are constantly coordinated as members pursue multiple and often contradictory goals.

Institutional positioning. Finally, the last flow links the organization to its environment (i.e., customers, suppliers, regulators, competitors, etc.). Communication that spans the organizational boundary comprises this flow, whether cast as representing an individual, a group, or the organization as a whole. This communication must establish the organization's presence, inclusion, and image in its environment, as well as its relation to other organizations and pre-existing social, cultural, or political structures.

Montreal School. So-called because of its association with scholars affiliated with the University of Montreal, this body of theory relies on a core set of ideas first formulated by Taylor, Cooren, Giroux, & Robichaud (1996) and more in depth by Taylor and Van Every (2000). Following the European and American pragmatist traditions, Montreal CCO theory focuses on the organizing properties of linguistic forms. Analysis centers on the inherent organizing properties of communication, positing these properties as the basis for communication's constitutive force. The foundation of Montreal theory is coorientational theory—the recursive interplay between *conversation* (interaction) and *text* (discourse). Text is both content and outcome of interaction. Conversation is interaction itself. Text is meaning and outcome, and can be tangible; conversation is activity. Conversation is about text and produces/reproduces text. For example, a work group who encounter a problem with tracking client orders has a meeting (conversation). In that meeting they collaborate to create a set of standard procedures (text) for training salespeople, as well as a standard online tracking sheet (text) for processing orders. Later, the sales managers convene their employees in a training session (conversation), during which they provide the procedures and new tracking sheet (texts). After the training, salespeople discuss (conversation) the relative merits of the new procedures (text) among themselves and comment (conversation) on how boring they found the training session (text). And so on.

Based on Weick, conversations must be interpreted through processes of punctuation and bracketing (sensemaking), and bracketing will depend on the interactant's interpretive frames (see Chapter 2). Organization, then, emerges *in* (not through or from) communication. Organization is not seen through communication; rather it is in the communicational lens (Taylor & Van Every, 2000). Once it has emerged, organization becomes an object to which organizational actors *coorient* their activities as they engage in coordination. Organization is thus enacted only through interaction and meaning negotiation (Taylor & Van Every, 2000). Communication is thus conceptualized as a mediating process, as conversations and texts are translated into one another. Communication is constitutive in two ways, as a sensemaking process and through the creation of an organizational entity for which actors speak (Schoenenborn & Vasquez, 2017).

Montreal scholars also point out that the organization communicates through *non-human* agents (documents, policies, organizational units). For example, individuals commonly act by following instructions given by a document, without any thought as to the human actions that resulted in that document. Agency, therefore, is attributed to the document; it gave instructions—note the language here: the document (the "it," not any human) gave instructions. The organization itself is non-human, and it speaks through humans and non-humans alike.

Montreal CCO theory also explores materiality and agency (Cooren, 2010) as texts and conversations are converted to material forms in which organization finds its expression. Yet, a conceptual gap arises between social construction and materialization, as early analyses commonly examined one or the other, but rarely the hybrid processes by which material and the discursive aspects of organizing are conjoined in CCO phenomena. Cooren (2006) defines organization as a *plenum of agencies*, positing that all action is hybrid—mobilizing participation of multiple entities in a wide variety of types (human, non-human, material, and discursive). Actors, thus, do not need to be human, or even material, to be mobilized with and through.

Montreal theory is far more complex than can be explained here. Other important concepts include imbrication (Taylor, 2011), coorientation (Taylor, 2009), presentification (Benoit-Barné & Cooren, 2009), and ventriloquism (Cooren, Matte, Brummans, & Benoit-Barné, 2013). *Imbrication* refers to the layering of communicative practices that *scale up* to constitute the organization. Individuals and groups then *coorient* to one another in relation to that object (the organization). *Presentification* is speaking and acting to make present in interaction things and beings (that are not physically present) in ways that influence the unfolding of a situation. *Ventriloquism* refers to the positioning of agents (both human and non-human) by their need to act as compelled by the structures that have been constituted—the organization speaks through its agents.

Luhmann's social systems theory. Luhmann's (2003) sociology of organizations rests on the assumption that society is comprised of a complex and dynamic interplay of numerous social systems. Similar to self-organizing systems theory (see Chapter 2), Luhmann's theory draws on the concept of *autopoiesis*. Communication constitutes the social systems that produce the very elements of communication. Organizations are constituted by these self-recursive communication events. Luhmann distinguishes organizations from other forms of social system because they are specifically constituted by *decisional communication*. Literally, organizations are made of decisions and, further, have the capability to make the decisions that constitute them. Hence, this branch of theory is noted for its focus on self-referential CCO. Organizations are created and continue to exist through the continuous perpetuation of interconnected decisions. Moreover, decisions are nonpermanent events. The identification of an organizational entity provides the common reference point, or *social address*, that allows agents to make decisions on its behalf (Schoenenborn & Vasquez, 2017).

Six commitments of CCO theory. Cooren, Kuhn, Cornelissen, and Clark (2011) articulate six premises on which all CCO theory relies, regardless of ontological and epistemological differences among schools of thought. First, CCO scholarship explicitly studies communication events. Second, CCO scholarship should be as inclusive as possible in its definition of communication. Third, CCO scholarship acknowledges the co-constructed nature of communication. Fourth, CCO scholarship holds that who or what is acting is an open question, explicitly questioning agency. Fifth, CCO scholarship never leaves the realm of communication events, maintaining the centrality of communication as the primary organizationally constitutive force. Finally, CCO scholarship favors neither organizing nor organization; the body of theory examines processes (O_1), the organization of structures (O_2) and the creation of entities (O_3).

2010s: Institutional Theory and Postcolonial Theory

In addition to theoretic advancements, important topics of research gaining popularity in this decade include materiality, agency, bullying, knowledge management, health organizing, relationship management, and organizational justice. Theoretically, the contemporary period (as of this writing) is marked by the expansion of CCO into more broad applications of institutional and postcolonial theory, deepening the influence of sociological concepts. Both bodies of theory are related to the study of discourse: Institutional theory and postcolonial theory. Like previous generations of theory, both have roots that are far earlier than the turn of the 21st century; however, both are gaining unprecedented attention from organizational communication scholars. Inherently critical, organizational communication applications of postcolonialism examine the ways in which structures and practices created and sustained by colonialism persist in contemporary organizational life (see Chapter 14). Because Chapters 12 and 14 provide in-depth attention to postcolonial theory, only institutional theory will be covered here.

Institutional Theory

Institutional theory has its roots in the late 19th century, with the works of Max Weber often cited as seminal (see Chapter 5). Institutional theorists (mostly in sociology, organizational theory, political science, and economics) have long examined the ways in which large social structures influence daily life. In its application to organizations, institutional theory gained great popularity in the 1970s, as organizational theorists sought to examine why organizations of the same type (e.g., hospitals, schools, public agencies) were so much alike in form, function, and practices even when they exist in isolation from one another. In the 2000s organizational communication scholars began contributing to that literature (e.g., Cheney & Ashcraft, 2007; Green, Babb, & Alpaslan, 2008; Lammers, 2011; Lammers & Barbour, 2006; Lammers & Garcia, 2009; Taylor, Flanagin, Cheney & Seibold, 2001). For organizational communication, institutional theory is necessarily related to CCO, as the challenge is to examine how human interaction carries the social arrangements of institutions, especially through generations (Lammers & Garcia, 2017). Lammers and Barbour (2006) summarize the need for an institutional theory of organizational communication as the field's neglect of *macrophenomena*, defined as forms of social structure that are larger than interaction, that appear to be outside the direct control of organizational members, and that persist to constrain and manipulate that interaction and perceptions of organizational members.

According to Scott (2008, third edition, widely considered to be the primary authority on institutional theory in organizational studies) "institutions are comprised of regulative, normative and cultural-cognitive elements that, together with associated activities and resources, provide stability and meaning to social life" (p. 48). While there is no one single agreed-upon definition of *institutions*, Lammers and Garcia (2017) identify persistence, reproduction, stability, or establishment as characteristic across definitions. Organizational communication institutional theorists grapple with the interplay between external institutional forces and internal organizational interaction. Moreover, organizations themselves can be examined as actors in an institutional environment, investigating both their adaptation to and influence over their institutional environments. Institutional theory overlaps with a number of other research traditions in the social sciences. Within organizational communication, institutional theorists have much in common with rhetoricians, cultural theorists, critical theorists, structuration theorists, and CCO theorists as they examine symbolic interaction, belief systems, systems of domination, and other broad social structures. However, institutional theorists do not attempt to explicate internal organizational behavior at the individual level (labelled *microphenomena* by Lammers & Barbour, 2006). For an institutional theorist, any individual-level analysis would examine the internalization of social norms for conduct (similar to concertive control theory, see Chapters 7, 11, and 12) because the focus is on the organizational environment itself, its nature, and its force.

Rather than study organizational communication from an interpersonal or a cognitive approach, institutional theory looks to the institutional environment to contextualize and explain communication behavior (e.g., decision-making, message formation, change strategies, management tactics, conflict management strategies, etc.). By the 1980s,

> concerns with individual organizations becoming institutionalized, or particular institutions' fate or relevance, were replaced with recognition that organizing was persistently influenced by institutional ideas. Meyer and Rowan (1977) referred to these ideas as rational myths or untestable beliefs about what organizations should

look like. DiMaggio and Powell (1983) contributed a way of thinking about institutional fields as continually structured by isomorphic forces that shaped organizations within a recognized area of institutional life, including the industry as well as regulating, supply, and market organizations. These concepts, the rational myth and field forces, laid the foundation for what has come to be known as *neo-institutionalism*, the study of external forces that influence organizational strategy, change, and behavior.

(Lammers & Garcia, 2017, pp. 2–3)

Organizational communication scholars continue to work in neo-institutional theory, with significant contributions over the past decade. Organizational communication neo-institutionalists study how organizational behavior and these field forces mutually influence one another and how individuals communicate to create or alter institutions.

Lammers and Barbour (2006) proposed an institutional theory of organizational communication based on five propositions:

- Communication sustains institutions.
- Communication aligns organizing with institutions.
- Institutions operate in organizing through formal communication.
- The success of boundary-spanning communication depends on the presence of institutions.
- Institutional hierarchy is manifested in organizing.

The links between institutional theory and organizational communication are quite clear, with communication-focused examinations of numerous processes: institutional logics that pattern organizational practices; deliberate attempts to create, maintain, or disrupt institutions; rhetoric that reveals institutionalization of activities, norms, beliefs, and rules; the logic and operation of professions as both an institutional and an organizational communication phenomenon; organizations themselves as actors in an institutional environment; and, finally, messages and message framing, where institutional messaging can be seen to manifest at institutional, organizational, and interactional levels (Lammers & Garcia, 2017).

The most recent development in organizational communication institutional theory is the articulation of *communicative institutionalism* (Cornelissen, Durand, Fiss, Lammers, & Vaara, 2015). Institutional theory's traditional approaches to communication were the conduit (SMCR) or performative approaches, which are very limited, linear, and not conceptually rich. The conceptual advancement of *communicative institutionalism* is to adopt organizational communication's meaning-centered and constitutive view, with institutions and organizations seen as mutually constitutive. Communication is defined as a dynamic manipulation of symbols that create, maintain, transform, and destroy meaning. Moreover, that meaning process is considered central to all organizational processes. Thus, interaction can be conceptualized at the institutional level as complex, rich, ambiguous, and diverse. Communicative institutionalism can account for the communicative constitution of institution, the institutional constitution of organization, and the organizational constitution of institution. Similar to CCO, the perspective breaks down traditional distinctions between structure and action and between micro- and macro-levels of analysis. However, it goes further than CCO in its ability to examine patterns that transcend organizations (Lammers & Garcia, 2017).

Summary: Organizational Communication Trends from the 1960s to 2010s

Organizational communication is a diverse and rich field. Early research approaches and topical areas continue to be pursued, even as new conceptual and methodological approaches emerge and gain popularity. Table 3.1 summarizes these developments. Over the past 50 years, numerous other social science and humanities disciplines have influenced the field. Figure 3.1 summarizes these influences and illustrates the multidisciplinary field that is organizational studies.

Conceptual Frameworks for this Book: Structuration Theory and CCO

This book takes an approach based in structuration theory and CCO theory, grounding an understanding of the field and its contents as mutually constitutive with organizational practices. Foundational management theories are conceived as having significant constitutive power in the creation of both the field and the contemporary organizational landscape that we study. The foundational theories of management you will study in Chapters 5, 6, and 7 are important conceptual foundations for organizational communication theory, but they are also bodies of prescriptive principles that functioned to create particular organizational phenomena that we study in organizational communication today (e.g., hierarchies, bureaucratic structures, labor protections, etc.). Hence structuration theory and CCO allow us to consider the conceptual foundations of our field as forces that created the common organizational structures and practices we study today. Structuration theory is a sociological explanation for the ways that

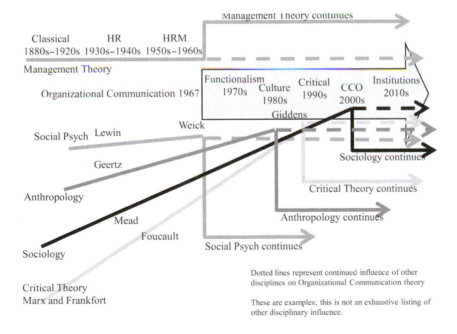

Figure 3.1 Disciplinary influences on the field of organizational communication over time

Table 3.1 Summary of developments in organizational communication

	1970s	1980s	1990s	2000s	2010s
Defining Feature	Variables	Process	Naturalism	Discourse	Communicative constitution
Dominant Paradigm	Structural-functionalism	Interpretivism	Critical-interpretivism	Pluralism	Pluralism
Theoretic Advances	Systems theory	Structuration theory	Concertive control theory	CCO theory	Institutional theory
Research Trends	Variable-analytic studies	Qualitative and ethnographic methods	Bona fide groups	Discursive approaches	Postcolonial approaches
Popular Topics	Message contents, channels, flows, barriers, and interpretations; communication rules and roles; rumors/grapevine; networks; nonverbal communication; communication load; communication audits; symbolism and shared meaning systems; superior-subordinate communication and leadership; socialization; climate; productivity; participative decision-making; effectiveness and efficiency; rationality; control and coordination; innovation; gender	Networks; gender; organizational culture; organizing; systems; conflict; strategic ambiguity; technology; satisfaction; organizational rhetoric; identification	Teamwork; globalization; leadership; concertive control; self-organizing systems; organizational democracy; stories; metaphors; gender; feminist theory; conflict; technology; identity; race; diversity; work–life balance; ethics	Paradox; restructuring; institutions; terrorism; virtual organizing; framing; alternative organizations; diversity; corporate social responsibility; work–life balance; spirituality	Materiality; agency; bullying; knowledge management; health organizing; relationship management; organizational justice

daily social practices produce and reproduce deep structures of meaning (societal, institutional, and organizational). Meaning structures provide knowledge so that we know how to make sense of our daily interaction and can act appropriately in social settings. Our social actions are thus constrained and to some extent dictated by these structures, but our actions can also change structures and create new ones. CCO theory is not in itself a theory, but rather is a genre of theory. CCO scholars seek to explain the ways in which organizing and organizations are constituted (accomplished, created, maintained, and/or changed) in interaction.

We theorize and practice in a field that has been constituted by theoretic constructions. We live in and act upon an organizational world that has been created and maintained, in significant part, by organizational theory. Contemporary organizational forms, structures, policies, procedures, practices, and so on, are communicatively constituted—largely by our own theories. Both structuration and CCO theory are prominent contemporary approaches to the study of organizational communication phenomena that examine the ways that social structures (such as organizations) and social practices enable and constrain one another. Thus, as you study organizational communication theory, this text asks you to also consider the ways in which that theory creates cultural structures that become the thing that we study. To accomplish this, this text takes a structurational CCO perspective.

Recommended Supplementary Readings

Canary, H. E., & Tarin, C. A. (2017). Structuration theory. In C. R. Scott & L. Lewis (Eds.), *The international encyclopedia of organizational communication* (online edition). Hoboken, NJ: Wiley-Blackwell.

This essay provides an accessible and thorough overview of structuration theory as it has been developed in organizational communication.

Cooren, F., Matte, F., Benoit-Barné, C., & Brummans, B. H. J. M. (2013). Communication as ventriloquism: A grounded-in-action approach to the study of organizational tensions. *Communication Monographs*, 80(3), 255–277.

Using fieldwork case studies from an extensive ethnographic study, Cooren and colleagues examine how organizational tensions are communicatively constituted and how they can be managed through awareness of everyday constitution.

Fairhurst, G. T., & Putnam, L. L. (2004). Organizations as discursive constructions. *Communication Theory*, 14(1), 5–26.

Putnam, L. L., & Fairhurst, G. T. (2015). Revisiting "Organizations as discursive constructions": 10 years later. *Communication Theory*, 25(4), 375–392.

The initial essay provides a deep analysis of the various discursive approaches in the field. The subsequent piece discusses the impact of the original and traces the ideas in CCO theory.

Lammers, J. C., & Garcia, M. A. (2017). Institutional theory approaches. In C. R. Scott & L. Lewis (Eds.), *The international encyclopedia of organizational communication* (online edition). Hoboken, NJ: Wiley-Blackwell.

This essay provides an accessible and thorough overview of structuration theory as it has been developed in organizational communication.

Schoeneborn, D., & Blaschke, S. (2014). The three schools of CCO thinking: Interactive dialogue and systematic comparison. *Management Communication Quarterly*, 28(2), 285–316.

This essay provides a unique view of CCO theory, through a dialogue among the major theorists from each school of thought.

Important Concepts: Define and Discuss

Discourse/discourse (big D, little d)
Organization as object
Organization as becoming
Organization as grounded in action
Structuration

> Duality of structure
> Rules and resources
> Modalities of meaning

Agency
Communicative constitution of organization

> McPhee's four flows
> Montreal school
> Luhmann's social systems theory

Institutional theory

Discussion Questions

1. What is discourse? Why is it important to contemporary organizational communication theory?
2. Choose a common organizational practice (e.g., budget requests, annual performance reviews) and trace its structuration. Identify the practice, its place in a system of practices, the underlying structure, rules, resources, and other structurational concepts. Can you trace the structurational C-O cycle through this practice?
3. How are the three theoretical traditions of CCO consistent with one another? How do they disagree?
4. What is the role of social construction in structuration theory and CCO?
5. What is the difference between CCO theory and institutional theory? How do they intersect?

Practitioners' Corner

At first glance, it may seem that developments in organizational communication in the 21st century have been more philosophical than practical. Yet, as always, organizational communication remains centered on daily experiences of organizational life. The structuration and CCO perspectives exemplify contemporary organizational communication theory as both abstract and immediately applicable. The central explanations of both emphasize the mutually enabling and constraining relationship between communicating and organizing. This basic understanding can empower organizational leaders and members to enact positive changes in daily activities to purposefully create repetitive structures that are more efficient and effective. Introducing new practices that can be communicatively linked to an existing structure (values, norms, goals, practices, etc.) can create new conventions for tomorrow. Working to eliminate ineffective practices can likewise open opportunities for positive permanent change as their underlying dysfunctional structures die away.

What we do every day, including how we communicate, is drawn from the conventions of yesterday and perpetuates those conventions. This understanding can create a fundamental self-awareness at the deepest level in how we frame, define, and approach our relationships with others. An understanding of the mutually enabling and constraining relationship between structures (or texts, for a Montreal approach) and communication helps us understand such things as applications of technology (AST), negative behavior cycles (SDT), and development of policy (SAT), and thus how to contribute to such things productively. As revealed by Cooren et al. (2013) and Nicotera et al. (2014), awareness of the underlying CCO processes that constitute our everyday realities improves individual and group organizational functioning.

References

Ballard-Reisch, D., & Turner, P. K. (2017). Contradictions, tensions, paradoxes, and dialectics. In C. R. Scott & L. Lewis (Eds.), *The international encyclopedia of organizational communication* (online edition). Hoboken, NJ: Wiley-Blackwell. doi:10.1002/9781118955567.wbieoc043.

Barker, J. R. (1993). Tightening the iron cage: Concertive control in self-managing teams. *Administrative Science Quarterly, 38*(3), 408–437. doi:10.2307/2393374.

Baxter, L. A. (1988). A dialectical perspective of communication strategies in relationship development. In S. Duck (Ed.), *Handbook of personal relationships* (pp. 257–273). New York: Wiley.

Benoit-Barné, C., & Cooren, F. (2009). The accomplishment of authority through presentification: How authority is distributed among and negotiated by organizational members. *Management Communication Quarterly, 23*(1), 5–31. doi:10.1177/0893318909335414.

Burke, K. (1965). *Permanence and change*. Indianapolis: Bobbs-Merrill. (Original work published 1954.)

Canary, H. E. (2010). Structurating activity theory: An integrative approach to policy knowledge. *Communication Theory, 20*(1), 21–49. doi:10.1111/j.1468-2885.2009.01354.x.

Cheney, G., & Ashcraft, K. L. (2007). Considering "the professional" in communication studies: Implications for theory and research within and beyond the boundaries of organizational communication. *Communication Theory, 17*(2), 146–175. doi:10.1111/j.1468-2885.2007.00290.x.

Cheney, G., Speirs-Glebe, L., Stohl, C., DeGooyer, D., Whalen, S., Garvin-Doxas, K., et al. (1998). Democracy, participation and communication at work: A multi-disciplinary review. In M. E. Roloff (Ed.), *Communication yearbook 21* (pp. 35–91). Thousand Oaks, CA: SAGE.

Connaughton, S. L., Linabary, J. R., & Yakova, L. (2017). Discursive construction. In C. R. Scott & L. Lewis (Eds.), *The international encyclopedia of organizational communication* (online edition). Hoboken, NJ: Wiley-Blackwell. doi:10.1002/9781118955567.wbieoc063.

Cooren, F. (2006). The organizational world as a plenum of agencies. In F. Cooren, J. R. Taylor, & E. J. Van Every (Eds.), *Communication as Organizing: Practical Approaches to Research into the Dynamic of Text and Conversation* (pp. 81–100). Mahwah, NJ: Lawrence Erlbaum Associates.

Cooren, F. (2010). Figures of communication and dialogue: Passion, ventriloquism and incarnation. *Intercultural Pragmatics, 7*(1), 131–145. doi:10.1515/IPRG.2010.006.

Cooren, F., Matte, F., Brummans, B., & Benoit-Barné, C. (2013). Communication as ventriloquism: A grounded-in-action approach to the study of organizational tensions. *Communication Monographs, 80*(3), 255–277. doi:10.1080/03637751.2013.788255.

Cooren, F., Kuhn, T., Cornelissen, J., & Clark, T. (2011). Communication, organizing and organization: An overview and introduction to the special issue. *Organization Studies, 32*(9), 1149–1170. doi:10.1177/0170840611410836.

Corman, S. R., & Poole, M. S. (2000). *Perspectives on organizational communication: Finding common ground*. New York, NY: Guilford Press.

Cornelissen, J. P., Durand, R., Fiss, P., Lammers, J. C., & Vaara, E. (2015). Putting communication front and center in institutional theory and analysis. *Academy of Management Review*, *40*(1), 10–27. doi:10.5465/amr.2014.0381.

DeSanctis, G., & Poole, M. S. (1994). Capturing the complexity in advanced technology use: Adaptive structuration theory. *Organization Science*, *5*(2), 121–147. doi:10.1287/orsc.5.2.121.

DiMaggio, P. J., & Powell, W. W. (1983). The iron cage revisited: Institutional isomorphism and collective rationality in organization fields. *American Sociological Review*, *48*(2), 147–160. doi:10.2307/2095101.

Fairhurst, G. T., & Putnam, L. L. (2004). Organizations as discursive constructions. *Communication Theory*, *14*(1), 5–26. doi:10.1111/j.1468-2885.2004.tb00301.x.

Foot, K. A. (2001). Cultural-historical activity theory as practice theory: Illuminating the development of a conflict-monitoring network. *Communication Theory*, *11*(1), 56–83. doi:10.1111/j.1468-2885.2001.tb00233.x.

Frey, L. (1995). Magical elixir or what the top tells the middle to do to the bottom? The promises and paradoxes of facilitating work teams for promoting organizational change and development. In R. Cesaria & P. Shockley-Zalabak (Eds.), *Organization means communication: Making the organizational communication concept relevant to practice* (pp. 173–188). Rome, Italy: Servizio Italiano Pubblicazioni Internationali Sri.

Giddens, A. (1979). *Central problems in social theory: Action, structure, and contradiction in social analysis*. Berkeley: University of California Press.

Giddens, A. (1984). *The constitution of society: Outline of the theory of structuration*. Berkeley, CA: University of California Press.

Giddens, A. (1987). *The nation-state and violence*. Berkeley, CA: University of California Press.

Green, S. E., Jr., Babb, M., & Alpaslan, C. M. (2008). Institutional field dynamics and the competition between institutional logics: The role of rhetoric in the evolving control of the modern corporation. *Management Communication Quarterly*, *22*(1), 40–73. doi:10.1177/0893318908318430.

Janis, I. (1982). *Groupthink* (2nd ed.). Dallas: Houghton Mifflin.

Krone, K. (2005). Trends in organizational communication research: Sustaining the discipline, sustaining ourselves. *Communication Studies*, *56*(1), 95–105. doi:10.1080/0008957042000332269.

Lammers, J. C. (2011). How institutions communicate: Institutional messages, institutional logics, and organizational communication. *Management Communication Quarterly*, *25*(1), 154–182. doi:10.1177/0893318910389280.

Lammers, J. C., & Barbour, J. B. (2006).An institutional theory of organizational communication. *Communication Theory*, *16*(3), 356–377. doi:10.1111/j.1468-2885.2006.00274.x.

Lammers, J. C., & Garcia, M. A. (2009). Exploring the concept of "profession" for organizational communication research: Institutional influences in a veterinary organization. *Management Communication Quarterly*, *22*(3), 357–384. doi:10.1177/0893318908327007.

Lammers, J. C., & Garcia, M. A. (2017). Institutional theory approaches. In C. R. Scott & L. Lewis (Eds.), *The international encyclopedia of organizational communication* (online edition). Hoboken, NJ: Wiley-Blackwell. doi:10.1002/9781118955567.wbieoc113.

Luhmann, N. (2003). Organization. In T. Bakken & T. Hernes (Eds.), *Autopoietic organization theory: Drawing on Niklas Luhmann's social systems perspective* (pp. 31–52). Oslo, Norway: Copenhagen Business School Press.

McPhee, R. D., & Zaug, P. (2000). The communicative constitution of organizations: A framework for explanation. *Electronic Journal of Communication*, *10*(1–2). Retrieved from www.cios.org/EJCPUBLIC/010/1/01017.html.

Meyer, J. W., & Rowan, B. (1977). Institutionalized organizations: Formal structure as myth and ceremony. *American Journal of Sociology*, *83*(2), 340–363. doi:10.1086/226550.

Montgomery, B. (1988). A dialectical analysis of the tensions, functions and strategic challenges of communication in young adult friendships. In J. A. Anderson (Ed.), *Communication yearbook 12* (pp. 157–189). Newbury, CA: SAGE.

Nicotera, A. M., & Clinkscales, M. J. (2003). *Understanding organization through culture and structure: Relational and other lessons from the African-American organization*. Mahwah, NJ: Erlbaum.

Nicotera, A. M., & Clinkscales, M. J. (2010). Nurses at the nexus: A case study in structurational divergence. *Health Communication*, 25(1), 32–49. doi:10.1080/10410230903473516.

Nicotera, A. M., & Mahon, M. M. (2013). Rocks and hard places: Exploring the impact of structurational divergence in nursing. *Management Communication Quarterly*, 27(1), 90–120. doi:10.1177/0893318912458214.

Nicotera, A. M., Mahon, M. M., & Wright, K. B. (2014). Communication that builds teams: Assessing a nursing conflict intervention. *Nursing Administration Quarterly*, 38(3), 248–260. doi:10.1097/NAQ.0000000000000033.

Nicotera, A. M., Mahon, M. M., & Zhao, X. (2010). Conceptualization and measurement of structurational divergence in the healthcare setting. *Journal of Applied Communication Research*, 38(4), 362–385. doi:10.1080/00909882.2010.514001.

O'Connor, E. (1993). *Paradoxes of participation: A textual analysis of case studies documenting employee involvement efforts*. Unpublished manuscript.

Poole, M. S., & DeSanctis. G. (1990). Understanding the use of group decision support systems: The theory of adaptive structuration. In J. Fulk & C. W. Steinfield (Eds.), *Organizations and communication technology* (pp. 172–193). Newbury Park, CA: SAGE.

Poole, M. S., Seibold, D. & McPhee, R. D. (1985). Group decision-making as a structurational process. *Quarterly Journal of Speech*, 71(1), 74–102. doi:10.1080/00335638509383719.

Poole, M. S., Seibold. D., & McPhee. R. D. (1986). A structurational approach to theory-building in group decision-making research. In R. Y. Hirokawa & M. S. Poole (Eds.), *Communication and group decision-making* (pp. 237–264). Beverly Hills, CA: SAGE.

Putnam, L. L. (2013). Primary and secondary contradictions: A literature review and future directions. *Management Communication Quarterly*, 27, 623–630. doi:10.1177/0893318913504139.

Putnam, L. L., & Fairhurst, G. T. (2015). Revisiting "Organizations as discursive constructions": 10 years later. *Communication Theory*, 25(4), 375–392. doi:10.1111/comt12074.

Putnam, L. L., Fairhurst, G. T., & Banghart, S. S. (2016).Contradictions, dialectics, and paradoxes in organizations: A constitutive approach. *Academy of Management Annals*, 10(1), 65–171. doi:10.1080/19416520.2016.1162421.

Schoenenborn, D., & Vasquez, C. (2017). Communicative constitution of organizations approaches. In C. R. Scott & L. Lewis (Eds.), *The international encyclopedia of organizational communication* (online edition). Hoboken, NJ: Wiley-Blackwell. doi:10.1002/9781118955567.wbieoc030.

Scott, W. R. (2008). *Institutions and organizations* (3rd ed.). Thousand Oaks, CA: SAGE.

Sewell, W. H. (1992). A theory of structure: Duality, agency, and transformation. *The American Journal of Sociology*, 98(1), 1–29. doi:10.1086/229967.

Stohl, C. (1995). Paradoxes of participation. In R. Cesaria & P. Shockley-Zalabak (Eds.), *Organization means communication: Making the organizational communication concept relevant to practice* (pp. 199–215). Rome, Italy: Servizio Italiano Pubblicazioni Internationali Sri.

Stohl, C., & Cheney, G. (2001). Participatory processes/paradoxical practices: Communication and the dilemmas of organizational democracy. *Management Communication Quarterly*, 14(3), 349–407. doi:10.1177/0893318901143001.

Stohl, C., & Sotirin, P. (1989). Absence as workplace control: a critical inquiry. In J. Anderson (Ed.), *Communication yearbook 13* (pp. 59–68). Newbury Park, CA: SAGE.

Taylor, J. R. (2009). Organizing from the bottom up? Reflections on the constitution of organization in communication. In L. L. Putnam & A. M. Nicotera (Eds.), *Building theories of organization: The constitutive role of communication* (pp. 153–186). New York, NY: Routledge

Taylor, J. R. (2011). Organization as an (imbricated) configuring of transactions. *Organization Studies*, 32(9), 1273–1294. doi:10.1177/0170840611411396.

Taylor, J. R., Cooren, F., Giroux, N., & Robichaud, D. (1996). The communicational basis of organization: Between the conversation and the text. *Communication Theory, 6*(1), 1–39. doi:10.1111/j.1468-2885.1996.tb00118.x.

Taylor, J. R., Flanagin, A. J., Cheney, G., & Seibold, D. R. (2001). Organizational communication research: Key moments, central concerns and future challenges. In W. B. Gudykunst (Ed.), *Communication yearbook 24* (pp. 99–137). Thousand Oaks, CA: SAGE.

Taylor, J. R., & Van Every, E. J. (2000). *The emergent organization: Communication as its site and surface*. Mahwah, NJ: Lawrence Erlbaum Associates.

Trethewey, A., & Ashcraft, K. L. (2004). Special issue introduction. *Journal of Applied Communication Research, 32*(2), 81–88. doi:10.1080/00909880042000210007.

Vygotsky, L. S. (1978). *Mind in society: The development of higher psychological processes*. Trans. M. Cole, V. John-Steiner, S. Scribner, & E. Souberman. Cambridge, MA: Harvard University Press.

Watzlawick, P., Beavin, J., & Jackson, D. (1967). *Pragmatics of human communication*. New York: W. W. Norton & Co.

Weber, M. (1978). *Economy and society: An outline of interpretive sociology*. Eds. G. Roth & C. Wittich. Berkeley: University of California Press.

4 Paradigms: Ways of Knowing in Organizational Communication

Anne M. Nicotera

A *paradigm* is a metatheoretical framework adopted by scholars as a perspective from which to approach the study of phenomena: a way of knowing. A *phenomenon* is an occurrence, circumstance, or process in the world that theory seeks to explain, such as *leadership, productivity, teamwork*, or *conflict*. Scholars across the social disciplines adopt a variety of assumptions about phenomena; these assumptions drive empirical research questions and research methods. A paradigm is a complex and internally consistent set of assumptions that constitute a conceptual stance. The most important criteria for evaluating the soundness, or rigor, of a theory or a piece of research are the internal consistency of its paradigmatic assumptions and the consistency of those assumptions with the claims of a theory, the methodologies used in research, and the conclusions drawn.

Organizational Communication Paradigms

The field of organizational communication is characterized by three major paradigms. These are summarized and compared in this chapter, to provide a summary of the paradigmatic state of the field from the detail provided in previous chapters. The first is the *positivist* approach, sometimes called *post-positivist*, which relies heavily on deductive reasoning. This paradigm is associated with structural-functionalism, as described in Chapter 2. The second approach is the *interpretivist* approach, which uses disciplined subjectivity as an important source of knowledge and understanding and relies heavily on inductive reasoning. The third is the *critical-interpretive* approach, usually called simply *critical theory*. In the field of organizational communication, the critical approach grew as an extension of interpretivism. However, in other social disciplines you may find critical theory based on positivist assumptions. So it is important to remember that in our field, critical theory presumes a critical-interpretive framework.

Deductive theory-building generates a theory from existing knowledge before doing empirical observation; whereas inductive theory-building does the opposite. It is important to take a moment here to clarify the basic distinction between the terms *deductive* and *inductive*. Deductive logic begins with a general statement and applies that statement to a specific observation. The general statement can be thought of as the theory, based on things we already know, and the observation (research) is application of the theory. The theory comes first; then observation tests it. Deductive reasoning starts with an abstraction and concludes a concrete statement from it. For example, existing knowledge (from our literature) tells us that aligning organizational goals with employee development goals improves productivity. Applying deductive logic, a researcher might hypothesize that managers using strategies based on employee development will have more productive departments than managers using strategies based on externally derived reward/punishment systems. To test that hypothesis, an empirical study would need to measure the managerial system (coding each manager according to which system s/he seems to follow), productivity, and other differences between the groups. For deductive logic, the conclusion—in this case a hypothesis—is the specific concrete statement. In *post-positivist* theory-building, which is largely deductive, abstract theories are developed from the existing literature on the topic and then are tested with empirical observations.

On the other hand, inductive logic begins with a concrete observation and concludes with an abstraction. The observation comes first; then the theory is the general statement that is drawn from the observation. Grounded theory follows this general approach, in addition to other strict methodological requirements. For example, a scholar may divide managers into groups based on the productivity of their units, and then observe the managers and units to discern differences between high- and low-performing units. Applying inductive logic, the research may conclude that the observable and consistent differences between the high- and low-performing groups explain their different outcomes. The research may then turn to an existing theory of leadership or management to conceptualize an abstract and transferable explanation. With inductive logic, the conclusion is the general abstract statement. In *interpretivist* and *critical-interpretivist* theory-building, which are largely inductive, extensive empirical observations are made and then abstract theories are drawn from those data.

The actual practice of theory-building in all three paradigms combines deductive and inductive reasoning. For example, post-positivist researchers often use inductive logic and practices to generate hypotheses when existing knowledge is inconclusive or incomplete. In addition, when existing knowledge is inadequate to allow confident prediction, the researcher will employ empirical research questions rather than hypotheses. Interpretivists and critical-interpretivists may draw conclusions prior to data-collection, in the form of assumptions based on previous knowledge. The research at hand, then, builds on those assumptions, but generally allows the researcher to question them in the light of new data. When abstract theory and concrete data conflict, the post-positivist paradigm demands we first look for fault in the data; whereas the interpretivist paradigms demand we first question the theory. These rules of thumb are consistent with the respective emphasis on the abstract or concrete as the logical origin.

Overview of the Three Paradigms in Organizational Communication

Post-Positivism

The post-positivist approach assumes, first of all, that there are objective truths about communication. For post-positivists, the research process must strive to be value-neutral. The fundamental positivist goal is to discover the general laws (principles, axioms, etc.) governing human interaction, with an emphasis on prediction and scientific control. This is a deductive approach that attempts to mirror scientific method as it is used in the physical sciences. Post-positivists seek to generalize their findings and claims as much as possible. To do so, they use reductionist methods—breaking the concepts of interest into increasingly smaller and more concrete conceptual units that can be then be operationalized into forms of observation and objectively observed, usually with quantitative measurement (Berger, 1977; Chaffee & Berger, 1987). The post-positivist approach is the most traditional in organizational communication research, largely due to the influence of social psychology on the study of interaction.

From the advent of the field through the 1970s, this deductive, variable-analytic approach to theory and research dominated the field of organizational communication. The label *post-positivism* was adopted by organizational communication scholars in the 1980s to clarify that its positivistic practice reflects adjustments to early 20th century *logical positivism*, which called for pure objectivity in an entirely value-free process of observation that verifies hypotheses. The *hypothetico-deductive* framework of logical positivism relies on strictly causal reasoning, which was largely rejected by the end of the 1960s for a number of reasons. Primarily, the verifiability principle came under serious question. This principle dictates that to be counted as knowledge, a theoretic claim must be empirically verifiable. The impracticality of creating perfect measurements for intangible human cognitive and behavioral phenomena, in addition to the impossibility of eliminating all potential unknown factors, made verifiability itself an impossible goal. Further, because it cannot be proven, the verifiability principle is itself unverifiable.

In practice, scholars realized that observation is necessarily theory-laden rather than value-free. It became clear under scrutiny that logical positivism was detached from the actual practice of social science. Daniels and Frandsen (1984) pointed out that the actual practice of communication science utilized a *hypothetico-constitutive* framework, rather than objectivity in a *hypothetico-deductive* framework. In other words, hypotheses are constituted from existing knowledge by conjecture, rather than deduced from it. Also, objectivity is actually practiced as *intersubjectivity*, which allows discussion of the adequacy of measures used for observation. Finally, in practice, positivist research is carried out through probability. Rather than verification, probability assesses the extent to which a claim is *not falsified*—the statistical null hypotheses.

Interpretivism

The interpretivist approach is subjective, assuming that truth is co-created by people. Interpretivists reject objectivity, instead privileging subjectivity as a more valuable source of insight. The fundamental interpretivist goal is to provide rich descriptions of human phenomena. This is an inductive approach that rejects the deductive scientific method, instead mirroring humanities methods. It is important to note that interpretivists do often seek to transfer knowledge across situations, but are careful not to generalize. Interpretivists expand their conceptual units rather than reducing them. Interpretivist methods begin with concrete observations, creating increasingly larger and more abstract conceptual units that can then be applied across situations. Two important publications launched this paradigm with a number of essays by leading scholars: A book, entitled *Communication and Organizations: An Interpretive Approach*, edited by Putnam and Pacanowsky (1983) and a special issue of the *Western Journal of Speech Communication* (Pacanowsky & Putnam, 1982). In these collections of essays, which also included some of the seminal treatises on the critical paradigm in organizational communication, comprehensive conceptual arguments for the interpretive paradigm were introduced to the field. (See Chapter 2 for an overview of the historical roots of interpretivism and the conceptual shifts it accomplished in organizational communication.)

Critical-Interpretivism

Critical-interpretivists in the field of organizational communication follow the interpretivist approach but add a particular focus on power and domination in society. Like interpretivists, critical-interpretivists assume that reality is subjective and co-created, but they go further to examine the ways in which some societal groups are able to create realities that dominate other groups. Critical scholars assume that those in power shape knowledge in ways that oppress the powerless. Critical feminist theory and critical race theory are commonly used to explore these phenomena. The goal of critical theory is to reveal societal structures of such oppression and work to change them. In organizational communication, the critical movement arose from the interpretivist movement, so even though we often drop the term *interpretivist* to simply call it the *critical paradigm*, we must always remember this is a shorthand reference, and presume that interpretivist assumptions are made by critical theorists in the field of organizational communication. (See Chapter 2 for more detail on the historical influences on the critical turn and the conceptual shifts it accomplished in organizational communication.)

Basic Comparison

The assumptions of the two main paradigms, positivism and interpretivism, are not discrete categories, but rather exist on a continuum. All social scientific scholars sit somewhere along a continuum between these two positions. There are very few scholars who practice either of the pure forms. Most scholars tend to stay toward one side or the other, embracing the assumptions of one but acknowledging that the other has merit for certain questions. Some scholars use one or the other for different projects for relevant tasks, taking the pluralist stance making the assumption that different kinds of questions demand different approaches. It must be emphasized that mixing paradigms in a single research project is not sound because it is internally inconsistent. Mixed-methods research uses the techniques of both paradigms while adhering to the underlying assumptions and ultimate goals of one or the other. Table 4.1 contains a comparison of basic assumptions for post-positivism and interpretivism. As deductive and inductive, these two schools of thought pursue theoretic goals differently. Both describe phenomena as a basis for their other goals. Beyond description, positivist theory strives to explain, predict and control; whereas, interpretivist theory strives to understand and transfer knowledge, and—if critical—to create deep structural social change.

Critical theory. To fully grasp how critical theory fits this continuum, we need to consider a *similarity* of positivism and interpretivism. Although positivist and

Table 4.1 Basic comparison of post-positivism and interpretivism

	Post-positivism	*Interpretivism*
View of reality	Objective	Subjective
Overall goal of research	To find regularities	To understand meaning-creation
Approach to method	Linear	Nonlinear (reflexive)
Path to knowledge	Deductive	Inductive

interpretivist theorists differ in many ways, both hold the general goal of representing aspects of the social world. Critical theorists, however, want to move beyond representation to be active agents of societal reform. Whereas interpretivist theory might be applied to change a phenomenon in a particular situation for particular people, critical theorists want to change oppressive practices in societal structures on a broad scale. They often do this in communication studies by analyzing language use. Subtle uses of language can indicate deep societal structures of racism, sexism, discrimination, unearned privilege, oppressive micro-practices, and so on. For example, consider the label *woman engineer.* That we use such a phrase to indicate a woman in a scientific profession reveals an underlying societal structure for gender-sanctioned occupations. Engineering is embedded in Western societal structure as a masculine role, so when this deeply embedded societal value is violated, the language people use to mark that practice reveals the underlying oppressive structure. Critical theorists strive to identify these underlying structures and sensitize people to the practices that reveal and perpetuate them. Changing day-to-day practices, such as our language use, is a first step to altering the underlying structures.

Metatheory

Metatheory is a body of philosophy and assumptions about the nature of theory and research—theory of theory. There are four basic sets of metatheoretical assumptions relevant to all communication theory: *ontology, epistemology, axiology,* and *praxeology. Ontology* is concerned with the nature of human reality. *Epistemology* is a set of assumptions about knowledge. *Axiology* is about values and their place in theory and research. Finally, *praxeology,* which is sometimes characterized as a subset of axiology, is principally concerned with what can and should be done with the outcomes of theory and research. Each of these will be examined in turn by examining the basic questions posed by each and how positivists and interpretivists make assumptions that answer those questions very differently.

Ontology. *Ontology* is concerned with the nature of human reality, of being and nonbeing. Ontological assumptions form the fundamental background for theorizing because they characterize the phenomenon of interest, defining the object of study (leadership, productivity, conflict, etc.). Ontology is explained here with four basic ontological questions. For each, the purely post-positivist and interpretivist answers should be seen as opposite ends of a continuum.

Ontological question 1: What is the human relationship with social reality? This question fundamentally addresses whether reality is external or internal. The *post-positivist* assumes we live in an external social reality we receive by observation (referred to as *the received view*). The *interpretivist,* on the other hand, assumes that our social reality lives in us—is internal. Because the interpretivist assumes that social reality is constructed by human interaction and human interpretation, it is often referred to as *the social constructionist view.*

Ontological question 2: Do human beings make real choices? Although Western culture is very heavily invested in the assumption—and value—of human free will, post-positivists generally see human action as driven by forces beyond the individual's control. For example, Lester and Bower (2003) conducted post-positivist research on supervisor–subordinate communication. (This research also presents an example that also nicely illustrates the deductive reasoning and reductionism of post-positivism.) Their focused literature review allowed them to create a theoretical structure linking trust to outcomes. They first note that the literature provides ample evidence that *trust* is a key factor in effective leadership. Their first reductionist move is to focus on the subordinate. Then, they reduce *trust* to two variables: trust in the supervisor and the extent to which the subordinate feels trusted by the supervisor. Finally, three specific outcomes are identified: performance, organizational citizenship behaviors (effective activities above and beyond job duties), and job satisfaction. These five variables were measured with existing well-researched scales, either self-report or reported by the supervisor. All aspects of measurement were thoroughly theoretically reasoned using the literature. They hypothesized that the extent to which a subordinate feels trusted will be associated with their performance, organizational citizenship behavior, and job satisfaction. Further, they hypothesized that feeling trusted would be a significant predictor of these three outcomes even after their trust of their supervisor had been accounted for. Statistical analyses were performed that included mathematically controlling for other variables, such as managerial level of the subordinate, primary language, education, and age. The results support all hypotheses. The theoretical explanations expressed in the hypotheses are thus accepted.

You may be asking what this example has to do with choice. Consider organizational citizenship behaviors. These are voluntary behaviors beyond the job description. They contribute to organizational effectiveness, but are neither dictated by the supervisor nor reflected in the organizational reward system. So, why do people choose do them? According to this research, we choose to do them when we feel trusted by our supervisors. If feeling trusted by the supervisor predicts these behaviors, and feeling trusted is attributable to the supervisor's behavior toward the subordinate (which the theoretic structure constructed here dictates), then the "choice" is not internally driven but externally determined. Post-positivists assume that human choices can be predicted by culture, upbringing, experiences, and a host of other factors (including interpretations in an acknowledgement of human subjectivity). The post-positivist looks for *regularity* in human behavior that is *externally* determined, thus negating the ontological question of personal choice. Under positivism, our choices are driven by predictable factors, and prediction of those choices is dependent on discovering those factors.

An interpretivist, on the other hand, looks at the highly individualized factors of meaning-creation and social construction and assumes humans do make real choices. While an interpretivist would not ignore the pattern of relationship between trust and outcomes, the theorist would ask very different kinds of questions that focus on social constructions of meaning that lead to individuals' choices and on the situational richness of the specific contexts. An interpretivist would be interested in individual meaning differences in what constitutes the interpretation of *feeling trusted* and how we, as individuals, make sense of that. The interpretivist would be interested in how that sensemaking contextualizes our choice of action.

Ontological question 3: Which is more important, the ways in which human individuals are alike or the ways in which they are unique? Post-positivist theory, which is interested in regularities, will assume that human similarities are the most important things to examine. For post-positivism, consistency is the music, but uniqueness is the noise—the phenomena of most importance lie in the regularities of human behavior. Individual differences are examined for how they predict behavior in regular fashion. On the other hand, interpretivist theory assumes that individuals' uniqueness is the most important feature for examination—distinctive meaning-creation and individual sense-making are where the phenomena of importance lie. This difference between the paradigms leads to the last question.

Ontological question 4: Is human behavior predictable? Post-positivists assume human choice is driven by factors beyond the actor's control to the point that regularities in human behavior occur, and further, that those regularities are the most important phenomena to examine. Hence, the assumption of *predictability* in human behavior follows. Conversely, interpretivists assume that humans do make their own choices because they are individually and situationally unique in the ways they create meaning and make sense of the world. Hence, interpretivists presume that behavior is not predictable. It is very important to note the internal consistency within each paradigm in the assumptions for each question. See Figure 4.1.

Epistemology. *Epistemology* addresses questions about knowledge, both the nature of knowledge and how we achieve it. *Post-positivist* epistemology is objectivist, assuming that it is possible to explain the social world and that knowledge is discovered through the researcher's objectivity. *Interpretivist* epistemology is subjectivist, assuming that the social world is relativistic and thus unexplainable, and further, that knowledge is created through the disciplined use of the researcher's subjectivity. Epistemology translates directly to research methods—how the theorist goes about empirical observation and data analysis. It is important to note here not only the internal consistency in each paradigm in their epistemological assumptions, but also the consistency of those assumptions with each paradigm's ontology as well. Epistemology is explained here with four basic epistemological questions. Like ontology, the purely positivist and interpretivist answers should be seen as opposite ends of a continuum. Most scholars sit somewhere in between, generally more toward one end than the other.

Epistemological question 1: Is knowledge objective or subjective? Post-positivist theory assumes knowledge is objective, consistent with an ontology presuming reality is external, human behavior is predictable, and so on. Interpretivist theory assumes knowledge is subjective, consistent with an ontology presuming socially constructed reality.

Epistemological question 2: Does knowledge exist before human experience? In other words, is knowledge external (waiting out there to be discovered) or is it internal—only coming to exist when we as human beings create it? This fundamental philosophical question ponders whether anything can be called *knowledge* before a human being possesses or experiences it. If knowledge is objective and reality is

Post-positivist	What is the human relationship with social reality?	Interpretivist/ Critical-interpretivist
SOCIAL REALITY IS EXTERNAL	What is the human relationship with social reality?	SOCAL REALITY IS INTERNAL
NO	Do humans make real choices?	YES
ALIKE	Are humans mostly alike or mostly unique?	UNIQUE
YES	Is human behavior predictable?	NO

Figure 4.1 Summary of ontological assumptions

external, then knowledge is separate from human thinking. As such, post-positivism assumes knowledge is external and discovered. Scientists do not create scientific knowledge—they make scientific discoveries, and those discoveries comprise a body of knowledge. On the other end of the continuum, if the interpretive paradigm assumes knowledge is subjective, that means knowledge is defined as something internal that human beings create. It is not knowledge until it is experienced, which is part of its creation.

Epistemological question 3: Can knowledge be certain? In post-positivism, knowledge is objective, external, and discovered, so it can also be certain. If knowledge is external and objective it can be verified with external objective standards. On the other hand, in the interpretivist paradigm knowledge is subjective, internal, and created, so it cannot be certain because it is deeply embedded in unique persons and contexts.

Epistemological question 4: How does knowledge come to exist? The answer to this question is very nuanced because, as previously discussed, the pure logical positivist ideal was rejected long ago—the impossibility of verification being the most problematic issue for practice. As you recall, this is the reason for the label *post-positivism*. Ideally, for the post-positivist, knowledge is objective, external, discoverable, and certain. Hence, *rationalism*—the process of pure deductive logic—is considered by positivism to be the purest path to knowledge. A sequence of pure deductive logic begins with a major premise of abstract fact presumed to be true, such as *all men are mortal*. It then introduces a minor premise of concrete fact presumed to be true, such as *Socrates is a man*. Then, we can draw a concrete conclusion, such as *Socrates is mortal*. If the major and minor premises are both true, the conclusion must also be true. We do not have to make Socrates drink hemlock to test whether he is mortal, we can know that he is mortal purely through rationalism. In the actual practice of social science theory and research, however, the availability of premises in whose truth we can place full confidence is lacking. So, post-positivists cannot function at the purely positivist end of our continuum. They must take an epistemological stance that is more toward the middle, in the form of *empiricism*. In the practice of post-positivist research, knowledge comes to exist through hypothesis-testing—the heart of scientific method in the physical sciences. Rationalism is used to generate hypotheses, but because we cannot have full confidence in the truth of the premises, empiricism must be used to test them. Making Socrates drink hemlock would test the hypothesis that Socrates is mortal. Together, rationalism and empiricism comprise the scientific method, which drives the methodological choices of post-positivism. Because positivism is objective, the knower (researcher) must be separated from the known (phenomenon). To separate themselves, post-positivists refer to the people observed as *subjects* or *respondents*.

At the interpretivist end of the paradigmatic continuum, knowledge is subjective, internal and created, and uncertain. Given those assumptions, knowledge comes to exist through human subjective construction. The knower *cannot* be separated from the known. To unite themselves with the people observed, interpretivists refer to them as *participants* or *co-researchers*, whose points of view and interpretations are a crucial part of creating scholarly knowledge. Further, interpretivists often engage in *participant-observation*, to immerse themselves in the experience they are observing. Interpretivist knowledge-creation can be individual or social. *Constructivism* is individual interpretation. Scholars come to an understanding of phenomena by observing them, participating in them, and reflecting on that experience. An individual scholar or theorist interprets the observations they make of phenomenon according to the framework and knowledge that they already have about that phenomenon. The purest form of interpretivist knowledge-creation is *social constructivism*, which is when interpretations are co-created among multiple people rather than one person alone. A key technique of interpretivist researchers is the *member-check*, asking the participants themselves to review the researcher's conclusions to assess whether they reflect their own experience and interpretations.

Constructivism and social constructivism together comprise humanistic methods, which drive the methodological choices of interpretivism. Whereas post-positivism uses scientific methods following the traditions of physical sciences, interpretivism uses humanistic methods following the traditions of the humanities (such as history, literature, and art), in addition to anthropological methods of cultural ethnography. For an overview of epistemology and a graphic representation of internal consistency in these paradigmatic assumptions, see Figure 4.2.

Axiology. The third branch of metatheory, *axiology*, is the study of values. The post-positivist paradigm assumes that the theorist's values will bias the research. Like dust from the air that will contaminate a laboratory experiment, the scholar's own values are extraneous variables that must be controlled and excluded from the research process. Whereas logical positivism dictated that research must be value-free, post-positivists acknowledge that this is not possible and, rather, that values must be controlled. The interpretivist paradigm dictates the opposite—that values are an important tool for research that should be closely examined and used to drive research design and data interpretation. In the middle of the continuum, scholars acknowledge values and try to understand how they influence the process of theory and research. Axiology can be explained here with two simple questions. As usual, the purely post-positivist and interpretivist answers should be seen as opposite ends of a continuum. Axiological assumptions for each paradigm are consistent with its ontology and epistemology.

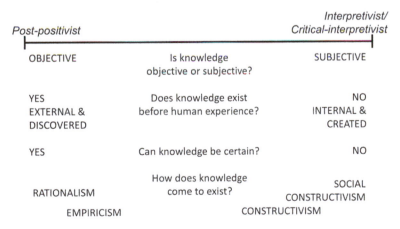

Figure 4.2 Summary of epistemological assumptions

Axiological question 1: Should values be part of our research? The post-positivist paradigm assumes values should be controlled so that they do not contaminate research. If knowledge is external, objective, and certain, then values can only obstruct our view of the phenomenon. Post-positivists use their values to inform their research interests, guiding their selection of phenomena that are the most important for us to understand. They also use their values to guide the ethics of their research (so no one would actually empirically test Socrates' mortality). Finally, they use their values to inform their praxis— how they use and apply their conclusions.

Under the interpretive paradigm, if knowledge is seen as subjective, internal and created, and uncertain, then we need to use our values to create knowledge. Like post-positivists, interpretivists' values drive their research interests and ethics, but interpretivists' values also drive their formation of research questions, data analysis decisions, and interpretations of data. Interpretivists use a disciplined process called *bracketing* to examine and understand their own values so that those values can be used as tools for research, rather than biasing the research.

Axiological question 2: Does observation influence the phenomenon? The logical positivist paradigm assumed that since the phenomenon is external to human experience, observing it cannot change it. However, post-positivists do assume that their presence as an observer may introduce an uncontrolled variable. Post-positivists are careful not to let their observations introduce uncontrolled variables into the phenomena under study—or at the very least, to identify these variables and control for them in the research design and data analysis.

On the other end of the continuum, the interpretivist paradigm assumes that since knowledge is humanly created, the process of observation necessarily changes the phenomenon observed. The interpretivist makes note of the influences observation may have on the phenomenon and uses that to better understand it. See Figure 4.3, and note how the assumptions on the left and right sides of Figures 4.1, 4.2, and 4.3 are consistent.

Praxeology. Finally, *praxeology* is the study of human conduct. It is here that the distinction between *interpretivism* and *critical-interpretivism* is made. *Praxis* is translating theory into action, designing practical applications of a theory. The *post-positivist* tradition accomplishes praxis by using scholarly knowledge to create prescriptive principles to follow, applying the principle of scientific control. The *interpretivist* tradition might apply theory by creating a set of guidelines by which to subjectively analyze a situation and plan a course of action.

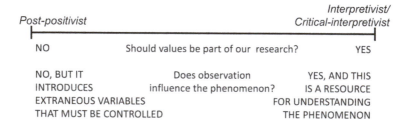

Figure 4.3 Summary of axiological assumptions

For the *critical* tradition, however, praxis is far more central. Critical theory by definition must change the social world by working toward the eradication of dominance and oppression. Critical-interpretivists define praxis as the process of shedding false consciousness or ideologies that serve ruling-group interests so as to develop individual and social change. Two simple questions help explain praxeology. As usual, the purely positivist and interpretivist answers should be seen as opposite ends of a continuum. Here, however, critical theory is seen as building upon interpretivism.

Praxeological question 1: Should research attempt to alter phenomena? Here, *social change* is defined as a fundamental altering of the phenomenon in question. Under the post-positivist paradigm this is not even possible because phenomena are external, objective, and certain. Scientific control of an outcome is not the same thing as fundamentally changing a phenomenon. At the other end of the continuum, however, such change is possible. Under interpretivism, social phenomena are assumed to be humanly created. Therefore, they can be humanly changed and should be when doing so is beneficial. For *critical-interpretivists*, however, effecting such social change is a fundamental principle. Critical-interpretivist theory is specifically committed to changing phenomena of oppression and dismantling social structures of domination. The distinction between interpretivism and critical-interpretivism lies in the predominance of this goal for critical-interpretivism.

Praxeological question 2: What should we do with theory? Across paradigms, all scholars seek to describe the social world to promote a deeper understanding of human social life. *Post-positivists* seek to apply theory by identifying predictable patterns that can be controlled by manipulating influential factors. For example, if research shows that employee perceptions of mutual trust improve organizational outcomes, a post-positivist would recommend teaching managers how to manifest their trust in their employees. *Interpretivists* seek to understand the social world, especially as it is situated in particular contexts. Interpretivists seek to apply theory by sensitizing actors to these contexts and teaching them to examine the patterns in ways the research has shown to be insightful. *Critical-interpretivists* specifically seek to apply theory by promoting consciousness-raising about underlying structures of domination that play out in day-to-day interaction, teaching actors to recognize and change the actions that perpetuate dominance and oppression—thus eventually altering the underlying structures (see Figure 4.4).

Implications for Organizational Communication Theory

At its inception, the field of organizational communication was dominated by post-positivism, with the popularity of interpretivism and critical-interpretivism supplanting this dominance in the 1980s and 1990s, respectively. Similar paradigm shifts have taken place at various times in other sub-disciplines of communication studies, as well as in other social sciences. Today, the field of organizational communication has achieved a pluralism characterized by mutual respect among the paradigms, with scholars who subscribe to different paradigms seeking to better understand one another rather than to establish dominance (Corman & Poole, 2000). The three paradigms assume different stances that have profound implications for theorizing. Each creates a distinct approach to conceptualizing communication, theorizing the relation between communication and organization, understanding authority, and approaching culture.

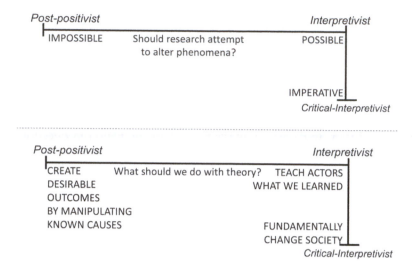

Figure 4.4 Summary of praxeological assumptions

Approach to Communication, Authority, and Culture

Positivism uses causal reasoning, although post-positivists are very careful to avoid deterministic thinking and causal explanations, instead relying on explanations of prediction or influence among variables. Under post-positivism, both communication and organization must be conceptually reduced to measurable *variables*. Communication and organization are treated as mutually influential sets of variables. Organizational variables influence communication, and manipulation of day-to-day communication variables can effect changes in organizational variables. Hence, the interplay between communication and organization is accounted for with reductionist conceptualizations of both. This reductionism is deepened by the necessity of quantifiable observations to achieve the precision demanded by post-positivist research. Post-positivists do not deny the social constructionist function of communication. However, they do not examine those meaning-creating processes; such a research question would not be driven by a post-positivist ontology. Rather, post-positivist research accounts for meaning-creation by examining quantified, self-reported perceptions.

On the other hand, the social-constructivist ontology and epistemology of interpretivism and critical-interpretivism provide the opportunity for a more processual approach to communication and organization. Meaning-creation can be foregrounded and directly theorized. Interpretivist perspectives are well-suited for generating research questions to examine the mutually constitutive relationship between communication and organization. See Table 4.2 for a comparison of the three paradigms in their approach to central organizational communication phenomena.

Table 4.2 Paradigmatic approaches to central organizational communication phenomenon

	Post-positivism	Interpretivism	Critical-Interpretivism
Communication-Organization Interplay	mutually causal linear/circular variable-analytic	mutually constitutive processual/reflexive meaning-creation	
Authority	… is a set of variables.	… is a socially constructed process.	… is a socially constructed process used by the dominant class to maintain their power over meaning.
			… is internalized by the oppressed, who are complicit in their own domination.
Culture	… is a set of variables.	… is socially-constructed.	
	… can be used as a management tool.	… emerges from interaction.	
	… is something organizations *have*.	… is something organizations *are*.	

Recommended Supplementary Readings

Buzzanell, P. M. (1994.) Gaining a voice: Feminist organizational communication theorizing. *Management Communication Quarterly*, 7, 339–383.

This article provides a comprehensive overview of feminist theory in organizational communication at the height of its growth.

Chaffee, S. H., & Berger, C. R. (1987). What communication scientists do. In C. R. Berger & S. H. Chaffee (Eds.), *Handbook of communication science* (pp. 99–122). Newbury Park, CA: SAGE.

This chapter provides a detailed summary of the activities and objectives of traditional positivist researchers in communication.

Corman, S. R., & Poole, M. S. (Eds.). (2000). *Perspectives on organizational communication: Finding common ground.* New York: Guilford.

This volume was the outcome of a conference panel discussing ways to bridge gaps among paradigms. This volume ushered in the era of healthy and mutually respectful paradigmatic pluralism that we continue to enjoy.

Craig, R. T. (2013). Constructing theories in communication research. In P. Cobley & P. J. Schulz (Eds.), *Theories and models of communication* (pp. 39–57). Berlin and Boston: De Gruyter Mouton.

This reading could be assigned to advanced students for detailed overviews of the theory-building processes employed in each of the three major paradigms.

Important Concepts: Define and Discuss

Phenomenon
Paradigm
Deductive vs. inductive reasoning
Metatheory
Ontology

Epistemology
Axiology
Praxeology
Post-positivism
Interpretivism
Critical-interpretivism

Discussion Questions

1. Discuss the consistency within paradigms of the answers to basic ontological, epistemological, and praxeological questions.
2. What is the difference between scientific control and social change?
3. Can a study truly achieve the ideals of its paradigm? How so?
4. What would happen if a researcher mixed paradigmatic assumptions in a single piece of research?

Practitioners' Corner

What value does an in-depth understanding of research paradigms have for a practitioner? After all, the production of original research is not what they do. Yet, successful practitioners must apply research findings to their organizational settings. Flipping to the conclusions section of an article, or pulling applicable content from an abstract, is ill-advised. The best applications of research are accomplished through the lens of a critical consumer.

First, understanding and recognizing the paradigm guiding a piece of research provide crucial criteria by which to evaluate its quality. It is naïve to assume publication of the piece of research can assure us of its perfection. Rather, a practitioner should have the ability to apply an evaluative eye to the findings, critiquing the quality of the research and finding its faults, thereby assessing its value for application. Metatheoretically sound research is internally consistent.

Second, paradigmatic understanding provides the knowledge from which to judge generalizability or transferability of research. Conventional wisdom is incorrect in its presumption that positivist research can be more confidently applied than interpretivist research. It depends on each piece of research. Generalizability of positivist research is limited to the parameters of the research setting and the population from which participants are drawn. For example, there may be a connection between trust perceptions and performance, but if the research was conducted in a manufacturing environment, can it be applied to a healthcare setting? Likewise, transferability of interpretivist research is limited by factors such as context and participant characteristics. Yet, interpretivist research that reveals fundamental human processes of social construction may actually be widely applicable when the conditions of that social construction are broadly defined to transcend the research setting. For example, ethnographic field studies that demonstrate fundamental processes of meaning construction and organizing behavior are not limited to the specific setting in which they were conducted.

In short, the best applications of research are grounded in a good understanding of theory and metatheory. A wise practitioner is a critical consumer of research, and understanding paradigm is inordinately helpful in achieving that goal.

References

Berger, C. R. (1977). The covering law perspective as a theoretical basis for the study of human communication. *Communication Quarterly, 25*(1), 7–18. doi:10.1080/01463377709369243.

Buzzanell, P. M. (1994). Gaining a voice: Feminist organizational communication theorizing. *Management Communication Quarterly, 7*(4), 339–383. doi:10.1177/0893318994007004001.

Chaffee, S. H., & Berger, C. R. (1987). What communication scientists do. In C. R. Berger & S. H. Chaffee (Eds.), *Handbook of communication science* (pp. 99–122). Newbury Park, CA: SAGE.

Corman, S. R., & Poole, M. S. (Eds.). (2000). *Perspectives on organizational communication: Finding common ground.* New York: Guilford.

Daniels, T. D., & Frandsen, K. D. (1984). Conventional social science inquiry in human communication: Theory and practice. *Quarterly Journal of Speech, 70*(3), 223–240. doi:10.1080/00335638409383693.

Lester, S.W., & Bower, H. (2003). In the eyes of the beholder: The relationship between subordinates' felt trustworthiness and their work attitudes and behaviors. *Journal of Leadership and Organizational Studies, 10*(2), 17–33. doi:10.1177/107179190301000203

Pacanowsky, M., & Putnam, L. L. (Eds.). (1982). Interpretive approaches to the study of organizational communication. *Western Journal of Speech Communication, 46*(2), 114–207. doi:10.1080/10570318209374071.

Putnam, L. L. (1982). Paradigms for organizational communication research: An overview and synthesis. *Western Journal of Speech Communication, 46*(2), 192–206. doi:10.1080/10570318209374077.

Putnam, L. L. (1983). The interpretive perspective: An alternative to functionalism. In L. L. Putnam & M. Pacanowsky (Eds.), *Communication and organizations: An interpretive approach* (pp. 31–54). Newbury Park: SAGE.

Putnam, L. L. & Pacanowsky, M. (Eds.). (1983). *Communication and organizations: An interpretive approach.* Newbury Park: SAGE.

Part II
Foundational Organizational Theory

In this section, the traditional/historical organizational theories treated in previous generations as foundations of organizational communication are reviewed—not just as conceptual foundations for the field, but also as societal forces that shaped (and continue to shape) organizational forms, practices, and management. One cannot adequately understand contemporary organizations as communicatively constructed and constituted without appreciation of the constitutive power of these foundational bodies of theory. As prescriptions, these theories quite literally wrote the scripts that contemporary organizations follow.

5 Classical Management Theory

Anne M. Nicotera

Industrialization and the Advent of the Large Organization

Human organizing is, of course, as old as human social groups. Large organizations (e.g., shipbuilders, religious orders, militaries) have likewise existed for centuries, but became the norm only with industrialization (Perrow, 1991). The shift in society to commonplace large organizations heralded the introduction of formal organizational theory to the mainstream. The postindustrial body of organizational theory (particularly management theory) was of course influenced by ancient texts—such as Kautilya's *Arthashastra* (Rangarajan, 1992, original circa 300 BCE), 1992), Sun Tzu's 6th-century *Art of War*, or Machiavelli's (2005, original 1515) *The Prince*. Such texts, however, were intended for the heads of nations, religions, and armies; whereas postindustrial organizational and management theory were written for heads of commercial entities and their agents—and eventually for everyone, as employment by and membership in large organizations became increasingly more commonplace.

Industrialization brought *wage dependency*—surviving by "working for someone else (and their profit) and receiving compensation in the form of money" (Perrow, 1991, p. 729). Perrow notes that by 1820, 20 percent of the U.S. population was wage dependent, surging to well over 80 percent by 1950 and continuing to rise thereafter. Other industrialized nations saw similar trends. As wage dependency became more widespread, the complexity and size of organizations increased, to the largely impersonal world of organizations we know today. Perrow's argument that contemporary society is an *organizational society* is compelling, as is his theory that organizations have, in fact, *absorbed society* through wage dependency and two other ensuing developments. First, the social costs of large organizations (e.g., increased crime rates and decreased sanitary conditions) were externalized to the community. Second, factory bureaucracy accomplished unobtrusive control.

> Activities that once were performed by relatively autonomous and usually small informal groups (e.g. family, neighborhood) and small autonomous organizations (small businesses, local government, local church) are now performed by large bureaucracies. This is the "pure" case of absorption—the large organization with many employees. As a result, the organization that employs many people can shape their lives in many ways, most of which are quite unobtrusive and subtle, and alternative sources of shaping in the community decline.
>
> (Perrow, 1991, p. 726)

Prior to the Industrial Revolution (roughly 1760–1820), society was largely agrarian, and goods were produced by artisans working as individuals or in small groups. Individuals and families, in small communities, subsisted on their own production, consuming based on what they produced, trading their surplus among themselves, and providing services to one another in exchange for goods. Then, technological advances created a workforce who, instead, sold their *labor* for *currency* that could be exchanged for goods and services. This shift disrupted the direct interdependency that had existed within communities, created dependency on organizations, and depersonalized the exchange of goods and services.

The European and American railroads, in particular, hastened the shift by allowing a wide distribution of products that created demand for increasing levels of mass production—resulting in even more large organizations to support that demand for distribution. As demand for mass-produced goods increased, the workforce to be managed became larger and less individualized, requiring more impersonal methods of controlling that production. Salaried managers, as an identifiable group, were fully in place by 1900 (Khurana, 2010). This group's need for management skills created a demand for management theory to teach them how to accomplish organizational tasks through managing a massive and depersonalized workforce. At the same time, the consequences of large-scale industrial production were externalized to the community (Perrow, 1991), creating more need for more large organizations to manage problems such as unemployment, industrial accidents, pollution, and overcrowding in cities—further requiring assistance in the development of techniques to manage large workforces in the accomplishment of large-scale goals.

The classical management theory reviewed in this chapter is best described as postindustrial management theory and is the precursor to organizational communication theory. An appreciation of the prescriptive nature of classical management theory is exceedingly important for a full understanding of contemporary organizational communication phenomena and theory. Management theory generally, and early management theory in particular, is constructed with the express purpose of discovering and promoting practices that maximize effectiveness and efficiency for goal-attainment. Unlike social science theory (like that in the field of organizational communication), which seeks to describe and understand human social phenomena as they exist, management theory is intended to instruct managers on what to do to maximize their achievement of organizational objectives. The implications are profound: Classical management theory was a set of instructions for early managers. *Early classical management theory thus actually created and perpetuated practices that have fashioned the very phenomena studied by organizational theorists a century later.* Structures and systems for authority, formal and informal communication, power relationships, organizational form and design—all things organizational that are now the subject of our descriptive theorizing—were formed by the implementation of prescriptions from these early theories. Our social construction of organizing today is thus profoundly shaped by early management theory. As you will see, presumptions about such things as formalization, division of labor, chains of command, formal authority, and appropriate communication practices are rooted in the instructions given by classical management theory. As prominent writers told us (as a society), "this is how it is done well," social constructions of organizing followed these directives to become entrenched and self-propagating.

Classical Economists, Industrial Innovators, and the Rise of the Salaried Manager

Classical management theory did not arise from a vacuum. Statesmen and scholars have been writing about society and its concerns for time immemorial—in earnest since the Enlightenment. Treatises on the human condition, moral living, and public success abound throughout history. For postindustrial management practices, classical economists Adam Smith and John Stuart Mill most influentially shaped how we think about organizing. Even if you have never heard of Adam Smith, you have probably heard reference to his treatise on economics, entitled *An Inquiry into the Nature and Causes of the Wealth of Nations* (1776) but often shorthanded as *Wealth of Nations*. Because of this work, Smith is widely regarded as the father of modern economics. The work contains two central messages. First, marketplace competition improves economic prosperity. His other main point is more directly applicable to the management of workers (and thus to organizational communication): Each person, by working industriously for his own interests, promotes the economic interests of the group and of society. Productive labor at the individual level is the fundamental unit of production on a wide societal (or organizational) scale. *In classical management theory, the very purpose of managerial effort is to increase and maintain individual-level worker productivity.*

John Stuart Mill's treatise, *On Liberty* (1859) is a central foundation of our own discipline in its passion for the importance of free and ethical speech to individual and societal growth. However, it his writings on economics, primarily *Principles of Political Economy* (1848), that set the ground for management theorists. Mill wrote extensively about the relationship between labor and production, remuneration to workers for their labor, the nature of productivity (material and immaterial products of labor), and capital as a stock produced by labor. These ideas, too, greatly influenced the way management theory later defined labor, laborers, and productivity.

At the same time as these philosophies of economy were being produced, the actual work of industry progressed quickly. Prominent industrialists, such as Eli Whitney and James Watt, shaped industrial practices for production and efficiency (e.g., standardization, product quality control, cost-accounting, etc.) that management theorists examined in the search for the best way to manage labor. In these early days, worker productivity was the chief concern of management theorists. This often led to exploitation and inhumane treatment of workers.

Classical Management Theorists

Three theorists are commonly identified as comprising the classical era in management theory. *Max Weber*, a German sociologist, taught us how to understand authority and bureaucracy, their ties to sociological phenomena (such as religion and economics), and their social and political implications. The work of *Henri Fayol*, a French industrialist, is largely responsible for how we design organizational structures and forms to achieve managerial control and for identifying managerial imperatives. Finally, *Frederick Taylor*, an American mechanical engineer and management consultant, espoused the scientific study of labor to determine the most efficient means of productivity and the resolute separation of management from labor in both theory and practice.

Max Weber's Legal-Rational Model of Bureaucracy

Writing in the late 19th century, sociologist Max Weber was neither the first nor last scholar to theorize bureaucracy. Weber did, however, provide the most well-known and widely influential scholarly treatise on the sociological functions of bureaucracy, *Economy and Society* (published posthumously in 1922), positing that bureaucracy was the most efficient and rational form of organizing, providing a form of authority "indispensable to the modern world" (Swedberg & Agevall, 2005, pp. 18–19). Because authority is a form of domination, it was of central concern for Weber as a sociologist. According to Weber (1978, translation of *Economy and Society*, p. 215), the legitimacy of domination may be validated in three ways. First, *legal authority* rests on rational grounds—"a belief in the legality of enacted rules and the right of those elevated to authority under such rules to issue commands." Second, *traditional authority* rests on "established belief in the sanctity of immemorial traditions and the legitimacy of those exercising authority under them." Finally, *charismatic authority* rests on "devotion to the exceptional sanctity, heroism and exemplary character of an individual person, and of the normative patterns of order revealed or ordained by him." Weber viewed the first of these, *legal-rational authority*, as superior in its function for modern society. Legal-rational authority constitutes the basis of modern bureaucracy.

Bureaucracy can be defined most simply as a system of legal-rational authority, accomplishing organizational administration of tasks through the implementation of departments with specialized functions. The bureaucratic form imbues each of these departments with legal-rational authority over the processes in its domain, and arranges them so that work is processed sequentially by each—the output of one department becoming the input of another. Individual managers, then, hold the legal-rational authority afforded to them by the bureaucratic system over their own specialized territories.

Weber (1978) outlined six interrelated characteristics of the modern bureaucracy. First, there is the principle of official *jurisdictional areas* ordered by rules, laws or administrative regulations. Within each area, three elements constitute a bureau (referred to as an *agency* in the public sector or an *enterprise* in the private sector):

1. Regular activities are assigned as official duties.
2. The authority to give commands is stably distributed and "strictly delimited by rules" (p. 956) governing the means that may be used to ensure compliance.
3. Individuals are hired based on general rules of qualification; the performance of duties and exercise of corresponding rights are ensured by methodical provisions.

The jurisdictional principle prescribes a division of labor dictating the creation of multiple bureaus, each with its own domain of specialization. Bureaus are traditionally categorized according to their functions as line and staff. *Line* departments are directly involved in the central purpose of the organization; whereas, *staff* departments perform functions that support the line departments. For example, in an automobile manufacturing corporation, we will have divisions and departments responsible for work products related to the organization's central function—the manufacturing of automobiles (e.g., engine parts fabrication and engine assembly, body parts and body assembly, paint shop, etc.). The work products of these units are the inputs for other units, so that all perform tasks in sequential fashion (hence, the "line" function) to produce the final output or product. The line bureaus rely on the work of staff bureaus to provide support functions, such as an accounting office responsible for overseeing all things financial. Further, each bureau has sub-bureaus; for example, the accounting office may oversee a purchasing department to approve vendors and process purchases of goods and services and an accounts payable department responsible for receiving and paying invoices to those vendors. Each department employs people assigned to specifically defined positions that further divide the labor. Bureaucracy is thus a set of embedded systems and sub-systems of divided labor, arranged in rigid prescribed sequences-within -sequences that allow work to be completed efficiently through the routinization of tasks and chains of tasks.

Weber's (1978) second principle is *office hierarchy and channels of appeal* (chain-of-command). This principle reflects the operation of authority central to the rational-legal bureaucratic form. Hierarchy and command channels

> stipulate a clearly established system of super- and sub-ordination in which there is a supervision of the lower offices by the higher ones. Such a system offers the governed the possibility of appealing, in a precisely regulated manner, the decision of a lower office to the corresponding senior authority.
>
> (Weber, 1978, p. 957)

The work is administered by this hierarchy of supervisory authority according to Weber's third principle, that management is based upon *written documents*. It is with this standard that the modern bureaucracy achieved the separation of official business from private life.

> In principle, the modern organization of the civil service separates the bureau from the private domicile of the official and, in general, segregates official activity from the sphere of private life. Public monies and equipment are divorced from the private property of the official. ... In principle, the *Kontor* (office) is separated from the household, business from private correspondence, and business assets from private wealth.
>
> (Weber, 1978, p. 957)

The remaining three principles are far simpler, and provide the means by which the first three are achieved. The fourth is that all managers are *thoroughly trained in their areas of specialization*. This is an important source of legitimate rational authority. Fifth, bureaucratic managers are expected to devote their *full working capacity* to official activity. The separation of private life from organizational life mutually necessitates and cultivates this expectation. Finally, Weber observes that modern bureaucracy stipulates management of the office according to *general rules*, "which are more or less stable, more or less exhaustive, and which can be learned. Knowledge of these rules represents a special technical expertise which the officials possess" (1978, p. 958). This last principle represents a dramatic departure from previous organizational norms of patrimonialism, which operated according to bestowals of favor. This last principle also provides the means by which the bureaucracy can achieve the degree of impersonalism necessary for the equal treatment of individuals. Weber's principles are summarized in Table 5.1.

Table 5.1 Summary: Weber's principles of modern bureaucracy

The Principle of Jurisdictional Areas
*Domains of specialization, each ordered by rules, laws, regulations. A **bureau** is constituted by*

1. *Regular activities assigned as official duties;*
2. *Stably distributed and strictly regulated authority to give commands and ensure compliance;*
3. *Hiring based on rules of qualification, with performance ensured by methodical provisions.*

The Principle of Office Hierarchy and Channels of Appeal
Chain-of-command is clear and implements rational-legal authority.

The Principle of Written Documents
Documentation serves to separate official and personal business, correspondence, and assets.

The Principle of Trained Specialization
All managers are thoroughly trained in their jurisdictional areas.

The Principle of Full Working Capacity
All managers devote full capacity to official activity (cultivated by the separation of business life from private life).

The Principle of Rules
Office management is stipulated by stable, exhaustive, and learnable general rules, knowledge of which represents the expertise of the bureau's officials.

Weber (1978) particularly noted that bureaucracy's ability to govern "without regard to persons" (p. 975) or *sine ira et studio*—"without hatred or passion and hence without affection or enthusiasm" (p. 225) is both required by capitalism and a "threat to humanity" (Swedberg & Agevall, 2005, p. 19) that must be counter-balanced by business and government leaders. In *Economy and Society*, Weber argues that bureaucracy is the necessary form of organizing in a capitalist economy, but he also clearly advocates for the necessity of regulating and controlling bureau-cracy's inherent domination. While Weber is usually depicted in summaries and textbooks as a cheerleader for bureaucracy, it is more accurate to describe his work as keenly observing the fit between the organizational needs of governance and commerce in capitalistic Western culture and the organizational form and control provided by bureaucracy. Weber predicted the increasing bureaucratization of society, noting both its organizational benefits and sociological dangers. "It is especially in his discussion of the future of bureaucracy that Weber was not simply an advocate of bureaucracy and its efficiency, but also fundamentally critical and fearful of it" (Swedberg & Agevall, 2005, p. 20). He coined the term *iron cage* as a metaphor for the system of rationality created and perpetuated by bureaucratic structures. Teleological, or means to end, reasoning produces efficiency because it affords control from the basis of rational logic, dispassionate to the individual and thus depersonalizing and dehumanizing. Weber warned that this threat to human freedom would create a "polar night of icy darkness and hardness" (Weber, 1994, p. 368). Contemporary organizational communication theory continues to explore these ideas. Because bureaucracy, as a rational system of organizing, is socially constructed, we are complicit in structuring our own iron cages.

Henri Fayol's Theory of Administration

Henri Fayol was a French industrialist and mining engineer who worked as managing director of *Compagnie de Commentry-Fourchambault-Decazeville*—a mining company with more than 10,000 employees that was one of the largest French producers of iron and steel by 1900 (Witzel, 2003). From his own experience, he developed a comprehensive theory of administration, which became widely known through a 1949 translation. Fayol identified six categories of activity necessary for industrial administration: technical, commercial, financial, security, accounting, and managerial (Lamond, 1998), with management being his chief concern. Fayol contributed three fundamental management concepts: Elements of management, principles of management, and the organizational chart to display bureaucratic structure.

Fayol's five elements, or functions, of management endure as a standard in management education: Planning/forecasting, organizing, commanding, coordinating, and controlling. First, managers must forecast a direction and *plan* methods for the attainment of organizational goals. Second, managers must *organize* human resources in an arrangement designed to meet those goals and must formulate and implement methods for evaluating the work of those employees. This element is accomplished by the box-and-line organizational chart displaying organizational units and vertical chains of authority that remains a ubiquitous feature of organizational design. Third, managers *command* the execution of tasks that will meet organizational goals. The fourth managerial function is to *coordinate* those activities of multiple units into a coherent whole. Finally, the manager must enact some degree of *control* over organizational processes so that the planned activities and their outcomes can be evaluated against the goals to assess organizational functioning and success. It is important to note Fayol's underlying presumption of Weber's legal-rational bureaucratic form. While Fayol pioneered the organizational chart as a graphic depiction of the bureaucratic form, he did not invent the form itself.

Fayol's elements of management are supported by 14 principles through which the five functions should be carried out. First, reflecting the Weberian dictum, Fayol advocated work specialization in a strict *division of labor* as the most desirable application of worker activity. Second, also reflecting Weber, managers are granted *authority*, manifesting in the right to give orders. Fayol particularly noted that authority must be accompanied by responsibility. Third, Fayol identified employee *discipline* as a crucial principle. Respect and obedience of organizational rules must be enforced, and effective management accomplishes that. *Unity of command* dictates that every employee reports to, and should receive orders from, only one manager or supervisor. This is accompanied by the principle *unity of direction*, organizing activities with similar objectives under the direction of one manager who implements a single plan for the achievement of the common goal. A great deal has been written about span of control as a central concern. Fayol cautioned that managers must not be granted authority over more employees or functions than the limits of their abilities allow, with fewer direct reports at higher levels of the hierarchy.

Subordination dictates that the interests of the organizational whole should take precedence over the interests of any individual or group of individuals. Yet, the principles of *remuneration* and *equity* specify the necessity of fair wages and equitable treatment of employees. Decision-making should be *centralized* so that management has control, with the understanding that organizational size and the characteristics and skills of managers and employees should temper the degree of centralization to max-imize the achievement of organizational goals. The principle of *initiative* dictates that employees' efforts will be improved when they are allowed to originate and carry out plans. The *scalar chain* principle requires a clear and enforced line of authority from top to bottom of the hierarchy, again reflecting Weber. Fayol specifically discussed prescriptions for communication, advocating limited horizontal interaction so as to minimize its interference with managerial control. Direct communication of employees among themselves was subject to prior managerial approval and formalization as a procedure. (This came to be known as *Fayol's bridge*.)

Order dictates that all people, machines, materials, and activities have an appointed place and a specified function in the organizational design. Correspondingly, orderly personnel planning should be used to ensure the principle of *tenure stability*—the avoidance of employee turnover—and the efficient filling of any vacancies that do occur. Finally, Fayol advocated the promotion of *esprit de corps* to build harmony and unity among employees. Table 5.2 summarizes Fayol's prescriptions.

Fayol also addressed interpersonal communication at the management level, specify-ing (in a departure from Weber's dictum) that verbal communication should be emphasized over written whenever possible to avoid the interdepartmental animosity

Table 5.2 Summary: Henri Fayol's theory of administration

ELEMENTS OF MANAGEMENT

Planning	Organizing	Commanding	Coordinating	Controlling

PRINCIPLES OF MANAGEMENT

Division of labor	Authority	Discipline	Unity of Command	Unity of Direction
Work specialization is the most desirable application of worker activity.	*Managers have the right to give orders, and are accountable for the outcomes.*	*Effective manage-ment enforces respect for and obedience to organizational rules.*	*Every employee reports to and receives orders from only one manager.*	*Activities with similar objectives are under the direction of one manager.*
Subordination	Remuneration	Equity	Centralization	Initiative
Organizational interests take precedent over individual interests.	*Employees need fair wages.*	*Employees should be treated equitably.*	*Decision-making is controlled by management.*	*Workers' efforts improve when they are allowed to originate and carry out plans.*
Scalar chain	Order	Tenure stability	Esprit de corps	
A clear and enforced vertical line of authority with limited horizontal interac-tion, which is assumed to interfere with managerial control.	*All resources, human and nonhuman, have an appointed place and speci-fied function.*	*Employee turnover should be avoided and vacancies filled efficiently.*	*Managers should promote harmony and unity among employees.*	

engendered by the impersonal nature of the customary memorandum. He went so far as to recommend that corporations "forbid all communication in writing which could easily and advantageously be replaced by verbal ones (Fayol, 1949, pp. 40–41, cited in Parker & Ritson, 2005, p. 184).

Fayol's theory is entirely prescriptive, based on his own experience. Fayol was not a social scientific scholar in the traditional sense, and his work has long been criticized as lacking the empirical basis to meet the rigorous standards of social science. However, recent analysis (Parker & Ritson, 2005) has pointed out that Fayol was trained as a research scientist in geology and metallurgy and that his naturalistic methods for deriving management theory closely resemble the grounded theory approach espoused by Glaser and Strauss (1967) decades later. Fayol's theory of administration, as it has been widely presented in secondary sources, is largely uncontroversial, and despite complaints about its lack of empirical evidence, has been widely applied, although there has been some debate about whether the actual activities of practicing managers reflect Fayol's principles (e.g., Mintzberg's, 1973, classic study).

Parker and Ritson (2005) provide an interesting analysis of the primary sources, concluding that Fayol's writing actually advocated a far less authoritarian approach than is attributed by most scholars and textbooks. They contend that the Fayol who is taught in contemporary management schools is far more rigid than the original texts would suggest the real Fayol was in actuality. Rather than a strict adherence to authoritarian bureaucracy, Fayol advocated management practices that would later come to be known as *human relations* or *human resource management* (see Chapters 6 and 7 in this volume). Fayol is, however, wholly depicted by secondary sources as a classical management theorist and an advocate of strictly formal vertical authority. Fayol's theory of administration, as presented in the literature, has had a profound effect on management and leadership education and training.

Frederick Taylor's Scientific Management

Frederick Taylor was an American businessman, a mechanical engineer, and one of the first management consultants. Taylor (1911) identified two pervasive problems in industrial workers' productivity: uneven work quality and "soldiering" (deliberate "underworking") (p. 13). Piece-work—paying workers according to the number of pieces produced (e.g., the number of bricks laid or pounds of pig iron toted, or the number of shoes or shirt sleeves made)—had become standard practice to avoid soldiering, as paid-by-the-hour workers would naturally slow their pace to match the slowest among them. However, piece-work had not solved the problem. When fast workers produced more pieces, the economic dynamic created a system whereby the pay rate-per-piece was reduced (or *busted*). Workers put great pressure on one another to slow down—so as to avoid this *rate-busting* phenomenon. Taylor (1911) provides numerous anecdotes that illustrate both the problems and the ways his system solves them. Taylor's *scientific management* advocated a system of determining, through scientific study, the best and most efficient way to do every task, followed by the requirement that every worker strictly follow that procedure. Taylorism, as it came to be known, ushered in the industrial efficiency movement of the early 20th century.

Scientific management espoused four tenets. First, rigorous empirical investigation through time and motion studies can determine the most superior procedure (highest quality and efficiency) for every job. Second, workers should be matched to jobs through a scientific analysis of their skills and characteristics. Every worker assigned to the same job should be thoroughly trained to the standard procedure and required to follow it. Third, management should closely supervise and cooperate with workers to ensure that all work is done in accordance with the standard procedure that has been scientifically determined. Finally, the labor should be equally divided between laborer and manager, so that the laborer is relieved of the responsibility of planning and is responsible only for carrying out the job in the prescribed way. Table 5.3 summarizes these tenets.

Taylor has been criticized as viewing workers as fundamentally lazy, motivated to provide quality work only by monetary reward. Even a cursory reading of the original source material reveals this bias, but it is equally clear that Taylor did not intend to mistreat workers—although others' applications of his methods often led to worker exploitation. Taylor stipulated that management's planning of workers' tasks should specify

> not only what is to be done but how it is to be done and the exact time allowed for doing it. And whenever the workman succeeds in doing his task right, and within the time limit specified, he receives an addition of from 30 per cent, to 100 per cent, to his ordinary wages. These tasks are carefully planned, so that both good and careful work are called for in their performance, but it should be distinctly understood that in no case is the workman called upon to work at a pace which would be injurious to his health. The task is always so regulated that the man who is well suited to his job will thrive while working at this rate during a long term of years and grow happier and more prosperous, instead of being overworked. Scientific management consists very largely in preparing for and carrying out these tasks.
>
> (Taylor, 1911, p. 39)

Taylor's viewpoint is both paternalistic and elitist. He saw his system as relieving workers of the burdensome responsibility for planning their work that had been "thrown upon" (1911, p. 37) them, and for which they were naturally ill-suited, so as to allow them to more freely, efficiently, and effectively carry out that work.

> Even if the workman was well suited to the development and use of scientific data, it would be physically impossible for him to work at his machine and at a desk at

Table 5.3 Summary: Tenets of Taylor's scientific management

Tenet 1: A superior procedure for every task can be discovered through scientific study of the task. Once discovered, one standard procedure for each task should be adopted.

Tenet 2: Scientific analysis of workers' skills and characteristic should be used to match them to tasks. Every worker should then be trained to the standard procedure and required to follow it.

Tenet 3: Management must closely supervise workers to ensure standard procedure is followed.

Tenet 4: Work should be strictly divided between management and labor. Management is responsible for planning and prescribing procedures; labor is responsible for carrying out procedures in the prescribed manner.

the same time. It is also clear that in most cases one type of man is needed to plan ahead and an entirely different type to execute the work.

(Taylor, 1911, p. 38)

The planning accomplished by managers was likewise designed scientifically. Henry Gantt (1910, 1916, 1919) provided such innovations as the Gantt chart for project management, prescriptions for scheduling, and remuneration (including that of managers, linking management bonuses to worker improvement).

Workers, however, did not respond positively, resisting Taylorism as unfriendly to them. Taylor experienced difficulties in implementation, complicated by the rapidly changing technological environment and others' faulty applications of his methods (Mullins, 2004). Alternatives to Taylorism were advocated by Taylor's contemporaries, who offered a more respectful view of the worker and highlighted the importance of taking human psychology into account in the management of employees. James Hartness (1912) a fellow mechanical engineer, wrote extensively about the importance of habit, employee relations, and human factors in mechanical design (George, 1968). Frank Bunker Gilbreth, Jr., an industrial efficiency consultant, with his business partner (and spouse), Dr. Lillian Moller Gilbreth, worked very closely with Taylor devising implementations for scientific management. Like others at the time, however, they criticized Taylorism for its failure to seriously consider psychological factors.

Frank Gilbreth pioneered motion studies. Although Taylor focused more on time as a factor (producing quickly), F. Gilbreth emphasized motion (producing efficiently). His method broke a task into discrete motions, dubbed *therbligs* (Gilbreth backwards with the *th* transposed). Using a motion picture camera calibrated in fractions of seconds to capture the minute motions of workers, F. Gilbreth scientifically examined tasks to determine the *one best way* (George, 1968). Lillian Moller Gilbreth was one of the first women working engineers with a doctorate—reputed to be the first conferred in the field of industrial psychology. While her partner focused on motion studies, Lillian Gilbreth examined human factors—most notably fatigue. Together, the Gilbreths' work provided the foundations for the continuous quality improvement movement and the field of ergonomics.

Worker Exploitation as a Negative Consequence of Classical Management

The fundamental flaw in classical management theory is the depersonalization of work, and thus the dehumanization of the worker. This is particularly true of Taylorism, which relied on replacing the craft knowledge of workers with management-controlled systematic methods of production (Lasch, 1987). The depersonalization of the industrial worker led to an implicit machine metaphor for the organization generally, and its workers in particular, who were viewed as, and treated like, cogs in a machine (Morgan, 1986). Explicating the machine metaphor reveals three fundamental presumptions: standardization, replaceability, and predictability. The standardization of process and the corresponding depersonalization of work often led to a callous treatment of workers as disposable—resulting in sweatshop conditions and the exploitation and mistreatment that led to the advent of labor unions. Worker abuse was common but only rarely subjected to public scrutiny, usually only in the face of tragedy, such as the Triangle Shirtwaist factory fire in 1911, which killed over 100 workers (most of them young immigrant women). The fire resulted in large-scale loss of life because exit doors had been locked to prevent unauthorized breaks and thefts (Hoenig, 2005). Public outcry led to legislation and oversight—and accelerated the formation of labor unions.

Yet, we must not presume to relegate these abuses to the archives of history. Contemporary industrial corporate cultures are equally as subject to the abuses of dehumanization, despite regulation and the protection of unions. In 1991, too recent for comfort, a fire at the Hamlet chicken processing plant in North Carolina killed more than 20 workers, due to exits that were locked or blocked (Kilborn, 1992). More recently, a fire chillingly similar to the Triangle fire killed over 100 workers in Bangladesh at the Tazreen Fashion factory—likewise because of inadequate fire exits (Ahmed & Paul, 2012).

Classical Management's Contemporary Influence

Classical management theory continues to have profound influences on contemporary organizing. A cursory glance through the annual report of a corporation of any size will reveal the continued grip of Fayol's organizational chart that guides how we arrange organizational forms and conceive of authority as vertical. The inefficiencies we decry in government can be directly traced to the depersonalization inherent in bureaucracy (which ironically is designed to create efficiency)—for example, a social worker's inability to save a child because the immediate actions needed violate regulations and required standard processes. Taylor's strict division of management from labor created an elitist corporate class system that is even felt outside the industrial setting, in the office environment—for example, the cultural divide between *the suits* and *the cubicle dwellers*.

It is easy to see the negative aspects of classical management ideals, but we also enjoy benefits as well. Because of Fayol's emphasis on control in relation to his other four elements, large-scale projects run with accountability. Bureaucratic sequencing creates efficient processes for reporting hours worked and processing our pay—and the bureaucratic structure of the banking industry allows the funds to simply appear in our personal accounts through direct deposit. Finally, Taylor's insistence that managers scientifically standardize tasks has made possible great strides in efficiency that free capital for innovation and expansion—bringing new products to market and creating jobs for unskilled laborers. Bureaucracy is here to stay. Later developments in management theory, by mitigating its negative impact, have entrenched it.

Implications for Organizational Communication Theory

Before we turn to the next era in the management theory, however, we must take a moment to assess the implications of classical management theory to our thinking about communication, organization, authority, and culture. In so doing, we will create a basis for critical comparison of theoretical approaches, as well as an understanding of our implicit assumptions about organizing and organizational communication—both as scholars and as human organizers.

Approach to Communication

Classical management theory examines the formal aspects of communication, with control and standardization as primary concerns. Communication is treated mechanistically with a transmissive presumption of one-way and linear messaging from manager to laborer. In classical management theory, communication, with a focus on clear messaging, is cast as a management tool to accomplish worker productivity by establishing and maintaining organizational control vested in persons who hold authority. In so doing, the function of communication is nearly completely informational—its only acknowledged relational functions being to establish and maintain the authority chain and to offset the impersonal nature of written channels.

For example, Taylor's treatment of the worker is paternalistic, elitist, and dehumanized. By ignoring craft knowledge, and thus eliminating it from organizational process, Taylorism's one-way, transmissive, and mechanistic treatment of communication denies the human relationship as a function of the organization (and vice versa) and ignores meaning-creation and the constitutive properties of communication. The failure of pure Taylorism can be directly attributed to its denial that workers feel and think in equal capacity as do managers—and that the emotional and cognitive capacities of workers are essential forces in the organizational meaning created, and thus the outcomes achieved. Through his writing on the relational aspects of communication, Fayol actually delved into these meaning-centered and constitutive aspects of communication. This is so little-known that it had marginal effect on either theory or practice, but these principles are contributed later by human relations and human resources theories (Chapters 6 and 7 in this volume, respectively). Finally, Weber (as a sociologist) was well-versed in the constitutive power of communication and human relating. He warned us of the cold and harsh world that would be created by the dehumanizing nature of bureaucracy, but he left it to later thinkers to prescribe methods to ameliorate these phenomena.

Approach to Organization and Authority

Classical management theory treats the organization as a machine (Morgan, 1986), an external authoritative entity that is conceptually removed from the social collectivity that comprises its membership. The managerial class is ascribed with the authority to dictate the actions required of the labor class. Fayol's organizational chart, so powerfully ingrained in our conception of organizational structures, has reified our thinking—even to this day—of organizations as concrete, physical structures and of organizational authority as vertical. Certain positions in that vertical hierarchy, and thus the individuals who occupy those positions, have authority *over* those in *lower* positions. The vertical metaphor originates from religious texts, the first use of the word *hierarchy* (from the ancient Greek) referring to systematic orders of angels and heavenly beings. Heaven being conceptualized as above Earth leads to a concomitant verticality in conceptions of authority.

Regardless of its origin, the vertical metaphor for authority is entrenched in Western bureaucracy. We speak of *moving up the ladder*, of executives occupying *high-up positions*, and of *low-level employees*. We even arrange the occupation of architectural structures accordingly so that those with greater authority have offices on higher floors in our buildings. The reification of verticality in our conception of authority is quite profound. This is one concrete way that the communication/organization spiral (Figure 1.4) can be seen in action. We actually arrange people physically to match the metaphor of vertical authority, then that arrangement perpetuates verticality in our thinking. Every day, we enact organizing principles internalized from classical management theory. We create organizational charts, put all manner of things in writing to institutionalize them, standardize tasks into sequential routines, and generally follow the lessons of Fayol as they are currently taught in management degree programs everywhere. Even the most cursory glance at a fast-food establishment or manufacturing facility shows classical management principles in action. We choose to do things this way consciously as much as we do them by habit, and the more we put them into practice the more habitual they become. We do so because they replicate patterns that have been successful before and are thus drawn upon for our current intentions. There are many sociological and social psychological theories that explain this human process of drawing on our collective societal knowledge base for organizing and structuring our collective actions, such as sensemaking (Weick, 1995) and structuration (Giddens, 1984), both of which were discussed in previous chapters.

Cultural Implications

The question of what this all means culturally is profound. First, classical management theory has enculturated a pattern of organizing that defines organizational authority concretely: as something one can *have* and *use*—a concrete tool that can be owned and operated tangibly. Further, classical management theory inculcated a cultural presumption that centralizes power and authority with fewer individuals at the top of a hierarchy holding more power than the many individuals at the bottom. Contemporary culture also embraces class structures based on the division of the management classes into upper, middle and lower levels, and the working classes as *white-* or *blue-collar* based on the nature of the work as the planning or implementing of labor. Finally, the absorption of contemporary society by large organizations (Perrow, 1991) is driven by the cultural internalization of classical management assumptions about the nature of work and its practices.

Recommended Supplementary Readings

Gotcher, J. M. (1992). Assisting the handicapped: The pioneering efforts of Frank and Lillian Gilbreth. *Journal of Management, 18,* 5–13.

This piece is highly recommended to link contemporary work in human factors, ergonomic design, and workplace accommodation to early management theory. The pioneering work of the Gilbreths and others (e.g., Gantt and Hartness) during the classical management period are usually glossed over in our field's textbook treatments of the era (if they are included at all). Yet, a great deal of current work traces its roots to those working in support of scientific task design.

Hough, J. R., & White, M. A. (2001). Using stories to create change: The object lesson of Frederick Taylor's "pig-tale." *Journal of Management, 27,* 585–601.

The criticism of Frederick Taylor as elitist and classist often obscures the brilliant insights of his work on scientific task design and worker assignment. This article focuses on one story told by Taylor to advocate for his methods, underscoring its continuing relevance for organizational science.

Parker, L. D., & Ritson, P. A. (2005). Revisiting Fayol: Anticipating contemporary management. *British Journal of Management, 16,* 175–194.

This article should be of interest, not just for its reconsideration of Fayol, but as a sobering reminder that reliance on secondary, tertiary, and subsequent generations of sources inevitably misrepresents the original. Much of what is "common knowledge" of Fayol is incomplete and misinterpreted.

Perrow, C. (1991). A society of organizations. *Theory and Society, 20,* 725–762.

This is a thought-provoking article for advanced readers to contemplate the nature of contemporary society as absorbed by organizations; highly recommended for students interested in organizations and democracy.

Taylor, F. (1911). *The principles of scientific management*. New York: Harper & Brothers. (digitized and in public domain, available from https://archive.org/details/principlesofscie00taylrich)

The original voice of Frederick Taylor provides a rich understanding of his scientific management as it was benignly intended; it also reveals the paternalistic and elitist distinction between management and labor that pervaded the time period.

Wren, D. A. (1972). In memoriam: Lillian Moller Gilbreth (1878–1972). *Academy of Management Journal, 15,* 7–8.

The contributions of women in early social science are obscured. This, and other readings about pioneering women in organizational studies, are highly recommended.

Important Concepts: Define and Discuss

Industrialization
Organizational society
Postindustrial management
Bureaucracy
Authority
Line vs. staff functions
Fayol's bridge
Scientific management
Control
Standardization

Discussion Questions

1. How (and where) can we see classical management principles operating in our contemporary organizational world? Name and discuss a few principles and give contemporary examples. What are the positive and negative consequences of these principles?
2. Weber was very concerned about the chilling effects of bureaucracy on the quality of human existence/society. If he were to appear today, a century later, to observe our 21st century organizational world, what would he say?
3. Given what we have learned about classical approaches to management and organizational design, how might we advise Taylor, Fayol, and their peers to do things differently? How might things have turned out if they did?
4. Scientific management was developed to counter the problems of uneven work quality and soldiering. How might we see these same problems among office workers, particularly those who telecommute? How might today's managers utilize Taylor's ideas for improving productivity in the face of a more skilled, specialized, and distant workforce conducting intellectual (rather than physical) labor?
5. Consider the principles and tenets of classical management theories from an ethical perspective. For example, how might an individual's decision based upon her own ethics violate or support the principle of subordination?
6. Is it possible to maintain order without using vertical authority? Can you find some contemporary organizational examples?

Practitioners' Corner

All contemporary work environments are rooted in formal organizational designs heavily influenced by classical management principles. Any person in a position of authority can enhance their unit's effectiveness by paying close attention to domains of responsibility for work groups. Better work products result from a clear shared understanding of the objectives for which the unit is responsible, careful analysis of what tasks are required to meet those objectives and how those tasks might best be done, and a clear shared understanding of who is responsible for each. Fayol's goal of a free flow of information and good relations between work groups is a worthy objective, so that everyone is kept apprised of one another's efforts and can share knowledge and other resources. Positive outcomes can come from simple techniques such as a regular short Monday morning meeting, where each group updates one another on their efforts. Coworkers who are well-informed about each other's labor are more likely to support one another and to produce better and more consistent work products.

Communication professionals can uniquely benefit from a deep understanding of the roots of organizational design. Whether representing the organization to internal or external publics, quality of that representation is enhanced by a deep understanding of the organization's design and function. Further, such understanding can inform an analysis of the organization's communication practices to create better, more effective policies and procedures. Communication practitioners are often well-trained in the principles of effective messaging, but few are knowledgeable about effective communication within organizational structures. There are obvious professional advantages, personally and organizationally, in being able to advise one's employer not only about effective formal messaging to audiences, but also about effective communication in day-to-day operations that supports the organization's design and function.

References

Ahmed, A., & Paul, R. (2012). More than 100 die in garment factory fire, the deadliest in Bangladesh's history. *Christian Science Monitor*, November 25. www.csmonitor.com/World/Latest-News-Wires/2012/1125/More-than-100-die-in-garment-factory-fire-the-deadliest-in-Bangladesh-s-history.

Fayol, H. (1949). *General and industrial management*. Trans. C. Storrs. London: Sir Isaac Pitman & Sons.

Gantt, H. L. (1910). *Work, wages, and profits: Their influence on the cost of living*. New York: Engineering Magazine Company.

Gantt, H. L. (1916). *Industrial leadership*. New Haven: Yale University Press.

Gantt, H. L. (1919). *Organizing for work*. New York: Harcourt, Brace, and Howe.

George, C. S., Jr. (1968). *The history of management thought*. Englewood Cliffs, NJ: Prentice Hall.

Giddens, A. (1984). *The constitution of society: Outline of the theory of structuration*. Berkeley, CA: University of California Press.

Glaser, B. G., & Strauss, A. L. (1967). *The discovery of grounded theory*. Aldine Publishing, Chicago.

Hartness, J. (1912). *The human factor in works management*. New York and London: McGraw-Hill.

Hoenig, J. M. (2005). The Triangle fire of 1911. *History Magazine*, April/May.

Khurana, R. (2010). *From higher aims to hired hands: The social transformation of American business schools and the unfulfilled promise of management as a profession*. New Jersey: Princeton University Press.

Kilborn, P. T. (1992). North Carolina is told to improve safety role. *The New York Times*, January 9.

Lamond, D. (1998). Back to the future: lessons from the past for a new management era. In G. Griffin (Ed.), *Management theory and practice: moving to a new era* (pp. 3–14). South Melbourne: Macmillan.

Lasch, C. (1987). Technology and its critics: The degradation of the practical arts. In S. E. Goldberg & C. R. Strain (Eds.), *Technological change and the transformation of America* (pp. 79–90). Carbondale: Southern Illinois University Press.

Machiavelli, N. (2005). *The Prince with related documents*. Trans. & Ed. William J. Connell. Bedford: St. Martins.

Mill, J. S. (1848). *The principles of political economy: With some of their applications to social philosophy*. London: John W. Parker & Son.

Mill, J. S. (1859). *On liberty* (2nd ed.). London: John W. Parker & Son.

Mintzberg, H. (1973). *The nature of managerial work*. New York: Harper & Rowe.

Morgan, G. (1986). *Images of organization*. Thousand Oaks, CA: SAGE.

Mullins, L. J. (2004). *Management and organisational behaviour* (7th ed.). Upper Saddle River, NJ: FT Press Pearson.

Parker, L. D., & Ritson, P. A. (2005). Revisiting Fayol: Anticipating contemporary management. *British Journal of Management*, 16(3), 175–194. doi:10.1111/j.1467-8551.2005.00453.x.

Perrow, C. (1991). A society of organizations. *Theory and Society*, 20(6), 725–762. doi:10.1007/BF0067.

Rangarajan, L. N. (Trans.). (1992). *Kautilya: The Arthashastra*. New Delhi, India: Penguin Books.

Smith, A. (1776). *An inquiry into the nature and causes of the wealth of nations*. London: W. Strahan and T. Cadell.

Swedberg, R., & Agevall, O. (2005). *The Max Weber dictionary: Key words and central concepts*. Redwood City, CA: Stanford University Press.

Taylor, F. (1911). *The principles of scientific management*. New York: Harper & Brothers.

Weber, M. (1978). *Economy and society: An outline of interpretive sociology*. Eds. G. Roth & C. Wittich. Berkeley: University of California Press.

Weber, M. (1994). *Weber: Political writings*. Ed.P. Lassman. Trans. Ronald Speirs. Cambridge: Cambridge University Press.

Weick, K. (1995). *Sensemaking in organizations*. Thousand Oaks, CA: SAGE.

Witzel, M. (2003). *Fifty key figures in management*. New York: Routledge, 2003.

6　Human Relations Theory

Anne M. Nicotera

Human relations (HR) theory and the HR movement in the U.S. are often misunder-stood as a revolution against the dehumanizing nature of classical management theory and an attempt to overthrow it. However, this depiction is somewhat inaccurate. First, the ideals of HR theory were discussed by both theorists and practitioners far earlier than the onset of the HR movement (Bruce, 2006), and many businesses practiced this way (although it was certainly not mainstream). Second, early applications of HR theory supplemented and revised rather than replaced classical management, shifting the focus of management strategy from the *work* to the *worker* while the fundamental management goal remained to be maximizing productivity. Third, the practices of classical management remain alive and well in 21st-century America, as anyone work-ing in the fast food industry (for example) can confirm. The advent of HR theory is evolutionary rather than revolutionary; the roots of the HR movement sit squarely in the center of scientific management. Moreover, HR-like industrial practices stretch back well into the 19th century.

HR theory broadens the theoretic treatment of productivity to include motivation, satisfaction, and other humanizing elements in the design of management strategies. Worker satisfaction in HR theory is seen as a means to an end: A happy worker, it was presumed, is a productive worker. However, while the empirical connection between HR practices and satisfaction are well-evidenced, the link between satisfaction and productivity is tenuous at best. While HR theory's prescribed practices do indeed reduce worker turnover and create a more humane and ethical workplace, both of which improve the quality of the working environment, the HR movement's success in enhancing workers' quality of life did not result in the productivity gains anticipated. Significant advances in management strategies to improve productivity were not rea-lized until the next generation of thinking, human resources management (HRM) theory, expanded management strategy to include workers' cognitive and intellectual contributions (see Chapter 7).

Distinguishing Classical Theory, HR, and HRM

We might simplify the differences between the three schools of thought (classical, HR, and HRM) by reducing the definition of a human being to three domains: working, thinking, and feeling. In classical management, emotion and other human psychological factors were acknowledged as an outcome of good management that served to ease worker acceptance of managerial control practices. For example, Frederick Taylor surmised that having managers think for them would make workers happy, but that was seen only as a positive side-effect that enhanced workers' acquiescence to their prescribed role. Worker happiness was not seen as a tool in itself to enhance their productivity. Classical management restricted *thinking* to management and *working* to labor, with a focus solely on formal communication. *Feeling* was hardly considered at all, and certainly not as central to management strategy. In HR theory, however, human emotion and other psychological factors were seen as essential tools for management strategy, with motivation being the central concern. Workers and managers alike were seen as both working and feeling beings, with informal communication taking on increased significance as a strategy for enhancing productivity through enhancing human relationships. In HR theory, however, *thinking* is still the domain of management alone.

Later, applications of HRM theory (Chapter 7) emphasized worker intellect as a powerful resource for process improvement. Participatory management is thus a central tenet of HRM theories, but not HR theories. With HRM, both workers and managers are seen as equally multidimensional sources for management strategy: Regardless of their place in the hierarchy, all human organizational members are seen as working, feeling, and thinking; HRM theory posits that it is this combination of human resources that improve processes and increase organizational value. Moreover, *thinking, working* and *feeling* are essential elements of one another. HR theory, with its focus on human motivation and worker satisfaction, is an important step in the evolution of management theory, as a conceptual bridge between classical and contemporary management theory. It is important to keep this in mind while we review HR theory, so as to understand not only where it came from (classical management) but where it then led (HRM).

Birth of HR: The Hawthorne Studies

HR theory was born of the Hawthorne Studies, a series of scientific management experiments and research studies conducted from 1924 to 1932 at the Hawthorne Works, a Western Electric factory near Chicago. The way this refrain is commonly repeated in most textbooks is, however, inaccurate in several ways (Bruce, 2006). First, most texts report that HR principles were an outcome of the studies, but the ideas about human motivation and human factors that underlie HR thinking were prevalent long before the Hawthorne Studies (as we saw from such theorists as Henri Fayol and Lillian Gilbreth in Chapter 5). Moreover, these ideas were a driving force for much of the *design* of the studies, not just a product of their results. Another inaccuracy is that Elton Mayo and collaborators from Harvard are commonly credited as the originators of the studies. Yet, they actually joined the project in 1928, several years after its inception. The Harvard academic team is indeed responsible for the design of later phases of research, and especially for impact of the Hawthorne Studies on academia and on the development of management theory through the HR movement. However, the Hawthorne Studies themselves were initiated by industry practitioners and industrial psychologists to establish a scientific basis for the claim, made by electric manufacturing companies, that increasing the level of electrical lighting was essential to increasing factory worker productivity. In short, businessmen (including Thomas Edison) in the electric light industry made the claim that their products would increase industrial output. Since this claim has an obvious bias, the studies were initiated by an organized group who sought to resolve any debate (see Wrege, 1976). The illumination studies found that increases in electric lighting, and manipulating other physical factors, did not in fact increase productivity. So, in that sense the studies were a failure, but like most historic discoveries something unintended and unanticipated was revealed—something that revolutionized the American workplace.

The analyses and interpretations of Mayo and his associates (most notably Roethlisberger, Dickson, & Wright, 1939) launched the HR movement. The studies consisted of several phases, beginning with the Illumination Studies, a series of experiments that controlled physical conditions (such as temperature) in the factory while varying the level of lighting to find the ideal level of illumination for maximum productivity. The general finding was that changes in the lighting resulted in higher productivity, regardless of the direction of change (brighter or dimmer). These findings did not provide evidence that would sell more lighting, but they did raise many questions about the explanations for the change in productivity, which led to a set of studies involving direct observations, interviews, and the manipulation of other factors (e.g., length of shifts, length of breaks, pay differentials, etc.) in addition to objective measurements of environmental conditions and productivity. (See Wrege, 1976, and Greenwood & Wrege, 1986, for a detailed description of the original studies drawn directly from the archival historical documents.) The Harvard team's conclusion that spurred the HR movement was that workers, due to the level of attention they were getting for the creation of ideal conditions, felt cared for by management and that this engagement increased their motivation to be more productive. (The term *Hawthorne Effect* was later coined to denote the idea that being observed is in itself an explanation for the behavior of research subjects.)

A very large literature chronicles the history and impetus for the Hawthorne Studies and their original interpretations, as well as a number of debates, reinterpretations and new analyses of the original data, including a gendered analysis (Acker & Van Houten, 1974). While a thorough review of this literature would be an interesting and worthwhile endeavor, it would distract from our central purpose in reviewing this history of management theory. Our purpose is to discuss the major theoretical advances and their translation into practice, concentrating on the HR movement's fundamental tenets and its major theories (and theorists), so that we can examine their implications for the early development of organizational communication theory and continuing influence on contemporary organizational communication theory.

Human Relations Theory and Theorists

The fundamental paradigm shift from the classical era to the HR era was from *mechanism* to *humanism*. Because the HR theory literature is far too broad and too large to fully review here, a set of theories is presented here—chosen for their historical prominence, influence on the field, and representativeness of HR principles. The fundamental assumption underlying HR theory is simple: Human beings have emotional and social needs, and attention to those needs is a key factor to improving motivation and thus productivity. HR theories focus on motivation through recognition/appreciation, feelings/emotions, informal relations, job security and job satisfaction, effective communication, self-supervision, and participative decision-making (although it must be noted that neither self-management nor fully collaborative decision-making was widely practiced until the HRM era).

Mary Parker Follett: A Century Too Soon

Mary Parker Follett was a visionary. She was a social worker and the first person to implement the operation of community centers in impoverished neighborhoods. She was also a very successful management consultant. Follett was a social and managerial philosopher who advocated for workplace democracy and self-governance through the power of the group. Her 1918 book, *The New State*, advocated a form of naturalistic democracy grounded in the emergence of organization from organic interaction among neighborhood residents. She theorized that group interaction and personal relations carry immense capacity to create power, authority, and freedom (Follett, 1919). (This is remarkably similar in character to 21st-century organizational communication theory; see Chapter 3.) In *Creative Experience* (1924), Follett applies her ideas to industrial management and labor relations. Her many papers and books, well-versed in scientific management, gained her a successful career in the 1920s as a lecturer to business scholars, practitioners, and government leaders in the U.S. and England. Her work continues to influence the field of public administration nearly a century later.

While Follett is commonly categorized as an HR theorist, her work is difficult to place because of its timing and character. In character, her work is more HRM theory than HR theory, with its application of human motivation and interpersonal communication to collaborative decision-making, organizational democracy, and self-governance. She gained attention among management theorists for her work on interpersonal relations and personnel management at the same time that the Hawthorne Studies were being conducted. However, even though she has long been heralded as a pioneer of the HR movement, her work failed to gain enduring traction in the U.S. until the 1960s. It achieved far earlier and more enthusiastic attention among European management scholars. Conceptually, Follett's work is a better fit for the late 20th and early 21st century, which may explain both its early marginalization and later resurgence.

As a member of the Taylor Society, Follett expressed support and appreciation for Taylorism's adherence to scientific objectivity and logic. However, "in contrast to Taylor's focus on engineering worker performance, Follett's focus is on the webs that connect workers to one another and to management and vice versa. Her work provided the groundwork for participatory management, total quality management, and team-building" (Newman & Guy, 1998, p. 294). Follett's chief focus was on *coordination*, using group and interpersonal relations as a primary source of managerial effectiveness. Follett's principles of organization are summarized as four degrees of coordination (Sethi, 1966, p. 13):

1. Coordination by direct contact of the responsible people concerned,
2. Coordination in the early stages,
3. Coordination as the reciprocal relating of all the factors in a situation, and
4. Coordination as a continuing process.

The successful progression of coordination through this sequence depends on direct and timely communication, positive and creative thinking, a reciprocally shared vision across levels and roles, and the integration of the group and its accomplishments to continually perpetuate progressive organizational growth. Follett's ideas are quite contemporary, envisioning leadership as a function of the skills of all organizational members, the manager's job being to coordinate and integrate the contributions of the group members, accomplishing control from within group communication rather than imposed upon it.

Her sequential principles of coordination have a number of important implications in Follett's body of theory, which reads more like a set of texts on teamwork and flattened organizing written in the 1990s than it does management theory discourse from the 1920s. The departure from classical management and Taylorism is quite profound. (The following summary is adapted from Sethi, 1966.) First, coordination refers to unity rather than conformity, and unity presupposes organic and emergent groups (as opposed to a crowd or a collection of individuals). Second, collaborative conflict management is explicitly advocated, integrating opposing interests rather than compromising any. Such integration requires "dexterity and intelligence" (Sethi, 1966, p. 14). Moreover, coordination cannot be imposed, but must be driven from within the group, and coordinated values should assimilate one another. Of utmost importance is Follett's definition of coordination as an interpenetrating process of organizing (Sethi, 1962). The organizational environment is seen as dynamic, requiring progressive adjustment leading to increased coordination. Such adjustment, in turn, creates a new sense of interrelatedness, rather than mere capitulation. For Follett, then, every social process is threefold: interacting, unifying, and emerging. She also discusses *synthesis* as a natural process arising from coordination, emphasizing that all members, expert workers and executives alike, bring unique knowledge and experience. This equalizing notion allows authority to flow horizontally as well as vertically. Further, coordination does not subjugate any unit to another, but rather integrates the integrity of the organization (seen by each unit from its own view). Perhaps the most radical departure from classical management theory is Follett's requirement that coordination start at the bottom rather than the top of the structure. Finally, coordination's growth-sequence is reflected in direct contact, early awareness of the vision, reciprocal relationships, and the self-perpetuating mechanism of the process.

From this brief summary, it is easy to understand both why Follett gained such early accolades and why her work was marginalized after her death in 1933. The landscape of management theory at the time was just beginning to recognize the humanity of workers, and Follett's thinking was far more advanced than that. Her ideas were exciting and visionary, and that very visionary nature made them difficult to implement onto a reality of practice that was only just beginning to adjust to a humanistic rather than a mechanistic view of laborers and the nature of work. It was not until after Chester Barnard (1938) published *The Functions of the Executive* that Follett's role as an HR pioneer was established, and it was not until the full advent of collaborative practices under HRM that her teachings could effectively be implemented. The mainstream organizational world simply was not ready to allow workers to share authority with executives, although there are some examples of companies instituting Follett's recommended lateral processes very early (e.g., the matrix structuring of DuPont in the 1920s). Moreover, the state of theoretical advancement in the field was not ready to conceptualize the kind of interdependence she advocated until very late in the 20th century.

Chester Barnard: The First Organizational Communication Theorist?

Chester Barnard was a business executive, most notably the president of the New Jersey Bell Telephone Company, who published the first book on management that did not take a prescriptive approach. Rather, *The Functions of the Executive* (1938) was a descriptive account of how organizations actually function, through the presentation of a theory of formal organizations as cooperative systems with communication as the chief coordinating force. While Barnard was not an academic, he was well-read in political science, philosophy, sociology, anthropology, and psychology (as evidenced by the citations in his work). The book is often labelled as the first text on organizational communication because it focused on human relating and communication, with communication being the source of authority, and cooperation being a result of good communication. A high and consistent degree of cooperation, according to Barnard, is the key to organizational success and longevity. Barnard covers a comprehensive range of topics to create a well-integrated theoretic explanation of how organizations operate and, in turn, how executives can use this knowledge to ensure their organizations operate successfully. We will focus here on the elements of his theory that are most directly influential on management theory and later organizational communication theory, omitting those elements of the work that speak more directly to business operations (such as the specifics of incentives, decision environments, opportunism, and the importance of moral leadership).

Effectiveness and efficiency. Barnard (1938) was the first to use *effectiveness* and *efficiency* as primary metrics of organizational success. Effectiveness is defined as the attainment of desired ends. Efficiency is twofold. First, an action is defined as efficient by its "unsought consequences" (p. 19), an efficient action being one whose unanticipated outcomes are outweighed by its achievement of desired outcomes. Second, an efficient action is one that satisfies the motives of the actors without creating dissatisfaction. "This often happens; we find we do not want what we thought we wanted" (p. 20). Barnard explicitly defines *ends* as both material and social. What is most important to our purposes is the centrality of communication and human relating to both organizational existence and success:

> Although effectiveness of cooperative effort relates to accomplishment of an objective of the system and is determined with a view to the system's requirements, efficiency relates to the satisfaction of individual motives. Efficiency of a cooperative system is the resultant of the efficiencies of the individuals furnishing the constituent efforts, that is, as viewed by them. If the individual finds his motives being satisfied by what he does, he continues his cooperative effort; otherwise he does not. If he does not, this subtraction from the cooperative system may be fatal to it. If five men are required and the fifth man finds no satisfaction in cooperating, his contribution would be inefficient. He would withhold or withdraw his services, so that the cooperation would be destroyed. If he considers it to be efficient, it is continued. Thus, the efficiency of a cooperative system is its capacity to maintain itself by the individual satisfactions it affords. This may be called its capacity of equilibrium, the balancing of burdens by satisfactions which results in continuance.
> (Barnard, 1938, pp. 56–57)

Barnard also provides a lengthy discussion about the economy of incentives.

Informal organization. The notion of the *informal organization* is Barnard's (1938) most notable influence on the field of organizational communication. Informal organization refers to "the aggregate of the personal contacts and interactions and the associated groupings of people" (p. 115). Barnard posits *informal organization* not only as a powerful source of organizational success, but as the very stuff of the organization. This idea that interaction is the very center of organizing processes is the core of contemporary organizational communication theory. Barnard (1938, p. 116) posits that informal organization has two classes of effects: the establishment of "certain attitudes, understandings, customs, habits, institutions" (which would later also be used as the basis of theories of organizational culture in the 1980s); and the creation of "the conditions under which formal organizations may arise." He also points out that formal and informal organization are mutually constitutive (although not using that language). Formal organization requires informal association as its basis, and the persistence of informal organization depends on the motives for action provided by formal organization. "Formal organizations arise out of and are necessary to informal organization; but when formal organizations come into operation, they create and require informal organizations" (p. 120). Informal organization is essential to both authority and the functioning of the executive, or leader.

Authority. For Barnard (1938), individual compliance and willingness to contribute to the organization are rooted in individual responsibility, and authority is rooted in communication. Authority is defined as "the character of a communication (order) in a formal organization by virtue of which it is accepted by a contributor to or 'member' of the organization as governing the action he contributes" (p. 163). This definition is a significant departure from classical management. Authority is defined, not by a position that dictates the right to give orders, but rather by the extent to which the recipient of the order accepts its legitimacy. Communication is authoritative under four conditions. These conditions predict the assent of the individual to accept authority: (1) the individual understands the communication; (2) when deciding to act, the individual believes the communication is consistent with the purpose of the organization; (3) that it is likewise consistent with his/her own personal interests; and that (4) he/she is able (both mentally and physically) to comply. Barnard also provides in-depth consideration of grey areas in these four conditions.

While authority resides in communication, Barnard does specify the conditions under which persons can be said to *hold* authority. First, the communication of the person must lie in the *potentiality of assent* defined by organizational membership. A manager does not issue directives to the employees of another organization, after all. Second, there is a presumption of authority when the communication originates from a *center of communication* (a position or office) in the formal organization's structure, rather than from an individual (i.e., from *a manager* rather than just *a person*). This *authority of position* is lost under two conditions: the directive is outside the scope of the position's function in the formal structure or the directive is not adjusted to the actual situation. *Authority of leadership* is quite different. The communication of individuals whose knowledge and understanding command respect will hold authority regardless of their positions because others will impute that authority. Barnard is one of the first theorists to differentiate *positional authority* from *leadership* in this way. Finally, authority and responsibility are inseparable, as those to whom authority is imputed are then obligated to submit to the dominance of organizational ends, to *organization action* rather than *individual action*.

Several factors dictate the organization communication system's function as an authority system. First, channels of communication must be clear and known to all. This is similar to Fayol's chain-of-command, except that Barnard situates authority in the communication rather than the persons or positions. Second, objective authority requires that every individual member of the organization be positioned in a clear and formal communication channel (a reporting relationship, again similar to Fayol but again focused on communication and not persons). Third, these channels should be as short and direct as possible. Fourth, the complete line of communication must be used, not skipping over reporting relationships. This avoids conflicting communication and maintains responsibility. Fifth, persons serving as communication centers (officers, supervisors, heads, etc.) must be competent. Competence requires both personal skills (e.g., to assess situations and communicate clearly) and technical expertise. When the landscape is so complex that a single individual cannot be expected to personally hold the expertise or technical mastery of all processes involved, a staff may be relied on to provide that mastery. Here, we can see clearly that the *communication center* is the position or office, and not the person. Sixth, the line of communication should not be interrupted in times when the organization is expected to function. The line of authority must never be broken; this can be seen in operation when an interim manager is appointed during times that the regular manager must be absent and the organization must still function. Finally,

> every communication should be authenticated. This means that the person communicating must be known actually to occupy the 'position of authority' concerned; that the position includes the type of communication concerned—that is, it is 'within its authority;' and that it actually is an authorized communication from this office.
>
> (Barnard, 1938, p. 180).

The executive. The communication system creates a system of coordination whereby individual actions are interlocked as organizational actions that achieve organizational goals.

> Such a system of communication implies centers or points of interconnection and can only operate as these centers are occupied by persons who are called executives. It might be said, then, that the function of executives is to service channels of communication so far as communications must passed through central positions. But since the object of the communication system is coordination of all aspects of organization, it follows that the functions of executives relate to all the work essential to the vitality and endurance of an organization so far, at least, as it must be accomplished through formal coordination. ... Executive work is not that *of* the organization, but the specialized work of *maintaining* the organization and operation.
>
> (Barnard, 1938, p. 215, emphasis in original)

Barnard (1938) is clear to explain that the executive must maintain a system of cooperative effort, not manage people. He explicitly states that the organization as a whole "is managed by itself, not by the executive organization, which is a part of it" (p. 216). He likens the executive organization to the body's nervous system, including the brain, which maintains the body by directing actions necessary for survival but is part of the body, and "can hardly be said to manage the body, a large part of whose functions are independent of it and upon which it in turn depends" (p. 217). Executives must provide three essential, and highly complex, functions. First they must provide the system of communication. Second, they must secure the efforts essential to its success. Third, they must formulate and define the organization's purpose.

The first function, the system of communication, is quite massive—the entirety of organizational design, what Barnard calls the *scheme of organization*—organization charts, division of labor, duty specifications, etc. The executive must also specify the types and quantity of personnel that are needed and can be obtained, the incentives required, and the times and places for the work to be conducted. Once the organization is designed, personnel must be defined, identified, and secured. Finally, the informal organization requires maintenance of informal executive organization by careful selection of executives.

> The functions of informal executive organizations are the communication of intangible facts, opinions, suggestions, suspicions, that cannot pass through formal channels without raising issues calling for decisions, without dissipating dignity and objective authority, and without overloading executive positions; also to minimize excessive cliques of political types arising from too great divergence of interests and views, to promote self-discipline of the group; and to make possible the development of important personal influences in the organization.
>
> (Barnard, 1938, p. 225)

In short, Barnard is referring to what contemporary theorists would study as the political dimensions of organizational communication.

The second function of the executive is to secure essential services from the individuals who have been secured as members, bringing individuals into the organization in a cooperative relationship and then eliciting services from them. The distinction from *managing persons* is subtle but important. The executive must function to define roles, attract individuals to fulfill those roles, and maintain an authoritative communication system that ensures a cooperative system of actions. It is the communication that must be managed, not the organization and not the people. Finally, the third essential function of the executive is to formulate and design the organization's purpose (i.e., goals, objectives, desired ends). The organization's general purpose is comprised of goals and objectives formulated in the cooperative system, as the organization has previously been defined. The formulation and design of purpose is therefore abstract and made up of smaller and increasingly more concrete goals and objectives. As such, the continual creation of the organization's purpose must be accomplished by the delegation of objective authority to positions in the communication system. At the lowest and most concrete levels of the organization, desired ends (which demand action) must be articulated with the more abstract objectives with which they correspond on up the chain; it is the executive's function to achieve these articulations. For example, a factory worker might be tasked with a target production goal—to produce x number of widgets per week. Because (1) his job is to produce widgets, (2) he has the skills and materials to do so, and (3) he is directed to do so by a manager with acceptable authority, his cooperation is secured and he sets himself to work. Whether he is aware of it or not, his widgets are part of the larger set of production goals, matched with a larger set of sales goals, which correspond with corporate-level competitive goals (such as increasing market share), which in turn create a higher trading value for company stock, and so on. While the worker on the floor may or may not be aware of the connections that align his concrete personal production targets with such abstract things as market share of the product or value of the company's stock, his cooperation must be secured by an authoritative communication system designed and maintained by executives who, together, do perceive and understand all those connections.

Barnard's (1938) book was widely acclaimed, and helped to launch the HR movement. He was heavily influenced by Mayo, Roethlisberger, and Follett, and his ideas about motivation and communication were revolutionary. Barnard's ability to cross disciplines, and particularly his psychological approach to leadership and employee motivation, were highly influential on management practices. The influence of his theory of the organization as a self-perpetuating communication system can still be seen in contemporary organizational communication theory.

Barnard's clear mandate to examine the human motivation to act toward organizational goals based on individual needs was not unique at the time, but it did serve to inspire broad application of psychological theories of motivation to the theory and practice of management. As managers and theorists sought ways to motivate employees to cooperate, and thus be more productive, they turned to the psychology literature on human motivation. The most notably influential theory of human motivation cited by HR theorists is Maslow's (1943b) hierarchy of needs.

Abraham Maslow's Theory of Human Motivation

Maslow's (1943b) hierarchy of needs is one of the most commonly known theories of human motivation, most likely because of its ubiquity in the HR movement. Consistent with consensus among psychologists of its time, the model is based on a number of propositions derived from the literature (including the writings of Kurt Lewin, Paul Thomas Young, Max Wertheimer, and other prominent thinkers). Maslow rejected basing human motivation theory on animal studies, largely because scholars (Young, for example), excluded the concept *goals* from motivation theory because goals are unmeasurable in studies of rats. Maslow (1943a, p. 89) queries, "Is it necessary to point out that we can ask a human being for his purpose?" Goal-driven behavior is a central proposition underlying Maslow's theory, which explains motivations for behavior rather behavior itself. The fundamental propositions are (Maslow, 1943a):

1. theories of motivation must conceptually maintain the integrated wholeness of the human organism;
2. somatically based and localizable needs are atypical and should not be the center of any understanding of motivation;
3. ultimate goals (ends rather than means) should be the center, explicitly including unconscious motivations;
4. basic, unconscious goals are primary over local specific desires (explicitly acknowledging culture as an explanation for varying paths to the same goal);
5. motivated behavior has multiple motivations and is a channel through which many basic needs are expressed and satisfied;
6. all states of the organism are motivated and motivating;
7. perhaps most importantly, *human needs are arranged in a hierarchy of prepotency* (the appearance of one resting on the prior satisfaction of another) and are not discrete or isolated (every drive is related to the state of others);

8. lists are useless theoretically and practically, and classifications of needs must encompass specificity and generalization of motives;
9. such classification must be based on goals;
10. motivation theory must be human, not based on animal research;
11. the situation (field) must be accounted for in the way that it is interpreted by the organism (but field theory is not motivation theory);
12. both integration and segmented reactions of the organism must be accounted for;
13. motivation theory is not behavior theory, motivations being just one class of behavioral determinant (others including biology, culture, and situation).

Based upon these propositions, Maslow (1943b) classified human motivation into five basic classifications of needs, each prepotent to the next—gratification of a need low in the hierarchy creates the condition for the next higher-order need's appearance. *Potency* here means capability to motivate. We do not feel a higher-order need, such as creative expression, when a lower-order need, such as need for warmth, is potent. This is an important distinction that accounts for variations. It is the *potency* of needs and their *prepotency* in relation to each other that explain their motivational function, not the nature of the needs themselves. Maslow posits that his classification of basic human needs is universal, but that needs only motivate behavior when their potency rises—which cannot occur in the face of an unmet prepotent need.

Deprivation and gratification are both important concepts. When a prepotent need is unsatisfied, it will dominate to the point that other (higher) needs are disregarded or nonexistent. Gratification "releases the organism from the domination" of the prepotent need, "permitting the emergence of" higher goals (Maslow, 1943b, p. 375). For example, if hunger is prepotent to physical safety, starving people will disregard their physical safety to obtain food—but the potency of the unmet lower need must be such that the deprivation is sufficient to drive behavior. I will not run through a rain of bullets for food until the need for food reaches a level of potency that pushes my safety need to the background. Once the hunger is gratified to a certain (but variable) extent, my chief drive will be to meet my safety need. The higher need (safety) cannot be potent until the lower and prepotent need (hunger) is gratified sufficiently.

Maslow's five categories of needs are, in order of typical prepotency: physiological, safety, love, esteem, and self-actualization.

- The most prepotent category, *physiological*, is not as simple as it would seem. Maslow is quick to point out that things that meet physiological needs, such as food and eating, also meet cultural and emotional needs, so he cautions against universal generalizations. Such needs as sleepiness, physical activity, sexual desire, and maternal behavior are also subject to localizations and should not be considered definitively physiological.
- *Safety* needs include emotional and psychological safety as well as physical, and must be defined by the individual's interpretation. In other words, the motivation is to *feel* safe; it is not measured by some objective assessment of actual safety. For example, sudden loud sounds may threaten a young child's feelings of safety in the absence of actual danger.
- *Love* includes affection, belongingness, and emotional intimacy—the need to have friends, be near family, or cultivate a romance. This last is an excellent example of the reason Maslow cautions against localized needs. Since emotional intimacy is

often achieved and expressed sexually, the sexual drive may be operating at either the physiological or love level of need, so localized expression cannot be generalized.

- *Esteem* is the need to attain stable positive evaluations of the self and others, and may be analyzed with a number of subcategories, such as achievement, independence, recognition, and appreciation.
- Finally, *self-actualization* "refers to the desire for self-fulfillment ... to become more and more what one is, to become everything that one is capable of becoming" (Maslow, 1943b, p. 382). The form and expression of self-actualization needs are highly individualized and deeply engrained in identity and culture.

Maslow discusses at length several very important points that are often glossed over in summaries of the theory. First, the hierarchical order of the need categories themselves is not universal but varies by person. For some, esteem may be prepotent to love, for example. He claims only that the prepotent order of his hierarchy is typical for the individuals observed in the research literature. While Maslow does claim that he has identified categories of basic human need that transcend culture, the universality of the theory is found most powerfully in the claim of hierarchical prepotency and the way deprivation and gratification of needs continually creates a new state of need. Thus, for some individuals, love may be prepotent to safety or creativity to hunger, but all individuals exist perpetually in a state of need, the gratification of which brings another (higher-order) need into prominence.

While behavior is universally driven by need gratification and deprivation, individualized prepotency variations can be explained by individual experience (such as a lifelong residence in a war zone that deadens the prepotency of safety), by culture, by personality, or by pathology. Second, multiple-level need fulfillment is simultaneous and need not be total to reach the next-higher need's level of potency. A family meal, for example, may simultaneously fulfill physiological and love needs, but the hunger need will be prepotent until it reaches a state of sufficient gratification to open a place for the love need (assuming the prepotency of hunger). Partial satisfaction of a prepotent need is sufficient to create a state of potency for the next-level need, and this too can vary individually. For example, an impoverished artist accustomed to chronic hunger may develop such an atypically low level of sufficiency to satisfy that physiological need that she is able to crave creative expression. Need gratification predicts the emergence of other needs, but *how much* gratification does so is not universal.

The unconscious character of needs and motivations is particularly important to an understanding of human drive. Culture is also clearly accounted for, and is the chief reason that basic human drives are used as the explanatory concept for motivation, rather than localized needs. Additionally, Maslow does not attempt to specify how needs are fulfilled. Maslow's discussion of other characteristics of basic needs includes the assertions that a single behavior has multiple motivations and that motivation is not the only determinant of behavior. Finally, Maslow's rejection of surface-level or fleeting desires as an explanation of motivation is important in applying the theory to psychopathology. "Thwarting of unimportant desires produces no psychopathological results; thwarting of a basically important need does produce such results" (1943b, p. 393).

The attention paid by management scholars and practitioners to Maslow's hierarchy (and other psychological treatments of human motivation) was a revolutionary departure from classical management. The recognition of the worker as a complex human being with needs, rather than a mechanistic component of the organizational machine, is the hallmark of the HR movement. Whether HR-theory-era managers actually personally cared about workers and their individual needs as humans is debatable, but the ubiquitous nature of their attention to Maslow's hierarchy is undeniable.

Douglas McGregor: Theory X and Theory Y

Douglas McGregor was a psychologist working as a professor of management. His summaries of Theory X and Theory Y are brilliant synopses of the managerial assumptions underlying traditional classical management philosophies and HR philosophies, respectively. McGregor (1957, 1960) offered an important distinction to Maslow's hierarchy between *lower-order needs* (physiological and safety) and *higher-order needs* (social, ego, and self-fulfillment). McGregor argued that traditional, external methods of control can only work when the level of employee development is confined to the drives of lower-order needs, but he is also quick to point out that while satisfaction of those needs may keep people working, it will not motivate increased productivity. Further, once the higher-order needs are in play, classical forms of management are actually detrimental because they offer deprivation rather than gratification. This is because traditional methods of managerial control rely on direction and command, with the means and methods of production dictated to the worker in conditions designed for them by management to serve organizational ends without regard to higher-order individual needs. McGregor argued that once the lower-order needs are satisfied, and workers are driven by their social (and higher) needs, direction and control actually create conditions that are oppositional to human motivational needs. Thus, the current organizational condition was such that management was no longer directing a workforce acting out of fear for their subsistence and survival, but rather needed to motivate a workforce for whom those things had already been assured. His fundamental point was that the industrial workforce had developed to the point where traditional forms of management were not only useless, but were actively thwarting worker need gratification and thus actually sabotaging organizational goals.

Theory X: The conventional view of management's task. McGregor (1957) identified three basic propositions for traditional management, which he called *Theory X*. First, it is the responsibility of management to organize money, materials, equipment, and people—the elements of productive enterprise—in the interest of economic ends. Second, organizing people is "a process of directing their efforts, motivating them, controlling their actions, modifying their behavior to fit the needs of the organization" (p. 23). Finally, in the absence of such management intervention, people would be passive and resistant to meeting organizational needs. This means that they must be directed—persuaded, rewarded, punished, controlled. McGregor goes on to identify several implicit beliefs commonly held by managers that underlie the propositions. First, people are fundamentally indolent with a desire to work as little as possible. People by nature lack ambition, dislike responsibility, want to be led, and are self-centered, indifferent to the needs of the organization, resistant to change, gullible, dull-witted, and easily duped. McGregor takes the position that conventional organization structures—as well as managerial policies, practices, and programs—are reflections of such assumptions.

Theory Y: The contemporary requirement. For Theory Y (which is essentially HR theory), McGregor identifies four fundamental propositions. The first one does not change: It remains the responsibility of management to organize the elements of productive enterprise (money, materials, equipment, and people) in the interest of economic ends. However, the remaining propositions recommend a revolution in the attitude of management. McGregor argues in his second Theory Y proposition that people are not *by nature* resistant to organizational needs, but rather have been led to be so from their organizational experiences. Third, McGregor posits that the motivation and capacity to develop, assume responsibility, and direct activities toward organizational goals are innate. Further, it is management's responsibility to create conditions in which people recognize and develop these human qualities in themselves. Finally, management's most fundamental task is to create organizational conditions and practices that allow people to achieve their own goals (satisfy their higher-order needs) by working toward organizational ends. McGregor explicitly acknowledges that creating such a system of management would face many obstacles, but should not be perceived as a "soft" approach, which was a common criticism of HR practices at the time. Managers, he argues, must find ways to create opportunities and encourage growth in ways that release workers' potential. He sought not an abdication of management or lowering of standards, but a wholly reinvented philosophy of leadership based on objectives rather than control.

HR in Practice: Did It Work?

By 1960, management theorists, industrial psychologists, and practitioners had internalized the notion that people are motivated to act on the organization's behalf when doing so meets their own needs. Unfortunately, they still had not fully grasped two fundamental ideas. First, the link between individual and organizational needs holds only when the individual needs under consideration are at the level of *esteem/ego* or *self-actualization/self-fulfillment*. Second, the motivation in question can only be *internally* generated. A manager cannot provide motivation, only the conditions in which motivation will thrive. Further, higher-order needs cannot be met by external pressure to produce, only by internal motivation to act on goals. HR practices continued to focus on worker's social needs and to be driven by the philosophy that management's goal was to drive employee compliance. However, although social needs are considered higher-order, they are simply the means through which ego (and then self-fulfillment) needs are activated.

Although McGregor's Theory Y was an excellent push in the right direction, scholars and practitioners still had not learned that human beings do not work harder because they are satisfied, rather it is the opposite. They are satisfied when their work fulfills their needs. Human beings work harder when they have an internalized need that is met through that effort, and that hard work then results in satisfaction. Maslow's theory of motivation is very clear on that point: Motivation is the *desire* to achieve an ungratified need, not the fulfillment derived from a previously met need. Yet, it is the previously met need that creates the appearance of the unmet need. So, motivation does not thrive by meeting needs, but rather by meeting needs in a way that provides both the next-level need and a path to achieve it. Furthermore, individual *social* needs simply do not align directly with *organizational* needs, so motivation to meet social needs does not translate to action that meets organizational needs. HR practices that created a friendlier and more social humane workplace were just a start, but for several decades, HR practices had stalled there—creating the complaint that HR management was "soft" (to which McGregor's Theory Y was in part a response).

Because the link between individual *development* and organizational goals had still not been made, HR practices focused on creating a positive climate and an enjoyable workplace that would lead to satisfied employees, under the faulty assumption that motivation to work harder would then follow from this satisfaction. While the first half of this linear sequence—from enjoyable workplace to worker happiness does indeed seem borne out by empirical research (e.g., Muchinsky, 1977), the second half—that improved productivity will be the final result—yields very mixed results (Brief, 1998), with the causal patterns among affect, job satisfaction and productivity being neither linear nor clear (Côté, 1999; Herzberg, 1968). Moreover, HR practices were often used unethically as managerial manipulation (Argyris, 1964) rather than as a genuine attempt to motivate.

Chris Argyris and Worker Alienation

Chris Argyris was a management scientist with a background in psychology and economics who closely examined the fit between personality and organizational work and the ways that organizational work might be designed to facilitate human development through alignment with higher-order needs. His work was foundational for the fields of organizational development, action research, and organizational learning, but had only marginal direct influence on organizational communication theory. His work is nonetheless important to organizational communication scholars, however, because it created revolutionary organizational practices that have profoundly shaped the phenomena we study in contemporary organizational communication research and because it deeply influenced the multidisciplinary field of organizational studies of which organizational communication is part.

Argyris' (1964) theory of personality and organization is an extension of Maslow's model. Like McGregor, he was particularly concerned with the ways in which hierarchical and bureaucratic organizational structures frustrate the needs of human development (Conrad, 1989). Argyris made several observations that led to his central point that a fundamental shift in organizational design, management philosophy, and management practices was necessary. First, higher-order human needs are inconsistent with the dehumanizing external control exacted by vertical hierarchies, and such organizational structures are thus unhealthy for human development. Formal control structures, lack of attention to internal motivations and drives, specialized jobs, and paternalistic HR practices exacerbate these frustrations. Furthermore, bureaucratic structures and practices that create a competitive climate foster hostile rivalry and selfish employee attitudes focused on the short term, rather than cooperative attitudes focused on the long-term organizational good. As a result, human beings, as adaptive organisms, naturally adjust to the stultifying environment of the vertical bureaucratic hierarchy with defensiveness, aggression, withdrawal, and apathy. They form social relationships with other alienated workers that feed on their common frustrations and dilute their attention to work and to organizational goals. They often leave the organization or attempt to advance to less frustrating positions, but with their individual goals so displaced from the organization's goals, such advancement benefits neither the employee nor the organization. In the end, organizations lose the very employees they most need to retain—those who are most mature and psychologically healthy. Those who do stay become less and less effective over time.

Argyris' work is based on the presumption that human beings are driven according to Maslow's hierarchy of needs and will enact their drive to achieve more higher-order needs in ways that are appropriate to the situation at hand. Therefore, if the organization provides opportunities for development that gratify employees' self-actualization needs, this basic human drive will lead to actions that will also serve the organization's needs. However, if the organization creates an environment in which self-actualization needs are frustrated and deprived, human behavior will fail to meet the needs of the organization. Argyris' observations are the fulfillment of Weber's admonition that bureaucracy would create a "polar night of icy darkness and hardness" (Weber, 1994, p. 368), as discussed in Chapter 5. Argyris went on to produce a prodigious library of books and articles, with many collaborators, that launched the field of organization development (OD). OD theory and practices unite the internal drives and needs of human development with the needs of the organization, positing that like individual human beings, organizations need to learn, grow, and develop.

Herzberg's Theory of Job Satisfaction

Frederick Herzberg was a psychologist who applied mental health principles to industrial and organizational settings. Herzberg (1968) sharply criticized popular HR practices as enacting a poor understanding of actual HR principles. He devised an explanation of worker motivation that both explicates the murky waters of the mixed results of HR practices and serves as a launching point for HRM. Like Argyris, Herzberg focused on individual *development* rather than simple need-fulfillment, uniting individual growth with organizational goals in the form of concrete practices.

Herzberg (1968) used the acronym KITA (kick in the "pants," p. 54) to describe pressure applied by managers externally. A negative KITA is a push or threat, whereas a positive KITA is a pull or reward. Quite obviously someone who viewed contemporary HR practices as "soft," he is contemptuously derisive in his description of common personnel practices intended to be motivating. For example, in his delightfully sarcastic critique of HR incentive programs that use time away from work as "an attempt to instill 'motivation'" he says,

> This represents a marvelous way of motivating people to work—getting them off the job! ... An interesting variant of this approach is the development of off-hour recreation programs. The philosophy here seems to be that those who play together, work together. The fact is that motivated people seek more hours of work, not fewer.
>
> (Herzberg, 1968, p. 55)

He goes on at length to skewer practitioners' attempts to create motivational programs, pointing out that while external forces may get employees to move, they do so under the energy of the manager, so it is the manager who is motivated rather than the worker. When that energy is withdrawn, movement stops.

> Similarly, I can charge a man's battery, and then recharge it, and recharge it again. But it is only when he has his own generator that we can talk about motivation. He then needs no outside stimulation. He *wants* to do it.
>
> (Herzberg, 1968, p. 55, emphasis in original)

Herzberg's central argument is that relying upon external management-driven techniques to exact performance from employees completely misses the point that true motivation stems from the employee's *desire to work* as a means to achieve his/her own *individual goals*. The fault lies in lack of attention to the individual worker's growth and development.

Herzberg's two-factor model of job satisfaction is based conceptually on Maslow's notion of lower- and higher-order needs and empirically on a number of comprehensive field observations. His data over these multiple studies (involving nearly 1,700 diverse participants across a broad range of organization and job types) clearly indicates that *dissatisfaction* and *satisfaction* are not opposite poles of a single linear continuum. Lack of dissatisfaction is not the same thing as satisfaction, and vice versa. Rather, gratification of lower-order needs, or *hygiene factors*, which relate to *job environment*, merely allows the employee to avoid dissatisfaction. It is important to note here that Herzberg quite explicitly lists *social* needs in the hygiene area, rather than the motivating area. Hygiene factors include company policy and administration, quality of supervision, relationship with supervisor, work conditions, salary, relationship with peers, personal life, relationship with subordinates, status, and security. These things are stimuli that induce pain-avoidance behavior. When hygiene factors are good, the employee is not dissatisfied.

On the other hand, gratification of higher-order needs, or *motivators*, related to *job content*, drives satisfaction. It is this latter class of factors that create the self-motivated employee whose job allows self-actualization. Motivators include achievement, recognition, challenge of the work itself, responsibility, advancement, and growth (Maslow's esteem and self-actualization). These factors induce individual development. When motivators are good, the employee is satisfied. Motivators create the employee's internal generator. In other words, Herzberg clearly points out that most HR applications had it backwards. Satisfaction is not the cause of motivation, but rather is its outcome.

Herzberg identifies a number of very specific practices management can adopt and a concrete sequence of steps to implement a job enrichment program built on his model. His system of job enrichment revolutionized the study of human motivation in industrial psychology. He cautioned against horizontal *job enlargement* practices, such as increased production targets, adding tasks, and rotating assignments—all of which simply enlarge the meaninglessness of the job. Successful *job enrichment*, on the other hand, increases the meaningfulness of the job to the employee's own growth and development. For example, vertical job enrichment practices that serve as motivators may include removing managerial controls while retaining employee accountability, increasing the individual's accountability for his/her own work, giving the employee complete responsibility for an entire unit of work (rather than distributing that unit's discrete tasks among several workers monitored by a supervisor), and introducing new and more difficult tasks as skills improve.

He gives the example of a secretarial pool required to produce a certain quota of letters each week, all of which were proofread, approved, and signed by the supervisor who was also consulted on specialized and difficult questions. Herzberg critiques this as mere *job enlargement*, which does not provide the opportunity for growth and is thus not motivating. The letters did not *belong to* the secretaries because they were given no accountability for the outcomes or control of the process; the processes in place were external—controlling work process and output by shaping the job's environment. *Job enrichment*, on the other hand, took a very different form, controlling work processes and output by shaping the job content—allowing the secretaries to internalize the job's demands and their drive to meet them by enacting all of Herzberg's motivators. Subject matter experts were appointed in each unit so that its members consulted with one another instead of with the supervisor. Those writing the letters signed their own names, and letters went directly to the mailroom rather than across the supervisor's desk first. Proofreading was gradually reduced from 100 percent supervisor verification to 10 percent, and was done at the secretary's desk rather than that of her supervisor. Specific quotas were eliminated in favor of an expectation for "a full day's work" (Herzberg, 1968, p. 61), and each correspondent was held personally responsible for the quality and accuracy of letters.

In summary, job enrichment is not a one-time practice, but should become a "continuous management function" (Herzberg, 1968, p. 62). Job enrichment allows the supervisor to spend less energy passively observing and correcting employees' performance and devote more time to administering thorough training and reviewing performance improvements. In this way, the organization develops in concert with the individual development of its employees. Moreover, job enrichment should progressively increase the challenge of the job to match the growing skills of the worker. This allows those with high ability to both better demonstrate that ability and improve it, opening up more opportunity for promotion. Because they promote individual development, motivators have a much longer-term effect on employees' attitudes than hygiene factors.

By the waning of the HR era, the thinking of both academics and practitioners about the nature of work, workers, organizations, and management had developed sophistication far beyond the mechanistic concerns of classical management. HR theory and practice had humanized the workplace, and management mandates were well into the transition from exacting worker compliance to fostering worker development. The commitment to provide a humane workplace that fostered the social needs of employees and took care of their social needs likewise shifted from a production-oriented demand to an ethically-oriented obligation.

Implications for Organizational Communication Theory

Before we discuss HRM, we must take a moment to assess the implications of HR theory to our thinking about communication, organization, authority, and culture. As the work of McGregor, Argyris, and Herzberg (among others) so clearly shows, classical management's bureaucratic structures and control practices remained in place throughout this era. HR theory should thus be seen as *highlighting* different aspects of communication, authority, and organization, but not in a way that replaced bureaucratic structures of authority or the priority of bureaucratic control.

Approach to Communication

HR theory examines the informal aspects of communication, with human psychology and emotion as primary concerns. Communication is treated relationally with a more transactional approach of two-way (but still linear) messaging between managers and employees. In HR theory, the treatment of communication is also enriched beyond mere messaging to also be seen as connecting and forging cooperative relationships. Communication, however, often remains cast as a management tool to accomplish worker productivity—but not by establishing and maintaining organizational control vested in persons who hold authority as it was in classical theory. Rather, communication is a management tool to accomplish employee cooperation. The function of communication is thus both informational and relational.

In HR, the reciprocal relationship between deep enduring structures and daily practices is clear in the revolutionary change in American organizational life that can be traced to their inception. The HR movement introduced new practices, encouraging managers to communicate in humanizing ways that manifest care for workers' humanity. Over time, these practices became institutionalized, to the point where entire bureaucratic units were deemed necessary to manage the HR function of the organization. HR has become such an enduring structure that *human resources* became a thriving profession with its own professional career path, credentialing processes, and specializations. In addition, complex systems of labor regulations (such as requirements to provide health insurance, fair hiring practices, etc.) also appeared—again creating thriving professions with their own internal structures. You can see here how daily practices constitute enduring organizational structures in many ways. The original organization itself evolves as new structures emerge, but new formal organizations can also trace their emergence to these initial practices. For example, organizational entities such as degree programs in human resources, law firms specializing in labor law, human resources consulting firms, and government regulatory agencies could not exist without the day-to-day HR practices initiated by the HR movement. HR theory also integrated our understanding of humans and organizations as mutually supportive and mutually constitutive, especially in the later theories (e.g., Herzberg). If daily practices that perpetuate organizational development also work for the individual's need satisfaction and growth, the communication/organization cycle is one that increasingly improves the development of both.

Approach to Organization and Authority

HR theory treats the organization more as an organism than a machine (Morgan, 1986), although the full extent of the organismic metaphor wouldn't be seen until HRM and the decades following it. In HR theory, especially as seen in Barnard, the organization is seen less as an external authoritative entity and more as a system of communication among its members. The managerial class is still somewhat ascribed with the authority to demand the actions required of the labor class, but the managerial class had become larger with more internal layers and divisions, and authority was treated more as negotiated than dictated. Yet, the vertical hierarchy of Fayol's organizational chart remained an engrained form for organizational structure. The shift is that the focus turned from persons to positions, with more fluidity and flexibility. Despite Follett's and Barnard's admonitions that authority should be construed as *power with* rather than *power over*, the vertical metaphor for authority remained entrenched. On the other hand, our current organizational practices also show free communication up and down that hierarchy, work groups that freely communicate with one another with management's full approval, and dehumanization of work as a chief concern.

Cultural Implications

The HR movement changed work environments profoundly and permanently. Concerns for worker wellbeing remain an organizational priority, and the social needs of workers garner the attention required for a humane and enjoyable work environment.

Today's legal mandates to provide health insurance, in addition to organizational incentive programs and employee wellbeing initiatives are all born of the HR movement. These programs are not just nice for employees, however, but also a means of meeting employees' lower-order needs as the foundation upon which management strategies for human development can foster the unification of individual and organizational needs, which has become a cultural imperative.

Recommended Supplementary Readings

Acker, J., & Van Houten, D (1974). Differential recruitment and control: The sex structuring of organizations. *Administrative Science Quarterly, 19,* 152–163.
This analysis provides an interesting and insightful gendered reading of the Hawthorne Studies, disrupting the common narrative about this piece of history.
Bruce, K. (2006). Henry S. Dennison, Elton Mayo, and human relations historiography. *Management and Organizational History, 1,* 177–199.
This article provides a thorough history of the Hawthorne Studies and the advent of the HR movement in management theory and practice.
Follett, M. P. (1919). Community is a process. *Philosophical Review, 28,* 576–588.
A reading of Mary Parker Follett's revolutionary ideas in their original source provides a first-hand experience of her visionary, ahead-of-her time ideas.
Herzberg, F. (1968). One more time: How do you motivate employees? *Harvard Business Review, 65,* 109–120.
Herzberg's irreverent style is interesting. The original had a sentence describing the motivation difference as that between rape and seduction (one "an unfortunate occurrence," the other a choice). Its 1968 acceptability, and subsequent deletion, can provoke a thoughtful classroom discussion.
Wrege, C. D. (1976). Solving Mayo's mystery: The first complete account of the origin of the Hawthorne Studies—the forgotten contributions of C. E. Snow and H. Hibarger. *Academy of Management Proceedings,* 12–16.
This article provides information on important contributors to the Hawthorne Studies who usually remain uncredited in contemporary accounts.

Important Concepts: Define and Discuss

Distinctions among management theory eras
Hawthorne Studies
Theory X and Theory Y
Alienation
Satisfaction vs. dissatisfaction
Motivators vs. hygiene factors
Job enlargement vs. job enrichment

Discussion Questions

1. Why should we classify the advancement of HR theory as an evolution from classical theory rather than a revolution against it?
2. Provide an example of a contemporary executive, and illustrate Barnard's three functions.

3. How does the contemporary landscape of electronic communication and social media accomplish the functions of informal organization?
4. How do contemporary communication media enhance the potential of implementing Follett's bottom-up coordination?
5. Why is it still so difficult to break away from top-down management to implement Follett's bottom-up thinking?
6. Discuss examples of contemporary programs and practices that have their roots in the HR movement. What functions do they serve?

Practitioners' Corner

Obvious applications of HR theories for communication practice include employee wellness and motivational programs. The distinction between hygiene factors and motivators based on an understanding of lower- and higher-order needs is particularly important both for designing programs that accomplish their intended purpose and for explaining those programs to organizational members and leaders. Clarity of expectations is key. A good understanding of what employee benefits and HR programs can accomplish is crucial to their success. Communication professionals have a role in providing this clarity to management.

More central to meeting organizational goals, however, is the important insight that managers and executives function as communication centers, and that employee performance is a direct function of the quality of that communication. Getting things done requires the exercise of authority rooted in communication. Communication professionals are well-suited to support managers, either as internal communication officers or as consultants, to meet Barnard's four criteria for effective management communication, ensuring that employees understand the message and feel capable of compliance, believe the message to be consistent with organizational purposes, and perceive their own personal interests to be aligned.

References

Acker, J., & Van Houten, D. (1974). Differential recruitment and control: The sex structuring of organizations. *Administrative Science Quarterly, 19*(2), 152–163. doi:10.2307/2393886.
Argyris, C. 1964. *Integrating the individual and the organization.* New York: Wiley.
Barnard, C. I. (1938). *The functions of the executive.* Cambridge, MA: Harvard University Press.
Brief, A. P. (1998). *Attitudes in and around organizations.* Thousand Oaks, CA: SAGE.
Bruce, K. (2006). Henry S. Dennison, Elton Mayo, and human relations historiography. *Management and Organizational History, 1*(2), 177–199. doi:10.1177/1744935906064095.
Conrad, C. (1989). *Strategic organizational communication* (2nd ed.). Fort Worth: Holt, Rinehart and Winston.
Côté, S. (1999). Affect and performance in organizational settings. *Current Directions in Psychological Science, 8,* 65–68. doi:10.1111/1467-8721.00016.
Follett, M. P. (1919). Community is a process. *Philosophical Review, 28*(6), 576–588. doi:10.2307/2178307.
Follett, M. P. (1924). *Creative experience.* New York: Peter Smith.
Greenwood, R. G., & Wrege, C. D. (1986). The Hawthorne Studies. In D. A. Wren & J. A. Pearce II (Eds.), *Papers dedicated to the development of modern management* (pp. 24–35). Briarcliff Manor, NY: Academy of Management.

Herzberg, F. (1968). One more time: How do you motivate employees? *Harvard Business Review*, 65(1), 53–62.

Maslow, A. H. (1943a). Preface to motivation theory. *Psychosomatic Medicine*, 5(1), 85–92. doi:10.1097/00006842-194301000-00012.

Maslow, A. H. (1943b). A theory of human motivation. *Psychology Review*, 50(4), 370–396. doi:10.1037/h0054346.

McGregor, D. (1957). The human side of enterprise. *Management Review*, 46(11), 22–28.

McGregor, D. (1960). *The human side of enterprise*. New York: McGraw-Hill.

Morgan, G. (1986). *Images of organization*. Thousand Oaks, CA: SAGE.

Muchinsky, P. (1977). Organizational communication: Relationships to organizational climate and job satisfaction. *Academy of Management Journal*, 20(4), 592–607. doi:10.5465/255359.

Newman, M. A., & Guy, M. E. (1998). Taylor's triangle, Follett's web. *Administrative Theory & Praxis*, 20(3), 287–297.

Roethlisberger, F. J., Dickson, W. J., & Wright, H. A. (1939). *Management and the worker: An account of a research program conducted by the Western Electric Company, Hawthorne Works, Chicago*. Cambridge, MA: Harvard University Press.

Sethi, N. (1962). Mary Parker Follett: Pioneer in management theory. *The Journal of the Academy of Management*, 5(3), 214–221.

Sethi, N. (1966). Coordination: The key to organizational engineering. *Industrial Management*, 8(8), 9–14.

Weber, M. (1994). *Weber: Political writings*. Ed. P. Lassman. Trans. R. Speirs. Cambridge: Cambridge University Press.

Wrege, C. D. (1976). Solving Mayo's mystery: The first complete account of the origin of the Hawthorne Studies—the forgotten contributions of C. E. Snow and H. Hibarger. *Academy of Management Proceedings*, 12–16. doi:10.5465/AMBPP.1976.4975490.

7 Human Resource Management Theory

Anne M. Nicotera

Human resource management (HRM) theory, as explained in Chapter 6, identified employee intelligence as a valuable resource. This was a natural extension to later HR theories' focus on human development, with Herzberg and Argyris as key scholars contributing to this shift in thinking. As managers strived to align employee developmental needs with organizational goals, and scholars sought better evidence on how to best do so, the importance of worker participation in decision-making became an important strategy, spurring the participation movement of the 1960s and 1970s, particularly in manufacturing. The humanism of the HR era functioned as an important transitional period from the mechanistic thinking and practices of the classical era to the more organismic thinking of HRM. As scholars and practitioners came to understand more about the nature of human motivation and human development, the need to unite individual and organizational development became progressively clearer. Rather than neutral and static entities, organizations were increasingly seen as fluid, growing, learning organisms. It was soon a commonly accepted assumption that the organization as a whole could thrive and develop only through the developmental progress of its employees. The work of Frederick Herzberg on job enrichment was very influential, as was Argyris' extensive work in organizational learning. In this chapter, we will focus on the early HRM theories that provide a conceptual link to the advent of organizational communication theory and research in the 1970s.

HRM had a profoundly democratizing effect on organizations. Participation strategies range from managers collecting employee input on decisions to fully delegating decision-making authority to employees. (See Tannenbaum & Schmidt, 1958, for one of the earliest analyses of determining the appropriate management strategy for decision-making on this continuum of autocratic to democratic to delegated). It was during this era in management theory that the field of organizational communication emerged as a separate and unique discipline from both management theory and other social sciences such as social psychology (see Chapter 1). As such, we will not continue to trace the development of management theory after HRM. It is important to note, however, that by the 1990s, the idea of participation had expanded in in the field of management to widespread prescriptions for organizational restructuring to flatten hierarchies, decentralize authority, and create team-based environments characterized by self-managed groups. This was particularly prevalent in the manufacturing environment.

The restructuring and teams movement in management is important for organizational communication scholars because it revolutionized the organizational environments we study, creating interesting communication phenomena, including paradoxes (Stohl & Cheney, 2001; see Chapter 3). There are sizable organizational communication literatures on groups, teams, leadership, and organizational democracy (in addition to numerous other areas) that document how the study of organizational communication shifted in response to the emergence of alternative organizational forms that for many organizations replaced the vertical authority hierarchy of traditional bureaucracy with flattened hierarchies encompassed by more circular organizational forms. The foundations of these sea changes lie in the mid-20th-century recognition of employee intelligence as a valuable organizational resource. HRM theory is most fruitfully described through three fundamental themes: The integration of formal and informal organization, contingency, and participation. Each theme is explicated here with overviews of theories and practices that provide striking illustrations of that theme. However, all HRM theories and practices resonate with all three themes. Before summarizing the implications of HRM theory, the chapter then looks ahead in time to management theory developments in restructuring that brought HRM ideals to fruition in the 1990s.

HRM Theme: Integrating Formal and Informal Organization

The integration of formal and informal organization is essential to HRM philosophy and practice. The two fundamental imperatives of HRM were to align individual and organizational development and to maximize the potential of employee intelligence. These could be accomplished only through fostering participative and collaborative relationships across hierarchical levels. While relational communication was attended to by HR theory, the manager–employee relationship remained paternalistic and authoritarian. Under HRM, the definition of that relationship transformed. While managers retained the legitimate positional authority embedded in the vertical hierarchy, the character of the manager–employee relationship became more egalitarian, with greater respect for employee opinion fueled by increased recognition of the perspective gained from direct experience. As shared authority over organizational decision-making and goal-setting became more expected, employee performance targets and reward systems likewise became negotiations rather than directives, and accountability became decentralized along with authority. These formal aspects of the manager–employee relationship could not have been reconfigured without a parallel reframing of the informal.

Rensis Likert: System IV

One of the earliest HRM theories was Likert's System IV. Rensis Likert was an organizational psychologist working in the U.S. Department of Agriculture in the 1940s, and later the director of the Institute for Social Research at the University of Michigan. Like McGregor, Likert (1961, 1967) provided descriptions of management systems he found undesirable in order to promote the system he advocated. Likert's primary focus was on decision-making.

System I: Exploitative authoritative. Rooted in the ideals and practices of classical management (see Chapter 5), exploitative authoritative management utilizes top-down decision-making and threat-based motivation based on fear of losing physical and economic security. Organizational goals, and the methods by which to achieve them, are dictated by management. In such a system, management feels responsible for meeting organizational goals; whereas employees do not and welcome opportunities to behave in ways that defeat organizational goals. Individual employee goals and needs are ignored. As a result, Likert (1961) warns that employee attitudes are hostile to organizational goals. Communication is almost entirely downward. Employees are thus subservient to managers with some hostility. Hostility is also cultivated downward and with peers, and distrust is widespread. The informal organization usually opposes the goals of the formal organization; productivity is mediocre; and employees are generally dissatisfied. In this way, Likert describes the undesirable outcomes of the exploitative authoritative management system.

System II: Benevolent authoritative. Still rooted in classical management ideals, but with a more considerate managerial attitude, System II is less controlling than System I, with employee motivation based on economic security and ego motives (e.g., a desire for status). While major decisions, such as setting organizational policies and goals, are made at the top, workers are afforded the opportunity to make some decisions within the limits of the framework provided by management. Organizational goals are set by management, with some employee opportunities for feedback. In this system, management feels responsible for organizational goals; whereas employees do not. Communication is mostly downward, but significant opportunities for upward communication do exist. Employees are subservient to and somewhat suspicious of managers, and the competition for managerial favor creates hostility among peers and condescension to subordinates. The informal organization partially opposes the goals of the formal organization; productivity is fair to good; and employees are only moderately satisfied. Likert's description of benevolent authoritative management shows how it begins to move management strategy in the right direction, but does not go far enough.

System III: Consultative. The consultative management system is fundamentally based in the ideals and practices of HR theory (see Chapter 6). Employee motivation is based in economic, ego, and other employee-centered motives, such as the desire for new experiences. While employee input is actively sought by management as a key source of information necessary for goal-setting and decision-making, major decisions and the setting of organizational goals remain the territory of management. Lower-level employees are afforded the freedom to make decisions only on specific things that directly impact their work. In this system, both managers and employees feel responsible for meeting organizational goals, and behavior counter to those goals is rare. Communication flows freely downward and upward, although upward communication is more limited. Employee attitudes are cooperative, albeit with some competition among peers. The informal organization is generally supportive of but somewhat resistant to the goals of the formal organization; productivity is good; and employees are moderately satisfied. Likert's description of System III shows it to be a vast improvement over Systems I and II, but not quite enough to maximize organizational goal-attainment.

System IV: Participative. Likert's System IV, which he argued was the most effective form of management, is an exemplar of HRM theory. System IV promotes full and genuine participation in decision-making and organizational goal-setting. Communication is free-flowing in all directions, with the skills, creativity, and intelligence of employees valued as key organizational resources. All organizational members feel responsibility for achieving organizational goals, and accountability is likewise high. Attitudes are favorable to organizational goals and foster cooperative relationships within and between levels. The informal and formal organizations are integrated; productivity is excellent; and satisfaction is high.

Likert (1967) provided detailed instructions for the successful implementation of System IV management. The achievement of System IV objectives is accomplished through shared authority, with clear systems of accountability in place. The role of management must shift to a facilitative function that monitors and coordinates rather than dictates. Data collection must be constant, and participation must be facilitated effectively in groups rather than individual-to-individual. The reframing of *the organization as a system of groups* is crucial to Likert's advancements in managerial thinking. Collaborative high-performance goal-setting with employees, coupled with supportive communication with managers, is crucial to both organizational and individual success. Fundamentally, the central innovation contributed by Likert was the redefinition of the manager from an *authority who translates* organizational goals to employee activities to a *mediator who facilitates* participation in organizational goal-setting and negotiates the articulation of those goals with employee activities.

Blake and Mouton's Managerial Grid

Blake and Mouton were management theorists and consultants. Their Managerial Grid model is one of several HRM-era depictions of management and leadership as a set of practices integrating the task and relational dimensions of organization—the formal and informal organizations. The Managerial Grid has remained popular in practice and managerial training, and as such there have been a number of updates in its terminology and the flexibility of its implementation. It was particularly influential as a way of examining conflict management (Blake, Shepard, & Mouton, 1964; also see Chapter 16). Many earlier considerations conceptualized leaders' task and relational behaviors as polar opposites, presuming that each took something away from the other. Blake and Mouton (1964) were among the first scholars to posit the task and relational behaviors of managers as independent dimensions, proposing five leadership styles according to the manager's *concern for production* and *concern for people*. Conceptualizations using this basic two-dimensional structure later became known as *dual-concern models*. In the Managerial Grid, each of these two dimensions is operationalized on a nine-point scale from low to high, with an accompanying self-report diagnostic scale covering numerous behavioral elements: Initiative, inquiry, advocacy, decision-making, conflict, critique, and resilience. Similarly to Likert, Blake and Mouton describe four of their five styles as less effective than their preferred HRM ideal, *team management* (9,9)—high concern for both production and people, and thus an integration of formal and informal organization.

Impoverished management (1,1), with its low concern for both production and for people, is seen as negligent, an abdication of managerial responsibility. *Authority-compliance management* (9,1), characterized by a high concern for production with a low concern for people, is traditional classical management—ignoring the informal organization and thus losing the contributions of employee experience, creativity, and intelligence. *Country club management* (1,9) is the opposite. Blake and Mouton describe it in a way that reveals their contempt for HR practices that presume job performance can be improved by attention to employee happiness without a concomitant focus on task productivity (similar to the posture assumed by both McGregor and Herzberg). *Middle of the road management* (5,5) is seen as ineffective—its compromising stance pitting the two concerns against one another as oppositional ideals rather than mutually influential processes that can enhance one another. *Team management* (9,9), however, is the *sine qua non* of HRM, uniting employees' need for development with organizational goals, seeking full employee participation in decision-making, and pursuing a collaborative relationship between management and employees. Like other HRM theorists, Blake and Mouton (and, after their deaths, the consulting company they founded) produced a large library of publications designed to assist practitioners in implementing their system of management.

HRM Theme: Contingency

Contingency is another central theme in HRM theory and practice. *Contingency theory* is an umbrella term for management theory claiming there is no "one best way" to manage. Rather, different managerial strategies and skill-sets fit different situations. One of the most pervasive assumptions of management theorists in this era (and since) was that one approach to managing employees was not advisable for all situations. Rather, the selection of appropriate and effective management strategies is presumed to be driven by contingent factors. As contingency thinking developed, flexibility of the leader emerged as a primary concern for the implementation of effective management strategies.

Fiedler's Situational Contingency Theory

One of the earliest contingency theories predicted group effectiveness from the match between leader style and situational demands, theorizing that leaders are most effective when the situation is modified to suit their strengths. Fiedler (1967) placed leader style into two categories, operationalized by the way the individual rates his or her *least preferred coworker* (LPC) on a number of bi-polar scales. Those who describe unfavorable coworkers in negative terms (low-LPC) are task-oriented; whereas, high-LPC leaders are more motivated to maintain good interpersonal relations. It is important to note that this is a less developed, bi-polar conceptualization of task and relational behavior than later HRM theories (such as Blake and Mouton's) would adopt. Fiedler also conceptually grounded leader style in personality traits, and therefore not subject to change. Rather than the leader's behavior, it is the contingent situational factors that are seen as malleable. Situational favorability (also called situational control) is defined by three contingencies: good leader–member relations (characterized by mutual trust and respect); clear task structures; and leader position power (ability to distribute resources) (Fiedler, 1967). Low-LPC leaders perform best in extreme situations—either highly unfavorable or highly favorable conditions. High-LPC leaders perform best in situations that are moderately favorable or unfavorable.

Later, the basic theory was expanded into *cognitive resource theory* (Fiedler, 1986). Two important leader cognitive resources—leaders' *intelligence* and *experience* (defined as knowledge and abilities gained over time in the organization) and an additional situational variable (*stress*) were included as leadership effectiveness contingencies. The theory predicts that a leader's direction is more likely to be followed when the leader has high intelligence and ability and when group members are supportive. In conditions of low stress (with leader's own supervisor, with the group members, or with the problem at hand) intelligence is applied more often and is more effective. On the other hand, in situations of high stress, leader experience (in the form of knowledge/skills gained over time) predicts high performance, and leader intelligence is either not important or can actually detract from the group's performance.

Fiedler's model was criticized because it neither accounted for nor advocated flexibility in the leader's style, presuming that leadership style was based in personality and was thus predetermined and stable. Fiedler, and those who joined his consulting practice, designed complex training programs to assist managers and executives in modifying organizational situational variables and matching leaders to appropriate assignments—but in the end the only reliable solution offered to a mismatch between leader and situation was to change the leader. Fiedler's models also conceptualized task and relational concerns as oppositional styles and persisted in the narrow presumption that leadership is defined as giving direction, so it did not keep pace with the increasing demand for multidimensional conceptualizations of leadership concerns, delegation of authority, and participative decision-making.

Hersey and Blanchard's Model of Situational Leadership

First introduced as the *life cycle theory of leadership* (Hersey & Blanchard, 1969), Situational Leadership theory is an exemplar of contingency thinking in HRM theory because it both advocates flexibility in management strategy and links such leadership behavior to employee development to maximize organizational outcomes. Situational Leadership theory is similar to Blake and Mouton's Managerial Grid in its two-dimensional structure of leader behavior. However, while Blake and Mouton focused on the concerns of the leader, Hersey and Blanchard concentrated on the type of support leaders offer to their followers. Hersey and Blanchard identified four main leadership styles, according to the extent of task and relationship support provided by the leader or manager, which should be adjusted contingent to the followers' task and relational needs. In early publications, these were referred to as *maturity* levels on the dimensions *ability* (task support need) and *willingness* (relational support need). Later versions of the theory (e.g., Blanchard, Zigarmi, & Zigarmi, 1985; Hersey, 1985) refined the conceptualization of follower needs to focus on *development* (sometimes referred to as *readiness*), operationalized on the dimensions *competence* and *commitment*. This was an important theoretical advance because this thinking introduced a dynamic character to the theory. The theory claims that the appropriate combination of task and relational support provided at levels adjusted over time—matched to followers' evolving needs—fosters follower development of independence and abilities that would, in turn, enable the leader to increasingly delegate responsibility in a way that advances organizational development and expansion. Further, the later iteration of the theory that replaced *willingness* with *commitment* provided a far more nuanced understanding of followers' relational support needs.

Followers with low competence but high commitment are the least developed, requiring the leader to practice a *Telling* (Style 1) leadership style that provides a high level of task direction and support and a low level of relational support. The initial version of the theory proposed the lowest level of employee maturity to be low on both ability and willingness, but data and field experience revealed that it was more typical for those new to a task to have initial enthusiasm that flags as their abilities increase. As they develop to the second level, followers remain less than fully competent and actually regress in their commitment level, realizing how much there is still to learn and feeling overwhelmed and/or disheartened. The second level of development is described as low competence and low commitment. This is the point when the manager needs to provide increasing relational support while maintaining high level of task support to continue building ability (Style 2, *Selling*). In the third level of development, competence is high. Followers now have the skills and abilities they need to perform independently. However, their commitment remains low or variable because they lack the confidence gained from independent performance, so the best leadership strategy reduces the level of task support while maintaining high relational support (Style 3, *Participating*). Finally, followers attain the highest level of development, with both the competence and commitment to perform independently. The leader can now greatly reduce both task and relational support, remaining involved to monitor and provide feedback, but distributing authority and accountability for the work to the follower (Style 4, *Delegating*). In a dynamic workplace, employees can be expected to repeat this process with each new set of tasks they encounter, as they increasingly develop to expand the domains of their ability to accomplish and expand organizational objectives. In this way, the Situational Leadership model demonstrates how attention to contingencies for appropriate management strategies also accomplishes the integration of individual and organizational development and champions the centrality of employee intelligence as an organizational resource.

HRM Theme: Participation

Finally, all HRM theorists advocate employee participation in decision-making (PDM). Unlike HR theory, which does so with employees' need for belongingness as a central concern, HRM applications of PDM highlight the value of employee intelligence as a valuable resource. Under HR, participation is used to benefit the employee; under HRM participation is used to benefit the organization. Whereas HR theory involves employees to help them feel good, HRM theory involves employees because of the value brought by their intelligence and experience. PDM can thus be seen as an important conceptual bridge from HR to HRM. As the organizational value of the employee perspective came to be more recognized and valued, PDM practices already in place for the purposes of building morale provided a basis for HRM management strategies. As mentioned at the outset of this chapter, HRM theory planted the conceptual seeds for the organizational restructuring movement several decades later that allowed numerous large organizations to dismantle vertical bureaucratic authority systems. PDM practices are at the heart of the ideas that manifested in such organizational redesign and the creation of new organizational forms. Decentralization of decision-making is fundamental to the flattening of hierarchies. As the authority to make decisions and the accountability for their outcomes were distributed horizontally, traditional authority structures in a significant number of industries were replaced by dynamic circular systems of independent business units comprised of self-managed teams.

The distinction between HRM-era decentralization and later large-scale restructuring efforts is the type and scope of decision-making authority that was distributed. Work-related decision-making, rather than policy-level strategic decisions, were the stuff of PDM programs in the HRM era. These early efforts built into more large-scale participation in strategic decision-making in large organizational systems, such a government bureaus (Bacharach & Aiken, 1977). According to Jablin (1987), early studies of participation in strategic decision-making leads to increased volume, frequency, and openness of communication across the organization (in all directions) and an increase in amount and quality of performance feedback. Siebold and Shea (2001) conducted a comprehensive summary of PDM programs, including the restructured or *new plant* approach. They analyzed the research literature on five voluntary formal participation systems, examining their effectiveness. The summary to follow is based on Seibold and Shea's (2001) analysis. The primary distinctions among PDM practices are the extent to which their influence on decisions ranges from consultative to full and the types of decisions involved (from concrete concerns of the work itself to organizational policy decisions).

Quality circles. *Quality circles* (QCs) are a continuous improvement strategy. A quality circle is a discussion group of workers with similar jobs who identify, analyze, and solve task-related problems. QCs have a consultative role. They are led by supervisors and must present proposals to management for approval. Ordinarily, the workers are expected to implement the approved actions that result from their discussion. Their discussions are limited to the work itself and the immediate work area. There is a low degree of involvement and a low degree of effectiveness.

Quality of work life programs. *Quality of work life* (QWL) is a broad term used to label structured programs that seek to involve employees in decisions affecting their work. QWL programs have a consultative role, functioning to provide important feedback to managers about the concerns of employees to inform their decision-making. The topics of discussion may be the work itself, working conditions, or even company policies. QWL programs can take many forms (e.g., employee surveys, town-hall type meetings) and can include union representatives, workers, and managers. The degree of participation is relatively low, and effectiveness varies. The Total Quality Management (TQM) fad of the 1980s, an effort to create an organization climate of continuous improvement, followed the QWL philosophy.

Employee stock ownership plans (ESOPs). ESOPs were instituted in the 1970s to provide incentives to employees by making company stock part of the employee compensation and benefits system. The fundamental philosophy underlying ESOPs is the assumption that employees will internalize corporate profitability as a personal goal because they own a piece of the corporation and reap personal financial benefit from the value of the stock. ESOPs may take many forms, but often allow voting among participating employees. The content of the decision-making varies, but normally involves sending representatives to the board of directors. The degree of participation varies from low to moderate, depending on the type of ESOP. The influence of participating employees can vary from consultative only to full participation in company policy decisions. Their effectiveness is moderate.

Scanlon plans. *Scanlon gainsharing plans* create a reward system linked to group and organizational performance. A Scanlon plan is a profit-sharing technique designed by Joseph Scanlon during the U.S. Great Depression to promote stability in labor-management relations during this volatile era. Employees share the financial rewards of cost savings and profit, based on their own effort according to a formalized incentive formula. Detailed periodic progress reporting and monitoring are necessary for implementation. Content of the decision-making can encompass the work itself, working conditions, company policy, and the design of financial bonuses. The degree of participation required is moderate to high. The influence can vary from consultative only to full participation in company policy decisions, and may even include the privilege of implementing some decisions without prior management approval. Their effectiveness is high.

Self-directed work teams (SDWTs). SDWTs manage themselves without the oversight of a traditionally authoritative manager. Teams are afforded full authority to make decisions over their own processes and production involving the work itself, working conditions, schedules, budgets, contracts, hiring (at the team level), and compensation. The degree of participation is very high, as is effectiveness when the program is implemented with appropriate training and is structured correctly. The use of SDWTs, or the *new plant* approach (Lawler, 1978, 1992), represents the most successful of the strategies that culminated in the restructuring movement of the 1990s. The new plant approach is reviewed in detail below to illustrate the kinds of large structural changes necessary to achieve the participation ideals of HRM. Research on the new plant approach provides evidence that the ideals of HRM are only fully attainable when formal structures are decentralized and hierarchies are flattened. However, without the appropriate cultural transition accomplished by thorough education and training, their implementation can result in adverse consequences (Barker, 1993; Stohl & Cheney, 2001; see Chapter 3).

Organizational Communication and Management Theory Developments

It is beyond the scope of this volume to provide full reviews of the ways that the ideas introduced by HRM theory were developed in management and organizational theory— as Organizational Communication had become an established and separate discipline by the end of the HRM era in the 1970s. Chapter 3 provided an overview of participation and democracy research in organizational communication that is directly related to the foundations laid by HRM (specifically, Stohl & Cheney's, 2001, paradoxes of participation). Here, it is important to diverge from our timeline momentarily and leap to the 1990s to provide an example of management theory that stems from HRM's implementation of employee participation programs.

Management Theory that Extended HRM: Organizational Restructuring

In the 1990s, Edward E. Lawler III and his colleagues at the Center for Effective Organizations, Marshall School of Business, University of Southern California (USC) generated a theoretically rich and empirically based body of prescriptive theory advocating the restructuring of vertical organizational designs with centralized authority structures to create flattened (or lateralized) participative designs with distributed authority. As a whole, this work (e.g., Galbraith, Lawler, & Associates, 1993; Lawler, 1991, 1992, 1999, 2000, 2001; Lawler, Mohrman, & Ledford, 1998; Mohrman, Cohen, & Mohrman, 1995; Mohrman, Galbraith, Lawler, & Associates, 1998) provides an exemplar of the eventual successful application of HRM ideals of human development and workplace democracy. In the interest of space, only Lawler's (1992) new plant approach is reviewed here. Lawler (1992) explicitly states that many of these "new" ideas and practices are not altogether new. In practice, what was new at the time were the business imperative that demanded such practices for survival, the wide scale with which they were being applied, and the flattening of organizational authority structures.

Lawler (2000) summarizes six *new logic principles* for organizing, conceptualizing *new logic organizing* as a new era of management thinking. His conceptualization of new logic emerges from the copious empirical description represented by the prolific body of research generated by the Center for Effective Organizations at USC, and thus provides a rich frame for the detailed overview of the new plant approach, established in practice prior to the articulation of these conceptual principles. Lawler (2000) contrasts his six new logic principles to the old logic principles of traditional bureaucratic organizing (see Table 7.1). Closely examined, it is clear that principles 2, 3, and 6 stem directly from

HRM ideals. Whereas, principles 1, 4, and 5 specify how presumptions about the design of the organizational structure must change to accomplish the promise of those ideals.

These are integrating principles that revolve around the dissemination of power, responsibility, and accountability—rooted in an explicit understanding that organizational form is the driving force. Lawler (1992) systematically reviews major structural features needed for high employee involvement. He then prescribes strategies to move beyond what had already been accomplished.

Lawler's high-involvement organization. Grounding his discussion in the assumption that a successful organization will have a management approach and design that is congruent with societal culture, Lawler (1992) begins by setting up a contrast between two managerial/organizational design approaches: the control-oriented approach (vertical authority) rooted in old logic principles and the involvement-oriented approach (lateral authority) rooted in new logic principles. He argues that the involvement-oriented approach is "highly congruent with democratic values about decision-making and respect for individual rights ... [And] directly aligned with the strong entrepreneurial bent in the American culture" (pp. 43–44). Conversely, he describes the control-oriented model as based on a set of principles that exist in opposition to such democratic ideals as participative decision-making, due process, freedom of speech, individual rights, and personal growth. Note, here, how all these ideals are rooted in the cultural shifts stimulated by the HR and HRM movements.

Lawler (1992) explains in detail features of organizational design that can achieve the high-involvement organization. These features include alternative work designs, work that is highly involving, organization/improvement groups, person-based pay (as opposed to position-based), and performance rewards. Next, he discusses structural features necessary for the management of information and human resources, including open information channels, high-involvement management practices, support for positive managerial behavior, and union involvement. He closes his book with a synthesis, providing a comprehensive view of the high-involvement organization and discussing change strategies. Lawler (1992) insightfully points out that a successful transition to

Table 7.1 Lawler's (2000) new logic principles

New logic principles	Old logic principles
1. Organization can be the ultimate source of competitive advantage.	1. Organization is a secondary source of competitive advantage.
2. Involvement is the most effective source of control.	2. Bureaucracy is the most effective source of control.
3. All employees must add significant value.	3. Top management and technical experts should add the most value.
4. Lateral processes are the key to organizational effectiveness.	4. Hierarchical processes are the key to organizational effectiveness.
5. Organizations should be designed around products and customers.	5. Organizations should be designed around functions.
6. Effective leadership is the key to organizational effectiveness.	6. Effective managers are the key to organizational effectiveness.

Reprinted from Nicotera & Clinkscales (2003)

a high-involvement organization is a massive change in organizational operation that completely replaces the bureaucratic form. This is, of course, a theme that is repeated throughout his later work (e.g., Lawler, 1999, 2000, 2001). Integrated into such change must be managers, employees, union leaders, board members, and government.

The new plant approach. The *new plant* is a description, based on actual cases, of business units that allow an existing organization to build from the ground up a new organizational unit that begins with the premise of participative management. There are five prescriptions to create the environment necessary for full employee participation: selection of employees, physical layout, job design, reward system and training, and organizational structure.

Selection of employees. Lawler prescribes full disclosure to prospective employees about the nature of the job(s) and of the management style. Employees are thus offered empowerment pre-employment, offering them a chance to decide for themselves whether they want to work in a participative environment, setting up an expectation of involvement, and accomplishing good fit between employee culture and organizational form. Furthermore, "a great deal of the selection process is handled by production employees. They interview and interact with the job applicants and ultimately make the decision as to who will join the organization" (Lawler, 1992, p. 308). Often, applicants are hired long before the actual start-up of the new unit "so that they can be involved in determining personnel policies and establishing various procedures and work methods" (Lawler, 1992, p. 308). Here, we can clearly see a deeply participative process engrained in the organizational authority structure.

Physical layout. Echoing Frederick Taylor's admonition that the job must be physically arranged for optimum employee performance, but with a much different aim, Lawler advocates newly designed physical facilities.

> The new plants are notable for the degree to which they have an egalitarian physical workplace. Employees and managers tend to park in the same parking lots, enter through the same doors and eat in the same cafeterias, and, in some cases, the managers have minimal offices or no offices. The physical layout of many new plants is designed to facilitate teamwork around particular products or services. For example, rather than having assembly lines, the plants often have manufacturing cells that build entire products.
>
> (Lawler, 1992, pp. 308–309)

Job design. Lawler's description of job design likewise emphasizes the egalitarian ideals of HRM.

> Employees perform jobs that are challenging, involving doing a whole piece of work, and allowing them to control how the work is carried out. Typically, this means that relatively self-managing work teams are responsible for the production of a whole product. They are self-managing in the sense that they make decisions about who performs which tasks on a given day; set their own production goals; and are often responsible for quality control, purchasing, and the control of absenteeism and employee behavior. Team members are expected to learn how to do all of the tasks that fall within the work area of the group.
>
> (Lawler, 1992, p. 309)

Reward system and training. As noted, Lawler's (1992) design requires person-based pay structures, increasing pay with individual learning that is relevant to the organization's mission—creating a direct link between individual development and financial compensation.

> Most plants that adopt the new plant approach evaluate the skills of each individual and pay each person based on the number and kind of skills they have. Typically everyone starts at the same salary, and as people learn more, they are paid more. All employees are considered salaried employees and no time clocks are used. Job security also is typically offered to all employees.
>
> (Lawler, 1992, p. 309)

Reward structures are linked to *training*:

> All the new plants place a heavy emphasis on training, career planning, and personal growth. This emphasis is usually backed up with extensive in-plant training programs and strong encouragement for employees to take part in training outside of work. A strong commitment to training and development of the workforce is a cornerstone of the management practices in the new plant approach and is supported by the skill-based pay system.
>
> (Lawler, 1992, p. 310)

Organizational structure. The new plant approach is successful where previous HRM-based participation programs were not because of fundamental shifts in organizational structure.

> One of the striking features of the new plants is their structure. These plants are characterized by very flat hierarchies and extremely wide spans of control. Typically, the traditional foreman's role is eliminated completely and multiple teams report to an area manager. Most plants have only two levels of supervision, although some large plants may have three levels. A flat structure is important because it helps assure that work teams will have the autonomy to manage themselves. ... The new plant approach is also characterized by relatively lean staff groups. Work team members are given responsibility for areas such as quality control, employee selection, inventory management, and production scheduling that typically are done by staff specialists in traditional organizations.
>
> (Lawler, 1992, pp. 309–310)

Moving beyond the new plant approach. Lawler (1992) emphasizes that such plants, although successful, "fall short of what can be done" (p. 313). Specifically, he identifies a *productivity involvement approach* to management that heavily emphasizes "being sure that individuals have control over and information about their piece of the production process" (p. 313). He recommends a significant step beyond this type of involvement to integrate individuals into the business process itself. In so doing, he recommends several organizational features.

He first identifies the required *organizational structure*: "a flat organizational structure and the extensive use of self-managing teams" (p. 314). He goes on to describe a structure in which teams operate as *mini-enterprises*, handling a full scope of business issues. This also requires integration of functions across the organization. It must be noted here that the term *flattened* is dated. The preferred terminology has shifted to *lateral*, so as to fully replace the presumption of verticality as the standard. Linguistically, *flat* connotes a vertical orientation; whereas *lateral* connotes a horizontal orientation.

In Lawler's model, a manufacturing team has responsibility for the entire process with respect to a particular customer. Customers order directly from the team, who deals directly with suppliers. Following delivery, the team deals directly with customers (e.g., via a toll-free telephone number printed on the product) regarding questions or problems with the product produced by the team. In addition, expertise on product development, design, manufacturing, marketing, and sales (for example) mutually inform one another in ways that enhance all of these areas. By linking team members directly to the business process from beginning to end, their productivity and the organization's mission drive one another. (This is precisely the kind of team-based organizing studied by Barker, 1993, who illustrated its potentially oppressive outcomes. See Chapter 3.)

Lawler also discusses *the total team environment* to expand the idea of teams beyond the production level to all parts of the organization.

> Managers, office personnel, and staff support individuals have different jobs than in a traditional plant because they have to deal with teams, but they are not in a team structure. This inconsistency has created some problems and, in some respects, has limited the effectiveness of the new plant approach because staff support groups do not have the same kind of flexibility and performance gains that are characteristic of the production area.
>
> (Lawler, 1992, p. 360)

Inherent in a total team environment is the application of *skill-based reward systems* across the organization as well. Lawler (1992) advocates reward systems based on organizational performance. For employees to achieve a high level of business involvement, they must be accountable for business performance. Such reward systems (gainsharing, profit-sharing, employee ownership, etc.) further deepen and strengthen convergences by integrating individuals with organizational structure and function.

Finally, Lawler (1992) discusses the use of new technologies to improve communication and quality. As information becomes widely available, and individuals across the organization become more interconnected, their integration with organizational performance is, of course, enhanced. Lawler (1992) could not have foreseen the burgeoning of such technologies that has occurred since, and so in this way this particular book is decidedly dated. In later works, this body of knowledge is vastly expanded in such areas as knowledge management (Lawler, 2001), organizational agility (Worley, Williams, & Lawler, 2014), and sustainability (Mohrman, O'Toole & Lawler, 2015). There are also copious works (e.g., Mohrman et al., 1995) detailing the specifics of designing a team-based organization to replace the bureaucratic form.

At the same time that Lawler and his associates were developing a body of prescriptive theory advocating wide-scale organizational restructuring, there was a burgeoning body of organizational communication scholarship examining participation (see Chapter 3). Whereas management theory is prescriptive with an overarching aim to improve organizational performance with a view from the top, organizational communication theory is descriptive and far more diverse both in purpose and vantage point, with recommendations for organizational improvement taking a more holistic view of the organization. It is particularly striking that many of Stohl and Cheney's (2001) paradoxes of participation, reviewed in Chapter 3, can be traced to the fundamental incongruity between the activities required to fulfill the ideals of participation and the constraints of organizational authority structures that subvert those activities—the same fundamental problem identified by Lawler (1992, 2000, 2001). These two theories illustrate the differences between disciplines in their prescriptive and descriptive approaches, but they also show that it took decades of intervening conceptual developments and empirical study to implement the ideals of HRM—which can only be fully accomplished with a total reconfiguration of organizational structure that, as organizational communication research reveals, can create troublesome paradoxes for organizational members (see Chapter 3).

It is also important to take note of the ways that the restructuring movement of the 1990s, and the corresponding trend to create and implement team-based organizational design, fundamentally altered the organizational landscape we study. Vertical hierarchy is central to our traditional understanding of formal organizations, and team-based organizing profoundly changes the nature of authority. As management theory and practice evolve, organizational communication theory and research must contend with these transformations in the objects of our scholarship. At heart, this is an ontological issue (see Chapter 4); team-based organizing and the disruption of vertical authority changes the nature of the phenomena, and our theory and research must develop to keep pace with and account for those changes.

Implications of HRM for Organizational Communication Theory

Prior to our brief review of restructuring in the 1990s, this chapter concluded our tracing of management theory to 1970, which was foundational to the field of organizational communication. Keep in mind, however, that the study of organizational communication, as you will see reflected in the reviews of topical areas in Part III of this book, is multidisciplinary. Organizational communication literature is not confined to the work of any one field. Before beginning our more focused examination of organizational communication literatures in Part III, we must take a moment to assess the implications of HRM theory for our thinking about communication, organization, authority and culture. While classical management's bureaucratic structures and control practices remain in place for many organizations across a multitude of industries, HRM heralded the advent of flattened, more democratic forms. These forms provide the ground for cultural changes highlighting different aspects of communication, authority, and organization.

Approach to Communication

HRM theory examines the intersections of formal and informal communication, with human intelligence and wellbeing as equally primary concerns for the benefit of the organization as a whole. Communication is treated holistically with a far more transactional, constitutive, and less linear approach than that espoused by earlier philosophies. In HRM theory, the treatment of communication is enriched beyond messaging and relationship-forming to a process of meaning-creation. In contrast to HR models, communication is no longer treated as a mere management tool to accomplish worker productivity and cooperation, but as a meaning-creation process to integrate individuals, groups, and processes. The function of communication is informational, relational, constitutive, and productive.

As it is for HR, in HRM the reciprocal relationship between deep enduring structures and daily practices is visible through its revolutionary changes to American corporate life. HRM practices introduced new expectations for all organizational members to be workers who think for themselves and contribute to leadership and the design of organizational plans, practices, and processing. Today's workers expect opportunities for growth and development and expect to contribute their intelligence to organizational process. An entire industry of training and development emerged and has developed into its own set of institutionalized structures and practices. Like human resources, organizational development became, and continues to be, a booming profession with its own professional career path, credentialing processes, and specializations. Organizational practices that did not exist prior to the 1970s are now commonplace, such as visioning, strategic planning, continuous improvement programs, team-based management, and the configuration of business units as independently operating profit centers.

Approach to Organization and Authority

HRM theory treats the organization as a living, learning organism and a brain (Morgan, 1986). The lines dividing the managerial and labor classes become blurred as authority is distributed. The traditional management/labor class system has been replaced by other classification systems—defining professions according to blue-collar and white-collar categories, for example. Still, the vertical hierarchy of Fayol's organizational chart remains presumed, with the focus on organizational functions rather than either persons or positions. Moreover, organizational communication practices remain open and far more egalitarian than ever, especially as communication technology has progressed.

Cultural Implications

The HRM movement democratized work environments. Concerns for worker development, and a corresponding expectation for employees to add value, have become organizational priorities. In large organizations, training and development opportunities abound in addition to the employee benefits for wellbeing and incentives instituted in HR. Employees are increasingly expected to think for themselves and for the organization. Contemporary employees demand a wide range of educational and training opportunities, and organizations who do not provide these opportunities often fail to attract the most qualified employees. Globally, workplace democracy is a vital concern (see Cheney & Cloud, 2006). Alternative organizational forms, such as worker collectives, are advocated by many scholars (e.g., Parker, Cheney, Fournier, & Land, 2014).

The HRM movement also fundamentally altered the typical employment trajectory. The traditional presumption that one would be employed for a lifetime by a single organization has been replaced by a cultural imperative to advance our careers with frequent job changes. This shift is directly traceable to the culture of continual employee development created by HRM ideals. Many large corporations provide expensive employee training and education under the protection of a contractual obligation to remain with the corporation for a specified period following the training, to ensure that the development opportunities provided benefit the organization rather than one of its competitors. At the same time, the culture of large organizations has also shifted to define the individual career advancements of former employees as an organizational accomplishment. In short, the meanings we now hold for career, employee development, meaningful work, and workplace democracy are a direct cultural consequence of HRM.

Recommended Supplementary Readings

Barker, J. R. (1993). Tightening the iron cage: Concertive control in self-managing teams. *Administrative Science Quarterly, 38*(3), 408–437.

This case study was the foundation for concertive control theory. Barker compellingly illustrates the potential for self-imposed oppressive practices in team-based organizing.

Berry, G. (2006). Can computer-mediated, asynchronous communication improve team processes and decision making? *Journal of Business Communication, 43*(4), 344–366.

This article reviews 25 years of business and management literature to draw conclusions about the effect of asynchronous communication technology on teamwork and decision-making.

Cheney, G. (1995). Democracy in the workplace: Theory and practice from the perspective of communication. *Journal of Applied Communication Research, 23*(3), 167–200.

Drawing from a multidisciplinary literature, this essay explores workplace democracy in the contemporary industrialized world, emphasizing issues that are particularly ripe for theoretical and practical contributions from a communication perspective. Cheney's now-classic case study of Mondragon worker cooperatives, in the Basque region of Spain, demonstrates the promise and problems of workplace democracy.

Cheney, G., & Cloud, D. L. (2006). Doing democracy, engaging the material: Employee participation and labor activity in an age of market globalization. *Management Communication Quarterly, 19* (4), 501–540.

The two leading organizational communication scholars of workplace democracy engage each other in a compelling discussion ranging from the metatheoretical to the practical. They examine the status of labor activity in organizational communication scholarship and consider important questions about workplace democracy in practice, with a goal of strengthening the field's engagement in robust democratic practices in a globalizing market economy, by using conceptualizations that venture beyond our comfortable discursive and symbolic constructionism to attend to practical and material concerns.

Coopman, S. J. (2001). Democracy, performance, and outcomes in interdisciplinary health care teams. *Journal of Business Communication, 38*(3), 261–284.

This study of hospice care interdisciplinary teams demonstrates the central importance of perceived involvement in decision-making to the success of team-based organizing, as evidenced by several outcomes (cohesiveness, productiveness, satisfaction with the team, satisfaction with team communication, desire to stay with the team, team involvement and job satisfaction).

Important Concepts: Define and Discuss

Formal organization
Informal organization
Participation
Contingency
Restructuring

Discussion Questions

1. Reflect on organizations of which you have been a part. Imagine you are a consultant who has been hired to align individual and organizational development

and to maximize the potential of employee intelligence. Drawing from the models/theories summarized in this chapter, how would you advise your new client to foster participative and collaborative relationships across hierarchical levels?

2. We have demonstrated that it took several decades for HRM ideals of participation to be implemented with the advent of team-based organizing in the 1990s. How do you see the themes of formal-informal integration and contingency expressed in the new plant approach?

3. What aspects of classical management do you see as most difficult to transcend in order to implement HRM ideals, and why?

4. In general, what aspects of HRM do you recognize in our contemporary organizations?

Practitioners' Corner

As with HR, obvious applications of HRM principles can be seen in today's large organizations. Training and other employee skill development programs, collaborative leadership, team-based structures, and other opportunities for growth and for collaborative decision-making are now commonplace. Yet, as Barker (1993) and Stohl and Cheney (2001) illustrated, the culture of vertical authority is difficult to transcend, even when organizations are designed to eliminate or reduce it. Classical management principles and presumptions run deep in the cultural mindset, manifesting in organizational life. For example, executive-level managers often fail to involve front-line employees in problem-analysis when planning for organizational change to solve problems. Commonly, upon getting feedback from employees about daily problems, well-intentioned executive-level management enter a new software contract for broad organizational processes without consulting the end-users of that software about its implementation or details about their experience of the problems it purports to solve. Organizational members are then faced with implementing a change intended to solve their problems that actually brings new and more difficult problems to their daily functioning. Many front-line employees can tell horror stories about new software implementation that could have been avoided if only someone had consulted them about precisely what was needed before making the decision. In other words, some unanticipated problems with solutions might be anticipated via participation of the right people in the analysis of the original problem.

Communication professionals, either as internal communication officers or as consultants, are well-suited to support managers in understanding how authority structures may impede employee development as they seek to improve employee participation in decision-making, integrate employee development with organizational goals, and implement flexibility into their own leadership skills repertoire. A communication consultant, using a graphic like the C-O dynamic, can aid managers in understanding (a) the degree of collaboration that can be supported by the organizational structure; (b) how the way they communicate matters in the implementation of team-based structures; (c) how to design and implement reward and accountability structures that facilitate goal-achievement in a team-based structure; and (d) how to guide employees to let go of vertical authority presumptions and habits to develop team-based skills. Internal communication officers who construct and disseminate messaging in a team-based environment are likewise benefited by an understanding of the interplay among organizational design structures, expectations for organizational members' responsibilities and performance, and the content of messaging about internal organizational decision-making.

References

Bacharach, S. B., & Aiken, M. (1977). Communication in administrative bureaucracies. *Academy of Management Journal, 20*(3), 365–377. doi:10.2307/255411.

Barker, J. R. (1993). Tightening the iron cage: Concertive control in self-managing teams. *Administrative Science Quarterly, 38*(3), 408–437. doi:10.2307/2393374.

Blake, R., & Mouton, J. (1964). *The managerial grid: The key to leadership excellence*. Houston, TX: Gulf Publishing Co.

Blake, R. R., Shepard, H., & Mouton, J. S. (1964). *Managing intergroup conflict in industry*. Houston, TX: Gulf.

Blanchard, K. H., Zigarmi, P., & Zigarmi, D. (1985). *Leadership and the one minute manager: Increasing effectiveness through Situational Leadership*. New York: Morrow.

Cheney, G., & Cloud, D. L. (2006). Doing democracy, engaging the material: Employee participation and labor activity in an age of market globalization. *Management Communication Quarterly, 19* (4), 501–540. doi:10.1177/0893318905285485.

Fiedler, F. E. (1967). *A theory of leadership effectiveness*. New York: McGraw-Hill.

Fiedler, F. E. (1986). The contribution of cognitive resources and leader behavior to organizational performance. *Journal of Applied Social Psychology, 16*(6), 532–548. doi:10.1111/j.1559-1816.1986.tb01157.x.

Galbraith, J. R., Lawler, E. E., & Associates. (1993). *Organizing for the future: The new logic for managing complex organizations*. San Francisco: Jossey-Bass.

Hersey, P. (1985). *The situational leader*. New York, NY: Warner.

Hersey, P., & Blanchard, K. H. (1969). *Management of organizational behavior: Utilizing human resources*. Upper Saddle River, NJ: Prentice Hall.

Jablin, F. M. (1987). Formal organizational structure. In F. M. Jablin, L. L. Putnam, K. H. Roberts, & L. W. Porter (Eds.), *Handbook of organizational communication: An interdisciplinary perspective* (pp. 389–419). Newbury Park, CA: SAGE.

Lawler, E. E. (1978). The new plant revolution. *Organizational Dynamics, 6*(3), 2–12. doi:10.1016/0090-2616(78)90044-X.

Lawler, E. E. (1991). *High-involvement management: Participative strategies for improving organizational performance*. San Francisco: Jossey-Bass.

Lawler, E. E. (1992). *The ultimate advantage: Creating the high-involvement organization*. San Francisco: Jossey-Bass.

Lawler, E. E. (1999). *Rewarding excellence: Pay strategies for the economy*. San Francisco: Jossey-Bass.

Lawler, E. E. (2000). *From the ground up: Six principles for building the new logic corporation*. San Francisco: Jossey-Bass.

Lawler, E. E. (2001). *Organizing for high-performance: Employee involvement, TQM, reengineering, and knowledge management in the Fortune 1000*. San Francisco: Jossey-Bass.

Lawler, E. E., Mohrman, S.A., & Ledford, G. E. (1998). *Strategies for high-performance organizations—the CEO report: Employee involvement, TQM, and reengineering programs in Fortune 1000 corporations*. San Francisco: Jossey-Bass.

Likert, R. (1961). *New patterns of management*. New York: McGraw-Hill.

Likert, R. (1967). *Human organization: Its management and value*. New York: McGraw-Hill.

Mohrman, S. A., Cohen, S. G., & Mohrman, A. M. (1995). *Designing team-based organizations: New forms for knowledge work*. San Francisco: Jossey Bass.

Mohrman, S. A., Galbraith, J. R., Lawler, E. E., & Associates. (1998). *Tomorrow's organization: Crafting winning capabilities in a dynamic world*. San Francisco: Jossey-Bass.

Mohrman, A. A., O'Toole, J., & Lawler, E. E. (Eds.). (2015). *Corporate stewardship: Achieving sustainable effectiveness*. Sheffield: Greenleaf Publishing.

Morgan, G. (1986). *Images of organization*. Thousand Oaks, CA: SAGE.

Nicotera, A. M., & Clinkscales, M. J. (2003). *Understanding organization through culture and structure: Relational and other lessons from the African-American organization.* Mahwah, NJ: Erlbaum.

Parker, M., Cheney, G., Fournier, V., & Land, C. (Eds.). (2014). *The Routledge companion to alternative organization.* London: Routledge.

Siebold, D. R., & Shea, B. C. (2001). Participation and decision-making. In F. M. Jablin, & L. L. Putnam (Eds.), *The new handbook of organizational communication: Advances in theory, research, and methods.* Thousand Oaks, CA: SAGE.

Stohl, C., & Cheney, G. (2001). Participatory processes/paradoxical practices: Communication and the dilemmas of organizational democracy. *Management Communication Quarterly, 14*(3), 349–407. doi:10.1177/0893318901143001.

Tannenbaum, R., & Schmidt, W. H. (1958). How to choose a leadership pattern. *Harvard Business Review, 36*(5), 95–101.

Worley, C. G., Williams, T. D., & Lawler, E. E. (2014). *The agility factor: Building adaptable organizations for superior performance.* San Francisco: Jossey-Bass.

Part III

Topics in Theory and Research

This section provides comprehensive literature reviews of 14 areas of theory and research, each of which explains the trends over time in the area, major traditions, and contributions of organizational communication scholars. Chapters are authored by established scholars with specialized expertise. While it is not possible to cover every possible topic in the field, literatures that comprise the core knowledge base in the field are provided here. Each chapter applies the general conceptual models provided in Chapter 1 to explore the conceptual approaches of scholars in the area and to illustrate the reciprocally enabling and constraining relationship between organization and communication.

8 Socialization

Patricia M. Sias and Yejin Shin

Organizations are an integral part of society. People join and leave organizations several times during their lifespan. Organizational socialization refers generally to the process by which an individual becomes a knowledgeable organizational member; it is one of the most frequently studied topics in organizational communication. Encompassing a lifelong process of learning about work and occupations, specific jobs and organizations, joining, and then leaving, organizations, the socialization process is part of everyday discourse and a system of meaning about work and work life (Clair, 1996). While theory and research in organizational socialization began in the management and sociology fields, socialization is fundamentally communicative. This chapter provides an overview of socialization research, with a focus on the role of communication throughout the process. We then note how socialization research comports with the conceptualizations of organization and communication that guide this book.

Organizational Socialization Models

First a Management Focus

Although scholarly interest in socialization began decades ago in the field of sociology (e.g., Giddings, 1897), it did not receive substantive attention in management and organizational studies until the 1970s. Van Maanen and Schein (1979) provided a seminal model of the organizational socialization process, conceptualizing it as the process of individuals joining, participating in, and leaving organizations. Specifically, organizational socialization refers to "the process by which an individual acquires the social knowledge and skills necessary to assume an organization role" (Van Maanen & Schein, 1979, p. 211).

Van Maanen and Schein's (1979) model addressed socialization primarily from an organizational or management perspective, delineating the various strategies organizations use to socialize new members. Their model includes six socialization strategies or pairs of strategies depending on the organization (Kramer, 2010). First, employees may be socialized using *formal* (e.g., formal training and orientation) or *informal* processes (e.g., begin tasks immediately with advice and feedback from interpersonal sources such as the supervisor and coworkers). Second, new employees may be socialized as a *group* (e.g., when cohorts are hired at the same time) or as *individuals*. Third, socialization may occur *sequentially* (e.g., a newcomer must master one skill before moving on to the next) or *randomly* (e.g., employees learn in order of what is important to them). Fourth, newcomer socialization can be *serial* (e.g., the new employee is trained by someone experienced in the role) or *disjunctive* (e.g., no experienced employee is specifically assigned to train the newcomer). Fifth, timing in the socialization process may be *fixed* (e.g., newcomers are given a specific amount of time to learn a particular aspect of their new role) or *variable* (e.g., newcomers spend as much time as needed to learn the various aspects of their new role). Finally, organizations may rely on *divestiture* (e.g., attempts to diminish the newcomer's unique individual characteristics, such as military boot camp) or *investiture* (e.g., the organization embraces the new employee's unique characteristics and talents and allows them to develop their new role) to socialize members.

Organizational Communication Enters

As exemplified by Van Maanen and Schein's (1979) model, much scholarship at the time approached socialization from an organizational (i.e., macro) perspective, conceptualizing the organization itself as an actor or agent. In 1984, Frederic Jablin provided a significant development by highlighting the important role of *communication* in individuals' socialization processes. His model brought socialization research squarely into the organizational communication field, and by so doing, brought attention to the micro-level communication practices and processes that characterize organizational socialization.

Shifting to broader terminology, Jablin conceptualized *assimilation* as a reciprocal process in which both individuals and organizational structures have power and influence (Myers & Oetzel, 2003). Specifically, assimilation entails two simultaneous processes: (1) *socialization*, via which organizations socialize newcomers, attempting to instill organizationally desired attitudes, values, and behaviors, and (2) *individualization*, via which employees simultaneously seek to individualize their roles in the organization or try to change the organization to meet their needs as they learn organizational norms and values (Jablin, 2001; Jablin & Krone, 1987). Mignerey, Rubin, and Gorden (1995) similarly argued that assimilation is an active process that requires involvement of organizational attempts to form the newcomer as well as the newcomer's efforts to influence the organization.

As Myers and Gailliard (2016) argue, Jablin is considered the patriarch of socialization research in the field of organizational communication. It is no exaggeration to say that Jablin's (1987) model is one of the most cited in the field. Since its introduction in 1984, Jablin's model has been widely used by scholars to examine the socialization experiences of a variety of organization members such as managers (King, Xia, Campbell Quick, & Sethi, 2005), policemen (Van Maanen, 1975), volunteers (Kramer & Danielson, 2016), students (Sollitto, Johnson, & Myers, 2013), soldiers (Levy & Sasson-Levy, 2008), firefighters (Scott & Myers, 2005), and even family members (Maccoby & Martin, 1983). In the following sections we explain the primary phases of Jablin's model and follow with an overview of research regarding each phase.

Jablin's Assimilation/Socialization Model

Scholars across disciplines have examined organizational socialization and, not surprisingly, have developed different terms for the process. For instance, Kramer (2010) noted that "scholars frequently use the term *socialization* to refer to the overall process of individual becoming organizational members, which Jablin terms *assimilation*" (p. 4, emphasis added). In this section, for ease of reading and to maintain consistency with terms used in most of the literature, we use the term *socialization* to refer to the overall process across the lifespan.

Jablin's model describes the socialization process across four phases: (1) anticipatory socialization, (2) encounter, (3) metamorphosis, and (4) exit/disengagement. Jablin (2001) emphasized that the model's phases should be understood as fluid and over-lapping instead of a set of linear phases as he pointed out, for example, that encounter and metamorphosis phases together can refer to one phase. Kramer and Miller (2014) also argued that despite the descriptions of these four phases appearing distinct from one another, they may not occur in separate, ordered sequences. With this caveat in mind, we address the phases in their most likely chronological order.

Even before entering a new organization, individuals formulate expectations about work and occupations generally, as well as specific jobs and organizations (Jablin, 1982). This comprises the *anticipatory socialization* process—the process of learning about work before an individual begins a specific job. Jablin (2001) divided this phase into *vocational anticipatory socialization (VAS)* and *organizational anticipatory socialization (OAS)*. VAS refers to the process of individuals learning about work careers, and occupations generally. OAS refers to the process of individuals learning about and choosing a specific job and organization to join. Kramer (2010) later used the term *role anticipatory socialization* for VAS, defining it as "the ongoing process of developing expectations for a role an individual wants to have in some organization" (p. 6).

The next phase, *encounter*, comprises individuals' experiences during first few days, weeks, or months of involvement in organizations through training or orientation (Feldman, 1976). Newcomers must learn the essentials of their organizational roles and responsibilities such as how to perform their jobs and maintain relationships with coworkers, as well as learn the organization's cultural norms (Ostroff & Kozlowski, 1992). *Metamorphosis*, the third phase, is the period during which individuals perceive themselves as established organizational members rather than newcomers (Jablin, 1987). This stage can be considered a long-term settling in, during which employees experience the transition to full members of the organization (Myers & Oetzel, 2003). Last, *exit/disengagement* occurs when individuals leave organizations (Jablin, 1987). Because all members eventually leave their organizations, it is an inevitable transition (Kramer, 2010). This phase can be divided into two different types: (1) voluntary exit when individuals initiate the process; or (2) involuntary exit when others initiate the process (Bluedorn, 1978).

Since the 1980s, communication scholars have given a significant amount of attention to the socialization process. Grounded on Jablin's (1984) model, many scholars have focused on the role of communication in each phase. We provide an overview of this research organized by each phase below.

Organizational Socialization Research

Anticipatory Socialization: VAS/OAS

Socialization is a *communicative* process that spans a variety of an individual's experiences from early childhood, education, and initial/full-time employment (Jablin, 2001). Jablin (2001) identified five major information sources that influence one's VAS via communication: family, education, friends, previous organization experience, and mass media. Most studies in this area focus on messages from different sources and how they are interpreted (Powers & Myers, 2017). Although VAS begins in early childhood and continues throughout one's lifetime, much research in this area focuses on children and adolescents. Along these lines, Levine and Hoffner (2006) found that messages from parents, school, and part-time job employment were the most influential to an individual's learning about work requirements such as responsibility, deadlines, and other performance-related behaviors. Parents and friends were also more likely to express negative, rather than positive, aspects of work. More recently, Powers and Myers (2017) found that college students perceive their mothers as the most influential and encouraging VAS source, followed by teachers/professors, friends, and fathers. Scarduzio, Real, Slone, and Henning (2018) examined messages college students remember receiving from their parents about work and that parents remember providing to their children (i.e., memorable messages). Such messages tended to center on importance of competence and hard work, autonomy, or interpersonal relations.

OAS begins when individuals consider specific jobs in specific organizations and take steps to join an organization. Unlike VAS, which is a lifelong process, OAS usually lasts only as long as the job search itself (Kramer, 2010). Much OAS research focuses on the recruitment and selection process including employment interviews and realistic job previews (RJPs) (Jablin, 2001). For example, Miller and Buzzanell (1996) noted that second interviews serve various purposes including finding qualified applicants and providing the organization with an opportunity to enhance their reputation (e.g., a public relations function), as well as providing applicants with information about the position and organization.

Although the employment interview is fundamentally communicative, Jablin, Miller and Sias (1999) noted that relatively little research in this area has examined the interview communication *process*. Those that do usually examine the interview from one of three approaches. Some studies identify patterns of "acts" (e.g., Babbitt & Jablin, 1985). Such studies identify general interaction patterns in employment interviews (e.g., "talk time" by interviewer and applicant, questions and answer patterns, etc.). A second approach examines "patterns of acts and interacts" (Jablin et al., 1999, p. 302) (e.g., Kacmar & Hochwarter, 1995). These studies focus on utterance types and interaction pairs to identify predictive patterns (e.g., how one person's dominance in the early part of an interview predicts overall control of the conversation). A third approach examines how the interviewer and applicant together enact the interview. Specifically, these studies conceptualize the employment interview "as a dynamic social system composed of interdependent beliefs and observable relations between recruiter and applicant that are produced and reproduced through the process of interaction" (Jablin et al., 1999, p. 305). These investigations examine how interactants exert mutual influence and socially construct their relationship, the interview structure, and various other outcomes. Cheepen (1988), for example, revealed how interviewers and applicants together socially constructed their relative status during employment interviews. Here, you can see the C-O dynamic (see Chapter 1), as the interaction constructs the structure of the interview, which then recursively enables and constrains that interaction.

Garnering more attention from scholars, much OAS research has focused on RJPs. Information provided to applicants during OAS tends to be positively skewed, giving applicants an inflated view of the position and organization by leaving out or minimizing drawbacks (Wanous, 1992). Such unrealistic previews lead to surprise and disappointment once an individual begins employment, in turn, leading to dissatisfaction and possibly turnover (Dugoni & Ilgen, 1981). To counter this, scholars argue for the use of RJPs as an alternative to the "seduction" method of recruiting. RJPs are designed to provide job candidates realistic information about the job and organization (Baur, Buckley, Bagdasarov, & Dharmasiri, 2014). Baur et al. (2014) argue that RJPs help organizations decrease turnover and increase both job satisfaction and stronger commitment. In a meta-analysis, Phillips (1998) found that RJPs were related to higher performance, lower recruitment attrition, and lower turnover.

Encounter

Perhaps the most often studied phase in Jablin's model, the *encounter* phase begins when an individual takes on a specific role or position in a specific organization. Research in this area is plentiful, examining a variety of issues and processes including uncertainty, information-seeking, and uncertainty management.

Van Maanen and Schein (1979) argued that newcomers need adequate information to understand their new roles and the organization to function effectively. The organizational encounter experience involves a high level of uncertainty and much research examines newcomers' experiences of uncertainty and strategies used to reduce or manage that uncertainty. This research is typically grounded in Uncertainty Reduction Theory (URT), which posits that when individuals experience uncertainty, they are motivated to seek information to reduce that uncertainty (Berger & Calabrese, 1975). This body of work addresses the types of uncertainty newcomers experience, tactics they use to seek information to reduce that uncertainty, and factors that influence information-seeking tactic use.

Types of uncertainty. Researchers have identified various types of newcomer uncertainty. Ostroff and Kozlowski (1992) identified the following four types of uncertainty: *task* (one's duties, assignments, and priorities), *role* (the boundaries of authority and responsibility, expectations and appropriate behaviors for different positions), *group* (coworker interaction, group norms and values, structure of the organization), and *organization* (the politics, power, mission/vision, leadership style, jargon). Similarly, scholars categorize newcomer uncertainty as (1) *referent uncertainty*, which refers to uncertainty about what one's tasks are and how they should be accomplished; (2) *appraisal uncertainty*, which refers to uncertainty regarding one's ability to do assigned tasks; and (3) *relational uncertainty*, which refers to uncertainty about relationships with other members of the organization and one's role in the group (Miller & Jablin, 1991; Sias & Wyers, 2001; Teboul, 1994).

Kramer (2010) organized uncertainty types into four main categories. *Task-related uncertainty* includes uncertainty about what tasks are expected, the norms regarding such tasks, and how such tasks are evaluated. *Relational uncertainty* involves uncertainty about who is in which workgroup, and how to develop relationships with others. *Organizational uncertainty* includes uncertainty about the organization's history, culture, norms, and rules. Finally, *political or power uncertainty* refers to uncertainty about who is influential in the organization and to whom one should talk in specific situations.

Information sources. Newcomers rely on several sources of information to reduce or manage their uncertainty and make sense of their new surroundings. As Katz (1980) argued, the "new employee reduces uncertainty primarily through interpersonal and feedback processes and interactions" (p. 95). Primary among interpersonal sources are the newcomer's supervisor and coworkers (Morrison, 1993). Teboul (1994) also found newcomers rely on broader messages from the organization and sources external to the organization such as friends, partner, and family members. Miller and Jablin's (1991) extensive list of sources includes information from others (e.g., peers, supervisors, other members, clients/customers) as well as written materials and the task itself.

As noted above, the newcomer's direct supervisor and coworkers are among the most important information sources during the encounter phase. This is due, in large part, to the fact that they possess information relevant to the newcomer's concerns. Specifically, coworkers, especially those who work in the same or similar job, have useful referent/task information. Coworkers and supervisors also have knowledge regarding the relational and cultural milieu of the workplace, and can likely provide useful appraisal information. Access to these important information sources, however, requires the development of functional relationships with coworkers and the supervisor. Indeed, Sias (2005) found strong positive relationships between the quality of information an employee receives (e.g., accurate, relevant, timely, and useful information) and the quality of that employee's relationships with their supervisor and their peer coworkers. Thus, it is important that new employees develop functional quality workplace relationships. (See Chapter 10 for a detailed review of workplace relationship research.)

Information-seeking strategies. In addition to relying on different sources, newcomers use a variety of methods to obtain information. Miller and Jablin (1991) identified seven newcomer information-seeking tactics. First, when newcomers feel comfortable with soliciting information, they use *overt questions* that involve direct interaction with information targets. On the other hand, if newcomers are not fully comfortable with the source, they may prefer *indirect questions*. Newcomers may prefer indirect questions because of their potential for saving face for both parties (Brown & Levinson, 1978). Specifically, the newcomer can mask the information-seeking intent of the message while the source can avoid responding to the request. Employees also use *third parties* to obtain information from a primary source. Newcomers tend to use this when the primary source is not available or when they feel uncomfortable in asking information from the primary source. *Testing limits or creating situations* in which the source must give information is the fourth tactic. In such cases, newcomers monitor sources' responses as an attempt to gain insight into sources' attitudes. This tactic is unique because of its more-or-less specific stimuli and confrontational nature.

Newcomers may also *disguise conversations* by embedding the information request as a natural part of conversation. While putting information sources at ease, newcomers subtly encourage the sources to talk about certain issues. However, this tactic does not guarantee that sources will reveal the information that newcomers seek because of the lack of control over sources' responses. The sixth tactic is *observing* information sources' behaviors. Newcomers use this tactic when they want to unobtrusively gain information. Observing discreetly provides information that may encourage newcomers to adjust their behaviors and attitudes. Last, *surveillance* involves retrospective sensemaking. Surveillance differs from observation in that observation is targeted—employees observe specific people or activities to acquire specific information, while surveillance involves indiscriminant attention to cues in the environment. In addition, surveillance involves integrating novel stimuli with past experiences (Miller & Jablin, 1991). As Weick (1979) pointed out, the accumulation of retrospective justifications can influence how one assigns meaning to present experiences and facilitates the new cognitive maps over time (see Chapter 2).

Factors affecting information-seeking. Various factors influence how newcomers seek information in the encounter phase (Miller & Jablin, 1991). First, seeking information entails *social costs*, such as harm to one's image by creating perceptions that one is incompetent or lacks confidence. Newcomers are fairly conscious of the rewards and costs of the exchange; they are concerned with negative relational consequences or costs associated with observable information-seeking requests and try to minimize damage to their images (Miller & Jablin, 1991). Research indicates that perceived social costs associated with information-seeking are negatively associated with the use of direct questions to obtain the information (Miller & Jablin, 1991; Morrison, 1993). In a longitudinal study, Sias and Wyers (2001) found that social cost perceptions increased over time, leading to a decrease in information-seeking as the employees adjusted to their role and organization. This is consistent with the notion of a "honeymoon" period that newcomers enjoy upon first joining the organization (Jokisaari & Nurmi, 2009). Coworkers understand and tolerate information-seeking from newcomers. But as the honeymoon comes to an end, coworkers expect the new employee to have developed competence and confidence; thus, continued information-seeking can be interpreted as problematic (Sias & Wyers, 2001).

Relatedly, the amount and importance of uncertainty influence information-seeking. As Miller and Jablin (1991) noted, "uncertainty is considered a basic catalyst for newcomers' information-seeking behaviors" (p. 95). In general, the more uncertainty an individual experiences and the more important that uncertainty is to them, the more likely they will engage in information-seeking. This indicates that people may ignore uncertainty rather than seek information to reduce it. Along these lines, Kramer (2004) introduced the Theory of Managing Uncertainty (TMU) as a contrast to the bulk of employee uncertainty studies that were grounded in Uncertainty Reduction Theory.

TMU (see Kramer, 2004) acknowledges that newcomers do not always want to reduce uncertainty or to gain certainty, instead they sometimes prefer to manage it. In contrast to the URT assumption that uncertainty is always negative, TMU contends that uncertainty may sometimes be preferable to certainty, similar to the concept of *strategic ambiguity*, which refers to situations in which organizations may purposefully use ambiguity as a tool to engender desired outcomes by manipulating how and when information is given to employees (Eisenberg, 1984). TMU entails two important points ignored by URT. First, TMU recognized that individuals often manage their uncertainty through internal or cognitive processes without seeking additional information. This is important to note, as TMU recognizes individuals' involvement as active participants. Second, TMU acknowledges competing motives that may reduce the impact of uncertainty on individuals' behaviors. Information-seeking will differ between individuals who are inherently inquisitive or less tolerant of uncertainty and those who are less inquisitive or more tolerant of uncertainty (Kramer, 2014). Therefore, TMU took a step forward in explaining how individuals *actively* participate in the socialization process; newcomers who successfully *manage* their uncertainty are more likely to be satisfied and to stay in the organization. TMU offers a more complex understanding of uncertainty as multilayered, interconnected, and temporal, so the responses used to manage it are likely to vary across contexts (Brashers, 2001).

Another theory used to address employee uncertainty during the encounter phase is Weick's sensemaking theory (1979, 1995). In contrast to the URT's assumption of direct links between uncertainty, information, and uncertainty reduction, sensemaking addresses how individuals retrospectively assign meaning to their experiences. Sensemaking also differs from uncertainty management in that sensemaking typically involves assigning meaning to something that has already occurred while uncertainty management involves proactively seeking information to reduce uncertainty, rather than explain past events. In addition, uncertainty management can be accomplished individually via cognitive processes such as rationalization. Sensemaking, in contrast, is an intersubjective and interactive process. As Weick (1995) noted, (1) sensemaking is not an individual process but an intersubjective process as individuals create "agreed-upon meaning" with others through communication, (2) sensemaking is driven by plausibility rather than accuracy because a group can agree with the meaning incorrectly, and (3) sensemaking creates a certain identity by establishing a commitment to a specific interpretation. Overall, sensemaking focuses on how employees (both newcomers and veterans) communicatively create meaning regarding organizational experiences. (See Chapter 2 for a detailed explanation of sensemaking theory.)

Metamorphosis

The third phase, *metamorphosis*, occurs when a newcomer "attempts to become an accepted, participating member of the organization by learning new attitudes and behaviors or modifying existing ones to be consistent with the organization's expectations" (Jablin, 1984, p. 596). In other words, this is the time when individuals no longer feel like they are newcomers but see themselves as established organizational members. Although uncertainty and information-seeking research tends to focus on newcomers in the encounter phase, Gallagher and Sias (2009) found that established members must adapt to new members and other organizational changes consistently; thus, members experience various types of uncertainty at varying levels throughout their membership. Metamorphosis involves *altering* one's attitudes and behaviors to be consistent with those of the organization, and this process is simultaneously coupled with individualization efforts by the member (Gibson & Papa, 2000). As Gibson and Papa (2000) noted, the metamorphosis phase is akin to actively adopting norms, rules, and behaviors, whereas the encounter phase could still be considered as a "feeling out" stage. Studies regarding metamorphosis phase have dealt with how organizational members experience the organization's particular culture, relationships, and transitions as established members (Kramer, 2010).

Exit

The final phase in Jablin's (2001) model, disengagement or exit, involves members leaving the organization. According to Bluedorn (1978), exit can be divided into two categories. Voluntary exit is when individuals perceive that they initiate the exit process by themselves, whereas involuntary exit is when individuals see that they have little or no choice because someone else forced them to leave. Lee, Mitchell, Wise, and Fireman (1996) suggested four different paths to voluntary exit: planned exit, shock resulting in quitting, shock resulting in a job search before quitting, and gradual disenchantment. On the other hand, the employer's gradual disenchantment with the employee's performance over time can result in involuntary exit through termination. According to Kramer (2010), the exit process is steeped in social exchange evaluations. Individuals deliberate whether the cost–benefit ratio justifies staying at the organization, they attempt to make sense of their leaving and the consequences of that departure for themselves, and stayers attempt to make sense of their coworker's exit, which creates uncertainty about whether they too should leave the organization (Krackhardt & Porter, 1986).

Socialization Outcomes

According to Modaff, Butler, and DeWine (2012), the socialization process is critical to maintaining a dedicated workforce, as "how seriously the organization takes its obligation to socialize new members may determine the degree of turnover, and ultimately, productivity" (p. 170). For instance, Chao, O'Leary-Kelly, Wolf, Klein, and Gardner (1994) noted that successful socialization results in high levels of performance proficiency, knowledge of organizational culture, understanding of organizational rules and language, and positive relationships with others. Saks, Gruman, and Cooper-Thomas (2011) found that proactive information-seeking was positively related to task mastery, role clarity, and intention to stay in the organization. Cooper-Thomas, Paterson, Stadler, and Saks (2014) found that newcomers' proactive behaviors (e.g., feedback-seeking) and outcomes (e.g., feedback) in socialization process are positively related to their levels of work engagement.

Socialization can also influence an individual's identification with organization (see Chapter 11 for more on identity and identification). Identification generally refers to the extent to which an individual shares the values and decision premises of the organization (e.g., Cheney & Tompkins, 1987) or feelings of oneness/shared identity (Mael & Ashforth, 1992). Bullis and Bach (1989), for example, found that identification with the organization tended to increase when employees experienced reduction in relational and appraisal uncertainty, while newcomers who experienced disappointment were less likely identify with the organization. More recently, Schaubroeck, Peng, and Hannah (2013) found that organizational identification increased as new employees developed relationships with their supervisor and coworkers during the encounter phase. Barge and Schlueter (2004) used a discursive approach to study communication during the encounter phase. Their analysis revealed how both socialization and individualization processes are accomplished discursively via memorable messages. Their results also demonstrated the role of informal communication in constructing the individual–organization relationship during entry.

Socialization Contexts

Lester (1987) argued that successful socialization depends on the member's ability to manage uncertainty and perform proper behaviors in an appropriate organizational context. The large majority of socialization research has centered on the more traditional workplace setting (e.g., full-time, permanent employees in an established organization). Increasingly, however, scholars have examined organizational socialization with different types of members and in different types of organizations, adding important insights to the literature.

For instance, Kramer (1993) examined uncertainty and information-seeking tactics of job *transferees*, rather than organizational newcomers. Although job transferees are unique, they in many ways become newcomers again as they adjust to a new position or a new location. Kramer (1993) found that, similar to newcomers, transferees used proactive strategies such as asking feedback from peers and supervisors to reduce uncertainties. However, transferees tended to use more proactive communication behaviors than newcomers. Transferees were also less likely to feel that they needed to prove themselves compared to newcomers. Sias, Kramer, and Jenkins (1997) compared the experiences of *temporary* and permanent employees and found temporary employees were less concerned about their impression, less frequently sought appraisal information, and were less involved in information-giving than newly hired, permanent employees.

In a case of *pilots* experiencing acquisition by another airline, Kramer, Dougherty and Pierce (2004) found that pilots experienced more uncertainty about specific job-related topics than broader organizational issues; they perceived that the acquisition changed their organization, but not their occupation. By focusing on their occupation instead of the company, pilots managed their uncertainty, but job satisfaction and commitment to their job remained constant. As a result, they experienced increases in job security while their attitude toward the acquisition declined.

Myers and McPhee (2006) examined socialization in a high-reliability organization— firefighting. High-reliability organizations (HROs) are those in which reliability is paramount because the consequences of mistakes are high or catastrophic (Jahn, 2016). Such organizations include firefighting, emergency medicine, and the like. Myers and McPhee (2006) found that high-reliability workgroup assimilation also follows a general sequence, including involvement, development of trustworthiness, commitment, and acceptance. The firefighters understood the importance of learning and following the norms of the culture that they believed were in place to protect them from harm.

Sias and Wyers (2001) examined socialization in newly formed organizations, asking the question, "What happens if everyone is a newcomer?" Specifically, they conducted a longitudinal study of several new branches that opened at the same in a retail organization's expansion (i.e., newly formed expansion organizations or NFEOs). They found NFEO employees experienced the same types of uncertainty as newcomers in established organizations (e.g., task requirements), but they also identified a new type of uncertainty—viability uncertainty, or uncertainty about the new organization's ability to survive. They also found that supervisors were the most frequent sources that NFEOs newcomers relied on and newcomers relied on their prior work experience to reduce uncertainty.

Gallagher and Sias (2009) reconceptualized the role of newcomer from someone who experiences uncertainty to someone who *creates* uncertainty for veteran employees. They found that veterans experience several types of uncertainty about new employees including uncertainty about the newcomers' competence, effect on the veteran employee's roles, and the possibility that newcomer may disrupt to the work environment's social milieu. They also found that veteran employees sought information to reduce such uncertainty via methods similar to newcomers (e.g., direct question, indirect questions, observation, etc.).

Critiques

While organizational socialization research is prolific, it is not free from critique. A primary criticism centers on the stages of the model. As Clair (1996, p. 265) argued, "the stage model leads researchers away from understanding work activities and occupational choice as communication practices." She also claimed that stage models can only be applied to mainstream corporations, ignoring occupations such as artists, painters, and the self-employed. In addition, as noted earlier, the four phases of the stage model are not as clear cut as the model suggests (Allen, 1996). For instance, some individuals go back and forth between phases. Furthermore, Feldman (1981) argued that there could be overlap between stages; that although the model suggests four stages occurring in the same way and order, socialization does not always occur that way. Some newcomers have different experiences from others, but this model offers the stage model as a generalized process.

Scholars have also criticized the literature for overlooking individual experiences and diversity in organizations. Bullis and Bach (1989) and Bullis (1993) argued that socialization theory and models tended to overemphasize the influence of the organization over the individual. In addition, Kramer and Miller (1999, p. 362) noted, "A particularly sensitive issue concerns stage models' inattention to women's voices or other specific groups." In this regard, some newcomers feel like they are "outsiders within" who never become established members of the organization (Bullis & Stout, 2000). Along these lines, Bullis and Stout (2000) argued that Jablin's model does not represent everyone's experiences. Allen (2004) similarly noted that the model does not address the unique experiences of individuals of different races, socio-economic status, religions, sexual identities, abilities, and ages. For example, Allen (1996) demonstrated how her socialization as a woman of color in academia differed from those of other men or women. Socialization research has given little attention to such situations.

Approach to Communication and Organizations

Organizational socialization research has focused largely on the member's experience throughout the socialization process. In general, scholars conceptualize the experience as one of uncertainty and information acquisition. Toward this end, the vast majority of research in this area is grounded in a *transmission model of communication*. The encounter phase has arguably received the most research attention with most studies grounded in uncertainty reduction theory (Berger & Calabrese, 1975). Specifically, newcomers seek and receive information that reduces their uncertainty; that is, information is transmitted from others to the newcomer.

Unlike other areas (e.g., workplace relationship research—see Chapter 10), the interpretive turn (Putnam & Pacanowsky, 1983; see Chapter 2) did not lead to a substantial paradigm shift in conceptualizing the role of communication and socialization. While Jablin's (1984) model highlighted the role of communication in organizational socialization, it and subsequent versions (e.g., Jablin, 1987, 2001) were still largely grounded in a transmission model (see Chapter 1), treating the organization as a neutral entity rather than as constituted by the communication of members and others.

Some studies, however, do reflect a constitutive approach to communication, examining how interaction constructs or constitutes organization. OAS studies of employment interviews from an enactment perspective, for example, do not examine the transmission of messages between applicant and interviewer. Rather they examine how the interactants together communicatively create interviews patterns and structures (i.e., the *organization*—organized structure, or O_2—of the interview). Shaw (1983), for example, examined how applicant and interviewer "taken-for-granted assumptions" about employment interviews emerged through and structured the interview process. Although the authors of these studies did not use the term "constitutive," their studies exemplify how communication constitutes the employment interview. Barge and Schlueter (2004) examined how informal communication constitutes the individual–organization relationship during the organizational encounter phase. While not explicitly grounded in CCO theory, their study's fundamental assumptions about communication represent a constitutive conceptualization by demonstrating how informal interaction constituted the organization and the newcomer's relationship to the organization. The C-O dynamic presented in Chapter 1 refers to how communication constitutes organizations and the organization, in turn, constitutes communication. Here, you can clearly see this cyclic relationship between day-to-day communication practices and structured organizational patterns that then enable and constrain communication practices. Overall, however, organizational socialization has been and continues to be largely grounded in a transmission approach to communication.

Organizational socialization research centers on links between individuals and the organizations they join and exit. This body of work tends to emphasize an O_2 approach to organization. O_2 refers to "the state of a social collective's coordination/order (Chapter 1, p. XX). For example, socialization research examines how individuals learn about/become part of the organization (i.e., social collective's order) via communication (e.g., information-seeking). Early work that approached socialization from a management or macro perspective by focusing on the strategies *organizations* use to socialize members represents an O_3 approach in which the organization is conceptualized as an entitative being or actor that acts upon its members (e.g., Van Maanen & Schein, 1979). The introduction of Jablin's model and subsequent focus on the communicative nature of socialization moved research toward an O_1 approach via research that "examines interaction processes by which members arrange themselves and manage their joint activities" (Chapter 1, p. 7). Such studies, for example, identified how new members become knowledgeable veterans via interaction with others such as their supervisor and coworkers (Miller & Jablin, 1991).

With respect to the three expressions of organization presented in Chapter 1, both O_1 and O_2 socialization research tends to emphasize structure over agency; that is, individuals learn about organizational structures and norms, rather than changing or reconstituting them. This is consistent with critiques that socialization research tends to emphasize the organization over the individual (Bullis, 1993). The relatively few studies grounded in a constitutive conceptualization of communication (e.g., Barge & Schlueter, 2004) address how newcomers' roles and relationship to the organization are socially constructed through discourse. Such work exemplifies a greater emphasis on mutual constitution—the individual's relationship to the organization is not static nor imposed on the individual; rather it is socially constructed (and mutually constituted) via interaction, so the C-O dynamic is explicitly examined in this body of work.

While the C-O dynamic and the three expressions of organization can clearly be seen in organizational socialization processes, the dearth of socialization research that directly addresses these phenomena highlights an opportunity for communication scholars to make substantive contributions to the organizational socialization literature. As noted above, for example, workplace relationships are crucial for newcomer socialization. In fact, newcomers socially construct their relationships as they seek information and communicate with coworkers and their supervisors during the encounter phase and beyond. Much research demonstrates the socially constructed nature of workplace relationships (e.g., Sias & Cahill, 1998). Research examining how such relationships, in turn, constitute the organization would provide important insights regarding how newcomers influence the organization. Moreover, understanding how pre-existing organizational structures both enable and constrain workplace relationship development, and, therefore, influence workplace relationship development could generate useful insights into functional and dysfunctional relationship dynamics.

Cultural Implications

Socialization research has given much attention to organizational culture. Becoming an established member of the organization requires learning the organizational culture as a successful socialization process. According to Van Maanen and Schein (1979), socialization "involves the transmission of information and values, it is fundamentally a *cultural* matter" (p. 210, emphasis added). Different organizations possess different cultures as members share substantially distinctive orientations to one another, their roles and missions of the organization (Louis, 1980). Along these lines, Alvesson (2002, p. 1) argues "the cultural dimension is central in all aspects of organizational life; how people in a company think, feel, value, and act are guided by ideas, meanings and beliefs of a cultural (socially shared) nature."

As noted earlier, however, socialization research has paid less attention to cultural diversity and intercultural communication. Instead, the body of research largely represents, at least implicitly, a white, Western perspective and experience, and gives little attention to cultural differences, diversity, and international culture in the organizational socialization process.

Conclusion

The organizational socialization process occurs repeatedly over a person's lifetime. Given its ubiquity in our lives, it is not surprising that socialization is one of the most frequently studied topics in organizational communication research. This overview highlighted how the field developed over time from a management focus on how organizations socialize members, to a communication focus on how socialization occurs communicatively. While we have learned much about socialization processes and practices, its complexities as people navigate increasingly global, diverse, and technologically complex organizational terrains remain much of a mystery. Examining how communication does not just play a role in socialization, but constitutes the process and the organization itself would provide important insights into this important and ubiquitous aspect of human existence.

Recommended Supplementary Readings

Allen, B. J. (1996). Feminist standpoint theory: A black woman's (re)view of organizational socialization. *Communication Studies*, 47(4), 257–271.
A feminist critique of organizational socialization research emphasizing the experience of a black, female academic as an "outsider within" a predominantly white organization.
Kramer, M. W., & Miller, V. D. (1999). A response to criticism of organizational socialization research: In support of contemporary conceptualizations of organizational assimilation. *Communication Monographs*, 66(4), 358–367.
Bullis, C. (1999). Mad or bad: A response to Kramer and Miller. *Communication Monographs*, 66 (4), 368–373.

Clair, R. P. (1999). Ways of seeing: A review of Kramer and Miller's manuscript. *Communication Monographs*, 66(4), 374–381.

Turner, P. K. (1999). What if you don't? A response to Kramer and Miller. *Communication Monographs*, 66(4), 382–389.

Miller, V. D., & Kramer, M. W. (1999). A reply to Bullis, Turner, and Clair. *Communication Monographs*, 66(4), 390–392.

The above five articles appeared the 1999 Volume 66, Issue 4, of Communication Monographs. The authors engage in a spirited debate about the state of organizational socialization research at the time. Together, they provide many useful insights into the primary conceptualizations and critiques of socialization theory and research.

Wanberg, C. (Ed.). (2012). *The Oxford handbook of organizational socialization.* New York: Oxford University Press.

A relatively recent broad overview of organizational socialization, from a management/organizational behavior perspective.

Important Concepts: Define and Discuss

Anticipatory socialization (VAS and OAS)
Uncertainty Reduction Theory (URT)
Theory of Managing Uncertainty (TMU)
Information-seeking tactics
Social costs
Organizational encounter
Metamorphosis
Exit/disengagement
Realistic job previews

Discussion Questions

1. Think about the last organization you joined (e.g., as an employee, student). How did you feel when you first became a member? What types of uncertainty did you experience and how did you deal with (e.g., information-seeking, uncertainty management, etc.)?
2. Who influenced your decision to pursue your current career choice? How did they influence you? What messages do you recall as particularly important?
3. Describe the process you used in your most recent job search. How did you learn about the position and company? To what extent did you rely on interpersonal communication and mediated communication (e.g., websites, online search companies, etc.).

Practitioners' Corner

Employee turnover is a fact of life in organizations—veteran members leave and newcomers take their places. Consequently, practitioners devote much time to recruiting, hiring, and socializing new members. The large body of research on organizational socialization provides many useful insights for practitioners.

First, practitioners should ensure their recruitment and interview practices provide applicants with realistic and accurate portrayals of the job and the organization. This means conveying the negative aspects (e.g., long hours, little opportunity for advancement) along with the positive. Such information can be communicated in recruitment materials such as job announcements and during interviews. Providing realistic job previews can minimize newcomer shock, surprise, disappointment, and potentially turnover.

Once a newcomer begins their new position, understand that they are likely experiencing a great deal of uncertainty—uncertainty about their new tasks, their ability to do those tasks, their role in the organization's social network, and the organizational culture. Understand also that they may be hesitant to ask questions for fear of making a bad impression. Rather than waiting for newcomers to come to you with questions, be sure to provide unsolicited information you think they may need. Also be sure to check in with them regularly to ask if they have any questions or need any information.

Practitioners are also encouraged to recognize the importance of functional workplace relationships during the socialization process and create an environment that encourages and supports the formation of quality coworker and supervisory relationships. One way to do this is provide opportunities for newcomers to communicate with others whenever possible (e.g., through collaborating on tasks, departmental lunches, etc.). See Chapter 10 for more regarding workplace relationships.

Finally, it is important to remember that uncertainty is not limited to newcomers. All employees throughout their time in an organization experience uncertainty about a variety of issues. We encourage practitioners to check in frequently with all employees to ensure they are adequately informed about departmental and organizational issues and concerns.

References

Allen, B. J. (1996). Feminist standpoint theory: A black woman's (re)view of organizational socialization. *Communication Studies*, 47(4), 257–271. doi:10.1080/10510979609368482.

Allen, B. J. (2004). *Difference matters*. Long Grove, IL: Waveland Press.

Alvesson, M. (2002). *Understanding organizational culture*. London: SAGE.

Babbitt, L. V., & Jablin, F. M. (1985). Characteristics of applicants' questions and employment screening interview outcomes. *Human Communication Research*, 11(4), 507–535. doi:10.1111/j.1468-2958.1985.tb00058.x.

Barge, J. K., & Schlueter, D. W. (2004). Memorable messages and newcomer socialization. *Western Journal of Communication*, 68(3), 233–256. doi:10.1080/10570310409374800.

Baur, J. E., Buckley, M. R., Bagdasarov, Z., & Dharmasiri, A. S. (2014). A historical approach to realistic job previews: An exploration into their origins, evolution, and recommendations for the future. *Journal of Management History*, 20(2), 200–223. doi:10.1108/JMH-06-2012-0046.

Berger, C. R., & Calabrese, R. J. (1975). Some explorations in initial interaction and beyond: Toward a developmental theory of interpersonal communication. *Human Communication Research*, 1(2), 99–112. doi:10.1111/j.1468-2958.1975.tb00258.x.

Bluedorn, A. C. (1978). A taxonomy of turnover. *The Academy of Management Review*, 3(3), 647–651. doi:10.5465/AMR.1978.4305918.

Brashers, D. E. (2001). Communication and uncertainty management. *Journal of Communication*, 51(3), 477–497. doi:10.1093/joc/51.3.477.

Brown, P., & Levinson, S. C. (1978). Universals in language usage: Politeness phenomena. In E. N. Goody (Ed.), *Questions and politeness: Strategies in social interaction* (pp. 56–311). Cambridge and New York: Cambridge University Press.

Bullis, C. (1993). Organizational socialization research: Enabling, constraining, and shifting perspectives. *Communication Monographs*, 60(1), 10–17. doi:10.1080/03637759309376289.

Bullis, C., & Bach, B. W. (1989). Are mentor relationships helping organizations? An exploration of developing mentee-mentor-organizational identifications using turning point analysis. *Communication Quarterly, 37*(3), 199–213. doi:10.1080/01463378909385540.

Bullis, C., & Stout, K. R. (2000). Organizational socialization: A feminist standpoint approach. In P. M. Buzzanell (Ed.), *Rethinking organizational & managerial communication from feminist perspectives* (pp. 47–75). Thousand Oaks, CA: SAGE.

Chao, G. T., O'Leary-Kelly, A. M., Wolf, S., Klein, H. J., & Gardner, P. D. (1994). Organizational socialization: Its content and consequences. *Journal of Applied Psychology, 79*(5), 730–743. doi:10.1037/0021-9010.79.5.730.

Cheepen, C. (1988). *The predictability of informal conversation.* London: Pinter.

Cheney, G., & Tompkins, P. K. (1987). Coming to terms with organizational identification and commitment. *Central States Speech Journal, 38*(1), 1–15. doi:10.1080/10510978709368225.

Clair, R. (1996). The political nature of the colloquialism, "a real job": Implications for organization socialization. *Communication Monographs, 63*(3), 249–267. doi:10.1080/03637759609376392.

Cooper-Thomas, H. D., Paterson, N. L., Stadler, M. J., & Saks, A. M. (2014). The relative importance of proactive behaviors and outcomes for predicting newcomer learning, well-being, and work engagement. *Journal of Vocational Behavior, 84*(3), 318–331. doi:10.1016/j.jvb.2014.02.007.

Dugoni, B. L., & Ilgen, D. R. (1981). Realistic job previews and the adjustment of new employees. *Academy of Management Journal, 24*(3), 579–591. doi:10.5465/255576.

Eisenberg, E. M. (1984). Ambiguity as strategy in organizational communication. *Communication Monographs, 51*(3), 227–242. doi:10.1080/03637758409390197.

Gallagher, E. B., & Sias, P. M. (2009). The new employee as a source of uncertainty: Veteran employee information seeking about new hires. *Western Journal of Communication, 73*(1), 23–46. doi:10.1080/10570310802636326.

Gibson, M. K., & Papa, M. J. (2000). The mud, the blood, and the beer guys: Organizational osmosis in blue-collar work groups. *Journal of Applied Communication Research, 28*(1), 68–88. doi:10.1080/00909880009365554.

Giddings, F. H. (1897). *The theory of socialization.* Oxford: Macmillan.

Feldman, D. C. (1976). A contingency theory of socialization. *Administrative Science Quarterly, 21* (3), 433–452. doi:10.2307/2391853.

Feldman, D. C. (1981). The multiple socialization of organization members. *The Academy of Management Review, 6*(2), 309–318. doi:10.5465/AMR.1981.4287859.

Jablin, F. M. (1982). Organizational communication: An assimilation approach. In M. Roloff & C. Berger (Eds.), *Social cognition and communication* (pp. 255–286). Newbury Park, CA: SAGE.

Jablin, F. M. (1984). Assimilating new members into organizations. *Annals of the International Communication Association, 8*(1), 594–627. doi:10.1080/23808985.1984.11678591.

Jablin, F. M. (1987). Organizational entry, assimilation, and exit. In F. M. Jablin, L. L. Putnam, K. H. Roberts, & L. W. Porter (Eds.), *Handbook of organizational communication: An interdisciplinary perspective* (pp. 679–740). Thousand Oaks, CA: SAGE.

Jablin, F. M. (2001). Organizational entry, assimilation, and disengagement/exit. In F. M. Jablin & L. L. Putnam (Eds.), *The new handbook of organizational communication: Advances in theory, research, and methods* (pp. 732–818). Thousand Oaks, CA: SAGE.

Jablin, F. M., & Krone, K. J. (1987). Organizational assimilation. In C. Berger & S. Chaffee (Eds.), *Handbook of communication science* (pp. 711–746). Newbury Park, CA: SAGE.

Jablin, F. M., Miller, V. D., & Sias, P. M. (1999). Communication and interaction processes. In R. W. Eder & M. M. Harris (Eds.), *The employment interview handbook* (pp. 297–320). Thousand Oaks, CA: SAGE.

Jahn, J. L. S. (2016). Adapting safety rules in a high reliability context: How wildland firefighting workgroups ventriloquize safety rules to understand hazards. *Management Communication Quarterly, 30*(3), 362–389. doi:10.1177/0893318915623638.

Jokisaari, M., & Nurmi, J. E. (2009). Change in newcomers' supervisor support and socialization outcomes after organizational entry. *Academy of Management Journal*, 52(3), 527–544. doi:10.5465/AMJ.2009.41330971.

Kacmar, K. M., & Hochwarter, W. A. (1995). The interview as a communication event: A field examination of demographic effects on interview outcomes. *Journal of Business Communication*, 32(3), 207–232. doi:10.1177/002194369503200301.

Katz, R. (1980). *Time and work: Toward an integrative perspective*. In B. M. Staw & L. Cummings (Eds.), *Research in organizational behavior* (Vol.2, pp. 81–121). Greenwich, CT: JAI Press Inc.

King, R. C., Xia, W., Campbell Quick, J., & Sethi, V. (2005). Socialization and organizational outcomes of information technology professionals. *Career Development International*, 10(1), 26–51. doi:10.1108/13620430510577619.

Krackhardt, D., & Porter, L. W. (1986). The snowball effect: Turnover embedded in communication networks. *Journal of Applied Psychology*, 71(1), 50–55. doi:10.1037/0021-9010.71.1.50.

Kramer, M. W. (1993). Communication and uncertainty reduction during job transfers: Leaving and joining processes. *Communication Monographs*, 60(2), 178–198. doi:10.1080/03637759309376307.

Kramer, M. W. (2004). *Managing uncertainty in organizational communication*. Mahwah, NJ: Lawrence Erlbaum.

Kramer, M. W. (2010). *Organizational socialization: Joining and leaving organizations*. Malden, MA: Polity Press.

Kramer, M. W. (2014). *Managing uncertainty in organizational communication*. New York, NY: Taylor & Francis.

Kramer, M. W., & Danielson, M. A. (2016). Developing and re-developing volunteer roles: The case of ongoing assimilation of docent zoo volunteers. *Management Communication Quarterly*, 30(1), 103–120. doi:10.1177/0893318915612551.

Kramer, M. W., Dougherty, D. S., & Pierce, T. A. (2004). Managing uncertainty during a corporate acquisition: A longitudinal study of communication during an airline acquisition. *Human Communication Research*, 30(1), 71–101. doi:10.1093/hcr/30.1.71.

Kramer, M. W., & Miller, V. D. (1999). A response to criticisms of organizational socialization research: In support of contemporary conceptualizations of organizational assimilation. *Communication Monographs*, 66(4), 358–367. doi:10.1080/03637759909376485.

Kramer, M. W., & Miller, V. D. (2014). Socialization and assimilation: Theories, processes, and outcomes. In L. L. Putnam & D. K. Mumby (Eds.), *The SAGE handbook of organizational communication: Advances in theory, research, and methods* (3rd ed., pp. 525–547). Thousand Oaks, CA: SAGE.

Lee, T. W., Mitchell, T. R., Wise, L., & Fireman, S. (1996). An unfolding model of voluntary employee turnover. *The Academy of Management Journal*, 39(1), 5–36. doi:10.2307/256629.

Lester, R. E. (1987). Organizational culture, uncertainty reduction and the socialization of new organizational members. In S. Thomas (Ed.), *Culture and communication* (pp. 105–113). Norwood, NJ: Ablex.

Levine, K. J., & Hoffner, C. A. (2006). Adolescents' conceptions of work. *Journal of Adolescent Research*, 21(6), 647–669. doi:10.1177/0743558406293963.

Levy, G., & Sasson-Levy, O. (2008). Militarized socialization, military service, and class reproduction: The experiences of Israeli soldiers. *Sociological Perspectives*, 51(2), 349–374. doi:10.1525/sop.2008.51.2.349.

Louis, M. R. (1980). Surprise and sense making: What newcomers experience in entering unfamiliar organizational settings. *Administrative Science Quarterly*, 25(2), 226–251. doi:10.2307/2392453.

Maccoby, E. E., & Martin, J. A. (1983). Socialization in the context of the family: Parent–child interaction. In E. M. Hetherington (Ed.), *Handbook of child psychology: Socialization, personality, and social development* (Vol.4, pp. 1–101). New York: Wiley.

Modaff, D. P., Butler, J., & DeWine, S. (2012). *Organizational communication: Foundations, challenges, and misunderstandings* (3rd ed.). Boston, MA: Allyn & Bacon.

Morrison, E. W. (1993). Longitudinal study of the effects of information seeking on newcomer socialization. *Journal of Applied Psychology, 78*(2), 173–183. doi:10.1037/0021-9010.78.2.173.

Mael, F., & Ashforth, B. E. (1992). Alumni and their alma mater: A partial test of the reformulated model of organizational identification. *Journal of Organizational Behavior, 13*(2), 103–123. doi:10.1002/job.4030130202.

Mignerey, J. T., Rubin, R. B., & Gorden, W. I. (1995). Organizational entry: An investigation of newcomer communication behavior and uncertainty. *Communication Research, 22*(1), 54–85. doi:10.1177/009365095022001003.

Miller, V. D., & Buzzanell, P. M. (1996). Toward a research agenda for the second employment interview. *Journal of Applied Communication Research, 24*(3), 165–180. doi:10.1080/00909889609365449.

Miller, V. D., & Jablin, F. M. (1991). Information seeking during organizational entry: Influences, tactics, and a model of the process. *Academy of Management Review, 16*(1), 92–120. doi:10.5465/AMR.1991.4278997.

Myers, K. K., & Gailliard, B. M. (2016). Organizational entry, socialization, and assimilation in health care organizations. In T. R. Harrison & E. A. Williams (Eds.), *Organizations, health, and organizations* (pp. 31–48). Mahwah, NJ: Routledge.

Myers, K. K., & McPhee, R. D. (2006). Influences on member assimilation in workgroups in high-reliability organizations: A multilevel analysis. *Human Communication Research, 32*(4), 440–468. doi:10.1111/j.1468-2958.2006.00283.x.

Myers, K. K., & Oetzel, J. G. (2003). Exploring the dimensions of organizational assimilation: Creating and validating a measure. *Communication Quarterly, 51*(4), 438–457. doi:10.1080/01463370309370166.

Ostroff, C., & Kozlowski, S. W. J. (1992). Organizational socialization as a learning process: The role of information acquisition. *Personnel Psychology, 45*(4), 849–874. doi:10.1111/j.1744-6570.1992.tb00971.x.

Phillips, J. M. (1998). Effects of realistic job previews on multiple organizational outcomes: A meta-analysis. *The Academy of Management Journal, 41*(6), 673–690. doi:10.2307/256964.

Powers, S. R., & Myers, K. K. (2017). Vocational anticipatory socialization: College students' reports of encouraging/discouraging sources and messages. *Journal of Career Development, 44* (5), 409–424. doi:10.1177/0894845316660627.

Putnam, L. L., & Pacanowsky, M. E. (Eds.). (1983). *Communication and organizations: An interpretive approach*. Beverley Hills, CA: SAGE.

Saks, A. M., Gruman, J. A., & Cooper-Thomas, H. (2011). The neglected role of proactive behavior and outcomes in newcomer socialization. *Journal of Vocational Behavior, 79*(1), 36–46. doi:10.1016/j.jvb.2010.12.007.

Scarduzio, J. A., Real, K., Slone, A., & Henning, Z. (2018). Vocational anticipatory socialization, self-determination theory, and meaningful work: Parents' and children's recollection of memorable messages about work. *Management Communication Quarterly, 32*(3). doi:10.1177/0893318918768711.

Schaubroeck, J. M., Peng, A. C., & Hannah, S. T. (2013). Developing trust with peers and leaders: Impacts on organizational identification and performance during entry. *Academy of Management Journal, 56*(4), 1148–1168. doi:10.5465/amj.2011.0358.

Scott, C., & Myers, K. K. (2005). The socialization of emotion: Learning emotion management at the fire station. *Journal of Applied Communication Research, 33*(1), 67–92. doi:10.1080/0090988042000318521.

Shaw, M. R. (1983). Taken-for-granted assumptions of applicants in simulated selection interviews. *Western Journal of Speech Communication, 47*(2), 138–156. doi:10.1080/10570318309374112.

Sias, P. M. (2005). Workplace relationship quality and employee information experiences. *Communication Studies*, 56(4), 375–395. doi:10.1080/10510970500319450.

Sias, P. M., & Cahill, D. J. (1998). From coworkers to friends: The development of peer friendships in the workplace. *Western Journal of Communication*, 62(3), 273–299. doi:10.1080/10570319809374611.

Sias, P. M., Kramer, M.W., & Jenkins, E. (1997). A comparison of the communication behaviors of temporary employees and new hires. *Communication Research*, 24(6), 731–754. doi:10.1177/0093650297024006006.

Sias, P. M., & Wyers, T. D. (2001). Employee uncertainty and information-seeking in newly formed expansion organizations. *Management Communication Quarterly*, 14(4), 549–573. doi:10.1177/0893318901144001.

Sollitto, M., Johnson, Z. D., & Myers, S. A. (2013). Students' perceptions of college classroom connectedness, assimilation, and peer relationships. *Communication Education*, 62(3), 318–331. doi:10.1080/03634523.2013.788726.

Teboul, J. B. (1994). Facing and coping with uncertainty during organizational encounter *Management Communication Quarterly*, 8(2), 190–224. doi:10.1177/0893318994008002003.

Van Maanen, J. (1975). Police socialization: A longitudinal examination of job attitudes in an urban police department. *Administrative Science Quarterly*, 20(2), 207–228. doi:10.2307/2391695.

Van Maanen, J., & Schein, E. G. (1979). Toward a theory of organizational socialization. In B. M. Staw (Ed.), *Research in organizational behavior* (pp. 209–264). Greenwich, CT: JAI Press.

Wanous, J. P. (1992). *Organizational entry: Recruitment, selection, orientation, and socialization of newcomers*. Upper Saddle River, NJ: Prentice Hall.

Weick, K. E. (1979). *The social psychology of organizing* (2nd ed.). Reading, MA: Addison-Wesley.

Weick, K. E. (1995). *Sensemaking in organizations*. Thousand Oaks, CA: SAGE.

9 Communication Networks

Lisa V. Chewning

Introduction

Throughout the text, we have focused on organizing as *the coordination of human activities for the purposes of achieving the accomplishment of tasks*. Such organizing is the foundation of network theory. Networks are the patterns of connection, called *ties*, among a set of actors (e.g., people, organizations), which are referred to as *nodes*. Put simply, networks are how we organize, and have implications for important social and organizational outcomes such as power, influence, access to resources, and collaboration. They can be defined in terms of the *ego*, or individual network of an actor, or as a *whole* network, which refers to all of the connections within a specific set of parameters, such as a neighborhood, organization, or supply chain. Networks can range from the individual level all the way to the societal level, as Castells (2000) claims that we have moved to a network society, which he defined as an "organizational arrangement of humans in relationships of production/consumption, experience, and power, as expressed in meaningful interaction framed by culture" (p. 5).

While traditional network theory positioned networks as collectives based on *connection* or *interaction*, it is through *communication* that connection is enacted and given meaning. That is, while interaction implies that something is being exchanged, a communication perspective moves beyond the idea of simple contact or unspecified exchange and encompasses the creation of shared meaning. As we emphasize throughout this text, a constitutive point of view posits that communication is about the creation of shared meaning. Thus, engaging in a network involves creating a series of connections with others through which shared meaning is negotiated and renegotiated though each instance of communicative action. Indeed, even as Castells (2000) talks about meaningful *interaction* framed by culture, because culture is socially and communicatively constructed, the basis of a network society is arguably communication.

There is a rich history of studying connections both within, and among, organizations as networks. According to Nohria (1998, p. 290), "all organizations are, in important respects, social networks." Returning to the idea of networks being embedded, organizations *are* networks consisting of multiple subgroups, which can also be considered networks. Additionally, organizations are part of multiple networks, including, but not limited to, industries, the communities in which they operate, supply chains, and trade organizations. Organizations can also be connected through the individual ties of organizational members, such as when members of a board of directors sit on the boards of other organizations, creating *interlocks*. Each level of connection, and the communication that flows through those connections, has implications for the individual organizational member, the organization as a whole, and often, the macro system within which the organization exists. Thus, networks represent the intersection of communication, social organization, and the organization.

Defining Networks

Network theory has its own vocabulary, so in order to understand how networks impact organizations, it is important to understand how to define and measure networks. As defined earlier, networks are the patterns of connection among a set of actors (e.g., people, organizations). Networks are not based on one-time communication, but rather on repeated communication between members of a specific population. Network communication evolves as a natural progression shaped by both internal and environmental forces. Accordingly, network development is typically fluid, changing as the needs and circumstances of participants change. While the nature and frequency of the communication can vary within and among networks, network formation is rooted in the idea that (a) participants already have an idea of what to expect and how the other partner works, (b) trust has already been established (or is anticipated if this is the initial interaction) so each party does not have to look out for opportunism, and (c) participants are more willing to accommodate special requests/circumstances because of intended future interactions (Powell, 1990).

Networks can be studied through the lens of *social network theory*, which refers to "the mechanisms and processes that interact within network structures to yield certain outcomes for individuals and groups" (Borgatti & Halgin, 2011, p. 1), by *using social network analysis*, which is the study of the nature of the shared social relations within a network using graph theory, or by studying the communication that takes place within a given network. Networks emerge organically though our social interaction and do not have natural boundaries (Borgatti & Halgin, 2011), so what constitutes a given network in social network analysis depends on the question being asked. In order to study a network, a researcher must identify what question they want to answer, and then choose a set of actors (e.g., population) and type of connection to study (Borgatti & Halgin, 2011). For example, if one wanted to learn about the advice network in organization, they could survey all organizational members about whom they turn to within the organization for advice, and then map the advice network. This network could then be studied in a variety of ways, including how it compares to the formal organizational chart or which members are most central in the network.

Networks can be studied from the ego, or individual, point of view or from a whole-network point of view. An ego network consists of all of the recurring contacts that an individual actor has. One actor's ego network often spans multiple other networks. For example, one person's network often includes family, friends, coworkers, members of their neighborhood, members of organizational affiliations (e.g., religious institutions, gyms, clubs, etc.). A whole network considers all of the contacts within a particular boundary, such as an organization. Within one organization there are often several smaller networks, or structural subgroups, that work together to keep the organization functioning. The composition and interaction of these subgroups are what create the overall organizational network.

Nodes and ties form the basis of the network. As mentioned earlier in the chapter, *nodes* are the actors in the network, and often represent individuals or organizations. However, some studies even consider hyperlinks and words as nodes, and examine how the co-occurrence of words in a body of text impact messages, or how hyperlinks among websites can create representational networks on the organizational level as organizations indicate affiliation with other organizations. *Ties* are the connections, or possible lines of communication, among network members. Ties can be conceptualized in terms of strength (*weak, strong, affiliative*), activity (*active, latent, dormant*), and symmetry (*symmetrical* or *asymmetrical*). Strength and activity of ties can affect everything from the resources that pass through the individual tie and the frequency of communication to the structure of the overall network. For example, *strong ties* are generally found among people such as friends and family, who have a long shared history, frequent communication, and communication around personal or intimate topics. Strong ties tend to be *homophilous*, or similar. Resources that typically flow through strong ties include personal advice, confidential information, social support, and even monetary or other types of tangible support. Homophily often breeds connection, meaning that individuals with strong ties within a network often have direct connections with the same alters (i.e., other actors). Thus, networks that consist of mainly strong ties tend to be closed and cohesive networks, meaning that all members of the network, or portion of a network, are directly connected. This can be helpful, such as in situations where trust is important, or when decisions have to be made quickly. However, it can stifle innovation and creativity, in that nodes who are similar often have access to similar resources, and see things in a similar way. This can lead to *groupthink*, or tendency toward group conformity that blinds group members to the importance of outside influence or alternative points of view. Groupthink can inhibit critical thinking and decision-making to the point of failure or even danger. For example, when organizational leadership fails to take into account environmental changes, the status quo is often maintained, causing the organization to innovate less and ultimately be left behind. (See Chapter 15 for more on groupthink.)

Conversely, *weak ties* are connections between people who share a smaller range of information and communication topics, and often do not have multiple contacts in common. This can lead to open networks, or networks that are not *densely connected*, meaning that members are "connected to many actors who are themselves unconnected" (Podolny & Baron, 1997, p. 673). Members of open networks often span several networks but are not deeply embedded in any given one, thus offering unique resources. While weak links and open network structures do not foster trust as quickly as a closed network, they may offer greater flexibility and innovation because of the diversity of their members, which provides easier access to a variety of resources. For individuals, having a large, sparse network of informal ties can lead to greater job mobility (Granovetter, 1984; Podolny & Baron, 1997, p. 673). However, while an actor's ego network may be primarily strong or weak ties, it is unlikely that any overall network will be one or the other. Rather, there is evidence that a mix of strong and weak ties within a network structure leads to the most efficacy in the ability to obtain and leverage resources (Capaldo, 2007; Doerfel, Lai, & Chewning, 2010). Given these findings, being able to strategically adapt networks depending on internal and external needs is critical to both individual and organizational success. Additionally, while tie strength and overall network structure create opportunities for trust, resource mobilization, and innovation, the content of communication flowing through the network ties ultimately determines network outcomes.

It is worth noting that not all members within a given network need to be connected, and that tie strength does not necessarily stay the same as networks evolve. Ties that connect two people are considered *active*. However, there is also the opportunity for *latent* ties, or ties for which a connection is possible but has not yet been activated, such as members of the same organization who have not met. Because they share the same boundary condition and are connected to others (either directly or indirectly) within that boundary condition, they still share the same social network. Additionally, because of the social identification that can come from being part of a shared social structure, unconnected members of the same network will likely still share a similar orientation to the overall network, although that orientation will be mediated by who they are connected to. Finally, *dormant* ties are those that were previously active, but through which communication no longer flows, such as old friends, or family members who have been out of communication for an extended period of time. However, dormant ties can be reactivated, start out as weak, and over time, evolve into strong ties. Conversely, two members of an organization can be part of the same work unit and share a strong tie, but when one gets transferred to another part of the organization or leaves altogether, their tie could become weak or dormant.

Network Roles, Access, and Power

The number and connections of ties that actors have within a network have implications for both individual and network level issues of access, efficiency, and power. *Centrality* is a measure of how connected one is to other members of the network, either directly or indirectly (Borgatti, Carley, & Krackhardt, 2006; Freeman, 1978). An actor with high centrality is generally one who is optimally connected within the network, either in terms of direct ties, or in their ability to connect other ties. Centrality is associated with power and influence, as one who is highly central has the most access to information and resources that flow throughout the network. This allows them not only to have high levels of institutional knowledge, both formal and informal, but also to become a "go-to" source of information or advice for coworkers. Briefly, there are four different types of centrality: degree, eigenvector, closeness, and betweenness (Borgatti et al., 2006; Borgatti & Everett, 1997).

Degree centrality measures the number of adjacent links to and from an individual, and is based solely on direct measures. *Eigenvector* centrality represents the degree measure of a node in terms of the centrality of adjacent nodes; that is, whether an actor is connected to other highly connected actors. *Closeness* centrality measures how close one is to all other members of a network by summing the lengths of the shortest paths from an individual to all other network members. *Betweenness* centrality measures the extent to which individuals occupy the position between other actors on the shortest paths that connect them. Networks can also be studied in terms of their degree of centralization, or the degree to which the majority of nodes cluster around a specific node or set of nodes. Within organizations, highly centralized networks have been shown to be the most efficient organizational structure for completing tasks that are not complex, while less centralized networks are more efficient for tasks with higher complexity.

How many ties an actor has within the overall network and the composition of these ties in relation to the rest of the network have implications for the role they play within the network. The most common network roles are gatekeepers, liaisons, bridges, isolates, and stars. *Stars* are the network members with the most lines of communication, or highest degree centrality. As discussed earlier, they often have power and influence, and occupy the role of opinion leader. An opinion leader is not the leader according to the organizational chart, but rather the person that people seek out most for information or advice. While the designated leader can also be the opinion leader, the network star is most often the leader in emergent (e.g., advice, friendship) networks.

There are three different network roles that serve brokerage positions, or positions that connect and manage communication/resource flow among different parts of the organization. *Liaisons* connect groups without being a member of either group, such as a manager or coordinator who shares information among various workgroups contributing to the same project. *Bridges* play a similar role to liaisons, in that they connect otherwise unconnected groups, however, they share membership in one or more of the groups. An example of a bridge is someone who is a member of IT, but also working on building the company website with members from the communication department. Finally, *gatekeepers* control the flow of information by strategically choosing with whom to share messages. Gatekeepers can be critical in the flow of messages through the organization, for example, in power differentials (e.g., an administrative assistant is a gatekeeper between employees and managers), and between the network and its macro-level environment (e.g., a client representative brokers information and goods between the organization and external stakeholders). Gatekeepers can be beneficial because they filter messages and can therefore prevent information overload (Rogers & Agarwala-Rogers, 1976), but can also stymie or misdirect organizational communication by filtering or altogether withholding information. Thus, the role of gatekeeper can be a powerful one regardless of the number of direct or indirect ties a given gatekeeper has, and regardless of his or her official position. For example, the administrative assistant is the quintessential gatekeeper, as admins generally control the flow of information between a manager and her or his employees.

The ways that these various network concepts interact within a social setting is the basis of most social network studies. While this section has highlighted the general ways in which network concepts can be applied to the study of organizational communication, the following section will dig deeper into the advances in organizational network studies and what this means in terms of social organization (O_2) related to the organization (O_3).

Networks and Organizations

The development of network studies related to organizational communication has not been linear in the traditional sense of clear stages of progression. Rather, research has focused on applying the previously described network concepts in a variety of organizational settings with a focus on the interplay of formal and informal communication relationships and their effect on individual and organizational outcomes. Thus, while this section of the chapter attempts to develop a chronological timeline of network studies related to organizations, developments that are directly related to each other are grouped together even if they took place years apart.

There have been some shifts in network research that have taken place as society has changed, most markedly with the rise of information and communication technologies (ICTs) and the accompanying shift from traditional hierarchies to a more horizontal organizational structure (see Chapter 1). ICT has led to the ability to communicate across time and distance, allowing for organizations to operate on a global scale and a reconceptualization of how organizations communicate with both internal and external stakeholders. However, while the focus and scope of networks studies has changed, one could argue that advances in ICT only highlight the core concepts of social network theory.

The Origin of Social Network Theory

Network concepts are interdisciplinary, and have been adopted among a variety of fields, including biology, mathematics, social science, anthropology, and computer science. Network theory as related to social and communication networks has roots in social science, psychological sciences, mathematics, and management communication. Scott (2000) traces three traditions in the development of social network analysis. The first is a group of Harvard researchers in the 1930s who studied small groups and made advances in the mathematical basis of social network analysis, graph theory. These researchers were influenced by Gestalt theories in psychology, which stress "the patterns through which thought and perceptions are structured. These organized patterns are regarded as 'wholes' or systems that have properties distinct from those of their 'parts' which furthermore, *determine* the nature of those parts" (Scott, 2000, p. 8, emphasis in original). Although Gestalt psychology was rooted in the idea of perception, researchers Jacob Moreno, Kurt Lewin, and Fritz Heider applied the concepts to study the influence of social contacts on one's actions, psychological development, and shared perception of the environment in which the group exists (Scott, 2000). Moreno is credited with developing the sociogram, or diagram where actors are represented as points, with the lines connecting the nodes representing the relationships (Scott, 2000; Fredericks & Durand, 2005, p. 16). This led to the birth of sociometry, or the qualitative study of social relations. The sociogram, as seen in Figure 9.1, is still used in network theory and analysis today. From the 1930s to the 1940s, network concepts were applied to a number of settings, including organizational studies such as the Hawthorne Studies (see Chapter 6) and geographic communities of place (Fredericks & Durand, 2005). Out of this tradition came the articulation of foundational structural concepts such as *cliques*, the tightly connected subgroups that exist within many networks, and the idea that larger networks can be studied by analyzing the connections within and between the smaller groups that serve as the building blocks of these structures.

The second tradition of network studies, rooted in work conducted by Manchester anthropologists, considered the role of conflict and power in the development of social

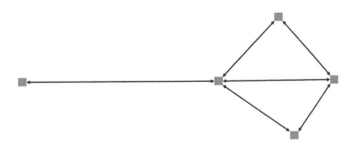

Figure 9.1 Example of a sociogram

structures. This work was heavily influenced by Radcliffe-Brown, whose theory of functionalism emphasized the interconnection of all aspects of society as vital to a functioning society, similar to the interdependence of biological functions. Using graph theory, researchers in this tradition used sociometrics to systemize the structural properties of social relations (Scott, 2000). Coining the term *network* as related to sociology, these researchers identified standard network properties such as *density* (the number of actual connections out of the total number of possible connections within a network), *content* (the meaning or basis of relations win a network), tie reciprocity and strength, and *reachability* (the degree to which all members can connect through a limited number of steps). Additionally, they formalized work on cliques and clusters and highlighted the importance of the *ego network* (Scott, 2000).

The third tradition, born out of work at Harvard, expanded the analytical capabilities of network studies through the inclusion of algebraic models and multidimensional scaling, allowing researchers to provide value and direction to the connections among actors, as well as calculate relationships in terms of social distance and map them in a social space (Scott, 2000). These advances allowed for a study of network properties regardless of context, thus moving network analysis out of purely interpersonal relations and into the study of other (nonhuman) actors such as organizations. As technology advanced, so did the ability to analyze larger networks from different perspectives, eventually leading to network analysis in its current form, in which networks are both a sociological construct and a mathematical object (Borgatti & Halgin, 2011).

Early social network studies conceptualized connection in terms of interaction. Arguably, interaction implies communication, as communication is the primary way that humans affect each other and exchange the information and relational content around which networks are built. Indeed, at its simplest, communication has been defined as "process by which individuals interact and influence each other" (Craig, 1999, p. 143). While many of the studies that frame network formation in terms of interaction articulate a topic of the interaction, such as research and development projects, informal social communication, or supply chain partnerships, they do not necessarily focus on what is being said. Any focus on message was often treated as transactional, rather than socially constituted (Chapter 1). Thus, while the act of communicating has always *implicitly* undergirded social network formation, it has often been reduced to the idea of patterns of interaction among partners, how those patterns of interaction contribute to social structure, and the implications of the resulting structure on both individual and whole-network levels. However, as we have discussed throughout this text, communication is more than contact or even simple information exchange, and involves the creation of shared meaning. Thus, in order to truly understand networks, it is important to know *who talks to whom*, as well as *what they talk about* and *why they are talking*.

As network theory spread into the field of communication, networks scholars began to pick up this thread and formally articulate communication as the underlying process of network building (Monge & Contractor, 2003), tying why and how we communicate to how networks are formed. For example, in studying network rebuilding after Hurricane Katrina, researchers found that communication was enacted as an adaptive strategy, as shifts in how and why organizational leaders were communicating at different points in time affected network composition (Doerfel et al., 2011). Directly after the hurricane, organizational leaders reported communicating about safety and emergency needs, leading to networks composed primarily of personal contacts.

However, once those needs were established, communication shifted outward to acquiring the resources to get organizations functional, which included reaching out to partners outside of the immediate area, relying in indirect and weak ties, and then eventually returning to a new state of normalcy consisting of primarily pre-disaster ties with some post-disaster ties integrated into the network.

Formal and Emergent Networks in Organizations

Network research in organizational communication has focused on how a combination of the formal and informal ties in and between organizations can lead to power, influence, identification, innovation, alliances, and productivity. Formal and emergent networks coexist and complement each other (Monge & Contractor, 2003) on multiple, interdependent levels, including personal, group, organizational and interorganizational (Stohl, 1995). Networks can take many forms related to organizations, such as personal contact networks, information flows within and between groups, strategic alliances among organizations, global network organizations, or employee networks supported by enterprise network software (Monge & Contractor, 2003, p. 3). According to Krackhardt and Hanson (1993, p. 104), while "the formal organization is the skeleton of a company, the informal is the central nervous system driving the collective thought processes, actions, and reactions of its business units."

The formal/informal dichotomy in network studies in some ways represents the implicit idea that the formal network is a predesignated entity. While the organization (O_3) is formed and sustained through communication links, the configuration of those links is often (but not always) treated as both a context for and direct result of the organizational communication. As we have discussed throughout this text, anytime there is O_3, O_1 and O_2 must be present. From this perspective, all organizational structures begin with rules for interaction designated by the individual(s) who conceptualize the organization. For example, the formal structure of the Ford motor plant was created through officially sanctioned rules for communication (i.e., the organizational hierarchy) established by Henry Ford. These rules constituted the formal structure. When enacted and re-enacted by Ford and his employees, formal structure was "created" and reinforced. Because industries are also networks through which influence flows, it is worth noting that Ford's ideas were likely influenced by classical management theories, which were a common characterization of organizational structure during this timeframe, and adopted by many different organizations (see Chapter 5).

Studies in intra-organizational networks primarily focus on how the O_1 and O_2 that take place "within" the organizations impact employees, as well as supporting or changing the overall organizational structure. Such studies focus on O_3 as the antecedent for organizational communication, while simultaneously acknowledging that the organizational structure can be reinforced or changed by the communication that takes place within it. The main drivers for change in organizational networks are agency (motivation of actors to engage with the old/new partners), opportunity, inertia (e.g., pressures to stay the same or change) and external or random factors (Ahuja, Soda, & Zaheer, 2012).Driven by these factors, organizational actors make decisions to create, maintain, or dissolve ties, which then changes both ego and whole-network structures. The ability to affect structural change can be enabled or constrained by issues such as organizational culture regarding who "can" talk to whom, individual preferences, and other factors.

A good example of the interplay of formal and emergent structure in organizational communication is found in early organizational communication network literature focused on how the informal communication patterns engaged in by employees and managers often did not follow the organizational chain of command, but rather created new, and sometimes more powerful, connections. For example, the *grapevine* is an emergent network that is temporarily created around specific messages, often gossip or informal organizational information (Davis, 1953). Despite the fact that the information is informal, it is often integral to both employee and management sensemaking within the organization, and can serve as an important feedback mechanism for organizational management (Davis, 1953, 1978; Goldhaber, 1993). Emergent networks within organizations can be mapped in several ways, including advice networks (alters that employees turn to for advice), trust networks (other organizational members that employees report trusting), and communication networks (all other organizational members with whom an ego employee reports communicating with) (Krackhardt & Hanson, 1993). Ties in such networks are often stronger and more durable, because they are based in personal connection, as opposed to formally designated organizational lines. As we tend to share more sensitive information with those to whom we are emotionally close, ties in emergent networks such as the grapevine or trust networks may provide access to exclusive or proprietary information that may not reach the same actors through formal network linkages.

Network Components, Overall Structure, and Organizational Outcomes

However, not all ties in emergent networks are strong and durable, and not all strong and durable ties are advantageous. Mark Granovetter (1973, 1985) introduced the importance of weak ties, arguing that within networks, weak ties, or ties with those actors with whom individuals have *loose connections that are not connected to many similar contacts*, are most advantageous in that they offer access to novel resources and new contacts. Weak ties often fill a brokerage role between two densely connected (well-interconnected) groups, thus being in a potentially powerful position of providing information that would not otherwise be available to members within the dense subgroups. Granovetter (1973) showed that such ties can be useful in terms of providing job leads, as they may know about opportunities outside of an individual's immediate group, and also can provide the impetus and connections to galvanize collective action. Being a weak tie connecting two other groups provides power to the individual occupying the brokerage position, which benefits individuals within the connected groups by providing them with access to information or tangible resources they would not otherwise have. Weak ties benefit the overall network structure by creating formerly absent pathways for the information and resources to flow through. Granovetter's work on weak ties has become a standard in organizational communication research, applied to areas such as job advancement, social capital development, innovation and knowledge transfer, and power. While this body of work largely underscores the value of weak ties, it also suggests that weak ties are not helpful in all situations. For example, weak ties between work units have been shown to speed up projects when knowledge is not complex, but slow down work as knowledge increases in complexity (Hansen, 1999). In a study of interorganizational research and development, Michelfelder and Kratzer (2013, p. 1159) found that a combination of strong and weak ties can have a "mutually reinforcing effect on innovation outcomes if combined rather than considered separately."

Tichy, Tushman, and Fombrun (1979) identified three network properties as relevant to organizational communication: transactional content, the nature of links, and structural characteristics. Transactional content is what is exchanged among actors; for example, exchange of affect (such as friendship), exchange of power, exchange of information, and exchange of goods or services. Tichy et al. (1979) argue that networks can be developed for each of these types of content, that an individual's position or membership in each network may vary, and that these networks may or may not overlap. The nature of the links is the strength and qualitative nature of the ties, which can be conceptualized in terms of intensity (i.e., strength of the tie), reciprocity (whether ties are one-way or reciprocal), clarity of expectations (link agreement on overall network goals), and multiplexity (the degree to which links share one or more roles, such as friend *and* coworker vs. friend *or* coworker). Structural characteristics include the external network, the *total* internal network, *clusters* (subsections) within the organizational network, and individual roles within the network.

Similar to Granovetter's work on weak ties, Burt's (1982) theory emphasizes the importance of *structural holes*, or parts of the social structure in which people can serve as a broker between network clusters that would be otherwise unconnected. Burt argues actors who bridge structural holes have a "vision advantage that can translate into social capital" (Burt, 2004, p. 351). *Social capital* is a concept distinct from but directly related to networks, which captures the idea that benefits accrue from being part of a social network. Burt argues that position in the network can affect one's access to social capital. The actor's ability to broker information gives the actor the advantages commonly associated with weak ties: less amplified reciprocity, less inclination toward groupthink, and more access to novel information. Additionally, an actor filling a structural hole can enjoy the power that comes from connecting those who are otherwise unconnected. While many bridges spanning structural holes are also weak ties, Burt's theory posits that their power comes not from tie strength, but from the fact that they are non-redundant (i.e., filling a position that no other actor in the network fills). In fact, he suggests that if one can bridge a strong tie, there may be more advantage in the form of interpersonal influence. Similar to Granovetter's assertion regarding the strength of weak ties, Burt's theory of structural holes underscore the importance of brokerage roles and non-redundancy of contacts. Multiple studies have underscored the importance of structural holes for power, innovation, and knowledge sharing (Ahuja, 2000; Gargiulo & Benassi, 1998), but also highlight the importance of balance between network closure and opportunities for brokerage.

Organization and the Environment

In attempting to answer the question of how social relations impact the behavior and economics of organizations, Granovetter (1985) articulated the concept of embeddedness—the idea that organizations are so constrained by social relations that the traditional, rational view of organizational behavior does not accurately characterize organizational reality. Granovetter (1985) argued that embeddedness is ongoing and socially (re)constructed during each interaction. Embeddedness guards against market opportunism as participants build relationships rooted in trust and reciprocity. Over time, these relationships are guided by a general knowledge of what one can expect from another partner, further embedding the actors within their shared network.

In 1990, Powell formalized the idea that the network as an organizational form is neither market nor hierarchy. His work distinguished the contemporary organization as something distinct from the traditional governance structure of the hierarchy, which wards off opportunism at the cost of bureaucracy, and the opportunism of the market. Powell (1990) identified as the basic assumption of network relations the idea that "one party is dependent on resources controlled by another, and that there are gains to be made by the pooling of resources" (p. 303). This dependency enters parties in a series of "reciprocal, preferential, [and] mutually supportive" interactions by which they are able to accomplish their own goals without sacrificing the goals of network partners (Powell, 1990, p. 303). As actors repeatedly interact in the same social patterns to drive resource acquisition and mutual gain, they create organizational and interorganizational structures. Unlike traditional hierarchies, these structures do not represent predetermined lines of communication, but rather socially constructed pathways. Such structures are more flexible than traditional conceptualizations of the organization, because they can be altered by changing communication to accommodate changing needs or conditions. Although he did not focus on communication per se, Powell's articulation of the organization as a network form was an articulation of the process of the CCO (Chapter 3) approach related to organizations.

Organizations can also develop networks with other organizations, which can be studied in the same way as internal organizational networks. Interorganizational network scholarship that considers cooperation or competition across organizational boundaries developed alongside traditional organizational network research. The basic premise of interorganizational networks research is that organizations form relationships in order to manage environmental uncertainty, share or leverage resources, and work together to address macro-level issues that affect their shared environment (Doerfel et al., 2010; Hannan & Freeman, 1977; Monge, Heiss, & Margolin, 2008). Interorganizational networks studies often examine how the connections among organizations lead to benefits for the involved organizations. Supply chains, or the network of organizations involved in the shared production and distribution of a product or other commodity, are a common example of interorganizational networks. Other examples include the contacts that organizations have in the community in which they operate, including community organizations, professional organizations, and the local government, as well as organizations that come together for a shared cause to advance macro-level interests. For example, nongovernmental organizations (NGOs) worked together, creating interorganizational networks to promote democratic election in Croatia (Doerfel & Taylor, 2004). Although the NGOs normally competed for monies from the same agencies, they found that the benefits of promoting democracy in Croatia outweighed their individual needs for funding. Such interorganizational networks can be more temporary than interorganizational alliances formed around industry needs during stable times, as they are likely to return to at least some of their regular networking patterns after they accomplish their joint task, as was the case with the NGOs in Croatia.

Toward the end of the twentieth century, network studies began a natural shift toward examining the effect of information and communication technology on network development and evolution. As early as the 1990s, organizations were beginning to adopt email and other communication technologies to facilitate organizational communication (see Chapter 19). Recognizing this shift, network studies started to focus more on theoretical motives for network emergence that play out on multiple levels (e.g., Monge & Contractor, 2003; Monge et al., 2008; Su, Huang, & Contractor, 2010). As the development of ICT progressed to offer more communicative capabilities, it became clear that the use of such technologies had a dramatic impact on both communication (O_1) and the process of social organizing (O_2), consequently affecting the organizational form (O_3).

Social Networks and Organizations in the 21st Century

Information and communication technology, such as the Internet, social media sites, and mobile phones, have dramatically altered the way that individuals communicate. We are no longer bound by geography, and can use technology to *disembed* from traditional, geographically based networks and *re-embed* in new networks based on interest and opportunity. ICT affects network structure in many ways, in that it allows for the creation of networks that are loosely coupled and flexible, with potentially unlimited boundaries. Strong ties can be reinforced by the communication redundancy offered by ICT, while weak ties can be created and maintained, and even strengthened over time, by the structural opportunity provided by each medium (Haythornewaite, 2002). Additionally, latent, dormant, and indirect ties can be easily (re)activated via ICT. Online platforms offer the structure to alter communication patterns in terms of increased frequency, the ability to direct communication to specific individuals, groups, or a mass audience, and often serve as a repository for information. Within organizations, the social and organizing capabilities offered by ICT have affected everything from organizational design (Fulk and DeSanctis, 1995), to employee communication (Ellison, Gibbs, & Weber, 2014), and how organizations view and communicate with external stakeholders (Brodie, Ilic, Juric, & Hollebeek, 2013).

Shifting organizational patterns supported by ICT have given rise to the workforces that are no longer co-located and must rely on technology to accomplish work tasks. For example, incorporation of ICT into organizational communication has given rise to the *teleworker*, or employee who works from home or another space rather than in the office. Teleworkers rely on ICT including email, videoconferencing, intranets, and other enterprise management systems to stay connected with management and coworkers and to facilitate work processes. While a teleworker is still part of the organizational network, they are less likely to be part of the emergent networks that come from informal organizational communication. This can impact employee identification with both the organization and its values, and the employees' work group (Scott & Timmerman, 1999). Thus, ICT facilitates the ability to be part of the organizational network, but often at the risk of not sharing the same level or types of relationships that co-located employees share with each other and organizational leaders. Conversely, ICT can create and/or strengthen connections that would be otherwise unavailable, potentially providing the opportunity for more, not less, engagement.

Whether or not ICT engages or distances people in organizations depends, in part, on how it is enacted. Although ICTs have established technological features, user agency comes into play because each user may decide to enact technology differently, influenced by a combination of the materiality of the technology, individual schema, and socio-cultural norms (e.g., organizational norms, group norms, etc.), thus determining the capabilities of the technology. In doing so, users can reinforce technical structures by continuing to use ICT in designated ways, or reinvent existing technological structures by reimagining the ICT use for new or novel purposes (Orlikowski, 2008). Thus, social organization dependent on ICT becomes a *socio-technical* structure by which actors are connected via the shared enactment of technology.

Technologies through which organizations and employees can enact socio-technical structures include email and videoconferencing, intranet sites, knowledge management (KM) systems and enterprise social network systems (ESNS). Intranet sites are the least interactive type of communication tool, and generally serve as information repositories. While smaller organizations often have only one intranet site, larger organizations can have several intranet sites that represent different branches of the organization, operating groups, or organizational initiatives. KM systems integrate multiple technologies, including data warehousing, decision support systems, project management systems, expert systems, expert directories, intranets and extranets, and groupware (Fulk & Yuan, 2013). While more interactive than intranets alone, and beneficial for coordinating workflow, KM systems do not enable the interpersonal coordination that is important to building relationships across organizational boundaries. ESNS enable organizations to communicate with employees and foster communication among employees as they allow users to easily create, edit, and link content, as well as include the familiar social media features such as wikis, blogs, social tagging systems, social bookmarking systems, and microblogs (Fulk & Yuan, 2013). As such, ESMS enable knowledge sharing, the creation of social capital, context, and network interaction (Ellison et al., 2014).

ICTs have also changed the nature of external stakeholder communication. Stakeholder networks are the social structure through which institutions both influence and are influenced by stakeholders. While traditional models of stakeholder networks position the organization at the center of a network of stakeholders who have no direct connections with each other, ICT enables the ability for various stakeholder groups to *see* communication between the organization and other stakeholder groups, thus shifting the conceptualization of stakeholder networks to one where the focal organization is one node in an interconnected network of various stakeholders who also have connections with each other. Thus, ICT has shifted power to stakeholder groups because organizations must now be cognizant of the fact that their communication with each stakeholder group is equally visible to all other groups, and even to potential stakeholders (latent ties) who are currently only a passive audience to the public communication.

Additionally, social media has become an increasingly necessary communication tool for organizational public relations and marketing, enabling organizations to further develop their brand through content and engage in more "informal" communication with stakeholders, both one on one, and as a mass audience. ESMS also allow stakeholders to communicate directly with each other. This can help strengthen ties with the organization, as stakeholders come to the social media sites and comment, or even dialogue with each other and the organization. It also enables stakeholders to form coalitions and pressure organizations, such as when the CEO of Barilla Pasta said Barilla would only use "traditional families" in Barilla advertising (Chewning, 2015, p. 139). Barilla received backlash, much of it in the form of stakeholder protests on their Facebook page that led to an apology and the creation of advisory board to promote diversity. The company then planned a new, more inclusive advertising campaign. Using hashtags and hyperlinks, stakeholders can also organize around a specific cause related to an organization, either in protest (e.g., when detractors of Paula Deen used #Paula'sBestDishes to mockingly named potential Deen meals such as *White's Only Rice* and *KKKesadillas* after she revealed she had used racial epitaphs) or in support (e.g., adopting organizational hashtags, such as when stakeholders adopted and shared Unilever's #ClearAPlate to promote their efforts providing half a million meals through a partnership with Oxfam).

Communication and Organizing in Social Networks

Communication and organizing are the building blocks of networks because, as stated in Chapter 1, it is through communication that we organize into social collectives. It is through our communication choices that we draw people into our networks. While sometimes this is based on convenience, such as proximity, we often make these communication choices strategically. Returning to the C-O dynamic explored throughout the text, human agency is integral within networks because it is through actively seeking out others for specific purposes that networks are created. Related to organizations, this happens on both the intra- and interorganizational level. For example, emergency networks emerged after the Exxon Valdez oil spill that consisted of already existing organizations whose interactions were altered as a result of working together to respond to the Alaskan crisis (Topper & Carley, 1999). Some formed new alliances, while others altered their former relationships to fit the context of the new crisis. Such emergency interaction led to the creation of alternative network forms that best accommodated the parties involved.

Within social science, Burt's (1982) theory of structural action is a seminal approach to network studies that both illustrates and defines the interplay of network communication and structure. Earlier approaches to network studies, such as Blau's (1977) theory of macrosocial interaction, focused on the distributions of people in social positions. Blau (1977) argued that the relations between and among people of different positions is influenced by the frequency distributions of these people in the overall population. Alternatively, Burt's (1982) theoretical perspective of a structural theory of action posited both relational and positional motivations for social interaction. Burt (1982) based his theory on the premise that action is purposive. Actors are motivated by resources offering the greatest utility as revealed by evaluation of the alternatives. Structural action, the concept underlying Burt's theory, assumes that an actor evaluates the utility of alternatives based independently and in regard to others. These actors, alternatives, and actions are all patterned by the context in which they exist. Thus, Burt's theory focuses on the idea of human agency as enabled or constrained by the macro-level environment in which the individual was embedded, and therefore, individuals are constrained by the very structure that their choices serve to reinforce. Similarly, Granovetter's view of embeddedness (discussed earlier) focuses on the reciprocal relationship that human agency and social structure share, through which communication choices both create, and are guided by, social organization.

Monge and Contractor's (2003) multi-theoretical multi-level (MTML) theorizing underscores this concept across social settings, as they argued for the application of a theoretical lens to examine the *why* behind the *how* actors come together to create networks within the context of broader, global systems. Such theorizing highlights the idea that "global organizations are processes, not places" (Monge & Contractor, 2003, p. 4) underscoring the connection between O_1 and O_2 both coincident with, and distinct from, O_3.

Conclusion

Networks richly illustrate the connections among O_1, O_2, and O_3. The interplay of formal and informal communication inherent to networks creates both bottom-up and top-down social structures that can be reified into organizations. The changing nature of the organizational landscape, fueled by the rise of ICT and an emphasis on employee feedback and collaboration has loosened both internal and external organizational boundaries, highlighting the ways in which individual connections create pathways for collaboration, innovation, and change.

As networks are driven by our human communication choices, they are flexible and adaptive, changing as individual-, group-, and organization-level needs change. While traditional network literature was primarily concerned with the social structures resulting from these choices, focusing on the communication processes that underlie the choices provides richer understanding of why organizational networks emerge and evolve, and how organizational members and leaders can create networks that maximize benefits on individual, organizational, and interorganizational levels.

Recommended Supplementary Readings

Krackhardt, D., & Hanson, J.R. (1993). Information networks: The company behind the chart. *Harvard Business Review*, July–August, 104–111.
This is an easy to follow article that explains the importance of informal networks in the organization.
Putnam, R. D. (2000). *Bowling alone: The collapse and revival of American community.* New York, NY: Simon & Schuster.
Bowling Alone *demonstrates the importance of social ties to the creation of social capital. While Putnam does not go into depth about organizational networks, he does demonstrate the importance of participation in community organizations to stronger relations on both the individual and community levels, thus implicitly connecting micro-, meso-, and macro-structure.*
Cheseboro, J. L. (2014). Networking. In *Professional communication at work: Interpersonal strategies for career success.* New York, NY: Routledge.
This chapter nicely illustrates both network concepts, and the importance of networking for professionals both in and out of the workplace. Will help students orient themselves to the idea of networking.
Monge, P. R., & Contractor, N. S. (2003). *Theories of communication networks.* New York, NY: Oxford University Press.
This book provides a comprehensive overview communication networks directly ties communication and social science theories to network formation.

Important Concepts: Define and Discuss

Bridge
Centrality
Density
Formal network
Emergent network
Gatekeeper
Grapevine
Groupthink
Interorganizational Networks
Liaison
Homophily
Nodes

Ties
Sociogram
Star
Strong tie
Weak tie

Discussion Questions

1. There is an old adage that says: "It's not what you know, but who you know." Given what you learned about network structure, what do you think that means? How can you build and leverage networks that are advantageous to your future career plans?
2. Think about your own networks in terms of your strong and weak ties. What benefits do you glean from each? In what ways do they inhibit you?
3. How can organizational leaders purposely structure organization communication to avoid groupthink and spur innovation and diversity, while at the same time building relationships and trust among members? (Hint: think about the interplay of emergent and formal networks and open/closed network structures.)
4. Think about where you currently work, or somewhere you have worked in the past. Was there a difference between the formal network and the way that information really traveled throughout the organization? If so, which had a stronger influence on workflow: the formal or emergent network? If there was an emergent network, did it undermine or complement the formal network?
5. What are some communicative ways that you can combat groupthink?

Practitioners' Corner

Social network theory provides direction for organizational leaders who want to increase overall network benefits, and individual organizational members who want to maximize their organizational advantage. The following suggestions provide direction for how network theory can provide direction when creating organizational level opportunities for interaction:

- Create opportunities for social interaction: Organizational communication research supports the importance of "watercooler" talk (informal communication). Company picnics, parties, and other social events provide opportunities for organizational members to strengthen their ties, which can increase personal and organizational social capital. An added advantage is that members have the opportunity to socialize across position and division boundaries.
- Strategically balance strong and weak ties: Network research has demonstrated the importance of both strong and weak ties for success in organizations. Dense, cohesive clusters, such as departmental work units, tend to develop strong ties based on frequent communication around shared goals. This often leads to trust and cooperation, which can be conducive to productivity. However, as mentioned earlier in the chapter, it can also lead to groupthink, which can stymie innovation and change. Research has shown that dense, closed networks are more useful in times of change and uncertainty (Krackhardt, 1992), while weak ties are better at providing exposure to new information and resources. However, the usefulness of weak ties can be mitigated by the complexity of the information being transferred

(Hansen, 1999). Ultimately, the optimal structure of network relations can be affected by the overall goals of the network members (Ahuja, 2000), emphasizing the need for making strategic communication choices on both the individual and organizational levels.

- Work with emergent networks: Organizational leaders should pay attention to emergent communication practices such as who department/organizational members turn to for advice and where work gets done or stalls. If there is an emergent leader to whom people turn instead of the formally designated leader, consider giving that person a larger role in the organization. If the formal workflow is less productive or followed than an employee created workaround, consider redesigning the process.

- Focus on the link between the micro and macro: It is important to remember that micro (individual) level change leads to macro (large-scale) level change. Returning to the network drivers of agency and opportunity (Ahuja et al., 2012), people naturally select ties that satisfy one or more important criteria. While these choices can be enabled and constrained by formal rules, they are the drivers for change and evolution in organizational networks.

- Bring in outside influences: social network theory emphasizes the importance of weak ties to combat groupthink and spark innovation. Bringing in organizational consultants and speakers and being part of a trade organization or community business council are effective ways to bring weak ties into the organizational network.

- Remember the importance of communication: While a communication network point of view focuses on the advantages or disadvantages offered by a given network structure, the content that flows through the links has implications that go beyond structural advantages. Kind words, helpful information, genuine interest, collegiality, and emotional intelligence all play a large role in the success and happiness of the individual employee and overall network.

References

Ahuja, G. (2000). Collaboration networks, structural holes, and innovation: A longitudinal study. *Administrative Science Quarterly*, 45(3), 425–455. doi:10.2307/2667105.

Ahuja, G., Soda, G., & Zaheer, A. (2012). The genesis and dynamics of organizational networks. *Organization Science*, 23(2), 434–448. doi:10.1287/orsc.1110.0695.

Borgatti, S. P., & Everett, M. G. (1997). Network analysis of 2-mode data. *Social Networks*, 19, 243–269. doi:10.1016/S0378-8733(96)00301-2.

Borgatti, S. P., Carley, K. M., & Krackhardt, D. (2006). On the robustness of centrality measures under conditions of imperfect data. *Social Networks*, 28, 124–136. doi:10.1016/j.socnet.2005.05.001.

Borgatti, S., & Halgin, D. (2011, May). On network theory. *Organizational Science*. Papers in Advance, pp. 1–24. doi:10.2139/ssrn.2260993.

Blau, P.M. (1977). A macrosocial theory of social structure. *American Journal of Sociology*, 83(1), 26–54. www.jstor.org/stable/2777762.

Brodie, R. J., Ilic, A., Juric, B., & Hollebeek, L. D. (2013). Consumer engagement in a virtual brand community: An exploratory analysis. *Journal of Business Research*, 66(1), 105–114. doi:10.1016/j.jbusres.2011.07.029.

Burt, R. S. (1982). *Toward a structural theory of action: Network models of social structure, perception, and action.* New York, NY: Academic Press.

Burt, R. S. (2004). Structural holes and good ideas. *American Journal of Sociology, 110*(2), 349–399. doi:10.1086/421787.

Castells, M. (2000). *The rise of the network society*. Chichester, West Sussex: Wiley-Blackwell.

Capaldo, A. (2007). Network structure and innovation: The leveraging of a dual network as a distinctive relational capability. *Strategic Management Journal, 28*, 585–608. doi:10.1002/smj.621.

Chewning, L.V. (2015). Measuring the enactment of IRT via social media: What are organizations and stakeholders saying during crisis? In J. Blaney and L. Alwine (Eds.), *Putting Image Repair to the Test*. Lanham, MD: Lexington Books.

Craig, R. T. (1999). Communication theory as a field. *Communication Theory, 9*(2), 119–161. doi:10.1111/j.1468-2885.1999.tb00355.x.

Davis, K. (1953). Management communication and the grapevine. *Harvard Business Review, 31* (5), 43–49.

Davis, K. (1978). Methods for studying informal communication. *Journal of Communication, 28* (1), 112–116. doi:10.1111/j.1460-2466.1978.tb01572.x.

Doerfel, M., Lai, C-H., & Chenwing, L. (2010). The evolutionary role of communication: Modeling social capital in disaster contexts. *Human Communication Research, 36*(2). doi:10.1111/j.1468-2958.2010.01371.x.

Doerfel, M., & Taylor, M. (2004). Network dynamics of interorganizational cooperation: The Croatian civil society movement. *Communication Monographs, 71*(4), 373–394.

Ellison, N. B., Gibbs, J. L., & Weber, M. S. (2015). The use of enterprise social network sites for knowledge sharing in distributed organizations: The role of organizational affordances. *American Behavioral Science, 59*, 103–123. doi:10.1177/0002764214540510.

Freeman, L. C. (1978). Centrality in social networks conceptual clarification. *Social Networks, 1*, 215–239. doi:10.1016/0378-8733(78)90021-7.

Fredericks, K. A., & Durand, M. M. (2005). The historical evolution and basic concepts of social network analysis. *New Directions for Evaluation, Special Issue: Social Network Analysis in Program Evaluation, 107*, 15–23. https://onlinelibrary.wiley.com/doi/abs/10.1002/ev.158.

Fulk, J., & DeSanctis, G. (1995). Electronic communication and changing organizational forms. *Organization Science, 6*(4), 337–349. doi:10.1287/orsc.6.4.337.

Fulk, G., & DeSanctis, G. (1999). Articulation of communication technology and organizational form. In G. DeSanctis and J. Fulk (Eds.), *Shaping organizational form: Communication, connection, and community* (pp. 5–32). Thousand Oaks, CA: SAGE.

Fulk, J., & Yuan, Y. (2013). Location, motivation, and social capitalization via enterprise social networking. *Journal of Computer Mediated Communication, 19*, 20–37. doi:10.1111/jcc4.12033.

Gargiulo, M., & Benassi, M. (2000). Trapped in your own net? Network cohesion, structural holes, and the adaptation of social capital. *Organization Science, 11*(2), 183–196. www.jstor.org/stable/2640283.

Goldhaber, G. (1993). *Organizational communication* (5th ed.). Madison, WI: Brown and Benchmark.

Granovetter, M. (1973). The strength of weak ties. *American Journal of Sociology, 6*, 1360–1380. doi:10.1086/225469.

Granovetter, M. (1984). *Getting a job*. Chicago, IL: University of Chicago Press.

Granovetter, M. (1985). Economic action and social structure: The problem of embeddedness. *American Journal of Sociology, 91*(3), 481–510. www.jstor.org/stable/2780199.

Hannan, M. T., & Freeman, J. (1977). The population ecology of organizations. *American Journal of Sociology, 82*(5), 929–964. www.jstor.org/stable/2777807.

Hansen, M. T. (1999). The search-transfer problem: The role of weak ties in sharing knowledge across sub units. *Administrative Science Quarterly, 44*(1), 82–111. doi:10.2307/2667032.

Haythornewaite, C. (2002). Strong, weak, and latent ties and the impact of new media. *Information Science, 18*, 385–401. doi:10.1080/01972240290108195.

Krackhardt, D. (1992). The strength of strong ties. In N. Nohria & R. G. Eccles (Eds.), *Networks and organizations: Structure, form, and action* (pp. 216–239). Boston, MA: Harvard Business School Press.

Krackhardt, D., & Hanson, J. R. (1993). Information networks: The company behind the chart. *Harvard Business Review*, July–August,104–111. https://hbr.org/1993/07/informal-networks-the-company-behind-the-chart.

Michelfelder, I., & Kratzer, H. (2013). Why and how combining strong and weak ties within a single interorganizational R&D collaboration outperforms other collaboration structures. *The Journal of Product Innovation Management, 30*(6), 1159–1177. doi:10.1111/jpim.12052.

Monge, P. R. & Contractor, N. S. (2003). *Theories of communication networks.* New York, NY: Oxford University Press.

Monge, P., Heiss, B. M., & Margolin, D. B. (2008). Communication network evolution in organizational communities. *Communication Theory, 18*(4), 449–477. doi:10.1111/j.1468-2885.2008.00330.x.

Nohria, N. (1998). Is a network perspective a useful way of studying organizations? In G. H. Hickman (Ed.), *Leading organizations: Perspectives for a new era* (pp. 287–301). Thousand Oaks, CA: SAGE.

Orlikowski, W. (2008). Using technology and constituting structures: A practice lens for studying technology in organizations. In M. S. Ackerman, C. A. Halverson, T. Erickson, & W. A. Kellogg (Eds.), *Resources, co-evolution and artifacts: Computer supported cooperative work.* London: Springer.

Podolny, J. M., & Baron, J. N. (1997). Resources and relationships: Social networks and mobility in the workplace. *American Sociological Review, 62*, 673–693. www.jstor.org/stable/2657354.

Powell, W. W. (1990). Neither market nor hierarchy: Network forms of organization. *Research in Organizational Behavior, 12*, 295–336. www.jstor.org/stable/2657354.

Rogers, E. M., & Agarwala-Rogers, R. (1976). *Diffusion of innovations.* New York, NY: Free Press.

Scott, J. (2000). Social network analysis: a handbook (2nd ed.). Thousand Oaks, CA: SAGE.

Scott, C., & Timmerman, C. E. (1999). Communication technology: Use and multiple workplace identifications among organizational teleworkers with varied degrees of virtuality. Paper presented at the International Communication Association Convention, May, San Francisco.

Stohl, C. (1995). *Organizational communication: Connectedness in Action.* Thousand Oaks, CA: SAGE.

Su, C., Huang, M., & Contractor, N. (2010). Understanding the structures, antecedents, and outcomes of organizational learning and knowledge transfer: a multi-theoretical and multilevel network analysis. *European Journal of International Management, 4*(6), 576–601. doi:10.1504/EJIM.2010.03559.

Tichy, N., Tushman, M., & Fombrun, C. (1979). Social network analysis for organizations. *The Academy of Management Review, 4*(4), 507–519. doi:10.5465/amr.1979.4498309.

Topper, C. M. & Carley, K. M. (1999). A structural perspective on the emergence of network organizations. *Journal of Mathematical Sociology, 24*(1), 67–96. doi:10.1080/0022250X.1999.9990229.

10 Workplace Relationships

Patricia M. Sias and Yejin Shin

Workplace relationships are central to organizational processes. In fact, some scholars conceptualize organizations as essentially systems of relationships (e.g., Wheatley, 1999). Thus, the quality of an organization is inextricably linked to the quality of the relationships among its members (Sias, 2014). The more functional the relationships among organizational members, the more functional the organization and vice versa. As interpersonal relationships, workplace relationships are ongoing social entities characterized by patterned interdependent interaction (Keyton, 2017). Communication is, therefore, fundamental to workplace relationship dynamics (Sias, 2014). While there are many different types of workplace relationships, this chapter addresses the workplace relationships that have been the primary focus of organizational communication research—supervisor–subordinate, peer, friendship, and romantic workplace relationships. For each relationship type, we provide a brief overview of how research in that area has developed over time, highlighting the contributions of communication scholars. Consistent with the broader theme of this book, we conclude the chapter with a discussion of how workplace relationship research has approached communication, organization, and culture.

Supervisor–Subordinate Relationships

Supervisor–subordinate relationships are one of the most frequently studied topics in organizational research (Sias, 2009). In fact, the organizational communication discipline arguably began with the study of these relationships. As seen in Chapter 1, organizational communication can trace its roots to the 1940s, when research in management, industrial relations, and industrial psychology turned attention to supervisory communication (Redding, 1985). The goal of such research was to improve communication between supervisors (at that time referred to as *superiors*) and their employees in the service of organizational efficiency and effectiveness.

The Beginning: Supervisor–Subordinate Communication and Leadership

Early research on supervisor–subordinate relationships was conducted by leadership and management scholars and mainly focused on the supervisor (see Chapter 18 for more on leadership), conceptualizing, at least implicitly, subordinate employees as passive recipients of leadership (Sias, Krone, & Jablin, 2002). Early theories, for example, centered on a leader's traits (e.g., intelligence, extroversion, attractiveness) and assumed leaders are born, not made (e.g., Ghiselli, 1963). Later theories centered leadership in behavior or styles rather than traits, but still positioned employees as passive partners in the relationship (e.g., Blake & Mouton, 1964). Theoretical development eventually acknowledged individual employees as relevant to leadership. For instance, situational leadership theory conceptualized employee readiness (i.e., ability and willingness) as central to effective leadership (Hersey & Blanchard, 1982). The supervisor, however, remained the dominant partner responsible for matching his or her leadership style to the employee.

A Turning Point: Leader–Member Exchange Theory

Vertical Dyad Linkage theory, introduced by Graen and Cashman in 1975, recognized the *dyadic relational* nature of supervisor-subordinate relationships. Unlike previous theories, it emphasized the employee's active and central role in the mutual negotiation of the supervisor-subordinate relationship. Later renamed leader–member exchange (LMX) theory (Graen & Scandura, 1987), the theory has had a significant impact on research about leadership and the supervisor–subordinate relationship. The majority of supervisor–subordinate relationship research since then has been grounded in LMX theory.

LMX's primary contribution was conceptualizing the supervisor–subordinate (i.e., leader–member) relationship as an exchange relationship in which the partners mutually exchange resources—conceptualizing the dyad, not just the supervisor, as active agents. Different types of exchanges create different types of relationships. Thus, LMX theory introduced the notion that supervisors do not have an overall leadership style, but rather treat their employees differently and develop different types of relationships with their various subordinate employees (Graen & Scandura, 1987). LMX research indicates that supervisors form two primary types of relationships with their employees. *Leadership exchange* (high-quality exchange) relationships are characterized by open communication, trust, support, and negotiating latitude for the employee. *Supervisory exchange* (low-quality exchange) relationships, in contrast, are characterized by low levels of trust and support, less open communication, and direct supervision. Not surprisingly, employees who report having leadership exchange relationships enjoy many positive outcomes including access to higher-quality information (Sias, 2005), higher job satisfaction (Turban, Jones & Rozelle, 1990), and better job performance (Michael, Leschinsky, & Gagnon, 2006), than those who report having supervisory exchange relationships.

Another Turning Point: Communication and LMX

While much LMX research was, and continues to be, conducted by management scholars, communication scholars provided an important development by conceptualizing supervisor–subordinate relationships as socially constructed. Fairhurst and Chandler (1989), for example, studied how supervisor–subordinate relationships were distinguished communicatively. They found that higher-quality LMX relationships were characterized by mutual persuasion while lower-quality relationships were characterized by authority and accentuation of power distance. In a subsequent study, Fairhurst (1993) found low-quality LMX relationships were characterized by accentuation of power distance via monitoring, face-threatening acts, and conflict. In contrast, high-quality LMX relationships are characterized by insider talk, value convergence, and non-routine problem-solving.

Subsequent studies yielded similar insights. Yrle, Hartman, and Galle (2003), for example, found high-quality LMX relationships are characterized by two distinct communication patterns: *Coordination* (i.e., interaction that enables mutual coordination of activities) and *participation* (i.e., interaction by which subordinates participate in decision-making processes). Similarly, Fix and Sias (2006) found that high-quality LMX relationships are characterized by *person-centered communication*, which encourages employees to consider the complexities of situations, recognize themselves as autonomous agents, and participate in decision-making and problem-solving. Low-quality relationships, in contrast, are characterized by *position-centered communication*, which accentuates authority and direct supervision. They also found that employees whose supervisor used person-centered communication reported higher levels of job satisfaction than those whose supervisor used position-centered communication. Jian and Dalisay (2017) found that high-quality LMX relationships are associated with higher-quality communication (i.e., communication characterized by efficiency, coordination, and accuracy) and that quality LMX communication is positively associated with employee commitment to the organization. In sum, communication research indicates LMX relationships are distinguished by communication patterns and practices and that this differential communication is associated with different outcomes for employees.

Supervisor–Subordinate Relationship Functions

In addition to leadership, research has centered on three other primary functions of the supervisor–subordinate relationship—information exchange, feedback, and mentoring. Studies consistently identify the supervisor–subordinate relationship as an important site of *information exchange*. Employees rely on their supervisor for important information about tasks, their performance, and organizational issues (Sias, 2009). Similarly, supervisors rely on their employees for information, using them as extra sets of eyes and ears in the organization (Ramaswami, Srinivasan, & Gorton, 1997). The quality of a supervisor–subordinate relationship is positively associated with the quality of information exchanged by the relationship partners (Sias, 2005).

Employees also rely on their supervisor for constructive *feedback* about their job performance, which is key to professional and technical development (Ashford, 1993; Fedor; 1991). Research suggests that high-quality supervisor–subordinate relationships are associated with effective performance feedback. Steelman and Rutkowski (2004), for example, found that employees with high-quality relationships with their supervisors (e.g., high levels of trust, likability) are more likely to listen to and accept negative feedback from them, and supervisors who maintain high-quality relationships with their employees tend to give constructive feedback. More recently, Lam, Peng, Wong, and Lau (2017) found that because an employee's performance information needs tend to be met by supervisors with whom they have a quality LMX relationship, the employee engages in less frequent feedback-seeking behavior. These studies highlight the importance of developing high-quality supervisor–subordinate (LMX) relationships to performance and professional development.

Because of their experience, knowledge, and positions of authority, supervisors are often important mentors for their employees. Mentoring is "a specific type of relationship in which the mentor functions as a type of 'guide' for the development and career advancement of the protégé/mentee" (Sias, 2009, p. 29). Mentoring relationships are unique in two ways—(1) they emphasize unidirectional information flow from mentor to protégé; and (2) they focus on the protégé's (rather than the mentor's) career. Organizations vary in whether they implement formal mentoring programs in which protégés are assigned to specific mentors or whether mentoring emerges informally. Regardless of whether the mentor is formally assigned or the relationship develops informally, research consistently demonstrates that mentoring is associated with a number of benefits for the protégé, including high levels of adjustment/satisfaction, career guidance, and role modeling (Jablin, 2001; Ragins & Scandura, 1997). LMX research indicates that mentoring is characteristic of high-quality leadership exchange relationships (Thibodeaux & Lowe, 1996; Thomas & Lankau, 2009), highlighting another way in which employees who lack such relationship are disadvantaged.

Supervisor–Subordinate Relationship Development

As noted earlier, supervisor–subordinate relationships are dynamic entities and much research has examined how and why such relationships develop. Much of this work is grounded in LMX theory and several factors influence the likelihood that a supervisor–subordinate relationship will develop into a leadership exchange (high-quality) relationship. Among these are the employee's job competence (e.g., Bauer & Green, 1996) and the supervisor's ability to train and help employees (e.g., Cogliser & Schriesheim, 2000). Employees with an internal, rather than external, locus of control are also more likely to enjoy a high-quality relationship with their supervisor, while supervisors with authoritarian personalities are more likely to maintain supervisory (low-quality) LMX relationships (Kinicki & Vecchio, 1994). High-quality LMX relationships are also more likely to develop between supervisors and subordinate who are demographically similar (e.g., Foley, Linnehan, Greenhaus & Weer, 2006).

In sum, the supervisor–subordinate relationship is central to individual experiences and organizational processes. As such, it has been a primary focus of management and communication scholars over the past several decades and continues to hold its place as a central topic. Communication scholars were important in moving this literature forward by identifying and emphasizing the role of communication in constituting these relationships, enhancing our understanding of supervisor–subordinate relationships as dynamic entities. While most employees have one supervisor and several peer coworkers, the latter have received comparatively less research attention. They are, however, crucial to the organizational process.

Peer Coworker Relationships

Peer coworker relationships are relationships between employees at the same hierarchical level in the organization, neither of whom have formal authority over the other. With the large focus on supervisor–subordinate relationships, peer relationships have received comparatively less research attention (Sias, 2014). However, given the number of peers an employee works with and the large amount of time peer coworkers generally spend with one another, they are an important workplace relationship type.

The Beginning: Alternatives to Formal Mentoring

Peer relationship research began with Kram and Isabella's (1985) study, which focused on identifying alternatives to formal mentors (i.e., supervisors) for employees. Their research revealed peer relationships as an important alternative to the traditional supervisor–subordinate mentoring relationship. Kram and Isabella (1985) identified three primary types of peer workplace relationships: information peers, collegial peers, and special peers. Most peer relationships are *information* peer relationships characterized by sharing superficial information regarding work-related topics, low levels of trust, and low levels self-disclosure (Odden & Sias, 1997). While, in general, all peer relationships begin as information peers, some develop into closer relationships characterized by friendship. Among these are *collegial* peers characterized by moderate levels of trust, self-disclosure, emotional support, career feedback, and friendship. Finally, some collegial peer relationships evolve into *special* peer relationships characterized by high levels of trust, self-disclosure, emotional support, career and personal feedback, and close friendship. According to Kram and Isabella (1985), informal mentoring is an important function of collegial and special peer relationships.

In addition to mentoring, peers are important sources of information and support for one another. Studies indicate, for example, that employees exchange higher-quality information with their special and collegial peers than with their information peers (Sias, 2005), and that employees tend to seek information more frequently from special peers than from information or collegial peers (Myers et al., 2018).

With respect to social support, Odden and Sias (1997) found that collegial peer relationships are related to cohesive workplace climates in which employees like one another and help each other. Sollitto and Myers (2015) found that the peer types vary in the extent to which they express lateral dissent (to employees at the same hierarchical level). Specifically, they found special and collegial peers engage in greater amounts of lateral dissent expression than do information peers, likely due to the higher levels of trust that characterize those relationships. Similarly, Myers, et al. (2018) found that employees believe it is more appropriate to seek task, appraisal/performance, and social information from special peers than from information peers.

Peers are also important sources of information and support for new employees during the organizational socialization process (see Chapter 8 for more information). Miller and Jablin (1991) found that coworkers help newcomers "learn the ropes," by teaching them the unwritten rules, providing insights into the unit's and the organization's distinctive cultural jargon and behavior patterns. Peers are also important sources of social support because they share a unique understanding of workplace issues that others (e.g., family and friends outside of work) cannot (Ray, 1993). Hence, when employees face work-related stress, they tend to seek social support from their coworkers first (Cahill & Sias, 1997).

Peer relationships can be challenging and associated with negative experiences and outcomes (Fritz & Omdahl, 2006). Peer relationships are sometimes sites of destructive communication such as incivility, harassment, and abuse of power (Lutgen-Sandvik, Namie, & Namie, 2009). Another form of destructive communication that occurs among peers is bullying. Bullying refers to several destructive communication practices including "verbal abuse; offensive conduct and behaviors (including nonverbal) that are threating, humiliating, or intimidating; or work interference and sabotage that prevent work from getting done" (Lutgen-Sandvik et al., 2009, p. 27). Workplace bullying can impair productivity, decrease worker commitment and satisfaction, harm the organization's image, and increase operating costs (Lutgen-Sandvik et al., 2009). Similarly, Duffy (2018) argues that bullying leads to decreased communication, which not only damages relationships, but also harms the work environment and culture.

Because of the amount of time they spend together, and their important roles as sources of information and social support, peers often develop into friendships. These unique relationships are important for individual attitudes and adjustment, performance, and organizational processes.

Workplace Friendships

As noted above, both supervisor–subordinate relationships and peer relationships can develop into friendships. Unlike formally assigned relationships, workplace friendships are informal, voluntary workplace relationships. Workplace friendships develop and thrive in all types of organizations, at all hierarchical levels, and between all types of employees (Bridge & Baxter, 1992; Sias, 2009). Although workplace friendships are not represented in an organization's formal structure and are not mandated by management, they are crucial to organizational functioning and employee experiences (Sias, 2009). As Lincoln and Miller (1979) noted early on, friendship networks are "systems for making decisions, mobilizing resources, concealing or transmitting information, and performing other functions closely allied with work behavior and interaction" (p. 196).

The Beginning: "Blended Relationships"

Little research examined workplace friendship explicitly until the 1990s. Bridge and Baxter (1992) were among the first to focus on workplace friendships. Their study conceptualized workplace friendship as a *blended* relationship—a relationship that blends the coworker role with the friend role. They argued that the two roles carry unique expectations that conflict with one another. Guided by dialectic theory (Baxter, 1988), Bridge and Baxter (1992) identified five dialectical tensions in blended relationships. Dialectical tensions are pairs of oppositional coexisting desires or pressures that characterize relationships. The *equality-inequality* tension refers to tensions between possible equality in friendship and inequality that characterizes workplace constraints and expectations. *Impartiality-favoritism* refers to tensions between organizational moral order without personal bias and friendship expectations of special treatment. The *openness-closedness* tension refers to expectations of openness and honesty as friends while honoring organizational expectations for confidentiality and caution about sharing information. The *autonomy-connection* tension refers to the advantages of contact for friends and the possibility that ongoing and daily contact among coworkers may provide too little autonomy or separation for the relationship parties. Last, *judgment-acceptance* refers to tensions between organizational requirements of critical evaluation process and mutual affirmation and acceptance as friends. These tensions threaten the stability of the relationship and, if not managed, the individuals may choose to terminate the friendship either by one of them quitting their job or by returning the relationship to "just coworkers" (Sias, Heath, Perry, Silva, & Fix, 2004).

Turning Point: Workplace Friendship

While Bridge and Baxter (1992) called scholars' attention to workplace friendship as a blended relationship, Sias and Cahill (1998) were among the first to study workplace friendship in its own right as a unique and uniquely important workplace relationship.

They noted that workplace friendships are unique in two ways. First, they are not imposed but *voluntary*. While supervisors and coworkers are typically assigned, employees voluntarily choose which of those they will befriend and voluntarily spend time with beyond what is required for task completion. Second, a *personalistic focus* characterizes workplace friendships. Workplace friends communicate with and understand one another as whole persons, not just role occupants.

Workplace friendship fulfills several important functions for the partners. These functions center primarily on information exchange and support. Workplace friendships are sites of quality information exchange. As Sias (2005) found, employees reported receiving higher-quality information (i.e., accurate, timely, relevant, and useful) from their workplace friends than from non-friend coworkers. Friends are also important sources of social support, providing advice and feedback regarding both work and personal problems and challenges. As Kahn (2001) explained, "what ideally occurs between coworkers is similar to what occurs between sophisticated adult friends when one turns to the other for support" (p. 265). Constructive workplace friendships also help employees cope with uncertainty, stress, and anxiety (Sias & Cahill, 1998). Similarly, Kruger, Bernstein, and Botman (1995) found workplace friends help one another to avoid burnout and emotional exhaustion.

Friendships can also be associated with negative outcomes. Sias and Cahill (1998), for example, found that high proportions of very close friendships in a workplace can be indicative of problems such as a problematic supervisor—the work-related problems draw coworkers into close friendships as they lean on one another for support. Methot, Lepine, Podsakoff, and Christian (2016) found that an employee's number of workplace friendships was positively associated with job performance, but also found that emotional exhaustion resulting from the difficulty of maintaining such relationships offset the effect on job performance. Similarly, Shah, Parker, and Waldstrom (2017) found a curvilinear relationship between friendships (i.e., multiplex relationships) and job performance, such that such relationships were associated with improved job performance to a point, after the excessive attention required to maintain relationships had a negative impact on performance.

Workplace Friendship Developmental Processes

Due to their important role in employee experiences and organizational processes, scholars have examined how and why employees become friends with one another. In the first study to examine workplace friendship development, Sias and Cahill (1998) identified two primary types of developmental factors. *Individual* factors derive from the individual employees and include personality, perceived similarity, sex, race, and important life events. *Contextual* factors derive from the workplace context and include physical proximity, shared tasks, work-related problems, and socializing. Personality, proximity, shared tasks, and similarity are more important to the initiation of a friendship (i.e., moving from coworkers to friends). Life events, work-related problems, and socializing appear to have greater influence in transitioning from friends to close or best friends.

Recent studies have reconsidered the role of physical proximity to friendship initiation, given the increased use of information and communication technologies (ICTs) and telecommuting. Sias, Pedersen, Gallagher, and Kopaneva (2012) examined the role of the developmental factors described above and found that, in contrast to Sias and

Cahill (1998), respondents rated physical proximity as the *least* important factor to initiate a workplace friendship by participants. Thus, new technologies that allow coworkers to communicate and work together virtually have removed the necessity of physical proximity and face-to-face interaction for friendship initiation.

Conceptualizing relationships as socially constructed, Sias and Cahill (1998) and Sias et al. (2004) examined how communication enabled relationship transitions from coworkers to friends and close friends. Specifically, they found that the transformation of a coworker relationship into a friendship is accomplished by increasingly frequent communication about a broader array of both work and personal topics, at increasingly intimate levels. The relationship partners also engage in less editing of their communication as the relationship grows closer. These results demonstrate how the coworkers communicatively produce the personalistic focus that characterizes friendship.

Although research emphasizes the positive side of workplace friendships (e.g., Feeley, Hwang, & Barnett, 2008; Song, 2006), as noted earlier, maintaining these relationships can be difficult and complex. When the partners are unable to manage these challenges, the friendship may deteriorate or even terminate. Sias et al. (2004) examined employees' narrative accounts of workplace friendship deterioration. They identified five primary causes of friendship deterioration. *Conflicting expectations* refer to the events in which coworkers behave differently than their partner expected (e.g., an employee may not support their coworker's proposal, but the coworker expects such support because they expect friends to support one another). This reflects the dialectical tensions that challenge workplace friendships that blend the coworker and friend role (e.g., Bridge & Baxter, 1992). A *problem personality* can result in friendship damage when one finds he or she can no longer deal with another's annoying personality trait. While life events can bring coworkers closer together (Sias & Cahill, 1998), when those life events *distract* the employee to the point that their coworkers have to pick up the slack, the friendship can be harmed. Given that trust is central to friendship development and maintenance, *betrayal* of trust is another threat to workplace friendship. Finally, a workplace friendship may deteriorate if one of the relationship partners is *promoted* to a position of formal authority over the other.

Again conceptualizing relationships as socially constructed, Sias et al. (2004) and Sias and Perry (2004) examined strategies individuals use to communicatively accomplish the deterioration of a workplace friendship. The most commonly used strategy is *depersonalization*, which refers to limiting communication to work-related topics only. Recall that a personalistic focus characterizes workplace friendship and communicating about non-work topics helps coworkers develop friendships (Sias & Cahill, 1998). The depersonalization strategy effectively removes the relationship's personalistic focus, while enabling the employees to communicate as needed for task completion. Another form of depersonalization is *avoidance*. However, this strategy involves avoiding any contact with the coworker, not just contact unrelated to work. This is effective for ending the friendship, but less functional for the employees and the organization because it harms the coworkers' ability to accomplish their tasks. Individuals may also use *cost escalation* to end the friendship. *Cost escalation* involves intentional negative acts toward the coworker such as criticism, snubbing, or talking to them in a condescending tone. Finally, individuals may address the issue *directly* with their coworker, explaining that they want to end the friendship or decrease the level of closeness in the relationship.

In sum, workplace friendship research has grown since the early 1990s. Studies have identified the unique nature of these relationships and their impact on individual experiences and organizational processes. Communication research has contributed to this body of research by conceptualizing workplace friendship as socially constructed, and developing our understanding of the important and constitutive role of communication in workplace friendship dynamics. As noted earlier, workplace friendships are informal and voluntary relationships. We turn next to another type of informal and voluntary workplace relationship—the romantic relationship.

Romantic Workplace Relationships

In a 2013 Society for Human Resource Management (SHRM) survey on workplace romantic relationship, 43 percent of human resource professionals reported current incidences of romance in their organization, and 25 percent of employees reported they are currently or have been involved in a workplace romance. As this survey indicates, workplace romantic relationships are not unusual. However, relative to the other relationships we address in this chapter, they have received little attention from organizational communication scholars (Sias, 2009). Romantic workplace relationship research was spurred into action in the 1970s when feminist movements led to an increase of women workers in U.S. organizations, leading to an increase in workplace romantic relationships (Sias, 2014).

Pierce, Byrne, and Aguinis (1996) defined a workplace romantic relationship as "any relationship between two members of the same organization that entails mutual attraction" (p. 6). (Hence, in this literature, any relationship with a sexual component is defined as romantic.) Similar to workplace friendship, romantic relationships are also voluntary and personalistic in nature. Compared to other relationships in workplace, romantic relationships are also characterized by their emotional and affective nature, incorporating love, affection, and intimacy. Thus, romantic workplace relationships are unique in that they are emotional, physiological, and consensual (Sias, 2009). The *consensual nature* of these relationships distinguishes them from sexual harassment. There has been a great deal of research on sexual harassment (e.g., Burke & McKeen, 1992; Clair, 1993; Dougherty & Hode, 2016; Dougherty & Smythe, 2004; also see Chapter 13). However, here we focus on consensual romantic relationships.

Motives, Types, and Consequences

Early research centered on identifying the motives and types of workplace romantic relationships. Quinn (1977) identified three primary motives for engaging in a romantic relationship at work. The *job motive* refers to situations in which individuals engage in a romantic relationship for utilitarian reasons including job advancement and security, financial rewards (e.g., promotion, bonuses), and more efficient or easier tasks. The *ego motive* reflects personal desire such as excitement, ego gratification, and adventure. Finally, the *love motive* reflects genuine affection, respect, love and companionship. Mainiero and Jones (2013, p. 188) argued "most romantic relationships at work are sincere, love-motivated, and of the long-term companionate variety as opposed to the short-lived flings or job-motivated utilitarian relationships."

Quinn (1977) found that different motives lead to different types of romantic relationships. Partners motivated by ego gratification and adventure tend to form *fling* relationships. Those who enter a romantic relationship due to the love motive form *companionate love* relationships. And when one partner (usually male) is motivated by ego gratification and the other engages in the relationship due to the job motive, the partners form a *utilitarian* relationship. As Sias (2009, p. 134) noted, this relationship type "represents the 'sleeping up the ladder' stereotype that has persisted over the years."

Romantic workplace relationships have a number of consequences for relationship partners and their coworkers. Much research in this area centers on how coworkers perceive the romantic relationship of others. This research indicates that when employees become aware of a romantic relationship between coworkers, that relationship becomes a topic of gossip, as the employees interpret and make attributions about the romance, particularly with respect to the relationship partners' motives (Michelson & Mouly, 2000). According to Dillard (1987), employees tend to make negative attributions about relationships that they perceive were formed for job motives. In contrast, romances motivated by love tend to generate more positive attributions. An important factor in coworker perceptions of a romantic relationship is whether or the relationship is between employees of same or different hierarchical status. Specifically, employees tend to hold negative attitudes toward hierarchical romances (i.e., between supervisor and subordinate employee) (Jones, 1999). Consistent with this, while not all organizations have policies forbidding workplace romance, those that do tend to forbid hierarchical romantic relationships, but are more lenient regarding non-hierarchical relationships (Wilson, Filosa, & Fennel, 2003).

Engaging in a workplace romance can have consequences for the relationship partners as well. Some studies indicate that employees are happier, have higher job satisfaction, and better motivation when they are in a romantic workplace relationship (Pierce et al., 1996; Dillard & Broetzmann, 1989; Mainiero, 1989). This may result from looking forward to seeing one another, as well as putting in extra effort to avoid coworker perceptions that the relationship may hinder the partners' performance (Sias, 2009). Of course, the consequences depend in part of the nature of the relationship. An unhappy or unsatisfying relationship can, instead, harm the partners' morale, satisfaction, and performance (Pierce et al., 1996).

Romantic Workplace Relationship Development

Studies of romantic relationship development have focused on identifying factors that encourage relational development. As Sias (2009), noted, such research tends to conceptualize the organization as an "incubator" in which romantic relationships form and grow. Similar to the other voluntary relationship discussed in this chapter—friendship—physical proximity is a primary influence on the initiation and development of a romantic workplace relationship; Quinn (1977) identified three types. *Geographical proximity* refers to individuals' physical closeness to one another in work spaces or office. *Ongoing work requirement proximity* refers to proximity resulting from various work-related activities such as employees working together on projects, business trips, and other requirements of the job that bring the individuals close to one another. Finally, some situations cause *occasional contact* with one another via riding the elevator together or running into each other in different locations other than work spaces because they work in the same organization.

Attitude similarity is an important contributor to liking that can lead to workplace romance (Sias, 2009). This factor reflects the homophily principle which refers to people being attracted to others who are similar to them (i.e., birds of a feather flock together). Pierce et al. (1996) argue that the homophily principle helps explain why romantic relationships are likely to develop in organizations because hiring and selection processes tend to filter in individuals with similar attitudes and interests and filter out those who are dissimilar to the origination's general population.

The organizational *culture* or *climate* can also influence romantic relationship development. For instance, studies suggest that workplace romances are more likely to form in "liberal" organizations where people are more fast-paced, action-oriented, and dynamic than in in "conservative" organizations, where such relationships tend to be discouraged (Mainiero, 1989; Pierce et al., 1996). Likewise, Mano and Gabriel (2006) examined workplace romantic relationships in "cold" and "hot" organizational climates. Cold climates are characterized by impersonal, formal organizational structures, while hot climates involve an emphasis on employees' physical appearance. They found that employees who work in hot workplace climates tend to talk more about romantic stories in the workplace with more passion compared to those in cold climates.

Communication and romantic relationship development. As noted earlier, organizational communication scholars have paid relatively little attention to romantic workplace relationships. Thus, much is unknown about the role of communication in romantic relationship dynamics. Along these lines, Yelvington (1996) identified flirting as key to romance initiation. They note that flirting is an indirect behavior and the initiator risks the communication being misinterpreted as sexual harassment and/or risks rejection. Nonetheless, flirting tends to be "the first step in the initiation of a romantic relationship" (Sias, 2009, p. 135).

Scholars have also examined the role of information and communication technology (ICT) in workplace romantic relationships. Hovick, Meyers, and Timmerman (2003), for example, found that employees tend to rely on face-to-face interaction to initiate a romantic relationships, then rely more on email or other technologies as the relationship develops. More recently, Cowan and Horan's (2014) model suggests the important role of technology in the initiation, maintenance, and termination of workplace romantic relationships. They found employees tend to use ICT differently at the various stages. For example, employees tended to avoid ICT during initiation and maintenance due to privacy concerns, but used ICT to terminate the relationship.

In sum, romantic relationships are common in organizations and, like the other relationships addressed in this chapter, play an important role in both employee experiences and organizational processes. Relative to other relationship types, however, they have received scant attention. In particular, we know little about the role of communication in romantic workplace relationships including the communication patterns that characterize romantic relationships and that characterize interaction between the partners and their coworkers. We also know little about how communication functions in romantic relationship initiation, development, and deterioration.

Approach to Communication

We now turn to a consideration of how organizational relationships literature approaches communication. Organizational communication as a discipline began, in part, with the study of workplace relationships; in particular, supervisor–subordinate relationships. As noted earlier, the goal was to identify supervisory practices that led to more effective organizational functioning (Redding, 1985). At that time, and consistent with other social science disciplines, research was grounded in a transmission model of communication, focusing largely on messages and message exchange. Jablin's (1979) review of the literature, for example, revealed that supervisor–subordinate communication research centered on identifying message exchange patterns such as openness in message sending and receiving, upward distortion (i.e., an employee's propensity to misrepresent information sent upward or withhold information from their supervisor), and semantic information distance (the extent to which supervisor and employees understanding of the employee's role responsibilities and knowledge are congruent). Later, Kram and Isabella's (1985) introduction of peer relationships to the literature examined message exchange between peers, particularly mentoring and advice-giving messages.

The interpretive turn (Putnam & Pacanowsky, 1983) introduced a different perspective on communication and social reality that, in turn, led to a shift in our understanding of workplace relationships. As noted in Chapter 2, the interpretive turn was grounded in a constructionist perspective that conceptualized social reality as socially constructed. This laid the foundation for constitutive approaches to communication and organizations. (See Chapter 3 for more on CCO theory.) At this point, organizational communication scholars began focusing on relationship dynamics, examining how workplace relationships are communicatively created, maintained, and transformed. Fairhurst and Chandler's (1989) study of LMX relationships was grounded in such an approach, conceptualizing leader–member (i.e., supervisor–subordinate) relationships as socially constructed. That study and others that followed (e.g., Fairhurst, 1993; Sias & Cahill, 1998) centered on communication not as message exchange in the context of relationships, but as constitutive of relationships themselves.

Conceptualizing workplace relationships as dynamic communicative entities, Bridge and Baxter (1992) studied the role of communication in the dynamic management of dialectical tensions in "blended" relationships that combine work and friend roles. Sias and colleagues followed suit with respect to peer relationships. Sias and Cahill (1998), for example, examined how friendship development is accomplished communicatively. Sias et al. (2004) and Sias and Perry (2004) similarly studied the constitutive role of communication in friendship deterioration. Finally, Sias et al. (2012) conceptualized workplace relationships as dynamic even in times of stability, demonstrating how relationship maintenance requires continual communication to constitute a relationship at a desired level of closeness. While these studies were not explicitly grounded in CCO theory, nor did they often use the terms *constituted* or *constitutive*, their fundamental assumptions were squarely in the constitutive camp.

Approach to Organization

As micro-level phenomena, it is not surprising that the bulk of workplace relationship uses an O_1 approach to organizations. As noted in Chapter 1 of this book, O_1 research "examines interaction processes by which members arrange themselves and manage their joint activities" (p. XX).

Although the vast majority of workplace relationships center on dyadic interpersonal relationships, recent research on relationship networks has broadened our understanding of the role of workplace relationships in broader organizational structure, processes, and practices. Such studies represent an O_2 approach to organizations, i.e., "the state of a social collective's coordination/order. Organizational communication theory and research might explicate the structuring of said coordination" (Chapter 1, p. 7). Feeley et al.'s (2008) study of peer relationship networks, for example, examines the broader network of workplace friendships and how such friendship networks are linked to turnover (an organization outcome). Shah et al. (2017) demonstrated how the nature of peer relationships (i.e., uniplex or multiplex) embedded in organization networks was linked to the organization's performance and capacity for creativity. Such studies illuminate the social order of an organization and the role of relationships in coordinating activities to maintain social order. (For more on networks, see Chapter 9.)

Workplace relationship research that uses a constitutive/social construction approach tends to explicitly emphasize the examination a mutually constitutive communication-organization (C-O) dynamic, as described in Chapter 1. That is, communication constitutes relationships and those relationship structures enable and constrain communication. For example, peer relationships are communicatively transformed into a friendship (via more personal, intimate, and frequent communication). Once the relationship becomes a friendship, the structures that characterize friendship (e.g., personalistic focus, openness, etc.) enable and constrain partner communication. The friendship structure, for instance, enables open discussion of broad topics and at the same time constrains employees from withholding information from one another that the organization prohibits them from sharing. This is just one example of the C-O dynamic as explicated in organizational relationship research.

Cultural Implications

Early management and organizational communication theories and research centered on formal communication and formal reporting relationships. In fact, classical theories (e.g., bureaucracy, administrative management, and scientific management; see Chapter 5) intentionally excluded informal relationships and informal communication from their design of organizational processes. The focus on interpersonal relationships and informal relationships such as friendship was accompanied by cultural changes in business practices (compare, for example, IBM in the 1960s to Google today). Peer relationships and friendships are now central to an organization's culture and climate, with many organizations becoming less authority-centered and instead more decentralized. (See Chapter 7 for more on decentralization.)

Despite globalization and increased multinational businesses (see Chapter 20), workplace relationship research has barely touched on cultural and intercultural concerns. Intercultural approaches to workplace relationships are few and far between. In one exception, Sergeant and Frenkel (1998) found that expatriate managers working with Chinese employees in an American subsidiary in China had difficulties developing high-quality LMX relationships due, in part, to Chinese cultural norms of respect for hierarchy and authority, which hindered the open communication, autonomy, and role negotiation that constitutes leadership exchange relationships. Although not focused on workplace relationships explicitly, Stage's (1999) study of American subsidiaries in Thailand found that expatriate and Thai employees rarely formed close friendships with one another due to cultural differences and differing time horizons (i.e., Thai employees had a long-term view of working in the subsidiary, while expatriates had a short-term view of their assignments). (See Chapter 14 for more on difference and diversity.)

Workplace relationship research has also largely ignored other forms of difference. For example, as Sias (2014) noted, organizations are becoming increasingly populated by multiple generations, each with different cultural expectations regarding communication and relationships. Yet studies of intergenerational workplace relationships are nonexistent. Similarly, few scholars have addressed links between sexual orientation and workplace relationships. An exception is Rumens (2013) who examined the important role of workplace friendship as a site of social support for gay male employees.

Conclusion

As this overview demonstrates, workplace relationships matter. The field of organizational communication was founded on the study of supervisor–subordinate communication, and scholars over the following decades recognized workplace relationships' central role in organizations. As noted earlier, organizations are fundamentally systems of relationships. There is still much to learn, however. We encourage future scholars to examine workplace relationships in new and innovative ways, such as studies of relationships as they relate to O_2 and O_3 conceptualizations of organizations. Such studies would address, for example, how relationships structure the broader organization (O_2) and how relationships constitute organizations as entities (O_3). We also encourage studies that incorporate culture in all its forms (e.g., organizational culture, occupational culture, national culture, as well as demographic cultural features such as race, gender, and sexual orientation, as well as their intersections).

Recommended Supplementary Readings

Fritz, J. M. H., & Omdahl, B. L. (2006). *Problematic relationships in the workplace*. New York: Peter Lang.

A thorough resource addressing the "dark side" of workplace relationships, covering cause and outcomes of negative workplace relationships, as well as how individuals experience such relationships.

Graen, G. B., & Uhl-Bien, M. (1995). Relationship-based approach to leadership: Development of a leader–member exchange (LMX) theory of leadership over 25 years—applying a multi-level multi-domain perspective. *Leadership Quarterly*, 62(2), 219–247.

An excellent review of the first 25 years of LMX theory development.

Jablin, F. M. (1979). Superior–subordinate communication: The state of the art. *Psychological Bulletin*, 86(6), 1201–1222.

This is a classic article in the field of organizational communication, summarizing supervisor–subordinate communication research.

Kahn, W. A. (2001). Holding environments at work. *Journal of Applied Behavioral Science*, 37(3), 260–279.

An interesting conceptualization of workplace relationships as sites of social support.

Omdahl, B. L., & Harden Fritz, J. M. (2012). *Problematic relationships in the workplace: Volume 2*. New York: Peter Lang.

A follow-up to Fritz and Omdahl (2006) referenced above.

Rumens, N. (2013). *Queer company: The role and meaning of friendship in gay men's work lives*. London: Routledge.

An important book covering an under-studied area in organizational communication/management research.

Rumens, N. (2017). Researching workplace friendships: Drawing insights from the sociology of friendship. *Journal of Social and Personal Relationships*, 34(8), 1149–1167.

A useful overview of workplace friendship research and agenda for future research examining workplace friendship from a sociological perspective.

Important Concepts: Define and Discuss

Blended relationship
Bullying
Information, collegial, and special peers
Mentoring
Personalistic focus
Leader–member exchange theory

Discussion Questions

1. Reflect on a current or past workplace friendship. What dialectical tensions did you experience and how did you manage them?
2. How might social media influence an employee's various workplace relationships?
3. Today's organizations are increasingly populated by employees from several different generations (e.g., Z generation, millennials, late and early baby boomers, etc.). How might generational differences impact coworker communication and workplace relationships?
4. Reflect on your current or most recent job. How would you characterize your relationship with your supervisor (i.e., supervisory exchange or leadership exchange)? Explain your choice.

Practitioners' Corner

As this chapter demonstrates, workplace relationships matter. Employees are happier, more motivated, and more successful when they have functional high-quality relationships at work. Organizations reap many rewards from such relationships including lower turnover and better performance. Practitioners would be wise to recognize the important role workplace relationships play in organizational practices and processes and ensure the work environment is conducive and supportive of functional relationships.

Key to creating such an environment is understanding how and why relationships develop and deteriorate. LMX theory and research indicates the important of high-quality (leadership exchange) relationships and indicates that supervisors tend to form such relationships with some, but not all, of their direct reports. However, as Graen and Uhl-Bien (1995) argued, there is no reason such relationships should be limited and supervisors should make efforts to forge and maintain leadership exchange relationships with all employees. Research on LMX relational development provides advice on how to do so. First, employee competence is key to leadership exchanges. To warrant the trust and autonomy that characterizes such relationships, employees must demonstrate their ability and initiative. Hiring competent and responsible individuals, therefore, is the first step to a quality LMX relationship. The supervisor's ability to mentor, train, and help employees is also important. Managers should recognize their role as mentor and coach, rather than simply supervisor, to help employees, both newly hired and veterans, with their professional development. Research also indicates that authoritarianism hinders LMX development. Supervisors must recognize that leadership exchange relationships require the sharing of power and authority with employees. Employees can also enable development of such relationships by demonstrating competence and responsibility and being open in their communication and information-sharing with their manager.

Practitioners can also encourage the development of quality relationships among the employees themselves. HR professionals and managers should work collaboratively to provide opportunities for the kinds of interaction among coworkers that foster the development of collegial relationships. Managers can, and should, be aware of relationship quality among their employees, foster good quality communication, and find ways to allow those good relationships to support organizational goals (and vice versa). Providing employees with opportunities to work together on tasks and collaborate with one another can help the coworkers initiate and maintain friendships. It is also important to provide opportunities for coworker interaction via physical proximity or virtual media such as information communication technologies and social networking systems.

Finally, we note that workplace romantic relationships are a fact of life. Despite their challenges and potential to disrupt organizational processes, they can also contribute to employee morale and performance. Practitioners are encouraged to review existing policies regarding workplace romance to ensure they are appropriate and effective with respect to differentiating between workplace romance and sexual harassment. This is especially important given recent societal changes spurred by the #MeToo movement. All employees should receive regular training in the organization's sexual harassment and consensual relationship policies, including mandatory reporting and disclosure, respectively. Employees who are unsure of policies are less likely to report or disclose, leaving the organization vulnerable.

References

Ashford, S. J. (1993). The feedback environment: An exploratory study of cue use. *Journal of Organizational Behavior, 14*(3), 201–225. doi:10.1002/job.4030140302.

Bauer, T. N., & Green, S. G. (1996). Development of leader–member exchange: A longitudinal test. *Academy of Management Journal, 39*(6), 1538–1567. doi:10.5465/257068.

Baxter, L. (1988). A dialectical perspective on communication strategies in relationship development. In S. Duck (Ed.), *Handbook of personal relationships* (pp. 257–273). New York, NY: John Wiley & Sons.

Blake, R., & Mouton, J. (1964). *The managerial grid*. Houston, TX: Gulf.

Bridge, K., & Baxter, L. A. (1992). Blended relationships: Friends as work associates. *Western Journal of Communication, 56*(3), 200-225. doi:10.1080/10570319209374414.

Burke, R. J., & McKeen, C. A. (1992). Social-sexual behaviours at work: Experiences of managerial. *Women in Management Review, 7*(3), 22–31. doi:10.1108/09649429210011354.

Cahill, D. J., & Sias, P. M. (1997). The perceived social costs and importance of seeking emotional support in the workplace: Gender differences and similarities. *Communication Research Reports, 14*(2), 231–240. doi:10.1080/08824099709388665.

Clair, R. P. (1993). The bureaucratization, commodification, and privatization of sexual harassment through institutional discourse: A study of the Big Ten universities. *Management Communication Quarterly, 7*(2), 123–157. doi:10.1177/0893318993007002001.

Cogliser, C. C., & Schriesheim, C. A. (2000). Exploring work unit context and leader–member exchange: A multi-level perspective. *Journal of Organizational Behavior, 21*(5), 487–511. doi:10.1002/1099-1379(200008)21:5%3C487::AID-JOB57%3E3.0.CO;2-P.

Cowan, R., & Horan, S. (2014). Love at the office? Understanding workplace romance disclosures and reactions from the coworker perspective. *Western Journal of Communication, 78*(2), 238–253. doi:10.1080/10570314.2013.866688.

Dillard, D. (1987). Money as an institution of capitalism. *Journal of Economic Issues, 21*(4), 1623–1647. doi:10.1080/00213624.1987.11504717.

Dillard, J. P., & Broetzmann, S. M. (1989). Romantic relationships at work: Perceived changes in job-related behaviors as a function of participant's motive, partner's motive, and gender. *Journal of Applied Social Psychology, 19*(2), 93–110. doi:10.1111/j.1559-1816.1989.tb00047.x.

Dougherty, D. S., & Hode, M. G. (2016). Binary logics and the discursive interpretation of organizational policy: Making meaning of sexual harassment policy. *Human Relations, 69*(8), 1729–1755. doi:10.1177/0018726715624956.

Dougherty, D. S., & Smythe, M. J. (2004). Sensemaking, organizational culture, and sexual harassment. *Journal of Applied Communication Research, 32*(4), 293–317. doi:10.1080/0090988042000275998.

Duffy, M. (2018). The psychosocial impact of workplace bullying and mobbing on targets. In M. Duffy & D. C. Yamada (Eds.), *Workplace bullying and mobbing in the United States* (Vol. 1, pp. 131–150). Santa Barbara, CA: ABC-CLIO.

Fairhurst, G. T. (1993). The leader–member exchange patterns of women leaders in industry: A discourse analysis. *Communications Monographs, 60*(4), 321–351. doi:10.1080/03637759309376316.

Fairhurst, G. T., & Chandler, T. A. (1989). Social structure in leader–member interaction. *Communication Monographs, 56*(3), 215–239. doi:10.1080/03637758909390261.

Fedor, D. B. (1991). Recipient responses to performance feedback: A proposed model and its implications. In G. R. Ferris & K. M. Rowland (Eds.), *Research in personnel and human resources management* (Vol. 9, pp. 73–120). Greenwich, CT: JAI.

Feeley, T. H., Hwang, J., & Barnett, G. A. (2008). Predicting employee turnover from friendship networks. *Journal of Applied Communication Research, 36*(1), 56–73. doi:10.1080/00909880701799790

Fix, B., & Sias, P. M. (2006). Person-centered communication, leader-member exchange, and employee job satisfaction. *Communication Research Reports, 23*(1), 35–44. doi:10.1080/17464090500535855.

Foley, S., Linnehan, F., Greenhaus, J. H., & Weer, C. H. (2006). The impact of gender similarity, racial similarity, and work culture on family-supportive supervision. *Group & Organization Management, 31*(4), 420–441. doi:10.1177/1059601106286884.

Fritz, J. M. H., & Omdahl, B. L. (2006). *Problematic relationships in the workplace*. New York: Peter Lang.

Ghiselli, E. E. (1963). Intelligence and managerial success. *Psychological Reports, 12*(3), 898. doi:10.2466/pr0.1963.12.3.898.

Graen, G. B., & Cashman, J. F. (1975). A role-making model of leadership in formal organizations: A developmental approach. In J. G. Hunt & L. L. Hunt (Eds.), *Leadership frontiers* (pp. 143–165). Kent, OH: Kent State University Press.

Graen, G. B., & Scandura, T. (1987). Toward a psychology of dyadic organizing. In B. Staw & L. L. Cummings (Eds.), *Research in organizational behavior* (Vol. 9, pp. 175–208). Greenwich, CT: JAI.

Graen, G. B., & Uhl-Bien, M. (1995). Relationship-based approach to leadership: Development of a leader-member exchange (LMX) theory of leadership over 25 years – Applying a multi-level multi-domain perspective. *Leadership Quarterly, 6*(2), 219-247. doi:10.1016/1048-9843(95)90036-5

Hersey, P., & Blanchard, K. H. (1982). *Management of organizational behavior* (4th ed.). Englewood Cliffs, NJ: Prentice Hall.

Hovick, S. R. A., Meyers, R. A., & Timmerman, E. (2003). E-mail communication in workplace romantic relationships. *Communication Studies, 54*(4), 468–482. doi:10.1080/10510970309363304.

Jablin, F. M. (1979). Superior–subordinate communication: The state of the art. *Psychological Bulletin, 86*(6), 1201–1222. doi:10.1037/0033-2909.86.6.1201.

Jablin, F. M. (2001). Organizational entry, assimilation, and disengagement/exit. In F. M. Jablin & L. L. Putnam (Eds.), *The new handbook of organizational communication: Advances in theory, research, and methods* (pp. 732–818). Thousand Oaks, CA: SAGE.

Jian, G., & Dalisay, F. (2017). Conversation at work: The effects of leader–member conversational quality. *Communication Research*, 44(2), 177–197. doi:10.1177/0093650214565924.

Jones, G. E. (1999). Hierarchical workplace romance: An experimental examination of team member perceptions. *Journal of Organizational Behavior*, 20(7), 1057–1072. doi:10.1002/(SICI)1099-1379(199912)20:7≤1057::AID-JOB956≥3.0.CO;2-O.

Kahn, W. A. (2001). Holding environments at work. *The Journal of Applied Behavioral Science*, 37 (3), 260–279. doi:10.1177/0021886301373001.

Keyton, J. (2017). Communication in organizations. *Annual Review of Organizational Psychology and Organizational Behavior*, 4, 501–526. doi:10.1146/annurev-op-04-030217-100001.

Kinicki, A. J., & Vecchio, R. P. (1994). Influences on the quality of supervisor–subordinate relations: The role of time-pressure, organizational commitment, and locus of control. *Journal of Organizational Behavior*, 15(1), 75–82. doi:10.1002/job.4030150108.

Kram, K. E., & Isabella, L. A. (1985). Mentoring alternatives: The role of peer relationships in career development. *Academy of Management Journal*, 28(1), 110–132. doi:10.2307/256064.

Kruger, L. J., Bernstein, G., & Botman, H. (1995). The relationship between team friendships and burnout among residential counselors. *The Journal of Social Psychology*, 135(2), 191–201. doi:10.1080/00224545.1995.9711423.

Lam, L. W., Peng, K. Z., Wong, C., & Lau, D. C. (2017). Is more feedback seeking always better? Leader–member exchange moderates the relationship between feedback-seeking behavior and performance. *Journal of Management*, 43(7), 2195–2217. doi:10.1177/0149206315581661.

Lincoln, J. R., & Miller, J. (1979). Work and friendship ties in organizations: A comparative analysis of relational networks. *Administrative Science Quarterly*, 24(2), 181–199. doi:10.2307/2392493.

Lutgen-Sandvik, P., Namie, G., & Namie, R. (2009). Workplace bullying: Causes, consequences, and corrections. In P. Lutgen-Sandvik & B. D. Sypher (Eds.), *Destructive organizational communication: Processes, consequences, and constructive ways of organizing* (pp. 27–52). New York, NY: Routledge.

Mainiero, L. A. (1989). *Office romance: Love, power and sex in the workplace*. New York, NY: Rawson Associates.

Mainiero, L. A., & Jones, K. J. (2013). Sexual harassment versus workplace romance: Social media spillover and textual harassment in the workplace. *Academy of Management Perspectives*, 27(3), 187–203. doi:10.5465/amp.2012.0031.

Mano, R., & Gabriel, Y. (2006) Workplace romances in cold and hot organizational climates: The experience of Israel and Taiwan. *Human Relations*, 59(1), 7–35. doi:10.1177/0018726706062739.

Methot, J. R., Lepine, J. A., Podsakoff, N. P., & Christian, J. S. (2016). Are workplace friendships a mixed blessing? Exploring tradeoffs of multiplex relationships and their associations with job performance. *Personnel Psychology*, 69(2), 311–355. doi:10.1111/peps.12109.

Michelson, G., & Mouly, S. (2000). Rumour and gossip in organisations: A conceptual study. *Management Decision*, 38(5), 339–346. doi:10.1108/00251740010340508.

Michael, J. H., Leschinsky, R., & Gagnon, M. A. (2006). Production employee performance at a furniture manufacturer: The importance of supportive supervisors. *Forest Products Journal*, 56 (6), 19–24.

Miller, V. D., & Jablin, F. M. (1991). Information seeking during organizational entry: Influences, tactics, and a model of the process. *The Academy of Management Review*, 16(1), 92–120. doi:10.5465/AMR.1991.4278997.

Myers, S. A., Cranmer, G. A., Goldman, Z. W., Sollitto, M., Gillen, H. G., & Ball, H. (2018). Differences in information seeking among organizational peers: Perceptions of appropriateness, importance, and frequency. *International Journal of Business Communication*, 55(1), 1–14. doi:10.1177/2329488415573928.

Odden, C. M., & Sias, P. M. (1997). Peer communication relationships and psychological climate. *Communication Quarterly, 45*(3), 153–166. doi:10.1080/01463379709370058.

Putnam, L.L., & Pacanowsky, M.E. (1983). *Communication and organizations.* Beverly Hills, CA: SAGE.

Pierce, C. A., Byrne, D., & Aguinis, H. (1996). Attraction in organizations: A model of workplace romance. *Journal of Organizational Behavior, 17*(1), 5–32. doi:10.1002/(SICI)1099-1379-(199601)17:13.0.CO;2-E.

Quinn, R. E. (1977). Coping with cupid: The formation, impact, and management of romantic relationships in organizations. *Administrative Science Quarterly, 22*(1), 30–45. doi:10.2307/2391744.

Ragins, B. R., & Scandura, T. A. (1997). The way we were: Gender and the termination of mentoring relationships. *Journal of Applied Psychology, 82*(6), 945–953. doi:10.1037/0021-9010.82.6.945.

Ramaswami, S. N., Srinivasan, S., & Gorton, S. A. (1997). Information asymmetry between salesperson and supervisor: Postulates from agency and social exchange theories. *Personal Selling and Sales Management, 17*(3), 29-51. doi:10.1080/08853134.1997.10754098.

Ray, E. B. (1993). When the links become chains: Considering dysfunctions of supportive communication in the workplace. *Communication Monographs, 60*(1), 106–111. doi:10.1080/03637759309376301.

Redding, C. W. (1985). Stumbling toward an identity: The emergence of organizational communication: Past and present tenses. In R. D. McPhee & P. K. Tompkins (Eds.), *Organizational communication: Traditional themes and new directions* (pp. 15–54). Newbury Park, CA: SAGE.

Rumens, N. (2013). *Queer company: The role and meaning of friendship in gay men's work lives.* London: Routledge.

Sergeant, A., & Frenkel, S. (1998). Managing people in China: Perceptions of expatriate managers. *Journal of World Business, 33*(1), 17–34. doi:10.1016/S1090-9516(98)80002-3.

Shah, N. P., Parker, A., & Waldstrom, C. (2017). Examining the overlap: Individual performance benefits of multiplex relationships. *Management Communication Quarterly, 31*(1), 5–38. doi:10.1177/0893318916647528.

Sias, P. M. (1996). Constructing perceptions of differential treatment: An analysis of coworker discourse. *Communication Monographs, 63*(2), 171–187.

Sias, P. M. (2005). Workplace relationship quality and employee information experiences. *Communication Studies, 56*(4), 375–395. doi:10.1080/10510970500319450.

Sias, P. M. (2009). *Organizing relationships: Traditional and emerging perspectives on workplace relationships.* Thousand Oaks, CA: SAGE. doi:10.1080/03637759609376385.

Sias, P. M. (2014). Workplace relationships. In L. L. Putnam & D. K. Mumby (Eds.), *The SAGE handbook of organizational communication: Advances in theory, research, and methods* (3rd ed., pp. 375–399). Thousand Oaks, CA: SAGE.

Sias, P. M., & Cahill, D. J. (1998). From coworkers to friends: The development of peer friendships in the workplace. *Western Journal of Communication, 62*(3), 273–299. doi:10.1080/10570319809374611.

Sias, P. M., Heath, R. G., Perry, T., Silva, D., & Fix, B. (2004). Narratives of workplace friendship deterioration. *Journal of Social and Personal Relationships, 21*(3), 321–340. doi:10.1177/0265407504042835.

Sias, P. M., Krone, K. J., & Jablin, F. M. (2002). An ecological systems perspective on workplace relationships. In M. L. Knapp & J. Daly (Eds.), *Handbook of interpersonal communication* (3rd ed., pp. 615–642). Thousand Oaks, CA: SAGE.

Sias, P. M., Pederson, H., Gallagher, E. B., & Kopaneva, I. (2012). Workplace friendship in the electronically connected organization. *Human Communication Research, 38*(3), 253–279. doi:10.1111/j.1468-2958.2012.01428.x.

Sias, P. M., & Perry, T. (2004). Disengaging from workplace relationships: A research note. *Human Communication Research, 30*(4), 589–602. doi:10.1111/j.1468-2958.2004.tb00746.x.

Society of Human Resource Management. (2013). *SHRM survey findings: Workplace romances*. Retrieved from www.shrm.org/hr-today/trends-and-forecasting/research-and-surveys/pages/shrm-workplace-romance-findings.aspx.

Sollitto, M., & Myers, S. A. (2015). Peer coworker relationships: Influences on the expression of lateral dissent. *Communication Reports, 28*(1), 36–47. doi:10.1080/08934215.2014.925569.

Song, H. (2006). Workplace friendship and employees' productivity: LMX theory and the case of the Seoul City Government. *International Review of Public Administration, 11*(1), 47–58. doi:10.1080/12294659.2006.10805077.

Stage, C.W. (1999). Negotiating organizational communication cultures in American subsidiaries doing business in Thailand. *Management Communication Quarterly, 13*(2), 245–280. doi:10.1177/0893318999132003.

Steelman, L. A., & Rutkowski, K. A. (2004). Moderators of employee reactions to negative feedback. *Journal of Managerial Psychology, 19*(1), 6–18. doi:10.1108/02683940410520637.

Thibodeaux, H. F., & Lowe, R. H. (1996). Convergence of leader–member exchange and mentoring: An investigation of social influence patterns. *Journal of Social Behavior and Personality, 11*(1), 97–114.

Thomas, C. H., & Lankau, M. J. (2009). Preventing burnout: The effects of LMX and mentoring on socialization, role stress, and burnout. *Human Resource Management, 48*(3), 417–432. doi:10.1002/hrm.20288.

Turban, D. B., Jones, A. P., & Rozelle, R. M. (1990). Influences of supervisor liking of a subordinate and the reward context on the treatment and evaluation of that subordinate. *Motivation and Emotion, 14*(3), 215–233.

Wheatley, M. (1999). *Leadership and the new science: Discovering order in a chaotic world* (2nd ed). San Francisco, CA: Berrett-Koehler Publishers.

Wilson, R. J., Filosa, C., & Fennel, A. (2003). Romantic relationships at work: Does privacy trump the dating police? *Defence Counsel Journal, 70*(1), 78–88.

Yelvington, K. (1996). Flirting in the factory. *The Journal of the Royal Anthropological Institute, 2* (2), 313–333. doi:10.2307/3034098.

Yrle, A. C., Hartman, S. J., & Galle Jr, W. P. (2003). Examining communication style and leader–member exchange: Considerations and concerns for managers. *International Journal of Management, 20*(1), 92–100.

11 Identity and Identification

Craig R. Scott[1]

It is difficult to imagine a broader topic than *identity* when it comes to the study of humans. Identity research has exploded across the social sciences in the past 30 years, in part due to the rise of the individual self in society where unique identities become increasingly possible in a globalized, diversified, mobile, media-intensive, and often consumption-driven world (Larson & Gill, 2017). A focus on communicative views of this construct still leaves a sizable body of research to examine—because communication and language play significant roles in how we construct identities in interaction and how we manage our often multiple and fragmented identities.

Considering how fundamental identity is, it should not be surprising that it is especially relevant when talking about the organization (Gioia, 1998). Without question, our identities are linked to the organizations we work for, belong to, and buy from. "Identity is increasingly constituted by public, profit-driven, and institutionalized discourses" (Tracy & Trethewey, 2005, p. 173). Deetz's (1992) arguments that multinational corporations have substantial influence on people's daily lives ring even more true today. Not only do various organizational narratives shape individual identity, but organizations themselves spend considerable resources on their own identities. "During the past 150 years especially, identity has become a focused and professionalized enterprise, adopted by organizations in all sectors through the successive development of advertising, public relations, and marketing" (Cheney, Christensen, & Dailey, 2014, p. 696). Identity issues have become even more central for organizations today (Albert, Ashforth, & Dutton, 2000) amid the explosion of communication in our world and additional pressures promoting organizational transparency and openness. As Schultz, Hatch, and Larsen (2000, p. 1) claim, "increasingly organizations compete [for customers and members] based on their ability to express who they are and what they stand for."

Inevitably, linkages between individual and organizational identities become of great importance. This connection is usefully examined as part of organizational identification, which refers to the attachment between organizational members and the organization itself (Larson, 2017). These connections are shaped by and in turn influence various messages and broader discourses surrounding organizations and their members. These organizational memberships and affiliations become significant aspects of who we are as

1 *I wish to acknowledge two graduate students, Maria Zhigalina and Hajar Shirley, for their hard work in tracking down resources and preparing the final version of this chapter.*

people (especially in a world where work organizations demand much of our time); but that identification also depends heavily on the identity of the organization and its values.

Thus, questions about *who am I?* and *who are we?* are not fully understood without also asking how those questions relate to one another. Cheney et al. (2014) have argued:

> Any comprehensive discussion of identity, identification, and organizational communication must consider at once (1) the grounds for and resources of identity construction and transformation in contemporary global society; (2) the articulation and promotion of corporate identities by institutions and organizations of all sorts; and (3) the individual linkages to and bonds with organizations, industries, professions, brands, and other features.
>
> (Cheney et al., 2014, p. 695)

Thus, it is useful to not only consider individual identity, organizational identity, and organizational identification together but also recognize the powerful role of communication in shaping and revealing individual and organizational identities as well as in influencing identification processes between members and various collectives.

This chapter attempts to provide an overview of individual identities as relevant to contemporary organizations, organizational identities, and organizational identifications. For each, an effort is made to describe them generally, examine relevant (meta) theoretical views and approaches, and highlight the constitutive role of communication. Given the size of these literatures, we cannot even begin to review all the research about each; however, we can forefront some of the major issues and connections as we take a communicative focus on organizational identity and identification. The chapter closes with discussion about identity and identification as they pertain to organizing and communicating.

Individual Identity

At first glance, the construct of individual identity with its philosophical and psychological understandings may seem somewhat distant from a discussion of identity and identification as they link to communicating and organizing. However, a significant amount of organizational communication research focuses on aspects of individual identity. Organizations play a significant role in answering questions about *who am I?* even though those organizations are often themselves struggling with that question (Larson & Gill, 2017).

One communication-focused definition comes from Kuhn (2006, p. 1340): "the conception of the self reflexively and discursively understood by the self." As Larson and Gill (2017) note, this definition is valuable because it positions discourse as central to identity construction and because it suggests ongoing construction of the self. Cruz (2017), who describes core identity as a set of enduring and stable characteristics, suggests that "identity is a complex concept that captures the multiple facets of the individual including personality, values, beliefs, roles, and, ultimately, how one perceives oneself in relation to others" (p. 1). She adds that organizational communication scholars have contributed to our understanding by accounting for various organizational and societal discourses (e.g., what it means to be a good worker or how to balance work and life) that impact how members view their identities generally and their organizational roles/jobs specifically.

Approaches/Perspectives

The relationship between identity and organizations can be examined through several metatheoretical lenses (Larson & Gill, 2017). *Post-positivism* views identity as an essential, enduring set of traits or properties that distinguish one person from the next; this identity is measurable and managers' communication helps shape these identities. Their *social construction* perspective (an interpretive view) suggests language constructs reality, with identities created through, and reflected in, communication. *Critical* approaches see identities as something that organizations and other powerful actors seek to control; communicative discourses make certain identities possible and allow for resistance. *Rhetorical* approaches provide explanation for how persuasive communication shapes identity and identification (discussed below). A *postmodern* perspective draws special attention to identities as fragmented, multiple, and contested where the experience of the self is constructed through language (although most other metatheoretical views also allow for multiple identities). Finally, *feminist* approaches emphasize the role of gender and other categories of sameness/difference; here again, identity is accomplished and (re)produced through communication and discourse.

Cutting across many of these perspectives is what Larson and Gill (2017) describe as a *discursive* approach, where the goal is to "consolidate the contributions of communication approaches as something that helps scholars to understand identity and organizations in ways that bring to the surface new insights" (p. 30). This discursive approach distinguishes little-d discourse (e.g., speech acts) from big-D Discourse (representing broader social narratives; see Chapter 3). For those authors, this discursive approach views identities as discursively constructed and mediated, investigates the relationship between discourse and Discourse, considers the role of power, treats communication as constitutive, and sees identity and organizations as mutually constituted. Thus, a constitutive view of communication is highlighted here. The methods used in such an approach include historical analyses, textual analysis of relevant materials, case studies focused on one or a small group of individuals, often with the use of multiple methods, participant observation, ethnographic-type approaches, interviews, biographical/life narratives, and emerging methods such as photovoice (where one provides visual images relevant to their life and then comments on them with the researcher).

Communication and Individual Identity

This discursive approach to identity highlights several overlapping areas where identity and organizations intersect. These include ideas related to *identity work, organizational/ societal discourses* about certain identities, and work on the *crystallized self* as it pertains to organizational members.

Identity work. Identity work describes how personal identities are formed and reformed through our interactions. The interest of many organizational scholars in issues of "work" provides some connection to identity management as part of the "work" organizational members perform. Identity work is contextual and shaped by broader organizational and professional contexts; thus, organizational members are regularly engaged in identity work (Larson & Gill, 2017). Definitions of the self are continuously formed, repaired, maintained, strengthened, or revised when a person's sense of self is challenged (Alvesson, Ashcraft, & Thomas, 2008). Larson and Gill

(2017) also point to organizational changes (e.g., restructuring job assignments) and destructive practices (e.g., workplace bullying) that create identity crises requiring even more identity work.

As Cruz (2017) explains, many potential challenges to self-identity (e.g., various face threatening acts, role changes, etc.) require identity work. Statements challenging a person's job or occupational identity (e.g., female pilots being addressed as flight attendants; male nurses misidentified as doctors) also demand identity work. Negative statements about one's employer or occupation, especially if engaged in any form of "dirty work" (see also Ashforth & Kreiner, 1999), may also necessitate identity work. Meisenbach (2010) proposed several measures individuals take to negotiate these identity challenges—including denying negative statements, reframing messages into something more positive, or even transcending the identity threat. Cruz (2017) offers the example of firefighters dispatched somewhere for medical reasons such as a spider bite. Although technically within the realm of their job responsibilities, such assignments threaten their "hero" identity (Tracy & Scott, 2006). Thus, identity work done here may well involve the firefighters highlighting discourses about rescuing a victim and dismissing identity threatening interpretations. Although much identity work seems to be reactive to identity threats/challenges, it can also be proactive in helping to reduce/limit potential challenges. The above examples illustrate the constitutive role of communication—which can threaten and challenge an organizational member's identity but also (re)establish and (re)negotiate one's sense of self through communicative forms of identity work.

Organizational/societal discourses. Another way of framing research about individual identity and organizing concerns broader societal/professional/organizational discourses drawn upon in identity creation. "A useful way of framing what individuals draw upon when forming and managing their identities is the concept of *discursive resources*" which "function as the building blocks for identity, the substance from which people imagine various possible identities and form the narrative they do for themselves" (Larson & Gill, 2017, p. 65, emphasis in original). A discursive resource is a "concept, phrase, expression, trope, or other linguistic device that (a) is drawn from practices or texts, (b) is designed to affect other practices and texts, (c) explains past or present action, and (d) provides a horizon for future practice" (Kuhn et al., 2008, p. 162). Formal organization is a key context supplying these resources. Overarching macro-discourses enable and constrain identity construction (Cruz, 2017).

A number of these resources have been linked to individual identities. Clair (1996) discusses what it means to be a professional; others have talked about broader discourses of professional image (see Cheney & Ashcraft, 2007). Conversations around what it means to be an "entrepreneur" (see Gill, 2013) and broad Discourses about "enterprise" (with its focus on everyone as consumers) are also useful examples (see Larson & Gill, 2017). Of course, organizational cultural narratives and socialization messages influence those identities as well.

These discursive resources enable and constrain identity for organizational members, who may also resist these broader discourses. Mumby (2005) argues for a dialectic approach to identity control and resistance, using tensions and contradictions as a way to better understand control and resistance related to identity work. Holmer Nadesan's (1996) study of female service workers shows how resistance to identity regulation is enacted—but also how that resistance can itself be controlling. Others have noted that responses to broader narratives about what makes for a "good mother" or a "good worker" can be integrated in creative ways as we construct identities as organizational members (e.g., good working mother; Turner & Norwood, 2013).

Crystallized self. Work on real, fake, and crystallized selves is also relevant to a discursive approach to individual identity and organizing. "Organizations play a prominent role in both creating identity choices and in sanctioning certain identities as more prestigious or desirable" (Larson & Gill, 2017, p. 94). Tracy and Trethewey (2005) argue that an employee's position in the organizational hierarchy offers unique, although often problematic, possibilities for identity construction. Their analysis suggests that some employees take extreme measures to align their seemingly real self with a preferred organizational self (with one's best self reserved for work at the likely expense of nonwork relations and activities). In other cases, members in certain job roles perform a seemingly fake, but organizationally preferred, identity (e.g., in emotional labor; see Chapter 18). Tracy and Trethewey claim that these understandings of the real-self and the fake-self pervade both popular understandings of identity and more scholarly discourse—to the detriment of organizational members.

Tracy and Trethewey (2005) challenge past conceptualizations of identity construction with the metaphor of the "crystallized self" to describe a unique whole that has many facets and appears different depending on how one looks at it. "Crystallized selves have different shapes depending on the various discourses through which they are constructed and constrained" (p. 186). In this perspective, organizational members can begin to alter identities across work, home, and the spaces between through language—suggesting a constitutive role for communication in shaping identities. "Rather than privileging work as the only productive realm of everyday experience, individuals might begin to elevate their nonprofessional selves alongside those that intersect with work" (e.g., home, community, or leisure; Tracy & Trethewey, 2005, p. 187).

Intersectionality is relevant here because it highlights how multiple identities (e.g., race, gender, class, etc.) entwine rather than looking at each separately (Larson & Gill, 2017; see also Chapter 14). This work has relevance to organizational communication where so many relevant identity categories come together (see Allen, 2011). Both the crystallized self and intersectionality invite organizational scholars to consider multiple facets of identities and the role of communication in their construction and expression.

Organizational Identity

Sizable literatures from fields such as management, organization studies, and communication have examined organizational identity, described as a root construct addressing an essential question of existence (Pratt, Schultz, Ashforth, & Ravasi, 2016). Albert and Whetten (1985) classically define organizational identity as that which is central, distinct, and enduring about the collective. Questions of identity essentially ask, "Who are we?" or "Who is [organization]?" An organization's identity is revealed through its values and mission—as well as its name, products/services, physical location, and/or the people it employs (see Cheney, Christensen, Zorn, & Ganesh, 2004). Furthermore, an organization's visual identity (i.e., names, logos, colors, fonts, slogans/taglines, and even architecture and product packaging) provides visibility and recognizability (Van den Bosch, de Jong, & Elving, 2006).

Several constructs are commonly linked to and overlap with organizational identity. Corporate identity focuses on how management represents the organization's identity symbolically to external audiences (see Hatch & Schultz, 2000). Balmer (2001) distinguishes between an organization's actual, communicated, and conceived identities, noting the desire for alignment among them. Brown, Dacin, Pratt, and Whetten (2006) consider four constructs: Organizational identity (who we are as an organization), intended image (what does the organization want others to think about it), construed image (what does the organization believe others think about it), and reputation (what do stakeholders actually think). Relations between identity, image, and reputation have been explored in a variety of theoretical models (Dukerich & Carter, 2000; Hatch & Schultz, 2000, 2003; Whetten & Godfrey, 1998). Identity and image issues have been linked to Goffman's (1959) concept of facework as we manage how others see us (suggesting a parallel with individual identity work). Image matters because it represents our assessment of what others see when they look at the organization (Dutton & Dukerich, 1991), which may encourage the organization to adapt its identity to change its image. Reputations (perceptions of outsiders about the organization) are associated with how well an organization communicates (Fombrun & Rindova, 2000). Reputations are revealed to the organization and others in a number of ways (company rankings, analysts' comments, media coverage, and direct consumer feedback)—and negative feedback threatens core identity and creates high likelihood of response (Dukerich & Carter, 2000).

Wieland (2017) argues that organizational communication scholars have "approached organizational identity in three primary ways: (1) as a resource for individual identity; (2) as a collective sense of self that enables interpretation and action; and (3) as external stakeholders' interpretations of who the organization is" (p. 1). The first strand of research relates to processes of organizational identification, covered later in the chapter. The second approach views organizational identity similar to individual identity but at a higher level—answering questions about "who are we?" and "what do we care about?" (Wieland, 2017). The third strand emphasizes the communication of organizational identity for external stakeholders (e.g., consumers, competitors, and the media).

Approaches/Perspectives

Organizational identity can be examined in many ways. "It shouldn't be surprising that a subject that is so central to our field's conceptions of organizing and organizations would attract a diverse set of interests and perspectives" (Foreman & Whetten, 2016, p. 56). Whetten and Godfrey (1998) review functionalist, interpretive, and postmodern views of organizational identity. Other efforts have taken more critical approaches (see Alvesson & Robertson, 2016). A wide range of approaches has been used to investigate organizational identity: narrative discourse analysis, ethnographic methods and grounded theory, case study approaches, survey data, and secondary data analysis—with slightly more qualitative than quantitative approaches overall and much more qualitative work in recent years (Foreman & Whetten, 2016).

Wieland (2017) describes key tensions in conceptualizations of organizational identity. The first tension centers on organizational identity as an entity (an essential or inherent property that can be measured) or as a social construction. In the former, identity is expressed and made visible through communication. In the constructionist view, identity itself is fundamentally communicative as it is constructed and negotiated. Gioia and Hamilton (2016) characterize this tension from a social actor perspective—which "provides insights into organizational phenomena by treating organizational identity as a set of overt claims that conveys consistent expectations to both internal and external stakeholders regarding how the organization should be seen and how it should conduct itself" (p. 24)—and a social construction perspective—which views identity as more subject to revisions as members interact and negotiate with others. These authors advocate structurational thinking to overcome tensions in potentially competing perspectives.

A second related tension asks whether organizational identity is something advanced by organizational leaders or emergent from various stakeholders. As Scott (2013) contends, both exist; there is a preferred identity based on organizational leadership strategies and an emergent identity resulting from the involvement of many others assessing who the organization seems to be over time. A focus on strategy inevitably emphasizes the role of organizational leaders in managing and communicating the organization's identity; whereas a more emergent perspective aligns again with constructionist and constitutive views that pay attention to various organizational stakeholders (Wieland, 2017).

Wieland's (2017) third conceptual tension focuses on internal vs. external audiences. Although several definitions privilege internal audiences, others have defined organizational identity as a view shared by internal and external stakeholders (e.g., Henderson, Cheney, & Weaver, 2015). As more external views are considered, image and reputation become increasingly important. Yet, if we are to understand organizational members' constructions and interpretations of organizational identity, we need to consider communication with both internal and external audiences (Cheney & Christensen, 2001). Institutional perspectives on organizational identity also consider larger institutional forces at play in the broader social context in which organizations are embedded (Gioia & Hamilton, 2016).

Organizations, like individuals, have multiple identities that reflect different views about what is central, distinctive, and enduring (Cheney, 1991; Pratt & Foreman, 2000). Views of organizations and identities as fragmented, fleeting, and conflicting reinforce the utility of a multiple-identities perspective. Pratt and Foreman (2000) offer a useful framework on management of multiple (sometimes conflicting) identities. *Deletion* involves abandoning all but one main identity. *Integration* fuses several existing identities into a distinct new identity. *Compartmentalization* is when the organization and its members retain all identities but keep them separate (e.g., different identities for different audiences). *Aggregation* maintains all identities and integrates them together. Pratt (2016) claims that a view emphasizing multiple organizational identities is aligned with social constructionist views and pays attention to a wider range of (mostly external) stakeholders.

Communication and Organizational Identity

Communication is central to organizational identity. Organizational identity management has focused on communicating identity consistently and frequently—sometimes with *integrated marketing communications*, which seeks to create a unified impression via a single organizational voice. This is difficult when an organization has multiple identities and/or is in a complex environment. Such communication may involve the practical deployment of various vehicles (public relations, marketing, etc.) used to disseminate identity features. Schinoff, Rogers, and Corley (2016) argue that identity is communicated through *saying, showing*, and *staging*. Their typology of organizational identity communication is based on clarity of identity content and intentional communication of that content. With low clarity and low intention, an organization may not know its identity, so cannot *say, show,* or *stage* it. With high clarity but low intent an organization may not need to communicate its identity—and to the extent it does, it is mostly just *shown.* With low clarity but high intent, an organization may communicate who it wants to be, mostly through what is *said.* Finally, with high intent and high clarity, an organization can communicate who it is through what it *says, shows,* and *stages* (see Figure 11.1).

When identity is viewed in less essentialist and more processual/constructivist terms, the relevance of communication shifts considerably; communication is better understood in more constitutive terms focusing on how identities are regularly (re)negotiated based on interactions with various relevant others (see Cheney & Christensen, 2001). As Cheney et al. (2014) explain, in this sense organizations enact their identities through the stories they tell about themselves; organizational identities are seen as "volatile social constructions based in large part on the interpretive capabilities and preferences of their audiences" (p. 698). Cooren, Kuhn, Cornelissen, and Clark (2011) argue that because communication constitutes organizations, "it only becomes possible to conceive and talk of an 'organizational identity' as grounded in language and as having no existence other than in discourse" (p. 1159).

Several empirical connections between organizational identity and constitutive views of communication have been offered by organizational communication scholars in recent years. For example, Dobusch and Schoeneborn's (2015) study of the hacktivist group Anonymous extends work on organizational identity "by emphasizing the fundamental and formative role of identity claims in the communicative constitution

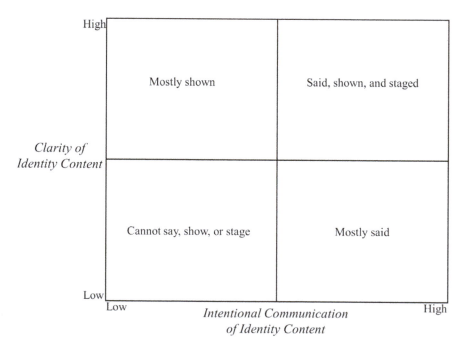

Figure 11.1 Typology of organizational identity communication (adapted from Schinoff et al., 2016)

of social collectives as organizational entities" (p. 1006). Kopaneva and Sias (2015) take a constitutive view of identity in examining how organizational mission statements are constructed. Madsen's (2016) study of interactions in a Danish bank illustrates how members use internal social media (ISM) to challenge and negotiate organizational identity: "Discussing *who we are* as an organization and *how we should act* as members of this organization are closely related and ISM introduce a new communication arena for negotiating rules, norms, and organizational identity" (p. 202, emphasis in original). Dawson's (2018) recent work also examines how organizational identity is constituted through conversation/interaction in a social media brand-based community—noting both identify-confirming and identity-disconfirming messages from various stakeholders involved in the "social co-construction of organizational identity" (p. 8). Koschmann (2013) investigates the closely related notion of how communication constitutes collective identity among a collaboration of social service agencies.

These examples illustrate that multiple communicators may be involved in the construction of organizational identity. "Identity management is carried out not only by managers with communication responsibilities but also by rank-and-file members who identify with the organization" (Cheney et al., 2004, p. 126). We next turn to a discussion of identification by organizational members.

Organizational Identification

Pratt (1998) suggests that identification involves an individual seeing some "other" as being definitive of one's self when beliefs about that other become self-referential or self-defining (through either a recognition of affinity or a changing of identity to emulate the other). Identification relates to specific aspects of identity more so than any other form of attachment. Our desire for identification stems from needs for safety, affiliation, self-enhancement, and more holistic (almost spiritual) goals.

Organizational identification refers to associations formed between people (usually organizational members or employees) and the organization itself (Larson, 2017). Indeed, organizational identification may help meet many basic needs described previously. Organizational identification is commonly defined as "the perception of oneness with or belongingness to [a collective], where the individual defines him or herself in terms of the [collective] in which he or she is a member" (Mael & Ashforth 1992, p. 104). Barker (1998) argues identification "is not just a Western phenomenon; instead, it is *a characteristic of any organizing practice*" (p. 261, emphasis in original). Organizational identification may describe both the process of becoming attached and the outcome of that process (see Tompkins & Cheney, 1985).

Strong identification has been linked to a wide range of benefits for organizations and their members—such as increased satisfaction and reduced turnover (see Ashforth, Harrison, & Corley, 2008). Organizational identifications are a key part of who we are, evidenced by the fact that many people mention their work or employer in initial encounters. Affiliation with a highly regarded organization reflects positively on the organizational member. Given these and other benefits, many organizations take deliberate efforts to induce members to identify with the organization. Such efforts take on particular significance in contemporary societies where people spend increasing amounts of time at their work organizations (Larson, 2017). Organizational identification can also come with downsides—most notably the control it may exert on organizational members.

Considering multiple identities of individuals and organizations, individuals also have multiple identifications. People might identify—in general or in specific situations—with a work organization, a project team, a specific department, or even a certain occupation/profession—in addition to a host of external identifications (religious organizations, family, etc.). Talk about multiple identifications often refers to *targets* of identification (where we aim to attach with various "others") and/or *resources* for identification (where we draw on those identities to shape our attachment) (Larson, 2017). Others have used the term identification *sources* to signify that identifications are simultaneously about targets and resources (Morgan et al., 2004). Although most research identifies specific targets/resources as other groups, organizations, or broader collectives, individuals may also identify with an organization's ideas, beliefs, and values. Regardless, organizational identity serves as a key source for our identifications.

Approaches/Perspectives

Scholarship on organizational identification comes primarily from two different disciplinary traditions (Scott, 2013). First, management scholars (e.g., Dutton & Dukerich, 1991; Mael & Ashforth, 1992, 1995; Pratt, 1998) have emphasized how individuals come to see themselves in terms of the organization's identity. The focus here is on a more cognitive view of identification based on a member's beliefs and knowledge about the organization's identity. Some research and theorizing from the management tradition has linked organizational identification to image and reputation issues. For example, the link between attractiveness of an organization's image and the strength of member identification depends on visibility of affiliation—with more visible/public roles in prominent organizations increasing organizational identification (see Dutton, Dukerich, & Harquail, 1994). Management scholars have also paid attention to the dark side of member identification—including disidentification, apathetic identification, deidentification, underidentification, overdisidentification, and schizo-identification (see Dukerich, Kramer, & Parks, 1998). Another aspect of this work has examined identification among members engaged in "dirty work," where the tasks have a physical, social, or moral taint associated with them (see Ashforth & Kreiner, 1999). Some of the work in this area suggests that if the dirty work is central to what the organization does, stronger identification may occur as compared to organizations where the dirty work aspects are less central to the overall identity (Kreiner, Ashforth, & Sluss, 2006).

Much of the work in the management tradition draws on Social Identity Theory (SIT), a social-psychological approach to identification focusing on cognitive processes related to self-categorization (Tajfel & Turner, 1985). This prominent approach has been described as one of the three primary schools of thought on organizational identification (Larson, 2017). SIT posits that people have two aspects to their identities: a *personal identity* that concerns individual characteristics and beliefs and a *social identity* that includes associations with various groups including organizations. Organizational scholars primarily use SIT to better understand how organizational members come to identify with a collective (Pratt, 2001). Two processes are at work according to SIT and related theories. *Categorization* involves clarifying in- and out-group boundaries and is more likely when the target organization is distinctive, outgroups are salient, and competition exists with other organizations. *Self-enhancement* suggests identification is more likely when an organization is prestigious, has an attractive image, and has an identity that increases members' esteem. SIT combines psychological and organizational views (Pratt, 2001)—but rarely mentions the role of communication.

A second disciplinary-based research tradition examining organizational identification comes from organizational communication. Here we find Larson's (2017) other two research perspectives: rhetorical and structurational. Indeed, identification has frequently been traced back to the rhetorical strategies of Burke (1937), who described identification as part of the natural human desire to overcome divisions in society (see especially Cheney, 1983; Tompkins & Cheney, 1983, 1985). In this approach, organizations use specific rhetorical strategies to induce that sense of attachment and persuade members they are alike or have similar interests. This may involve the use of specific strategies such as unified "we" terms when communicating about the organization, uniting against a common enemy, and the common ground technique. Concertive control theory (Tompkins & Cheney, 1985) is also linked to this rhetorical tradition, providing a comprehensive explanation for how identification creates organizational control. Members who are highly identified with the organization act "in concert" to hold each other accountable; control is unobtrusive because it comes from peers rather than management (see Chapter 12).

In addition to SIT and rhetorically based views, Scott, Corman, and Cheney's (1998) structurational approach offers a way to conceptualize the mutually influential ways in which identification and identity relate. As they note, "most important indicators and expressions of identification are found in language. Thus, communicative manifestations of identification are emphasized as they occur in social interaction with others" (p. 305). Expressions of belonging or positive statements of membership represent important forms of member identification with the organization. They define identification as the "process of emerging identity," which implies "the forging, maintenance, and alteration of linkages between persons and groups" (p. 304). Scott et al. (1998) draw on several features of structuration theory in their model. The *duality of structure* suggests that structures (identities) are enabling and constraining when appropriated in the expressions of identifications that in turn serve to (re)create those identities. Additionally, the *regionalization of structure* helps to explain the ways in which multiple identities and identifications might relate to one another. *Situated activity* suggests that the identification process depends on what one is doing (and with whom they are doing it) and thus should be understood as changing based on the context. "Overall, the structural model of identification has proven useful in articulating the relationship between identity and identification as well as conceptualizing the complex, contextual, and communicative nature of identification" (Larson, 2017, p. 4) (see also Chapter 3).

Researchers have used varied methods to study organizational identification, including survey questionnaires, interviews, observations, and rhetorical analyses. In organizational communication, Cheney's Organizational Identification Questionnaire (OIQ) was widely used until critiques of its considerable overlap with measures of organizational commitment (Miller, Allen, Casey, & Johnson, 2000). Mael and Ashforth's (1992) measure is prominent across fields as a way to quantitatively measure organizational identification. Scott and others have used select items from these two measures and sometimes extended them to other identification targets to assess multiple identifications (see Scott, 1997; Scott & Stephens, 2009). Qualitative approaches have begun to gain traction—focusing on interviews and textual analysis (Larson, 2017). We are beginning to see more sophisticated approaches when it comes to reconsidering organizational membership, challenging the desirability of identification, and questioning unitary expressions of identity. Future approaches should be culturally and historically informed, sensitive to time, multi-level, multi-methodological, and practical—but also critical/reflective and ethically aware (Cheney et al., 2014).

Communication and Organizational Identification

Each of the perspectives discussed in the previous section has implications for connecting communication to identification processes. In SIT, "direct reference to communication has been remarkably absent" (Postmes, 2003, p. 88); yet, even here, communication may play an important, if sometimes covert, role. In SIT, simply talking about the collective or wearing a sign that signifies group membership can make group identity salient and foster a sense of identification. As Postmes explains, communication is possible because of our social identities and commonalities; it also helps shape those identities. Bartel and Dutton (2001) argue for the need to move beyond psychic/cognitive views of identification to consider more interactional and relational views to better understand "how a sense of membership in an organization is constituted through daily interactions with others" (p. 116). Scott (2007) has specifically noted five key linkages between communication and SIT that are relevant to organizational identification and identity: salience of dual/multiple identifications, computer-mediated communication and virtual work related to identification, relationally focused work identities, organizational-level identities, and disidentification and related forms.

As already discussed, rhetorical and structurational perspectives clearly highlight the role of communication and its relationship to organizing. They have been used to describe how communication is used to create identification, how that identification may be expressed, and how those interactions then influence identity and future identification processes. More recent efforts build significantly on those traditions by specifically looking at how organizational identification communicatively constitutes organization. Chaput, Brummans, and Cooren (2011, p. 253) view organizational identification as a "communicative process through which people develop a common basis for collective action and argue that this process of 'consubstantialization' is of central importance for the constitution of an organization." Their study shows how identification (and dis/mis-identification) occurs through communication and how that plays into the coproduction of a Canadian political organization.

Communication is important for managing multiple identifications. Research has moved from simply studying multiple identifications to examining how communication influences the management of those multiple identifications (Larson, 2017). Scott (1997) found that in decentralized, geographically dispersed organizations, members identify more strongly with local offices with whom they have greater interaction than with the larger organization. Kuhn and Nelson (2002) found that those with more central places in a communication network tended to have stronger identification with multiple targets/sources. Larson and Pepper (2003) found three broad strategies for communicatively managing tensions between identifications: comparison (which uses rhetorical juxtaposition of competing identification targets to compare identity options), logic (which involves constructions of situationally and culturally logical arguments for identification choices), and support (which consists of communicative strategies referencing support from others to justify identifications).

Other work has looked more at externally directed communication as it relates to identification. For example, Bartel, Baldi, and Dukerich (2016) note that stakeholder identification is fostered through expressions of organizational identity. How identity is expressed through websites and other channels is part of the effort to craft a desired organizational image. This identification is similar to how members identify, even though the stakeholders are not formal members. Cheney et al.'s (2014) notion of *auto-communication*—or communication with self—is especially intriguing. This concept explains how communication about organizational identity influences internal audiences and their sense of identification even though it is largely externally directed. Consider, for example, messages about corporate social responsibility that are presumably directed to external stakeholders but that may also strongly influence identification with one's workplace (see Morsing, 2006). As Cheney notes, while potentially useful, auto-communication can also be dysfunctional when members become too obsessed with identity concerns.

Other strands of work suggest a need to reconsider some thinking about how communication relates to identification. For example, efforts to communicatively manage multiple identifications challenges arguments favoring a "unified voice" when it comes to issues of identity and identification. Additionally, organizational members may have to reframe their thinking and their talk when dealing with stigma surrounding dirty work or managing identifications with low-prestige organizations. Even recent work on hidden organizations suggests expressions of identification do not always suggest strong attachment—indeed, in some cases even silence may reflect a stronger identification that does not reveal the hidden organization or its members (Scott, 2013).

Conclusion

As we think about individual identity, organizational identity, and organizational identification, it is clear that communication is a vital element for all three interrelated constructs. Clearly, various societal discourses influence the construction of identity at all levels and our interactions with various others influence the development of identity as we organize. More practically, communication is how we manage multiple identities and identifications as organized structures; it allows for the induction of identification through various rhetorical strategies, and it is a vehicle for conveying and expressing identity to both external and internal audiences. Thus, identity and identification are constructed as we organize (O_1), they are organized structures (O_2), and organizational identity is crucial for entitative being (O_3; see Chapter 1).

To illustrate, imagine a member of a large company who considers taking part in a corporate volunteering effort. Corporate communication about its identity as a good corporate citizen influences development of a volunteer identity in employees and identification of members with the corporate identity. How members talk to others shapes their own identification and influences the organization's identity. Although communication enables the development of various identities and identifications, it also constrains such efforts (e.g., when the company's volunteering-related messages seem hypocritical and lead members to avoid certain individual identities and resist organizational identification).

Communication is also seen in constitutive terms—implicitly and explicitly—in some of this work as well. Larson and Gill (2017) see communication as constitutive in discursive approaches to identity development. Organization identity is clearly constructed and negotiated through communication (Wieland, 2017). Cooren et al. (2011) argue for a constitutive view of communication in the construction of organizational identity grounded in language; indeed, as noted in earlier sections, constitutive approaches among organizational communication scholars appear to be more common in studies of organizational identity than for the other constructs examined in this chapter. Having said that, Chaput et al. (2011) offer a very constitutive view of the organizational identification process. Even Scott et al. (1998), while not explicitly adopting a constitutive view, clearly argue for what can be recognized as constitutive-like processes related to communication and identity in their structurational model of organizational identification.

The C-O cycle (see Chapter 1) is also clear in this literature, as it is, of course, nearly impossible to separate out organization and organizing from the communicative processes surrounding identity and identification in organizations. Indeed, a communication as constitutive of organization view understands both constructs in terms of the other. In many ways, this aligns with a process view of organizing, where the organization is best viewed as an ongoing construction composed largely of interactions with various others. Thus, it is organizing that helps to (re)create and (re)negotiate a fluid sense of identity at multiple levels. Views of organizational identification that emphasize its ongoing development in situated interactions with others fit here as well.

However, it is also useful to consider the ways in which organizations are understood as entities and structures when it comes to issues of identity and identification. As entities, organizations are a pervasive aspect of our society, and each organizational entity has its own identity. This entity perspective is highlighted in one of Wieland's (2017) key tensions surrounding organizational identity. The view of organizations as entities also aligns with many views of organizational identification, where the organization is the "thing" we attach to. Organizations are often treated as the storytellers, narrators, and sources of discourse that influence identity and identification. These collective entities are often powerful actors that strategically shape identity and identification and that may unobtrusively control members through such processes. As a form of structure, organizations provide important resources (discursive and otherwise) for members to draw from in the creation of multiple identities/identifications. Those structures may also sanction some identities as more or less preferred and can create challenges for identity (e.g., because of the nature of some forms of work). SIT is relevant here when it comes to organizational-based social identities. Structurational views (Scott et al., 1998) also highlight some ways in which organizations are structures that may enable and constrain identity and identification.

Approaches that more closely consider the interplay between communicating and organizing are especially important for understanding personal identity, organizational identity, and organizational identification. As Larson and Gill (2017) conclude, "a discursive identity lens offers researchers an avenue to uncover necessary understandings about a fundamental factor and process of organizational life and to link identity to other important organizational constructs" (p. 171). Pratt et al.'s (2016) advice that future research should focus on process and deepen understanding of plurality and complexity also points to the importance of communication explicitly and constitutive views at least implicitly. It is important to consider not only the more positive ways that organizations and communication construct identity and identification, but also the ways in which communication deconstitutes organization as we resist, reframe, disidentify, detach, and otherwise challenge certain identities and identifications (see Chapter 12). Organizational communication scholars are in a position to continue offering valuable insights, useful theory, and informed research about identity and identification.

Recommended Supplementary Readings

Ashcraft, K. L. (2013).The glass slipper: "Incorporating" occupational identity in management studies. *Academy of Management Review, 38,* 6–31.
This article redefines the current division of scholarly labor and, through the use of the glass slipper metaphor, theorizes collective occupational identity and its relation to other social identities.
Barker, J. R., & Tompkins, P. K. (1994). Identification in the self-managing organization: Characteristics of target and tenure. *Human Communication Research, 21*(2), 223–240.
This study examines worker identification with two targets simultaneously: one's self-managing team and the larger organization that employees the individual.
Meisenbach, R. J., & Kramer, M.W. (2014). Exploring nested identities: Voluntary membership, social category identity, and identification in a community choir. *Management Communication Quarterly, 28*(2), 187–213.
This study explores how individuals articulate identities and identification sources in the context of joining or continuing to participate in a community choir.
Russo, T. C. (1998). Organizational and professional identification: A case of newspaper journalists. *Management Communication Quarterly, 12*(1), 72–111.
This study was one of the very first to study multiple targets of organizational identification by examining organizational and professional identification among a group of professional journalists.
Scott, C. R., Connaughton, S. L., Diaz-Saenz, H., Maguire, K., Ramirez, R., Richardson, B., Shaw, S. P., & Morgan, D. (1999). The impacts of communication and multiple identifications on intent to leave: A multi-methodological exploration. *Management Communication Quarterly, 12*(3), 400–435.
This study examines multiple targets of identification and how they influence turnover intentions— revealing a rather complex relationship between three different types of identification and intent to leave.

Important Concepts: Define and Discuss

Identity
Organizational identity
Organizational identification
Discursive resource
Multiple identities/identifications

Discussion Questions

1. How do issues like work–life balance, corporate colonization, and calls for transparency relate to identity and identification in organizations?
2. Can a transmission view of communication (in how we strategically convey messages to induce identification or use various communication channels to convey identity) exist alongside a constitutive view of identity and identification in organizations?
3. How stable are identities and identifications as they relate to organizations? Do situational views better account for any changes that may occur with identity and identification?
4. How are individual identities (as discursively constructed) constituting and constituted by organizational identities (which are themselves discursively constructed)?
5. How might communication serve to deconstitute identities and identifications related to organizations?

Practitioners' Corner

Tips for Effectively Managing Organizational Identities and Identifications

The responsibility for identity management falls not only to organizational leadership and those in professional communication roles, but every member plays a potential role in the creation and management of their own identities, the organization's identity, and the identifications they have with various parts of the organization. Recognition of that dispersed responsibility and power is important. A few additional key tips are suggested by the literature as they relate to communication:

- Individual and organizational identities are better thought of as fluid than stable. Thus, it is vital to think about how we communicate a tentative identity to various audiences in different situations and how interactions with those stakeholders influence those identities—recognizing that the identity is more emergent than fixed (and thus requires regular attention).
- Individual and organizational identities are almost always multiple. Thus, part of our identity work is about communicatively managing what are sometimes competing and sometimes compatible identities for individuals and organizations.
- Identity and reputation are different issues, but they are intimately tied when we remember that identity is communicatively constructed through our interactions with various others. Our identity and our reputation are mutually influential and consideration of either requires efforts to manage and appreciate both in our messages.
- We should be conscious about ways in which organizational practices (e.g., certain job tasks, bullying and harassment, organizational change) as well as broader societal discourses about work can challenge the self-identity of members and threaten the identity of the organization in the process. The creation and communication of policies and practices that are sensitive to identity concerns are essential.
- Strong bonds of identification from employees, customers, and others depend in part on the organizational identity being one that people find attractive and something with which they can align their own identity. Thus, organizations and their members should strive to co-construct mutually beneficial identities.
- Members and organizational leaders should recognize that there are downsides to obsessing too much about communicating identity or to creating unobtrusive forms of control based on identifications. Even disidentifications and deidentifications may serve as important feedback about how people see themselves in relation to the organization.
- Our identity messages to external audiences may also be heard by internal members in ways that influence their sense of identification. This "auto-communication" can be used strategically—or we can at least recognize the challenges in creating entirely distinct messages for different audiences in a media-rich world where messages are increasingly available to all.

If we always keep in mind that issues of identity and identification can be quite consequential for organizations and their members, we can help remain alert to threats that challenge identity and opportunities for constructing strong identities and identifications.

References

Albert, S., & Whetten, D. A. (1985). Organizational identity. In L. L. Cummings & B. M. Staw (Eds.), *Research in organizational behavior* (Vol. 7, pp. 263–295). Greenwich, CT: JAI Press.

Albert, S., Ashforth, B. E., & Dutton, J. E. (2000). Organizational identity and identification: Charting new waters and building new bridges. *Academy of Management Review, 25*(1), 13–17. doi:10.5465/AMR.2000.2791600.

Allen, B. J. (2011). *Difference matters: Communicating social identity* (2nd ed.). Prospect Heights, IL: Waveland Press.

Alvesson, M., Ashcraft, K. L., & Thomas, R. (2008). Identity matters: Reflections on the construction of identity scholarship in organization studies. *Organization, 15*(1), 5–28. doi.org/10.1177/1350508407084426.

Alvesson, M., & Robertson, M. (2016). Organizational identity: A critique. In M. G. Pratt, M. Schultz, B. E. Ashforth & D. Ravasi (Eds.), *Organizational identity* (pp. 160–180). Oxford: Oxford University Press.

Ashforth, B. E., & Kreiner, G. E. (1999). "How can you do it?" Dirty work and the challenge of constructing a positive identity. *Academy of Management Review, 24*(3), 413–434. doi:10.5465/amr.1999.2202129.

Ashforth, B. E., Harrison, S. H., & Corley, K. G. (2008). Identification in organizations: An examination of four fundamental questions. *Journal of Management, 34*(3), 325–374. doi:10.1177/0149206308316059.

Balmer, J. M. T. (2001). From the Pentagon: A new identity framework. *Corporate Reputation Review, 4*(11), 11–21. doi.org/10.1057/palgrave.crr.1540129.

Barker, J. R. (1998). Managing identification. In D. A. Whetten & P. C. Godfrey (Eds.), *Identity in organizations: Building theory through conversations* (pp. 257–267). Thousand Oaks, CA: SAGE.

Barker, J. R. (1999). *The discipline of teamwork: Participation and concertive control*. Thousand Oaks, CA: SAGE.

Bartel, C. A., Baldi, C., & Dukerich, J. M. (2016). Fostering stakeholder identification through expressed organizational identities. In M. G. Pratt, M. Schultz, B. E. Ashforth & D. Ravasi (Eds.), *Organizational identity* (pp. 474–493). Oxford: Oxford University Press.

Bartel, C. A., & Dutton, J. (2001). Ambiguous organizational memberships: Constructing organizational identities in interactions with others. In M. A. Hogg & D. J. Terry (Eds.), *Social identity processes in organizational context* (pp. 115–130). Philadelphia, PA: Psychology Press.

Brown, T., Dacin, P., Pratt, M., & Whetten, D. (2006). Identity, intended image, construed image, and reputation: An interdisciplinary framework and suggested methodology. *Journal of the Academy of Marketing Science, 34*(2), 95–106. doi:10.1177/0092070305284969.

Burke, K. (1937). *Attitudes toward history*. New York, NY: The New Republic Press.

Chaput, M., Brummans, B. H., & Cooren, F. (2011). The role of organizational identification in the communicative constitution of an organization: A study of consubstantialization in a young political party. *Management Communication Quarterly, 25*(2), 252–282. doi:10.1177/0893318910386719.

Cheney, G. (1983). The rhetoric of identification and the study of organizational communication. *Quarterly Journal of Speech, 69*(2), 143–158. doi:10.1080/00335638309383643.

Cheney, G. (1991). *Rhetoric in an organizational society: Managing multiple identities*. Columbia: University of South Carolina Press.

Cheney, G., & Ashcraft, K. L. (2007). Considering "the professional" in communication studies: Implications for theory and research within and beyond the boundaries of organizational communication. *Communication Theory, 17*(2), 146–175. doi:10.1111/j.1468-2885.2007.00290.

Cheney, G., & Christensen, L. T. (2001). Organizational identity: Linkages between internal and external communication. In F. M. Jablin & L. L. Putnam (Eds.), *The new handbook of organizational communication: Advances in theory, research, and methods* (pp. 231–269). Thousand Oaks, CA: SAGE.

Cheney, G., Christensen, L. T., & Dailey, S. L. (2014). Communicating identity and identification in and around organizations. In L. L. Putnam & D. K. Mumby (Eds.), *The SAGE handbook of organizational communication* (pp. 695–716). Thousand Oaks, CA: SAGE.

Cheney, G., Christensen, L. T., Zorn Jr., T. E., and Ganesh, S. (2004). *Organizational communication in an age of globalization: Issues, reflections, practices.* Prospect Heights, IL: Waveland.

Clair, R. P. (1996). The political nature of the colloquialism, "a real job": Implications for organizational socialization. *Communication Monographs, 63*(3), 374–381. doi:10.1080/03637759609376392.

Cooren, F., Kuhn, T., Cornelissen, J. P., & Clark, T. (2011). Communication, organizing and organization: An overview and introduction to the special issue. *Organization Studies, 32*(9), 1149–1170. doi:10.1177/0170840611410836.

Cruz, D. (2017). Identity, individual. In C. R. Scott & L. Lewis (Eds.), *The international encyclopedia of organizational communication* (online edition). Hoboken, NJ: Wiley-Blackwell. doi:10.1002/9781118955567.wbieoc101

Dawson, V. R. (2018). Fans, friends, advocates, ambassadors, and haters: Social media communities and the communicative constitution of organizational identity. *Social Media + Society, 4*(1), pp. 1–11. doi:10.1177/2056305117746356.

Deetz, S. (1992). *Democracy in an age of corporate colonization: Developments in communication and the politics of everyday life.* Albany, NY: SUNY Press.

Dobusch, L., & Schoeneborn, D. (2015). Fluidity, identity, and organizationality: The communicative constitution of Anonymous. *Journal of Management Studies, 52*(8), 1005–1035. doi:10.1111/joms.12139.

Dukerich, J. M., & Carter, S. M. (2000). Distorted images and reputation repair. In M. Schultz, M. J. Hatch & M. H. Larsen (Eds.), *The expressive organization: Linking identity, reputation, and the corporate brand* (pp. 97–112). Oxford: Oxford University Press.

Dukerich, J. M., Kramer, R., & Parks, J. M. (1998). The dark side of organizational identification. In D. A. Whetten & P. C. Godfrey (Eds.), *Identity in organizations: Building theory thorough conversations* (pp. 245–256). Thousand Oaks, CA: SAGE.

Dutton, J. E., & Dukerich, J. M. (1991). Keeping an eye on the mirror: Image and identity in organizational adaptation. *Academy of Management Journal, 34*(3), 517–554. doi:10.5465/256405.

Dutton, J. E., Dukerich, J. M., & Harquail, C. V. (1994). Organizational images and member identification. *Administrative Science Quarterly, 39*(2), 239–263. doi:10.2307/2393235.

Fombrun, C., & Rindova, V. (2000). The road to transparency: Reputation management at Royal Dutch/Shell. In M. Schultz, M. J. Hatch & M. H. Larsen (Eds.), *The expressive organization: Linking identity, reputation, and the corporate brand* (pp. 77–96). Oxford: Oxford University Press.

Foreman, P. O., & Whetten, D. A. (2016). Measuring organizational identity: Taking stock and looking forward. In M. G. Pratt, M. Schultz, B. E. Ashforth & D. Ravasi (Eds.), *Organizational identity* (pp. 39–64). Oxford: Oxford University Press.

Gill, R. (2013). The evolution of organizational archetypes: From the American to the entrepreneurial dream. *Communication Monographs, 80*(3), 331–353. doi:10.1080/03637751.2013.788252.

Gioia, D. A. (1998). From individual to organizational identity. In D. A. Whetten & P. C. Godfrey (Eds.), *Identity in organizations: Building theory through conversations* (pp. 17–31). Thousand Oaks, CA: SAGE.

Gioia, D. A., & Hamilton, A. L. (2016). Great debates in organizational identity study. In M. G. Pratt, M. Schultz, B. E. Ashforth, & D. Ravasi (Eds.), *Organizational identity* (pp. 21–38). Oxford: Oxford University Press.

Goffman, E. (1959). *The presentation of self in everyday life.* New York: Anchor.

Hatch, M. J., & Schultz, M. (2000). Scaling the Tower of Babel: Relational differences between identity, image, and culture in organizations. In M. Schultz, M. J. Hatch & M. H. Larsen (Eds.),

The expressive organization: Linking identity, reputation, and the corporate brand (pp. 11–35). Oxford: Oxford University Press.

Hatch, M. J., & Schultz, M. (2003). Bringing the corporation into corporate branding. *European Journal of Marketing*, 37(7/8), 1041–1064. doi:10.1108/03090560310477654.

Henderson, A., Cheney, G., & Weaver, C. K. (2015). The role of employee identification and organizational identity in strategic communication and organizational issues management about genetic modification. *International Journal of Business Communication*, 52(1), 12–41. doi:10.1177/2329488414560278.

Holmer Nadesan, M. (1996). Organizational identity and space of action. *Organization Studies*, 17 (1), 49–81. doi:10.1177/017084069601700103.

Kopaneva, I., & Sias, P. M. (2015). Lost in translation: Employee and organizational constructions of mission and vision. *Management Communication Quarterly*, 29(3), 358–384. doi:10.1177/0893318915581648.

Koschmann, M. A. (2013). The communicative constitution of collective identity in interorganizational collaboration. *Management Communication Quarterly*, 27(1), 61–89. doi:10.1177/0893318912449314.

Kreiner, G. E., Ashforth, B. E., & Sluss, D. M. (2006). Identity dynamics in occupational dirty work: Integrating social identity and system justification perspectives. *Organization Science*, 17 (5), 619–636. doi:.1287/orsc.1060.0208.

Kuhn, T. (2006). A "demented work ethic" and a "lifestyle firm": Disclosure, identity, and workplace time commitments. *Organization Studies*, 27(9), 1339–1358. doi:10.1177/0170840606067249.

Kuhn, T., Golden, A. G., Jorgenson, J., Buzzanell, P. M., Berkelaar, B. L., Kisselburgh, L. G., Kleinman, S., & Cruz, D. (2008). Cultural discourses and discursive resources for meaning/ful work constructing and disrupting identities in contemporary capitalism. *Management Communication Quarterly*, 22(1), 162–171. doi:10.1177/0893318908318262.

Kuhn, T., & Nelson, N. (2002). Reengineering identity: A case study of multiplicity and duality in organizational identification. *Management Communication Quarterly*, 16(1), 5–38. doi:10.1177/0893318902161001.

Larson, G. S. (2017). Identification, organizational. In C. R. Scott & L. Lewis (Eds.), *The international encyclopedia of organizational communication* (online edition). Hoboken, NJ: Wiley-Blackwell. doi:10.1002/9781118955567.wbieoc100.

Larson, G. S., & Gill, R. (2017). *Organizations and identity*. Cambridge, UK: Polity Press.

Larson, G. S., & Pepper, G. L. (2003). Strategies for managing multiple organizational identifications: A case of competing identities. *Management Communication Quarterly*, 16(4), 528–557. doi:10.1177/0893318903251626.

Madsen, V. T. (2016). Constructing organizational identity on internal social media: A case study of coworker communication in Jyske Bank. *International Journal of Business Communication*, 53(2), 200–223. doi:10.1177/2329488415627272.

Mael, F. A., & Ashforth, B. E. (1992). Alumni and their alma mater: A partial test of the reformulated model of organizational identification. *Journal of Organizational Behavior*, 13(2), 103–123. doi:10.1002/job.4030130202.

Mael, F. A., & Ashforth, B. E. (1995). Loyal from day one: Biodata, organizational identification, and turnover among newcomers. *Personnel Psychology*, 48(2), 309–333. doi:10.1111/j.1744-6570.1995.tb01759.x.

Meisenbach, R. M. (2010). Stigma management communication: A theory and agenda for applied research on how individuals manage moments of stigmatized identity. *Journal of Applied Communication Research*, 38(3), 268–292. doi:10.1080/00909882.2010.490841.

Miller, V., Allen, M., Casey, M., & Johnson, J. (2000). Reconsidering the organizational identification questionnaire. *Management Communication Quarterly*, 13(4), 626–658. doi:10.1177/0893318900134003.

Morgan, J. M., Reynolds, C. M., Nelson, T. J., Johanningmeier, A. R., Griffin, M., & Andrade, P. (2004). Tales from the fields: Sources of employee identification in agribusiness. *Management Communication Quarterly, 17*(3), 360–395. doi:10.1177/0893318903258169.

Morsing, M. (2006). Corporate social responsibility as strategic auto-communication: On the role of external stakeholders for member identification. *Business Ethics: A European Review, 15*(2), 171–182. doi:10.1111/j.1467-8608.2006.00440.x.

Mumby, D. K. (2005). Theorizing resistance in organization studies: A dialectical approach. *Management Communication Quarterly, 19*(1), 19–44. doi:10.1177/0893318905276558.

Postmes, T. (2003). A social identity approach to communication in organizations. In S. A. Haslam, D. Van Knippenberg, M. J. Platow, & N. Ellemers (Eds.), *Social identity at work: Developing theory for organizational practice* (pp. 81–97). New York, NY: Psychology Press.

Pratt, M. G. (1998). To be or not to be? Central questions in organizational identification. In D. A. Whetten & P. C. Godfrey (Eds.), *Identity in organizations: Building theory thorough conversations* (pp. 171–207). Thousand Oaks, CA: SAGE.

Pratt, M. G. (2001). Social identity dynamics in modern organizations: An organizational psychology/organizational behavior perspective. In M. A. Hogg & D. J. Terry (Eds.), *Social identity processes in organizational context* (pp. 13–30). Philadelphia, PA: Psychology Press.

Pratt, M. G. (2016). Hybrid and multiple organizational identities. In M. G. Pratt, M. Schultz, B. E. Ashforth & D. Ravasi (Eds.), *Oxford handbook of organizational identity* (pp. 106–120). Oxford: Oxford University Press. doi:10.1093/oxfordhb/9780199689576.013.28.

Pratt, M. G., & Foreman, P. O. (2000). Classifying managerial responses to multiple organizational identities. *Academy of Management Review, 25*(1), 18–42. doi:10.5465/amr.2000.2791601.

Pratt, M. G., Schultz, M., Ashforth, B. E., & Ravasi D. (2016). Introduction: Organizational identity, mapping where we have been, where we are, and where we might go. In M. G. Pratt, M. Schultz, B. E. Ashforth & D. Ravasi (Eds.), *Oxford handbook of organizational identity* (pp. 1–18). Oxford: Oxford University Press. doi:10.1093/oxfordhb/9780199689576.013.23.

Schinoff, B. S., Rogers, K. M., & Corley, K. G. (2016). How do we communicate who we are? Examining how organizational identity is conveyed to members. In M. G. Pratt, M. Schultz, B. E. Ashforth & D. Ravasi (Eds.), *Oxford handbook of organizational identity* (pp. 219–238). Oxford: Oxford University Press. doi:10.1093/oxfordhb/9780199689576.013.8.

Scott, C. R. (1997). Identification with multiple targets in a geographically dispersed organization. *Management Communication Quarterly, 10*(4), 491–522. doi:10.1177/0893318997104004

Scott, C. R. (2007). Communication and social identity theory: Existing and potential connections in organizational identification research. *Communication Studies, 58*(2), 123–138. doi:10.1080/10510970701341063.

Scott, C. R. (2013). *Anonymous agencies, backstreet businesses, and covert collectives: Rethinking organizations in the 21st century.* Stanford, CA: Stanford University Press.

Scott, C. R., Corman, S. R., & Cheney, G. (1998). Development of a situated-action theory of identification in the organization. *Communication Theory, 8*(3), 298–336. doi:10.1111/j.1468-2885.1998.tb00223.x.

Scott, C. R., & Stephens, K. K. (2009). It depends on who you're talking to... Predictors and outcomes of situated measures of organizational identification. *Western Journal of Communication, 73*(4), 370–394. doi:10.1080/10570310903279075.

Schultz, M., Hatch, M. J., & Larsen, M. H. (Eds.). (2000). *The expressive organization: Linking identity, reputation, and the corporate brand.* Oxford: Oxford University Press.

Tajfel, H., & Turner, J. C. (1985). The social identity theory of intergroup behavior. In S. Worchel & W. G. Austin (Eds.), *Psychology of intergroup relations* (2nd ed., pp. 7–24). Chicago, IL: Nelson-Hall.

Tompkins, P. K., & Cheney, G. (1983). Account analysis of organizations: Decision-making and identification. In L. L. Putnam & M. E. Pacanowsky (Eds.), *Communication and organizations: An interpretive approach* (pp. 123–146). Beverly Hills, CA: SAGE.

Tompkins, P. K., & Cheney, G. (1985). Communication and unobtrusive control in contemporary organizations. In R. D. McPhee & P. K. Tompkins (Eds.), *Organizational communication: Traditional themes and new directions* (pp. 179–210). Beverly Hills, CA: SAGE.

Tracy, S. J., & Scott, C. (2006). Sexuality, masculinity, and taint management among firefighters and correctional officers: Getting down and dirty with "America's heroes" and the "scum of law enforcement." *Management Communication Quarterly*, 20(1), 6–38. doi:10.1177/0893318906287898.

Tracy, S. J., & Trethewey, A. (2005). Fracturing the real-self–fake-self dichotomy: Moving toward "crystallized" organizational discourses and identities. *Communication Theory*, 15(2), 168–195. doi:10.1111/j.1468-2885.2005.tb00331.x.

Turner, P. K., & Norwood, K. (2013). Unbounded motherhood: Embodying a good working mother identity. *Management Communication Quarterly*, 27(3), 396–424. doi.org/10.1177%2F0893318913491461.

Van den Bosch, A. L. M., de Jong, M. D. T., & Elving, W. J. L. (2006). Managing corporate visual identity: Differences between profit and non-for-profit, and manufacturing and service organizations. *Journal of Business Communication*, 43, 138–157.

Whetten, D. A., & Godfrey, P. C. (Eds.). (1998). *Identity in organizations: Building theory through conversations*. Thousand Oaks, CA: SAGE.

Wieland, S. M. B. (2017). Organizational identity. In C. R. Scott & L. Lewis (Eds.), *The international encyclopedia of organizational communication* (online edition). Hoboken, NJ: Wiley-Blackwell. doi:10.1002/9781118955567.wbieoc156.

12 Power and Resistance

Heather M. Zoller and Zhuo Ban

Looking at organizations through the critical lens of power and resistance challenges some traditional approaches to understanding organizational communication. Rather than focus primarily on the development of shared meaning and cooperation, critical research views organizations as sites of conflict, both apparent and hidden. Critical studies built on the interpretive turn in organizational communication, questioning how certain meanings become dominant in the organizing process and whose interests are served by those symbolic constructions (see Chapter 2). Critical researchers adopt a discourse of suspicion (Mumby, 1997), often focused on structural inequalities. As a result, critical researchers theorize organizations "as social historical creations accomplished in conditions of struggle and power relations" (Deetz, 2001, p. 25), and as "political sites where various organizational actors and groups struggle to 'fix' meaning in ways that will serve their particular interests" (Mumby, 2004, p. 237). From this viewpoint, apparent consensus can hide conflicting interests.

To begin the chapter, we talk more about how scholars have theorized the role of power in communication processes, and the implications for our understanding of organizations. This discussion is followed by a description of the concept of resistance. We follow this with a description of some major areas of research investigating power and politics.

Defining Power in Organizational Communication: Historical Approaches

Researchers conceptualize *power* in different ways. Foundational organizational communication scholars drew from other disciplines to develop communication-centered perspectives that emphasize the politics of the organizing process. Early conceptualizations of power include psychologists French and Raven's (1959) bases of social power. Their model theorized sources of social influence including reward, coercive, legitimate, referent, and expert power. Although useful in some ways, research in this area tended to theorize communication as legitimizing already existing relations of power rather than as productive of power relations.

Another source of theorizing power came from political scientists. Dahl (1957) theorized a "one-dimensional" pluralist model of power, which construed power as a person's or group's direct influence over the behavior of others (an ability to make someone do something they would not otherwise do). Bachrach and Baratz (1962) introduced a two-dimensional model highlighting how elite groups can also control agendas in ways that impede or suppress discussion of issues that might threaten their interests and preferences. Lukes'(1974) three-dimensional model added an even more complex view of communication by observing that power operates not only through visible decision-making and apparent conflict, but through its absence, as the ability to shape and articulate the desires of others.

Organizational communication scholars built on the three-dimensional model of power to advocate for understanding power as a centrally communicative phenomenon. As described in Chapter 2, scholars integrated critical theories with hermeneutic theories of interpretation and social constructionist epistemologies. Their work highlighted how struggles over meaning are constitutive of organizational life (Clair, 1993; Conrad, 1983; Deetz, 1992; Mumby, 1993) and led to alternate definitions of power.

For example, Hardy and Phillips suggested that dominant groups establish and maintain power by

> articulating meaning in ways that legitimate their particular views as "natural" and "inevitable," link the actions and preferences of other actors to the achievement of their interests, and make particular socially constructed structures take on a neutral and objective appearance.
>
> (Hardy & Phillips, 2004, p. 304).

Communication-centered approaches also highlighted the construction of subjectivity as a central component of relations of power (Holmer Nadesan, 1996). Mumby and Clair theorized that

> The most effective use of power occurs when those with power are able to get those without power to interpret the world from the former's point of view. Power is exercised through a set of interpretive frames that each worker incorporates as part of his or her organizational identity.
>
> (Mumby & Clair, 1997, p. 184)

As we will discuss, researchers also began to address the relationship between power and *resistance*.

Power and the Communicative Constitution of Organization

As these definitions demonstrate, critical scholars have long theorized organizing as a fundamentally communicative as well as power-laden process. This orientation reflects the *organization as grounded in action* perspective (Fairhurst & Putnam, 2004) because it views organizational action and structure as mutually constitutive. Through everyday communication interactions, taken-for-granted assumptions become sedimented into cultural norms, rules, and routines, and potentially enduring organizational policies, contracts, and practices. These social constructions serve some interests over others, resulting from and contributing to power relationships.

Critical organizational communication was influenced by sociologist Anthony Giddens' (1979) theory of structuration (see Chapter 3). Giddens emphasized the role of power and ideology in the recursive (mutually defining) processes of constituting individual agency and social structures, describing how social structures can take on "objective" status. Contemporary structuration and CCO perspectives bring attention to how micro-level, relational communication processes constitute and are constituted by organizational structures. However, this research does not always address Giddens' focus on power and ideology, stopping short of considering how certain constructions favor the interests of some groups over others in systematic ways. For example, some have argued that much CCO research sometimes treats workers and managers as equally capable of discursively constructing the organization (Cloud, 2005). Others have argued that authors drawing from this perspective tend to "delimit the examination of power in communication to issues such as: the competencies of individual actors; the effects of organizational structure on actors; or the concentration of power in authority figures" (Kwon, Clarke, & Wodak, 2009).

Like the institutional theorists (see Chapter 3) who consider the ways that organizations are both influenced by broader organizational structures and are actors in those structures, critical scholars consider how organizing processes are embedded in larger cultural and political systems. For example, workplace policies about sexual harassment are influenced by larger cultural and public policy discourses about gender (and changes in workplace policies recursively influence larger cultural discourses). Although institutional structures are constituted through communication, they often become enduring patterns that appear to be outside of our control. We describe later in this chapter how critical scholars investigate these micro-macro issues.

Conceptual Development of Power Though Multiple Theoretical Lenses

Drawing from multiple theoretical perspectives, researchers have created a rich conceptual repertoire for understanding relationships among communication and power. In the following section, we describe concertive control, ideology and hegemony, systematically distorted communication, discipline, difference and intersectionality, and colonialism.

Concertive Control

Normative and interpretive perspectives on power address the relationship between shared beliefs and systems of control. Theorizing may promote (normative) or describe (interpretive) control systems. For example, Barker (1993) and Barker and Cheney (1994) expanded on Edwards' (1981) theorizing about simple (direct, authoritative), technological, and bureaucratic control (rules and hierarchical structures) to develop the concept of *concertive control* (see also Chapter 7). Barker studied the creation of self-managing work teams, which allowed organizations to reduce layers of supervision, promote more flexible production practices, and arguably increase the speed of production. Barker observed the development of "concertive" forms of control in which team members come to control themselves more powerfully than supervisors had previously. Barker argued that as workers internalized organizational values, they created and enforced stricter work expectations for themselves and their fellow teammates because employees felt a stronger commitment to deliver on goals that they had set themselves. These goals appeared to be more voluntary and less directed. In Barker's study, team members used guilt and peer pressure to encourage conformity. Newcomers to the team complained about the stress of self-management.

Management in many organizations attempts to foster concertive control. In the movie *Office Space*, a manager in an Applebee's-type restaurant questions a server (played by Jennifer Aniston) about her *flair* (quirky buttons on her uniform suspenders): "I only see 15 pieces." He asks, "What do you think of someone who only does the bare minimum?" Aniston's character suggests that he should change the minimum to 30 if that is what he wants. The manager responds, "I thought you wanted to express yourself." Management hopes that employees will desire to "express themselves" in ways that support organizational goals. (You can search "Joanna Quits" to see the scene.)

Ideology and Hegemony

Many critical theorists trace their roots to Karl Marx (1967). Marx was a German theorist who identified capitalism as the primary source of inequality and exploitation. In the 19th-century factory economy, capitalists received a return on their financial investment, whereas the source of profit comes from paying the laborer less than the value of what the worker produces. Marx described the ways in which ideologies served to hide workers' exploitation in this system, but he also theorized this exploitation as the source of a worker revolution aimed at the development of socialism. German scholars in the Frankfurt School (Institute for Social Research) sought to understand why workers continued to consent to exploitation. As they did so, they expanded Marx's approach to address multiple sources of inequality and the economic, ideological, and cultural basis of power relationships (see Chapter 2).

Contemporary critical research critiques a range of situations of domination and asymmetry with the goals of understanding, critique, and reformation. *Ideology* critique is often central to this work. Critical researchers are particularly interested in the ways that ideologies, or shared belief systems, construct and reinforce the power of dominant groups. Anthony Giddens (1979) theorized three functions of ideology, including:

1. Representing the interests of particular group as universal (e.g., "what is good for GM is good for America").
2. Denying contradictions in society (e.g., politicians saying "we have the best healthcare in the world" in the U.S. ignores high costs and lack of access for many low and middle-income Americans).
3. Reifying social relations (e.g., treating social hierarchies and inequities as natural and inevitable—"the rich got that way because they work hard.").

Gramsci (1971) was an Italian Marxist theorist who theorized linkages between ideology and *hegemony*. Hegemony is a relationship in which a social group accepts subordination to a dominant group or groups as the norm. These groups "consent to and support belief systems and structures of power relations that do not necessarily serve – indeed, may work against – those groups' interests" (Mumby, 1997, p. 344). Dominant groups are able to articulate their own interests in ways that lead other groups to identify with those interests. For example, in the wake of the #MeToo movement addressing sexual harassment, we have seen many women criticize victims who have shared stories of harassment for being *too sensitive*, or failing to come forward sooner. Such perspectives identify with and support the dominant, masculine perspective. Hegemony is not a matter of simple domination, however. It involves active struggles over meaning among multiple groups. For example, many women disagree about what constitutes harassment, or how to achieve equality in the workplace, and we have seen both improvements and setbacks in women's status in the workplace over time.

Systematically Distorted Communication

A different strain of critical research focuses on the role of power in enabling or constraining participatory, democratic participation in meaning construction and decision-making. Researchers draw from the German philosopher Jurgen Habermas (1984) to investigate *systematically distorted communication*. Habermas posited an ideal speech situation in which communication follows a set of norms that facilitate open deliberation. In particular, participants:

- are able to evaluate each other's assertions on the basis of reason and evidence;
- are free from non-rational or coercive influences (physical or psychological sources);
- are motivated by the desire to achieve a rational consensus.

Deetz (1992) drew from the ideal speech situation to theorize about organizational practices of *discursive closure*. Communication may be distorted so that rational and open deliberation does not take place, often because full evaluation of the interests and claims of participants is prevented or certain people/groups/perspectives are not able to participate. Deetz argues that it is not enough for people to participate in sets of choices others have already constructed for them. Rather, people should be able to actively participate in constructing meaning (contributing to the choices themselves). As he says, "Democratic communication in these terms must be about the formation of knowledge, experience, and identity, not merely their expression" (Deetz, 1992, p. 47).

Communication becomes systematically distorted when discursive closure is hidden from assessment. Groups with social and political power can use systematically distorted communication to silence certain groups and ideas/positions over long periods of time. Forms of systematically distorted communication include: neutralization, treating a value-based decision as though it were objective or value-free (*we had no choice but to downsize the company*); disqualification, using a rationale to rule out someone's ability to speak (*you are too emotional about this topic*); and meaning denial, refusing to accept valid interpretations of speech acts or events (*that was flirting, not harassment, I am not shouting!*). Lyon (2007) described how the pharmaceutical company Merck trained salespeople to use discursive techniques to prevent physicians from questioning the safety of Vioxx despite the well-established risks of the drug.

Disciplinary Power

As described in Chapter 2, a critical discourse of suspicion can be contrasted with a postmodern "discourse of vulnerability" (Mumby, 1997), which questions foundational concepts and master narratives such as objective truth, knowledge, and the unitary self, emphasizes contradiction and paradox (Ganesh, 2009), and treats power as shifting and diffuse. Organizational communication scholars have drawn from Michel Foucault (1979, 1980) to theorize the productive role of power in forming the self, social norms, and structures of knowledge. Foucault addresses individuals as subjects in two ways: (1) in the sense of actively making choices, and (2) in the sense of objects of cultural and institutional efforts to shape knowledge and meaning (subject to). Foucault addresses both elements as he theorizes about *disciplinary power*. Discipline can be understood in terms of areas of expertise, as we define what counts as knowledge and constitutes professional practices in particular areas (e.g., the discipline of communication, medical licensing). Discipline can also be understood in terms of efforts to shape behavior and define our sense of self. Foucault emphasized the role of historically situated discourses in developing disciplinary power. For example, as disciplinary institutions develop, they use surveillance technologies (e.g. tests, supervision, technologies) to observe and control the body, and Foucault detailed how this surveillance is internalized by those controlled. He described Bentham's panopticon as a prison in which the guard is positioned to see all of the prisoners. The prisoners internalize this gaze so that they discipline themselves even in the absence of the guard's direct observation. Discipline functions to make power both hidden and dispersed while the individual becomes highly visible.

If, for example, we think about disciplinary power in the classroom, we have to consider how layers of meaning evolve over time. Students are subject to the constructions of what counts as knowledge by different disciplinary areas (history, science). Students are also subject to different forms of surveillance including testing and grading technologies that encourage some forms of learning and behavior over others. However, in order for testing to have an effect, we first had to develop meaning systems that translated learning into numeric or letter grades, and students had to come to see high grades as a way to judge the self and achieve desired outcomes. Disciplinary discourses work to create *docile bodies* that are ideal for particular economic/social arrangements, such as factories and military regiments. In the modern classroom, we might view the rise of more flexible class structures conducive to small group work and technology use as a way to produce workers who can contribute to our rapidly changing *knowledge economy*.

Otherness and Intersectionality

Research addresses the ways that differences, particularly as they relate to identity, are connected with relations of domination. As you will see in Chapters 13 and 14, researchers call for greater attention to *intersectionality*, viewing identity as a crystallization of multiple discourses of race, class, age gender, and other forms of difference. For example, as Chapter 13 will discuss, feminist research provides a lens for understanding power, foregrounding gender and sexuality as constitutive of organizing and relations of domination, increasingly with attention to the ways that ethnicity, class, nationality, and other points of distinction work together to create inequalities (Allen, 1995; Buzzanell, 1994; Buzzanell & Liu, 2005). Feminist research questions binary distinctions that are embedded in organizational life such as subject/object, masculinity/femininity, public/private, emotionality/rationality that often devalue women's experiences and feminine characteristics more broadly (Ashcraft, 2009). For example, airlines historically treat the role of pilot as male (rationale/mind) and flight attendants as female (emotional/body) (Ashcraft, 2007).

Feminist perspectives tend to share an emancipatory goal, critiquing *patriarchy* (a system privileging male leadership) and reclaiming or revaluing women's voice. For instance, Trethewey's (2001) investigation of women's narratives about aging and work suggested that, "To at once critique and possibly begin to transform a patriarchal capitalist system that denigrates older working women, we need to first hear from those women and learn from their experience" (p. 185). Dougherty and Goldstein Hode (2016) investigated sexual harassment at the confluence of gender and power. They observed, for example, that organizations often treated sexual harassment claims as dangerous to men rather than systematically addressing the effects on women. Further, dominant constructions of gender often reinforce *heteronormativity*, the assumption that heterosexuality is fundamental and natural, through everyday communication (Fleming, 2007; Lewis, 2009). Lewis (2009) notes that LGBTQ individuals are not covered under civil rights laws, and that discrimination can lead to quitting, depression, and even suicide.

As Chapter 14 addresses, understanding organizational power also entails recognition that organizations have been constituted in and through racial hierarchies (Ashcraft & Allen, 2003; Parker, 2013; Parker & Mease, 2009). For example, Brenda Allen (2009) observed that theories of socialization have ignored racial hierarchies by assuming that organizations seek to transition members from outsider to insider. This assumption ignores the experiences of racial minorities, who are often treated as outsiders throughout their time in an organization. She also addressed the role of power in silencing dissent, as white people generally determine what count as "real" incidents of racial harassment when they are (infrequently) reported.

Intersectional research recognizes that class distinctions influence multiple forms of difference. Although some researchers argue that our "new" information economy outmodes class analysis, Cloud (2001) countered that class antagonism remains fundamental to the economy, and that such perspectives ignore the material aspects of production including worker and environmental impacts of technology (Cheney & Cloud, 2006). We saw these effects vividly when workers at the Chinese Foxconn plant that makes iPads and other communication technologies committed suicide in response to sweatshop conditions (Barboza, 2010). In the next section, we describe how questions of otherness play out in international contexts.

Colonialism

As mentioned in Chapter 3, many critical theorists have recognized the multifaceted influence of colonialism on global social structures. From the perspective of power and control, colonialism can be understood as an all-encompassing form of subjugation. Colonialism involves an assemblage of technologies and practice of control over the economic, political, and social processes in the colonies. Colonialism entails the creation of history and knowledge about the colony that justifies domination and exploitation. Critical research investigates the influence of these knowledge systems as they become an integral part of contemporary language and modernist systems of representation, thus problematizing the relationship between colonialism and modernity (Shome & Hegde, 2002) (see also Chapter 14).

Postcolonial studies represent an emancipatory agenda that investigates marginalization resulting from projects of colonization and decolonization (Guha, 1983; Shome, 2002; Spivak, 1988). The postcolonial tradition investigates the relationship between colonialism and institutionalized knowledge. In organizational communication, postcolonial researchers interrogate the neocolonial assumptions of European management styles exported to the Global South (Broadfoot & Munshi, 2007). For example, Hall (2010) observed in his investigation of Jamaican managers in a multinational bank a need for organizational theories that address colonial power, history, geopolitical power, and national culture.

Subaltern studies focus "on rewriting history from below, based on the argument that dominant narratives of colonial histories have systematically represented the interests of the colonizers and the national elite" (Dutta & Pal, 2010). Spivak (1988) encouraged aligning disciplinary agendas to recover the erased voices of the global *subaltern* or marginalized communities. Researchers address the context of globalized capitalist frameworks. For instance, Dutta and Pal (2010) extended organizational frameworks of dialogue and participation to accommodate perspectives of the marginalized communities of the Global South. Postcolonial organizational studies offer critiques "against the grain" (Prasad, 2012, p. 21) of standard management and organizational studies texts, offering alternative articulations of non-Western, indigenous, grassroots experiences of organizational processes. Ban and Dutta (2012) explored how neocolonialist discourses around China are prevalent in trade publications about doing business in China, as well as within mainstream news discourse (Ban, Sastry, & Dutta, 2013).

Engaging Resistance

Having described organizational communication approaches to power, we now turn to different ways that researchers have theorized and applied the concept of resistance.

A Dialectical Approach

Early theories of power were critiqued for failing to adequately address resistance. Some researchers also critique postmodernism, and Foucault in particular, for failing to adequately theorize agency, and therefore resistance to power. Some approaches to theorizing organizations as discourse go too far, as Conrad (2004b) described, to the point that "there is no agency and there are no oppressors" (p. 429).

To address these concerns, researchers, often drawing from neo-Gramscian perspectives, investigate a *dialectical* relationship between power and resistance (Mumby, 2005; Mumby & Ashcraft, 2004). Dialectical perspectives emphasize the simultaneity of control and resistance, domination and subordination. Resistance and power are interlinked (after all, there is no need for power without resistance and vice versa). Rather than view power as a relatively fixed and one-way relationship, a dialectical view investigates struggles over meaning among individuals and groups within shifting relations of power (Fleming & Spicer, 2007). The perspective avoids privileging either control or resistance. Scholars who privilege control tend to see resistance as ineffectual, merely reproducing existing power relations, while those who privilege resistance may romanticize the concept by overestimating the potential for change (Mumby, 2005). By contrast, "a dialectical approach examines the inherent tensions and contradictions between agency and structure, between the interpretive possibilities that exist in every discourse situation and institutional efforts to impose or fix meaning" (Mumby & Ashcraft, 2004, p. 53). A dialectical viewpoint is consistent with CCO approaches because it takes a structurational perspective linking structure and agency (see Chapter 2). Some examples of dialectical theorizing:

- Knight and Greenberg (2002) described how Nike's promotionalism (advertising, public relations, etc.) celebrating athletes from marginalized groups deflected public concerns about factory conditions in their supply chain (arguably a form of domination). However, that discourse also made the company a target for activists who asked Nike to live up to these promotional claims to care about the marginalized.
- Real and Putnam (2005) observed that unions are often positioned to advocate for the working class, but they also are systems of power and hierarchy in themselves.

- Carlone and Larson (2006) found that although self-help groups fashioned after Steven Covey's "7 Habits of Highly Effective People" exerted significant influence on the identities of employees and managers, employees also used the program to resist organizational demands. One employee used the habit "put first things first" to argue for spending fewer hours at work and more with his family.

Complications in Understanding Resistance

Researchers have to make difficult choices about how to interpret resistance and control dynamics within specific contexts. For example, Larson and Tompkins (2005) observed that what appears to be resistance may reflect employee uncertainty about what management actually wants. In another example, some scholars view employee cynicism as a form of resistance to managerial directives and the colonization of employee identity (e.g., *the customer is always right, service with a smile, we are a family*). Others, including Fleming and Spicer (2003), argued that although employee cynicism demonstrates the partial and incomplete nature of managerial influence, many cynical employees still follow organizational rules and norms in their behaviors. For example, a Disneyland cast member who gives a highly enthusiastic greeting to park guests is fulfilling the company's goals, even if she believes the greeting is silly and her performance is ironic. In this way, cynicism actually can be the vehicle through which behavioral consent is achieved, because the cynical attitude allows employees to view themselves as liberal, choosing subjects even as they comply with management. As Fleming pointed out, management ultimately cares about employee behaviors rather than internal attitudes.

Another complication in theorizing resistance relates to the partial and often-unanticipated consequences of resistance. For example, Lutgen-Sandvik (2006) found that bullied employees may exit the organization as sign of defiance to bullies and their enablers, but the departure may be the outcome desired by the bully. Another unanticipated consequence occurs when resistant efforts become their own forms of hegemony or discipline (Freire, 1970). Dempsey's (2007) research into transnational advocacy networks cautions us to address potential tensions and inequalities that develop within advocacy groups and among such groups and the communities with which they work (see also Papa, Singhal, & Papa, 2006).

Scholars also differ in how they theorize the scope of resistance. Scholars may focus on relatively overt (public and visible) or covert (hidden and indirect) and individual or collective forms of resistance (Putnam, Grant, Michelson, & Cutcher, 2005). Researchers have reclaimed the significance of relatively covert and everyday forms of resistance, attending to behaviors that once may have been dismissed by critical scholars because they were incapable of really disrupting capitalism (Zoller & Fairhurst, 2007). Organizational communication researchers have adopted Scott's concept of "hidden transcripts" (1990) to examine employee nonconformist discourse like humor or bitching that occurs *backstage* outside the purview of management (Murphy, 1998; Tracy, 2000), along with employee disengagement (Prasad & Prasad, 2000) and even sabotage and theft (Morrill, Zald, & Rao, 2003). This research uncovers hidden forms of conflict through which less powerful groups assert agency and autonomy.

Recently, however, scholars have questioned whether the bulk of research on subtle, everyday forms of resistance has adequately investigated the relationship between these relatively hidden forms and more confrontational challenges and efforts to promote social change (Ganesh, Zoller, & Cheney, 2005). Tracy (2000) addressed the limitations of hidden transcripts in her study of cruise ship workers, observing that private forms of "bitching" gave employees the impression of control, but largely left disciplinary expectations in place that made employees vulnerable to harassment and burnout. Contu (2008), a critical management scholar, critiqued researchers for sidestepping Marxist concerns with capitalist relationships, describing cynicism and misbehavior as *decaf resistance* versus *real resistance*, which she defined as an effort involving existential risks and material losses in its aim for transformation. Ganesh et al. (2005) called for work that explicitly theorizes or documents pathways between relatively individual and more coordinated forms of collective resistance. Gossett and Kilker's (2006) analysis of the website "radioshacksucks" found that "hidden transcripts" of employee complaints on the site facilitated more overt, collective resistance by making complaints visible to management and encouraging members to participate in an ongoing lawsuit against the company. Zoller and Fairhurst (2007) described how discursive leadership can connect hidden transcripts of resistance with the development of collective shows of solidarity and social movements.

Further in this vein, Ganesh et al. (2005) called for renewed attention to larger-scale efforts at transformative change including public policy and social movements. Cloud's (2005) study of Staley's union argued for more confrontational economic strategies for labor versus a discourse of victimhood and moralizing. Social movement and activist research investigate struggles among grassroots organizing, more formal social movement organizations, union campaigns, and corporate issue management strategies (Kendall, Gill, & Cheney, 2007; Knight & Wells, 2007; Weaver, 2010). Research into collective resistance to neoliberal institutions, including New Zealand activists (Ganesh & Stohl, 2010) and the transnational Zapatista model (Dutta & Pal, 2010) demonstrate the challenges of coordinating networked and transnational activism.

Linking collective resistance with policy outcomes, Conrad and McIntush (2003) theorized a rhetorical approach to the punctuated equilibria model (from political science). Conrad (2004a) argued that business elites can maintain policy monopolies—situations in which the policy status quo serves their interests—because they have knowledge, resources and connections that other groups do not have. For example, for many years, gun manufacturers, often working through the NRA, successfully influenced state and federal legislators to avoid restrictions on gun ownership. However, non-dominant groups *can* assert their influence and interrupt elite control of policy making when three things occur:

(1) long-standing sociopolitical conditions become visible to the public and are defined as *"problems"* of sufficient import to demand action by policymakers, (2) potential *solutions* are made available to policymakers, and (3) *political pressures* are sufficiently intense to overcome the dominance by political and economic elites.
(Conrad, 2004a, p. 312, emphasis in original)

For example, in the wake of several high-profile school shootings, parents and high school students organized to define gun policies as a major cause of school shootings, promote increased background checks for gun purchases, and used their retail power to pressure stores such as Field & Stream to stop selling certain guns like AR-15 rifles. So far, the policy impact has been low, but these groups may be able to build momentum for change.

The punctuated equilibrium model represents a third way between elite theories that focus on policy domination by powerful groups (elites control our system) and pluralist models that emphasize equality of competition among social groups (no single groups control our system). A rhetorical perspective highlights how groups attempt to frame issues in ways that are beneficial to their interests in this dialectical struggle between political/economic elites and non-elites (Conrad & McIntush, 2003). Non-elites can outflank more powerful groups by exploiting differing interests among elites or capitalizing on events that bring their issues to the public's attention (see also Mann, 1986). At the same time, Conrad (2004a) described how financial industry elites used the issue management strategy of containment in the wake of the Enron scandal to delay action until public anger receded.

Power and Resistance in Context: Areas of Research

In this section, we describe how research into power and politics has revised our thinking about some major areas of the field. We will focus on three areas of research: organizational culture, workplace health, and corporate influence. In all three cases, researchers have recognized the central role of communication in the way power is enacted in organizational contexts and interpret communicative events from the perspective of power and politics.

Communication, Power, and Organizational Culture

The 1980s witnessed a shift in thinking about managerial–employee relations. Theorists and practitioners began to address the importance of culture to organizational outcomes and employee experiences. Cultural elements include narratives, metaphors, rituals and ceremonies, humor, and organizational norms. Normative and managerial scholars, along with practitioners, treated culture as a variable that could be managed to encourage employees to meet managerial goals. Peters and Waterman (1982) promoted the development of Excellent Cultures, Deal and Kennedy (1982) advocated for "strong cultures." Interpretive scholars, on the other hand, emphasized the organic nature of culture as the product of everyday interactions (see Chapter 2). Critical researchers built on that interpretive perspective, but specifically addressed the ways that organizational cultures may constitute and reinforce the power of dominant groups. Many organizations use cultural strategies of management to influence the behavior of employees. For example, some businesses in China line up all personnel in front of the store every morning before opening for business —rather like when servants line up outside a mansion to welcome guests in *Downton Abbey*, the award-winning television show set in the early 20th century. Management believe that a ritual like that can build a "service attitude" among the employees, which will help increase sales revenues.

Power, Resistance, and Workplace Health

Many scholars and practitioners promote the benefits of workplace health promotion (WHP) programs (Geist-Martin, Horsley, & Angele, 2003; Stephens, Goins, & Dailey, 2013). Initiatives may include on-site gyms or gym membership, health education and wellness topics, and/or medical testing and services (Geist-Martin & Scarduzio, 2011). However, critical scholarship questions whose interests these programs serve.

Critical scholars (Conrad, 1987; Zoller, 2003) argue that WHP expands managerial control of employee lives. These programs construct knowledge about what health is and how it should be achieved, but this advice can be problematic given uncertainties and shifting evidence about how to be healthy (for example, promoting low-fat diets contributed to rising obesity rates; Ebbeling et al., 2012). WHPs shape knowledge about *risk* in ways that protect managerial interests (for example, WHPs rarely warn against the dangers of working long hours or exposure to workplace toxins but do focus on things like salt intake). Programs often moralize about behaviors such as having a poor diet and smoking, which can contribute to stigmatizing certain identities such as smokers or overweight individuals. Fitness promotion may further isolate employees perceived as unfit (Dale & Burrell 2013). At a U.S.-based Japanese auto-mobile manufacturing plant, Zoller (2003) observed that a wellness initiative led some employees to label non-participants as "fat" or "[not] really car[ing] about themselves" (p. 195). Moreover, attributing illness primarily to lifestyle "choices" can lead to victim-blaming (Zoller, 2003) by ignoring the economic roots of health status.

WHP can be viewed as a form of disciplinary power (Foucault, 1979) and biopower in particular (Foucault, 1980). Initiatives represent a governing technique aimed at producing docile, productive, and *less costly* bodies for work. Employees may inter-nalize ideas that equate health with hard work (*working out*), self-control, and surveillance in contrast to discourses that associate health with pleasure or release from worry (Crawford, 1984; Zoller, 2003). Workplaces encourage participation by providing incentives like health insurance discounts, while others penalize some work-ers with a surcharge for certain employees (e.g., Walmart and PepsiCo charged workers deemed to have high cholesterol or be overweight). Newer forms of WHPs promote compliance through discourses of religion and spiritually and may entail more extreme and cult-like fitness regimes such as CrossFit (James & Zoller, 2017).

Management hopes to reduce health care costs, despite unclear return on investment (James & Zoller, 2017). Employees are concerned about loss of income, privacy, discrimination, and autonomy within these programs (Ford & Scheinfeld, 2016; Zoller, 2004). Employees may resist WHP initiatives when the programs are not perceived to meet their needs and when they are not given choices about participation (James & Zoller, 2017). Resisting health promotion can increase employee autonomy and create space for more personalized health behaviors. It can also have a boomerang effect in which employees identify more strongly with habits such as smoking that may put them at greater risk for illness or premature death (James & Zoller, 2017).

Corporate Influences: Corporate Colonization and Corporate Social Responsibility

Addressing the political role of organizations, critical scholars address the role corpora-tions play in influencing other parts of civil society. Deetz (1992) theorized *corporate colonization*, arguing that corporate values come to dominate non-work life within modern society, largely by extending the language, values, and practices of business to the everyday life of members of society. Corporations have in some ways eclipsed the power of the state, and government regulations and restrictions on business have largely given way to state subsidy of corporations. In addition, corporations have transformed the structure and dynamics of families and communities, as work increas-ingly extends into and redefines people's relationship with their families and commu-nities. Corporate values and practices are also adopted by schools and training centers, as the principle goal of education has gradually shifted from preparing for citizenship to preparing for employment. Furthermore, centralized private ownership of media raised questions about the ability of mass media institutions to truly represent and serve public interest.

Corporate social responsibility (CSR) is one form of harnessing the enormous power of corporations toward social good. The dominant "win-win" school of CSR (Porter & Kramer, 2011) believes that corporations can/should use their economic prowess to create positive social change by pursuing policies beneficial to both business and society. Critical engagement with CSR, however, points out that various CSR initiatives and programs further expand corporate power. Viewing CSR discourse as "an ideological movement that intend[s] to legitimize and consolidate the power of large corporations," Banerjee (2008, p. 51) argued that CSR programs are only concerned about stakeholders in the sense of "stakeholder colonialism," a strategy to regulate stakeholder behaviors for the benefit of the business interests. CSR discourse normalizes capitalist governmentality. For example, promoting corporations' commitment to social welfare (ranging from compiling supplier codes of conduct to organizing a marathon to cure cancer) may give the impression that corporations can take over the role of government and other social institutions. CSR discourse may justify a socio-political structure with limited government intervention on social issues and reduced regulations on corporate activities. In short, CSR discourses may not make corporations more socially responsible, but they can prevent other social actors from effective engagement in social issues.

Conclusion

In this chapter, we demonstrated the pervasive nature of power in organizations, and surveyed some key literature on the complex ways that power is exercised in organizational context. Power is central to organizational communication theorizing because both power and communication are constitutive of the organizing process. Organizational communication researchers interested in the issues of power and resistance understand communication in various ways. These different approaches largely depend on the particular lens taken to examine power in an organizational setting.

One view examines power as an organizational tool and conceptualizes communication in terms of messages. For scholars interested in the way power manifests and is exercised in an organization, communication may be treated as linguistic events (transmission of messages) that are conditioned by pre-existing social structures. Another approach treats power as an outcome and conceptualizes communication as constituted of organization. These scholars seek to understand how institutions and formations of power emerge as the outcome of communication. These scholars may be interested in the origin of power—how power emerges from/within/concurrent to the organizing process. A third approach views power as self-reproductive. Here, communication is understood as the process in which systems of meaning and social structure are in a mutually constitutive relationship. Scholars are interested in how groups gain and maintain power through control of meaning-making processes.

Many scholars covered in the chapter have captured the way power is produced, reproduced and contested in communicative practices, whether through the lens of ideology and hegemony, disciplinary discourses, or concertive control. This chapter has also shown the different ways communication research conceptualizes organization vis-à-vis issues of power and resistance. As we have seen in other chapters in this book, the conceptualization of organization is often associated with how communication is understood in the organizing process. The message transmission view of communication is typically associated with the entitative understanding of organizations (O_3), in which power and resistance emerge as the result of/in response to pre-existing organizational conditions. The constitutive approach to communication, on the other hand, recognizes the role that communication plays in shaping the organizational structure (O_2); for example, when dominant ideologies reify in the form of social structures and institutions. Moreover, researchers that view communication as a meaning-making process often see power and resistance in a dialectic relationship. As organizational actors compete in the meaning-making process, their interaction drives the organizing process (O_1) forward.

From the CCO perspective, organizations are grounded in action. This includes communicative practices that are shaped by, and further reify the existing power structures. In this chapter, we have demonstrated how day-to-day communication/interaction and deep enduring processes/structures enable and constrain one another in spiraling fashion in the context of power and resistance. From a dialectical approach, we have emphasized the simultaneity of control and resistance, domination and subordination, and have discussed how ideological control is never complete, but is always embedded in everyday interactions and discursive struggles. As such, resistance in the form of day-to-day interactions may challenge, disrupt, or eventually rupture dominant system of meaning, and bring about change at the institutional or structural level. Therefore, we highlight the importance of observing power in the communicative tug and tow between control and resistance, and refrain from focusing on only one side of the struggle, which may underestimate or overestimate the potential for resistance to bring about change.

In this chapter, we focused on three areas of research—organizational culture, workplace health, and corporate influence—to demonstrate how the issues of power and politics has revised our thinking in these areas. We have demonstrated how research in the three areas addresses the ways that power structures (e.g., managerial control in workplace, corporate dominance in contemporary society) influence and are influenced by organizational discourses, rituals, and value system. Work in these areas and others covered in this chapter demonstrates that organizational communication is embedded in the dialectical relationship between control and resistance, and that power is a central feature of the way organizations are communicatively constituted.

Recommended Supplementary Readings

Ashcraft, K. L., & Allen, B. J. (2003). The racial foundation of organizational communication. *Communication Theory, 13*, 5–38.

This journal article is one of the first to reflect on the racial nature of organizations. It made pertinent critique on the ways core organizational communication texts frame race, and pointed out that these ironically reproduce normative white power.

Broadfoot, K. J., & Munshi, D. (2007). Diverse voices and alternative rationalities: Imagining forms of postcolonial organizational communication. *Management Communication Quarterly, 21*(2), 249–267.

This forum article explores the alternative ways of conceptualizing organizational communication from a postcolonial perspective. This is done in the form of a dialogue between the two authors on their professional experience as organizational communication scholars.

Buzzanell, P. M. (2000). *Rethinking organizational and managerial communication from feminist perspectives.* Thousand Oaks, CA: SAGE.

This is an edited book that brings multiple feminist perspectives to the field of organizational and managerial communication. The emphasis of the book is the ongoing dialogues and negotiations among diverse voices.

Conrad, C. (2011). *Organizational rhetoric: Strategies of resistance and domination.* Cambridge: Polity.

This book critically engages with the ideological nature of corporate discourse, arguing that organizational rhetoric has been used strategically to manipulate public opinion and influence public policies. It also examines resistance to these ideological constructions.

Fleming, P., & Spicer, A. (2007). *Contesting the corporation: Struggle, power and resistance in organizations.* Cambridge: Cambridge University Press.

The authors examined the various ways power operates in a corporate setting, and argue that contemporary corporations are driven by political struggle, power plays, and resistive practices.

Ganesh, S., Zoller, H. M., & Cheney, G. (2005). Transforming resistance: Critical organizational communication meets globalization from below. *Communication Monographs, 19*(2), 169–191.

This essay argues that organizational communication studies should pay more attention to collective (rather than individual) forms of resistance in order to study the transformative movement of "globalization from below."

Mumby, D. K. (2004). Discourse, power and ideology: Unpacking the critical approach. In D. Grant, C. Hardy, C. Oswick, & L. L. Putnam (Eds.), *The SAGE handbook of organizational discourse* (pp. 237–258). London: SAGE.

This handbook chapter conducts a survey on critical organizational discourse research, focusing on the relationship among organizing, discourse, and power.

Zoller, H. M. (2013). Power and resistance in organizational communication. In L. Putnam & D. K. Mumby (Eds.), *The SAGE handbook of organizational communication* (3rd ed.). Thousand Oaks, CA: SAGE.

This book chapter overviews recent approaches to studying power and resistance in organizational communication, including multiple theoretical perspectives.

Important Concepts: Define and Discuss

Power
Concertive control
Ideology
Hegemony
Systematically distorted communication
Disciplinary power
Patriarchy
Heteronormativity
Colonialism
Dialectical approach
Resistance
Resistance, covert form of
Social movement
Punctuated equilibrium model

Discussion Questions

1. What is the difference between concertive control and other types of control? Have you had experience when you internalize the value and objectives of the organization you are in? Please reflect on how some socially accepted values (e.g., efficiency and rationality) work to regulate the behavior of social actors.
2. How do you see the dialectical approach to power and resistance playing out in your university? Do you see examples of ways that undergraduate and graduate students both comply with and resist relationships of power on campus?
3. What are some examples of everyday form of resistance that you see operating in places where you have worked?
4. What are some examples of how corporate values influence your educational experience?

Practitioners' Corner

Due to the pervasive nature of power in organizations, everyone in the organization, including communication practitioners, is surrounded by various power dynamics and relationships, with or without consciously recognizing and responding to them. Communication practitioners have to navigate the power dynamics and relationships inside (and outside) the organization in designing, executing, and evaluating communication programs. We have identified two problematic tendencies within which power is dealt with among communication practitioners. The first tendency is to ignore or elide over power issues in communication events and programs. The second tendency is to treat power and control as absolute, and therefore resign to totally conform to the established power structure even when positive change is possible. Like we have discussed earlier about systematically distorted communication, communication practitioners with these tendencies may treat value-based communication practices as though it were objective or value-free, and may design campaigns that exclude or discredit some people's voices.

While many communication practitioners consider these as the "pragmatic approach" to organizational communication, many have observed problems with this approach in practice. For example, a marketing campaign based on assumed "generally accepted" normative values may trigger vehement objections from underrepresented social groups. While communicating with internal audiences, communication efforts can be challenged by employees' covert, subtle forms of resistance. The best practice is to consciously incorporate a power perspective in the designing, executing, and evaluating communication programs that anticipate and proactively deal with the issue of power. In doing so, communication practitioners may have the potential to be part of positive change toward a more power-equitable society. To that end, we will offer some strategic and tactical considerations.

Strategic considerations:

- Understand the power aspects of communicative situations. Is the target audience a historically disempowered group? If some form of persuasion is used in the communication, is the target audience empowered to make sound and independent judgments about the promoted position? Whose voice is represented in the communication?

- Design power-sensitive communication plans. Does the plan involve discursive closure and systematically distorted communication in the form of neutralization, disqualification, and meaning denial? When trying to reach agreement with a target group, is the objective of the plan to realize mutual benefit or exert concertive control? Has the plan been checked for normative assumptions (e.g., in some Asian countries, many skin product commercials highlight the "skin-lightening" functions, assuming that lighter skin tone is more desirable)? Is there plan for resistance, either in collective or individual, overt or covert forms?
- Critically evaluate communication programs. This means evaluating the output and outcome of communication programs beyond economic indicators. Does the plan result in discursive closure and systematically distorted communication? What kind of relationship is built? Is the relationship marked by power domination? Is the relationship mutually beneficial?

Tactical considerations:

- At the planning stage, it is important to conduct research on the real power structure and relationship in the organization context. Communication network analysis often helps you to more accurately identify the real influencers in the organization.
- Invite or form minority/diversity teams to check for normative assumptions in the communication plan.
- At the execution stage, it is important to reach out to audience members that keep silent, and make sure that they feel empowered enough to voice their concerns if they have any. Organizational member who feel disempowered to disagree openly may use more covert forms of resistance.
- Treat humor and gossip seriously.

References

Allen, B. J. (1995). "Diversity" in organizations. *Journal of Applied Communication Research, 23,* 143–155. doi:10.1080/00909889509365420.

Allen, B. J. (2009). Racial harassment in the workplace. In P. Lutgen-Sandvik & B. Davenport Sypher (Eds.), *Destructive organizational communication* (pp. 164–183). New York: Routledge.

Ashcraft, K. L. (2007). Appreciating the "work" of discourse: Occupational identity and difference as organizing mechanisms in the case of commercial airline pilots. *Discourse & Communication, 1*(1), 9–36. doi:10.1177/1750481307071982.

Ashcraft, K. L. (2009). Gender and diversity: Other ways to "make a difference." In M. Alvesson, T. Bridgman & H. Willmott (Eds.), *The Oxford handbook of critical management studies* (pp. 304–327). Oxford: Oxford University Press.

Ashcraft, K. L., & Allen, B. J. (2003). The racial foundation of organizational communication. *Communication Theory, 13,* 5–38. doi:10.1111/j.1468-2885.2003.tb00280.x.

Bachrach, P., & Baratz, M. (1962). Two faces of power. *American Political Science Review, 56,* 947–952. doi:10.2307/1952796.

Ban, Z., & Dutta, M. J. (2012). Minding their business: Discourses of colonialism and neoliberalism in the commercial guide for U.S. companies in China. *Public Relations Inquiry, 1*(2), 197–220. doi:10.1177/2046147X11435079.

Ban, Z., Sastry, S., & Dutta, M. J. (2013). "Shoppers' Republic of China": Orientalism in neoliberal U.S. news discourse. *Journal of International and Intercultural Communication*, 6 (4), 280–297. doi:10.1080/17513057.2013.792941.

Banerjee, S. B. (2008). Corporate social responsibility: The good, the bad and the ugly. *Critical Sociology*, 34(1), 51–79. doi:10.1177/0896920507084623.

Barboza, D. (2010). After suicides, scrutiny of China's grim factories. *The New York Times*. Retrieved from www.nytimes.com/2010/06/07/business/global/07suicide.html?pagewanted=all.

Barker, J. (1993). Tightening the iron cage: Concertive control in self-managing teams. *Administrative Science Quarterly*, 38, 408–437. doi:10.2307/2393374.

Barker, J., & Cheney, G. (1994). The concept and practices of discipline in contemporary organizational life. *Communication Monographs*, 61, 19–43. doi:10.1080/03637759409376321.

Broadfoot, K. J., & Munshi, D. (2007). Diverse voices and alternative rationalities: Imagining forms of postcolonial organizational communication. *Management Communication Quarterly*, 21(2), 249–267. doi:10.1177/0893318907306037.

Buzzanell, P. (1994). Gaining a voice: Feminist organizational communication theorizing. *Management Communication Quarterly*, 7, 339–383. doi:10.1177/0893318994007004001.

Buzzanell, P., & Liu, M. (2005). Struggling with maternity leave policies and practices: A poststructuralist feminist analysis of gendered organizing. *Journal of Applied Communication Research*, 33, 1–25. doi:10.1177/0893318994007004001.

Carlone, D., & Larson, G. S. (2006). Locating possibilities for control and resistance in a self-help program *Western Journal of Communication*, 70(4), 270–291. doi:10.1080/10570310600992087.

Cheney, G., & Cloud, D. (2006). Doing democracy, engaging the material: Employee participation and labor activity in an age of market globalization. *Management Communication Quarterly*, 19 (1), 1–40. doi:10.1177/0893318905285485.

Clair, R. P. (1993). The bureaucratization, commodification, and privatization of sexual harassment through institutional discourse. *Management Communication Quarterly*, 7, 123–157. doi:10.1177/0893318993007002001.

Cloud, D. L. (2001). Laboring under the sign of the new: Cultural studies, organizational communication, and the fallacy of the new economy. *Management Communication Quarterly*, 15(2), 268–278. doi:10.1177/0893318901152006.

Cloud, D. L. (2005). Fighting words: Labor and the limits of communication at Staley, 1993 to 1996. *Management Communication Quarterly*, 18(4), 543–592. doi:10.1177/0893318904273688.

Conrad, C. (1983). Organizational power: Faces and symbolic forms. In L. L. Putnam & M. E. Pacanowsky (Eds.), *Communication and organizations: An interpretive approach* (pp. 173–194). Beverly Hills, CA: SAGE.

Conrad, C. (2004a). The illusion of reform: Corporate discourse and agenda denial in the 2002 "corporate meltdown." *Rhetoric & Public Affairs*, 7(3), 311–338. doi:10.1353/rap.2005.0003.

Conrad, C. (2004b). Organizational discourse analysis: Avoiding the determinism voluntarism trap. *Organization*, 11, 427–439. doi:10.1177/1350508404042001.

Conrad, C., & McIntush, H. G. (2003). Organizational rhetoric and healthcare policymaking. In T. L. Thompson, A. M. Dorsey, K. I. Miller & R. Parrott (Eds.), *Handbook of health communication* (pp. 403–422). Mahwah, NJ: Lawrence Erlbaum Associates.

Conrad, P. (1987). Wellness in the workplace: Potentials and pitfalls of work-site health promotion. *Milbank Quarterly*, 65(2), 255–275. doi:10.2307/3350022.

Contu, A. (2008). Decaf resistance: On misbehavior, cynicism, and desire in liberal workplaces. *Management Communication Quarterly*, 21(3), 364–379. doi:10.1177/0893318907310941.

Crawford, R. (1984). A cultural account of health: Control, release and the social body. In J. B. McKinlay (Ed.), *Issues in the political economy of health care* (pp. 60–103). New York: Tavistock.

Dahl, R. (1957). The concept of power. *Behavioral Science*, 2, 201–215. doi:10.1002/bs.3830020303.

Dale, K., & Burrell, G. (2014). Being occupied: An embodied re-reading of organizational "wellness." *Organization, 21*(2), 159–177. doi:10.1177/1350508412473865.

Deal, T. E., & Kennedy, A. A. (1982). *Corporate cultures: The rites and rituals of corporate life.* Reading, MA: Addison Wesley Publishing Company.

Deetz, S. (1992). *Democracy in an age of corporate colonization: Developments in communication and the politics of everyday life.* Albany, NY: SUNY Press.

Deetz, S. (2001). Conceptual foundations. In F. M. Jablin & L. L. Putnam (Eds.), *The new handbook of organizational communication* (pp. 3–47). Thousand Oaks, CA.: SAGE.

Dempsey, S. (2007). Towards a critical organizational approach to civil society contexts: A case study of the difficulties of transnational advocacy. In B. J. Allen, L. A. Flores & M. P. Orbe (Eds.), *The international and intercultural communication annual* (pp. 317–339). Washington, D.C.: National Communication Association.

Dougherty, D. S., & Goldstein Hode, M. (2016). Binary logics and the discursive interpretation of organizational policy: Making meaning of sexual harassment policy. *Human Relations, 69*(8), 1729–1755. doi:10.1177/0018726715624956.

Dutta, M. J., & Pal, M. (2010). Dialog theory in marginalized settings: A subaltern studies approach. *Communication Theory, 20*(4), 363–386. doi:10.1111/j.1468-2885.2010.01367.x.

Ebbeling, C. B., Swain, J. F., Feldman, M. A., Wong, W. W., Hachey, D. L., Garcia-Lago, E., & Ludwig, D. S. (2012). Effects of dietary composition on energy expenditure during weight-loss maintenance. *JAMA, 307*(24), 2627–2634. doi:10.1001/jama.2012.6607.

Edwards, R. C. (1981). The social relations of production at the point of production. In M. Zey-Ferrell & M. Aiken (Eds.), *Complex organizations: Critical perspectives* (pp. 156–182). Glenview, IL: Scott Foresman.

Fairhurst, G. T., & Putnam, L. (2004). Organizations as discursive constructions. *Communication Theory, 14*(1), 5–26. doi:10.1111/j.1468-2885.2004.tb00301.x.

Fleming, P. (2007). Sexuality, power and resistance in the workplace. *Organization Studies, 28*(2), 239–256. doi:10.1177/0170840606068307.

Fleming, P., & Spicer, A. (2003). Working at a cynical distance: Implications for power, subjectivity and resistance. *Organization, 10*(1), 157–179. doi:10.1177/1350508403010001376.

Fleming, P., & Spicer, A. (2007). *Contesting the corporation: Struggle, power and resistance in organizations.* Cambridge: Cambridge University Press.

Ford, J. L., & Scheinfeld, E. N. (2016). Exploring the effects of workplace health promotions: A critical examination of a familiar organizational practice. *Annals of the International Communication Association, 40*(1), 277–305. doi:10.1080/23808985.2015.11735263.

Foucault, M. (1979). *Discipline and punish: The birth of the prison* (Trans. A. Sheridan). New York: Vintage.

Foucault, M. (1980). *The history of sexuality: An introduction* (Trans. R. Hurley, Vol. 1). New York: Vintage.

Freire, P. (1970). *Pedagogy of the oppressed.* New York: Herder and Herder.

French, J., & Raven, B. (1959). The bases of social power. In D. Cartwright (Ed.), *Studies in social power.* Ann Arbor, MI University of Michigan Press.

Ganesh, S. (2009). Organizational communication: Postmodern approaches *Encyclopedia of Communication Theory* (pp. 1–5). Thousand Oaks, CA: SAGE.

Ganesh, S., & Stohl, C. (2010). Qualifying engagement: A study of information and communication technology and the global social justice movement in Aotearoa New Zealand. *Communication Monographs, 77*(1), 51–74. doi:10.1080/03637750903514284.

Ganesh, S., Zoller, H. M., & Cheney, G. (2005). Transforming resistance: Critical organizational communication meets globalization from below. *Communication Monographs, 19*(2), 169–191. doi:10.1080/03637750903514284.

Geist-Martin, P., Horsley, K., & Angele, F. (2003). Working well: Communication and individual and collective wellness initiatives. In T. L. Thompson, A. M. Dorsey, K. I. Miller & R. Parrott (Eds.), *Handbook of health communication* (pp. 423–443). Mahwah, NJ: Erlbaum.

Geist-Martin, P., & Scarduzio, J.A. (2011). Working well: Reconsidering health communication at work. In T. Thompson, R. Parrott, & J. Nussbaum (Eds.), *Handbook of health communication* (2nd ed., pp. 117–131). Mahwah, NJ: Erlbaum.

Giddens, A. (1979). *Central problems in social theory: Action, structure and contradiction in social analysis*. Berkeley: University of California Press.

Gossett, L., & Kilker, J. (2006). My job sucks: Examining counterinstitutional web sites as locations for organizational member voice, dissent, and resistance. *Management Communication Quarterly, 20,* 63–90. doi:10.1177/0893318906291729.

Gramsci, A. (1971). *Selections from the prison notebooks* (Trans. Q. Hoare & G. N. Smith). New York, NY: International Publishers.

Guha, R. (1983). *Elementary aspects of peasant insurgency in colonial India*. Delhi: Oxford University Press.

Habermas, J. (1984). *The theory of communicative action: Reason and the rationalization of society* (Trans. T. McCarthy, Vol. 1). Boston: Beacon Press.

Hall, M. L. (2010). Constructions of leadership at the intersection of discourse, power, and culture: Jamaican managers' narratives of leading in a postcolonial cultural context *Management Communication Quarterly, 25*(4), 612–643. doi:10.1177/0893318910389432.

Hardy, C., & Phillips, N. (2004). Discourse and power. In D. Grant, C. Hardy, C. Oswick & L. L. Putnam (Eds.), *The SAGE handbook of organizational discourse* (pp. 299–316). London: SAGE.

Holmer Nadesan, M. (1996). Organizational identity and space of action. *Organization Studies, 17,* 49–81. doi:10.1177/017084069601700103.

James, E. P., & Zoller, H. M. (2017). Resistance training: (Re)shaping extreme forms of workplace health promotion. *Management Communication Quarterly, 32*(1), 60–89. doi:10.1177/0893318917696990.

Kendall, B., Gill, R., & Cheney, G. (2007). Consumer activism and corporate social responsibility. In S. May, G. Cheney & J. Roper (Eds.), *The debate over corporate social responsibility* (pp. 241–266). Oxford: Oxford University Press.

Knight, G., & Greenberg, J. (2002). Promotionalism and its subpolitics: Nike and its labor critics. *Management Communication Quarterly, 15*(4), 571–600. doi:10.1177/0893318902154002.

Knight, G., & Wells, D. (2007). Bringing the local back in: Trajectories of contention and the union struggle at Kukdong/Mexmode. *Social Movement Studies, 6*(1), 83–103. doi:10.1080/14742830701251369.

Kwon, W., Clarke, I., & Wodak, R. (2009). Organizational decision-making, discourse, and power: Integrating across contexts and scales. *Discourse & Communication, 3*(3), 273–302. doi:10.1177/1750481309337208.

Larson, G., & Tompkins, P. (2005). Ambivalence and resistance: A study of management in a concertive control system. *Communication Monographs, 72*(1), 1–21. doi:10.1080/0363775052000342508.

Lewis, A. (2009). Destructive organizational communication and LGBT workers' experiences. In P. Lutgen-Sandvik & B. Davenport Sypher (Eds.), *Destructive organizational communication* (pp. 203–226). New York: Routledge.

Lukes, S. (1974). *Power: A radical view*. London: Macmillan.

Lutgen-Sandvik, P. (2006). Take this job and... Quitting and other forms of resistance to workplace bullying. *Communication Monographs, 73*(4), 406–433. doi:10.1080/03637750601024156.

Lyon, A. (2007). "Putting patients first": Systematically distorted communication and Merck's marketing of Vioxx. *Journal of Applied Communication Research, 35*(4), 376–398. doi:10.1080/00909880701611052.

Mann, M. (1986). *The sources of social power* (Vol. 1). New York: Cambridge Press.

Marx, K. (1967). *Capital* (Trans. S. Moore & E. Aveling). New York: International Publishers.

Morrill, C., Zald, M., & Rao, H. (2003). Covert political conflict in organizations: Challenges from below. *Annual Review of Sociology, 29,* 391–415. doi:10.1146/annurev. soc.29.010202.095927.

Mumby, D. K. (Ed.). (1993). *Narrative and social control: Critical perspectives.* Newbury Park, CA: SAGE.

Mumby, D. K. (1997). The problem of hegemony: Rereading Gramsci for organizational communication studies. *Western Journal of Communication, 61,* 343–375. doi:10.1080/10570319709374585.

Mumby, D. K. (2004). Discourse, power and ideology: Unpacking the critical approach. In D. Grant, C. Hardy, C. Oswick & L. L. Putnam (Eds.), *The SAGE handbook of organizational discourse* (pp. 237–258). London: SAGE.

Mumby, D. K. (2005). Theorizing resistance in organizational studies: A dialectical approach. *Management Communication Quarterly, 19*(1), 19–44. doi:10.1177/0893318905276558.

Mumby, D. K., & Ashcraft, K. L. (2004). *Reworking gender: A feminist communicology of organization.* Thousand Oaks, CA: SAGE.

Mumby, D. K., & Clair, R. P. (1997). Organizational discourse. In T. A. van Dijk (Ed.), *Discourse studies, volume 2: Discourse as social interaction* (Vol.2, pp. 181–205). London: SAGE.

Murphy, A. G. (1998). Hidden transcripts of flight attendant resistance. *Management Communication Quarterly, 11,* 499–535. doi:10.1177/0893318998114001.

Papa, M., Singhal, A., & Papa, W. (2006). *Organizing for social change: A dialectic journey of theory and praxis.* Thousand Oaks, CA: SAGE.

Parker, P. S. (2013). Difference and Organizing. In L.L. Putnam & D. K. Mumby (Eds.), *Handbook of Organizational Communication* (pp. 619–641). Los Angeles, CA: SAGE.

Parker, P. S., & Mease, J. (2009). Beyond the Knapsack: Disrupting the Production of White Racial Privilege through Organizational Practices. In L. A. Samavor, R. E. Porter, & E. R. McDaniel (Eds.), *Intercultural Communication: A Reader, 12th Edition.* Belmont, CA: Wadsworth.

Peters, T. J., & Waterman, R. M. (1982). *In search of excellence.* New York: Harper & Row.

Porter, M. E., & Kramer, M. R. (2011). Creating shared value. *Harvard Business Review, 89*(1/2), 62–77. doi:10.1007/978-94-024-1144-7_16.

Prasad, A. (2012). *Against the grain: Advances in postcolonial organization studies* (Vol. 28). Copenhagen: Business School Press DK.

Prasad, P., & Prasad, A. (2000). Stretching the iron cage: The constitution and implications of routine workplace resistance. *Organization Science, 11*(4), 387–403. doi:10.1287/orsc.11.4.387.14597.

Putnam, L. L., Grant, D., Michelson, G., & Cutcher, L. (2005). Discourse and resistance: Targets, practices, and consequences. *Management Communication Quarterly, 19*(1), 5–18. doi:10.1177/0893318905276557.

Real, K., & Putnam, L. L. (2005). Ironies in the discursive struggle of pilots defending the profession. *Management Communication Quarterly, 19*(1), 91–119. doi:10.1177/0893318905276561.

Scott, J. C. (1990). *Domination and the arts of resistance: Hidden transcripts.* New Haven, CT: Yale University Press.

Shome, R. (2002). Postcolonial approaches to communication: Charting the terrain, engaging the intersections. *Communication Theory, 12,* 249–270.

Shome, R., & Hegde, R. S. (2002). Postcolonial approaches to communication: Charting the terrain, engaging the intersections. *Communication theory, 12*(3), 249–270. doi:10.1111/j.1468-2885.2002.tb00269.x.

Spivak, G. C. (1988). Can the subaltern speak? In C. Nelson & L. Grossberg (Eds.), *Marxism and the interpretation of culture* (pp. 271–313). Urbana, IL: University of Illinois Press.

Stephens, K., Goins, E., & Dailey, S. (2013). Organizations disseminating health messages: The roles of organizational identification and HITs. *Health Communication, 29*(4), 398–409. doi:10.1080/10410236.2012.759896.

Tracy, S. J. (2000). Becoming a character for commerce: Emotion labor, self-subordination, and discursive construction of identity in a total institution. *Management Communication Quarterly*, *14*(3), 90–128. doi:10.1177/0893318900141004.

Trethewey, A. (2001). Reproducing and resisting the master narrative of decline. *Management Communication Quarterly*, *15*(2), 183–226. doi:10.1177/0893318901152002.

Weaver, C. K. (2010). Carnivalesque activism as a public relations genre: A case study of the New Zealand group Mothers Against Genetic Engineering. *Public Relations Review*, *36*, 35–41. doi:10.1016/j.pubrev.2009.09.001.

Zoller, H. M. (2003). Working out: Managerialism in workplace health promotion. *Management Communication Quarterly*, *17*(2), 171–205. doi:10.1177/0893318903253003.

Zoller, H. M. (2004). Manufacturing health: Employee perspectives on problematic outcomes in a workplace health promotion initiative. *Western Journal of Communication*, *68*(3), 278–302. doi:10.1080/10570310409374802.

Zoller, H. M., & Fairhurst, G. T. (2007). Resistance leadership: The overlooked potential in critical and leadership studies. *Human Relations*, *60*(9), 1331–1360. doi:10.1177/0018726707082850.

13 Gender and Feminist Theory

Patrice M. Buzzanell

Gender and Feminist Theory

Gender and feminist theory has changed markedly over the past several decades. People engaged in *consciousness-raising* activism to make visible gender inequalities to larger groups in efforts to gain support for redressing issues. Today, *networked feminism* takes up current political, economic, societal, and cultural manifestations of inequality through online social movements and mobilization of numerous groups through social media. For instance, *hashtag feminisms* is an umbrella term made up of varied social movements that document and provide a virtual space for gender justice organizing and promotion of tactics for combating these inequalities, such as #MeToo and the "Time's Up" campaign that encourage women to act against sexual harassment and assault. Current organizing spans the globe with different names, agendas, and politics befitting local concerns by women and men. Yet there are several commonalities. These commonalities capture actions and fears about men's and women's safety, violence, economic sustainability, and other aspects. They bring together scholarship on sex, gender, feminisms, and organizing from local grassroots to global Internet-enabled networked movements.

At the heart of this chapter are questions about what gender equality means. The meaning has shifted over time. Early rights to vote and attention to laws focused on persuasive messages and institutional structures (also known as First and Second Wave Feminisms, respectively as discussed below) have now shifted to subtle nuances, ambiguities, and contractions in the sensemaking, constitutive, and iterative nature of organizing processes. Gender equality is one of numerous contemporary movements labeled as social justice focused on distribution of privilege (advantages) and individual–societal relationships.

Regardless of what era and meaning of gender equality to which individuals subscribe, this chapter maintains that equality is advantageous for everyone. On the personal level, we might consider how we would feel if we knew that our own family members, neighbors, and friends were not paid fairly, could not earn educational degrees or attend school, and could not own property, have credit, speak in public, drive cars, obtain the job titles commensurate with what they do in their jobs, and so on. On broader levels, gender equality is advantageous so that men and women can participate fully in personal and work life. These rights include the opportunities both to contribute meaningfully to the organizations with which they identify, and to choose what careers they want and how they might best "balance" work and personal life considerations. These reasons align with human agency, choice, and dignity presented in other chapters of this book (see Chapters 2, 3, 12, 14, and 20).

The current chapter discusses why and how agency is constrained and enabled in ways that align with sex (biological difference) and gender (psychological and socially constructed identities). The earliest research on gender and feminisms sought to understand the many different reasons why sex and gender were and continue to be primary ways of organizing societies and individual identities. Put simply, this research sought to uncover why, how, and in what contexts traditional sex and gender prevail (i.e., women should act feminine and do women's work of caring at home and in the office, just as men should act masculine and do men's work of leading, directing, being breadwinners, and forming governments). Early gender and feminist scholarship and activism focused on finding strategies to enable women's voice to enter into governmental policies and decisions (such as rights to vote in elections) and on rewriting scientific, literary, and communication histories. The process of rewriting and including women is ongoing. For instance, it was only recently that films such as *Hidden Figures* (2016, the story of black mathematicians and engineers, Katherine Johnson, Dorothy Vaughan, and Mary Jackson) and *Bombshell: The Hedy Lamarr Story* (2017) depicted contributions made by these women decades earlier. Their insights and hard work were crucial for humans orbiting the earth and for "frequency hopping" techniques that became the basis of Wi-Fi and Bluetooth.

Ironically, when women did accomplish work or discoveries, their efforts and outcomes were considered unusual, irregular, and non-normative. In these ways, women and men maintained the current gendered order, an order and set of gendered stereotypes codified in the Bem Sex Role Inventory (BSRI; Bem, 1974), which enabled researchers to test how and in what contexts conventional gender stereotypes were associated with particular behaviors, values, and attitudes. U.S. Supreme Court judge Ruth Bader Ginsburg built her career arguing that gender-based discrimination on pay, partner benefits for men, ability of women to buy beer at the same age as men, and other cases were unconstitutional (for overview and videos, see Blakemore, 2018). Today men's activities in the home or private realm still are applauded and treated as special although there is nothing inherently gendered in who changes diapers and does household tasks (Buzzanell & D'Enbeau, 2009).

Our discussion explores the myriad and complicated considerations through which sex and gender are intertwined with how people do their everyday lives and structure their worlds. Over time, these relationships between sex and gender have explored the contradictions, ironies, and tensions in research and everyday practice. Despite extensive documentation, *sexism* or gender-based stereotyping and discrimination persists. The Everyday Sexism Project (ESP) invites and catalogues women's (and some men's) accounts of sexism to promote feminist solidary and resistance to such acts; the ESP reports that the largest number of entries into this transnational global Internet-enabled platform report and promote individual and collective agency against assault, harassment, and discrimination in the workplace (Vachhani & Pullen, in press). In explicating the complex challenges embedded in managing and investigating agency, our discussion is informed by Brummans' (2018) tensions formed around individual–collective, action–structure, control–resistance, and human–non-human actants. Each tension is complicated by gender and acknowledges that choice often is limited by norms in everyday lives such that we do not even imagine—let alone become agents in constituting—a different and more fulfilling world (see Buzzanell & Lucas, 2013).

We begin this chapter by differentiating among sex, gender, and feminisms in communication and interdisciplinary studies on gender and feminist theory. We do so to establish fundamental conceptualizations for discussion in this chapter. We present studies in these areas and show where there are continuities and discontinuities, such as sustained attention to sex differences and messages that equate sex (biology) with gender (social construction). We discuss current expansion beyond binary male-female models prominent in earlier studies, such as transgender scholarship that disrupts sex=gender equations. We also discuss how scholarship and organizing has expanded to online organizing that encourages politicized action in ways that reconstitute particular forms of masculinity and networked feminisms.

In the second part, we explore organizational communication scholars' contributions to gender studies and feminisms. In this section, we describe how organizational communication scholars have contributed to, or advanced, gender studies and feminisms in three main ways. In each of these three areas, we attend to theoretical developments and new insights from empirical studies as well as strategies for research-to-practice considerations.

Sex, Gender, and Feminisms

To begin, we differentiate among sex, gender, and feminisms. In doing so, we lay out the continuities of traditional assumptions and everyday practices based on beliefs that sex and gender are equivalent, meaning for example that someone who is female is also feminine (and heterosexual). Second, we elaborate upon core feminist values and how they manifest differently over time, space, and organizational research. We close this section by noting that the present is a time of profound contestations centering on sex, gender, and feminisms that call into question how women and men enact agency, choice, and dignity.

Differentiating categorizations. First, we *differentiate among sex, gender, and feminisms*, and provide an example of organizational communication research that touches upon these categorizations. *Sex* is the traditional biological classification into male and female, as assigned through genitalia, genetics, and hormones. Sex categories on surveys have expanded to include "other" for those whose bodies exhibit prominent anatomical and physiological factors that are both male and female. The Mindset List 2018 that describes incoming university student members of the Class of 2022 notes that "When filling out forms, they are [the first entering college cohort] not surprised to find more than two gender categories to choose from" (Jaschik, 2018). In contrast, *gender* conveys the wide range of socially constructed grouping associated with masculinity and femininity, as well as LGBTQ, that result from socialization, identity, norms, and cultural processes about appropriate roles, communication, and expectations. To understand how gender is socially constructed, we might consider how what is feminine or masculine and normative for people in the United States today is vastly different in appearance and roles from what would be appropriate in China during the Ming Dynasty, in rural vs. urban and Northern vs. Southern alignments during the U.S. Civil War, and in other contexts. Gender scholars in communication continue to include *sex* as a demographic variable or means of comparing and contrasting practices (activities) and enduring structures (see Figure 1.4, p. XX, this volume) without politicizing sex=gender difference by engaging in discussions about choice and human agency. Feminist scholars maintain that sex and gender are central organizing structures and *modus operandi* in societies. Feminist organizational communication scholars seek to disrupt the linear depiction of privilege that accords male=masculine with benefits such as advancement, leadership, status, power, and control. This privilege does not happen in all situations, as we discuss later in this chapter. Instead, privilege is always co-constituted with marginalization, which means that based on our social identities we might accrue advantages (e.g., given the benefit of the doubt about our competence before we even open our mouths) or might be disadvantaged (e.g., automatically dismissed as not the person in power) as a group member.

Feminisms explore gender with pragmatic and advocacy approaches called *praxis* (see Chapter 4) both to create and change awareness of how gender organizes everyday life in ways that are inequitable for both women and men and that require transformation in all processes of the communication-organization dynamic cycle (Figure 1.4). For individuals, these change mechanisms might involve men and women's identification, or acknowledgement of orientation, as *feminist* to produce activist solidarity (Frederick & Stewart, 2018). In their case study of organizations trying to raise and change consciousness about the gendering of institutions and corporate social responsibilities, McCarthy and Moon (2018, p. 1174) urge making the "invisible visible" by encouraging "diverse stakeholders to reflect on strategies, rules, decisions and the very nature of what it is they wish to change."

These awareness and advocacy approaches known as praxis are the basis of many feminist transformational models, although the areas and levels that are targeted for change differ in specific feminist approaches (for overview, see Buzzanell, 1994; see also Ashcraft & Mumby, 2004). For instance, *liberal feminists* find that the root of women's subordination lies in exclusion from legal and policy (structural) equality, with the idea that showing how and where such exclusions occur can then lead to equalizing rules (laws, policies, and practices). *Radical feminists*, believing that change to existing structures is too difficult, advocate the revamping of society and alternative organizing structures based on feminist values. Still other feminists, known as *standpoint feminists*, study how groups of women and men are systematically advantaged and disadvantaged by the socio-political-cultural and material aspects of their lives such that they construct knowledge from their awareness of these commonalities to make change. The advantage of understanding the different feminisms is that they provide insight into how and why gender inequality exists and is so complex—insight that cannot be obtained by referencing only one feminism or promoting only one set of strategies to benefit women and men. Instead, a feminist metatheoretical matrix enables dialogue within and across the different feminisms for a rich and powerful basis for studying organizations and proposing changes (Buzzanell, 1994).

Combining these feminist approaches, Harris (2017) analyzed how federal laws and institutional policies and procedures coalesce around "mandated reporting" of sexual violence on U.S. universities in ways that prioritize (or privilege) masculinity, whiteness, and heteronormativity. In discussing a first-year student orientation skit, Harris described how the audience and skit actors ironically constructed understanding of sexual violence and its reporting from white heterosexist and homophobic positions through techniques of humiliation and humor, thus continuing to "prioritize privileged perspectives" (p. 274). Methods of reporting violence also may buffer colleges against more complete knowledge. For example, she overheard students talk about date rape but lacked names and details. This lack of detail meant that she was not mandated to report the occurrence to officials, thus legitimating non-responsiveness. Furthermore, organizational members' knowledge depended on the production of power as associated with their social locations (e.g., student vs. administrator, a standpoint feminist approach) and difference (e.g., interlocking systems of power and inequality predicated on discourses and structures of difference such as race, class, gender, sexuality, an intersectional feminist approach; see also Chapter 14). Although not stated in Harris' article, a radical feminist implication based on her findings might be to scrap current mandated reporting practices and start from the ground up, or everyday experiences and feminist values, to generate more viable procedures. These examples combine messages and meaning such that procedures of mandated reporting are contradictory in process and in their institutionalization as policy.

Core feminist values. Second, we *elaborate upon core feminist values* and how they manifest differently over time, space, and organizational research. To do so, we provide an overview of feminist waves (phases of theoretical advancements). Then, we delve more fully into feminist communication research to note how communication theories and research about everyday organizing extend and enrich ideas about sex, gender, and feminisms.

Like our earlier discussion about gender, feminisms have shifted over time and space both in political contestations and in communication theory and research. As can be seen in the example of Harris' (2017) study on mandated reporting of sexual violence, one feminist approach often is inadequate to describe and remedy situations that preclude women's and men's full participation in organizational life. As a result, we use *feminisms* rather than the singular form, *feminism*, to indicate the numerous movements and theoretical bases for feminist organizational communication theory. However, core feminist commitments transcend these individual approaches. Core commitments include: analyses of how local and global conditions can be changed to create greater equality (research for praxis), engagement in ongoing and mindful self- and other-critique (self-reflexivity and analyses), and moral obligations to advocate for change (Buzzanell, 1994). Seeing these commitments through a spatio-temporal lens can indicate how and why individuals and collectivities have acted as agents in the past and how people continue to advocate for constituting an organizational world predicated on equality.

Feminist waves. In taking a spatio-temporal lens to feminisms, we note how feminist waves have made changes in our worlds and in organizing processes. Starting with social movements to incorporate women's voice in public venues, the suffrage movements around the world fought to gain the right to vote in political elections. Suffrage movements differed nationally and globally in time periods based on activism, demands, and effectiveness. They differed (and still do differ) for particular groups of women such as members of indigenous tribes and minority groups (Örtenblad, Marling, & Vasiljević, 2017). This U.S. feminist First Wave ended in 1920 after decades of activism when women achieved the right to vote. However, black women in the southern United States often could not exercise this right until the 1960s because of threats and actual physical violence. Saudi Arabian women voted in the 2015 municipal elections for the first time because King Abdullah issued a proclamation in 2011 granting women the right to vote (see BBC News, 2015).

In the United States, the Second Wave began in the 1960s and expanded activism in the 1970s and later for women's rights, inclusion in public and private arenas, incorporation of color and sexualities, and protections against discrimination and harassment (e.g., acts against pregnancy discrimination in the workplace; rights to education, equal pay, and ability to have one's own credit). Consistent with Second Wave politics and practices, organizational communication scholars engaged in examination and critique of doing gender and structuring gendered institutions, as well as policies and laws formed to promote gender equality. Ashcraft and Kedrowicz's (2002) ethnographic analysis of staff and volunteers' relations in a feminist nonprofit organization displayed ironies in members' investments, emotions, and contexts that resulted in both empowerment and disempowerment tensions. Buzzanell's (e.g., Buzzanell & Liu, 2005; Buzzanell et al., 2017; Buzzanell, Waymer, Tagle, & Liu, 2007) research program on maternity leave demonstrated the struggles that women in different occupations, organizations, and racial or ethnic and class structures face in both complying with and resisting worker-mother ideals and with being able to actually use leave policies. These studies examine everyday micro-practices of inequity and macro-discourses of gendered organizing (e.g., masculine ethics of equal treatment and policy use that privilege work over family in tension with feminine ethics of care, nurturing, and family and fairness) and societal notions of gendered identities and relations (e.g., traditional gender roles in and boundaries between family and work or career).

Although much of this discussion has been about gendered and feminist analyses of women's subordination and resistance, Ashcraft (2005) described how male airline pilots utilize conventional gender and organizational roles, power, and authority as father and protector to advance their own interests in organizational restructuring efforts. Duckworth and Buzzanell (2009) described how men talk about and organize their personal and work lives to fulfill their many obligations to children, partners, other family members, neighbors, and their communities in a complex web of responsibility whereby they constitute their fatherhood and masculinities. Discussed later in this chapter is how gendered organizational communication and interdisciplinary scholars examine how men engage in online messages to work together in constituting masculinity in today's economically and politically changing world.

Moreover, race, class, sexuality, and other forms of difference emerged during (and affected the transition from) Second Wave Feminist organizational communication studies to challenge normative linear models of newcomer socialization (e.g., Allen, 2000), gender-neutrality of organizational relationships, policies, and ideal (male) worker bodies (e.g., D'Enbeau & Buzzanell, 2014; Trethewey, 1999), and the nature of communication itself in feminist activism (e.g., Harris, 2018). These studies have developed new theoretical insights about organizational communication. Embedded within and extending Second Wave organizational communication studies are investigations about the paradoxical organizational relationships and structures established to provide gender equality that often fail to achieve goals (see summary, Putnam & Ashcraft, 2017).

The Third Wave and subsequent iterations expand upon activism for women's and men's rights and have enriched feminisms through explicit incorporations of, and theorizing about, paradox, ambiguity, embodiment, ethics, culture, and online and global feminist organizing. Current scholarship aligns with the structurational process depicted in Figure 1.4. Postmodern sensibilities are destabilizing notions of sex, gender, feminisms, sexuality, organizing, and organization. These recent feminist manifestations are discussed in the next section of this chapter.

In summary, throughout these different waves, notions about sex, gender, and feminisms have become more complicated. They have been contested in different ways in politics, in the home, in workplaces, and in the communication discipline. Organizational communication scholars continue to investigate sex differences because there still exists a need to demonstrate inequitable treatment and material consequences for those men and women who both conform to and violate sex role expectations. Contemporary sex difference research conducted on micro- (individuals), meso- (workplaces, project teams, organizations), and macro-levels (societal, global) has uncovered complex dynamics of privilege and marginalizations that defy easy conclusions, invalidating assumptions that women always experience disenfranchisement and men always are privileged or benefit in the public sphere.

Contestations. Third, organizational communication scholars are addressing *profound contestations centering on sex, gender, and feminisms* that call into question how women and men enact agency, choice, and dignity. These contestations surface in scholarship on work, occupations, and careers, and on online organizing, including local and transnational social movements.

Gendered scholarship on work, occupations, and careers. Instead of the somewhat simplistic notions about different behaviors, qualities, and styles aligned with the sex=gender equation, current sex and gender difference research contributes complicated and contradictory or paradoxical insights about difference and intersectionalities in work, occupations, and careers. For instance, privilege–marginalization, ideal–real, "majority"–difference are politicized tensions that erupt in discursive and material ways. Whereas meritocracy beliefs (namely, that the cream rises to the top, everyone has an equal chance, hard work and competence can insure employability) form the core of organizational rules, structures, and advancement, the reality is that meritocracy does not account for difference. Fatherhood bonuses such as higher pay and promotions with greater remuneration offer advantages to men already privileged by society (typically white, middle- or upper-class professionals; see Hodges & Budig, 2010). Attempts to shape fatherhood identities of low-income men tend to reinforce inequality by promoting inaccessible hegemonic masculinities associated with well-paid work and breadwinner status (Randles, 2018).

Furthermore, wage-earning mothers across nations work and live within contradictory policies and results. Countries and organizations that provide family-friendly benefits such as extended parental leaves, flexible work arrangements, and publically funded childcare assistance find lower gender equality. Women opting out of the workforce with even temporary labor force detachments incur long-term wage inequalities and lower-value retirement amounts (e.g., Budig, Misra, & Boeckmann, 2016; Cukrowska-Torzewska, 2017; Fuller & Hirsch, 2018). A 2014 Pew Research Center documents the growing trend for fathers to stay at home and care for children (Livingston, 2014). Yet the long-term economic and familial consequences are unknown, especially in a society that equates masculinity with success in the public realm of work and career. Interdisciplinary scholars have looked at labor force trends through sociological, cross-national and global, gendered, economic, and political lenses. Organizational communication researchers have begun to delve deeply into contradictions and disparities in their examinations of messages, meanings, and the constitution of organizing in labor force trends.

These literatures portray the tangled relationships among gender identities and hegemonic conceptualizations of career and personal life in processes of doing and undoing gender. Medved (2017) described how women breadwinners engage in doing-undoing gender in several ways: Resisting career-primary assumptions of breadwinning; creating parallel obligations that primary obligation need not be "earner" for men or "caregiver" for women; positioning themselves as fitting their roles invoking masculine qualities and language; and challenging traditional gendered relationships by disrupting power-money associations and identities. In these disruptive and reintegrative communication strategies, women and men struggle with the meanings and boundaries of career and personal life. They engage in tension-filled change for themselves through language, social interaction, and reformulations of social institutions:

> While they may, more often than not, perpetuate the ideal worker norms, some women also paradoxically leverage these same ideal worker expectations to gain power in their relationships. These women, even if in contradictory ways, likewise are doing social change and helping, at times, to undo gender in their everyday interactions.
>
> (Medved, 2017, p. 249)

Likewise, McDonald (2013) takes a different tactic from the usual studies of men in women-dominated occupations, such as nursing, by exploring how both women and men construct and resist gender norms during their occupational socialization. In their doing-undoing gender, these women and men perform and resist gender norms:

> The future nurses therefore do not see nursing as a feminized occupation where no masculine gender norms can be enacted ... enacting masculine norms is even sometimes seen as necessary in order to promote the patients' needs. As such, men and women—not just men—recognize and perform aspects of their job that are culturally coded as both more masculine and more feminine. The male and female nursing students in this study thus conform to the gender norms that are expected of them (by doing gender in culturally expected and privileged ways) and resist these same norms (by undoing culturally expected and privileged ways of performing gender).
>
> (McDonald, 2013, p. 576)

This research by Medved (2017) and McDonald (2013) extends past scholarship by transcending complicated and tension-filled sex and gender differences in individual, workplace, work-family, occupational, and societal sites. These articles are theoretically based, problem-centered in orientation, and strategic in implications for everyday life.

Online organizing and social movements. This section on online organizing and social movements discusses organization and organizing centered around hashtag activism and network feminisms discussed at the start of this chapter with attention to women's and men's rights, dignity, choice, and wellbeing. To these we add *material feminisms* that seek to understand the confluence of social arrangements that result in particular forms of gender relations and structures in a specific time and place.

As of this writing, sex, gender, and feminist contestations depicted in this section are being played out in national and global social media and in scholarship with the #MeToo movement focused on gender harassment and with other media exposing transgender inequities in U.S. military membership, blocked access to bathroom facilities in high schools and other public spaces, and frustrations and poverty associated with inabilities to secure employment (e.g., Eger, 2018; Philipps, 2018). These are feminist organizational communication issues because they affect the abilities of men and women to participate fully in different organizations—thus affecting membership, activity, organizing, and organizational structure.

Moreover, online organizing for men trying to protect masculinities in a world where traditional gender markers, economic advantages, and other benefits of mainstream (white) hegemonic masculinity seem to have eroded is creating an uneasy space of contestation. These alt-right movements from the manosphere (clusters of numerous Internet-enabled men's rights organizing spaces) attempt to reconcile and establish a male-dominated order that is technologically sophisticated, anti-feminist, misogynist, pro-fathers' rights, and founded in precarious labor markets locally and globally (Marwick & Caplan, 2018), such as The Red Pill. There are many different readings for what is happening and why. However, most discuss the alt-right's perspective that they need to redress political correctness and discriminations against straight white men and their rights, so that men can resume their places at the heads of the tables at home and in the public sphere (Nicholas & Agius, 2018).

The means for alt-right men's activism is online gender harassment—networked harassment—framed against feminists and depicted as men's moral obligations (Marwick & Caplan, 2018). These networked organizing movements serve as digital micro-publics, or "safe havens and support for those from marginalized groups or with minority viewpoints, and facilitate collaboration among participants as they work to expand mainstream discursive space to create room for their issues and voices" with outreach labeled as "hashtag activism" (e.g., #blacklivesmatter and #alllivesmatter; Sobieraj, 2018, p. 1702). These online collectivities self-organize to promote particular activities and ideologies through social network platforms, conventional mass media, and face-to-face organizing. For instance, a two-year interview study of digital sexism (processes and practices of online abuse based on gender) uncovered three patterns that mitigate against women's safety: Strategies designed to limit women's impact in digital publics (intimidating, discrediting, and shaming); invocation of femininity to undermine women's contributions; and attention directed to women's physicality in exchanges to divert attention and develop fear (Sobieraj, 2018). These patterns are instantiated in verbal messages, visual imagery, online organizing, and embodiment (e.g., physical responses to hostility and online and offline attacks on women's bodies).

This global crisis of masculinity is coupled with women's feminist activity: Network feminisms in which men and women dedicated to women's safety and retention of women's rights have formed online organizing processes and collectivities. *Transnational feminist* network scholars engage in problem-centered research and practice that cross national boundaries but manifest differently depending on women's regional concerns, human rights, labor organizing, not-for-profit and nongovernmental organizing, effects of global neoliberalism, and other activities (e.g., Moghadam, 2005; Shome, 2006). In organizational communication, this work has focused on how men and women organize online and globally to construct and sustain safe spaces for women who have experienced violence (Linabary, 2017). The constitution of contested terms like "safety" and attention to materialities have been incorporated into these hybrid social movement-self-organizing collectivities. For instance, how do women living under the threat of sexual violence and death self-organize and reach out to others for support when there exist possibilities for identification even with privacy safeguards?

Regarding this last point, *material feminism* reincorporates the body and other physical conditions of everyday life both as "real", not entirely constituted through language and interaction, and as agentic (Alaimo, Hekman, & Hekman, 2008). It is here that the organizing and organization online and offline are interrelated theoretically and practically. Violence against women and men is not only symbolic, it has material consequences for wellbeing. Thus material feminist organizational communication scholars explore knowledge developed through epistemologies (or ways of knowing through social constructionism) and ontologies (or ways of being and connections with the physical as grounded in nature, technologies, bodies, places, and spaces) to indicate how our relationships and organizing are co-constituted discursively and materially.

In short, the present is an exciting time to explore sex, gender, and feminisms as communication scholars and students, but also as members of societies that are dealing with the tensions and paradoxes about what it means to be men and women of varied sexual orientations and organizations. Simply because businesses are relatively new, decentralized, agile, Internet-enabled, and labeled as part of the "share economy"—such as Uber's ridesharing and Airbnb's lodging sharing—or simply because businesses promote social justice through presumably "gender-free" technologies, does not mean that people constitute businesses and other organizing efforts that exhibit equality. Simply because gender normative patterns become replicated does not mean that the practices/activities (communication) and enduring structures (organization, see again Figure 1.4) are deterministic. Instead, this chapter highlights how choice/strategy and human agency are explored in gender and feminist organizational communication theory and research about how the kind of world that could and does move more toward gender equality for men and women is constituted.

Organizational Communication Scholars' Contributions to Gender Studies and Feminisms

Gender and feminist organizational communication scholars have explored and advanced gender studies and feminisms in particular ways. These ways include the focus on: (a) the communication-organization interplay, (b) enactment of gender in in/equitable ways materially and discursively, and (c) contradiction- and/or tension-based lens.

Communication-organization interplay. First, gender and feminist organizational communication scholars focus on the *communication-organization interplay* or *how* agents constitute organization (structure) and organizing (process) as relatively enduring systems and practices that are gendered and that affect the welfare of individuals, communities, and ecological systems (see Figure 1.4).

With regard to structure, Mumby and Putnam's (1992) now-classic piece on bounded emotionality (see Chapter 18), deconstructed how organizational practices deemed rational and normal were based on masculine underpinnings that replicated traditional hierarchies, reward structures, and ideal worker norms (24/7 white male employee without caregiving responsibilities) to exert control and benefit few. In exploring feminist ways of knowing, being, and valuing the world as organizing principles, they constructed an organizational framework that could thrive on contradiction and construct businesses and other types of organizations based on care, mutual respect, reflexivity, empathy, and other values. Similarly, Putnam and Kolb (2000) constructed viable ways of reconstructing negotiation from ideals of empathic and collaborative dialogue in which sharing of perspectives and asking of questions rather than posturing and positioning could establish feminist ways of changing conflicts to result in mutually beneficial solutions.

In gendered and feminist organizing-organization, alternative typically means that these organizations are defined through their opposition or resistance, as well as their desire, to offer choice amid dominant ways of structuring tasks and work relationships (Buzzanell et al., 1997). In a typology of gendered alternative organizing, choice means that alternative organizations position themselves as possibilities or as contrastive forms, relationships, and ideologies. By definition, then, alternative organizations include those that: Are structurally different from traditional bureaucratic and hierarchical organizations; operate as relationally oriented; and are ideologically focused, communal, cooperative, and socially responsible rather than as primarily competitive entities interested in bottom-line financial outcomes. They may provide alternative services, such as cooperatives for foods, medical care, sexual assaults, birth control, and other services for which governmental privatization provides insufficient or no funding. They may also be organized around relationships and activities, such as quilting guilds and reading groups. These organizations may operate on donations and "soft money" or grant-based funding that can be embedded in larger bureaucratic structures such as U.S. federal agencies, nonprofit governmental organizations, and social enterprises that link nonprofit missions with commercial units or businesses. These social enterprises assist victims of sexual assault, domestic violence, human trafficking, and so on.

In these contra-bureaucratic, relationally oriented, and value-rational or ideologically focused organizations, leadership and membership often are not distinct, making the mechanisms by which these organizations work to be systems of shared responsibilities and series of agreements (Buzzanell et al., 1997). Leadership also is embodied insofar as leadership is performed in everyday acts of invitation to participate. For instance, invitations to participate may come without pressures to conform to singular food preferences (e.g., food co-op) or may involve physical movement of bodies in particular settings (e.g., the foregrounding of members onto a "stage" for expressing voice as those formally designated as leaders remove themselves physically from the central focus; e.g., quilting guild) (Buzzanell et al., 1997).

As a final example of organizing-organization co-constitution, Cruz (2015) contends that "feminist organizational communication scholarship remains rooted in Western assumptions in the ways in which it approaches organizational forms, values, and subjectivities of organizational members" (p. 23). She discusses classic Western bureaucratic structures, rationalities in terms of audit mentalities and accountabilities, and which communication and identities are valued. In contrast to Western organizing, she describes African feminist organizing as rooted in praxis or change in terms of economic agency, immediacy with regard to material conditions for survival, and foundations of holism, collectivity, and situationality. Holism counters Western dualistic worldviews, including work–family boundaries. Collectivity is oriented to group or communal life and harmony, whereas situationality portrays the shifting meanings and nature of relationships including flexible categories such as a "'male daughter' institution, [in which] a daughter could become an honorary male if her father did not have a male heir" (Cruz, 2015, p. 29). Greater incorporation of feminist organizational communication scholarship from around the globe can help people to locate different ways of constructing messages, meanings, and organizing around gender.

In summarizing this section, whereas many members of other organizational disciplines focus upon distinctions between female and male managers and leaders, and between employees in terms of horizontal (occupational) and vertical (advancement) sex segregations and career content and trajectories, organizational communication scholars often explore how difference itself is constituted communicatively in organizing processes and structures as well as how alternative ways of theorizing and embodying gender individually and organizationally, such as that found in African feminisms, can be produced.

Moreover, gender and feminist organizational communication scholars working in alternative organizational space confront assumptions that: Organization must be done a particular way; organizing and organization are and should be designed around particular values or else they are not serious or legitimate; and survival, profit, and growth are the ultimate indicators of organizational success. Some of these assumptions seem outdated given corporate social responsibility (CSR). But the organizing-organization tensions remain and become replicated in the hopes and ideals surrounding online organizing, sharing economy, and even feminist transnational networks that strive to disrupt and resist deeply embedded patterns of relating, structuring, and valuing members and organizations as a whole. In these ways feminist organizing has the burden of proof against the normalization or presumption of mainstream organizing and organization even as network and material feminisms provide proof of concept. Of interest in these Internet-enabled feminist collectives are challenges about whether these are simply social movements in online (and often offline hybrid) formats or whether they are new organizational forms predicated on feminist solidarity and resistance.

Gender enactment. Second, besides the focus on the communication-organizational interplay in general, most gender and feminist organizational communication scholars attend to the *enactment of gender in in/equitable material and discursive ways*. In other words, they focus on *how* gender and feminist change takes place within and through linguistic choices, interactions, and (relational network and institutional) structures as well as *what* is changed (discursive-material). For instance, Long (2016) challenges notions of good work through examination of how women's identities, Chinese values, and the material conditions of the Chinese workplace exert agency to elevate and/or diminish gender equality in contemporary mainland China. Long, Selzer King, and Buzzanell (2018) focus on the interplay of three figures that exerted human and nonhuman agency to construct graduate student parents' experiences. Figures of the ideal graduate student worker norms, gendered work-family ideologies, and cultural values of family form a system that encourages, perhaps even forces, students to act in particular ways. Women are particularly disadvantaged because of childcare responsibilities.

Figures act upon men and women in ways that are not obvious but are accepted as parts of space and place. For example, a whiteboard in a hospital birthing room pulled a male doctoral student toward writing algorithms and studying for an exam that his female professor would not postpone even though the student's wife was giving birth around the same time as the exam (Long et al., 2018). The subordinate (feminine) position of graduate students in the higher education power regime meant that students often neither challenged nor expected advisors or the system as a whole to be supportive of or helpful in their non-academic pursuits and life events. Professors treated students fairly according to equal treatment (justice, masculine) but not according to expected accommodations (care, feminine), just as supervisors sometimes speak, manage, and enact policy through ethics of justice even when pregnant subordinates medically require accommodations for their own and their babies' health (Liu & Buzzanell, 2004). It is as if these people are talking right past each other in voicing their behavioral intentions and interests. None of the graduate student-parent participants in our study even considered invoking laws designed to protect students from situations resulting from parenthood that could negatively impact their degree completion. They wanted to be perceived as understanding the rules, as fulfilling the hardworking and focused ideal graduate student, and as worthy of advisors' career development and sponsorship. Likewise, the pregnant employees could not seem to find the "right" language to encourage their supervisors to disrupt the value and figure of equal treatment and policy enactment (e.g., needing to perform all job duties, including break times, as specified in standard operating procedures). In other words, the graduate students did not even consider that they had choice in disrupting the orientations to which the figures directed their attention and action. Likewise, the supervisors and employees in our project were bound by their orientations toward justice and care, as indicated by their organizational roles.

In these cases and in other research, organizational communication scholars delve into gendered embodiment (birth, male and female bodies, breastfeeding), work and personal life spaces (hospital rooms, classrooms, labs, apartments), and artifacts (grades, computers, lab equipment, project timetables, bottles, toys, play areas) that reproduce and disrupt traditional organizing in particular spaces and institutions.

Contradiction and tension. Third and finally, many gender and feminist organizational communication scholars leverage a *contradiction- and/or tension-based lens* to develop practices and processes that can have value in how people make sense of a chaotic world. For instance, D'Enbeau (2017) wanted to know how organizational members confronted with dilemmas of sexual violence on U.S. university campuses came to understand how such complex behaviors, policies established for clarity in ambiguous and threatening situations, and stakeholder roles and practices were constituted ironically in specific socio-material conditions. Occupation and action orientations to dilemmas with their advocacy-compliance and proactive-reactive tensions provided insight into how viable strategies for approaching sexual assault on campuses could be constructed. These strategies go well past mandatory reporting regulations and encourage diverse response and prevention procedures.

Furthermore, typical models for changing the gendered status quo have been "fix the women"/"change the culture" or sameness/difference, and control/resistance strategies —all rational, coherent, and ultimately unsatisfying models for change. These models reflect the kinds of dilemmatic thinking about which D'Enbeau (2017) and Harris (2015) write. Harris combines material feminism and a tension-centered approach to describe persistent dilemmas in feminist theory. These dilemmas include: desires to explain and change the world, to demarcate biological sex and socially constructed gender, to preserve and trouble identity categories, to celebrate agency while noting constraints, to envision and use the personal as political, and to depict feminisms, particularly the waves, as linear and less complex than they were and are. She situates communication as a site for agency. This move is picked up by Putnam and Ashcraft (2017) who encourage innovative both/and mergers to deal with multiple dilemmas in organizing.

So what does feminist dilemmatic scholarship mean for organizations? In particular, what does it mean for organizational difficulties in fostering talent regardless of difference, encouraging innovation that comes from integration of diverse opinions and knowledge, and embedding creative logics and difference into corporate boards and the C-suite? The two main strategies for incorporating women and people of color has been "fix the woman" and "fix the culture" with their contradictory sameness and difference orientations. We explore these strategies to challenge readers and scholars to engage in dilemmic—material and tension-based—feminisms for change.

In particular, "fix the woman" strategies are based on deficit models, meaning that women are different from men, but this movement strives to signal key similarities that could affect desired individual and organizational outcomes. In other words, these models are based on what women were lacking—they lack masculine bodies, single-minded devotion to work and organization because they do not have "wives" (caretakers and caregivers), and sometimes prioritized relationships and family. The male developmental model strove to break free of relationships and be autonomous, independent, strong, and self-reliant (Marshall, 1993). To be successful, namely, to advance in organizations and industry and to attain leadership positions, means that women (and communal men) supposedly need to emulate hegemonic males. They need to leave anything feminine and collectively oriented behind to pursue success. Even so, they could never be what they are not (Buzzanell, 1995). They could not meet the criteria for success because the criteria advantage careerist men by making excuses for lack of qualifications or by shifting criteria (Van den Brink & Benschop, 2012). "Fix the woman" orientations are based on the notion that awareness of inequities would be sufficient to make changes without fully addressing how deeply sedimented the categorical male=masculine and female=feminine equations are (even with acknowledgement of variations within and between these equations; see Buzzanell, 1995).

"Fix the woman" strategies seek rational solutions to the "problems" called by various names: Glass ceiling, vertical and horizontal sex segregation in occupations, gender pay gaps, motherhood penalty and fatherhood bonus, family-friendly (originally women-friendly) policies, lack of mentoring, clarity and reporting in sexual assault policies and procedures, and other inequalities. Even as gains were made in terms of laws, policies, and formulated standard operating procedures, as for which liberal feminists advocated, the gains were relatively small because they often did not achieve goals and/or were not sustainable or alienated men. However, they were significant because they established the foundations for equality. They named inequality and they legitimized the need for interventions. In "fix the woman" strategies, however, the interventions made women different but not equal.

The contradictions in "fix the culture" surface some of the same arguments. The culture is deficient and can be readily fixed, thus ignoring a vast literature of organizational communication scholarship that indicates just how difficult changing cultures is and how long such change would take. In "fix the culture" (as in "fix the woman"), celebrating difference as a message strategy assumes that all women (or communal men) are similar. Creating equal opportunities, as discussed earlier in this chapter, again assumes that all men and women are fundamentally the same. It also assumes that the structure—and not people—create gender inequalities. Gendered and feminist organizational communication scholarship indicates that this locus of change (structure) is not the case, or at least not the whole means of creating change. Instead, using the process, structure, organization model (O_1, O_2, and O_3,) depicted in Chapter 1 enables us to understand how language, social interaction, structuring activities, and organization can recreate and offer opportunities to challenge the status quo (e.g., through alternative settings or organizational forms, authority and community processes, and diverse organizational membership; see Buzzanell, 1995).

Conclusion

The most outrageous contribution of feminist organizational communication theorists is overlying lenses that *call into question everyday organizing and organization*. When taking a feminist analytic lens, everything looks different—because the lens confronts everyday normative assumptions about organizing and organization. This lens is not just about critique but about building a new vision, with the vision of gender equality involving ethics, embodiment, and multiple pathways for constructing better-quality lives for women and men. In recognizing feminist contributions to everyday practice and scholarship, we return to the core feminist values, particularly the one that says that gender equality is a moral obligation (Buzzanell, 1994). It is a moral obligation to engage in the constitution of organizing and structuring of organization in ways that are in women's and men's best interests overall and in their particular socio-political and economic locations. Core feminist values and individual feminisms formed a metatheoretical matrix, or structure that enabled dialogue about feminist theory, root causes for and strategies for agency, and praxis in organizational communication (Buzzanell, 1994) bringing together process, structure, and entity (O_1, O_2, and $O_{3,}$).

Recent work in network and material feminisms promise to engage in these discussions in local through global spaces, online and off. Networked feminisms can be viewed organizing processes or online mobilizing (O_1). It is through these processes that structures are organized or assembled (O_2) to form the entities that we call organization. Hashtag feminisms function as organizations (entities or O_3) insofar as they operate as social collectives that focus on specific issues and that have the authority and agency to speak out on behalf of members and offer remedies or strategies for combatting particular forms of gender violence. As noted in Chapter 1, ethical considerations about who and what is represented, whether the organization fairly represents members' concerns, and how accountability for actions can be assessed are important questions. To address these questions, material feminisms offer insights today into the social and material conditions that recreate, modify, and disrupt gendered arrangements in any particular gendered spatio-temporal-cultural location. These locale-specific inquiries and activisms can be linked transnationally through online affordances to continuously engage in generating feminist processes, structures, and organization. It is an exciting time to learn how to enact choice, agency, and dignity for self and others from gender and feminist organizational communication.

Recommended Supplementary Readings

Ashcraft, K., & Harris, K.L. (2014). "Meaning that matters": An organizational communication perspective on gender, discourse, and materiality. In S. Kumra, R. Simpson, & R. Burke (Eds.), *Gender in organizations* (pp. 130–150). Oxford: Oxford University Press.
This chapter extends the constitutive approach for gender and organization studies. The authors discuss how discursive approaches contribute to the social construction of realities, how constitutive approaches integrate materialities, and how organizational communication adds greater complexity and insight into work and organization.

Budgeon, S. (2015). Individualized femininity and feminist politics of choice. *European Journal of Women's Studies*, 22, 303–318.
Early feminist scholarship and activism focused on how aspects of everyday life and gender relations constrained women's agency or abilities to realize that they had choice and to strategies ways to act upon choice. This article argues that "choice feminism" presumably frees women

from prescriptions about how they should live their lives by showing how today's women are even more constrained by the very ideologies of choice to which they are directed to undertake.

Putnam, L., Myers, K., & Gailliard, B. (2014). Examining the tensions in workplace flexibility and exploring options for new directions. *Human Relations, 67,* 413–440.

Taking a contradiction-centered approach, these authors demonstrate why work–life balance initiatives designed for workplace flexibility tend to fail. They advocate organizational cultural change, framing flexibility as a right rather than choice for workers, and encouraging adaptability as the principle for making work–life organizational decisions and structures.

Van den Brink, M., & Stobbe, L. (2014). The support paradox: Overcoming dilemmas in gender equality programs. *Scandinavian Journal of Management, 30,* 163–174.

This article features discussions about equality policies and merit or advancement practices. In academic careers, men's support is taken for granted whereas women's support challenges their ability to advance on their own. This "support paradox" undermines efforts toward gender equality in the workplace.

Important Concepts: Define and Discuss

Core feminist commitments
Hashtag feminism
Liberal feminism
Material feminism
Network feminism
Radical feminism
Standpoint feminism

Discussion Questions

1. What communication strategies and organizing processes could enable people to transcend the dilemma of "fix the woman" and "fix the culture" strategies?
2. Please debate the different sides of alt right men's online movements and network feminisms? How could different stakeholders' needs and interests be addressed?

Practitioners' Corner

Gender and feminist organizational communication has always been both theoretical and practical. Because praxis is based in understanding and change, there are multiple ways in which gender inequality has been discussed to raise and/or change consciousness about equality for men and for women. There also have been multiple ways to redress causes and promote action. The practical applications of gender and feminist organizational communication has been flexible work arrangements, parental leave and anti-discrimination and anti-harassment policies, and services on the corporate grounds to help manage work–life considerations (e.g., childcare, eldercare, clinics, take home dinners, technologies to work from home). Particularly with regard to services, some experts contend that corporations have included these services to better control workers and increase productivity. Still others point out that use of these policies and services is considered a choice, meaning that those who request them need special treatment to do their work and that their top priority is not paid labor but some other aspect of their lives. The implications are that gender and feminist organizational communication scholarship ironically can both enable and constrain choice, agency, and dignity.

Xandra was a top student in her major and was encouraged by her engineering instructors and undergraduate advisors to consider graduate school. To help build her application, her professor offered her an opportunity to do research in his lab. Xandra was thrilled by this chance to understand more about what graduate school and, perhaps, a professorial career would entail. She also was excited about contributing to papers that might be published from her lab contributions. After a few weeks in the lab, Xandra's best friend tweeted her wedding and pregnancy announcement. Xandra immediately Facetimed with her friend and accepted the invitation to be the "person of honor" at the ceremony a few weeks later. The ceremony and her person of honor duties would require that she miss school and her lab work for a week. Xandra was shocked when her professor questioned her commitment to the lab project and to an academic career. If you were Xandra, how would you handle this situation?

References

Alaimo, S., Hekman, S., & Hekman, S.J. (Eds.). (2008). *Material feminisms*. Bloomington, IN: Indiana University Press.

Allen, B.J. (2000). "Learning the ropes": A black feminist standpoint analysis. In P. M. Buzzanell (Ed.), *Rethinking organizational and managerial communication from feminist perspectives* (pp. 177–208). Thousand Oaks, CA: SAGE.

Ashcraft, K. (2005). Resistance through consent? Occupational identity, organizational form, and the maintenance of masculinity among commercial airline pilots. *Management Communication Quarterly, 19*, 67–90. doi:10.1177/0893318905276560.

Ashcraft, K., & Kedrowicz, A. (2002). Self direction or social support? Nonprofit empowerment and the tacit employment contract of organizational communication studies. *Communication Monographs, 69*, 88–110. doi:10.1080/03637750216538.

Ashcraft, K., & Mumby, D. (2004). *Reworking gender: A feminist communicology of organization*. Thousand Oaks, CA: SAGE.

BBC News (2015, December 12). *Saudi Arabia's women vote in election for first time*. www.bbc.com/news/world-middle-east-35075702.

Bem, S. L. (1974). The measurement of psychological androgyny. *Journal of Consulting and Clinical Psychology, 42*, 155–162. doi:10.1.1.472.52.

Blakemore, E. (2018). Ruth Bader Ginsburg's landmark opinions on women's rights. *History*, May 30. www.history.com/news/ruth-bader-ginsburgs-landmark-opinions-womens-rights-supreme-court.

Brummans, B. H. J. M. (Ed.). (2018). *The agency of organizing: Perspectives and case studies*. New York, NY: Routledge.

Budig, M., Misra, J., & Boeckmann, I. (2016). Work–family policy trade-offs for mothers? Unpacking the cross-national variation in motherhood earnings penalties. *Work and Occupations, 43*, 119–177. doi:10.1177/0730888415615385.

Buzzanell, P. M. (1994). Gaining a voice: Feminist organizational communication theorizing. *Management Communication Quarterly, 7*, 339–383. doi:10.1177/0893318994007004001.

Buzzanell, P. M. (1995). Reframing the glass ceiling as a socially constructed process: Implications for understanding and change. *Communication Monographs, 62*, 327–354. doi:10.1080/03637759509376366.

Buzzanell, P. M. (Ed.). (2000). *Rethinking organizational and managerial communication from feminist perspectives*. Thousand Oaks, CA: SAGE.

Buzzanell, P. M., & D'Enbeau, S. (2009). Stories of caregiving: Intersections of academic research and women's everyday experiences. *Qualitative Inquiry, 15*, 1199–1224. doi:10.1177/1077800409338025.

Buzzanell, P. M., Ellingson, L., Silvio, C., Pasch, V., Dale, B., Mauro, G., Smith, E., Weir, N., & Martin, C. (1997). Leadership processes in alternative organizations: Invitational and dramaturgical leadership. *Communication Studies, 48*, 285–310. doi:10.1080/10510979709368509.

Buzzanell, P. M., & Liu, M. (2005). Struggling with maternity leave policies and practices: A poststructuralist feminist analysis of gendered organizing. *Journal of Applied Communication Research, 33*, 1–25. doi:10.1080/0090988042000318495.

Buzzanell, P. M., & Lucas, K. (2013). Constrained and constructed choice in career: An examination of communication pathways to dignity. *Annals of the International Communication Association, 37*, 3–31. doi:10.1080/23808985.2013.11679144.

Buzzanell, P. M., Remke, R. Meisenbach, R., Liu, M., Bowers, V., & Conn, C. (2017). Standpoints of maternity leave: Discourses of temporality and ability. *Women's Studies in Communication, 40*, 67–90. doi:10.1080/07491409.2015.1113451.

Buzzanell, P. M., Waymer, D., Tagle, M. P., & Liu, M. (2007). Different transitions into working motherhood: Discourses of Asian, Hispanic, and African American women. *Journal of Family Communication, 7*, 195–220. doi:10.1080/15267430701221644.

Cruz, J. (2015). Reimagining feminist organizing in global times: Lessons from African feminist communication. *Women & Language, 38*(1), 23–41.

Cukrowska-Torzewska, E. (2017). Cross-country evidence on motherhood employment and wage gaps: The role of work–family policies and their interaction. *Social Politics: International Studies in Gender, State & Society, 24*, 178-220. doi:10.1093/sp/jxx004.

D'Enbeau, S. (2017). Unpacking the dimensions of organizational tension: The case of sexual violence response and prevention among college students. *Journal of Applied Communication Research, 45*, 237–255. doi:10.1080/00909882.2017.132056.

D'Enbeau, S., & Buzzanell, P. M. (2014). Intimate, ambivalent, and erotic mentoring: Popular culture and mentor–mentee relational processes in *Mad Men. Human Relations, 67*, 695–714. doi:10.1177/0018726713503023.

Duckworth, J., & Buzzanell, P.M. (2009). Constructing work–life balance and fatherhood: Men's framing of the meanings of *both* work *and* family. *Communication Studies, 60*, 558–573. doi:10.1080/10510970903260392.

Eger, E. K. (2018). Transgender jobseekers navigating closeting communication. *Management Communication Quarterly, 32*, 276–281. doi:10.1177/0893318917740226.

Frederick, J. K., & Stewart, A. J. (2018). "I became a lioness": Pathways to feminist identity among women's movement activists. *Psychology of Women Quarterly, 42*, 263–278. doi:10.1177/0361684318771326.

Fuller, S., & Hirsh, C. (2018). "Family-friendly" jobs and motherhood pay penalties: The impact of flexible work arrangements across the educational spectrum. *Work and Occupations*. doi:10.1177/0730888418771116.

Harris, K. L. (2015). Feminist dilemmatic theorizing: New materialism in communication studies. *Communication Theory, 26*, 150–170. doi:10.1111/comt.12083.

Harris, K. L. (2017). Re-situating organizational knowledge: Violence, intersectionality and the privilege of partial perspective. *Human Relations, 70*, 263–285. doi:10.1177/0018726716654745.

Harris, K. L. (2018). Yes means yes and no means no, but both these mantras need to go: Communication myths in consent education and anti-rape activism. *Journal of Applied Communication Research, 46*, 155–178. doi:10.1080/00909882.2018.1435900.

Hodges, M., & Budig, M. (2010). Who gets the daddy bonus? Organizational hegemonic masculinity and the impact of fatherhood on earnings. *Gender & Society, 24*, 717–745. doi:10.1177/0891243210386729.

Jaschik, S. (2018). Mindset 2018: Want to know what the new frosh have never experienced? Or have always known? Want to feel old? It's that time of year again. *Inside Higher Education*, August 21. www.insidehighered.com/news/2018/08/21/mindset-list-reminds-you-what-new-students-have-and-have-never-experienced?utm_source=Inside+Higher+Ed&utm_cam

paign=0fff53d6ba-DNU_COPY_03&utm_medium=email&utm_term=0_1fcbc04421-0fff53d6ba-233780849&mc_cid=0fff53d6ba&mc_eid=20a7214035.

Linabary, J. (2017). *Constructing digital "safe" space: Navigating tensions in transnational feminist organizing online.* Doctoral dissertation, Purdue University.

Liu, M., & Buzzanell, P. M. (2004). Negotiating maternity leave expectations: Perceived tensions between ethics of justice and care. *Journal of Business Communication, 41,* 323–349. doi:10.1177/0021943604268174.

Livingston, G. (2014). Growing number of dads home with the kids: Biggest increase among those caring for family. *Pew Research Center,* June 5. www.pewsocialtrends.org/2014/06/05/growing-number-of-dads-home-with-the-kids/.

Long, Z. (2016). A feminist ventriloqual analysis of "Hao Gongzuo" (good work): Politicizing Chinese post-1980s women's constructions of meanings of work. *Women's Studies in Communication, 39,* 442–441. doi:10.1080/07491409.2016.1224991.

Long, Z., Selzer King, A., & Buzzanell, P. M. (2018). Ventriloqual voicings of parenthood in graduate school: An intersectionality analysis of work–life negotiations. *Journal of Applied Communication Research, 42,* 223–242. doi:1080/00909882.2018.1435901.

Marshall, J. (1993). Viewing organizational communication from a feminist perspective: A critique and some offerings. *Annals of the International Communication Association, 1,* 122–143. doi:10.1080/23808985.1993.11678848.

Marwick, A., & Caplan, R. (2018). Drinking male tears: Language, the manosphere, and networked harassment. *Feminist Media Studies, 18,* 543–559. doi:10.1080/14680777.2018.1450568.

McCarthy, L., & Moon, J. (2018). Disrupting the gender institution: Consciousness-raising in the cocoa value chain. *Organization Studies, 39*(9), 1153–1177. doi:10.1177/0170840618787358.

McDonald, J. (2013). Conforming to and resisting dominant gender norms: How male and female nursing students do and undo gender. *Gender, Work and Organization, 20,* 561–579. doi:10.1111/j.1468-0432.2012.00604.x.

Medved, C. (2017). The new female breadwinner: Discursively doing and undoing gender relations. *Journal of Applied Communication Research, 44,* 236–255. doi:10.1080/00909882.2016.1192286.

Moghadam, V. (2005). *Globalizing women: Transnational feminist networks.* Baltimore, MD: John Hopkins University Press.

Mumby, D., & Putnam, L. (1992). The politics of emotion: A feminist reading of bounded rationality. *Academy of Management Review, 17,* 465–486. doi:10.2307/258719.

Nicholas, L., & Agius, C. (2018). #Notallmen, #menenism, manospheres and unsafe spaces: Overt and subtle masculinism in anti-"PC" discourse. In L. Nicholas & C. Agius, *The persistence of global masculinism* (pp. 31–59). Cham, Switzerland: Palgrave Macmillan

Putnam, L., & Kolb, D. (2000). Rethinking negotiation: Feminist views of communication and exchange. In P. M. Buzzanell (Ed.), *Rethinking organizational and managerial communication from feminist perspectives* (pp. 76–106). Thousand Oaks, CA: SAGE.

Örtenblad, A., Marling, R., & Vasiljević, S. (Eds.). (2017). *Gender equality in a global perspective.* New York, NY: Routledge.

Philipps, D. (2018). Ban was lifted, but transgender recruits still can't join up. *The New York Times,* July 5. www.nytimes.com/2018/07/05/us/military-transgender-recruits.html.

Putnam, L., & Ashcraft, K. (2017). Gender and organizational paradox. In M. Lewis, W. Smith, P. Jarzabkowski, & A. Langley (Eds.), *Handbook of organizational paradox: Approaches to plurality, tensions, and contradictions* (pp. 333–352). Oxford: Oxford University Press.

Putnam, L., Fairhurst, G., & Banghart, S. (2016). Contradictions, dialectics, and paradoxes in organizations: A constitutive approach. *Academy of Management Annals, 10,* 65–171. doi:10.1080/19416520.2016.1162421.

Randles, J. (2018). "Manning up" to be a good father: Hybrid fatherhood, masculinity, and U.S. responsible fatherhood policy. *Gender & Society.* doi:10.1177/0891243218770364.

Shome, R. (2006). Transnational feminism and communication studies. *The Communication Review, 9,* 255–267. doi:10.1080/10714420600957266.

Sobieraj, S. (2018). Bitch, slut, skank, cunt: Patterned resistance to women's visibility in digital publics. *Information, Communication & Society, 21,* 1700–1714. doi:10.1080/1369118X. 2017.1348535.

Trethewey, A. (1999). Disciplined bodies: Women's embodied identities at work. *Organization Studies, 20,* 423–450. doi:10.1177/0170840699203003.

Vachhani, S., & Pullen, A. (in press). Ethics, politics and feminist organizing: Writing feminist infrapolitics and affective solidarity into everyday sexism. *Human Relations.* doi:10.1177/0018726718780988.

Van den Brink, M., & Benschop, Y. (2012). Gender practices in the construction of academic excellence: Sheep with five legs. *Organization, 19,* 507–524. doi:10.1177/1350508411414293.

14 Difference and Intersectionality

Jamie McDonald

On the surface, the claim that "people are different than each other" (Sedgwick, 2008, p. 22) seems relatively banal. Of course, people are different from each other. However, behind this claim lie enormous complexities that scholars across many disciplines seek to understand. In organizational communication, difference scholars explore these complexities in relation to questions such as: How are people different from each other? Which differences matter and shape our organizational experiences? How do these differences intersect with each other? How are some differences privileged in organizational settings? How are other differences marginalized and/or stigmatized? How are work and occupations organized around these differences? How do certain organizations seek to "manage" difference? And how is difference a constitutive feature of organizing?

As we shall see in this chapter, there is a rich body of research that addresses the above questions. Although difference has been addressed in some way by organizational communication scholars since the field's origins (Parker, Jiang, McCluney, & Rabelo, 2017), it was arguably the publication of the first edition of Brenda J. Allen's (2004) *Difference Matters* that institutionalized difference in organizational communication scholarship (McDonald, 2015). Since then, scholarship on difference and organizing has made its way into the field's main journals, as well as the most recent *SAGE Handbook of Organizational Communication* (Parker, 2014). Most textbooks today also have chapters that are dedicated to this line of research—a far cry from what Ashcraft and Allen (2003) found less than 20 years ago. Indeed, it is likely that if this book had been published at that time, it would not have contained this chapter.

Difference is conceptualized broadly in organizational communication scholarship, most often being used as an umbrella term "to refer to the ways in which people differ from each other along the lines of socially significant identities such as gender, race, and sexuality" (McDonald, 2015, p. 310). Difference can also be conceptualized in terms of behaviors or characteristics in addition to identities (Buzzanell, 2018). As such, all forms of difference that "matter"—that is, forms of difference that shape organizational interactions and experiences, as well as work itself—are within the purview of organizational communication scholarship on difference (Allen, 2011). Examples of forms of difference that organizational communication scholars have examined include gender, race, class, sexuality, (dis)ability, age, nationality, and citizenship status. However, there is a much longer tradition of scholarship on gender than on any of the other aforementioned forms of difference, which explains why the previous chapter was explicitly devoted to reviewing scholarship on gender and feminist theory.

Importantly, forms of difference intersect with each other in ways that shape organizational interactions and experiences. This is the main premise of intersectionality, a concept first coined by legal scholar Kimberlé Crenshaw (1991) when analyzing a case of discrimination where women of color were discriminated against not on the basis of either gender or race alone, but simultaneously by both gender and race. Referring to this case, she used the term *intersectionality* to describe how multiple forms of difference—including but not limited to gender and race—are experienced in relation to each other and cannot be neatly separated. Since it was first developed, the concept of intersectionality has been extensively taken up in interdisciplinary circles, so much so that Cho, Crenshaw, and McCall (2013) have suggested that intersectionality studies is becoming its own field of inquiry. Intersectionality is also a central concept to contemporary difference research in organizational communication, as we shall see later in this chapter.

This chapter reviews how difference and intersectionality have been conceptualized in organizational communication research, the key theoretical frameworks that have informed this research, and how this research conceptualizes communication, organization, and the communication/organization spiral. As you read this chapter, I encourage you to think of difference as a constitutive feature of organizing (Mumby, 2011). Thinking about difference in this way underscores that just like communication, difference is relevant to and can help us understand all organizing processes. In this sense, much of what you learn in this chapter can help enhance your understanding of topics covered in other chapters, such as socialization, relationships, leadership, emotion, and conflict, as all of these processes are shaped by relations of difference. Rather than considering difference as merely one topic to examine among others, difference can thus be seen as an overarching theme that can be engaged across all topics pertaining to organizational communication (Alvarez, Bauer, & Eger, 2015).

Theorizing Difference as a Social Construction

As has been discussed earlier in the book, the field of Organizational Communication has functionalist roots. Unsurprisingly then, a strong managerial bias was apparent in early organizational research that addressed difference. Rather than interrogate difference as it relates to power and privilege, this research, mostly conducted by management scholars, sought to examine how difference could best be controlled and/or suppressed in organizations (O_3) (Parker et al., 2017). For instance, research in this area typically treated race as a demographic variable and sought to explain differences between different racial groups, as well as whether different racial groups "have what it takes to succeed in organizations" (Nkomo, 1992, p. 499). As such, this research largely presupposed a transmissive model of communication and conceptualized organizations through the container metaphor (see Chapter 2), in addition to treating categories of difference as objective and stable features of social life.

Nkomo (1992) offered a landmark critique of the early organizational research on difference described above. Taking race as her focus, she noted that this research relied heavily on racial stereotypes, assumed that race was only relevant if it could be objectively measured, presumed organizations (O_3) to be race-neutral entities, viewed discrimination only as a function of personal bias, and often relied on a black/white racial binary. Nkomo's (1992) critique largely explains why organizational communication scholars have now largely eschewed functionalist approaches to difference in favor of approaches more attentive to both power dynamics and the socially constructed nature of difference.

Rather than assuming categories of difference to be objective and pre-existing as functionalist approaches do, social constructionism approaches difference as emergent through both large societal Discourses and everyday communication practices. A social constructionist approach is thus very much in line with a constitutive view of communication, as communication is viewed as constituting difference. For instance, a social constructionist approach examines how categories of difference emerge in particular socio-historical contexts and how meanings of difference vary across time and space (Allen, 2011). In this regard, a social constructionist lens underscores that the concept of "race" was invented by European colonizers and the categories that are used to denote race are arbitrary, constantly evolving, and contextually specific (Parker et al., 2017). Although arbitrary, socially constructed meanings of difference have real and sometimes devastating consequences. Indeed, socially constructed meanings of race have been deployed throughout history to justify horrific practices such as colonialism, slavery, and genocide.

Since the institutionalization of difference as a key area of research in organizational communication, scholars have drawn extensively from social constructionism to examine how socially constructed categories and meanings of difference shape everyday experiences of work; that is, how difference matters *in* organizations (O_3) (e.g., Allen, 1996, 2011; P. S. Parker, 2001, 2003; Trethewey, 2001). More recently, organizational communication scholars have also begun to examine how difference operates as a key organizing (O_1) principle that shapes, in Ashcraft's (2011, p. 4) terms, the "meaning, structure, practice, and economy of work" (O_2). Conceptualizing difference in this way turns our attention to the ways in which difference shapes the character of work as we know it and how difference is a constitutive feature of work (Mumby, 2011). This line of research investigates how certain lines of work become, through communication, symbolically associated with bodies that are gendered, raced, classed, and sexualized—as well as how these associations shape the value and meaning of this work (Ashcraft, 2011).

Ashcraft's (2013) metaphor of the *glass slipper* explains how arbitrary and socially constructed meanings of work become associated with embodied forms of difference. The glass slipper serves as a metaphor about occupational identity; that is, the identity *of* work. Ashcraft's (2013) work in this area shows how particular occupations have been discursively and strategically associated with certain forms of difference in order to shape the meaning and value of this work. As such, some work is made to "fit" certain people but not others, just like, in line with the glass slipper metaphor, shoes are designed to fit some people's feet but not others. This is particularly apparent in her research on airline pilots, which shows that in order to bolster claims to professionalism and secure higher salaries, pilots' associations post-World War II sought to associate the occupational identity of the pilot with a particular form of white, heterosexual masculinity (Ashcraft, 2007; Ashcraft & Mumby, 2004). In this case, we see that socially constructed meanings of difference and occupational identity arise through communication. Put differently, communication is constitutive and shapes the processes through which work is organized (O_2) and understood in relation to difference (Ashcraft, 2011).

Understanding difference as a social construction is consistent with viewing difference through an intersectional lens. As such, we now examine how intersectionality informs organizational communication research on difference.

Intersectionality in Difference Research

As mentioned previously, intersectionality is a central concept in organizational communication research on difference. In fact, the tradition of difference scholarship that is being reviewed in this chapter emerged in part from the recognition that early organizational communication research on gender needed to become more intersectional and problematize additional forms of difference in addition to gender (Ashcraft, 2014). However, with some exceptions (e.g., Adib & Guerrier, 2003; P. S. Parker, 2001; Trethewey, 2001), it's only relatively recently that a substantial body of empirical intersectional research has emerged in the fields of both Organizational Communication and Organization Studies (e.g., Cruz, 2015; Harris, 2013, 2015, 2017; Malvini Redden & Scarduzio, 2017; Ressia, Strachan, & Bailey, 2017; Rodriguez, Holvino, Fletcher, & Nkomo, 2016; Wells, Gill, & McDonald, 2015).

It has been suggested that the inherent complexity involved in operationalizing what intersectionality means and how to study it is one of the reasons why empirical intersectional research was slow to emerge (McDonald, 2015). Indeed, tensions arise in intersectional research because it is a challenge to foreground particular forms of difference while at the same time not "negating or undermining the complexities and particular character of an individual, group, system of oppression, or culture" (Parker, 2014, p. 625). For instance, intersectional scholarship that attends to gender and race can inadvertently gloss over additional intersections that matter, such as those related to forms of difference such as sexuality, age, and nation (Holvino, 2010; McDonald, 2015; Rodriguez et al., 2016). Moreover, intra-group complexities exist within all categories of difference, which creates another tension for intersectional scholars: making political claims on behalf of marginalized groups without also falling into essentialism and reifying what it means to be part of a particular group (Harris, 2015).

Rather than seeking to resolve tensions inherent to intersectional scholarship, it is more productive to think about how they can be managed (Harris, 2015). One way to manage those tensions consists in practicing reflexivity; that is, reflecting upon why we are foregrounding the forms of difference that we do, what our analysis enables and does not enable us to claim, and recognizing both the merits and limitations of whatever approach to intersectionality we may be taking (Cunliffe, 2003). When conducting intersectional scholarship, it is also imperative to conceive of categories as fluid, changing, and interwoven with each other (Cho et al., 2013). Conceiving of categories in this way helps underscore that even as we may foreground particular intersections of difference, these categories should not be taken to be stable and fixed features of social life (Harris, 2015). Indeed, certain intersections of difference can be more or less salient in particular contexts and interactions (Wells et al., 2015).

Wells et al.'s (2015) study serves as an exemplar of research that focuses on how particular intersections of difference shape workplace interactions. Because of its focus on organizational interactions, this study focuses on how difference and intersectionality shape both organizing processes (O_1) and communication within organizations (O_3). In their study, Wells et al. explore how nationality intersects with multiple forms of difference to shape the experiences of highly skilled foreign-born workers at a scientific organization in the U.S. They show that nationality is a driving discourse in scientific work that significantly shapes how other forms of difference, such as gender, are experienced. Indeed, their analysis shows that among their participants, "national origin and alignment with western modes of organizing and communication were more salient in constructing workplace privilege and inequalities than characteristics such as education, occupational tenure, and/or gender" (Wells et al., 2015, p. 547).

Another exemplar of intersectional scholarship in organizational communication is Harris' (2017) study, which adopts a constitutive perspective to communication and organizing (O_1) by viewing organizational knowledge as created and sustained through power-laden organizing processes that have implications for difference. In her study, Harris (2017) uses an intersectional approach to show how organizational knowledge is shaped by power dynamics at the intersections of gender, race, and sexuality. By focusing on the mandated reporting of sexual violence at a university, she shows how whiteness, masculinity, and heteronormativity are embedded into the what the university knows about incidents of sexual violence. Harris' (2017) research thus responds to Holvino's call to study intersectionality not solely at the level of everyday interactions, but also at the level of institutional practices by examining how "meanings of gender, race, class, ethnicity, sexuality, and nation are built into and manifested in organizational structures and policies, dominant societal beliefs and ideologies, and everyday work interactions" (Holvino, 2010, p. 262).

Although there are different ways of conceptualizing and operationalizing intersectionality, its main premise—that multiple forms of difference shape social life and must be examined as they relate to each other—is well accepted among organizational communication scholars of difference. Intersectionality is also an overarching theme that cuts across the critical frameworks through which organizational communication scholars approach difference, which we now turn to.

Critical Approaches to Difference

As mentioned previously, most contemporary research on difference in organizational communication is rooted in critical approaches that seek to understand how multiple intersecting forms of difference are embedded within power relations. In this section, we examine some of the key critical frameworks that have informed organizational communication research on difference: feminist standpoint theory, whiteness, queer theory, and postcolonial theory.

Feminist Standpoint Theory

Some of the earliest research that examined difference critically in organizational communication scholarship is rooted in feminist standpoint theory. According to feminist standpoint theory, knowledge about the social world is political, embedded within power relations, and always partial. Feminist standpoint theory posits that non-dominant groups have access to knowledge about the social world that dominant and privileged groups do not. This is because knowledge is believed to be rooted in collective experience and in the material and social conditions that shape the lives of non-dominant groups. Standpoint theory is thus premised on the assumption that to function in the social world, non-dominant group members must understand the dominant group, as well as their own experiences. Dominant groups, by contrast, do not need to understand the knowledge of non-dominant and marginalized groups to function in everyday life. As such, non-dominant groups are said to have more complete knowledge about the social world than dominant groups (Collins, 1991; Harding, 1991; Smith, 1987).

Although feminist standpoint theory has been used to explain the experiences of women more generally (Harding, 1991; Smith, 1987), it is a particularly prominent framework through which to explore the intersections of gender and race (Collins, 1986, 1991). In this regard, organizational communication scholar Brenda J. Allen (1996, 1998, 2000) drew extensively from standpoint feminism in her pioneering work that brought race into the purview of organizational communication scholarship. One way through which she did this was by rereading existing research on organizational socialization in light of her own standpoint as a black woman in the academy. Her work demonstrated that scholarship in this area reflected the knowledge of the dominant groups (e.g., white men), but not the experiences and standpoints of black women, as existing theories of organizational socialization did not resonate with her experiences (Allen, 1996, 2000). P. S. Parker's (2001) work on African-American female executives also drew from feminist standpoint theory to demonstrate how their standpoints as black women informed and shaped their experiences of leadership.

Whiteness

Much critical research on race in organizational communication has problematized the concept of *whiteness*. The aim of whiteness studies is to examine and critique the ways in which white privilege is maintained through everyday practices that subtlety construct whiteness as the dominant, taken-for-granted norm (Grimes, 2002). Because of these practices, white racial identity becomes invisible and race becomes associated with what is *not* white. As such, white people tend to be seen as just people in dominant societal and organizational contexts, whereas people of color tend to be seen as people of a particular racial group (Nkomo, 1992). White racial identity thus enables the development of a unique standpoint through which one understands the world—a standpoint from which individuals are not likely to think about their race and from which race appears to be a non-issue (Allen, 2007). Whiteness scholars contend that this is a standpoint of privilege and that to fully understand how power operates in all aspects of social life, whiteness must be investigated and problematized. In line with the principles of intersectionality, whiteness scholars also suggest that it is crucial to examine how whiteness is intertwined with other oppressive regimes, such as patriarchy (Grimes, 2002).

Because whiteness tends to be invisible, whiteness studies proceed in part by rereading existing bodies of literature in order to identify the ways through which whiteness is implicitly reified, taken for granted, and organized (O_2) (Parker, 2014). In this regard, Ashcraft and Allen's (2003) rereading of key organizational communication textbooks exposed how whiteness is subtlety embedded into organizational communication research, partially by the absence of race from much of this scholarship. Since the publication of Ashcraft and Allen's (2003) article, race has become more problematized in many organizational communication textbooks (e.g., Eisenberg, Tretheway, LeGreco, & Goodall, 2017; Miller & Barbour, 2018; Mumby, 2013), although much more work remains to be done to challenge the inherent whiteness of both organizational communication and the field of Communication more broadly (Chakravartty, Kuo, Grubbs, & McIlwain, 2018).

Grimes' (2002) analysis of the diversity management literature written by and for practitioners offers another exemplar of whiteness scholarship in organizational communication. Through her analysis, she identified three perspectives on whiteness that are found in this literature: interrogating whiteness, re-centering whiteness, and masking whiteness. The first perspective on interrogating whiteness represents the goal of whiteness studies, as this entails naming, unmasking, and de-centering whiteness as a privileged standpoint. As such, interrogating whiteness is a practice through which authors "take seriously the perspectives of people of color and bring to light the assumptions of white privilege" (Grimes, 2002, p. 390). Although some of the literature that Grimes (2002) analyzed interrogated whiteness, re-centering whiteness was also a prominent theme in her analysis. Unlike interrogating whiteness, re-centering whiteness relies on racial stereotypes and treats whiteness as a universal, taken-for-granted norm. Although racial difference is acknowledged, re-centering whiteness does not problematize the power relations that are embedded into whiteness. The third perspective that Grimes (2002) identified in her analysis is masking whiteness, which maintains the status quo by denying both racial difference and white privilege, thereby keeping whiteness invisible and treating race as a non-issue. Taken together, the three perspectives on whiteness that Grimes (2002) identified can serve as a helpful heuristic for future work that examines the ways in which whiteness is embedded into both organizational communication scholarship and organizational communication processes.

Queer Theory

Queer theory refers to a dynamic and heterogeneous body of thought that emerged in the early 1990s from the writings of theorists such as Judith Butler (1990), Eve Sedgwick (1990), and Teresa de Lauretis (1991). Although queer theory has had a presence in the field of Organization Studies for more than a decade (e.g., Brewis, Hampton, & Linstead, 1997; Harding, Lee, Ford, & Learmonth, 2011; M. Parker, 2001, 2002; Rumens, 2012, 2018) and has even been the topic of a special issue in the interdisciplinary journal *Gender, Work & Organization* (Pullen, Thanem, Tyler, & Wallenberg, 2016), it's only relatively recently that organizational communication scholars have begun to explore this body of thought. Indeed, it was only in 2018 that *Management Communication Quarterly*, widely considered to be the flagship journal of organizational communication scholarship, published its first article with the word "queer" in the title or abstract (Harris & McDonald, 2018). With few exceptions (e.g., Compton & Dougherty, 2017; McDonald, 2015), organizational communication scholars exploring queer theory have also published their work in interdisciplinary and organization studies journals (Ashcraft & Muhr, 2017; McDonald, 2013, 2016a, 2016b, 2017). That queer theory is more established in organization studies than in organizational communication is curious given that, as we will see below, queer theory is very consistent with the constitutive view of communication and organizing (O_1) that is predominately espoused by organizational communication scholars.

A comprehensive summary of queer theory is out of the purview of this chapter, but one of the defining features of this body of thought is its performative and fluid approach to difference. Rather than take identity categories such as gender and sexuality as stable and objective features of social life, queer theory views them as emerging through the performative (re)enactment of the normative practices that are said to constitute these identities (Butler, 1990). Because identities are contingent upon their performative (re)enactment, they are also fluid and shifting. Butler (1990) cites *drag* as a practice through which the fluidity of gender becomes evident, as through drag individuals who may be usually recognized as a "man" can become recognized as a "woman" because of their enactment of the normative practices that are said to constitute this very category. Conceptualizing identity through a queer lens thus compels a constitutive understanding of communication, as communication practices are seen as performatively (re)constituting identity in everyday life.

Another defining feature of queer theory is its critique of (hetero)normativity, broadly defined. Heteronormativity refers to the localized and systemic practices that function to cast heterosexuality as the dominant and taken-for-granted norm, while casting all other forms of sexuality as deviant and non-normative (Yep, 2003). Because these practices are often taken-for-granted and invisible, heteronormativity functions in a similar way to whiteness, which also maintains its dominance through its invisibility. Although queer theory has sexuality as its point of reference, many queer theorists suggest that queer theory must also go beyond the realm of sexuality and can serve as a framework through which to critique all forms of normativity (Butler, 2004; Cohen, 2005; Halperin, 2003; Warner, 1999). In this view, queerness refers to a whole host of non-normative practices that resist dominant societal norms. The goal of queer theory is thus to critique the ways in which multiple normalizing regimes are intertwined, including but not limited to those related to sexuality, gender, and race (McDonald, 2015).

The implications of adopting a queer theoretical lens can be seen particularly well when applied to the concept of diversity management. Diversity management refers to practices through which organizations (O_3) seek to value and increase diversity among its members, often because of the assumption that enhancing organizational diversity is good for business (Özbilgin & Tatli, 2011). Although organizational attempts to value diversity are laudable because they can potentially lead to greater equality and inclusion, tensions are a constitutive feature of diversity management practices (Mease, 2012, 2016). One of these tensions revolves around operationalizing diversity, particularly as it relates to which groups to include within the purview of diversity management discourse (Mease, 2016). In this regard, diversity management discourse identifies particular groups that are said to be diverse (e.g., women, people of color, people with disabilities) and, in line with a representational view of communication, assumes these groups to be pre-existing, fixed, and stable. A queer perspective on diversity management discourse challenges these assumptions by adopting a constitutive and performative view of communication (Bendl, Fleischmann, & Walenta, 2008; Bendl & Hofmann, 2015). As such, diversity management discourse is not viewed as merely representing diverse subjects, but as actively constituting certain individuals and groups as the "subjects of diversity" (Just & Christiansen, 2012, p. 321). Queer analyses of diversity management discourse thus examine how this practice can accept and re-inscribe binary notions of identity, as well as constrain individuals within fixed subject positions (Bendl et al., 2008; Bendl & Hofmann, 2015).

To date, the majority of research drawing from queer theory in both organization studies and organizational communication has been primarily conceptual. However, empirical research that uses queer theory as a theoretical and analytical framework is making its way into the field. In this regard, Compton and Dougherty's (2017) analysis of co-sexuality processes in Midwestern organizations (O_3) offers an exemplar of such empirical research. The authors conceptualize co-sexuality as referring to various forms of sexuality that coexist, some of which are socially constructed as normative while others are cast as deviant. In their analysis, the authors show how participants discipline themselves to discuss sexuality only in ways that align with heteronormative understandings, thereby silencing any discussion of sexuality that challenges dominant understandings and reifying norms about how sexuality can be discussed at work. In line with the political impetus of queer theory, the authors critique these normalizing processes and show how they uphold heteronormativity in organizational contexts (Compton & Dougherty, 2017).

In addition to Compton and Dougherty's (2017) work on co-sexuality, a 2018 forum in *Management Communication Quarterly* sought to bring queer theory into empirical organizational communication research through a focus on the closet. Although the closet is most commonly associated with the experiences of those who identify as lesbian, gay, bisexual, and queer (LGBQ), the forum conceptualizes the closet in a broader way and as it relates to a whole host of forms of difference that can potentially be concealed and that are subject to some type of social stigma such that revealing a particular difference can come with negative consequences (Harris & McDonald, 2018). As such, the forum consists of essays that consider the closet and closeting processes as they relate to forms of difference, such as transgender identity (Eger, 2018), family structures (Dixon, 2018), communities of origin (Ferguson, 2018), citizenship status (McDonald, 2018), and health and lifestyle characteristics (Romo, 2018). Together, the forum essays contribute to queer research in organizational communication by adopting a fluid and performative approach to difference and intersectionality, pushing the scope of difference research beyond identity categories, and critiquing normalizing processes that stigmatize multiple forms of difference (Harris & McDonald, 2018; McDonald, 2015).

Postcolonial Theory

Like queer theory, postcolonial theory is associated with a broad interdisciplinary body of thought. Some of the foundational texts of postcolonial theory include contributions from authors such as Edward Said (1978, 1993), Gayatri Spivak (1985, 1988a, 1988b, 1999) and Homi Bhabha (1994). Postcolonial theory explores how contemporary social relations are embedded within macro structures of power and domination that are linked to the legacy of colonialism. What distinguishes postcolonial scholarship on difference from other frameworks is thus "a historical and international depth to the understanding of cultural power" (Shome & Hegde, 2002, p. 252), as well as analyzing relations of difference within geopolitical and historical arrangements. Postcolonial theory is especially concerned with challenging the pervasive ideology of Western-centrism, which assumes Western modes of being and knowing to be universal (Shome, 1996; Shome & Hegde, 2002). Postcolonial theorists posit that the legacy of colonialism lives on through Western-centric logics, knowledges, and forms of representation and that it is necessary to both challenge Western-centric ways of engaging with the world and explore alternative, indigenous possibilities (Kalonaityte, 2010).

Postcolonial theory was first explicitly introduced to organizational communication scholars in an essay by Broadfoot and Munshi (2007) in *Management Communication Quarterly*. There is thus a longer history of organizational communication engagement with postcolonial theory than with queer theory, as well as a chapter devoted to postcolonial approaches in the most recent *SAGE Handbook of Organizational Communication* (Broadfoot & Munshi, 2014). Nevertheless, the field of Organization Studies has shown a more substantial interest in postcolonial approaches than Organizational Communication, which explains why there is a more substantial body of research on postcolonial approaches to organizing in interdisciplinary journals than in Communication journals (Broadfoot & Munshi, 2014).

In their foundational essay, Broadfoot and Munshi (2007) critique the Euro-American dominance of organizational communication on several fronts. For instance, they note that the field of organizational communication scholarship overwhelmingly draws on Euro-American theory, cites Euro-American scholarship, and studies Euro-American contexts without considering alternative possibilities. They also argue that engaging with postcolonial approaches is a key way by which organizational communication scholars can challenge the Western-centric nature of the field and thus make room for diverse voices and alternative rationalities that aren't currently given a place in the field (Broadfoot & Munshi, 2007).

In a later piece, Broadfoot and Munshi (2014) suggest that conducting postcolonial research in the field of Organizational Communication entails espousing three broad commitments. The first of these commitments is to disrupt and reimagine organizing space(s) by exploring organizing outside of dominant Western contexts. The second commitment entails resisting colonial discourse by advancing alternative non-Western understandings of organizational concepts. Examples of concepts that have been interrogated through a postcolonial lens include career success (Hanchey & Berkelaar 2015), dirty work (Cruz, 2015), and resistance (Pal & Buzzanell, 2013). The third commitment that Broadfoot and Munshi (2014) suggest for postcolonial organizational communication scholarship consists in interrogating the dominant ways through which we generate, organize, and represent knowledge, as well as exploring alternative methodologies and modes of representation. Importantly, each of these three commitments has both deconstructive and reconstructive elements. That is, postcolonial scholarship in organizational communication should not just deconstruct dominant understandings of organizational life, but also imagine alternative forms of organizing that foreground indigenous epistemologies, philosophies, and methodologies (Broadfoot & Munshi, 2014).

Cruz's (2017) study of visibility and invisibility in alternative organizing serves as an exemplar for postcolonial research in organizational communication and espouses each of the three postcolonial commitments identified by Broadfoot and Munshi (2014). In her study, she draws from African feminisms to explore indigenous organizing (O_1) by women's susu groups in post-conflict Liberia. Cruz's (2017) analysis shows how susu groups communicatively negotiate invisibility and visibility in their organizing practices, as well as how these organizing practices advance alternative understandings of the concepts of invisibility and visibility that Western-centric understandings do not consider. As such, Cruz's (2017) work responds to Broadfoot and Munshi's (2007) call to center diverse voices and alternative rationalities that organizational communication scholarship rarely accounts for. The field certainly stands to benefit by additional work that enacts the commitments of postcolonial scholarship and thereby challenges Western-centric understandings of organizational communication processes.

Approaches to Communication, Organization, and the Communication/Organizational Spiral

As has been suggested throughout this chapter, contemporary organizational communication research on difference and intersectionality approaches communication through a constitutive lens. Rather than seeing communication as merely representing difference, this area of scholarship views communication as actively constituting difference. Put differently, it is through communication that difference becomes socially significant and that we come to know and understand difference.

This chapter has also shown that organizational communication research on difference conceptualizes organization in multiple ways. In one sense, we saw that this research examines organizing processes (O_1); that is, how members of a social collective coordinate meaning. This approach to understanding organization is particularly evident in research that examines how work is organized around difference and how particular intersections of difference come to matter in everyday organizational interactions. In addition, scholarship on difference conceptualizes organization as a coordinated entity and thus as a noun (O_3). Conceiving of organizations in this way is especially salient in research on diversity management that seeks to understand how greater diversity and inclusion can be fostered within the coordinated entities that we call organizations. Research on diversity management also conceives of organization as the state of a social collective's coordination (O_2) because it is concerned with the state of diversity within organizations at particular times. Ultimately then, organizational communication research on difference needs to conceive of organization in these three ways—O_1, O_2, and O_3—in order to account for how meanings of difference are embedded into organizing processes, the state of diversity in organizational contexts, and how organizations seek to "manage" diversity.

As this chapter has shown, organizational communication research on difference views the relationship between communication and organization as a complex and ongoing process. For instance, communication is seen as shaping organizing processes and structures in ways that are consequential for difference and power relations. Humans can thus be seen as exercising agency through communication by actively shaping the meanings of difference that are embedded into organizing processes and organizational structures. However, the critical frameworks that we examined in this chapter—feminist standpoint theory, whiteness, queer theory, and postcolonial theory—also view human agency as constrained within deep power structures and ideologies such as patriarchy, white supremacy, heteronormativity, and Western-centrism. As such, these ideologies shape the ways through which individuals think about difference in the first place, thereby constraining human agency. Put differently, ideologies and power structures shape communication in ways that uphold these very ideologies and power structures. In this sense, action and structure are mutually constitutive, as action is shaped by structure and structure is shaped by action. Importantly, however, the ultimate goal of organizational communication research on difference is emancipatory; that is, challenging the power structures that constrain the ways through which we think about and organize around difference, thereby carving out a stronger place for human agency.

In conclusion, this chapter has served as an introduction to the ways in which difference matters in both Organizational Communication as a discipline and organizational communication as a process. We have seen that organizational communication processes cannot be understood without attending to how relations and meanings of difference are embedded into these processes; difference is thus a constitutive feature of organizing (Mumby, 2011). Compared to some of the other topics being covered in this book, the critical study of difference is a relatively new area of inquiry for organizational communication scholars. However, organizational communication research on difference and intersectionality has been rapidly expanding over the past 20 years, and it is exciting to think about what this chapter would look like if it were written 20 years from now. Ideally, the chapter would show that organizational life has transformed in emancipatory ways and that organizations have become more just and inclusive. That is, after all, the primary goal that difference scholars seek to achieve with their research.

Recommended Supplementary Readings

Allen, B. J. (2011). *Difference matters: Communicating social identity* (2nd ed.). Long Grove, IL: Waveland.

This is a foundational book that has helped institutionalized difference as a key area of concern for organizational communication researchers.

Allen, B. J. (2017). Diversity. In L. K. Lewis & C. R. Scott (Eds.), *International encyclopedia of organizational communication* (online edition). Hoboken, NJ: Wiley-Blackwell.

This encyclopedia article provides an excellent overview of key concepts and theoretical frameworks that are engaged in organizational communication research on difference.

Mumby, D. K. (Ed.) (2011). *Reframing difference in organizational communication studies: Research, pedagogy, practice.* Thousand Oaks, CA: SAGE.

This edited collection contains influential contributions from key difference scholars and has helped shape the agenda for contemporary organizational communication research on difference.

Parker, P. S. (2014). Difference and organizing. In L. L. Putnam & D. K. Mumby (Eds.), *The SAGE handbook of organizational communication: Advances in theory, research, and methods* (pp. 619–643). Thousand Oaks, CA: SAGE.

This is the first chapter devoted to research on difference that has appeared in one of the three handbooks of organizational communication and provides an excellent and comprehensive overview of the key theoretical approaches to difference in organizational communication.

Parker, P. S., Jiang, J., McCluney, C. L., & Rabelo, V. C. (2017). Race, gender, class, and sexuality. *Oxford Research Encyclopedia of Communication.*

This recent encyclopedia article provides an excellent summary of organizational communication research on difference as it relates to race, gender, class, and sexuality.

Important Concepts: Define and Discuss

Difference
Diversity management
Essentialism
Glass slipper
Intersectionality
Race
Sexuality
The closet
Postcolonial theory
Queer theory
Social constructionism
Standpoint
Whiteness

Discussion Questions

1. How can you apply what you've learned in the chapter to what you've learned so far in this book? That is, how can scholarship on difference and intersectionality help us better understand topics such as classical management theory, human relations theory, human resource management theory, organizational socialization, workplace relationships, organizational identity, and power and resistance?

2. What does it mean to say that difference is socially constructed? What are some ways in which we can view categories such as gender, race, class, sexuality, (dis)ability, and

age as social constructions? How do these social constructions matter—that is, how do they shape experiences and interactions—in organizational settings?

3. What is the difference between researching difference within organizations (O_3) and researching difference as a key organizing (O_1) principle that shapes the meaning and structure of work?

4. What does it mean to say that difference is a *constitutive* feature of both work and organizing? How are meanings of difference embedded into the ways in which we know and understand work and organizing?

Practitioners' Corner

Organizations in the U.S. are increasingly diverse in regards to gender, race, sexuality, disability, age, and other forms of difference. With the changing demographics that are anticipated over the next several decades, they are poised to continue to become even more diverse (Lieber, 2008). Moreover, valuing diversity is increasingly seen as being "good for business" and organizations ranging from Fortune 500 companies to institutions of higher education now seek to demonstrate their commitment to diversity. To demonstrate this commitment, there has been a proliferation of organizations that employ diversity consultants and create positions for a Chief Diversity Officer.

In light of this context, imagine that you are interviewing for a position as Chief Diversity Officer for the university with which you're currently affiliated. If you land the position, you will be tasked with developing initiatives that will foster a diverse and inclusive environment for all faculty, students, and staff. Given your knowledge of critical approaches to difference, consider how you will answer the following questions during the interview:

- What are the key challenges that you expect to encounter as Chief Diversity Officer?
- What tensions do you envisioning encountering as Chief Diversity Officer? How do you envision managing these tensions?
- Describe some of the initiatives that you will implement as Chief Diversity Officer to foster a diverse and inclusive environment.
- How will the initiatives that you develop help challenge dominant ideologies related to whiteness, patriarchy, and heteronormativity on campus?
- How will your initiatives highlight particular forms of difference while at the same time not "negating or undermining the complexities and particular character of an individual, group, system of oppression, or culture" (Parker, 2014, p. 625)?
- How will your initiatives promote diversity and inclusivity in *everyday organizational interactions*?
- How will your initiatives promote diversity and inclusivity in *organizational structures and policies*?
- How will you assess the efficacy of the initiatives and the overall climate related to diversity and inclusion on campus?

Good luck with the interview!

References

Adib, A., & Guerrier, Y. (2003). The interlocking of gender with nationality, race, ethnicity and class: The narratives of women in hotel work. *Gender, Work & Organization, 10*(4), 413–432. doi:10.1111/1468-0432.00204.

Allen, B. J. (1996). Feminist standpoint theory: A black woman's (re)view of organizational socialization. *Communication Studies, 47*(4), 257–271. doi:10.1080/10510979609368482.

Allen, B. J. (1998). Black womanhood and feminist standpoints. *Management Communication Quarterly, 11*(4), 575–586. doi:10.1177/0893318998114004.

Allen, B. J. (2000). "Learning the ropes": A black feminist standpoint analysis. In P. M. Buzzanell (Ed.), *Rethinking organizational and managerial communication from feminist perspectives* (pp. 177–208). Thousand Oaks, CA: SAGE.

Allen, B. J. (2004). *Difference matters: Communicating social identity.* Long Grove, IL: Waveland Press.

Allen, B. J. (2007). Theorizing race and communication. *Communication Monographs, 74*(2), 259–264. doi:10.1080/03637750701393055.

Allen, B. J. (2011). *Difference matters: Communicating social identity* (2nd ed.). Long Grove, IL: Waveland.

Alvarez, W., Bauer, J. C., & Eger, E. K. (2015). (Making a) difference in the organizational communication undergraduate course. *Management Communication Quarterly, 29*(2), 302–308. doi:10.1177/0893318915571352.

Ashcraft, K. L. (2007). Appreciating the "work" of discourse: Occupational identity and difference as organizing mechanisms in the case of commercial airline pilots. *Discourse & Communication, 1*(1), 9–36. doi:10.1177/1750481307071982.

Ashcraft, K. L. (2011). Knowing work through the communication of difference: A revised agenda for difference studies. In D. K. Mumby (Ed.), *Reframing difference in organizational communication studies: Research, pedagogy, practice* (pp. 3–29). Thousand Oaks, CA: SAGE.

Ashcraft, K. L. (2013). The glass slipper: "Incorporating" occupational identity in management studies. *Academy of Management Review, 38*(1), 6–31. doi:10.5465/amr.2010.0219.

Ashcraft, K. L. (2014). Feminist theory. In L. L. Putnam & D. K. Mumby (Eds.), *The SAGE handbook of organizational communication: Advances in theory, research, and methods* (pp. 127–150). Thousand Oaks, CA: SAGE.

Ashcraft, K. L., & Allen, B. J. (2003). The racial foundation of organizational communication. *Communication Theory, 13*(1), 5–38. doi:10.1111/j.1468-2885.2003.tb00280.x.

Ashcraft, K. L., & Muhr, S. L. (2017). Coding military command as a promiscuous practice? Unsettling the gender binaries of leadership metaphors. *Human Relations.* doi:10.1177/0018726717709080.

Ashcraft, K. L., & Mumby, D. K. (2004). *Reworking gender: A feminist communicology of organization.* Thousand Oaks, CA: SAGE.

Bendl, R., Fleischmann, A., & Walenta, C. (2008). Diversity management discourse meets queer theory. *Gender in Management, 23*(6), 382–394. doi:10.1108/17542410810897517.

Bendl, R., & Hofmann, R. (2015). Queer perspectives fuelling diversity management discourse: Theoretical and empirical-based reflections. In R. Bendl, I. Bleijenbergh, E. Henttonen, & A. J. Mills (Eds.), *The Oxford handbook of diversity in organizations* (pp. 195–217). Oxford: Oxford University Press.

Bhabha, H. K. (1994). *The location of culture.* New York: Routledge.

Brewis, J., Hampton, M. P., & Linstead, S. (1997). Unpacking Priscilla: Subjectivity and identity in the organization of gendered appearance. *Human Relations, 50*(10), 1275–1304. doi:10.1177/001872679705001005.

Broadfoot, K. J., & Munshi, D. (2007). Diverse voices and alternative rationalities: Imagining forms of postcolonial organizational communication. *Management Communication Quarterly, 21*(2), 249–267. doi:10.1177/0893318907306037.

Broadfoot, K. J., & Munshi, D. (2014). Postcolonial approaches. In L. L. Putnam & D. K. Mumby (Eds.), *The SAGE handbook of organizational communication: Advances in theory, research, and methods* (pp. 151–172). Thousand Oaks, CA: SAGE.

Butler, J. (1990). *Gender trouble: Feminism and the subversion of identity*. New York: Routledge.

Butler, J. (2004). *Undoing gender*. New York: Routledge.

Buzzanell, P. M. (2018). Legitimizing and transforming the closet/closeting. *Management Communication Quarterly*, 32(2), 297–300. doi:10.1177/0893318917742518.

Chakravartty, P., Kuo, R., Grubbs, V., & McIlwain, C. (2018). #CommunicationSoWhite. *Journal of Communication*, 68(2), 254–266. doi:10.1093/joc/jqy003.

Cho, S., Crenshaw, K. W., & McCall, L. (2013). Toward a field of intersectionality studies: Theory, applications, and praxis. *Signs*, 38(4), 785–810. doi:10.1086/669608.

Cohen, C. J. (2005). Punks, bulldaggers, and welfare queens: The radical potential of queer politics? In E. P. Johnson & M. G. Henderon (Eds.), *Black queer studies: A critical anthology* (pp. 21–51). Durham, NC: Duke University Press.

Collins, P. H. (1986). Learning from the outsider within: The sociological significance of black feminist thought *Social Problems*, 33(6), s14–s32. doi:10.2307/800672.

Collins, P. H. (1991). *Black feminist thought: Knowledge, consciousness, and the politics of empowerment*. New York: Routledge.

Compton, C. A., & Dougherty, D. S. (2017). Organizing sexuality: Silencing and the push–pull process of co-sexuality in the workplace. *Journal of Communication*, 67(6), 874–896. doi:10.1111/jcom.12336.

Crenshaw, K. W. (1991). Mapping the margins: Intersectionality, identity politics, and violence against women of color. *Stanford Law Review*, 43(6), 1241–1299. doi:10.2307/1229039.

Cruz, J. M. (2015). Dirty work at the intersections of gender, class, and nation: Liberian market women in post-conflict times. *Women's Studies in Communication*, 38(4), 421–439. doi:10.1080/07491409.2015.1087439.

Cruz, J. M. (2017). Invisibility and visibility in alternative organizing: A communicative and cultural model. *Management Communication Quarterly*, 31(4), 614–639. doi:10.1177/0893318917725202.

Cunliffe, A. L. (2003). Reflexive inquiry in organizational research: Questions and possibilities. *Human Relations*, 56(8), 983–1003. doi:10.1177/00187267030568004.

de Lauretis, T. (1991). Queer theory: Lesbian and gay sexualities. *Differences: A Journal of Feminist Cultural Studies*, 1(2), 3–18.

Dixon, J. (2018). Looking out from the family closet: Discourse dependence and queer family identity in workplace conversation. *Management Communication Quarterly*, 32(2), 271–275. doi:10.1177/0893318917744067.

Eger, E. K. (2018). Transgender jobseekers navigating closeting communication. *Management Communication Quarterly*, 32(2), 276–281. doi:10.1177/0893318917740226.

Eisenberg, E. M., Tretheway, A., LeGreco, M., & Goodall, H. L. J. (2017). *Organizational communication: Balancing creativity and constraint* (8th ed.). Boston, MA: Bedford/St. Martin's.

Ferguson, M. W. (2018). (Re)negotiating organizational socialization: Black male scholarship and the closet. *Management Communication Quarterly*, 32(2), 282–286. doi:10.1177/0893318917741990.

Grimes, D. S. (2002). Challenging the status quo? Whiteness in the diversity management literature. *Management Communication Quarterly*, 15(3), 381–409. doi:10.1177/0893318902153003.

Halperin, D. (2003). The normalization of queer theory. *Journal of Homosexuality*, 45(2–4), 339–343. doi:10.1300/J082v45n02_17.

Hanchey, J. N., & Berkelaar, B. L. (2015). Context matters: Examining discourses of career success in Tanzania. *Management Communication Quarterly*, 29, 411–439. doi:10.1177/0893318915584623.

Harding, N., Lee, H., Ford, J., & Learmonth, M. (2011). Leadership and charisma: A desire that cannot speak its name? *Human Relations*, 64(7), 927–949. doi:10.1177/0018726710393367.

Harding, S. (1991). *Whose science? Whose knowledge? Thinking from women's lives*. Ithaca, NY: Cornell.

Harris, K. L. (2013). Show them a good time: Organizing the intersections of sexual violence. *Management Communication Quarterly, 27*(4), 568–595. doi:10.1177/0893318913506519.

Harris, K. L. (2015). Reflexive voicing: A communicative approach to intersectional writing. *Qualitative Research, 16*(1), 111–127. doi:10.1177/1468794115569560.

Harris, K. L. (2017). Re-situating organizational knowledge: Violence, intersectionality and the privilege of partial perspective. *Human Relations, 70*(3), 263–285. doi:10.1177/0018726716654745.

Harris, K. L., & McDonald, J. (2018). Introduction: Queering the "closet" at work. *Management Communication Quarterly, 32*(2), 265–270. doi:10.1177/0893318917742517.

Holvino, E. (2010). Intersections: The simultaneity of race, gender and class in organization studies. *Gender, Work & Organization, 17*(3), 248–277. doi:10.1111/j.1468-0432.2008.00400.x.

Just, S. N., & Christiansen, T. J. (2012). Doing diversity: Text-audience agency and rhetorical alternatives. *Communication Theory, 22*(3), 319–337. doi:10.1111/j.1468-2885.2012.01407.x.

Kalonaityte, V. (2010). The case of vanishing borders: Theorizing diversity management as internal border control. *Organization, 17*(1), 31–52. doi:10.1177/1350508409350238.

Lieber, L. (2008). Changing demographics will require changing the way we do business. *Employment Relations Today, 35*(3), 91–96. doi:10.1002/ert.20218.

Malvini Redden, S., & Scarduzio, J. A. (2017). A different type of dirty work: Hidden taint, intersectionality, and emotion management in bureaucratic organizations. *Communication Monographs*, 1–21. doi:10.1080/03637751.2017.1394580.

McDonald, J. (2013). Coming out in the field: A queer reflexive account of shifting researcher identity. *Management Learning, 44*(2), 127–143. doi:10.1177/1350507612473711.

McDonald, J. (2015). Organizational communication meets queer theory: Theorizing relations of "difference" differently. *Communication Theory, 25*(3), 310–329. doi:10.1111/comt.12060.

McDonald, J. (2016a). Expanding queer reflexivity: The closet as a guiding metaphor for reflexive practice. *Management Learning, 47*(4), 391–406. doi:10.1177/1350507615610029.

McDonald, J. (2016b). Occupational segregation research: Queering the conversation. *Gender, Work & Organization, 23*(1), 19–35. doi:10.1111/gwao.12100.

McDonald, J. (2017). Queer methodologies in qualitative organizational research: Disrupting, critiquing, and exploring. *Qualitative Research in Organizations and Management, 12*(2), 130–148. doi:10.1108/QROM-06-2016-1388.

McDonald, J. (2018). Negotiating the "closet" in U.S. academia: Foreign scholars on the job market. *Management Communication Quarterly, 32*(2), 287–291. doi:10.1177/0893318917740428.

Mease, J. J. (2012). Reconsidering consultants' strategic use of the business case for diversity. *Journal of Applied Communication Research, 40*(4), 384–402. doi:10.1080/00909882.2012.720380.

Mease, J. J. (2016). Embracing discursive paradox: Consultants navigating the constitutive tensions of diversity work. *Management Communication Quarterly, 30*(1), 59–83. doi:10.1177/0893318915604239.

Miller, K., & Barbour, J. (2018). *Organizational communication: Approaches and processes* (7th ed.). Stanford, CT: Cenage.

Mumby, D. K. (2011). Organizing difference: An introduction. In D. K. Mumby (Ed.), *Reframing difference in organizational communication studies: Research, pedagogy, practice* (pp. vii–xiii). Thousand Oaks, CA: SAGE.

Mumby, D. K. (2013). *Organizational communication: A critical approach*. Thousand Oaks, CA: SAGE.

Nkomo, S. M. (1992). The emperor has no clothes: Rewriting "race in organizations." *Academy of Management Review, 17*(3), 487–513. doi:10.5465/AMR.1992.4281987.

Özbilgin, M., & Tatli, A. (2011). Mapping out the field of equality and diversity: Rise of individualism and voluntarism. *Human Relations, 64*(9), 1229–1253. doi:10.1177/0018726711413620.

Pal, M., & Buzzanell, P. M. (2013). Breaking the myth of Indian call centers: A postcolonial analysis of resistance. *Communication Monographs, 80,* 199–219. doi:10.1080/03637751.2013.776172.

Parker, M. (2001). Fucking management: Queer, theory and reflexivity. *Ephemera, 1*(1), 36–53.

Parker, M. (2002). Queering management and organization. *Gender, Work & Organization, 9*(2), 146–166. doi:10.1111/1468-0432.00153.

Parker, P. S. (2001). African American women executives' leadership communication within dominant-culture organizations: (Re)conceptualizing notions of collaboration and instrumentality. *Management Communication Quarterly, 15*(1), 42–82. doi:10.1177/0893318901151002.

Parker, P. S. (2003). Control, resistance, and empowerment in raced, gendered, and classed work contexts: The case of African American women. *Annals of the International Communication Association, 27*(1), 257–291. doi:10.1080/23808985.2003.11679028.

Parker, P. S. (2014). Difference and organizing. In L. L. Putnam & D. K. Mumby (Eds.), *The SAGE handbook of organizational communication: Advances in theory, research, and methods* (pp. 619–643). Thousand Oaks, CA: SAGE.

Parker, P. S., Jiang, J., McCluney, C. L., & Rabelo, V. C. (2017). Race, gender, class, and sexuality. *Oxford Research Encyclopedia of Communication.* doi:10.1093/acrefore/9780190228613.013.204.

Pullen, A., Thanem, T., Tyler, M., & Wallenberg, L. (2016). Sexual politics, organizational practices: Interrogating queer theory, work and organization. *Gender, Work & Organization, 23*(1), 1–6. doi:10.1111/gwao.12123.

Ressia, S., Strachan, G., & Bailey, J. (2017). Operationalizing intersectionality: An approach to uncovering the complexity of the migrant job search in Australia. *Gender, Work & Organization, 24*(4), 376–397. doi:10.1111/gwao.12172.

Rodriguez, J. K., Holvino, E., Fletcher, J. K., & Nkomo, S. M. (2016). The theory and praxis of intersectionality in work and organisations: Where do we go from here? *Gender, Work & Organization, 23*(2), 201–222. doi:10.1111/gwao.12131.

Romo, L. K. (2018). Coming out as a non-drinker at work. *Management Communication Quarterly, 32*(2), 292–296. doi:10.1177/0893318917740227.

Rumens, N. (2012). Queering cross-sex friendships: An analysis of gay and bisexual men's workplace friendships with heterosexual women. *Human Relations, 65*(8), 955–978. doi:10.1177/0018726712442427.

Rumens, N. (2018). *Queer business: Queering organization sexualities.* New York: Routledge.

Said, E. W. (1978). *Orientalism.* New York: Vintage Books.

Said, E. W. (1993). *Culture and imperialism.* New York: Vintage Books.

Sedgwick, E. K. (1990). *Epistemology of the closet.* Berkeley, CA: University of California Press.

Sedgwick, E. K. (2008). *Epistemology of the closet.* Berkeley, CA: University of California Press.

Shome, R. (1996). Postcolonial interventions in the rhetorical canon: An "other" view. *Communication Theory, 6*(1), 40–59. doi:10.1111/j.1468-2885.1996.tb00119.x.

Shome, R., & Hegde, R. S. (2002). Postcolonial approaches to communication: Charting the terrain, engaging the intersections. *Communication Theory, 12*(3), 249–270. doi:10.1111/j.1468-2885.2002.tb00269.x.

Smith, D. E. (1987). *The everyday world as problematic: A feminist sociology.* Toronto, ON: University of Toronto Press.

Spivak, G. C. (1985). Three women's texts and a critique of imperialism. *Critical Inquiry, 12*(1), 243–261. doi:10.1086/448328.

Spivak, G. C. (1988a). Can the subaltern speak? In C. Nelson & E. Grossberg (Eds.), *Marxism and the interpretation of culture* (pp. 271–313). Urbana, IL: University of Illinois Press.

Spivak, G. C. (1988b). Subaltern studies: Deconstructing historiography. In R. Guha & G. C. Spivak (Eds.), *Selected subaltern studies* (pp. 3–34). Oxford: Oxford University Press.

Spivak, G. C. (1999). *A critique of postcolonial reason: Toward a history of the vanishing present.* Cambridge, MA: Harvard University Press.

Trethewey, A. (2001). Reproducing and resisting the master narrative of decline: Midlife professional women's experiences of aging. *Management Communication Quarterly, 15*(2), 183–226. doi:10.1177/0893318901152002.

Warner, M. (1999). *The trouble with normal: Sex, politics, and the ethics of queer life*. New York: The Free Press.

Wells, C. C., Gill, R., & McDonald, J. (2015). "Us foreigners": Intersectionality in a scientific organization. *Equality, Diversity and Inclusion, 34*(6), 539–553. doi:10.1108/EDI-12-2014-0086.

Yep, G. A. (2003). The violence of heteronormativity in communication studies: Notes on injury, healing, and queer world-making. *Journal of Homosexuality, 45*(2–4), 11–59. doi:10.1300/J082v45n02_02.

15 Groups, Teams, and Decision-Making

Dawna I. Ballard and Dron M. Mandhana

The research and theorizing on teamwork and decision-making in organizational communication has been shaped by multidisciplinary perspectives that intersect around the processual and structural aspects of group interaction. As such, the study of groups and teams across disciplines—such as psychology, sociology, management, information studies, education, social work, political science, public policy, and urban planning—reflects a deeply communication-focused site of scholarship. Indeed, Poole (1998) argues that the small group should be *the* fundamental unit of analysis in communication research because of its key characteristics related to interaction: Individual actors can be easily discerned (unlike at macro-levels of analysis) and yet social context comes into play (unlike at micro-levels of analysis). Poole's provocative argument is even more apt for organizational communication scholarship because groups are a site where organizational scholars and practitioners can discern agency, varying cultures, and see the constitutive aspects of communication in organizations up close. Notably, McPhee and Zaug (2000) highlight subgroup processes as central to activity coordination—one of the four message flows that constitute organizations (see Chapter 3).

In this chapter, we offer a broad overview of the group and teamwork literature, especially as it relates to decision-making. We begin by defining groups and teams, and pay particular attention to the theoretical developments over time, especially the contributions of communication theorists. Throughout, we consider the approaches taken to communication and to organization, noting the attention to culture, and trace how various literatures consider the communication-organization spiral and the role of agency that shapes groups, teamwork, and decision-making in organizational contexts.

Groups, Teams, and Decision-Making in Organizational Life

The description of an organization in Chapter 1 was *a culturally suffused, living system of interconnected communicative relationships among a conglomerate of interdependent coalitions, composed themselves of interconnected communicative relationships and bound together by their homage to a common mission and dependence on a common resource base, with multiple and often incompatible instrumental and interactive goals and objectives.* This description is a particularly helpful place to begin considering the role of groups, teams, and decision-making in organizational life. It highlights the role of smaller social collectives in organizing—like formal teams, informal coalitions, or entire departments—and the divergent objectives each may have that often require difficult decisions to be made about which goals to privilege, when to execute them, and how to do so. Various parts of this description also help us to trace the role of entity, process, and structure in defining groups and teams, as discussed below.

Across the literature, membership in a *group*—as entity—is determined based on shared *dependence on a common resource base* as described above. This dependence can arise through assignment to a formal team that holds a particular budget to fund members' activities. The common resources that members of a group share can also be informal. For example, members may seek social resources—perhaps they enjoy the same hobbies or like to talk about parenting—or skill-based resources—as when organizational members come together as communities of practice (Wenger, 1998) to solve a problem shared across various teams. In this chapter, we will discuss methods and approaches to studying each of these types of groups (i.e., formal and informal).

There is an additional process-related distinction between groups and *teams* that is reflected in their *homage to a common mission* as above: In addition to relying upon shared resources, team members' activities also evidence commitment to a shared purpose. So, all teams are groups—an entity designation (O_3)—but not all groups are teams—which reflects both structural (O_2) and processual (O_1) designations. Additionally, teams rely upon formal and informal structures to accomplish their tasks: This is observed, in popular parlance, as *teamwork*. Their communication is both task-oriented and concerned with managing the social and emotional needs of group members. In terms of these formal and informal communication structures and the processes that they enable and constrain, then we can also say—more precisely—that while not all groups carry out teamwork processes, all teamwork necessarily arises through group interaction.

The related decision-making focus that characterizes much of the group literature is owed to the fact that teams often face *multiple and often incompatible instrumental and interactive goals and objectives*. Nonetheless, not all of the literature focuses solely on decision-making in teams. Below we choose three prominent traditions in group and team communication research—one focused on decision-making and formal task-oriented groups, the other focused on the role of communication in creating the team itself, and the last one focused on both formal and informal team membership. Throughout, we pay particular attention to how the instrumental and interactive goals and objectives are communicatively managed. See Table 15.1 for an overview of the three perspectives—*functional approaches to group decision-making, symbolic-interaction perspective*, and *network approaches*.

Multiple Traditions of Group and Team Scholarship in Organizational Communication

The study of teamwork and group decision-making was highly influenced by early work at the Tavistock Institute in T-groups, or training groups, popularized within the human relations tradition of management scholarship (see Chapter 6). The focus originally centered on psychological variables, but interest among group scholars soon moved into decision-making and influence.

Based on this backdrop, we begin our review below with the earliest tradition and describe new developments in the study of groups, teams, and decision-making over time. However, this is not primarily a chronological review because the perspectives have origins in different disciplines that developed without reference to (or knowledge of) the other in some cases, often in parallel or overlapping fashion. (In fact, because so many different group and team scholars were working in similar areas without

Table 15.1 The treatment of communication, organization, agency, and culture across traditions

Tradition	Communication (message, meaning, constitutive)	Organization (process, structure, entity)	C-O spiral with agency	Culture
Functional perspective and decision-making	The focus on communication as message is reflected in early models of communication that were prominent at the time that this perspective emerged.	The primary focus is on the decision-making process, and structure is considered in the ways that it informs process.	Early treatments addressed agency; however, the focus in much research is on outcomes and not agency.	Culture is generally not considered.
Symbolic-interpretive perspective	This perspective pays special attention to meaning creation given its focus on symbol use. It also views the group as communicatively constituted through members' symbolic activities.	The interplay among structure, process, and entity is vital. The focus is on how the entity is (re)shaped through symbolic processes. This process (re)produces structures that enable and constrain members' interaction.	The role of agency is central to this perspective.	Culture is relevant as it is part of the lens we use to constitute meanings. It is one of the structural factors that enable and constrain agency.
Network perspective	The focus is on the tie among and between individuals and groups—rather than a particular message or meaning—as the constitutive feature of social collectives.	Structure and entity are considered simultaneously. Process is not the focus of the network perspective, with notable exceptions.	Communication and organization are highlighted. Agency is often overlooked in this perspective, with notable exceptions (e.g., MTML, Monge).	Culture is considered as one of the many factors which shapes networks and characterize different systems.

opportunities to learn or benefit from work in other fields, the Interdisciplinary Network of Group Research [INGRoup] was formed in 2006 to remedy this problem and integrate group research.) Thus, in the following pages, the prominent organizing principle for our review highlights differences in the treatment of communication (as message, meaning, or constitutive), organization (entity [O_3], process [O_1], and structure [O_2]), culture, and the communication-organization spiral with agency. Particularly, we begin with perspectives that historically took more limited conceptions of communication and organization and move on to perspectives that more clearly attend to the mutually constitutive nature of communication and organization.

Functional Approaches to Group Decision-Making

Origins. The functional perspective and interest in group decision-making can be traced over time through the early work of philosopher John Dewey (1910), sociologist

Robert Freed Bales (1950), and psychologist Irving Janis (1972). First, Dewey's reflective thinking method was used to teach group discussion. The method contained five steps—it begins with identifying a felt difficulty, determining its cause and definition, suggesting potential solutions, problematizing the solutions, and concluding the best course forward.

Next, Bales' work on problem-solving groups (which began in the 1940s) led to the development of Interaction Process Analysis (IPA) as a method to study group performance. IPA epitomizes the functional perspective and is still widely used by group researchers today. Bales proposed that groups strive for equilibrium and that varied communication acts—both verbal and nonverbal—indicate either a lack of equilibrium or are used by group members to (re)establish equilibrium. IPA was a means through which recorded group interaction could be classified into 12 different categories that reflect a variety of functions—including three categories concerning positive reactions, three concerning negative reactions, three concerning the task, and three concerning responses to questions—all of which supported this ultimate goal of equilibrium.

Finally, Irving Janis' popular work on groupthink centered on decision-making and, particularly, the reasons for faulty decision-making among governmental groups. Janis (1972, 1982) highlighted that groups often make faulty, unsound decisions even when they appear to be well-informed. Groups and teams are goal-oriented, information-processing entities. However, they are vulnerable to information processing failures (Schippers, Edmondson, & West, 2014). Herbert Simon (1982) found that individual members of groups or teams are restricted by their cognitive abilities to process all of the information and make decisions under the constraints of *bounded rationality*. Bounded rationality refers to the finding that—under conditions of limited processing capabilities, knowledge, and time—individuals are unable to behave and interact according to early models of problem-solving, such as Dewey's reflective thinking. Members' ability to follow models that suggest the idealized rational actor (one who carefully weighs all options, is fully informed and expert, and has unlimited time to make a decision) is, in fact, bounded by the limits of their processing capabilities, knowledge, and time) (Simon, 1982). While it seems logical that team or group members should be able to complement each others' information-processing lacunae, group dynamics such as withholding information, proclivity to seek consensus, and selective information-processing biases lead to groupthink and poor decision-making (Janis, 1972, 1982; Schippers et al., 2014).

Key assumptions. Together, these strands of scholarship helped to establish the functional approach to group decision-making. The core assumptions of a functional perspective are that groups are (a) goal-oriented entities (b) whose performance varies, and (c) this variation is a function of internal and external influences on group interaction. It is still the most common approach taken to the study of groups, and centers on discerning which inputs and processes shape team effectiveness in the form of particular outputs (or outcomes). Below, we offer an overview of three prominent theories that draw on this perspective.

Key scholarship. Some examples of this perspective include groupthink theory, the functional theory of group decision-making, and the social combination approach.

Groupthink theory. Groupthink is such a popular concept with mainstream purchase that you can find this term in the Oxford English Dictionary (among other dictionary sources). Irving Janis (1972) proposed a groupthink theory to explain the faulty and sound decision-making processes during global political and economic crises. Through a qualitative analysis, he compared the faulty decision-making processes that led to disasters such as the invasion of North Korea, the escalation of the Vietnam War, and the attack on Pearl Harbor with the effective decision-making processes that took place during the Cuban Missile Crisis and the Marshall Plan. Based on these comparisons, Janis (1972, p. 9) defined groupthink as "a mode of thinking that people engage in when they are deeply involved in a cohesive in-group, when the members' strivings for unanimity override their motivation to realistically appraise alternative courses of action." Janis (1972) further observed that groupthink occurs in a team when the drive toward unanimity leads to suppressing or discounting dissenting voices and perspectives. This loss of information weakens the inputs and processes needed for effective decision-making, and results in poor quality decisions. Groupthink is more likely in groups when three conditions are present: (1) high levels of cohesion; (2) high levels of insulation from outside ideas and information; and (3) high pressure (competitive or time-constrained) environments.

In 1982, Janis developed a unified, five-stage model of groupthink and proposed groupthink as a decision-making process. Although this model included certain organizational and situational conditions as antecedents to groupthink, Janis (1982) maintained that group cohesiveness was the primary predictor of groupthink (Cline, 1990). Per Janis, this concurrence seeking tendency resulted in eight symptoms of groupthink that led to faulty decision-making among groups. To loosely categorize these symptoms: the first two symptoms are outcomes of overconfidence in group's abilities; the next two symptoms are due to the lack of exploration of alternative views; and the remaining symptoms stem from the pressures of group conformity. Below we list the eight symptoms with a brief description of the resulting outcomes of each symptom:

1. *The illusion of invulnerability:* groups engage in reckless risk-taking due to optimistic biases.
2. *Belief in the inherent morality of the group:* individuals strongly believe in the rightness of their cause with a lack of regard for the moral consequences.
3. *Collective rationalization:* group members are unwilling to reconsider and operate based on their preconceived assumptions.
4. *Out-group stereotypes:* group members tend to respond to intergroup conflict ineffectively due to negative stereotypes of out-group members.
5. *Self-censorship:* individuals sway from raising concerns that tend to deviate from the perceived consensus of the group.
6. *Illusion of unanimity:* group members believe that the decisions made are agreed by all members.
7. *Direct pressure on dissenters:* group members are dissuaded from making counterarguments to the group's view.
8. *Self-appointed mindguards:* Members tend to keep the group and the leaders in the dark from problematic information.

Functional theory of group decision-making. The functional theory developed by Gouran and Hirokawa (1983, 1996, 2003) identifies five requisite functions needed for effective decision-making. First, *problem analysis* includes using available information to understand (a) the nature of the problem, (b) its magnitude or seriousness, (c) its probable cause, and (d) potential consequences of not resolving it. The second requisite function is to *establish evaluation criteria*. What standards does the group need to meet

—by its own and others' judgment? Herbert Simon's (1982) concept of satisficing is relevant here. Satisficing concerns making a decision that is adequate but not optimal. It typically occurs when resources (material or time-based) are low or when it is difficult to determine an optimal solution because of highly ambiguous or constantly changing events. The third requisite function is to *generate alternative solutions*. Groups should identify a number of potential resolutions, rather than limiting themselves to one idealized "best" choice. The fourth requisite function focuses on *evaluating the positive consequences of solutions*. What is the best-case scenario for each proposed decision? The fifth requisite function focuses on *evaluating the negative consequences of solutions*. What is the worst-case scenario for each proposed choice? The ability of a group to carry out each of these requisite functions predicts their ability to perform well.

Social combination approach. This approach is based on social decision scheme theory and centers on predicting how members of a group will combine their unique contributions for a given task type (Davis, 1973; Lorge & Solomon, 1955). It is only relevant for task settings in which a group must agree on a pre-specified set of possible decision alternatives. Studies also show that the best decision rule depends on the task (Davis, 1973, 1980). Thus, the findings are highly specific, making it useful to understand group decision-making in particular contexts, such as with jury decisions (Davis, Kameda, Parks, Stasson, & Zimmerman, 1989).

The social combination approach, or social decision schemes, has been utilized to study decision-making processes involved in the execution of a range of task types. For example, Laughlin and Ellis (1986) found that groups use a truth-wins decision scheme on tasks that have demonstrably correct responses (e.g., mathematical problems). For decision tasks that do not have explicitly visible correct solutions, a majority-wins decision scheme is used by group members (Davis, 1982). The social combination approach has also been used to explain how groups come to a decision based on the inputs from expert group members. For instance, Bonner (2004) studied the influence of expert members on decision-making and found that experts wield more influence than other group members.

Approaches taken to communication. The majority of research in this line of scholarship regards communication as a message and focuses on its role in making meaning, which shapes group process. This is consistent with its specific and narrow focus on task-oriented decision-making. For example, how does a given message fulfill any of the requisite functions needed for team success? Hirokawa and Poole (1996) explicitly delineate nine functions of communication in groups: information processing, analytical processing, procedural functions, goal-oriented functions, synergistic functions, rhetorical, conflict management, control, and creation and maintenance of group cultures and climates. This focus on messages and meaning is consistent with early models of communication that were prominent at the time this perspective emerged (see Chapter 1). Similarly, much of the work in this tradition ignores the role of culture except as it shapes the ability of the group to fulfill its requisite functions.

Approaches taken to organization and agency in the communication-organization spiral. Three core assumptions of the functional perspective are that groups are goal-oriented, group performance varies and can be evaluated, and internal and external factors influence group performance. Structure (seen as an input) is considered in the ways it informs process, which is viewed as a predictor of team performance. Theories that draw on a functional perspective mainly focus on communication and influence. However, some of the work from this perspective includes a deliberate focus on the role of agency in the communication-organization spiral. Homans' (1950) work on the External Systems Orientation highlights the dynamic construction of groups and teams. Rather than viewing groups as a static entity, Homan considers the continuing cycles of interaction with the environment and the ways in which positive or negative feedback loops shape groups through their ability to adapt to external conditions. This focus on interaction with the environment is unique among many group theories that draw on a functional perspective, and it illustrates the range of approaches that can be described as functional. Its view of the group as inherently dynamic and shapeshifting is consistent with the symbolic-interpretive perspective, described next.

The Symbolic-Interpretive Perspective

Origins. The symbolic-interpretive perspective has its origins in hermeneutics and phenomenology. Hermeneutics was founded based on a pre-20th-century concept called *verstehen*, or understanding. Similarly, phenomenology is the study of knowledge that arises from understanding, consciousness, and experience. Ultimately drawn from theoretical and methodological influences across a range of literatures and disciplines—including Shutz's social phenomenology, Heidegger's hermeneutic phenomenology, Garfinkel's ethnomethodology, as well as seminal work by Mead, Blumer, Langer, and Burke—the symbolic-interpretive approach takes communication to be the key social process that shapes our reality. Within a group perspective, it bears on team members' shared reality.

Key assumptions. A fundamental assumption of the symbolic-interpretive perspective is that groups are socially constructed and the group as an entity exists only through members' interaction. Following from this basic understanding of groups as communicatively constituted, groups are also readily acknowledged to be fluid in terms of their boundaries and to exhibit interdependence with the external environment. It shares this in common with Homans' (1950) work discussed in the functional perspective. However, it typically departs from the external systems orientation in terms of its empirical focus. Scholarship conducted from a symbolic-interpretive perspective focuses on group members' symbolic activities, ranging from the stories members tell to the written organizational rules they follow or reject in their daily interactions.

Key scholarship. Exploring symbolic convergence theory, structuration theory, the dialectic perspective, and adaptive structuration theory helps to further explicate the key assumptions and methods used in symbolic-interpretive research.

Symbolic convergence theory (SCT). SCT concerns how group consciousness is created through symbol use. The communication process that leads them to converge as a group around a given fantasy is a central point of investigation for this theory. Scholars drawing on this theoretical perspective study group fantasy chains, which derive from members' shared interpretations of events that fulfill particular social or psychological needs (Bormann, 1996). Fantasies reflect the creative and imaginative interpretations of everyday events that converge in a shared group understanding (i.e., chain reaction). Additionally, symbolic convergence theory highlights the ways in which group members' behavior is then shaped and guided by this shared understanding (Bormann, 1973, 1996).

An early example of a study based on symbolic convergence theory is Bormann's (1973) study of the Eagleton Affair. In this study, Bormann grounded the concept of fantasy to observable communication and looked at the resignation of Thomas Eagleton as a nominee for the Democratic party's vice-president position. In this case, Eagleton went through electric shock therapy to deal with depression. However, due to this participation in the shock therapy, Eagleton was referred to as "Electric Tom" by individuals in Missouri (Bormann, 1973; Bormann, Cragan, & Shields, 2001). These words became a symbolic cue (inside joke) for Missourians and triggered a sharing of the Eagleton Affair drama (Bormann et al., 2001).

Structuration theory. The focus of structuration theory extends well beyond the confines of the group as an entity or even topic of inquiry. A sociological theory, structuration is concerned with the role of larger societal structures in shaping human behavior. However, this theory found a home in group communication research as scholars from the functional perspective began to look further outside the boundaries of group process to consider the larger role of structure—the *rules* and *resources* that group members' draw on to accomplish everyday activities—as well as the role of human agency in decision-making. In terms of structure, examples of rules in an organization include an employee handbook or stories told to newcomers about what to do or not to do in order to succeed. Resources range from things like the raw materials used in production to the training and certification needed to obtain a job (see Chapter 3 for details).

Unlike a functional perspective, these structures alone are not viewed as determining group outcomes. Group members make decisions—implicitly or explicitly—about whether or not to draw on these structures in their daily practices. For instance, a meeting agenda is a structure designed to introduce a particular order to group interaction. Members may only loosely follow that agenda, however. This reflects human agency, which is enabled and constrained by structures (such as the agenda)—making some things more likely and others less likely—but is not solely determined by the structures. Therefore, structures are both the medium and the outcome of human interaction and symbolic activity.

Dialectic perspective. Continuing the example above about whether or not group members closely follow a meeting agenda, the dialectic perspective highlights the frustration members may feel about how their agenda item is treated or rushed or even skipped altogether. It concerns the inevitable tensions that will arise in group interaction because of the continual need to choose between two different, and seemingly, contradictory choices. The ways that team members manage these ever-present tensions through their symbolic activity is the focus of this perspective (Johnson & Long, 2002).

Adaptive structuration theory (AST). In the 1990s, associated with the rise of information and communication technologies (ICTs) adopted by organizations to facilitate the work of groups and teams, Poole and DeSanctis (1990) further refined aspects of structuration theory to bear on this process. AST theorizes that the influence of ICTs (on teamwork, for example) depends upon the structure built (i.e., designed) into the technology and the structures that emerge when users try to incorporate the ICTs in their work. Structure refers to both the *features* and the *spirit* of the ICTs. The features are made up of the specific rules and resources embedded in the material aspects of the ICT. The spirit is made up of the broader aim concerning the values and goals that underlie a certain feature.

The closer the alignment between the way a given technology is appropriated by its users and the spirit of the technology, the more likely it is that the technology may provide benefits. If the meeting agenda described above is delivered via any number of the popular digital meeting applications, its success will depend upon a combination of the structural features, the spirit of the app, and how members use it. For instance, in a healthy team, if members use it to keep the meeting moving and productive without regard to privileging the voices of particular people then it will be more likely to be adopted and used by members. If, however, it is appropriated to suppress dissent then it may become a contested ICT that some members refuse to use altogether (see Chapter 3 for details).

Approaches taken to communication. The symbolic-interpretive perspective pays special attention to meaning creation, given its focus on symbol use. It also views the group as communicatively constituted through members' symbolic activities. Group fantasy chains are key to the symbolic-interpretive perspective. They begin with dramatizing messages, which contain at least one of the following: analogy, anecdote, parable, allegory, fable, narrative, word play (including puns), double entendre, or a figure of speech (i.e., a comparison or personification of a nonhuman life form or object). If these messages elicit an affirmative response among members, a chain reaction (i.e., a fantasy chain) is created in which others join in and participate, shaping the group culture (Bormann, 1973, 1996; Bormann et al., 2001).

Cragan and Shields (1995) offer an illustrative example of a fantasy chain in their research on dentists. Based on the profit declines of their practices in light of the oversaturation of dentists, one dentist opined, "The days of drill, fill, and bill are over … I should have gone to medical school and specialized in plastic surgery. Then, I could cut, suck, and tuck for $3,000 a whack" (Cragan & Shields, 1995, pp. 35–36). The other dentists laughed, and then repeated and embellished the statement, reflected in a fantasy chain. This particular fantasy theme chained out because it highlighted a symbolic reality shared among members of the dentistry profession.

Approaches taken to organization and agency in the communication-organization spiral. The interplay between entity and process is vital to the symbolic-interpretive perspective. The focus is on how the entity arises and is (re)shaped through symbolic processes. These symbolic representations then structure future interactions. However, while symbolic representations enable and constrain group members' interactions, this perspective centers on the ways in which group members continually (re)create these representations through exercising their own agency. This reflects the concept of *duality of structure* in structuration.

The agentic nature of fantasy chains offers an illustrative example: Fantasy themes are never faithful representations of some past experience—they always project a particular experience that has a unique spin, thus recreating the group to suit their purposes. Also, multiple fantasy themes are often shared among group members as a way to account for different versions of the same experience and can develop into stock scenarios that are repeated over and over again. Sometimes these themes get integrated by characters into a larger rhetorical vision that captures the group's imagination. Thus, the group (and larger organization of which it is a part) is literally created through their members' everyday symbolic communication practices. Culture plays an important role in this perspective because organizational groups and teams are often sites of organizational subcultures. These fantasy themes and rhetorical visions often mark divisions across these subcultures and serve to bind members within a subculture even more tightly. This interest in the group as an entity and the ways each group differs from each other is consistent with the network perspective described below.

The Network Perspective

Origins. The network tradition of group scholarship dates back to at least the 1930s and was developed across multiple disciplines, including anthropology, social psychology, communication, sociology, mathematics, epidemiology, political science, and economics. It derives from theories of mutual or collective interest, theories of self-interest, theories of homophily, social exchange or dependency theories, and cognitive theories—all of which have contributed to the diverse schools of thought within the network approach. Two distinct lines of work emerged across time. The first line of work was conducted between 1930 and 1960, and a new line of research emerged in the 1990s that reflects strides made in network software as well as a burgeoning interest in social capital. Consistent with the timing and tradition of the functional perspective, in the 1950s, one of the earliest and most famous experiments that leveraged a network approach to small groups examined the ideal network structure to support group performance (Bavelas, 1950; Bavelas & Barrett, 1951). More centralized groups, those focused around a few primary group members, performed better than others on complex tasks. More decentralized groups performed better on simple tasks.

Key assumptions. Unity across the varied perspectives is found in five underlying principles identified by Wellman (1988). First, individuals' social networks—e.g., reflected in their group membership—are a better predictor of individual behavior than are their drives, attitudes, or demographic characteristics. Second, the relationship among units—such as among members of a group or among groups in an organization —should be the analytical focus of network research rather than characteristics of the units themselves, e.g., individual or group characteristics. Third, the methods used to study networks should not rely upon the assumption of independence among units or groups. Fourth, we cannot understand a social system, such as a group or a network of groups, through the dyadic ties within that system. All units within a system are interdependent; therefore, the whole system must be studied. Finally, organizations are not made up of clearly demarcated groups, but of overlapping networks. This is due to the fuzzy, permeable, and shifting boundaries of groups which is owed, in part, to the fact that individuals maintain multiple group memberships.

Within a network perspective, a group is considered either (a) an emergent characteristic of a network that reflects a particular structural "grouping" or (b) a formally imposed category or designation about a set of actors. Also frequently referred to as a clique, within the emergent view, a group reflects the connection among various nodes in a population. In this view, network analyses often focus on various types of connection among nodes within a system, based on any number of characteristics including culture, expertise, trust, collaboration, etc. In contrast, when a group is considered as an imposed designation or boundary, such as a political party, network analysis often focuses on comparing communication patterns within and outside of that network. (See Chapter 9 for details on network research.)

Key scholarship. Some examples of this perspective include theories of self-interest, social exchange and dependency, and theories of mutual or collective interest.

Theories of self-interest. This school of thought assumes that individuals are driven by a rational self-interest and form dyadic or group ties in order to pursue these interests. A central influence in this research tradition was the work of sociologist James Coleman (1988) who illustrated how dyadic interactions—where each actor tries to maximize his or her self-interest—form the basis of a social system (like a small group). Against this backdrop of self-interest, Coleman's work showed that the interdependence shared by the individuals acts as a limit or constraint on the extent to which each person will pursue their self-interests. Ultimately, each person receives access to more rewards by working together than could be obtained by unchecked self-seeking.

From a self-interest theoretical perspective, individuals also earn social capital from their investments in particular relationships that can be leveraged for a variety of rewards. Sociologist Pierre Bourdieu defines social capital as the "sum of the resources, actual or virtual, that accrue to an individual or group by virtue of possessing a durable network of more or less institutionalized relationships of mutual acquaintance and recognition" (Bourdieu & Wacquant, 1992, p. 119). One of the ways that people may gain further social capital is through filling structural holes, or places in a network where connections are missing. Making those connections for others can be a "profitable" way to invest one's social capital and earn returns on one's investment.

Social exchange and dependency. In addition to the external systems orientation discussed earlier as part of the functional school, Homans' (1950) work was also central to the social exchange school. He argued that people proactively seek to build ties to others with whom they can reap benefits through the exchange of valuable resources. Relationships are continued to the extent that they continue to yield such resources and ended when they no longer do so. Because of the explicit focus on external resources (and resource dependency) within the study of groups, Homans (1950) helped to link micro (i.e., individual) and macro (i.e., organizational) levels of analysis, and show how structure arises from interaction (as we discussed with regard to structuration theory). Emerson (1972a, 1972b) also studied the social exchange of resources and observed that it was enabled by a large-scale network of relationships in which individuals, dyads, and groups are embedded. Thus, he also considered the role of intergroup communication and relationships. In contrast to theories of self-interest, the social exchange and dependency perspective highlights how individuals are motivated to create ties in order to minimize their dependence on others and to maximize the dependence of others on them.

Theories of mutual or collective interest. Public goods theory is a well-developed theory of collective action by Samuelson (1954) that focuses on how the potential benefits that accrue from coordinated action typically outweigh individual self-interests. Its original focus centered on the economics of public versus private ownership of public goods, like material resources, but it has been applied to a range of public goods, including intellectual property (Fulk, Flanagin, Kalman, Monge, & Ryan, 1996). Research in this tradition identifies the conditions under which group members are more likely to aid collective action aimed at creating and maintaining public goods that benefit everyone. It addresses the *free-rider* problem, wherein all members of the group will benefit from this public good whether or not they help to create or maintain it. Findings suggest that individuals are motivated to act in ways that maximize their shared ability to use these resources, in spite of the free-rider problem. This runs counter to both the self-interest and social exchange theories.

Approaches taken to communication. Major network theories are concerned with how communication ties and networks are created rather than a particular message or meaning. For instance, public goods theory (discussed above) highlights the conditions under which group members are motivated to form ties and build networks.

Communication networks are also based on homophily, the finding that ties are more likely to form among group members who share things in common. Individuals strategically form ties with others who are similar in order to reduce conflict, foster trust, and offer predictability. Transactive memory systems is another theoretical perspective that concerns how group members develop communication networks to benefit from the expertise and skills of others in the group. For each of the varied network perspectives, while the focus is on the constitutive features of the ties within a network, scholars also consider the nature of the ties, which inheres in the messages or meaning associated with the tie. This includes:

> communication ties (such as who talks to whom, or who gives information or advice to whom), formal ties (such as who reports to whom), affective ties (such as who likes whom, or who trusts whom), proximity ties (who is spatially or electronically close to whom), and cognitive ties (such as who knows who knows whom).
>
> (Katz, Lazer, Arrow, & Contractor, 2004, p. 308).

Approaches taken to organization and agency in the communication-organization spiral. While structure and entity are considered simultaneously, process is typically not the focus of the network perspective. Therefore, in most survey network studies, network content is rarely a variable under investigation. Podolny and Baron (1997) are among the few who emphasize and explore the effects of network content and its interaction with network structure. Instead, a prominent—although contested—view is that formal organizational structure influences the communication interactions and the content of those interactions. These formal roles should determine the individuals with whom the member communicates, what s/he should communicate, and the operating procedure for communication. This view is debated because it fails to take into account the active part that individuals play in creating and shaping organizational structure.

Following the weaknesses and inconclusive findings relating formal networks to organizational behaviors (Johnson, 1992, 1993), there is growing interest in the role of informal networks. Informal networks are driven and shaped by factors such as expertise or friendship—variables not captured by formal organizational structure analysis. Informal networks involve more discretionary patterns of interaction, where the content of relationships may be work-related, social, or both. Several network researchers (e.g., Brass, 1984; Roberts & O'Reilly, 1979; Tichy, Fombrun, & Devanna, 1982) also take a relational approach to organizations, rooted in modern systems theory (see Chapter 2), and consider the emergence of structure as bottom-up, individually motivated, and dynamic. The impact of informal networks on various organizational outcomes, such as job effectiveness, commitment, turnover rate, career mobility, and satisfaction has been examined in this tradition.

Some scholars recommend studying formal and informal networks together in the context of each other as way of understanding the interdependencies between formal and informal networks. Not surprisingly, formal workplace interactions often develop into informal, friendship networks due to similarity, proximity, and constant interaction among organizational members (see Chapter 10). When these formal and informal networks overlap they create multiplex ties, which means they interact in multiple contexts. In addition to the idea that formal ties naturally lead to informal ones, the reverse is also true. For instance, we may recommend our friends for jobs within our organization, or we may befriend a colleague from another department and this informal tie may influence the way we vote on interdepartmental matters. The key issue with formal and informal ties is to explore each within the context of the other.

Conclusion

Across the varied research traditions focused on groups, teams and decision-making, the concept of organization is viewed and studied in diverse ways—including as process (O_1), as structure (O_2), and as entity (O_3). Beginning with the functional perspective, organization is largely treated as structure $(O_2$, seen as an input) and is investigated in terms of the ways it informs process (rather than organization being investigated *as* a process). While Homans' (1950) approach sheds light on the ways in which communication and organization are mutually constituted, most theories that draw on a functional perspective mainly focus on the relationship between communication and influence. In contrast, the symbolic-interpretive perspective highlights the communication-organization spiral through considering the interplay between entity and process. Research from this perspective considers how the entity (i.e., the group and/or organization) arises and is (re)shaped through symbolic processes as well as the ways in which group members continually (re)create symbolic representations through exercising their own agency. Finally, for research within the network perspective, structure and entity are considered simultaneously, but process is typically not studied.

The study of groups, teams, and decision-making in organizations is fundamental to the study of organizational communication processes. It is a multidisciplinary area of study, yet the varied fields coalesce around communication and interaction as the key driver of group formation and process, exhibiting the conceptual pattern of the C-O dynamic that is so prevalent in organizational communication theory.

Recommended Supplementary Readings

Functional Perspective

Cummings, J. N., & Ancona, D. G. (2005). The functional perspective. In S. A. Wheelan (Ed.), *Handbook of group research and practice* (pp. 107–117). Thousand Oaks, CA: SAGE.

Gouran, D. S., & Hirokawa, R. Y. (2003). Effective decision making and problem solving in groups: A functional perspective. In R. Y. Hirokawa, R. S. Cathcart, L. A. Samovar, & L. D. Henman (Eds.), *Small group communication* (pp. 27–38). Los Angeles, CA: Roxbury.

Hirokawa, R. Y. (1985). Discussion procedures and decision-making performance: A test of a functional perspective. *Human Communication Research, 12,* 203–224.

Orlitzky, M., & Hirokawa, R. Y. (2001). To err is human, to correct for it divine: A meta-analysis of research testing the functional theory of group decision-making effectiveness. *Small Group Research, 32*(3), 313–341.

Wittenbaum, G. M., Hollingshead, A. B., Paulus, P. B., Hirokawa, R. Y., Ancona, D. G., Peterson, R. S., Jehn, K. A. & Yoon, K. (2004). The functional perspective as a lens for understanding groups. *Small Group Research, 35*(1), 17–43.

These five readings provide a good overview of the functional perspective, specifically, as it relates to groups performing tasks. They include the early work in the area (Hirokawa, 1985), reviews of the work (Cummings & Ancona, 2005; Gouran & Hirokawa, 2003; Wittenbaum et al., 2004), as well as a meta-analysis of empirical research on functional groups (Orlitzky & Hirokawa, 2001).

Symbolic-Interpretive Perspective

Bormann, E. G. (1996). Symbolic convergence theory and communication in group decision making. In R. Y. Hirokawa & M. S. Poole (Eds.), *Communication and group decision making* (2nd ed., pp. 81–113). Thousand Oaks, CA: SAGE.

DeSanctis, G., & Poole, M. S. (1994). Capturing the complexity in advanced technology use: Adaptive structuration theory. *Organization Science, 5*, 121–147.

Frey, L. R., & Sunwolf. (2004). The symbolic-interpretive perspective on group dynamics. *Small Group Research, 35*, 277–306.

Poole, M., & DeSanctis, G. (1990). Understanding the use of group decision support systems: The theory of adaptive structuration. In J. Fulk & C. Steinfield (Eds.), *Organizations and communication technology* (pp. 175–195). Newbury Park, CA: SAGE.

Seibold, D. R., & Meyers, R. A. (2007). Group argument: A structuration perspective and research program. *Small Group Research, 38*, 312–336.

These readings focus on the key scholarship related to the symbolic-interpretive perspective and how it applies to the study of groups. Bormann (1996) uses symbolic convergence theory to explain how individuals create a common ground through a chain of fantasies. DeSanctis and Poole (1994) and Poole and DeSanctis (1990) explain the tenets of adaptive structuration theory and how it explains the relationship between the structures of advanced technologies and the emergent structures of social action that emerge using these technologies. Seibold and Meyers (2007) provide a review of research on group argument from a structuration perspective. Finally, Frey and Sunwolf (2004) reviews the foundations of the symbolic-interpretive perspective and propose a composite model of group processes, practices, products, and predispositions.

Network Perspective

Cummings, J. N., & Cross, R. (2003). Structural properties of work groups and their consequences for performance. *Social networks, 25*(3), 197–210.

Balkundi, P., & Harrison, D. A. (2006). Ties, leaders, and time in teams: Strong inference about network structure's effects on team viability and performance. *Academy of Management Journal, 49*, 49–68.

Contractor, N., & Su, C. (2011). Understanding groups from a network perspective. In A. Hollingshead & M.S. Poole (Eds.), *Research methods for studying groups and teams: A Guide to approaches, tools, and technologies* (pp. 284–310). New York, NY: Routledge.

Katz, N., Lazer, D., Arrow, H., & Contractor, N. (2004). Network theory and small groups. *Small Group Research, 35*, 307–332.

This set of readings focus on the study of small groups from a network perspective. They include pragmatic approaches to studying small groups from a network perspective (Contractor & Su, 2011), a detailed review of network research on small groups (Katz et al., 2004), a meta-analysis of research on the effects of network structures on team effectiveness (Balkundi & Harrison, 2006), and an empirical study on the effects of group network structure on team performance (Cummings & Cross, 2003).

Important Concepts: Define and Discuss

Bounded rationality
Cohesion
Duality of structure
Feedback loops
Free rider problem
Group fantasy chains
Homophily

Phenomenology
Problem analysis
Satisficing
Social capital

Practitioners' Corner and Discussion Questions:

Contributions to Multidisciplinary Teams (MDTs) at the Children's Advocacy Centers

In any given organizational context, each of the three major research traditions we describe here may be leveraged—sometimes simultaneously—to yield insights on teamwork and decision-making. Below, we describe a recent multi-year large scale research project undertaken by a team of researchers (which include the present authors) and ask you to consider how each of the scholarly traditions could assist in the study.

Background: The Children's Advocacy Center (CAC) Movement

More than a quarter of a century ago, the children's advocacy center (CAC) movement changed the individual and institutional landscape for child abuse investigations around the globe through leveraging the power of multidisciplinary teams (MDTs) in the service of children and their families. The CAC MDT refers to the various individuals from a myriad of core child abuse disciplines who provide the front-line and immediate supervisory services involved in child abuse investigations, assessment, intervention and prosecution. Those core disciplines include law enforcement, child protective services, prosecution, medical, mental health, and the CAC itself (forensic interviewers, family advocates, mental health clinicians, and MDT coordination staff).

Joint investigation of child abuse cases by MDTs is foundational to the mission of children's advocacy centers. The success of this approach is shaped by the quality and timeliness of communication among team members from different agencies and professions. A number of intra- and interorganizational factors come together to enable and constrain effective coordination in this setting. Our team—comprised of experts in communication, time-based coordination, team interaction, and organizational science—conducted a comprehensive analysis of the MDT model. Our objective was to determine what factors influence MDT performance in the complex environment they face.

Discussion Questions

PRACTITIONER LENS: *In an effort to better understand the teams you will study, what kinds of questions would you ask during initial meetings with the organizational leadership?*

RESEARCHER LENS: *Can each of the three research traditions described in this chapter be of assistance in a project of this nature? Describe specific contributions that each of the varied traditions can make to address this research objective.*

Fieldwork at the Children's Advocacy Centers

To understand the multiple factors that shape best practices for joint investigations, we took a multi-tiered approach to studying MDT communication dynamics. To offer a complete and exhaustive account of the life of MDTs, we systematically analyzed and compared three different—yet complementary—types of observations:

- MDT members' language and communication patterns as exhibited in focus group conversations (in both 10 intra-disciplinary settings and 17 multi-disciplinary settings);
- MDT members' shared views and considerations about the issues of greatest import to high quality work (discussed in concert with other members of their MDT during 17 multidisciplinary focus groups); and,
- MDT members' personal reports about a range of individual, team, and agency-related factors that shape their ability to be effective as an MDT member (as reflected in a statewide survey of 1,424 members).

Our primary objective was to identify systemic barriers to effective collaboration and information sharing. Through reviewing emergent themes from the participant observation, archival data, focus groups, and interviews, we developed a survey to assess MDT members' experiences around issues that included factors such as the role of task design and feedback, training, supervisory support, team psychological safety, task cohesion, social cohesion, individual attraction to the group, and work method autonomy in team performance.

Discussion Questions

PRACTITIONER LENS: *As a practitioner, how would you approach the fundamental question of what constitutes MDT performance? On what particular outcomes would you focus as you spoke with MDT members and as you reviewed relevant organizational documents?*

RESEARCHER LENS: *Taking the perspective of a researcher trained in each of the three traditions, which of the previous types of data would be of most interest to you? How would you design a study that collects the types of information needed to understand MDT performance?*

Culture at the Children's Advocacy Centers

Because the MDTs were made up of occupational groups with unique cultures—most notably law enforcement, doctors and nurses, therapists, child protective services, and prosecutors—we studied how members of each occupational group perceived the other occupational groups through both focus groups and survey data. In the occupational focus groups, each focus group was constituted entirely of members belonging to a given profession or from a given agency—i.e., where the members were largely homogenous in terms of their work focus. This allowed us to view differences in interagency perceptions of the MDT model.

Discussion Questions

PRACTITIONER LENS: *What questions would you ask participants in the occupational focus groups?*

RESEARCHER LENS: *What insights, if any, could each research tradition offer to help you better understand the impact of occupational culture on MDT performance?*

Research Findings About MDT Effectiveness

Based upon our triangulation of the multiple data sources, several prominent themes emerged about what shapes MDT effectiveness (both in terms of existing practices associated with strong case development and outcomes as well as existing barriers to effective collaboration and information sharing):

- *Social support predicts resilience and positive case outcomes.* We found positive case outcomes for child abuse investigations are associated with strong MDTs. At the same time, this social support not only leads to improved case outcomes but expressly allows MDT members to carry out their work more effectively and to have more longevity in their careers within an agency.
- *Institutional barriers weaken MDTs. Institutional support strengthens MDTs.* A number of structural and professional barriers exist inside the various partner agencies. These institutional barriers may serve to systematically weaken team processes and create impediments for team members' full participation on the MDT. When partner agencies support the model, MDTs are more effective.
- *Proximity facilitates information sharing and collaboration.* Proximity served as a powerful predictor of information sharing, collaboration, and identity, and diminished barriers associated with professional identity. Physical distance increased these barriers and reduced the ease of information sharing and collaboration.

Discussion Questions

PRACTITIONER LENS: *(a) Based on these findings, what advice would you offer to children's advocacy centers about how to foster social support among MDT members?*
(b) How can children's advocacy centers communicate and leverage these findings to cultivate greater institutional support among partner agencies?
(c) In settings without physical proximity, how can children's advocacy centers address the barriers we found associated with physical distance?

RESEARCHER LENS: *(a) Which of these findings would you predict based on extant research in any of the three traditions? Are any of the findings unexpected?*
(b) Based on these findings, can you design a follow-up study to collect more data to shed even greater insight into team dynamics at children's advocacy centers? What research tradition(s) would offer the most utility given these findings?

References

Bales, R. F. (1950). *Interaction process analysis.* Reading, MA: Addison-Wesley.
Bavelas, A. (1950). Communication patterns in task-oriented groups. *Journal of the Acoustical Society of America, 22,* 723–730. doi:10.1121/1.1906679.

Bavelas, A., & Barrett, M. (1951). An experimental approach to organizational communication. *Personnel, 27,* 386–397.

Bonner, B. L. (2004). Expertise in group problem solving: Recognition, social combination, and performance. *Group Dynamics: Theory, Research, and Practice, 8,* 277–290. doi:10.1037/1089-2699.8.4.277.

Bormann, E. G. (1973). The Eagleton affair: A fantasy theme analysis. *Quarterly Journal of Speech, 59,* 143–159. doi:10.1080/00335637309383163.

Bormann, E. G. (1996). Symbolic convergence theory and communication in group decision making. In R. Y. Hirokawa & M. S. Poole (Eds.), *Communication and group decision making* (2nd ed., pp. 81–113). Thousand Oaks, CA: SAGE.

Bormann, E. G., Cragan, J. F., & Shields, D. C. (2001). Three decades of developing, grounding, and using symbolic convergence theory (SCT). *Annals of the International Communication Association, 25,* 271-313. doi:10.1080/23808985.2001.11679006

Bourdieu, P., & Wacquant, L. J. D. (1992). *An invitation to reflexive sociology.* Chicago, IL: University of Chicago Press.

Brass, D. J. (1984). Being in the right place: A structural analysis of individual influence in an organization. *Administrative Science Quarterly, 29*(4), 518–539. doi:10.2307/2392937.

Cline, R. J. W. (1990). Detecting groupthink: Methods for observing the illusion of unanimity. *Communication Quarterly, 38,* 112–126. doi:10.1080/01463379009369748.

Coleman, J. (1988). Social capital in the creation of human capital. *American Journal of Sociology, 94,* S95–S120. Retrieved from www.jstor.org/stable/2780243.

Cragan, J. F., & Shields, D.C. (1995). *Symbolic theories in applied communication research: Bormann, Burke, and Fisher.* Cresskill, NJ: Hampton.

Davis, J. H. (1973). Group decision and social interaction: A theory of social decision schemes. *Psychological Review, 80,* 97–125. doi:10.1037/h0033951.

Davis, J. H. (1980). Group decision and procedural justice. In M. Fishbein (Ed.), *Progress in social psychology* (Vol. 1, pp. 157–229). Hillsdale, NJ: Erlbaum.

Davis, J. H. (1982). Social interaction as a combinatorial process in group decision. In H. Brandstatter, J. H. Davis, & G. Stocker-Kreichgauer (Eds.), *Group decision making* (pp. 27–58). London: Academic Press.

Davis, J. H., Kameda, T., Parks, C., Stasson, M., & Zimmerman, S. (1989). Some social mechanics of group decision making: The distribution of opinion, polling sequence, and implications for consensus. *Journal of Personality and Social Psychology, 57,* 1000–1012. doi:10.1037/0022-3514.57.6.1000.

Dewey, J. (1910). *How we think.* Boston, MA: D. C. Heath.

Emerson, R. M. (1972a). Exchange theory: Part I. A psychological basis for social exchange. In J. Berger, M. Zelditch, & B. Anderson (Eds.), *Sociological theories in progress* (pp. 38–57). Boston, MA: Houghton Mifflin.

Emerson, R. M. (1972b). Exchange theory: Part II. Exchange relations and networks. In J. Berger, M. Zelditch, & B. Anderson (Eds.), *Sociological theories in progress* (pp. 58–87). Boston, MA: Houghton Mifflin.

Fulk, J., Flanagin, A. J., Kalman, M. E., Monge, P. R., & Ryan, T. (1996). Connective and communal public goods in interactive communication systems. *Communication Theory, 6*(1), 60–87. doi:10.1111/j.1468-2885.1996.tb00120.x.

Gouran, D. S., & Hirokawa, R. Y. (1983). The role of communication in decision-making groups: A functional perspective. In M. S. Mander (Ed.), *Communications in transition* (pp. 168–185). New York, NY: Praeger.

Gouran, D. S., & Hirokawa, R. Y. (1996). Functional theory and communication in decision-making and problem-solving groups: An expanded view. In R. Y. Hirokawa & M. S. Poole (Eds.), *Communication and group decision-making* (2nd ed., pp. 55–80). Thousand Oaks, CA: SAGE.

Gouran, D. S., & Hirokawa, R. Y. (2003). Effective decision making and problem solving in groups: A functional perspective. In R. Y. Hirokawa, R. S. Cathcart, L. A. Samovar, & L. D. Henman (Eds.), *Small group communication* (pp. 27–38). Los Angeles, CA: Roxbury.

Hirokawa, R. Y., & Poole, M. S. (Eds.). (1996). *Communication and group decision making*. Thousand Oaks, CA: SAGE.

Homans, G. (1950). *The human group*. New York, NY: Harcourt, Brace.

Janis, I. L. (1972). *Victims of groupthink*. Boston, MA: Houghton-Mifflin.

Janis, I. L. (1982). *Groupthink: Psychological studies of policy decisions* (2nd ed.). Boston, MA: Houghton Mifflin.

Johnson, J. D. (1992). Approaches to organizational communication structure. *Journal of Business Research, 25*(2), 99–113. doi:10.1016/0148-2963(92)90010-9.

Johnson, J. D. (1993). *Organizational communication structure*. Norwood, NJ: Ablex.

Johnson, S. D., & Long, L. M. (2002). "Being a part and being apart": Dialectics and group communication. In L. R. Frey (Ed.), *New directions in group communication* (pp. 25–42). Thousand Oaks, CA: SAGE.

Katz, N., Lazer, D., Arrow, H., & Contractor, N. (2004). Network theory and small groups. *Small Group Research, 35*(3), 307–332. doi:10.1177/1046496404264941.

Laughlin, P. R., & Ellis, A. L. (1986). Demonstrability and social combination processes on mathematical intellective tasks. *Journal of Experimental Social Psychology, 22*, 177–189. doi:10.1016/0022-1031(86)90022-3.

Lorge, I., & Solomon, H. (1955). Two models of group behavior in the solution of eureka-type problems. *Psychometrika, 20*, 139–148. doi:10.1007/bf02288986.

McPhee, R. D., & Zaug, P. (2000). The communicative constitution of organizations: A framework for explanation. *The Electronic Journal of Communication, 10*, 1–15. Retrieved from www.cios.org/EJCPUBLIC/010/1/01017.html,

Podolny, J. M., & Baron, J. N. (1997). Resources and relationships: Social networks and mobility in the workplace. *American Sociological Review, 62*(5), 673–693. Retrieved from www.jstor.org/stable/2657354.

Poole, M. S. (1998). The small group should be the fundamental unit of communication research. In J. S. Trent (Ed.), *Communication: Views from the helm for the 21st century* (pp. 94–97). Boston, MA: Allyn & Bacon.

Poole, M. S., & G. DeSanctis (1990). Understanding the use of group decision support systems. In J. Fulk & C. Steinfield (Eds.), *Organizations and communication technology* (pp. 173–193). Beverly Hills, CA: SAGE.

Roberts, K. H., & O'Reilly, C. A. (1979). Some correlates of communication roles in organizations. *Academy of Management Journal, 22*(1), 42–57. doi:10.5465/255477.

Samuelson, P. (1954). The pure theory of public expenditure. *The Review of Economics and Statistics, 36*(4), 387–389. doi:10.2307/1925895.

Schippers, M. C., Edmondson, A. C., & West, M. A. (2014). Team reflexivity as an antidote to team information-processing failures. *Small Group Research, 45*, 731–769. doi:10.1177/1046496414553473.

Simon, H. A. (1982). *Models of bounded rationality*. Cambridge, MA: MIT Press.

Tichy, N. M., Fombrun, C. J., & Devanna, M. A. (1982). Strategic human resource management. *Sloan Management Review, 23*(2), 47–61.

Wellman, B. (1988). Structural analysis: From method and metaphor to theory and substance. In B. Wellman & S. Berkowitz (Eds.), *Social structures: A network approach* (pp. 19–61). Cambridge: Cambridge University Press.

Wenger, E. (1998). *Communities of practice: Learning, meaning, and identity*. New York, NY: Cambridge University Press.

16 Conflict

Jessica Katz Jameson

Robbie is a Certified Registered Nurse Anesthetist (CRNA) at a private hospital in North Carolina. Her job is to prepare patients, provide anesthesia during surgery, and stay with the patient through their post-op recovery. The rules of her state and hospital call for an anesthesiologist to supervise the anesthesia process. The anesthesiologist checks in during surgery in case complications arise or the CRNA needs assistance. Anesthesiologists and CRNAs meet at the beginning of each shift to review the patients for that day. One particular day, Robbie met with Dr. Don Dolan to discuss the anesthesia plan for patient Monica Jones. They agreed on the process and knew when the surgery was scheduled, but when the appointed time came, Robbie learned that Monica had eaten within the last two hours, and she recommended a change of plan and delayed start to adapt to this new information. The surgeon, Dr. Valerie Kent, was irritated that her surgical schedule was being thrown off and she immediately reprimanded Dr. Dolan. Dr. Dolan was embarrassed and furious that Robbie's actions were inconsistent with the plan they had agreed upon. Dr. Dolan lodges a complaint against Robbie to the Chief Nurse, who begins an investigation of the incident and will have to decide whether a new policy needs to be put in place to prevent this type of conflict in the future.

This anecdote demonstrates the interdependence among organizational members, teams, and organizational policies that construct an environment requiring constant negotiation of interests, work tasks, and relationships. The conflict between Robbie and Dr. Dolan is influenced by the patient's failure to follow instructions about fasting before surgery as well as the surgeon's frustration at having her schedule disrupted. Robbie's decision to change the plan without consulting Dr. Dolan plays a direct role in how this communication unfolds, and the conflict between Robbie and Dr. Dolan impacts their relationship while also having a ripple effect on the surgical team and future communication among CRNAs and anesthesiologists at this hospital. Yet this conflict is further influenced by (and influences) communication outside of this specific organization. There is nationwide tension between CRNAs and anesthesiologists due to ambiguous policies about the need for CRNA supervision. In some rural hospitals, for example, CRNAs give anesthesia without supervision as a matter of common practice. However, anesthesiologists often argue that the depth of medical expertise acquired by doctors is required to assure the safety of the patient. Given the uncertainties of surgery, potential drug interactions, or other unknowns that may develop during a surgical process, they contend that CRNAs must always be under the supervision of an anesthesiologist. The CRNAs often find this insulting to their knowledge and expertise. This conflict therefore plays out at several organizational and structural levels as hospital administrations must decide on policy that is consistent with the statewide healthcare policies, which must comply with federal legislation. In fact, the professional associations of each group, the American Society of Anesthesiologists and the American Association of Nurse Anesthetists, have actively lobbied legislators to support their views on the issue of supervision and members of each organization promote their positions with politicians, administrators, and colleagues (for more background on this conflict, see Jameson, 2003, 2004).

Consistent with the CCO perspective that underlies this organizational communication text, there is mutual influence between official conflict management policies and the everyday conflict interaction among organizational members. This vignette vividly illustrates the communication-organization spiral depicted in Chapter 1 as policy influences interaction among organizational members, while dyadic negotiation alters the interaction norms of anesthesiologists and CRNAs, enables and constrains future interaction, and influences changes to organizational culture and administrative policies.

As we begin this chapter on organizational conflict, it is interesting to note the overlap among the definitions of *organization* and *conflict*. As defined in Chapter 1, an *organization* is a:

> living system of interconnected communicative relationships among a conglomerate of interdependent coalitions ... bound together by their homage to a common mission and dependence on a common resource base, with multiple and often incompatible instrumental and interactive goals and objectives.

Conflict is often defined as "the interaction of interdependent people who perceive opposition of goals, aims, and values, and who see the other party as potentially interfering with the realization of these goals" (Putnam & Poole, 1987, p. 552). The emphasis on interdependence in conflict and in organizations suggests that conflict will be an omnipresent, even necessary, part of organizational life as people coordinate and negotiate activities to achieve individual, group, and organizational goals. The remainder of this chapter reviews the myriad ways conflict has been examined by organizational communication scholars and demonstrates the discipline's contributions to the larger field of conflict studies.

While the opening vignette demonstrates the interdependence among organizational levels of analysis, most research is conducted at a single level. Therefore, this chapter organizes several decades of research that has examined organizational conflict (1) in the interaction of *dyads* (such as between coworkers or a supervisor–supervisee relationship), (2) in communication both within and between *groups* (which might be departments, work teams, or professional or demographic identity groups), (3) in communication that takes place between *organizations* (such as conflict between a corporation and environmental group), and (4) in terms of alternative dispute resolution, or *institutional-level* conflict management systems. This review will emphasize the communication spiral in terms of how employee and management approaches to conflict communication influence future interaction, organizational relationships, and the co-construction of organizational culture.

Dyadic Conflict

Conflict Styles

Following the lead of other organizational communication research, early organizational conflict scholars tended to examine interpersonal communication in organizational settings, primarily from a post-positive perspective, and with a view of organization as an entity that serves as a container for conflict. Conflict scholars were interested in how employees and managers communicated to resolve conflict, and there was a lot of attention to conflict styles, defined as individual preferences for using some conflict management approaches more frequently than others (Thomas & Kilmann, 1974). Thomas and Kilmann (1974) adapted Blake and Mouton's (1964) dual concern model framework, described in Chapter 7, to describe conflict behavior on the two dimensions of *assertiveness*, the extent to which the person attempts to satisfy his own concerns, and *cooperativeness*, the extent to which the person attempts to satisfy the other person's concerns. The resulting five conflict management styles are avoiding, accommodating, competing, collaborating, and—in the middle—compromising. *Avoiding* is described as a conflict style used when an individual is unassertive and uncooperative, as they do not address the issue. *Accommodating* occurs when one has low assertiveness and high cooperativeness, and thus gives in to the other. High assertiveness and low cooperativeness is described as a *competing* style, where one party emphasizes getting their own needs met, even at the expense of the other. *Collaborating* is posited as the ideal style in which a party shows both high assertiveness and high cooperativeness, seeking to meet both or all parties' needs. Finally, the model suggests that when a party is moderately assertive and cooperative, this results in a *compromising* style that meets some of all parties' needs. Thomas and Kilmann developed the most widely used instrument for professional training and development in conflict management, known as the Thomas-Kilmann Conflict Mode Instrument, or TKI.

The conflict styles scale most widely used in academic research, the ROCI-II, was developed by Rahim and Bonoma (1979), who describe the dual concerns as *concern for self* and *concern for other*, resulting in the same five styles with slightly different names (avoiding, obliging, dominating, integrating, and compromising). Decades of organizational research using the ROCI-II instrument (Rahim, 1983) have demonstrated that integrating is most often perceived as the most appropriate and effective conflict style (Friedman, Tidd, Currall, & Tsai, 2000; Gross & Guerrero, 2000; Trudel & Reio, 2011).

Linda Putnam (1988) is credited for raising awareness of the relationship between communication and conflict styles when she edited a special issue on Communication and Interpersonal Conflict in Organizations in *Management Communication Quarterly* in February 1988. In that issue, for example, Womack (1988) pointed out that rather than having one dominant style, communication research revealed that organizational members are likely to use all five styles depending on the context. Putnam and Wilson (1982) addressed this concern directly by creating the Organizational Conflict Communication Index (OCCI) to measure conflict communication rather than style. Their research resulted in three communicative approaches to conflict management that result from collapsing the original five conflict styles found in the dual concern models: non-confrontation strategies (similar to avoidance and accommodating), solution-oriented strategies that focus on solving a problem (similar to compromising or collaborating), and controlling strategies (similar to a competing style). One important finding from the OCCI was the relationship between hierarchical position and conflict communication. Organizational members were more likely to use controlling strategies with subordinates than superiors, more likely to use non-confrontation strategies with superiors than peers or subordinates, and more likely to use solution-oriented strategies with peers and superiors than subordinates (Wilson & Waltman, 1988). These early studies elucidated the important relationship between power and organizational conflict communication.

Given the managerial bias of early organizational communication research, a significant body of research examines conflict communication between managers and employees. Weider-Hatfield and Hatfield (1995) examined the relationship between conflict styles, supervisor success, and subordinate satisfaction, and found that supervisors who used collaborative strategies were more likely to be promoted, receive raises, and have satisfied employees than those who used other styles. While employees in this study perceived there to be more conflict overall when supervisors used collaborative strategies, these results validate that the presence of conflict is not problematic when it is managed effectively.

Employee Satisfaction and Organizational Dissent

Moving away from conflict styles research, Infante and Gordon (1985) also found a positive relationship between conflict communication, managerial success, and employee satisfaction. Infante and Gordon contrasted *argumentativeness*, the use of facts and data to support one's position in conflict, with *verbal aggressiveness*, the tendency to attack the other personally. They found that the use of argumentativeness increased career satisfaction, achievement, and relationship satisfaction. Again, this line of research examined conflict as something that happens among individuals within an organization, defining organization as an entity or container (O_3).

This research paved the way for an important stream of research on *organizational dissent*, started by Jeffrey Kassing (1998, 2011). Organizational dissent is defined as the communication of disagreement with an organizational decision or policy. While dissent is not the same as conflict, the way in which members communicate dissent likely predicts how that dissent is received and responded to, and whether conflict occurs. Dissent may be communicated *upward* (i.e., to one's supervisor), *laterally* (to one's peers), or it may be *displaced* (communicated to someone external to the organization, such as a friend, partner, or the media, as in the case of *whistleblowing*) (Kassing, 2002). Specific to organizational communication is the discourse used, or dissent tactics. Kassing (2002) identified five common upward dissent tactics. The *direct-factual appeal* brings facts and evidence to support the employee's concerns, while a *solution-orientation* presents a problem and a solution. These are both considered the most likely to have positive outcomes, and are therefore referred to as *prosocial dissent*. The empirical evidence on the use of prosocial dissent strategies indicates they are consistent with *argumentativeness*, described above, and supports that prosocial dissent is most likely to create an environment that welcomes employee *voice* (the ability to speak up and participate) and collaborative conflict management. The remaining three upward dissent strategies identified by Kassing include *repetition*, *circumvention*, and *threatening resignation*. These strategies tend to be *face-threatening* to supervisors or management, and therefore have been found to have less positive results. (See Garner, 2012 for an extended list of additional dissent strategies.)

In a study of the relationship among conflict styles, dissent strategies, and leader–member relationships, Redmond, Jameson, and Binder (2016) found that prosocial dissent tactics were correlated with the use of a collaborative conflict style, while repetition, circumvention, and threatening resignation were correlated with a dominating conflict style. While no direct relationship was found between leader–member relationship and dissent strategies, the study confirmed previous studies that demonstrated higher superior–subordinate relationship quality was related to the use of an integrating conflict management style.

Intercultural Conflict

Because organizations are constituted by diverse members, conflict related to intercultural differences in communication represents another important stream of organizational conflict scholarship. Drawing from Erving Goffman's (1956) concept of *face*, the public persona or identity someone presents to others, Stella Ting-Toomey (1988) developed *Face Negotiation Theory* to explain intercultural communication in conflict (for more on identity, see Chapter 11). Ting-Toomey's theory integrates intercultural communication with conflict styles research by noting that (1) certain conflict styles are more face supportive or face threatening, and (2) an individual's conflict style and attention to face may be related to the culture in which they were raised. For example, people from collectivist cultures, typically found in the Eastern part of the world, may be more concerned with *other-face*, protecting the face of others, than *self-face*, or protecting their own identity needs, and thus tend toward conflict styles such as avoidance and accommodation. Oetzel and Ting-Toomey (2003) conducted a cross-cultural study of 768 students from four nationalities (China, Japan, Germany, and the US) in which participants were asked to recall a specific conflict and then answer a series of questions about this experience. This study confirmed the hypotheses that people who emphasize interdependence (collectivity), focus more on other-face and are more likely to use avoidance and accommodating conflict styles, while those who emphasize their independence are more focused on self- than other-face and more likely to use dominating conflict styles. Findings such as these demonstrate that organizations must pay attention to the role of cultural differences in organizational communication, both in terms of how culture impacts interpersonal communication as well as how it constitutes the organizational culture.

Interpretive Studies of Organizational Conflict

While the examples of conflict scholarship thus far have focused on post-positivist methods (see Chapter 4) that view the organization as an entity where conflict occurs (O_3), organizational communication scholars have also used interviews and observational methods to study dyadic conflict interpretivistically. These approaches typically view organization as a process (O_1) in which conflict is an inevitable and necessary aspect of communication among interdependent parties that constructs relationships and the organizational culture. In the example that introduced this chapter, Jameson (2004) interviewed anesthesiologists and certified registered nurse anesthetists to collect their conflict stories. This study revealed that face-saving communication that protected one's own and the other's identity had the best results for the patient, ongoing relationships, and the organizational culture. Nicotera and Clinkscales (2010) also used interviews and observation of nurses to discover the existence of *structurational divergence*, an organizational condition that occurs when members find themselves trying to follow the rules of multiple and incompatible rule systems (see Chapter 3). Organizations must understand and address conflicts that arise from different occupational roles and relationships (such as that between nurse and nurse, nurse and doctor, and nurse and patient) that require one person to adhere to different rules simultaneously.

There are many other examples of interpretive organizational conflict research at the dyadic level. One of the more notable examples used interpretive methods to examine organizational dissent. Garner (2013) observed that most research on organizational dissent viewed communication from the perspective of the dissenter (using the container model of organization), neglecting the continuous interaction among dissenters, coworkers, and managers that co-constructs the environment. Garner conceptualized dissent as "an organizational stream of interaction punctuated by particular moments" (2013, p. 377) and sought to demonstrate how ongoing organizational communication creates an organizational culture that either supports or obstructs employee voice and dissent effectiveness. Garner conducted interviews, observed meetings, and volunteered at a nonprofit organization for a year to illustrate how interaction, such as how managers responded to previous dissent, led to employees' future decisions regarding whether and how to dissent. This study further revealed important differences in how managers and coworkers talked about dissent, such as whether an employee was described as making a *valiant effort* versus being a *whiny employee*. The discourse of dissent results in *residual communication* that stays with organizational members and co-constructs a narrative that either supports or impedes future dissent. As can be seen in these few examples, interpretive scholarship tends to emphasize the communication-organization spiral, as the structures created by day-to-day communication and the ways that those structures then enable and constrain future communication are very clear. These examples demonstrate the benefits of diverse methodological approaches to organizational communication and conflict.

In summary, organizational communication research at the level of dyadic conflict has made important contributions to conflict studies through its emphasis on the communication employees and managers use during conflict as well as how organizational members talk about conflict. Whether conflict is framed as information/feedback versus complaining, for example, constructs an environment that either welcomes or silences employee voice—and thus influences perceptions of trust and organizational justice. Examining dyadic interaction among employees across occupational roles, hierarchical levels, and cultural differences has enabled organizational communication scholars to reveal how conflict impacts the communication-organization spiral that creates an environment for more or less productive conflict management.

Intra- and Intergroup Conflict

While *group communication* is a sub-discipline often considered distinct from organizational communication (see Chapter 15), organizations are made up of sub-systems such as work teams and committees, hierarchies (e.g., labor vs. management), occupation (nurses vs. doctors or accountants vs. account managers), and identity groups (North American vs. Japanese employees). Scholars interested in group communication generally see organizations as set of interdependent structures (O_2) and thus conflicts within and across groups both impact and are impacted by the larger organizational context. While teamwork is covered in greater detail in Chapter 15, some attention must be given to the phenomenon of group conflict here. Kuhn and Poole (2000) investigated the relationship between conflict styles and group decision-making. Their study of 11 naturally occurring workgroups across two U.S. organizations found that groups that developed norms of collaborative conflict management made better decisions than those who used competing or avoiding styles. They also found that collaborative teams performed better than groups that did not develop any consistent conflict style.

Computer-Mediated Support and Virtual Collaboration

Again examining organization from the viewpoint of structures, or how the organization is ordered (O_2), Poole and his colleagues made further contributions to the field by studying the role of computer-mediated support systems in group conflict. Poole, Holmes, and DeSanctis (1991) conducted a lab experiment to compare conflict management between standard face-to-face groups and groups using a group decision support system (GDSS). The authors found that differences in conflict management between the face-to-face and GDSS-supported groups were not predicted by the *presence* of the technology, but how the groups *used* the technology. For example, when groups used the GDSS to openly communicate about conflict management processes and communicate positive affect, they created more constructive conflict interaction than face-to-face groups. However, when groups used the GDSS to avoid discussion by reducing the number of alternatives examined or voting to make a decision more swiftly, these behaviors limited conversation and led to fewer instances of consensus than in face-to-face groups.

As the global workforce has resulted in more geographically dispersed work teams, organizational communication scholarship increasingly examines conflict in the context of virtual collaboration. The fact that virtual team members are separated by geography and time (and often language and culture) poses a challenge to the development of trust and effective conflict management. In a case study of one geographically dispersed team, Scott (2013) used a structuration theory framework (Giddens, 1984) and collected data via observation and interviews to describe how virtual teams develop communication routines that manage conflict and improve virtual collaboration. Scott's study had two interesting findings. One was that the software itself, called Scrum, had built-in rules and rituals that were adopted by group members. For example, members hold a brief, daily, stand-up video conference meeting for quick updates, and "sprint planning meetings" (Scott, 2013, p. 309) every four weeks to reflect on the previous weeks and plan ahead. Following these rituals facilitated communication and promoted the emergence of trust and direct conflict management. Scott notes, however, that rituals in and of themselves may not be enough. His second finding was that the emergence of common values such as a team identity, meeting halfway, and openness to multicultural communication were important factors in the effectiveness of this virtual collaboration (for more on organizational communication and technology, see Chapter 19).

Intergroup Conflict

Another body of group conflict research examines conflict that occurs not within, but between groups in organizations. Perhaps the most common form is conflict between labor and management. Smith and Eisenberg (1987) made an important contribution to organizational communication and conflict scholarship with their metaphor analysis of conflict at Disneyland. The authors conducted interviews with Disneyland employees and management, asking them to complete the sentence "Conflict at Disneyland is like..." Analysis of the responses resulted in the emergence of two unique root metaphors: management referred to Disneyland as a *drama* while employees relied on the metaphor of *family*. The authors concluded that one of the underlying causes of this labor relations conflict came from different expectations of how employees should be treated and how organizational members related to each other. This study opened the door to many more studies using metaphor and narrative analysis approaches to provide new insights into how organizations are co-constructed through the interactions among and discourse used by organizational members. As was noted in the section on dyadic conflict above, scholars who take this interpretive approach see organizational conflict as central to the communicative constitution of the organization and view organization as a process (O_1).

Another important examination of intergroup conflict was a study of bargaining between teachers and a school board (Putnam, 1990). Observing the interactions as they unfolded, she was able to analyze how participants framed their arguments and how they changed over time. For example, teachers' initial arguments emphasized harm and work environment and then moved toward proposed solutions and priorities. The school board's arguments focused on the cost barriers to proposed solutions. These differences in framing created a barrier to finding common ground. This research is another example of the value of looking at naturalistic interaction and taking more qualitative, discourse-based approaches that reveal the interactive nature of communication and environment.

Another type of intergroup conflict in organizations takes place between employees from different cultural identity groups. Acknowledging the need to better understand how identity impacts communication and behavior, Turner and Shuter (2004) conducted a metaphor analysis to explore differences in how African American and European (white) American women perceived the experience of organizational conflict. Based on interviews with 17 African American and 32 European American women employed in one geographic region, Turner and Shuter discovered a variety of metaphors that captured whether conflict behavior was more active or passive, the perceived likelihood of resolution, whether the women saw conflict as positive or negative, and the intensity of language used to describe conflict. The authors found significant differences in the experience of the two groups such that African American women were more likely to use passive metaphors. While the remaining differences were not statistically significant, they found that African American women were less likely to perceive that resolution was possible, more likely to use negative metaphors for conflict, and more likely to use intense language in their conflict metaphors than were the European American women. This study supports the importance of understanding intersectionality of race and gender as part of the organizational experience (see Chapter 14). This study suggests that organizational power imbalances that present conflict challenges for all women are even greater for African American women who may perceive addressing conflict as futile and unlikely to lead to improvements. Research on diversity and conflict reminds us that organizational members have different experiences that impact perceptions of trust, fairness, overall organizational satisfaction, all of which will impact organizational behavior and communication.

While not directly a study of conflict, Gallant and Krone's (2014) study of how organizational members talk about diversity further contributes to our understanding of how identity differences impact organizational communication and conflict. Gallant and Krone's case study examined the diversity policy, interviewed the diversity director, and interviewed 30 of the 96 employees of a diverse human services organization.

Consistent with Turner and Shuter's findings, the two key themes that emerged from the study were *fairness* and *apprehension*. When asked about affirmative action, for example, employees experienced a tension between seeing affirmative action as necessary to promoting equal opportunity while also expressing concerns about perceptions of differential treatment that complicated interracial communication. Relatedly, study participants were apprehensive about the possibility of violating social norms or customs, which caused them to avoid talking to people with different backgrounds. While the intricacies of differences and diversity are covered in more detail in Chapter 14, it is important to note the important role of diversity in the co-construction of an organizational environment that is more or less likely to promote trust and open conflict management.

This section has revealed several types of organizational conflict at the group level of interaction. Organizational communication scholars are interested in the role of conflict in how teams make decisions, collaborate, and achieve task goals. They have also made important contributions in examining how groups can use various technologies to support (or impede) the discussion and negotiation of conflict that leads to improved decision-making and collaboration. In the intergroup arena, organizational communication scholars have emphasized the importance of metaphors and framing to better understand how employees from different roles, hierarchical levels, and identity groups experience and express conflict and how these dynamics influence employee relationships, organizational culture, and future conflict management communication.

Interorganizational Conflict

The history of our discipline presented in Chapter 1 reveals that organizational communication emphasizes internal communication among organizational members. Research on interorganizational conflict is therefore more frequently found in the field of Public Relations, where organizations are defined as bounded entities that both influence and are influenced by other organizations. Interesting examples of interorganizational conflicts include those between Greenpeace and DuPont (Murphy & Dee, 1992) and Walgreens and drug retailer associations (Plowman et al., 1995). As described in the opening vignette, research describing the conflict between the American Society of Anesthesiologists and the American Association of Nurse Anesthetists reveals the mutual influence of communication that occurs both outside and within the organization (Jameson, 2003).

Given the complicated relationship between industry and environmental stakeholders, it should come as no surprise that environmental conflict has emerged as an area of interest to organizational scholars. Brummans et al., (2008) examined four discrete multiparty environmental conflicts covering water regulation, toxic waste, and/or natural resources. Like Putnam's (1990) study of bargaining, the authors examined how the framing of disputes impacted the conflict interaction. One frame, for example, included stories of *victimhood*, in which interviewees saw the conflict as a clear example of right and wrong behavior, in which the other party was behaving unfairly. A frame of *dispassion*, on the other hand, revealed stories that characterized the conflict parties in positive, albeit neutral ways that revealed the speaker's detachment from the conflict. If members of the *victim* framing felt a sense of hopelessness, those using a *dispassion* frame believed that logic and reason would rule the day and those with the appropriate power would resolve the conflict. A third frame included stories of *optimism* and *hope*. These stakeholders were not detached, they trusted the various parties, and they believed democracy and collaborative engagement would yield a mutually satisfactory resolution. A fourth framing category defined the conflict as a *power struggle* and tended to view those with more power and resources with cynicism. This study revealed that even when organizational members are having the same conflict, they do not experience it in the same way, and how we perceive and frame a conflict influences the unfolding conflict interaction, with implications for potential conflict transformation or intractability.

To summarize the research on interorganizational conflict, scholars in organizational communication have revealed how conflicts external to an organization can influence organizational communication and conflict as well as how conflict framing may lead to more collaborative or competitive conflict management tactics. While most of the research on this level of conflict is found in the Public Relations domain, the findings have important implications for organizational communication and conflict management.

Organizational Conflict Management

As conflict is a ubiquitous and important part of organizational communication, it is incumbent upon leaders to provide alternatives that help organizational members manage conflict. Most organizations have a formal policy for filing a *grievance* when an employee believes their rights have been violated, such as an act of discrimination or sexual harassment. Yet an area of scholarship focused on *alternative dispute resolution* (Ury, Brett, and Goldberg, 1988) has demonstrated that practices that enable employees to address conflicts early in the process, resolve conflict at lower cost, and come to a solution more quickly can promote a culture of organizational fairness and justice that also enables employees to resolve future conflicts more independently. Although *dispute system design* has traditionally been studied in the fields of management and public administration, organizational communication scholars have also made contributions to this area. Management scholars have revealed a variety of strategies managers use to intervene in employee conflicts (acting as advisers, mediators, or arbitrators, for example, see Kolb, 1986). Yet, a communication approach incorporates relational and environmental factors to describe the complexity of managerial intervention into organizational conflicts. For example, Putnam (1994) used a political frame to point out that rather than being a matter of personal choice, managers respond to a combination of organizational characteristics, coalitions, and employee networks as they decide how to intervene.

To further our understanding of how employees address conflict, Volkema, Bergmann, and Farquhar (1997) conducted a study of 396 individuals involved in interpersonal conflict in the workplace. The study examined the informal third parties employees were most likely to talk to as well as the impact of those conversations on conflict interaction and outcomes. A sizable majority of the study participants (78 percent) reported they spoke to coworkers about the conflict, while 58 percent spoke to someone outside of the workplace. Going to an external third party was most likely when individuals reported the conflict was intense, when conflicts were with supervisors rather than coworkers, and when the employee had less organizational tenure. Conversations with coworkers were found to reduce assertiveness, while talking to external third parties was more likely to increase assertiveness and reduce cooperativeness. These findings are supported by research on co-rumination (Boren, 2014), which found that venting without developing strategies for conflict resolution increased frustration and stress. The results of this research reinforce the importance of directly addressing rather than avoiding conflict.

Organizational communication scholars have also examined specific third-party roles such as ombuds, mediators, and conflict coaches. Ombuds (originally called ombudsmen) are found on many college campuses and have become more common across the business sector. The ombud is a neutral adviser who listens to employees and suggests options such as directly addressing the other party, entering into mediation, or filing a formal grievance. The advantage of an ombud is that they are not directly connected to human resources or the official chain of command, and therefore conversations are confidential and employees need not fear repercussions. Hopeck, Desrayaud, Harrison, and Hatten (2014) studied whether students' conflict styles predicted their decisions to use an ombuds process in a conflict with a professor. They found that students with a solution-orientation were more likely to perceive the ombuds process as fair and more likely to use the process, while those with controlling or non-confrontational styles were less likely to use this option. This is consistent with other conflict studies research finding a relationship between perceptions of organizational justice and willingness to use organizational conflict systems (Blancero & Dyer, 1996).

While organizational communication scholars have not examined mediation at length, studies of conflict management systems that include mediation reveal that employees often perceive mediators as fair, are satisfied with mediation agreements, and that participation in mediation increases perceptions of organizational justice (Jameson & Johnson, 2004; Jameson, Berry-James, Daley, and Coggburn, 2017). An experimental study in which students were disputants in a simulated organizational conflict revealed the potential for mediation to improve relationships between disputants and result in agreements that were transformative in nature (Jameson, Sohan, & Hodge, 2014). Unfortunately, organizational communication scholarship has not paid much attention to mediation. This may be due to its limited use in organizational settings outside of public administration (such as government agencies and universities). Paul and Putnam (2017a) revealed a common approach to organizational conflict management: To expect parties to try to work conflicts out on their own, followed by raising the conflict to an administrator who then decides how it will be handled. This *legalistic* model does little to promote perceptions of justice and workplace satisfaction, while a more *restorative* model that emphasizes collaborative approaches is more likely to have transformative long-term consequences. Due to the many positive outcomes that have been identified with organizational mediation (see, for example, Bingham, Hallberlin, Walker, & Chung, 2009), adopting this third-party option would be expected to have a positive impact on organizational culture and conflict management.

Conflict coaching, another alternative dispute resolution approach, is also gaining popularity. Conflict coaching is an integrative system that offers employees an opportunity to talk with someone who can help them analyze and appraise the conflict, determine the best process for moving forward, and provide the communication skills to enable employees to manage current and future conflicts more productively (Jones, 2016). Conflict coaching is a holistic approach taking multiple variables into consideration, including the nature of the conflict, the parties involved, and the organizational environment. In a hospital setting, Brinkert (2011) examined perceptions of coaching effectiveness among a nursing staff in which 20 nurse managers received 12 hours of conflict coaching training. Nurse managers reported that coaching skills were used to help nurses reflect on recurring difficult situations such as team conflict or interactions where nurses used inappropriate language. While there were some challenges noted, such as trying to play an advisory and supervisory role simultaneously and time constraints, the coaching model improved mentoring and social support as well as nurses' conflict management skills.

A final important trend in organizational conflict management scholarship is attention to forgiveness and restorative justice in the workplace (Paul, 2017; Paul & Putnam, 2017a, 2017b). This work focuses on the role of organizational values and communication norms in constructing an environment for positive conflict communication and organizational relationships. In a study of forgiveness, Paul and Putnam asked teachers and administrators in four educational settings (for students ranging in age from kindergarten to 12th grade) to describe how they coped with difficult interactions at work. Their analysis of interview transcripts revealed that many participants' first response to such encounters was to vent to trusted third parties either inside or outside the organization. This supports the work of Volkema et al. (1997) reported above, as well as the work on organizational dissent (Kassing, 2011). Employee talk about coping strategies revealed forgiveness as a complicated concept, as it may be used for the primary purpose of letting go and moving on or as part of a dialogue to achieve understanding and repair relationships. Importantly, forgiveness was tied to an underlying value of harmony, and those who practiced forgiveness tended to recognize the importance of accountability as well as their personal role in co-constructing the culture of the organization. The evolution of research on alternative dispute resolution and approaches to dispute system design follows the trend illustrated in other parts of this review, whereby scholars started with an interest in how organizational structures (O_2) influenced conflict and have moved toward examining processes through which the conflict practices (O_1) of organizational members constitute the organization (O_3).

To summarize the discussion of organizational conflict management, the communication-organization spiral from Chapter 1 illustrates the ways in which day-to-day communication constructs the organization and the norms, rules, and rituals that develop. This chapter reveals that how employees and managers address conflict is critical to how well the organization receives and accepts feedback, adapts to organizational and environmental changes, and to the narratives that develop around employee voice and organizational justice. While organizational hierarchy and power structures present a real threat to employee use of any conflict management system, having options may provide important resources that prevent employees from unproductive responses such as avoidance, venting and co-rumination, and complaining to external third parties. Third parties who are available to help employees analyze their conflicts, consider alternatives, and train them in more effective communication may have a significant impact on organizational communication.

Recommended Supplementary Readings

Bodtker, A. B., & Jameson, J. K. (2001). Emotion in conflict formation and its transformation: Application to organizational conflict management. *The International Journal of Conflict Management, 12*(3), 259–275.
This essay provides a conceptual argument for the role of emotion in organizational conflict and presents ideas for confronting emotions in organizations.
Gayle, B. M., & Preiss, R. W. (1998). Assessing emotionality in organizational conflicts. *Management Communication Quarterly, 12*(2), 280–302.

One of the few organizational communication studies to empirically examine emotion in organizational conflict, this study discusses the relationship between how conflicts are remembered and the impact on future communication. Unresolved conflicts and those with supervisors or administrators were remembered with greater emotional intensity.

Harrison, T. R., & Morrill, C. (2004). Ombuds processes and disputant reconciliation. *Journal of Applied Communication Research*, 32(4), 318–341.

This article presents another description of the role of ombuds in an organizational setting and Tyler Harrison is one of the few organizational communication scholars looking at third-party processes in organizations.

Jameson, J. K. (1999). Toward a comprehensive model for the assessment and management of intraorganizational conflict. *International Journal of Conflict Management*, 10(3), 268–294.

This article presents a model to illustrate the complexity of choosing among possible conflict management approaches based on whether one takes an interests-, rights-, or power-based approach, features of the conflict, the relationship between parties, and situational variables.

Kirby, E., & Krone, K. J. (2002). "The policy exists but you can't really use it": Communication and the structuration of work-family policies. *Journal of Applied Communication Research*, 30, 50–77.

This article speaks to the relationship between organizational policy and how employee interaction impacts how employees interpret the policy. This study has implications for conflict management systems as it points out that employee experiences with such systems will impact the narratives organizational members create and whether employees trust they can use organizational conflict management options.

Knapp, M. L., Putnam, L. L. and Davis, L. J. (1988). Measuring interpersonal conflict in organizations: Where do we go from here?, *Management Communication Quarterly*, 1, 414–429.

This article is credited for setting the initial research agenda for communication scholarship in organizational conflict.

Kolb, D. M., and Putnam, L. L. (1992). The multiple faces of conflict in organizations. *Journal of Occupational Behavior*, 13, 311–324.

This is one example of Linda Putnam's interdisciplinary work, which increased the visibility of organizational communication for the field of conflict studies. The article discusses the many manifestations of organizational conflict and is extended upon in the authors' chapter in another excellent read: Hidden Conflict in Organizations: Uncovering Behind-the-Scenes Disputes, edited by D. M. Kolb and J. M. Bartunek (1992), SAGE Publications.

Nicotera, A. M. (1995). *Conflict and organizations: Communicative processes.* New York, NY: State University of New York Press.

This edited volume features several prominent scholars of interpersonal and organizational communication and emphasizes constructive conflict management at interpersonal, organizational and international levels.

Putnam, L. L. (2005). Discourse analysis: Mucking around with negotiation data. *International Negotiation*, 10, 17–32.

This article defines discourse analysis and discusses insights scholars might glean from this and other qualitative, discourse-based approaches to the study of conflict and negotiation.

Putnam, L. L. (2010). Communication as changing the negotiation game. *Journal of Applied Communication Research*, 38(4), 325–335.

In this article Linda Putnam provides several points of practice for negotiators in all types of settings based on her research. She emphasizes the importance of using communication to differentiate conflict issues, frame and reframe, and engage collective sensemaking to generate creative solutions.

Oetzel, J. G., & Ting-Toomey, S. (Eds.). (2013). *The SAGE handbook of conflict communication: Integrating theory, research, and practice* (2nd ed., pp. 267–292). Thousand Oaks, CA: SAGE.

The organizational conflict section of this handbook includes several comprehensive literature reviews covering negotiation, work group conflict, bullying, conflict education, conflict in healthcare, and organizational conflict management systems.

Important Concepts: Define and Discuss

Alternative dispute resolution
Argumentativeness
Conflict
Conflict coaching
Conflict styles
Dissent
Face
Identity
Interdependence
Mediation
Ombud
Organizational dissent
Organizational justice
Restorative justice
Transformation
Verbal aggressiveness

Discussion Questions

1. Do you believe the individual styles of organization members or the actions of organizational leadership have a greater influence on organizational conflict communication? Discuss how official management policies and day-to-day communication practices are mutually constitutive of an organization.
2. You and a coworker are on the same project team and you rely on each other for information and task coordination to help the team achieve its goals. Your coworker is often unavailable as they have a tendency to arrive late, leave early, and take longer than usual lunch breaks. You once told this coworker that it would be helpful if you had a daily routine for touching base, but your coworker just said "yeah" and laughed it off. Based on ideas from this chapter, what would be your next step in trying to address this conflict?
3. Discuss a situation in which you or a coworker felt you were not being treated fairly by your supervisor or you disagreed with an organizational policy. Did anyone talk to the supervisor or a manager? Why or why not? Provide some examples of how you, as an employee, might voice your concerns in a constructive way. Describe what you would do as an organizational leader to promote a culture in which employees are able to come forward when they have concerns or complaints.
4. Describe any organizational conflict management systems you have seen or experienced. Provide possible explanations for why employees did or did not take advantage of these options.

Practitioners' Corner

When it comes to organizational conflict management, there are several ways in which one might become a practitioner. This section will discuss a variety of potential practitioner roles ranging from more official positions to informal conflict management responsibilities. This section will conclude with an example of how one organization conducted a needs-assessment of their organization to develop a comprehensive conflict management system.

Conflict Management Practitioners

Attorney: Attorneys who specialize in contract or employment law may find themselves working in-house for one specific organization or are available to counsel and represent organizations or employees. When conflict takes on a rights-based orientation, such as claims of breach of contract or violations of human rights (such as equal employment, discrimination, or harassment), attorneys are likely to get involved. Depending upon the nature of the issue and relevant state or federal employment laws, the attorney may recommend mediation or another alternative dispute resolution (ADR) process or the grievance may go through the legal process.

Arbitrator: An arbitrator acts like a judge in that parties to a conflict will present their case and evidence, and the arbitrator makes a decision about how to settle the case based on relevant organizational policies or legislation. Some organizations require the use of mediation or arbitration as a first step in any employee grievance. It is important to pay attention to any clause in an employment agreement (usually signed when one is first hired) to make sure you know your rights and whether you are agreeing to settle any dispute with your employer in arbitration. Arbitration decisions are usually final and not subject to appeal. Arbitrators are often attorneys or judges with expertise in employment law or the specific organizational context. Some organizations train employees in relevant policies, legislation, and precedent so that they can serve as internal arbitrators for employee grievances.

Mediator: A mediator is a neutral third party who does not make any decision regarding a conflict. The mediator's role is to help parties identify their underlying interests, brainstorm possible solutions for mutual gain, and develop a final agreement that satisfies all parties. Mediators typically have a minimum of 40 hours of mediation training. Training can be more generalized (for all types of conflict) or may be specific to employment conflict. While some attorneys are trained in mediation, many mediators are not attorneys, and there is no universally applied certification for mediators. It is useful for organizations to have employees trained in mediation; most commonly employee relations specialists. Some organizations train supervisors in mediation, and some train employees to serve as peer mediators. Organizations may also hire external mediators to help resolve employee conflicts. Typically mediation is voluntary in that both or all parties to a conflict must agree to participate. In some cases organizations or courts will mandate that parties try to reach agreement in mediation as a first step before filing a formal grievance or going to court.

Ombud: An ombud is a third party who is not part of the regular organizational hierarchy. While an ombud is employed by the organization, they typically maintain some distance from other employees, possibly even having an office off-site. This enables the ombud to reduce conflicts of interest and allows employees to maintain anonymity and confidentiality as coworkers do not see them going to the ombuds office. Ombuds should be well-versed in employment law as well as the policies of the organization(s) they work with. In some cases employees are trained to serve in an ombud role so that employees know there are certain people with expertise who have been designated to help them. This can be difficult, however, due to concerns about conflict of interest. Examples of this model include a university who created a cadre of ombuds specifically to help students or employees who made claims of sexual harassment. Other universities have created student ombuds to provide a place where students can go if they have a concern or a problem with a professor or administrator. An ombud may also be trained in mediation so they can offer those services to interested parties. There are two organizations for more information on ombuds: the United States Ombudsman Association and the International Ombudsman Association.

Conflict Coach: A conflict coach is a third party who takes on an advising role to help an employee examine their conflict, consider the underlying interests for all parties, and consider different ways to move forward with the conflict. While this sounds similar to an ombud, a conflict coach will also help the employee learn and practice communication and conflict management skills to prepare them to manage this and future conflicts. Conflict coaching can be a valuable alternative when both or all parties do not agree to mediate, as the coach can at least help one interested party prepare and improve their skills. Conflict coaching is a relatively new role. There are examples of organizations who train employees to be coaches for other employees and there are also practitioners who may do conflict coaching as part of a broader consulting practice.

Managers/Supervisors/Employee Relations Specialists: Any organizational member may take on a role as a conflict practitioner. As this chapter demonstrates, the first place employees often go when they experience conflict at work is to a peer. This is one reason it benefits organizations to offer conflict management training to all employees. Given the expense, however, it is more likely that managers, supervisors, and employee relations specialists will find themselves in a position to have to address conflict, either as a party to the conflict or as a third party. Many organizations have certain members who are known to be good at conflict management, whether by accident, personality, experience, or conflict management training. These organizational members may be highly sought after as advisers, while they may or may not get official recognition for the important role they play.

Example Organizational Dispute System Design

An organization called Unity Healthcare (a pseudonym) determined that their existing grievance process was not meeting their needs due to the length of the process and limited options for employees. They created a task force of approximately 23 employees representing staff and upper-level management. The needs assessment process included conversations with three employee focus groups. Fairness and equity surfaced as the primary procedural and ethical considerations. With those issues in mind, the task force began to examine the strengths and weaknesses of the current system. The review found that both the management and employees lacked confidence in the existing process. Specifically, management identified the time-consuming and adversarial nature of the process as key weaknesses. Employees viewed the existing program as management-biased. In addition, some employees avoided participation in the process out of fear of retaliation and being a part of subsequent legal proceedings. The Employee Relations department wanted to design an ADR program that would send a message to employees that they were not *pro-management* or *pro-employee*, but *pro-rules*.

The task force identified 18 characteristics of an excellent grievance and appeals process. Some of these included: a user-friendly documentation process, simplicity, a need to avoid unnecessary bureaucratic layering, and clear information about what the policy includes and excludes. In addition, they canvassed several other organizations for information on their respective grievance processes. These characteristics were used as a foundation for creating a new system.

A three-step grievance and appeals procedure was created and implemented that includes several alternative conflict management options. The first step involves the employee filing a grievance within 15 calendar days of the occurrence. The most senior departmental manager reviews the grievance and sends a written response within seven calendar days. If unsatisfied with the response, the employee has seven calendar days to file a written appeal. The second step begins with a review of the written appeal by an Investigating Officer who then submits a fact-finding report to a three-person, *coworker panel*. This panel reviews the grievance and provides a recommendation to the Chief Operating Officer within 21 days. The COO utilizes the recommendation to provide a written response to the parties. After receiving the decision, the grievant has seven days to appeal the decision. There are several interesting features of the Unity Healthcare ADR process: (1) The use of a coworker panel in the first appeal process, (2) agreement not to use an attorney if the employee chooses not to use one, and (3) either party may request mediation at any time during the process. When both parties agree to mediation, the parties are assigned an in-house mediator. Having options and providing for decision-makers external to top management empowers employees and may increase their trust in the program.

For discussion: Think about how Unity Healthcare's ADR system might impact how employees talk about conflict and how employee use of the system might impact the organizational culture. Can you trace the communication-organization spiral in your thinking about this process?

References

Bingham, L. B., Hallberlin, C. J., Walker, D. A., & Chung, W. T. (2009). Dispute system design and justice in employment dispute resolution: Mediation at the workplace. *Harvard Negotiation Law Review*, *14*(1), 1–50. www.hnlr.org/articles/archive/.

Blake, R., & Mouton, J. (1964). *The managerial grid: The key to leadership excellence*. Houston, TX: Gulf Publishing Co.

Blancero, D. & Dyer, L. (1996). Due process for non-union employees: The influence of system characteristics on fairness perceptions. *Human Resource Management*, *35*(3), 343–359. doi:10.1002.

Boren, J. P. (2014). The relationships between co-rumination, social support, stress, and burnout among working adults. *Management Communication Quarterly*, *28*(3), 3–25. doi:10.1177/0893318913509283.

Brinkert, R. (2011). Conflict coaching training for nurse managers: A case study of a two-hospital health system. *Journal of Nursing Management*, *19*, 80–91. doi:10.1111/j.1365-2834.2010.01133.x.

Brummans, B. H. J. M., Putnam, L. L., Gray, B., Hanke, R., Lewicki, R. J., & Wiethoff, C. (2008). Making sense of intractable multiparty conflict: A study of framing in four environmental disputes. *Communication Monographs*, *75*, 25–51. doi:10.1080/03637750801952735.

Friedman, R. A., Tidd, S. A., Currall, S. C., & Tsai, J. C. (2000). What goes around comes around: The impact of personal conflict style on work conflict and stress. *The International Journal of Conflict Management*, *11*(1), 32–55. doi:10.1108/eb022834.

Gallant, L. M., & Krone, K. J. (2014). Tensions in talking diversity. *Communication Reports*, *27*(1), 39–52. doi:10.1080/08934215.2013.837497.

Garner, J. T. (2012). Making waves at work: Perceived effectiveness and appropriateness of organizational dissent messages. *Management Communication Quarterly*, 26(2), 224–240. doi:10.1177/0893318911431803.

Garner, J. T. (2013). Dissenters, managers, and coworkers: The process of co-constructing organizational dissent and dissent effectiveness. *Management Communication Quarterly*, 27, 373–395. doi:10.1177/0893318913488946.

Garner, J. T. (2017). An examination of organizational dissent events and communication channels: Perspectives of a dissenter, supervisors, and coworkers. *Communication Reports, 30* (1), 26–38. doi:10.1080/08934215.2015.1128454.

Giddens, A. (1984). *The constitution of society*. Cambridge: Polity Press.

Goffman, E. (1956). *The presentation of self in everyday life*. Edinburgh: University of Edinburgh, Social Sciences Research Centre.

Gross, M. A., & Guerrero (2000). Managing conflict appropriately and effectively: An application of the competence model to Rahim's organizational conflict styles. *The International Journal of Conflict Management, 11*, 200–226. doi:10.1108/eb022840.

Hopeck, P., Desrayaud, N., Harrison, T. R., & Hatten, K. (2014). Deciding to use organizational grievance processes: Does conflict style matter? *Management Communication Quarterly, 28*(4), 561–584. doi:10.1177/0893318914549811.

Infante, D. A., & Gordon, W. I. (1985). Superiors' argumentativeness and verbal aggressiveness as predictors of subordinates' satisfaction. *Human Communication Research, 12*(1). 117–125. doi:10.1111/j.1468-2958.1985.tb00069.x.

Jameson, J. K. (2003). Transcending intractable conflict in health care: An exploratory study of communication and conflict management among anesthesia providers. *Journal of Health Communication, 8*(6), 563–582. doi:10.1080/716100415.

Jameson, J. K. (2004). Negotiating autonomy and connection through politeness: A dialectical approach to organizational conflict management. *Western Journal of Communication, 68*(3), 257–277. doi:10.1080/10570310409374801.

Jameson, J. K., Berry-James, R. M., Daley, D. M., & Coggburn, J. D. (2017). Benefits of including mediation in the state agency grievance process. In A. Georgakopoulos (Ed.), *The Handbook of mediation: Theory, research and practice*. London; Routledge.

Jameson, J. K., & Johnson, J. T. (2004). Bridging dispute system design theory and practice: The case of Unity Hospital. Paper presented at the annual meeting of the International Association for Conflict Management, awarded Outstanding Applied Conference Paper. June 6–9,2004, Pittsburgh, PA.

Jameson, J. K., Sohan, D., & Hodge, J. (2014). Turning points and conflict transformation in mediation. *Negotiation Journal, 30*(2), 225–237. doi:10.1111/nejo.12056.

Jones, T. S. (2016). Mediation and conflict coaching in organizational dispute systems. In K. Bollen, M. Euwema, & L. Munduate (Eds.), *Advancing workplace mediation through integration of theory and practice, industrial relations & conflict management* (Vol. 3, pp. 89–110). Switzerland: Springer. doi:10.1007/978-3-319-42842-0_13.

Kassing, J. W. (1998). Development and validation of the Organizational Dissent Scale. *Management Communication Quarterly*, 12, 183–229. doi:10.1177/0893318998122002.

Kassing, J. W. (2002). Speaking up: Identifying employees' upward dissent strategies. *Management Communication Quarterly*, 16(4), 187–209. doi:10.1177/089331802237234.

Kassing, J. W. (2011). *Dissent in organizations*. Malden, MA: Polity Press.

Kolb, D. M. (1986). Who are organizational third parties and what do they do? In R. J. Lewicki, B. H. Sheppard, & M. H. Bazerman (Eds.), *Research on negotiation in organizations* (Vol. 1, 207–227). Greenwich, CT: JAI Press.

Kuhn, T., & Poole, M. S. (2000). Do conflict management styles affect group decision-making? Evidence from a longitudinal field study. *Human Communication Research*, 26, 558–590. doi:10.1111/j.1468-2958.2000.tb00769.x

Murphy, P., & Dee, J. (1992). Du Pont and Greenpeace: The dynamics of conflict between corporations and activist groups. *Journal of Public Relations Research*, 4(1), 3–20. doi:10.1207/s1532754xjprr0401_02.

Nicotera, A. M., & Clinkscales, M. J. (2010). Nurses at the nexus: A case study in structurational divergence. *Health Communication*, 25(1), 32–49. doi:10.1080/10410230903473516.

Oetzel, J. G., & Ting-Toomey, S. (2003). Face concerns in interpersonal conflict: A cross-cultural empirical test of the Face Negotiation Theory. *Communication Research*, 30(6), 599–624. doi:10.1177/0093650203257841.

Paul, G. D. (2017). Paradoxes of restorative justice in the workplace. *Management Communication Quarterly*, 31(3), 380–408. doi:10.1177/0893318916681512.

Paul, G. D., & Putnam, L. L. (2017a). Emergent paradigms of organizational justice: Legalistic, restorative, and retributive justice in the workplace. In P. M. Kellett & T. G. Matyok (Eds.), *Transforming conflict through communication: Personal to working relationships*. New York: Lexington Books.

Paul, G. D., & Putnam, L. L. (2017b). Moral foundations of forgiving in the workplace. *Western Journal of Communication*, 81(1), 43–63. doi:10.1080/10570314.2016.1229499.

Plowman, K. D., ReVelle, C., Meirovich, S., Pien, M., Stemple, R., Sheng, V., & Fay, K. (1995). Walgreens: A case study in health care issues and conflict resolution. *Journal of Public Relations Research*, 7(4), 231–258. doi:10.1207/s1532754xjprr0704_01.

Poole, M. S., Holmes, M., & DeSanctis, G. (1991). Conflict management in a computer-supported meeting environment. *Management Science*, 37, 926–953. doi:10.1287/mnsc.37.8.926

Putnam, L. L. (1988). Communication and interpersonal conflict in organizations, *Management Communication Quarterly*, 1, 293–301. doi:10.1177/0893318988001003002.

Putnam, L. L. (1990). Reframing integrative and distributive bargaining: A process perspective. In B. H. Sheppard, M. H. Bazerman, & R. J. Lewicki (Eds.), *Research on negotiation in organizations* (Vol. 2, pp. 337–346). Greenwich, CT: JAI Press.

Putnam, L. L. (1994). Beyond third party role: Disputes and managerial intervention. *Employee Responsibilities and Rights Journal*, 7, 23–36. doi:10.1007/BF02621058.

Putnam, L. L. & Poole, M. S. (1987). Conflict and negotiations. In F. Jablin, L. Putnam, L. Porter, & K. Roberts (Eds.), *Handbook of organizational communication* (pp. 549–599). Beverly Hills: SAGE.

Putnam, L. L., & Wilson, C. (1982). Communication strategies in organizational conflicts: Reliability and validity of a measurement scale. In M. Burgoon (Ed.), *Communication yearbook* 6 (pp. 629–652). Beverly Hills, CA. doi:10.1080/23808985.1982.11678515.

Rahim, M. A. (1983). A measure of styles of handling interpersonal conflict. *Academy of Management Journal*, 26, 368–376. doi:10.5465/255985.

Rahim, A., & Bonoma, T. V. (1979). Managing organizational conflict: A model for diagnosis and intervention. *Psychological Reports*, 44(3), 1323–1344. doi:10.2466/pr0.1979.44.3c.1323.

Redmond, V., Jameson, J. K., & Binder, A. R. (2016). How superior–subordinate relationship quality and conflict management styles influence an employee's use of upward dissent tactics. *Negotiation and Conflict Management Research*, 9(2), 164–172. doi:10.1111/ncmr.12072.

Scott, M. E. (2013). "Communicate through the roof": A case study analysis of the communicative rules and resources of an effective global virtual team. *Communication Quarterly*, 61(3), 301–318. doi:10.1080/01463373.2013.776987.

Smith, R. C., & Eisenberg, E. M. (1987). Conflict at Disneyland: A root-metaphor analysis. *Communication Monographs*, 54, 367–380. doi:10.1080/03637758709390239.

Thomas, K. W., & Kilmann, R. H. (1974). *Thomas-Kilmann conflict MODE instrument*. Tuxedo, NY: Xicom.

Ting-Toomey, S. (1988). Intercultural conflict styles: A face-negotiation theory. In Y. Y. Kim & W. Gudykunst (Eds.), *Theories in intercultural communication* (pp. 213–235). Newbury Park, CA: SAGE.

Trudel, J., & Reio, Jr., T. G. (2011). Managing workplace incivility: The role of conflict management styles—antecedent or antidote? *Human Resource Development Quarterly, 22*(4), 395–423. doi:10.1002/hrdq.20081.

Turner, L. H., & Shuter, R. (2004). African American and European American women's visions of workplace conflict: A metaphorical analysis. *Howard Journal of Communications, 15*(3), 169–183. doi:10.1080/10646170490479787.

Ury, W. L., Brett, J. M., & Goldberg, S. B. (1988). *Getting disputes resolved.* San Francisco, CA: Jossey-Bass.

Volkema, R. J., Bergmann, T. J., & Farquhar, K. (1997). Use and impact of informal third party discussions in interpersonal conflicts at work. *Management Communication Quarterly, 11,* 185–216. doi:10.1177/0893318997112002.

Weider-Hatfield, D., & Hatfield, J. D. (1995). Relationships among conflict management styles, levels of conflict, and reactions to work. *Journal of Social Psychology, 135*(6), 687–699. doi:10.1080/00224545.1995.9713972.

Wilson, S. R., & Waltman, M. S. (1988). Assessing the Putnam-Wilson Organizational Communication Conflict Instrument (OCCI). *Management Communication Quarterly, 1*(3), 367–388. doi:10.1177/0893318988001003006.

Womack, D. F. (1988). A review of conflict instruments in organizational settings. *Management Communication Quarterly, 1*(3), 437–445. doi:10.1177/0893318988001003010.

17 A Communicative Approach to Leadership

J. Kevin Barge

This chapter focuses on two key questions, "What counts as leadership?" and "What is the relationship between communication and leadership?" A common definition used by communication scholars describes leadership as "a co-created, performative, con-textual, and attributional process where the ideas articulated in talk or action are recognized by others as progressing tasks that are important to them" (Barge & Fairhurst, 2008, p. 232). This definition suggests that leadership is a social activity aimed at progressing tasks that are important to individuals or groups of people. Moreover, it is within the flows of communication that social understandings of what counts as leadership and expectations regarding its effectiveness within particular situations are generated. At face value, this simple definition seems to provide solid answers to both questions, defining leadership as a collective activity that progresses tasks that are important to people and establishing that communication is the primary social activity that creates our understanding of what constitutes leadership within situations and facilitates organizing to accomplish tasks.

While conceptual definitions are useful for demarcating the domain of study for a particular area such as leadership, they oftentimes obscure important distinctions, differences, and issues that differentiate scholars who work within an area. For example, within recent years, a number of leadership scholars have identified them-selves as working within a social constructionist framework that examines the way that language, communication, and discourse constitute leadership within conversational episodes as well as the worldviews that inform what counts as leadership within organizations and societies. However, Fairhurst and Grant (2010) observe there is not a monolithic social constructionist approach to leadership. Rather, there are a number of dimensions that distinguish leadership scholars who take a social constructionist approach to leadership: Whether it focuses on the social construction of reality or the construction of social reality; whether communicative approaches to leadership should focus on theory or praxis; to what degree communicative leadership approaches should attend to issues of power; or whether leadership research should be monomodal (focusing on language) or multimodal focusing on both the symbolic aspects of leader-ship and other "means of generating meaning through, for example, the use of space, the body, clothing, technology, and so on" that are more material or institutional (Fairhurst & Grant, 2010, p. 190). While definitions may highlight commonalities among theorists and researchers, they can also obscure important distinctions.

The focus of this chapter is provide a sense of orientation to the two aforementioned questions. To answer the question, "What counts as leadership?" it is important to distinguish between individualistic and relational approaches to leadership that center on what counts as the appropriate unit of analysis for leadership theory and research. To answer the second question, "What is the relationship between leadership and communication?" it is crucial to differentiate between leadership communication as transmissive and leadership communication as the management of meaning. While such questions and distinctions are useful, the ultimate question is not whether an individualistic or relational approach to leadership is better or whether a transmissive or meaning-making approach to communication is superior, the ultimate question is how these distinctions can be employed by researchers and practitioners in useful ways to generate action. This is a question about judgment and is the focus of last section of the chapter.

Individualistic and Relational Approaches to Leadership

The study of leadership has been of interest to writers, philosophers, and researchers for over 2,000 years. Grint (2011) points out that some of the earliest written treatises on leadership focused on the conduct of war, such as Sun Tzu's *The Art of War*, as well as the importance of civic and political leadership as reflected in the writings of Plato and Aristotle. The focus of studying leadership within military and political contexts was expanded to organizational contexts in the late 1800s and early 1900s by scholars such as Max Weber, Frederick Taylor, and Elton Mayo, who were interested in the way that leadership influences the way individuals experience organizations (see Chapters 5 and 6). Contemporary leadership studies have continued to focus on the way that leadership is practiced in military, civic, governmental, and business contexts. While context can serve as one dimension to distinguish among leadership research and scholars, leadership studies may be more profitably distinguished by the unit of analysis it employs in its inquiry into leadership—whether it focuses on the characteristics of organizational leaders or whether it focuses on leadership as a relational practice that is accomplished through the interaction of organization actors.

Individualistic Leadership Approaches

Individualistic leadership approaches tend to focus on the individual traits, competencies, and actions that allow people to create and sustain leadership roles within organizations, communities and societies. Such individuals are typically viewed as being privileged and are often characterized as either being "heroes" that are able to engage the major problems confronting a human system or as imbued with particular authority by an organization or institution. The former is illustrated in the lectures by Thomas Carlyle, one of the first modern writers of leadership in the 1800s, who equated leadership with individualistic heroism. As Grint (2011, p. 8) observes, "In the beginning was perhaps not god, but rather the god-like creatures that peppered the 1840 lectures of Thomas Carlyle, whose fascination with the 'Great Men' of history effectively reduced the role of mere mortals to 'extras.'" The emphasis on individualistic heroism is reflected by the traditional focus of leadership studies and practice on military and political leaders such as Sun Tzu, Machiavelli, Napoleon, and Abraham Lincoln. While the traditional focus on military and political leaders has been broadened over the past few decades to include corporate and sports leaders such as Steve Jobs (founder of Apple), Jeff Bezos (founder of Amazon), Warren Buffett (a noted investor), John Wooden (former UCLA basketball coach), and Gregg Popovich (NBA basketball coach), "heroic" approaches to leadership still tend to focus on identifying men who seem to possess superhuman qualities and to a much lesser degree female business (e.g., Sheryl Sandberg), political (e.g., Susan Collins), and sports leaders (e.g., Pat Summitt).

In the early 1900s, the historical concentration on "heroic" leadership was complemented by a focus on administrative leadership that occurred within formal hierarchies. While both foci share an assumption that leadership should focus on individuals, the basis for leadership authority changes as administrative leadership: (1) is equated with the power and influence that are granted leaders given their roles as managers or administrators within organizational systems, and (2) places emphasis on rationality with a key concern for logically understanding the context to ensure that the leadership responds appropriately to the social and structural constraints of the situation. Grint (2011) observes that this emphasis on administrative leadership and its concern with rationality can be traced from early 1900s with its emphasis on scientific management, to the 1950s with the emergence of contingency analysis and systems analysis, to the 1970s and 1980s with its focus on Total Quality Management and Quality Circles, to contemporary leadership approaches that give attention to distributed leadership and followership (see Chapters 5–7).

Whether one ascribes to a "heroic" or administrative leadership model, both focus on leadership as an individually centered phenomenon. However, differences exist among specific leadership theories and models associated with an individualist leadership approach according to: (a) whether the theory or model focuses on identifying the traits or behaviors associated with leadership, (b) whether the theory or model assumes that a set of leadership traits and behaviors are universally effective across contexts or whether the effectiveness of a set of leadership traits and behaviors depends on the situation, and (c) whether the analytical focus should be placed on a single leader or a distributed set of leaders.

Traits versus behaviors. One way to distinguish among various individualistic leadership theories and models is whether they use traits or behaviors to explain how individuals create and sustain positions of leadership. Trait-based leadership theories focus on identifying the underlying communicative, social, physical, cognitive, or personality characteristics that explain how and why individuals create and sustain leadership positions. Behavior-based leadership theories focus on the overt verbal utterances or nonverbal behaviors that are performed by leaders and how they affect an individual's ability to act as a leader. Behavior-based leadership theories often rely on the concept of style, a pattern of messages and nonverbal acts that serve as a distinctive behavioral signature, to explain leadership. Regardless of whether a leadership theorist focuses on traits or behaviors, the underlying assumption is that individual differences should be correlated with various outcomes such as leadership effectiveness and emergence, follower motivation and satisfaction, and organizational productivity and efficiency.

Trait-based leadership approaches began by identifying the motives, traits, and abilities that distinguish leaders from non-leaders and contribute to leadership effectiveness. For example, Ensari, Riggio, Christian, and Carslaw (2011, p. 532) were interested in identifying the individual differences that predicted who would emerge as a leader and found that extraversion and authoritarian personality were strong predictors of leadership emergence. More recently, leadership researchers such as Hoffman, Woeher, Maldagen-Youngjohn, and Lyons (2011) have distinguished between trait-like and state-like individual differences where the former are viewed as more distal dispositional qualities such as motives, traits, and abilities that an individual is born with and that remain with a person for a lifetime, with the latter being viewed as proximal situated differences such as knowledge and skills that can be learned and are particularly relevant for specific kinds of tasks and contexts. Rather than get caught in a debate over "nature-nurture," whether leaders are born or made, more contemporary research adopts a "both-and" position where both trait-like and state-like individual differences are expected to influence leadership and organizational performance with the question becoming which one exercises the most influence and when.

Behavior-based leadership approaches have focused on identifying the behavioral styles associated with leadership and has taken three distinct paths. One path may be characterized as "two-factor" theories of leadership where the behavior leaders exhibit to others can characterized by two global dimensions—task and relational. Inspired by the 1950s Ohio State Leadership Studies, the task dimension focuses on behaviors that facilitated goal achievement while the relational dimension centers on behaviors that indicate trust, warmth, support, empathy, and two-way communication. "Two-factor" theories of leadership typically use these two dimensions to create a grid where the factors are integrated to differentiate among competing behavioral styles a leader may employ. For example, Blake and Mouton's (1994) Managerial Grid Theory identified five different styles of leadership including Country Club Management (high relationship, low task), Impoverished Management (low relationship, low task), Middle-of-the-Road Management (moderate relationship, moderate task), Authority-Compliance (low relationship, high task), and Team Management (high relationship, high task). Hersey and Blanchard (Hersey, Blanchard, & Dewey, 2012) identified four styles of leadership including Telling (moderate to high task, low to moderate relationship), Selling (moderate to high task, moderate to high relationship), Delegating (low to moderate task, low to moderate relationship), and Participating (low to moderate task, moderate to high relationship). While the names of a particular style may vary according to the particular theory or model, the assumption that leadership styles can be arrayed along the dual dimensions of task and relationship orientation remain the same (see Chapter 7).

A second stream of leadership style research can be traced to the 1930s Iowa Child Welfare Studies, which examined the consequences of autocratic, democratic, and laissez-faire leadership (Lewin, Lippitt, & White, 1939). Autocratic leadership is associated with leaders having high levels of power, who employ centralized decision-making, and who direct their followers' behavior through one-way communication. Democratic leadership is typically associated with shared power and decentralized decision-making where leaders and followers employ two-way communication to jointly make decisions and pursue particular lines of action. Laissez-faire leadership is typically viewed as a "hands off" approach to leadership, as leaders are relatively uninvolved with the activity of their followers. The notion that leadership styles can be differentiated along the dimensions of autocratic-democratic leadership has informed several approaches to leadership such as Likert's System IV, Vroom and Yetton's Contingency Theory of Leadership, and team leadership (see Chapter 7).

A third stream of research focuses on transformational leadership approaches. Initially conceptualized by James T. Burns (1978) and subsequently revised by Bernard Bass (1985), transformational leadership is concerned with explaining how leaders create changes in their followers' beliefs, needs, and attitudes through appeals to their higher-order needs using the strength of their personality and the creation of a compelling vision. Dimensions of transformational leadership include idealized influence, inspirational motivation, intellectual stimulation, and individualized consideration. Transformational leadership differs from transactional leadership as the latter is based on the notion that the relationship between leaders and followers is based on social exchange whereby leaders use contingent and noncontingent rewards to gain followers' compliance. Transformational leadership research has been interested in exploring the relationships between transformational leadership dimensions and outcomes such as performance, innovation, job satisfaction, organizational identification, and organizational citizenship behavior, yet the relationships between these individual behavioral dimensions and outcomes, as well as moderating and mediating variables that may influence these relationships, are not clear (van Knippenberg & Sitkin, 2013).

Universal versus contextual. A second way that individualistic leadership theories or models are differentiated centers on whether the theory or model assumes that a single set of traits or leadership style is universally effective or whether the traits or behaviors that are needed to help progress tasks varies according to the situation. For example, some two-factor leadership behavioral theories such as Blake and Mouton's Managerial Grid Theory suggest that a single leadership style such as Team Management is universally effective across situations, while Hersey and Blanchard's Situational Leadership Theory suggests that job and psychological maturity determines whether a Selling, Telling, Consulting, or Participating leadership style is most appropriate for the situation. Similarly, while "Great Man" theories of leadership presume that particular traits are effective across situations, situational trait-based theories such a Fiedler's Contingency Theory (1967) assumes that there needs to be a match between leader traits and the situation in order for leadership to be effective. Fiedler identified three situational variables that can be used to determine whether more task-oriented or relationship-oriented traits are needed: (a) Position power, (b) task structure, and (c) leader–member relationships. Depending on how these different dimensions are configured, they can generate different levels of favorableness where some situations are viewed as highly favorable, some highly unfavorable, and some in the middle. Fiedler's theory predicts that situations which are highly favorable or unfavorable requires leaders to have task-oriented traits and those that are moderately favorable/unfavorable require leaders to have more relationally oriented traits. More broadly, any number of contextual variables such as culture, leader and follower gender, economic conditions, task and job characteristics, temporal factors, and social networks can influence the type of leadership that is needed to manage situations as well as moderate or mediate the relationship between leadership traits or behaviors and outcomes (Oc, 2018) (see Chapter 7).

A contextual variable that has been a central focus for leadership researchers is national culture. Comparative leadership studies have focused on the differences and similarities between the kinds of traits, values, and behaviors that characterize leaders and followers among differing national cultures. The GLOBE (Global Leadership and Organizational Behaviour Effectiveness) Project has focused on the interrelationships among culture, leadership, and effectiveness developing a network of more than 200 researchers representing 62 countries to systematically explore these interrelationships (see https://globeproject.com/foundation). The GLOBE studies have focused on developing a culturally endorsed theory of leadership (CLT) that is based in implicit leadership theory (Dorfman, Javidan, Hanges, Dastmalchian, & House, 2012). Implicit leadership theories, "represent the cognitive structures or schemas that specify what people expect from leaders in terms of leader traits or attributes" (Offermann &

Coates, 2018, p. 513). The GLOBE studies are grounded in the belief that CLTs are an important phenomenon that cultures and societies rely on to socialize individuals into a particular set of values that make them more accepting of particular leadership practices than others. For example, if individuals have been socialized into a culture that is more egalitarian and emphasizes shared decision-making, they may prefer organizational leadership styles that are more democratic, emphasizing participatory and consultative decision-making.

The starting point for the GLOBE studies was to identify the key attributes that are perceived to facilitate or inhibit outstanding leadership, which could then be used to develop leadership profiles to characterize nations or clusters of nations. The six dimensions that were used to construct CLT leadership profiles were: (1) charismatic/valued-based, (2) team-oriented, (3) participative, (4) humane-oriented, (5) autonomous, and (6) self-protective. Differences among these dimensions were then used to create clusters of nations that have a distinctive profile such as Latin Europe, Confucian Asia, the Middle East, and sub-Saharan Africa.

The GLOBE studies suggest that there are particular leadership attributes that are universal facilitators and inhibitors of leadership effectiveness. For example, Dorfman et al. (2012, pp. 507–508) state that, "ideal leaders are expected to develop a vision, inspire others, and create a successful performance oriented team within their organizations while behaving with honesty and integrity" regardless of culture. At the same time, Javidan, Dorfman, Howell, and Hanges (2010) identified several dimensions that were culturally specific: status consciousness, bureaucratic, autonomous, face saving, humane, self-sacrificial/risk taking, and internally competitive. Culturally specific dimensions may be facilitative in some cultures, but inhibitive in others. Javidan, Dorfman, De Luque, and House (2006) offer a compelling example of the way that status consciousness may play out in different cultures observing, "While it may be a good idea in an American organization to directly contact anyone with the right information regardless of their level, such behavior may be seen as a sign of disrespect to those in formal positions in a Brazilian organization" (p. 76).

The GLOBE studies provide a nuanced analysis of culture that explores both similarities and differences among various cultures using multiple dimensions. For leaders who wish to work in different cultures than their home culture, Dorfman et al. (2012) offer the following advice. First, match and exceed the expectations that are associated with a particular culture. The idea is for leaders, at a minimum, to match their behaviors with cultural expectations, and if they are to be highly successful, exceed them. Second, given that some leadership attributes are universal, if a leader is not sure what to do, then a leader should focus on, "developing a vision, inspiring others, demonstrating integrity, being decisive, and creating a performance oriented culture" (Dorfman et al., 2012, p. 514).

Single versus distributed leadership. Individualistic approaches have tended to view leadership as either an individual-level phenomenon performed by a single individual or a distributed phenomenon performed by a group of individuals. The former attempts to identify the traits or behaviors that enable an individual to perform a leadership role. While studies of followership have grown in recent years as an attempt to conceptualize leadership as more a relational phenomenon (Uhl-Bien, Riggio, Lowe, & Carsten, 2014), they reinforce the notion that there are particular individuals who are leaders, and others who are followers and, further, that a person can be either a leader or a follower at a particular moment in time but not both. While some leadership approaches such as leader–member exchange theory (see Chapter 10) suggest that we need to look at the relationships leaders may form with followers, they still presume that there is an individual who is a leader within the network of relationships within an organization and others are non-leaders. Leaders may individualize their relationships with others, forming either in-group relationships with followers characterized by closeness, trust, and support or out-group relationships characterized by distance, a lack of trust, and low levels of support (Martin, Guillaume, Thomas, Lee, & Epitropaki, 2016), but they remain in a leadership position while others enact follower-ship roles.

In response to increasingly complex organizational systems, the notion that a single person can be a leader and direct the activities of an organization or team was complemented with the notion that leadership needed to be shared or distributed throughout members within a system. Denis, Langley, and Sergi (2012) refer to this as "leadership in the plural," where focus is placed on "the combined influence of multiple leaders in specific organizational situations" (p. 211). Although different approaches to shared and distributed leadership exist, many of these approaches focus on individual leaders and the pattern of distribution of particular leadership roles or functions within a system. Denis et al. (2012) observe that leadership may be shared to enhance team effectiveness; leadership may be pooled at the top of organizations (e.g., senior manage-ment teams) to lead others; and leadership may be shared sequentially where leadership is spread across levels over time. For example, Manz and Sims' (2001) concept of super-leadership is premised on the idea that the formal team leader needs to adopt an empowering style that enables others within the team to also act as leaders. Distributed approaches to leadership recognize that leadership can be distributed vertically throughout various levels of a hierarchy as well as horizontally within a particular level of grouping of individuals. The analytical interest is on how different configura-tions of distributed leadership generate different outcomes.

Key questions. An individualistic leadership approach has a specific mindset that focuses on the mechanisms that explain how and why individual leaders act the way they do, determines whether the traits and behaviors that are needed to progress tasks cut across situations or must be tailored to the unique qualities of situations, and explores the way that individual leaders or distributed leadership affect various out-comes. Individualistic leadership approaches tend to view organization as a structure (O_2) by focusing on the way leadership is coordinated within organizations, the way that leadership structures such as distributed leadership influence organizations, and how other aspects of an organization's structure such as task structure, leader–member relationships, and national culture moderate or mediate the relationships between leadership and organizational outcomes. Although an individualistic leadership approach is comprised by a large and varied set of specific theories and research initiatives, they rely on a shared set of common questions that create a distinctive focus for how to they theorize and research leadership which include:

- What are the personality and social traits, drives and motivations, and cognitive characteristics that distinguish leaders from non-leaders? That influence behavioral performance? That influence organizational outcomes such as productivity or job satisfaction?
- What are the behavioral characteristics that distinguish leaders from non-leaders? That influence organizational outcomes such as productivity or job satisfaction?

- What contextual variables moderate or mediate the relationship between leadership traits or behaviors and outcome variables?
- How are leadership and followership roles distributed within an organization?
- How does the distribution of leadership and followership roles influence organizational outcome variables?

Relational Approaches to Leadership

Starting in the early 2000s, relational approaches to leadership began to develop which offered a contrasting perspective to individualistic leadership approaches (Uhl-Bien & Ospina, 2012). Numerous lines of theorizing and research have emerged within a relational approach including discursive leadership (Fairhurst, 2007), systemic constructionist leadership (Barge, 2012), and leadership-as-practice (Raelin, 2016a). Although these lines of theorizing and research to leadership vary, relational leadership approaches tend to make one or more of the following assumptions: (1) Relational leadership focuses on mundane interaction and practices; (2) relational leadership focuses on the role of symbolic and material actors within organizational systems, and (3) relational leadership needs to take into account multiple agencies that constitute organizational systems.

Mundane interaction and practice. Rather than center attention on knowledge, skills, and actions that individual leaders need to possess to perform their role, relational approaches suggest leadership is located "in the ways actors engage, interact, and negotiate with one another to influence organizational understandings and produce outcomes" (Fairhurst & Uhl-Bien, 2012, p. 1044). This means that leadership theory and research should focus attention on the process and temporality of communication, recognizing that different configurations of messages and utterances among individuals and groups in organizations are likely to create various leadership arrangements. Both quantitative and qualitative methods can be used to examine the relationships among communication processes, leadership, and outcomes. For example, the former is illustrated by Fairhurst, Rogers, and Sarr (1987), who used relational control theory to conceptualize individual messages in leadership conversations as one-up (asserting a relational definition), one-down (accepting a relational definition offered by another), and one-across messages (neither offering or accepting a relational definition) that could be used to identify sequential control patterns and subsequently correlated with relational judgments regarding leadership. The latter is illustrated by Cooren and Fairhurst's (2004) use of discourse analysis to examine how control is exercised in conversations by the way that individuals initiate and close off sequences of interaction. Whether a quantitative or qualitative approach is employed, the focus is on unpacking the sequence and organization of talk using a variety of discourse analytic methods including interaction analysis, critical discourse analysis, conversation analysis, narrative analysis, and membership categorization (Fairhurst & Uhl-Bien, 2012).

The focus on leadership talk-in-interaction does more than simply dissolve the leader–follower binary by viewing leadership as a processual phenomenon where individuals may move in and out of leadership positions or share leadership positions several times over the duration of an interaction, it also views leadership interaction as culturally, historically, and temporally situated. Raelin (2016b) observes, "we can see that it [leadership] has a cultural and grammatical history that can be traced to an origin that is humanly constructed (Grint, 2005; Hersted and Gergen, 2013)" (p. 132).

Leadership talk acts from context and invites new contexts. Simply, pre-existing worldviews, perspectives, and stories as well as material realities exist, which create a context that shapes the way that individuals interact within conversation. At the same time, the way that individuals interact within conversation may alter and reframe the context, inviting new possibilities for meaning making and action. For example, Barge (2004) examined how leaders can use "systemic stories" to create an understanding of the context that they are engaging in order to make choices regarding how to intervene and reshape the context.

Human and nonhuman actants. Leadership studies have tended to focus on the way human actors create and sustain leadership. Inspired by approaches such as actor network theory (Latour, 1999), some relational approaches have argued that the creation of leadership cannot be solely reduced to the interactions among human actors, the influence of nonhuman actors must also be considered (Fairhurst & Cooren, 2009). For example, participative leadership involves more than leaders inviting others to give their opinion or jointly deliberate over important issues. The ability to create participative leadership also depends on nonhuman technologies that can be used to share data, poll organizational members, and make decisions as well as the physical or electronic space to convene meetings. Even if an individual wants to act as a participative leader, it would be difficult to pull off this performance unless other technologies and spaces are present that support this impulse. Actor network theory (ANT) uses the term *actants* as opposed to *actors* to capture both the human and nonhuman elements that contribute to the accomplishment of a social activity such as leadership.

Understanding a social activity requires articulating the network of human and nonhuman actants associated with the activity and how the actants' interrelationships contribute to its performance. For example, the authority presented by a university professor is composed by a number of human actants such as the professor's communication style and other professors and students collaborating with the professor on research, as well as nonhuman actants such as the professor's title (e.g., endowed professorship) and framed degrees and awards prominently displayed in the professor's office. The authority of a university professor is not simply an individual characteristic; rather, it is supported, created, and enabled by the configuration of a larger network of human and nonhuman actors.

The use of ANT to inquire into leadership is nicely illustrated by Fairhurst's (2007) analysis of Rudy Giuliani's performance of charisma in his response to the 9/11 attacks on New York's World Trade Center. Most studies of charismatic leadership tend to suggest that leadership charisma is a function of some combination of individual traits and behaviors that foster an impression that the leader is charismatic. From an ANT perspective, most studies of charismatic leadership tend to "black box" charisma attributing it to the contribution of a single actant, the individual leader, and ignore the other actants that are part of a network of human and nonhuman actants that contribute to the construction of charismatic leadership. Fairhurst (2007) demonstrates how the network of actants was orchestrated in such a way to create the attribution that Giuliani acted as a heroic and charismatic leader. Her analysis explored how human actants (e.g., needs and emotions of New York citizens) and nonhuman actants, such as architectural actants (e.g., where news conferences were held) and technological actants (e.g., telephone and geographical information systems), contributed to peoples' attribution that Giuliani was a charismatic leader.

Plurality and relational agency. Meindl, Ehrlich, and Dukerich (1985) observed over three decades ago that the agency of leaders to create change within organizations is exaggerated. They argued that that our fascination with the "romance of leadership" tends to move organizational members to ascribe important changes within an organization to the acts of leaders as opposed to other concepts such as organizational culture or technical systems. While it may be premature to dismiss completely the agency of individuals, the notion that human and nonhuman actors constitute networks that enable leadership suggests that agency is plural; that agency may best be located in the joint action among human and nonhuman actants in a network. What this means is that leadership researchers should not focus on the individual agency of organizational members and how their sense of agency enables or constraints available choices regarding actions and meaning making. Rather, the focus needs to be on the practice that emerges among individuals. Raelin (2016c, p. 125) argues that, "A practice is a coordinative effort among participants who choose through their own rules to achieve a distinctive outcome. It is, accordingly, less about what one person thinks or does and more about what people may accomplish together." This suggests that patterns of interaction become an actant when people talk and act together. Moreover, a distinct logic emerges from the interaction pattern that enables and constrains people from taking certain actions or making particular social choices. For example, sometimes when people engage in a heated argument that neither wants, they often feel that the argument itself acted as a third-party in the conversation that initiated and sustained the argument.

Raelin's (2016b, p. 137) notion of collaborative agency as aligning thoughts, actions, and interpretations reflects the notion that agency is an intersubjective accomplishment among people. Within his leadership-as-practice (LAP) framework, activities become attached to a practice, which cannot be reduced to single individuals, but instead focus on the relationality of leadership, making "the unit of analysis in collaborative agency … the intersubjective interaction among parties to the practice rather than the individuals who are presumably mobilizing the practice" (Raelin, 2016b, p. 142). For example, Raelin (2016b) has identified several leadership activities including task (scanning, signaling, weaving, stabilizing) and relational (inviting, unleashing, reflecting) whose performance are not associated with a particular individual, but rather with the activity of multiple actants and authorities. As a result, agency is not singular; it is plural as each actant carries its own sense of agency that intertwines with other actants to create a hybrid agency that reflects different elements of its network.

Key questions. A relational approach to leadership differs from an individualistic approach given its emphasis on everyday interaction, human and nonhuman actants, and the notion of collaborative agency. A relational approach to leadership clearly engages organization as a process (O_1) where the mundane interaction of human and nonhuman actants create and invite different patterns of organizing. These patterns of organizing may become institutionalized over time—in the form of ideologies, ritualistic or normative interaction, stories, and the like—which give rise to organized patterns within organizations such as networks and role structures (O_2). As organizational members interact, they may explicitly reference these organized patterns or these organized patterns may enter the interaction as silent actors who nonetheless exert influence within the ongoing conversation. For example, a team member may, "Call the question," in order to end discussion over an issue and take a vote. Other team members recognize this utterance as being tied to a historical nonhuman actant, Robert's Rules of Order, a normative parliamentary model for conducting meetings, that only has to be indirectly referenced in order to shape the discussion. The research focus of scholars operating within a relational approach is informed by a number of key questions that unfolds the relationships among patterns of interaction within networks of human and nonhuman actants and what consequences these interaction patterns and networks create. These key questions include:

- How do patterns of communication construct our understanding and attributions of leadership?
- How do interactional networks of human and nonhuman actants create different kinds of leadership practices and arrangements?
- How is agency enabled or constrained given particular interactional networks of human and nonhuman actants?
- How are patterns of leadership communication enabled and constrained by pre-existing cultural and organizational leadership stories?
- How can new patterns of leadership communication be created that alter people's existing understanding of leadership and create new possibilities for meaning making and action?
- How do flows of activity and communication intersect at particular moments to create particular patterns of leadership and position certain individuals as momentary leaders?
- How do interaction patterns and network create particular outcomes such as perceptions of leadership charisma, task coordination, and change?

Leadership and Communication

Fairhurst and Connaughton (2014a, 2014b) suggest that leadership research has viewed communication as both a transmissive and meaning-making phenomenon. These two conceptualizations of communication represent complementary alternatives regarding the function and purpose of leadership communication.

Leadership Communication as Transmission

A transmissive approach to leadership communication views communication as a form of information transfer where messages are encoded by a source, through a channel or conduit, and are decoded by a receiver. Communication effectiveness is judged according to message fidelity where effective communication is clear and that the message and the meaning the source intended to send are received and are clearly understood by the receiver. Barriers that may frustrate the ability to accurately decode the message may include obstacles that block or interfere with the transmission of the message as well as perceptual filters that may influence the interpretation of the message (see Chapter 1).

Transmissive models tend to use an input-process-output orientation with communication frequently conceptualized as a process. For example, Chaudhry and Joshi's (2018) model of transformational leadership and commitment to change identified transformational leadership as its key concept and then identified five types of transformative leadership communication—organizational vision, inspiration, change information, feedback, and emotional support. Moving from a focus on input-process to process-outcome, they then hypothesized that these types of communication would influence affective commitment to change and organizational identification. Studies that examine the process-outcome link operationalize communication in a variety of ways including interaction coding or self-report surveys that capture perceptions of communication processes. The former is illustrated by Lehman-Willenbrock, Meinecke, Rowold, and Kauffeld's (2015) study where they coded interaction within team meetings in terms of problem-solving and solution-focused communication and discovered that transformational leadership was positively related to problem-solving communication. The latter is represented by Men's (2014) study that revealed that transformational leadership influenced an organization's symmetrical internal communication channels and that transformational leaders tended to use rich face-to-face channels to communicate with employees.

Key questions. Fairhurst and Connaughton (2014a, 2014b) observe that leadership scholars who employ transmissional models of communication do not problematize the meaning-making process that leads them to focus on issues relating to message clarity, the frequency and timing of communication, informational adequacy, communication effectiveness, the way that messages are used to formulate and convey vision, and message characteristics such as message complexity. For example, they note that several studies relating to transformational leadership and visionary leadership focus on elements of communication that have a transmissional flavor such as idea density and grammatical complexity (Balthazard, Waldman, & Warren, 2009) and the importance of being careful encoders (transmitters) and decoders (listeners) of messages (Berson and Avolio, 2004). Leadership scholars who knowingly or unknowingly adopt transmissive models of communication view communication as a message that is encoded by a source, transmitted through a channel, and decoded by a receiver. Leadership communication scholars who operate within a transmissive model of communication, therefore, ask questions that center on the way that source, message, channel, and receiver characteristics influence the production and interpretation of communicative acts. These questions include, but are not limited to:

- How do source characteristics influence the construction and interpretation of messages?
- How can messages be constructed to enhance clarity and comprehension?
- How do message characteristics influence the construction and interpretation of messages?
- How can repeating or layering messages make sure that audiences correctly interpret messages?
- How does the timing of messages influence message reception?
- What are the consequences of using particular channels for distributing messages?
- Under what conditions is it effective to use single or multiple channels to disseminate messages?
- How do receiver characteristics influence the interpretation of messages?
- What are the key messages that need to be sent to key constituencies within and outside the organization?

Leadership Communication as the Management of Meaning

Leadership communication as the management of meaning focuses on the way communication is employed by individuals and organizations to make sense of situations and centers attention on the formative power of language and communication to shape meaning. For example, Grint (2005) argued that the kinds of situations that leaders must respond to are not separate from the actions they undertake. Rather than assume that situations dictate how leaders respond to contextual demands, Grint contended that leaders use communication to shape the very situation that they find themselves engaging. In an analysis of President Bush's rhetoric prior to the decision to invade Iraq, he concluded the Bush administration used communication in a way to frame the situation as a crisis that would mandate and legitimate his use of a command style of leadership. The appropriateness and effectiveness of leadership communication is both constrained by the pre-existing situation but can also be altered through communication.

Leadership communication research that operates within a communication as the management of meaning framework focuses attention on how individuals position themselves to make meaning from within the flow communication, the strategies that individuals may use to influence the meaning-making process, and the consequences of particular patterns of meaning-making. For example, Shotter (2011) and his associates have been interested in creating an approach to leadership grounded in social poetics that centers attention on how individual leaders may pick up on the way that meaning is made from within the flow of conversation and alter it. Rather than assume that leaders only cognitively plan their responses, Shotter argues for the importance of embodied ways of knowing and using preconscious feelings to explore how leaders use their body to notice important elements of the unfolding conversation as the basis for additional inquiry and to act in ways that both pick up on what has been previously uttered and gesture toward new possibilities for meaning making. Fairhurst's (Fairhurst & Sarr, 1996; Fairhurst, 2011) research program on leadership as framing has explored the ways that individual leaders may use frames such as spin, comparison/contrast, metaphors, and stories to create ways of interpreting and making sense of person, situations, and events. Her research not only examines the kinds of frames that leaders may employ to influence the meaning-making power but also the processes such as mental models that influence how leaders make sense of the situation and select particular frames as well as the consequences of employing particular frames on the way that future action and power relationships are constructed.

Key questions. Within recent years, there has been a growing interest in leadership studies that focus on the management of meaning. For example, Fairhurst's (Fairhurst & Sarr, 1996; Fairhurst, 2011) program of research has examined the variety of tactics that leaders may use to frame issues and problems and how that can facilitate organizing processes. Barge (2004) has explored how inquiry—through questioning and story-making—can shape the way that leaders and organizational members co-create meaning. Leadership scholars who operate from the communication as the management of meaning model focus on addressing questions that relate to the way that individuals make sense of situations and communication, how they can intervene into the process of meaning making, and the consequences that are generated by shaping the meaning-making process in particular ways. The following kinds of questions are central to scholars who work from a communication as the management of meaning framework:

- How do individuals orient to and make sense of situation through cognitive and embodied ways of knowing?
- How do patterns of communication invite and discourage particular forms of meaning making?
- How can individuals position themselves to pick up on and sense various possibilities for meaning making within a situation?
- How do linguistic devices such as myths, narratives, metaphors, arguments, and frames influence the meaning-making process?
- What are the power and control dynamics associated with various patterns of meaning making?
- How is meaning coordinated and co-managed among multiple human and nonhuman actants?

Integrating Questions of Leadership and Communication

This chapter is organized around two key questions: "What counts as leadership?" and "What is the relationship between communication and leadership?" The first question focuses on the appropriate unit of analysis for leadership studies with individualistic approaches focusing attention on individual organizational leaders or networks of organizational leaders and the personal qualities, traits, and behaviors that distinguish leaders from non-leaders and enable leaders to create and sustain leadership positions and achieve excellence. Individualistic approaches tend to view organization as a structure (O_2) focusing on the structure of leadership within organizations and how leadership structures interact with other organizational structures such as task and role structures. Relational approaches center attention on the everyday interactional processes of organizational members and how their symbolic interaction is connected with material actants within the organization to create varied forms of leadership. Relational approaches tend to focus on the process of organizing through everyday communicative practices (O_1) as well as how communicative practices give rise to and institutionalize particular structures (O_2) over time that can impinge and influence subsequent communicative practices. The second question focuses on the ways that leadership scholars have conceptualized communication and the perspectives of communication as transmissive message-centered process and communication as a meaning-making phenomena are both represented in the research.

It is tempting to want to answer these two questions by taking a side on whether an individualistic or relational approach to leadership is superior or whether a transmissive or meaning-making approach to communication is the best conceptualization of communication. However, these are false choices that move us to create overly simple answers when trying to explain and account for a complex phenomenon such as leadership. Taking a cue from Fairhurst (2007), it is more profitable to view these competing alternatives as complementary takes on what counts as leadership and its relationship to communication allowing that: (a) particular alternatives might be more appropriate given the kinds of research questions scholars pose or the types of problems that individual leaders engage; and (b) these competing alternatives may be integrated or blended in ways to address particular problems. The alternatives for both leadership and communication can be combined to generate four distinct approaches to leadership: (1) individualistic transmissive, (2) individualistic meaning-making, (3) relational transmissive, and (4) relational meaning-making. Each of these approaches illuminate different areas and questions that leadership scholars may want to investigate and highlight different ways that practitioners can orient themselves to the problems they face within their organizations. While an academic researcher or practitioner may have a strong preference for one alternative or combination of alternatives, it does not preclude an academic researcher or practitioner from drawing on or combining different alternatives given the situation.

The utility of using these different approaches can be illustrated through the way that administrative leaders may approach the practical problem of what they accomplish when using email. For most administrative leaders, email is about pushing information out to people so they are kept in the loop about changing events within the organization. Such an attitude reflects an individualistic transmissive approach to leadership where there is a belief that a single leader can make a difference in the organization and that it is incumbent on the leader to clearly transmit information to other organizational members.

But what occurs if the administrative leader thinks that the leader's role is not only to share information with other organizational members but also to shape people's meaning making about the kinds of relationships and culture that needs to be present within the organization? Adopting an individualistic meaning-making approach would mean the leader needs to not only pay attention the best ways to convey the needed information clearly to other organizational members, but also to give serious consideration to the relational and cultural implications of the message. For example, if the email is sent at 3am does that convey an expectation that the organizational culture views working around the clock as a chief priority? What is the tone of the email? Does it invite meaning making around what kind of relationship the leader envisions with other organizational employees? Does it convey a sense of support and trust or does it convey an attitude that other organizational members are lacking in some way and are unreliable? If there is a problem, how is the problem framed and who is positioned to take the blame? Relying on an individualistic-transmissive approach to leadership would ignore these kinds of questions, yet, viewing email as both an opportunity to transmit a message and make meaning would position the leader to think through these kinds of implications. In this case, using multiple approaches to orient to the challenges associated with the use of email allows administrative leaders to create emails that simultaneously share important information and shape the organization's culture. The approach or combination of approaches not only will influence how a practitioner or scholar reads the situation, but also how they respond to it.

Leadership has been a topic of interest for people for millennia. The purpose of this chapter has been to highlight alternative answers to central questions regarding what counts as leadership and what leadership's relationship to communication is. The leadership literature provides a number of possible answers to these questions and it is incumbent on academic researchers and practitioners to make wise choices from the available traditions and research regarding leadership theory, research, and practice to address the challenges, dilemmas, and problems they engage.

Recommended Supplementary Readings

Fairhurst, G. T., & Connaughton, S. L. (2014). Leadership. In L. L. Putnam & D. K. Mumby (Eds.), *The SAGE handbook of organizational communication* (pp. 401–423). Thousand Oaks, CA: SAGE.

Fairhurst, G. T. (2001). Dualisms in leadership communication. In L. L. Putnam & F. M. Jablin (Eds.), *The new handbook of organizational communication* (pp. 379–439). Newbury Park, CA: SAGE.

Jablin, F. M., Putnam, L. L., Roberts, K., & Porter, L. (1987). *The handbook of organizational communication: An interdisciplinary perspective*. Newbury Park, CA: SAGE.

These handbook chapters provide state-of-the-art reviews on the relationship between communication and leadership. They trace the historical evolution of leadership from being primarily grounded in leadership psychology (1987), to a dialectical view of communication and leadership (2004), to a complex view of leadership communication (2014) as a relational process that embraces both transmission and meaning centered models of communication, that needs to take into account human-material organizing, and recognizes that organizing is infused with power dynamics, reflexivity, and moral accountability.

Grant, D., Fairhurst, G. T., Grint, K., & Jackson, B. (Eds.). (2010). Social constructionist views of leadership. *Management Communication Quarterly, 24*(2).

This special issue focuses on the way that social constructionist approaches have been used to reconceptualize leadership. The opening essay by Gail Fairhurst and David Grant provides a valuable framework for teasing apart the many dimensions of social constructionism and highlighting the many faces that social constructionism may take in leadership studies.

Liden, R. C., Antonakis, J., & Fairhurst, G. (Eds.). (2009). The context of leadership. *Human Relations, 62*(11).

Context is a key concept in leadership studies that focuses attention on the ways that situations and environments may (or may not) influence what counts as leadership and the relationship between leadership and outcomes. This special issue explores how context is conceptualized within leadership psychology and discursive leadership approaches.

Uhl-Bien, M., & Ospina, S. M. (2012). *Advancing relational leadership theory: A conversation among perspectives*. Charlotte, NC: Information Age Publishing.

Relational leadership is an alternative perspective to traditional individualistic approaches to leadership. This book provides a wide-ranging overview of relational leadership from a variety of perspectives including communication, critical leadership studies, and psychodynamic theory, as well as examines the way that relational leadership engages with issues of social change, shared leadership, and working with diverse staff in organizations.

Bryman, A., Collinson, D. L., Grint, K., Jackson, B., & Uhl-Bien, M. (Eds.). (2011). *The SAGE handbook of leadership*. London: SAGE.

Provides an excellent overview of the history of leadership as well as coverage of macro and sociological perspectives, political and philosophical perspectives, and psychological perspectives on leadership. Fairhurst's chapter on discursive leadership helps situate what a communicative approach offers in relation to existing perspectives within leadership studies.

Grint, K. (2010). *Leadership: A very short introduction*. Oxford: Oxford University Press.

An excellent introduction to the study of leadership that is organized around key questions such as: What is leadership? Are leaders born or bred? What is followership? Is leadership important to organizations?

Northouse, P. G. (2016). *Leadership theory and practice* (7th ed.). Thousand Oaks, CA: SAGE.

An introductory text that provides an overview of general leadership approaches such as trait, skills, and behaviors as well as specific theories and types of leadership such as leader–member exchange, authentic leadership, and servant leadership.

Johnson, C.E., & Hackman, M. Z. (2018). *Leadership: A communication perspective* (7th ed.). Long Grove, IL: Waveland Press.

An introductory text to leadership with a distinctive communication approach that examines how leadership communication in terms of styles, behaviors, and messages relates to issues of power, influence, and crisis management within various contexts such as teams, organizations, and the public.

Important Concepts: Define and Discuss

Leadership
Individualistic approach to leadership
Relational approach to leadership
Heroic leadership
Administrative leadership
Trait-based leadership
Behavior-based leadership
Autocratic leadership
Democratic leadership
Transformational leadership
Transactional leadership
Distributed leadership
Actants
Collaborative agency

Discussion Questions

1. Compare and contrast individualistic and relational approaches to leadership. Imagine that you have been asked to design a leadership training program for mid-level managers in an organization. If you adopted a individualistic approach to leadership, what knowledge, skills, and abilities would you emphasize in your training program? What knowledge, skills, and abilities would you emphasize if you adopted a relational approach?

2. When is it more useful to view leadership as primarily a transmission or meaning-making process? Are there particular kinds of situations or problems where it may helpful to view communication through a transmission lens? A meaning-making lens? Both simultaneously?

3. Make a list of the various elements (e.g., task structure, culture, history, gender, etc.) that may serve as a context for leadership communication. What elements do you consider to be most important? Least important? When do particular elements become more or less important? Why?

4. Information and communication technologies (ICTs) have dramatically altered modes of organizing. How might the prevalence of ICTs in contemporary life alter our conceptualizations of individualistic and relational approaches to leadership? Our conceptualizations about leadership communication as a transmission or meaning-making process?

Practitioners' Corner

The study of leadership is marked by a number of varied approaches and perspectives, each generating a distinct take regarding what leadership activities need to be taken to facilitate organizing. For example, the GLOBE leadership studies move individuals to think about the importance of culture while Hersey and Blanchard's life cycle theory focuses attention on the maturity and capacity of the people we are leading and how that might affect the kind of leadership style that is needed to facilitate organizing. Distributed leadership approaches focus our attention on the configuration of individual leaders within an organization and how they are connected with the process of organizing. None of these approaches is necessarily incorrect and the advice that flows from a particular perspective is not inherently wrong. Taken collectively, these various approaches, perspectives, and theories simply provide different lenses to make sense of situations and determine what actions need to be performed.

It is more useful to think of these different perspectives as providing a variety of resources that organizational leaders may use to engage situations and make wise choices about how to act. Simply, organizational leaders need to be become mindful of the situation they are engaging, reflective of their ethical stance that they use when making decision about how to act, and endeavor to create lines of action that fit with the demands of the situation and align with their ethical stance. For example, Scharmer (2016) suggests that leaders need to engage in the activity of "presencing" versus "downloading" as the former directs leaders to attune to the unique qualities of situations and to be open to reconfiguring their perspective on the situation whereas the latter suggests that organizational leaders use a set of *a priori* fixed frameworks to understand and engage situations. Operating from a communication as design perspective, Barge (2012, 2015) suggests that leaders and individuals undertaking leadership activities need to determine what communication problem(s) they are trying to address in the situation, brainstorm various options that might address the problem(s), and select actions that reflect the leader's sensibility or core values regarding how to work working with people and manage the problem(s).

Differing leadership frameworks should not necessarily be viewed as competing; rather, they can be viewed as complementary, each providing a different way to read a situation and offering a different repertoire of actions to perform. From this perspective, organizational leaders need to ask themselves four important questions:

1. What values inform my approach to relating and organizing?
2. How do I frame the problems in the present situation?
3. What communicative actions can I make to address the problems I have named?
4. What communicative actions best fit with my value system and the needs of the situation in order to move the system forward and progress tasks?

The first question requires individuals to reflect on the key values that inform their approach toward relating to people and organizing activity. Questions 2–4 have people draw on their past experience as well as the theoretical frameworks to view the potential problems, actions, and solutions from a variety of perspectives. For example, what problems do I give attention to if I view the situation through Fiedler's leadership contingency theory? Raelin's practice theory? Fairhurst's leadership framing approach? Rather than rely on one's pet theories regarding leadership, an approach based on "presencing" has people examine a situation from multiple perspectives, assuming that the more alternative readings of situations that can be generated, the more likely it is that a leader will select one that fits with the unique characteristics of the situation and will progress tasks. By aligning potential actions simultaneously with a leader's core values and the unique particulars of a situation, leaders can create patterns of interaction over time that are both consistent with their core svalues yet uniquely adapted to the demands of the situation.

References

Balthazard P. A., Waldman, D. A., & Warren, J. E. (2009). Predictions of the emergence of transformational leadership in virtual decision teams. *Leadership Quarterly*, *20*, 651–663. doi:10.1016/j.leaqua.2009.06.008.

Barge, J. K. (2004). Antenarrative and managerial practice. *Communication Studies*, *55*, 106–127. doi:10.1080/10510970409388608.

Barge, J. K. (2012). Systemic constructionist leadership and working from within the present moment. In S. Ospina & M. Uhl-Bien (Eds.), *Advancing relational leadership theory: A conversation among perspectives* (pp. 107–142). Charlotte, NC: Information Age Publishing.

Barge, J. K. (2015). Consulting as collaborative co-inquiry. In G. Bushe & R. Marshak (Eds.), *Dialogic organizational development: Theory and practice* (pp. 177–196). San Francisco: Berrett-Koehler.

Barge, J. K., & Fairhurst, G. F. (2008). Living leadership: A systemic constructionist approach. *Leadership*, *4*, 227–251. doi:10.1177/1742715008092360.

Bass, B. M. (1985). *Leadership and performance beyond expectations*. New York: Free Press.

Berson, Y., & Avolio, B. (2004). Transformational leadership and the dissemination of organizational goals: A case of a telecommunication firm. *Leadership Quarterly*, *15*, 625–646. doi:10.1016/j.leaqua.2004.07.003.

Blake, R. R., & Mouton, J. S. (1994). *The managerial grid*. Houston: Gulf Publishing Company.

Burns, J. M. (1978). *Leadership*. New York: Harper.

Chaudhry, S., & Joshi, C. (2018). Effect of transformational leader communication on affective commitment to change. *International Journal of Leadership*, *6*, 27–35.

Cooren, F., & Fairhurst, G. T. (2004). Speech timing and spacing: The phenomenon of organizational closure. *Organization*, *11*, 797–828. doi:10.1177/1350508404047252.

Denis, J., Langley, A., & Sergi, V. (2012). Leadership in the plural. *The Academy of Management Annals*, *6*, 211–283. doi:10.1080/19416520.2012.667612.

Dorfman, P., Javidan, M., Hanges, P., Dastmalchian, A., & House, R. (2012). GLOBE: A - twenty year journey into the intriguing world of culture and leadership. *Journal of World Business*, *47*, 504–518. doi:10.1016/j.jwb.2012.01.004.

Ensari, N., Riggio, R. E., Christian, J., & Carslaw, G. (2011). Who emerges as a leader? Meta-analyses of individual differences as predictors of leadership emergence. *Personality and Individual Differences*, *51*, 532–536. doi:10.1016/j.paid.2011.05.017.

Fairhurst, G. T. (2007). *Discursive leadership*. Los Angeles: SAGE.

Fairhurst, G. T. (2011). *The power of framing: Creating the language of leadership*. San Francisco: Jossey-Bass.

Fairhurst, G. T., & Connaughton, S. L. (2014a). Leadership: A communicative perspective. *Leadership*, *10*, 7–35. doi:10.1177/1742715013509396.

Fairhurst, G. T., & Connaughton, S. L. (2014b). Leadership. In L. L. Putnam & D. Mumby (Eds.), *The SAGE handbook of organizational communication* (pp. 401–423). Thousand Oaks, CA: SAGE.

Fairhurst, G. T., & Cooren, F. (2009). Leadership as the hybrid production of presence(s). *Leadership*, *5*, 469–490. doi:10.1177/1742715009343033.

Fairhurst, G. T., & Grant, D. (2010). The social construction of leadership: A sailing guide. *Management Communication Quarterly*, *24*, 171–210. doi:10.1177/0893318909359697.

Fairhurst, G. T., Rogers, L. E., and Sarr, R. A. (1987). Management–subordinate control patterns and judgements about the relationship. In M. McLaughin (Ed.), *Communication yearbook 10* (pp. 395–415). Beverly Hills, CA: SAGE.

Fairhurst, G. T., & Sarr, R. A. (1996). *The art of framing: Managing the language of leadership*. San Francisco: Jossey-Bass.

Fairhurst, G. T., & Uhl-Bien, M. (2012). Organizational discourse analysis (ODA): Examining leadership as a relational process. *The Leadership Quarterly, 23*, 1043–1062. doi:10.1016/j. leaqua.2012.10.005.

Fiedler, F. E. (1967). *A theory of leadership effectiveness.* New York: McGraw-Hill.

Grint, K. (2005). Problems, problems, problems: The social construction of leadership. *Human Relations, 58*, 1467–1494.

Grint, K. (2011). A history of leadership. In A. Bryman, D. Collinson, K. Grint, M. Uhl-Bien, & B. Jackson (Eds.), *The SAGE handbook of leadership* (pp. 3–14). London: SAGE. doi:10.1177/0018726705061314.

Hersey, P., Blanchard, K. H., & Dewey, E. J. (2012). *Management of organizational behavior* (10th ed.). New York: Pearson.

Hersted, L. & Gergen, K. J. (2013). *Relational leading: Practices for dialogically based collaboration.* Chagrin Falls, OH: Taos Institute Publications.

Hoffman, B. J., Woeher, D. J., Maldagen-Youngjohn, R., & Lyons, B. D. (2011). Great man or great myth? A quantitative review of the relationship between individual differences and leader effectiveness. *Journal of Occupational and Organizational Psychology, 84*, 347–381. doi:10.1348/096317909X485207.

Javidan, M., Dorfman, P. W., De Luque, M. S., & House, R. J. (2006). In the eye of the beholder: Cross cultural lessons in leadership from Project GLOBE. *Academy of Management Perspectives, 20*(1), 67–90. doi:10.5465/AMP.2006.19873410.

Javidan, M., Dorfman, P. W., Howell, J. P., & Hanges, P. J. (2010). Leadership and cultural context: A theoretical and empirical examination based on Project GLOBE. In N. Nohria & R. Khurana (Eds.), *Handbook of leadership theory and practice* (pp. 335–376). Boston, MA: Harvard Business Press.

Lehman-Willenbrock, N., Meinecke, A. L., Rowold, J., & Kauffeld, S. (2015). How transformational leadership works during team interactions: A behavioral process analysis. *The Leadership Quarterly, 26*, 1017–1033. doi:10.1016/j.leaqua.2015.07.003.

Latour, B. (1999). *Pandora's hope: Essays on the reality of science studies.* Cambridge, MA: Harvard University Press.

Lewin, K., Lippitt, R., & White, R. K. (1939). Patterns of aggressive behavior in experimentally created "social climates." *Journal of Science Psychology, 10*, 271–299.

Manz, C. C., & Sims, H. P., Jr. (2001). *The new super-leadership: Leading others to lead themselves.* San Francisco: Berrett-Koehler.

Martin, R., Guillaume, Y., Thomas, G., Lee, A., & Epitropaki, O. (2016). Leader–member exchange (LMX) and performance: A meta-analytic review. *Personnel Psychology, 69*, 67–121. doi:0.1111/peps.12100.

Meindl, J. R., Ehrlich, S. B., & Dukerich, J. M. (1985). The romance of leadership. *Administrative Science Quarterly, 30*, 78–102. doi:10.2307/255897.

Men, L. R. (2014). Strategic internal communication: Transformational leadership, communication channels, and employee satisfaction. *Management Communication Quarterly, 28*, 264–284. doi:10.1177/0893318914524536.

Oc, B. (2018). Contextual leadership: A systematic review of how contextual factors shape leadership and its outcomes. *The Leadership Quarterly, 29*, 218–235. doi:10.1016/j.leaqua.2017.12.004.

Offermann, L. R., & Coats, M. R. (2018). Implicit theories of leadership: Stability and change over two decades. *The Leadership Quarterly, 29*, 513–522. doi:10.1016/j.leaqua.2017.12.003.

Raelin, J. A. (Ed.). (2016a). *Leadership-as-practice: Theory and application.* New York: Routledge.

Raelin J. A. (2016b). Imagine there are no leaders: Reframing leadership as collaborative agency. *Leadership, 12*, 131–158. doi:10.1177/1742715014558076.

Raelin, J. A. (2016c). It's not about the leaders: It's about the practice of leadership. *Organizational Dynamics, 45*, 124–131. doi:0.1016/j.orgdyn.2016.02.006.

Scharmer, O. C. (2016). *Theory U: Leading from the future as it emerges* (2nd ed.). Oakland, CA: Berrett-Koehler.

Shotter, J. (2011). *Getting it: Withness-thinking and the dialogical... in practice.* Cresskill, NJ: Hampton Press.

Uhl-Bien, M., & Ospina, S. M. (2012). *Advancing relational leadership theory: A conversation among perspectives.* Charlotte, NC: Information Age Publishing.

Uhl-Bien, M., Riggio, R. E., Lowe, K. B., & Carsten, M. K. (2014). Followership theory: A review and research agenda. *The Leadership Quarterly, 25*, 83–104. doi:10.1016/j.leaqua.2013.11.007.

van Knippenberg, D., & Sitkin, S. B. (2013). A critical assessment of charismatic-transformational leadership research: Back to the drawing board? *The Academy of Management Annals, 7*, 1–60. doi:10.1080/19416520.2013.759433.

18 The Structuration of Emotion

Sarah J. Tracy and Shawna Malvini Redden

Organizations and organizing processes are typically presented rationally, as focused on maximizing financial gains and efficient production (Fineman, 2010). The reigning Western discourse of rationality privileges reason, which in turn suggests that emotions interfere with goal-directed economical processes (Dougherty & Drumheller, 2006). Most workplaces expect employees to behave *professionally*, which includes practicing self-control and masking non-prescribed emotions on the job (Cheney & Ashcraft, 2007). Together, these expectations create a disease model of emotions that suggests strong feelings and expressed emotions threaten the health of the workplace and require management (Paul & Riforgiate, 2015).

Indeed, getting emotional is linked to being unprofessional, feminine, and/or even mentally unstable (Waldron, 2012), which helps explain why most early organizational research either ignored emotion or subsumed it under bland variables such as job satisfaction, morale, or commitment (Kramer & Hess, 2002). In the popular imagination, emotion is deemed useful when coupled with masculine characteristics like being tough or showing anger to control others (Lutgen-Sandvik & Tracy, 2012). When employees get upset, stressed, or burned out, discourses of rugged individuality and meritocracy suggest they deal with these issues on their own time, privately, without whining (Lutgen-Sandvik & McDermott, 2008). Indeed, emotional anguish is all but absent in society's grand narratives about work where successful employees gallantly "pull themselves up by their bootstraps" rather than admit feeling burned out due to unmanageable workloads or abusive bosses.

Through the 1990s, management research treated emotion as incompatible with desired behaviors in the workplace because managing emotion was viewed as damaging to productivity (Weiss & Cropanzano, 1996). Meanwhile, communication scholars in the areas of organizations and emotions pretty much ignored one another. Case in point, the index of the *Handbook of Communication and Emotion* (Andersen & Guerrero, 1998) did not include the word *organization*, and the index of the *Handbook of Organizational Communication* (Jablin, Putnam, Roberts, & Porter, 1987) did not include the word *emotion*.

Arguably the first and most influential communication article to question the rationality-emotionality duality was Mumby and Putnam's (1992) research on *bounded emotionality*. They offered bounded emotionality as an alternative to Herbert Simon's (1982) *bounded rationality* (see Chapter 15), suggesting that organizations should encourage employees to experience a range of emotions, including nurturance, care, and supportiveness. From a feminist perspective, Mumby and Putnam (1992) argued that emotion should not be simply used as a rational organizational instrument, but rather that we should examine *work feelings* as integral to organizing. Around this time, organizational psychologists and management scholars began to explore the concept of *emotional intelligence*. This literature suggested that well-timed emotional displays, empathy, and emotion regulation are important characteristics of good leadership and effective organizing (Salovey & Mayer, 1990). Most emotional intelligence research remains siloed in management and organizational psychology, with critical organizational and communication researchers arguing that emotional intelligence research is flavored with instrumental rationality (Murphy, 2014).

Returning to Mumby and Putnam's (1992) plea to revere a range of work feelings, communication scholars have only recently begun to highlight the value of desired emotions like compassion in the workplace (Miller, 2007; Tracy & Huffman, 2017; Way & Tracy, 2012). Most researchers studying emotions like kindness and nurturance have found that care work is undervalued and associated with private, unpaid labor that women have always done—work that is "not credentialed and is considered natural and instinctual rather than due to education or skill" (Tracy, 2008, p. 169). Most organizational communication emotion research has focused on the negative. In this frame, emotion is the problematic result of employee conditions (e.g., emotional exhaustion); something to be harnessed and used by the organization for rational ends (e.g., emotional labor); feminized care work that is naturalized and under-rewarded; and something that when turned into a weapon (e.g., emotional abuse) is considered an individual issue rather than an organizational one.

We begin this chapter by explaining the pragmatic impetus for emotion and organizing research. Second, we review organizing structures and macro-discourses that discipline workplace emotion. Third, we explain the central communicative actions of emotion at work. Fourth, we analyze how employees resist, reify, and sometimes transcend emotion rules and emotional constructions. Along the way, we highlight how organizational communication has extended parallel work from management, organizational psychology, and sociology, and discuss how culture intersects with emotion and organizing. The chapter closes with a structuration model of emotion and organizational communication.

Suffering at Work: The Impetus for Organizational Communication and Emotion Theorizing

"There is nothing so practical as a good theory" (Lewin, 1951, p. 169). For organizational communication and emotion, much related theory is designed to practically explain and ameliorate suffering at work including burnout, compassion fatigue, emotive dissonance, and emotional abuse.

Burnout

Chronologically, burnout was the first problem that motivated organizational communication theorizing related to emotion. Usually considered the general "wearing down" from work pressures, burnout is characterized by emotional exhaustion, depersonalization, cynicism, and decreased personal accomplishment. As a defense mechanism, emotionally exhausted employees distance themselves from work. But, as a result, they experience increased cynicism, callousness, and alienation, which results in decreased job performance and satisfaction (Tracy, 2017).

The most widely used inventory to measure burnout was developed by social psychologist Christina Maslach (1982). The earliest studies in organizational communication used this inventory to explore communication variables that might cause, mitigate, or ameliorate burnout (Miller, Stiff, & Ellis, 1988). Burnout research peaked in the 1990s, but the concept remains popular, with more than 6,000 related academic essays published through 2009 (Schaufeli, Leiter, & Maslach, 2009). Most burnout research has focused on caring professions—such as nursing (Way & Tracy, 2012), corrections (Tracy, 2009), and teaching (Zhang & Zhu, 2008)—that require high levels of client contact and managing the negative emotions of others, something called *toxin management* (Frost, 2004). Such work is typified by conflicting work expectations (e.g., to care for clients yet control or discipline them), work overload, and caring deeply for a job as a calling in the face of its increasing professionalization (Schaufeli et al., 2009).

Compassion Fatigue

Related to burnout is *compassion fatigue*, or the cost of caring. This concept emanated from nursing, sociology, and traumatology, and is similar to vicarious traumatization and secondary traumatic stress as it refers to discomfort resulting from caring for others experiencing traumatic events (Radey & Figley, 2007). Similar to second-hand smoke, certain types of workers regularly bear witness to trauma, and some are quite susceptible to its ill-effects. Past research cautions that when "our hearts go out to our clients through our sustained compassion, our hearts can *give* out from fatigue" (Radey & Figley, 2007, p. 207, emphasis in original). Concern about compassion fatigue has spurred organizational communication research with hospice nurses (Way & Tracy, 2012) and volunteers (McAllum, 2014).

Discomfort of Faking Emotions

A third source of organizational suffering is expressing inauthentic emotion as a requirement of work. Coined by sociologist Arlie Hochschild (1983), *emotive dissonance* is the discomfort that emanates when employees' inner feelings clash with inauthentic outward expression. Many jobs ask employees to amplify, suppress, or transform inappropriate emotions, such as when service employees are expected to smile and suppress irritation (Tracy, 2000), and security employees are expected to maintain stoicism and suspicion (Malvini Redden, 2013). Such work can be alienating when people feel as though they are creating false selves. Furthermore, the pain of emotion work is exacerbated when it conflicts with employees' preferred identities. For instance, most correctional officers prefer to perceive themselves as tough and masculine, and often find it difficult to show deference to convicted criminals (Tracy, 2005). Indeed, being kind or compassionate to stigmatized populations can be challenging, such as with border patrol officers whose work includes caring for undocumented immigrants (Rivera, 2015).

Emotional Abuse and Bullying

A fourth problem motivating emotion and organizational communication research involves emotional abuse at work. Workplace bullying refers to "persistent verbal and nonverbal aggression at work that includes personal attacks, social ostracism, and a multitude of other painful messages and hostile interactions" (Lutgen-Sandvik, 2006, p. 406). Up to 35 percent of employees experience bullying during their working lives, and 11 percent witness coworkers being bullied (Workplace Bullying Institute, 2010). Bullying is linked to psychosomatic illnesses, suicidal ideation, increased medical expenses, and reduced productivity (Lutgen-Sandvik & Tracy, 2012). Targets of workplace bullying describe it as feeling like they are enslaved children and tortured animals forced to suck up noxious substances as they battle demons and "little Hitlers" in an unending nightmare (Tracy, Lutgen-Sandvik, & Alberts, 2006). Moreover, bullying also harms the larger workgroup and bystanders who feel terrified, muted, guilty, and powerless (Lutgen-Sandvik, 2006).

In summary, four main areas of organizational suffering have motivated emotion and organizational communication theorizing—burnout, compassion fatigue, emotive dissonance, and workplace bullying. To address and ameliorate suffering, researchers have investigated the organizational and institutional norms that produce and discipline emotional problems, how problems manifest in employee interactions, and how employees resist, reify, or transcend them. Together, these processes make up the communication-organization spiral dynamic that frames this book. Next, we synthesize the organizational and institutional norms and structures that contribute to emotional suffering at work.

Organizational and Institutional Structures That Discipline and Construct Emotion

Organizations are typically considered to be rational and masculine enterprises where employees should be professional and succeed by their own merit. Discourses of rationality, masculinity, individuality, and meritocracy produce and shape organizational norms about emotions and their (im)proper place at work.

Feeling Rules

Many organizations institute blatant or subtle feeling rules that discipline employees' emotions (Hochschild, 1983). Governing most organizational settings is the expectation to suppress and restrict communication about stress and burnout, something called *communicatively restricted organizational stress* (Boren & Veksler, 2015). In such a model, employees simply put up with hard work and, if they feel stressed, deal with it privately or leave the organization. In addition to this blanket expectation that dominates a majority of workplaces, some employee roles have specific feeling rules, as described by Waldron (2012):

- boundary spanners, like receptionists, should show interest and patience;
- emotional believers, such as clergy, should show calm and faith;
- emotional elicitors, like stand-up comics, should create laughs;
- resilience builders, such as soldiers, should be tough and stoic;
- orchestrators, such as sales team leaders, should amplify their own emotion and motivate it in others;
- coolers and soothers, such as 911 call-takers, should suppress personal anxiety and neutralize others;
- moral emoters, such as activists, should show outrage.

These feeling rules show up formally and informally in employee recruitment materials (Rivera, 2015), socialization rituals (Scott & Myers, 2005), training manuals (Tracy & Tracy, 1998), and performance evaluations (Tracy, 2000).

Gendered and Raced Emotion Norms

Since Hochschild's (1983) groundbreaking research with flight attendants, feeling rules remain gendered and classed. Employees (especially women) in feminized occupations, such as teaching, nursing, social work, and service, are expected to express care and concern for their students and patrons. What's more, much care work goes unnoticed and under-rewarded (England & Folbre, 1999). The myth prevails that paying people too much to be a teacher or nurse, for instance, would attract only those who did the job for the money and did not truly care. Meanwhile, when jobs are associated with caring for low-status clients (e.g., children, the elderly, criminals, undocumented immigrants), those employees must manage contagious stigma and emotional taint (Rivera, 2015). Meanwhile, men (especially white men) typically enjoy a "status shield" that protects them from the "displaced feelings of others" (Hochschild, 1983, p. 163). Due to their greater social status, dominant group members (Razzante & Orbe, 2018) are more likely to be shielded from anger, verbal abuse, and complaints than are marginalized group members, such as women, children, or people of color.

Some in masculine professions, such policing, creative arts, and executive leadership, are allowed and even glorified for being angry, tough, and verbally abusive (e.g., an ex-reality television star turned U.S. president who got famous for yelling, "You're fired!") (Razzante, Tracy, & Orbe, 2018). However, even when marginalized group members hold masculinized or high-status positions, they are not afforded the same luxury as dominant group members in terms of expressing a range of emotion. Instead they are often sexualized, ignored, or exemplified as angry (Forbes, 2009). As Collins argues:

> Aggressive Black and Hispanic men are seen as dangerous, not powerful, and are often penalized when they exhibit any of the allegedly "masculine" characteristics. Working class and poor White men fare slightly better and are also denied the allegedly "masculine" symbols of leadership, intellectual competence, and human rationality. Women of color and working class and poor White women are also not represented [by universal gender symbolism], for they have never had the luxury of being "ladies."
>
> (Collins, 1998, pp. 217–218)

In sum, feeling rules along with racial and gendered discourses allow some employees more than others to freely perform a full range of emotions at work.

Empathy, Care, and Emotional Intelligence are Underrated

Empathy, care, and emotional intelligence are largely underrated and under-rewarded in organizational settings. *Emotional intelligence* refers to a set of capabilities that include emotional self-awareness, emotional self-regulation, motivating oneself and others, and empathizing with the emotions of others (Salovey & Mayer, 1990). These capabilities have been linked with stronger relationships, trust, and higher organizational productivity (Harvard Business Review, 2015). However, few organizations directly reward employees for these capabilities. Despite the fact that emotional intelligence and its attendant literature has put one of the few "positive faces" on emotions and organizing (see Goleman, 1995), the concept has come under critique due to its association with using emotions as a means to profit (Dougherty & Krone, 2002).

Emotional Abuse Is Enabled by Workplace Structures

Organizational structures produce and enable emotional abuse at work. Lutgen-Sandvik and McDermott argue that employee abuse emerges from the

> meanings inherent in contemporary workplaces [that] come from an amalgamation of economic theory, religious and secularized ideals of work, the merger of corporate interests and governing bodies, ... [belief in] rugged individualism, [the dogma of] meritocracy, and the ideology of entrepreneurialism.
> (Lutgen-Sandvik & McDermott, 2008, p. 317)

Such discourses penalize employees perceived as weak or thin-skinned, and link tough treatment to increased productivity and "just the way the world works." When bad behavior is too blatant to ignore, workplaces tend to focus on bad apples rather than organizational structures. However, individual "bad apple" behavior spills into larger work processes and, therefore, can spoil the barrel (Felps, Mitchell, & Byington, 2006).

Most workplace bullies are supervisors, and when targets seek help, human resource professionals are often at a loss because they view workplace abuse as competitive rather than objectively hostile (Cowan, 2012). Therefore, workplace policies (or lack thereof) often condone abusive behavior (Keashly & Jagatic, 2003). In more than 70 percent of cases, bullying targets believe that upper management is complicit in the abuse, whether due to inaction or through managerial intervention that worsens the situation (Namie & Lutgen-Sandvik, 2010). Indeed, human resource policies are largely ineffective for punishing "equal opportunity" workplace jerks who are abusive without obvious demographic-specific discrimination. And, even when companies institute well-being programs, they tend to focus on individual rather than collective concerns of employee health (Ganesh & McAllum, 2010). In short, numerous organizational and societal structures enable emotional suffering at work.

Employee Communicative Action in Relationship to Emotion and Organizing

Employees respond to organizational structures and larger societal discourses via emotional labor, care work, empathic concern, and workplace bullying.

Emotional Labor

Defined by sociologist Arlie Hochschild (1983), *emotional labor* is the commodification of emotion or the process of people managing their emotions in line with organizational expectations and training. In practice, emotional labor involves people shaping their emotional communication, frequently to suppress negative emotions and to amplify emotions that foster organizational goals. For instance, customer service workers are usually trained to conduct "service with a smile"—suppressing anger with rude customers while amplifying cheerfulness. However, in some occupations like law enforcement, organizationally preferred emotion management may look stoical, where people cultivate composure in difficult situations even when they feel anxious or scared.

Hochschild (1983) differentiated between types of emotional labor by discussing processes of deep and surface acting. Employees engage in *surface acting* when they force emotions they do not actually feel, like when airport security officers perform an intimidating "commanding presence" when they actually feel angry, bored, or compassionate (Scarduzio & Malvini Redden, 2015, p. 7). Discrepancies in felt and expressed emotions results in *emotive dissonance*, which is associated with tension and strain (Ashforth & Humphrey, 1993). When employees feel compelled to generate inauthentic emotions they do not agree with—what Rafaeli and Sutton (1987) call "faking in bad faith"—they are likely to experience more significant consequences, such as burnout, depression, and cynicism. On the contrary, when employees both feel and demonstrate the required emotional display, they may engage in *deep acting* which is an effortful process of changing internal feelings to match organizational requirements. Over time, however, deep acting can lead to alienation from personal feelings.

Examining power relations is vital to understanding whether employees will feel discomfort with emotional labor. Faking low-status emotions that conflict with preferred identities can be much more difficult than feigning those that line up with dominant, affirmative organizational discourses (Tracy, 2005). Simulating low-status emotions is easier when employees engage in acts of interpersonal resistance, something we return to in a following section about employee agency. Likewise, while most research focuses on employee experiences of emotional labor, some scholarship considers the complex interplay between organizational members and patrons. In compulsory interactions in airport security checkpoints, patrons in low-power positions are required to demonstrate emotional performances in line with organizational expectations, which are negotiated through interactions with security officers in positions of power rather than spelled out in policies (Malvini Redden, 2013). These emotional performances or *emotional taxes* are similar to financial penalties—required for everyone—but can vary depending upon factors such as interpersonal interactions and personal identity.

Compassion

Compassion is another important emotional process in organizations (Miller, 2007) and includes three primary components: (a) Recognizing verbal and nonverbal cues from others, as well as the context and subtext of interactions; (b) relating, which involves "identifying with, feeling for, and communicatively connecting with another to enable sharing of emotions, values, and decisions"; and (c) reacting, which involves communicating compassionately (Way & Tracy, 2012, p. 307). Compassion in organizations can improve relationships, customer service, productivity, and reputation (Men, 2014). However, some compassion work involves burnout-inducing toxin management (Frost, 2004).

Although the emotional labor literature suggests that feminized care work is low status and exhausting, some populations like hospice nurses seem to thrive. Rather than their hearts giving out due to strain, their hearts actually get stronger and more capable through work (Way & Tracy, 2012). This may be due to the hospice context, where the overall goal is to provide comfort (in contrast to hospitals where the goal is to cure). This also suggests that organizational visions and norms influence whether the same behavior (e.g., caring) is experienced as exhausting or enriching.

Workplace Emotional Abuse, Bullying, and Microaggressions

Employee communicative action becomes very difficult when organizational structures enable antisocial behaviors like microaggressions, emotional abuse, and workplace bullying. Defined as "subtle, intentional, or unintentional prejudicial or discriminatory words or behaviors" (Shenoy-Packer, 2015, p. 258), *microaggressions* are small actions that can cause serious emotional consequences as they are often tied to critical identity markers like race/ethnicity, gender, culture, size, and ability. For example, over time, questions and comments like, "What are you?" or "You speak such good English" can *other* racial minorities. Likewise, microaggressions often feature as tools leading to workplace bullying.

Bullying is a communicative process that involves ongoing, escalating, and repeated significant physical or psychological harm between a bully and target with disparate power positions in organizations (Lutgen-Sandvik & Tracy, 2012). Bullying comes in a variety of communicative forms, including spreading rumors, public humiliation, abusive language, and constant criticism. Furthermore, these behaviors are accomplished with a persistence that intensifies abuse, differentiating it from incivilities or microaggressions. For example, occasionally yelling at a coworker does not equate to bullying. However, screaming, swearing at, and isolating the same coworker day after day, week after week, does.

Targets of abuse usually perceive that bullies are acting on purpose (Tracy, Lutgen-Sandvik et al., 2006). Abusive behaviors—whispering, insults, gossip, sneering, eye-rolling—can be traumatizing over time. Bullying victims often have trouble describing the abuse, although narratives show that targets experience significant loss, isolation, and lack of social support from bystanders who are more likely to ignore bullying than intervene (Tye-Williams & Krone, 2015).

Employees Agentically Sediment, Resist, and Transcend Emotion Issues at Work

Despite the grim picture that emerges from much emotion research, organizational communication scholarship has also examined how employees agentically shape their emotional constructions and organizations' emotion rules. Employee action can involve (a) sedimenting and reinforcing, (b) resisting, and (c) transcending.

Sedimenting and Reinforcing

As structuration theory posits (Giddens, 1984), structures are constructed and reinforced by action. Organizational communication research shows that employees can also reinforce and sediment emotion norms and related discourses. For instance, employees tend to reinforce the dichotomy between emotionality and rationality by carefully controlling their emotions in organizations, denying emotions altogether, reframing experiences to depersonalize emotions, discussing emotions in rationalized ways, and relegating emotions to private spaces (Dougherty & Drumheller, 2006). By de-emphasizing emotion and repeating rationalist discourses about professionalism, prevailing norms are reinforced and sedimented.

Employees can also reinforce emotional labor expectations via cynicism and disidentification. For instance, the idea of distancing or making fun of one's work role may appear to be resistance. However, disidentification can ironically facilitate emotional labor expectations. Consider a disgruntled fast food worker who wears a "McShit" T-shirt under her uniform to show that her "real" self sees through the absurdity of minimum wage work. However, her secret act of rebellion might actually preclude more blatant or consequential resistance (Fleming & Spicer, 2003) and, therefore, may strengthen the organization's feeling rules. Likewise, correctional officers who view work as "just a job" and find confirmation of their identity and success outside of work appear to more successfully engage in emotion labor without undue discomfort (Tracy, 2005). As noted by Fleming and Spicer (2003, p. 160), "when we dis-identify with our prescribed social roles we often still perform them—sometimes better, ironically, than if we did identify with them."

Emotional abuse can also be sedimented through activity at the workgroup level. Consider bystanders to workplace bullying who join in to mock a colleague. Their actions reinforce problematic emotion cycles and make it difficult to change organizational culture. Hareli and Rafaeli (2008) describe emotion cycles as a "double-interact social process" (p. 37) where a person's emotion is communicated, shared, and made sense of by another, who then reciprocates with an emotional process that can continue or change the cycle. Emotion cycles can reinforce emotion norms or give sense about organizational processes to others (Scarduzio & Tracy, 2015). For instance, in municipal courtrooms, bailiffs function as intermediaries in the emotion cycle; for example, by downplaying a judge's anger to help a defendant, or by laughing at a judge's unfunny joke to keep a positive mood.

In the case of complex emotion cycles like workplace bullying, opportunities for agency and control are complicated. Followers are likely to endure abuse when the organizational climate tolerates or ignores negative leader behavior (Thoroughgood, Hunter, & Sawyer, 2011). Sometimes targets of bullying go through official channels to address the problem and find human resource professionals believe that bullying is a direct manager's issue and not an organizational problem (Cowan, 2012). Likewise, well-intentioned peers may offer bad advice by recommending that the bullied employee simply "keep calm" and "stay rational." Such advice discounts the severity of abuse, emphasizes the role of the individual over the organization, and constrains individual agency (Tye-Williams & Krone, 2017).

Resistance

Although employees themselves can sediment and reinforce feeling rules and emotional abuse, they also resist in ingenious ways. In stressful, stigmatized, and rule-bound work, employees can draw on larger discourses to create positive identities, as with restaurant workers who create identities of flexibility, empathy, and composure in the face of stigma (Hanners, 2018). Employees can also refuse to buy into feeling rules by blatantly ignoring them via emotional deviance, which is considered to be "the opposite of emotional dissonance because the organizational member expresses inner feelings and disregards feeling rules" (Rafaeli & Sutton, 1987, p. 33). Examples of emotional deviance include a pastor who giggles during a funeral or a food server who rolls her eyes at a customer's ridiculous request. Emotional deviance can serve several agentic purposes, including providing employees with distance, a break from emotion rules, and relief from monotonous tasks.

Some employees are able to deviate from emotion rules without penalty more than others. People in high-power professions associated with masculinity and whiteness, such as law, medicine, and academia, more easily deviate. Such is the case with judges who enact "robe-itis," and let the power of their formal black robe go to their heads. Via what Scarduzio (2011) calls *privileged deviance*, judges regularly break from expectations that they should be solemn and neutral, and instead joke with defendants. People with marginalized identities like women and people of color are more likely to feel compelled to play by the rules (Razzante & Tracy, 2019). Related, employees say they are more likely to resist and blow the whistle on abusive leaders when the leader is female (Thoroughgood et al., 2011).

Employees also find creative ways to resist workplace bullying and emotional abuse. Although ambiguous human resource policies can often discourage intervention (Cowan, 2012), bystanders, witnesses, and supervisors can intercede. In particular, traditionally powerful employees may impede and dismantle abuse (Razzante & Orbe, 2018). Some organizations have also instituted bystander training, where employees learn to increase affirmative communication, speak up when they witness problematic interactions, and re-source problematic behavior (Foss & Foss, 2011). Depending on the context, effective bystander intervention affirms positive behavior, corrects emotionally abusive behavior, and may include immediate intervention (Bowes-Sperry & O'Leary-Kelly, 2005). Interference could be employees saying, "Hey, stop being such a bully, dude" or redirecting to a new topic, something called *conversational pivoting* (Foss & Foss, 2011). A bystander could also comfort targets. This last type of action may not immediately change the behavior but would help the organization maintain high-quality connections (Dutton, 2003) and help employees cope—a topic we turn to next.

Coping

Employees engage in many coping techniques—another form of enacting agency in response to emotional pressures at work. To practice compassion without fatigue, employees balance involvement with detachment. This is accomplished by feeling *for* clients via empathic concern rather than feeling *with* clients via emotional contagion (Miller, 2007). Indeed, if a client is in deep despair, caregivers should generally avoid joining them. Showing concern without feeling clients' negative emotions is a balancing act, however. Some workers descend into depersonalization or aloofness that, while useful for self-protection, does not usually accomplish organizational goals (Miller et al., 1988).

Compassion is also best accomplished by setting boundaries, making sure the compassion-giver has privacy, and ensuring social support (Miller, 2007). Indeed, having the ability to talk through workplace stressors can help employees make sense of frustrating, identity threatening, or demanding work. When employees feel constricted in talking about workplace frustrations, this results in *communicatively restricted organization stress* (CROS) (Boren & Veksler, 2015). At the same time, excessive negative talk and co-rumination can exacerbate burnout when people focus on problems rather than potential solutions (Boren, 2014).

Similar to bystander intervention, the effectiveness of social support depends on context. As Tracy describes:

Instrumental support (an exchange of time, resources or labor) helps prevent emotional exhaustion and depersonalization, and as such, may enhance the care and treatment of clients. Informational support (related to role definition, general information about job, skills training) is related to increased retention. Emotional support (empathy, caring, acceptance and assurance) is directly related to retention, commitment and all dimensions of burnout.

(Tracy, 2009, p. 88)

Support from like-minded peers can be more effective than help from researchers, family, or friends (Lutgen-Sandvik, 2006). Organizational superiors also can help alleviate emotional exhaustion by decreasing workloads, providing recognition and rewards, fostering fairness, and increasing employee participation in decision-making (Leiter & Maslach, 2011). Indeed, employees who help "creat[e] their work environment feel more powerful and accomplished. Further, having a voice … helps them deal with rules or regulations that would otherwise be framed as debilitating constraints or irritating hassles" (Tracy, 2017, p. 5).

Social support is especially useful for workplace abuse targets because abusive interactions "linger in a hundred conversations as members of the original audience re-encounter one another and negotiate the meaning of the original event" (Waldron, 2000, p. 68). Rehashing can affect workplace productivity, re-victimize targets, and poison organizational climates (Lutgen-Sandvik & McDermott, 2008). However, when bullied employees make sense of their experience with coworkers or other bullying targets, they feel less isolated (Tracy, Lutgen-Sandvik et al., 2006). Some employees even construct elaborate collective revenge fantasies (Tye-Williams & Krone, 2015). Although these fantasies may not transform bullying, they help employees to reframe the problem and create preferred identities (Lutgen-Sandvik, 2008).

Thriving and Overcoming

Prosocial emotions can also be cultivated at work to help people not only overcome problems but thrive. Flourishing is different than simply surviving. It's an agentic activity that allows employees to transcend emotional suffering. For example, organizational members use humor to manage stress and bond with coworkers, which fosters organizational identification, and reduces job-related stress (Tracy, Myers, & Scott, 2006). Humor and affirmative behaviors like praise and acknowledgment create healthy organizational cultures (Bowes-Sperry & O'Leary-Kelly, 2005) and open the door for "high-quality interpersonal connections" characterized by trust and respect (Dutton, 2003). For instance, joking helps public safety employees make light of dangerous work and eases the tension of worrying family members (Bochantin, 2017). These communicative processes, when they involve regular, positive experiences, help people feel important and included, building resilience (Lutgen-Sandvik, Riforgiate, & Fletcher, 2011).

Psychologically speaking, resilience is an important skill involving the ability to bounce back from challenges or recover from crisis (Richardson, 2002). A social process "grounded in messages, d/Discourse, and narrative" (Buzzanell, 2010, p. 2), resilience involves maintaining social ties and creatively reframing difficulties. Cultivating resilience does not ignore related negative emotions but instead focuses on productive actions that help people work through challenges. One way people cultivate resilience is through mindfulness practices. Individually, this might include setting aside judgment to "practice acceptance, kindness, and openness, even when what is occurring … is contrary to deeply held wishes or expectations" (Shapiro, Carlson, Astin, & Freedman, 2006, p. 377). In organizations, an orientation of "nonattachment" encourages people to reframe their subject positions to reduce personal ego and see themselves and their coworkers as interdependent (Brummans & Hwang, 2010). This orientation can enable compassion, flexibility, attention, discipline, and wisdom.

Culture, Gender, and the Constitution of Organizing via Emotion

Chapter 1 defined communication as "a symbolic process of creating and sharing meaning." As illustrated in this chapter, emotion and organizational communication literature conceptualize communication as a method employees use to attend to an organization's feeling rules, a manner in which emotional abuse manifests due to larger structural norms that value rationality and expertise over emotional intelligence, and a way that organizations try to help employees know the meaning of their work through specific types of feeling rules. In this section, we return to issues of culture and gender, and examine emotion and the communicative constitution of organizing and organization.

Culture and Gender

Organizational emotion processes are embedded in and shaped by discourses of culture and gender. Emotional experiences can be spurred by cultural and identity differences such as gender, ethnicity, race, or class (Malvini Redden & Scarduzio, 2017) (see also Chapters 11–14). Meanwhile, organizational processes perpetuate discriminatory or difficult emotion practices such as racialized feeling rules in professional workplaces (Wingfield, 2010) and training that prioritizes cheerful Western emotion norms (Raz & Rafaeli, 2007).

Understanding emotional abuse at work requires consideration of identity, as gender, ethnicity, and race are historically stigmatizing markers that contribute to workplace bullying. Marginalized workforce members are easier targets for bullying and enjoy less flexibility in acceptable emotional displays (Meares, Oetzel, Derkacs, & Ginossar, 2004). Indeed, women and people of color regularly experience a range of negative social phenomena (Allen, 2009). Within the emotion and organizing literature, scholars examine culture and gender as they influence individual employees as well as larger organizational structures. So, how do these communicative practices constitute organizing and organization?

O_1—Organizing

Consider organizing as a verb or, as explained in Chapter 1, the process of coordinating/ ordering among members of a social collective. What does this look like in the emotion and organizational communication literature? Emotion research shows how work feelings cycle through collective groups (Hareli & Rafaeli, 2008). For example, judges sometimes express sarcasm to misbehaving defendants, and the defendants' response affects whether bailiffs amplify harsh emotion or compensate for it through comforting behavior (Scarduzio & Tracy, 2015). This cycling of emotion through organizational workgroups is accomplished through verbal and nonverbal messaging. Organizational communication scholarship shows how both negative and positive emotion is contagious, rippling through mentoring sessions, hushed hallway conversations, and employee training. For instance, teachers communicatively construct resilience in response to burnout via collective sensemaking and storytelling that frames organizational challenges as meaningful growth opportunities (Kamrath, 2018).

O_2—*Organized*

This chapter also illuminates O_2, *organized* (adj.), which is the "state of a social collective's coordination/order" (see Chapter 1). Emotion research explicates the structuring of workplace coordination showing, for example, that emotion rules are strongest when employees identify with and buy into organizational norms. Furthermore, emotion and organizing research has illuminated concepts like emotional intelligence, and now this term frequently appears in trainings and performance reviews (Harvard Business Review, 2015). Using the term *emotional intelligence*, employees are encouraged and rewarded for expressing emotion appropriately, listening, and empathizing with others.

Workplace bullying was an almost unheard-of term at the turn of the century. Now the term returns 702,000 Google hits in .36 seconds (as of Fall 2018). Increasing numbers of workplaces have policies about bullying, such as University of California, Berkeley's Workplace Bullying Prevention Policy, instituted in 2016 (University of California, Berkeley, 2016). This policy mirrors conceptualizations of workplace bullying that have emerged in a range of scholarship, including organizational communication. Indeed, years earlier, the Berkeley ombudsman office publicly posted a white paper, now book chapter, by communication scholars Tracy, Alberts, and Rivera (2007) called "How to Bust the Office Bully."

Emotional labor, despite its dominance in organizational communication research, is not as clearly powerful as the other research at constituting organizations. Despite calls to do so, emotional labor is curiously missing from most performance reviews (Poly, 2015). This may not be surprising; societal discourses tend to naturalize emotion work (especially feminized care work) so much that *emotional labor* may be an almost invisible concept to most organizational practitioners.

O_3—*Organizations*

Chapter 1 discusses organizations as nouns, or as coordinated and ordered entities arising from O_1 and O_2. Emotion and organizational communication scholarship tends to implicitly treat organizations as neutral environments. Much research studies interactional behavior at the individual and group level with the organization as a container or backdrop. That said, critical scholars have examined how organizational histories and genealogies affect emotion labor norms (e.g., Tracy, 2000) and organizational climates and policies affect workplace bullying (Cowan, 2012).

The research reviewed herein has also constituted academic organizations such as specialized emotion conferences, institutes, and LISTSERVs including the now 1,400-member Emonet. Likewise, research centers have sprung up such as the Center for Positive Organizing at the University of Michigan and the Greater Good Center at UC Berkeley. Organizational entities associated with workplace bullying have also emerged. Public scholarship has led to documentaries, specialized institutes like the Workplace Bullying Institute, and movement toward anti-bullying laws (Namie, Namie, & Lutgen-Sandvik, 2010).

Finally, the continued attention on burnout and stress in organizations has arguably contributed to wellness and employee assistance programs that feature a menu of activities ranging from fitness challenges to chair massages to anger management. Such programs, although popular, tend to focus on individual rather than collective concerns of employee health (Ganesh & McAllum, 2010), as do products like the "fidget cube," essential oils, and adult coloring books.

Conclusion

As demonstrated, the emotion and organizing literature exemplifies the C-O spiral in many ways. The literature shows how larger discourses, organizational policies, and employee talk create organizational feeling rules that enable and constrain emotional expression. Meanwhile, institutional human resource processes enable the destructive communication of "equal opportunity" jerks, and employee resistance can ironically result in even harsher or more stringent treatment in organizations.

Taken together, the complex and varied literature about emotion in organizations contributes to organizational practices and the way employees, supervisors, and the general public interpret such practices. The research hopefully has helped people see that emotion in the workplace is not only something that gets in the way of organizing but also as something that can enhance the workplace experience. Furthermore, a desired result is that when people are better able to name and define various types of emotional suffering (e.g., compassion fatigue, burnout, bullying, emotive dissonance), they know they are not alone and might even have avenues to survive or transcend the suffering.

Supplementary Readings

Bochantin, J. E. (2017). "Ambulance thieves, clowns, and naked grandfathers": How PSEs and their families use humorous communication as a sensemaking device. *Management Communication Quarterly, 31*(2), 278–296.
An exemplar of humor, sensemaking, and work–life balance among public safety employees.
Dougherty, D. S., & Drumheller, K. (2006). Sensemaking and emotions in organizations: Accounting for emotions in a rational(ized) context. *Communication Studies, 57*(2), 215–238.
Critiques the priority of rationality over emotionality in organizations.
Hareli, S., & Rafaeli, A. (2008). Emotion cycles: On the social influence of emotion in organizations. *Research in Organizational Behavior, 28*, 35–59.
The original discussion of emotion cycles in organizations, focusing primarily on negative emotion cycles.
Hochschild, A. R. (1983). *The managed heart: Commercialization of human feeling.* Berkeley, CA: University of California Press.
The book that coined key terms of emotional labor, surface and deep acting, and emotive dissonance.
Huffman, T. P. (2017). Compassionate communication, embodied aboutness, and homeless young adults. *Western Journal of Communication, 81*(2), 149–167.
Drawing upon experiences of homeless youth, Huffman depicts the embodied enactment of compassion.
Lutgen-Sandvik, P., & Tracy, S. J. (2012). Answering five key questions about workplace bullying: How communication scholarship provides a thought leadership for transforming abuse at work. *Management Communication Quarterly, 26*, 3–47.
A synthesis of the workplace bullying literature in organizational communication.

Malvini Redden, S., & Scarduzio, J. A. (2017). A different type of dirty work: Hidden taint, intersectionality, and emotion management in bureaucratic organizations. *Communication Monographs*, 1–21.
This study shows how professional occupations can involve difficult, identity- and emotion-related dirty work.
Miller, K. (2002). The experience of emotion in the workplace: Professing in the midst of tragedy. *Management Communication Quarterly, 15*(4), 571–600. doi:10.1177/0893318902154003.
Emotional labor is used as a lens to vividly and autoethnographically examine a workplace tragedy.
Rivera, K. D. (2015). Emotional taint: Making sense of emotional dirty work at the US Border Patrol. *Management Communication Quarterly, 29*(2), 198–228.
Rivera coins the term "emotional taint" to describe work that is "dirty" by virtue of the emotion it requires.
Tracy, S. J., & Huffman, T. P. (2017). Compassion in the face of terror: A case study of recognizing suffering, co-creating hope, and developing trust in a would-be school shooting. *Communication Monographs, 84*(1), 30–53.
This article provides a vivid picture for communicating compassion when sufferers are angry, threatening, or resisting help.
Tracy, S. J., Lutgen-Sandvik, P., & Alberts, J. K. (2006). Nightmares, demons and slaves: Exploring the painful metaphors of workplace bullying. *Management Communication Quarterly, 20*, 148–185.
Using drawing and metaphor analysis, this article shows what workplace bullying feels like.

Important Concepts: Define and Discuss

Bounded emotionality
Burnout
Compassion (fatigue)
Communicatively restricted organizational stress (CROS)
Deep acting, surface acting
Discourses of individualism, meritocracy, rationality, and masculinity
(dis)Identification
Emotional deviance
Emotional Intelligence
Emotional labor
Emotive dissonance
Emotional taint and dirty work
Emotional taxes
Feeling rules/emotion norms
Microaggressions
Resilience
Workplace bullying

Discussion Questions

1. Identify organizational and institutional discourses that shape emotional experiences for employees (e.g., rationality, individuality). How do these structures shape emotion at personal, organizational, and societal levels?
2. How have you resisted or participated in emotion management norms?
3. How can workplace policy and/or employee communication improve workplace emotional experiences?

4. What emotional cycles have you experienced? How does considering emotion socially, and in relationship to organizational and discursive structures, shape your understanding of how emotions influence organizing?

Practitioners' Corner

Emotion and Communication Go to the Airport

Since the September 11, 2001 terrorist attacks and subsequent creation of the Transportation Security Administration (TSA), airport security is steeped with Discourses about terrorism, safety, privacy, and authority. On one hand, macro-level conversations about security are rife with critiques of security policies. However, millions of people submit to TSA procedures daily in order to fly. In doing so, they are complicit in practices that curb personal freedoms.

For Transportation Security Officers (TSOs), emotional experiences are complicated by organizational training and mandates; many require difficult, sustained emotional performances of intimidation and composure. TSOs are trained to prevent terrorist attacks with the mantra "not on my watch" and are bombarded with pseudo-military and patriotic messaging regarding duty to country. However, the material reality of TSO work is physically processing thousands of people and constantly managing emotions. Furthermore, TSOs do not enjoy many affirmative discourses about their occupation outside of organizational training.

Consider a typical trip to the airport. People regularly worry about long lines, security screenings, and missing flights. It's not uncommon for people to be sleep deprived and anxious about getting through quickly. Imagine a tired, uncertain passenger—irritated by long, winding lines and fellow passengers who take forever loading their belongings on the conveyor belt—being confronted by a TSO who says they've done something wrong. They will need a bag search and full body pat-down. The passenger—now angry because they've flown before, know what they're doing, and are very worried about the extra time—starts rudely ranting to the TSO about feeling unfairly singled out. The TSO explains that something in the passenger's bag looked suspicious and protocol dictates extra screening.

The passenger belittles the officer, shouting about how their taxes pay TSO salaries and that TSOs are glorified security guards who couldn't make it into "real" law enforcement anyway. In turn, the officer stays outwardly neutral, sharing that they only enforce and do not create rules. But the TSO moves slower now, performing the pat-down with unnecessary thoroughness. The passenger runs to make the plane, careening through airport crowds while the TSO, still seething but amused that the passenger will probably miss the flight now, turns to face the next person in line. The passenger barely makes it, lucky to gain admittance as they were past the airline's boarding deadline. Instead of acting grateful, however, the passenger scans packed overhead bins and doesn't see a single available space. While trying to cram a duffel bag into an overfull bin, a flight attendant says the bag must be checked. The passenger laments that it is unfair since security caused the delay and tells the flight attendant to stop being such a "bitch" and just help already. The flight attendant keeps a placid grin plastered on and explains how it would be less fair to move the luggage of people who arrived on time. It's the fifth passenger meltdown today, and there are still two more legs before the flight attendant is off work. It's no wonder that a Jet Blue flight attendant lost it a few years ago and, after a profanity-laced rant over the PA system, grabbed a beer and exited the plane via an inflatable ramp (Newman & Rivera, 2010)!

In this mini case study, inspired by past research about airport security (Malvini Redden, 2013), it's easy to see how emotion influences communication at many levels, and is shaped by organizational and institutional structures. For passengers, emotional management is informed by personal experiences of airport security and air travel, as well as macro-level discourses like news about security. Likewise, the airport context is surrounded by broad social Discourses about terrorism and how airport security is meant to ensure national safety. Furthermore, the reality of flying involves significant anxiety and embodied time pressures. When passengers are primed to be unsettled, it's not surprising that security lines provoke further negative feelings and upsets.

Think about the downstream effects of interactions described in the case. Will the emotion cycle co-created in security promote many positive emotions? How will the passenger treat fellow travelers on the airplane or interact with flight attendants who might issue more directions that seem "unfair"? How will the TSO cope with passenger ranting? Will the officer seek social support from coworkers? If so, will those conversations involve excessive co-rumination that will just make the situation feel worse? Or, perhaps their talk will contribute to negative discourses about passengers who "check their brains with their baggage." What if the passenger complained to the TSO's manager who, unbeknown to the passenger, is an emotionally abusive bully? If the interaction had been racially charged, would the passenger or TSO perhaps feel singled out because of ethnicity? Now think about the organizational structures and processes that shape security interactions—the requisite emotional performances for TSOs and the processes purposefully meant to provoke anxiety in passengers (Malvini Redden, 2013). Certainly, these organizational processes constrain agency for patrons and employees alike.

References

Allen, B. J. (2009). Racial harassment in the workplace. In P. Lutgen-Sandvik & B. D. Sypher (Eds.), *Destructive organizational communication: Processes, consequences, and constructive ways of organizing* (pp. 164–183). New York: Routledge/Taylor & Francis.

Andersen, P. A., & Guerrero, L. K. (Eds.). (1998). *Handbook of communication and emotion: Research, theory, applications, and contexts.* San Diego, CA: Academic Press.

Ashforth, B. E., & Humphrey, R. H. (1993). Emotional labor in service roles: The influence of identity. *Academy of Management Review, 18,* 88–115. doi:10.2307/258824.

Bochantin, J. E. (2017). "Ambulance thieves, clowns, and naked grandfathers": How PSEs and their families use humorous communication as a sensemaking device. *Management Communication Quarterly, 31,* 278–296. doi:10.1177/0893318916687650.

Boren, J. P. (2014). The relationships between co-rumination, social support, stress, and burnout among working adults. *Management Communication Quarterly, 28*(1), 3–25. doi:10.1177/0893318913509283.

Boren, J. P., & Veksler, A. E. (2015). Communicatively Restricted Organizational Stress (CROS) I: Conceptualization and overview. *Management Communication Quarterly, 29,* 28–55. doi:10.1177/0893318914558744.

Bowes-Sperry, L., & O'Leary-Kelly, A. M. (2005). To act or not to act: The dilemma faced by sexual harassment observers. *Academy of Management Review, 30*(2), 288–306. doi:10.5465/AMR.2005.16387886.

Brummans, B. H., & Hwang, J. M. (2010). Tzu Chi's organizing for a compassionate world: Insights into the communicative praxis of a Buddhist organization. *Journal of International and Intercultural Communication*, 3(2), 136–163. doi:10.1080/17513051003611610.

Buzzanell, P. M. (2010). Resilience: Talking, resisting, and imagining new normalcies into being. *Journal of Communication*, 60, 1–14. doi:10.1111/j.1460-2466.2009.01469.x.

Cheney, G., & Ashcraft, K. L. (2007). Considering "the professional" in communication studies: Implications for theory and research within and beyond the boundaries of organizational communication. *Communication theory*, 17(2), 146–175. doi:10.1111/j.1468-2885.2007.00290.x.

Collins, P. H. (1998). Toward a new vision: Race, class, and gender as categories of analysis and connection. In M. L. Anderson & P. H. Collins (Eds.), *Race, class, and gender: An anthology* (pp. 213–223). Belmont, CA: Wadsworth.

Cowan, R. L. (2012). It's complicated: Defining workplace bullying from the human resource professional's perspective. *Management Communication Quarterly*, 26, 377–403. doi:10.1177/0893318912439474.

Dougherty, D. S., & Drumheller, K. (2006). Sensemaking and emotions in organizations: Accounting for emotions in a rational(ized) context. *Communication Studies*, 57(2), 215–238. doi:10.1080/10510970600667030.

Dougherty, D. S., & Krone, K. J. (2002). Emotional intelligence as organizational communication: An examination of the construct. *Annals of the International Communication Association*, 26, 202–229. doi:10.1080/23808985.2002.11679014.

Dutton, J. (2003). *Energizing your workplace*. Ann Arbor, MI: University of Michigan Press.

England, P., & Folbre, N. (1999). The cost of caring. *The Annals of the American Academy of Political and Social Science*, 561(1), 39–51. doi:10.1177/000271629956100103.

Felps, W., Mitchell, T., & Byington, E. (2006). How, when and why bad apples spoil the barrel: Negative group members and dysfunctional groups. *Research in Organizational Behavior*, 27, 175–222. doi:10.1016/S0191-3085(06)27005-9.

Fineman, S. (2010). Emotion in organizations—a critical turn. In B. Sieben & A. Wettergren (Eds.), *Emotionalizing organizations and organizing emotions* (pp. 23–41). London: Palgrave Macmillan. doi:10.1057/9780230289895_2.

Fleming, P., & Spicer, A. (2003). Working at a cynical distance: Implications for power, subjectivity and resistance. *Organization*, 10(1), 157–179. doi:10.1177/1350508403010001376.

Foss, S. K., & Foss, K. A. (2011). *Inviting transformation: Presentational skills for a changing world*. Long Grove, IL: Waveland Press.

Forbes, D. A. (2009). Commodification and co-modification: Explicating black female sexuality in organizations. *Management Communication Quarterly*, 22(4), 577–613. doi:10.1177/0893318908331322.

Frost, P. J. (2004). Handling toxic emotions: New challenges for leaders and their organizations. *Organizational Dynamics*, 33, 111–127. doi:10.1016/j.orgdyn.2004.01.001.

Ganesh, S., & McAllum, K. (2010). Well-being as discourse: Potentials and problems for studies of organizing and health inequalities. *Management Communication Quarterly*, 24(3), 491–498. doi:10.1177/0893318910370274.

Giddens, A. (1984). *The constitution of society: An outline of the theory of structuration*. Cambridge, MA: Polity.

Goleman, D. (1995). *Emotional intelligence: Why it can matter more than IQ*. New York: Bantam.

Hanners, A. (2018). *"Everyone should work in restaurants": How identity is enacted in the food and beverage service industry*. Unpublished Master's thesis. Sacramento State University, Sacramento, CA.

Hareli, S., & Rafaeli, A. (2008). Emotion cycles: On the social influence of emotion in organizations. *Research in Organizational Behavior*, 28, 35–59.

doi:10.1016/j.riob.2008.04.007.

Harvard Business Review. (2015). *HBR's 10 must reads on emotional intelligence*. Boston, MA: Harvard Business Review Press.

Hochschild, A. R. (1983). *The managed heart: Commercialization of human feeling*. Berkeley, CA: University of California Press.

Jablin, F. M., Putnam, L. L., Roberts, K. H. & Porter, L. W. (Eds.) (1987). *Handbook of organizational communication*. Newbury Park, CA: SAGE.

Kamrath, J. K. (2018). *L1. The social construction and reciprocity of resilience: An empirical investigation of an organizational context*. Tempe: Arizona State University.

Keashly, L., & Jagatic, K. (2003). By any other name: American perspectives on workplace bullying. In S. Einarsen, H. Hoel, & C. L. Cooper (Eds.), *Bullying and emotional abuse in the workplace: International perspectives in research and practice* (pp. 31–61). London: Taylor and Francis.

Kramer, M. W., & Hess, J. A. (2002). Communication rules for the display of emotions in organizational settings. *Management Communication Quarterly, 16*, 66–80. doi:10.1177/0893318902161003.

Leiter, M. P., & Maslach, C. (2011). *Banishing burnout: Six strategies for improving your relationship with work*. San Francisco, CA: Wiley.

Lewin, K. (1951). *Field theory in social science: Selected theoretical papers*. Ed. D. Cartwright. New York, NY: Harper & Row.

Lutgen-Sandvik, P. (2006). Take this job and… Quitting and other forms of resistance to workplace bullying. *Communication Monographs, 73*(4), 406–433. doi:10.1080/03637750601024156.

Lutgen-Sandvik, P. (2008). Intensive remedial identity work: Responses to workplace bullying as trauma and stigma. *Organization, 15*(1), 97–119. doi:10.1177/1350508407084487.

Lutgen-Sandvik, P., & McDermott, V. (2008). The constitution of employee-abusive organizations: A communication flows theory. *Communication Theory, 18*(2), 304–333. doi:10.1111/j.1468-2885.2008.00324.x.

Lutgen-Sandvik, P., Riforgiate, S. & Fletcher, C. (2011). Work as a source of positive emotional experiences and the discourses informing positive assessment. *Western Journal of Communication, 75*(1), 2–27. doi:10.1080/10570314.2010.536963.

Lutgen-Sandvik, P., & Tracy, S. J. (2012). Answering five key questions about workplace bullying: How communication scholarship provides thought leadership for transforming abuse at work. *Management Communication Quarterly, 26*, 3–47. doi:10.1177/0893318911414400.

Malvini Redden, S. (2013). How lines organize compulsory interaction, emotion management, and "emotional taxes": The implications of passenger emotion and expression in airport security lines. *Management Communication Quarterly, 27*, 121–149. doi:10.1177/0893318912458213.

Malvini Redden, S., & Scarduzio, J. A. (2017). A different type of dirty work: Hidden taint, intersectionality, and emotion management in bureaucratic organizations. *Communication Monographs*, 1–21. doi:10.1080/03637751.2017.1394580.

Maslach, C. (1982). *Burnout: The cost of caring*. Englewood Cliffs, NJ: Prentice Hall.

McAllum, K. (2014). Meanings of organizational volunteering: Diverse volunteer pathways. *Management Communication Quarterly, 28*(1), 84–110. doi:10.1177/0893318913517237.

Meares, M. M., Oetzel, J. G., Derkacs, D., & Ginossar, T. (2004). Employee mistreatment and muted voices in the culturally diverse workforce. *Journal of Applied Communication Research, 32*, 4–27. doi:10.1080/0090988042000178121.

Men, L. R. (2014). Strategic internal communication: Transformational leadership, communication channels, and employee satisfaction. *Management Communication Quarterly, 28*, 264–284. doi:10.1177/0893318914524536.

Miller, K. (2007). Compassionate communication in the workplace: Exploring processes of noticing, connecting, and responding. *Journal of Applied Communication Research, 35*, 223–245. doi:10.1080/00909880701434208.

Miller, K. I., Stiff, J. B., & Ellis, B. H. (1988). Communication and empathy as precursors to burnout among human service workers. *Communication Monographs*, *55*(3), 250–265. doi:10.1080/03637758809376171.

Mumby, D. K., & Putnam, L. L. (1992). The politics of emotion: A feminist reading of bounded rationality. *Academy of Management Review*, *17*, 465–486. doi:10.5465/amr.1992.4281983.

Murphy, K. R. (Ed.) (2014). *A critique of emotional intelligence: What are the problems and how can they be fixed?* New York: Routledge.

Namie, G., & Lutgen-Sandvik, P. E. (2010). Active and passive accomplices: The communal character of workplace bullying. *International Journal of Communication*, *4*, 343–373.

Namie, G., Namie, R., & Lutgen-Sandvik, P. (2010). Challenging workplace bullying in the United States: An activist and public communication approach. In S. Einarsen, H. Hoel, D. Zapf & C. L. Cooper (Eds.), *Bullying and harassment in the workplace: Developments in theory, research, and practice* (pp. 447–467). Boca Raton, FL: CRC Press. doi:10.1201/EBK1439804896-25.

Newman, A., & Rivera, R. (2010). Fed-up flight attendant makes sliding exit. *The New York Times*, August 9. www.nytimes.com/2010/08/10/nyregion/10attendant.html.

Paul, G. D., & Riforgiate, S. E. (2015). "Putting on a happy face," "getting back to work," and "letting it go": Traditional and restorative justice understandings of emotions at work. *Electronic Journal of Communication*, *25*(3/4). www.cios.org/getfile/025303_EJC.

Poly, A. (2015). Emotional labour and employee performance appraisal: The missing link in some hotels in south east Nigeria. *International Journal of Hospitality and Tourism Systems*, *8*(2). https://pdfs.semanticscholar.org/2263/7ac93bd9f255064a19f540238d70b7e1a695.pdf.

Radey, M., & Figley, C. (2007). The social psychology of compassion. *Clinical Social Work Journal*, *35*(3), 207–214. doi:10.1007/s10615-007-0087-3.

Rafaeli, A., & Sutton, R. I. (1987). Expression of emotion as part of the work role. *Academy of Management Review*, *12*(1), 23–37. doi:10.5465/amr.1987.4306444.

Raz, A. E., & Rafaeli, A. (2007). Chapter 8: Emotion management in cross-cultural perspective: "Smile training" in Japanese and North American service organizations. In C. E. J. Härtel, N. M. Ashkanasy, & W. J. Zerbe (Eds.), *Functionality, intentionality and morality* (pp. 199–220). Emerald Group Publishing Limited. doi:10.1016/S1746-9791(07)03008-8.

Razzante, R. J., & Orbe, M. P. (2018). Two sides of the same coin: Conceptualizing dominant group theory in the context of co-cultural theory. *Communication Theory*, *28*(3), 354–375. doi:10.1093/ct/qtx008.

Razzante, R., & Tracy, S. J. (2019). Co-cultural theory: Performing emotional labor from a position of exclusion. In C. J. Liberman, A. S. Rancer, & T. A. Avtgis (Eds.), *Casing communication theory* (pp. 117–130). Dubuque, IA: Kendall Hunt.

Razzante, R., J., Tracy, S. J., & Orbe, M. P. (2018). How dominant group members can transform workplace bullying. In R. West, & C. Beck (Eds.), *Routledge handbook of communication and bullying* (pp. 46–56). London: Routledge.

Richardson, G. E. (2002). The metatheory of resilience and resiliency. *Journal of Clinical Psychology*, *58*, 307–321. doi:10.1002/jclp.10020.

Rivera, K. D. (2015). Emotional taint: Making sense of emotional dirty work at the U.S. Border Patrol. *Management Communication Quarterly*, *29*, 198–228. doi:10.1177/0893318914554090.

Salovey, P., & Mayer, J.D. (1990). Emotional intelligence. *Imagination, Cognition and Personality*, *9*, 185–211. doi:10.2190/DUGG-P24E-52WK-6CDG.

Scarduzio, J. A. (2011). Maintaining order through deviance? The emotional deviance, power, and professional work of municipal court judges. *Management Communication Quarterly*, *25*, 283–310. doi:10.1177/0893318910386446.

Scarduzio, J. A., & Malvini Redden, S. (2015). The positive outcomes of negative emotional displays: A multi-level analysis of emotion in bureaucratic work. *Electronic Journal of Communication*, *25*(3/4).

Scarduzio, J. A., & Tracy, S. J. (2015). Sensegiving and sensebreaking via emotion cycles and emotional buffering: How collective communication creates order in the courtroom. *Management Communication Quarterly, 29*, 331–357. doi:10.1177/0893318915581647.

Schaufeli, W. B., Leiter, M. P., & Maslach, C. (2009). Burnout: 35 years of research and practice. *Career Development International, 14*, 204–220. doi:10.1108/13620430910966406.

Scott, C., & Myers, K. K. (2005). The socialization of emotion: Learning emotion management at the fire station. *Journal of Applied Communication Research, 33*(1), 67–92. doi:10.1080/0090988042000318521.

Shapiro, S. L., Carlson, L. E., Astin, J. A., & Freedman, B. (2006). Mechanisms of mindfulness. *Journal of Clinical Psychology, 62*(3), 373–386. doi:10.1002/jclp.20237.

Shenoy-Packer, S. (2015). Immigrant professionals, microaggressions, and critical sensemaking in the U.S. workplace. *Management Communication Quarterly, 29*(2), 257–275. doi:10.1177/0893318914562069.

Simon, H. A. (1982). *Models of bounded rationality: Empirically grounded economic reason* (Vol. 3). Cambridge, MA: MIT Press.

Thoroughgood, C. N., Hunter, S. T., & Sawyer, K. B. (2011). Bad apples, bad barrels, and broken followers? An empirical examination of contextual influences on follower perceptions and reactions to aversive leadership. *Journal of Business Ethics, 100*(4), 647–672. doi:10.1007/s10551-010-0702-z.

Tracy, S. J. (2000). Becoming a character for commerce: Emotion labor, self subordination and discursive construction of identity in a total institution. *Management Communication Quarterly, 14*, 90–128. doi:10.1177/0893318900141004.

Tracy, S. J. (2005). Locking up emotion: Moving beyond dissonance for understanding emotion labor discomfort. *Communication Monographs, 72*(3), 261–283. doi:10.1080/03637750500206474.

Tracy, S. J. (2008). Care as a common good. *Women's Studies in Communication, 31*, 166–174. doi:10.1080/07491409.2008.10162529.

Tracy, S. J. (2009). Power, paradox, social support and prestige: A critical approach to addressing correctional officer burnout. In S. Fineman (Ed.), *Le emozioni nell'organizzazione*. Milano: Rafaello Cortina Editore.

Tracy, S. J. (2017). Burnout. In C. Scott & L. Lewis (Eds.), *The international encyclopedia of organizational communication* (online edition). Hoboken, NJ: Wiley-Blackwell. doi:10.1002/9781118955567.wbieoc015.

Tracy, S. J., Alberts, J. K., & Rivera, K. D. (2007). *How to bust the office bully: Eight tactics for explaining workplace abuse to decision-makers.* https://staffombuds.berkeley.edu/sites/default/files/how_to_bust_the_office_bully.pdf.

Tracy, S. J., & Huffman, T. P. (2017). Compassion in the face of terror: A case study of recognizing suffering, co-creating hope, and developing trust in a would-be school shooting. *Communication Monographs, 84*, 30–53. doi:10.1080/03637751.2016.1218642.

Tracy, S. J., Lutgen-Sandvik, P., & Alberts, J. K. (2006). Nightmares, demons, and slaves: Exploring the painful metaphors of workplace bullying. *Management Communication Quarterly, 20*(2), 148–185. doi:10.1177/0893318906291980.

Tracy, S. J., Myers, K. K., & Scott, C. W. (2006). Cracking jokes and crafting selves: Sensemaking and identity management among human service workers. *Communication Monographs, 73*(3), 283–308. doi:10.1080/03637750600889500.

Tracy, S. J., & Tracy, K. (1998). Emotion labor at 911: A case study and theoretical critique. *Journal of Applied Communication Research, 26*, 390–411. doi:10.1080/00909889809365516.

Tye-Williams, S., & Krone, K. J. (2015). Chaos, reports, and quests: Narrative agency and co-workers in stories of workplace bullying. *Management Communication Quarterly, 29*(1), 3–27. doi:10.1177/0893318914552029.

Tye-Williams, S., & Krone, K. J. (2017). Identifying and reimagining the paradox of workplace bullying advice. *Journal of Applied Communication Research 45*(3), 218–235. doi:10.1080/00909882.2017.1288291.

University of California, Berkeley. (2016). *Workplace bullying prevention policy*. https://campuspol.berkeley.edu/Policies/Bullying.pdf.

Waldron, V. R. (2000). Relational experiences and emotions at work. In S. Fineman (Ed.), *Emotion in organizations* (pp. 64–82). Thousand Oaks, CA: SAGE. doi:10.4135/9781446219850.n4.

Waldron, V. R. (2012). *Communicating emotion at work*. Malden, MA: Polity Press.

Way, D., & Tracy, S. J. (2012). Conceptualizing compassion as recognizing, relating and (re)acting: An ethnographic study of compassionate communication at hospice. *Communication Monographs, 79*, 292–315. doi:10.1080/03637751.2012.697630.

Wingfield, A. H. (2010). Are some emotions marked "whites only"? Racialized feeling rules in professional workplaces. *Social Problems, 57*(2), 251–268. doi:10.1525/sp.2010.57.2.251.

Workplace Bullying Institute (n.d.). *History of the Workplace Bullying Institute*. www.workplacebullying.org/history-of-wbi/.

Workplace Bullying Institute. (2010). *Results of the 2010 and 2007 WBI U.S. Workplace Bullying Survey*. www.workplacebullying.org/wbiresearch/2010-wbi-national-survey/.

Weiss, H. M., & Cropanzano, R. (1996). Affective events theory: A theoretical discussion of the structure, causes and consequences of affective experiences at work. In B. M. Staw & L. L. Cummings (Eds.), *Research in organizational behavior: An annual series of analytical essays and critical reviews* (Vol. 18, pp.1–74). Greenwich, CT: Elsevier Science/JAI Press.

Zhang, Q., & Zhu, W. (2008). Exploring emotion in teaching: Emotional labor, burnout, and satisfaction in Chinese higher education. *Communication Education, 57*(1), 105–122. doi:10.1080/03634520701586310.

19 Technology and Organizational Communication

Keri K. Stephens and Kerk F. Kee

Technology is a vague term with multiple meanings. For example, a refrigerator is a technology, and now that many interface with smart devices, they can actually "communicate" with the humans who need to restock them. But to understand how technology functions in an organizational context, there needs to be a more specific definition that reflects issues relevant for our field. In keeping with the communicative constitution of organization (CCO) perspective, this chapter uses a definition that encompasses communication with technology but also considers that information (referred to as *data* in the discussion of *big data* later in the chapter) is a key structure found in organizational life. *Computer-mediated communication* (CMC) is a term commonly used in several communication fields. Although CMC does combine the concepts of communication and technologies, the term *information and communication technologies* (ICTs) is used throughout this chapter because it more closely aligns with organizational communication.

ICTs define the tangled nature of technologies that enable and constrain communication as well as various forms of organizational information. This approach assumes that ICTs—while not openly biased—are not necessarily neutral objects: Information and communication are inherently entwined with power and control (Beniger, 1989). This means that that ICT use can influence and be influenced by a host of organizational variables and processes, including organization/organizing type, hierarchies, policies, individual preferences, job roles, and coworkers.

In the past decade, exciting changes have occurred in how organizational communication scholars study technology: We have embraced prior calls to move beyond studying how communication happens *through* ICTs (Rice & Leonardi, 2014) and we now study how communication and organizing happen *around* ICTs (e.g., Bimber, Flanagin, & Stohl, 2012; Ganesh & Stohl, 2010; Leonardi, 2009; Stephens & Ford, 2016; Stephens, 2018). This has helped the sub-discipline of organizational communication contribute to the growing perspective that technology is an integral part of the communicative constitution of organizational life. When organizational communication scholars study technology, we use our field's theoretical assumptions and frameworks to guide our research, but we also build on theories found in other disciplines. Thus, today we focus less on specific technologies and their features, which will likely change over time, and more on structures and processes that will shape and are shaped by communication technologies.

Therefore, the frame used in this chapter to understand the role technology plays in organizational communication is the following: *Organizational life is lived, and communication is shaped, through and around ICTs.* This framework follows the communication-organization spiral guiding this book and reflects the mutual enabling and constraining relationship between communication and organization seen in ICTs. For example, in some organizations, email (an ICT) is understood by the communication practices that shape its use, but it also constrains communication because it is not feasible or advisable to copy many people on every email. Furthermore, email can be a flexible ICT for asynchronous communication; people can read and respond at their own leisure. However, users can become too dependent on the convenience of asynchronous email communication and thus use it as a substitute for much needed face-to-face communication, sometimes under the wrong circumstances. Here we can see how daily communication through and with ICTs and enduring organizational structures enable and constrain one another over time.

Because it was not always this way in studies of technology and organization, this chapter begins with a historical perspective on ICTs and organizational life. The early theorizing around ICTs began in the field of management, but organizational communication scholars quickly joined these efforts and created a robust set of early conversations to address the explosive growth in communication technology in organizational contexts.

This chapter is organized as follows. First, we provide an overview of the three foundational perspectives on understanding ICTs' use in organizational life. Second, we discuss organizational communication research in understanding the adoption and diffusion of ICTs into organizational practices at the individual and organizational levels. Third, we explore the various ways scholars have studied communication with and through ICTs in organizational processes. Fourth, we examine how cultures manifest in the integration of ICTs into organizational life. Finally, we conclude with a reflection of the ways organizational communication scholarship and ICTs help us answer the three central questions of communication, organization, and the communication-organization spiral guiding this book.

Historical Perspective on ICTs and Organization

Many organizational scholars have focused on how technology can structure communication (e.g., Barley's, 1986, work on CT scanners). With the 1980s growth in forms of communication technologies, it was also important to develop an understanding of how the material devices functioned for communication. Between the 1980s and early 2000s, developing theories and empirical studies progressed from viewing technology as being the key deciding factor in how communication *should happen* to a more social constructivist view, where other people are a dominant influence in using technology to communicate. This chapter adopts a waves metaphor (following Stephens & Mandhana, 2017) to explain these shifting perspectives. We begin with a focus on the technology-deterministic wave.

The Technology-Deterministic Wave

Imagine a time when organizations did not rely on email and smartphones to coordinate and communicate. Although ICTs like computers, documents, and landline phones have been a part of organizational life for more than 60 years, this is still a young and rapidly changing area of study. In the early 1970s the telecommunication field began explaining the presumed magic present in face-to-face communication that did not exist as fully when communicating over the telephone and videoconferencing. The theory of *social presence* (Short, Williams, & Christie, 1976) identified that magic and defined it as the "degree of salience of the other person in the interaction and the consequent salience of interpersonal relationships" (p. 65). More recently, Lee (2004) added to our understanding of presence as "a psychological state in which virtual objects are experienced as actual objects in either sensory or nonsensory ways" (p. 27). Short and his colleagues (1976) placed ICTs on a continuum of their ability to convey social presence. There was an assumption that some tasks required a high degree of social presence, so communicators should match their tasks and ICTs. Notice that this is not an organization-specific theory, but it forms the foundation for the next major theoretical development around ICTs in the field of management.

Many ICTs were not ubiquitous in the 1980s, and most of them had distinct features that allowed scholars to categorize these technologies into what was considered their inherent communication potentials. As these communication tools diffused into organizations, management scholars created new theories to help managers optimize their time and use them effectively, building theories around *information* and *media richness* (Daft & Lengel, 1984, 1986). Management scholars and social psychologists often focused on organizational environments as being uncertain (Weick, 1979), unpredictable, and having vast information-processing needs (Daft & Lengel, 1984). Media richness theory (MRT)—the popularized term from the original work on information richness—became a logical, structured roadmap for managers needing to make difficult ICT use decisions.

Richness is a set of properties that an ICT possesses, with four criteria that determine an ICT's richness (capability to convey robust details): (1) Feedback timeliness; (2) multiple cues available for interpretation; (3) language variety; and (4) personal focus. Face-to-face (FtF) communication is considered the richest medium because of access to immediate feedback, nonverbal cues, language variation, and emotional message tailoring to make the conversation more personal. Much like the continuum found in social presence theory, a continuum of ICTs ranges from richest (i.e., FtF) to leanest (i.e., print documents).

Since the goal of MRT was to help managers be more efficient in handling complex organizational realities, the theory also proposed that managers should match their communication needs with the ideal ICT, following an optimizing strategy. Imagine these two examples of a mismatch in communication needs and efficiency in communicating:

- You walk seven blocks to a person's office to ask for a copy of a report that is available online. When you get to her office, you spend 30 minutes chatting about a basketball game, and walk back to your office, spending an unnecessary hour.
- Your colleague sends you a text message asking why you are rejecting a proposal to restructure your department and lay off four of your staff. You roll your eyes and respond, "duh!" Seven text messages later you realize that your colleague was concerned about his friend losing her job.

MRT suggests considering two main things about the task before choosing the ICT to use. First, is the request meant to answer a question (reduce uncertainty)? If so, a leaner ICT, possibly email, would be the best match to optimize efficiency. Second, is the request complex enough that emotions will be involved and you will need to interact to determine how to respond (an equivocal task)? In this situation, using a richer medium, like FtF communication will likely be needed to take advantage of the features inherent in a rich ICT.

Building on MRT, Trevino, Lengel, and Daft (1987) expanded this theory to align with a symbolic interactionist framework, highlighting ICTs as carriers of symbolic meaning. For example, a written letter symbolizes formality. These types of extensions, and some of the early empirical comparison research, reveal the incompleteness of a rational task-matching ICT framework. Rice's (1992) comprehensive comparative studies provided direct tests of social presence theory and MRT. While FtF was consistently ranked the highest in richness and social presence, the continuum broke down with added gradations of new ICTs.

Multidisciplinary nature of early theorizing and empirical work. While much of the early research on ICTs was conducted in the field of management, organizational scholars across disciplines were regular contributors to these bodies of literature. For example, Rice conducted many empirical tests of early theories (e.g., Rice, 1992, 1993), and communication scholars Fulk and Poole were regular coauthors with management professor DeSanctis. Together, these partnerships created some of the most foundational theoretical works in organizational communication and technology, grounded in a multidisciplinary perspective. Fulk partnered with Steinfield to edit one of the most grounding books in this area: *Organizations and Communication Technology* (1990). She engaged in several additional partnerships that yielded a pivotal contribution with the social influence model (Fulk, 1993; Fulk & Boyd, 1991; Fulk, Schmitz, & Steinfield, 1990). DeSanctis and Fulk's (1999) edited book, *Shaping Organization Form: Communication, Connection, and Community*, set the stage for the explosive use of ICTs and how they shaped (and were shaped by) organizational life. DeSanctis and Poole (1994) embraced a more structurational approach, explaining that different groups use ICTs differently. This research developed into adaptive structuration theory (see Chapter 3). Therefore, it was natural to begin considering the social aspects of ICT use.

The Social Construction and Emergent Perspectives Wave

As more scholars began to question whether the richness and ICT-matching approach provides extensive explanatory value, new theories, models, and perspectives entered the field. These theories claimed that people and social considerations matter more than the ICTs themselves; thus, a wave of social-construction-oriented theories emerged. In their social influence model, Fulk and colleagues (1990) built their claims by relying on theories of social learning, organizational norms, and social-information processing. They certainly included ICT features as part of their model, but they also included considerations like peoples' experiences and skills in using the ICTs along with task features, and myriad situational factors. Of particular relevance for organizational communication, Fulk identified four social factors that influence ICT perceptions and use: (1) direct statements by coworkers in organizations; (2) vicarious learning—observing others; (3) organizational norms for how ICTs should be evaluated and used; and (4) social definitions of rationality. This socially oriented theory did not lend itself to then-popular quantitative methods and experimental research; yet it garnered support. For example, Fulk's (1993) measure of social influence was found to predict individuals' ICT attitudes as well as when they choose to use a particular ICT. Furthermore, research concluded that large enough groups of people need to use specific ICTs to reach *critical mass* (Markus, 1990) before the technologies will naturally diffuse widely. Yet, the general feeling was that something was still missing in this ICT-use puzzle.

There was growing evidence that individuals, groups, and organizations use what appears to be the exact same ICTs in very different ways. While the social influence model provided some suggestions for why this might be the case, other scholars began exploring this more deeply. DeSanctis and Poole (1994) drew from the macro, societal-level metatheoretical perspective of structuration theory, to develop what they called adaptive structuration theory (see also Chapter 3). They theorized that a combination of technologies and social influences explain why some groups adapt technology in unexpected, novel ways. Their theory has since been used extensively in organizational communication, information systems, and management. Most recently, Barrett and Stephens (2017) used this theory to explain how healthcare workers who create work-arounds in their electronic healthcare record (EHR) systems are more likely to view the technology more favorably.

Carlson and Zmud (1999) pivoted away from understanding how people select specific ICTs to expand Fulk and colleagues' notion of experience, arguing that users can expand their perception of a specific ICT. These scholars, along with researchers like D'Urso and Rains (2008) have tested the value of channel expansion theory and found that as users become more experienced with a given ICT, they will view it as richer. Other scholars, primarily in management, argued that the materiality of ICTs—like features—were so entwined with the social and organizational environment that it was impossible to examine them independently; thus, the concept of socio-materiality emerged (Orlikowski, 2007). In response to these claims, Leonardi (2009) and colleagues (Leonardi & Barley, 2010) pushed back to demonstrate that even though both material and social factors matter, materiality can play a key role in enabling and constraining organizational communication. Leonardi, Nardi, and Kallinikos (2012), in *Materiality and Organizing: Social Interaction in a Technological World*, present a set of edited chapters making the case that scholarship will suffer if we ignore materiality when considering the important role that social considerations play in organizational life.

Up to this point in ICT theorizing, most theories assumed that people used a single ICT for each task, but there was growing evidence that this assumption was false (e.g., Rice, Hiltz, & Spencer, 2004), especially when mobile devices appeared and included multiple ICTs in a single tool. For example, is a smartphone a telephone, email, an Internet-access device, or a texting tool? It serves all these functions, and how users draw from the affordances of these tools further explains ICT use.

Combinatorial ICT Use Wave

The third wave of understanding how ICTs are used in an organizational context focused on sequential and simultaneous use. Stephens (2007) developed ICT succession theory to illustrate how people build and expand on the material and social considerations of ICT use when they chain them over time. She and her colleagues further illustrated how this functioned with content analysis and cluster analysis of a large qualitative data set to explain patterns in sequential ICT-use pairs (Stephens, Sørnes, Rice, Browning, & Sætre, 2008). Browning, Sætre, Stephens, and Sørnes (2008), in *Information & Communication Technologies in Action: Linking Theory and Narratives of Practice*, present narratives collected between 1999 and 2003 of combinatorial ICT use in Norway and the U.S., connecting these narratives to organizational theories that explained and situated their interviewees' experiences with ICTs.

Simultaneous ICT use also began emerging as people multitasked and multicommunicated in various organizational contexts. Multicommunicating is a theoretically derived term describing what happens when people use technology to carry on multiple conversations simultaneously (Reinsch, Turner, & Tinsley, 2008). Simultaneous conversations are more cognitively taxing than multitasking, or doing two things at once (Reinsch et al., 2008). This practice is often on display during organizational meetings, whether in person or through an online conferencing system.

Cyberinfrastructure. Simultaneous and sequential ICT use also occurs in the emerging concept of cyberinfrastructure. Cyberinfrastructure can be understood as an interwoven collection of ICTs, specialized software, computing hardware, remote instruments, big data, high speed networks, virtual processes, organizational policies, and human experts (Kee, Cradduck, Bloggett, & Olwan, 2011; Kee & Browning, 2010). Scholars in this area argue that we need to understand the larger infrastructure in which the ICTs are embedded to avoid studying ICTs out of context. Furthermore, increasingly the use of one ICT is dependent on an infrastructure of many other ICTs and technologies available for combinatorial use. Therefore, to manage effective organizational infrastructure, particularly when organizing virtually, we need to understand when and how technologies are simultaneously and sequentially used to achieve organizational goals.

Affordances of communication technologies. Work on the affordances of communication technologies build on the ideas that materiality matters, social parameters are influential, and contemporary tools provide many options. Affordances are material features that individuals and groups can choose to use to accomplish relational communication objectives (Evans, Pearce, Vitak, & Treem, 2017). The concept of affordances did not originate in the field of communication, but organizational-, interpersonal-, and mobile-communication researchers have embraced it because it provides conceptual framing that helps technology discussions move beyond deterministic assumptions (e.g., Evans et al., 2017; Gibbs, Rozaidi, & Eisenberg, 2013; Leonardi, 2013, 2014; Rice et al., 2017; Schrock, 2015; Stephens, 2018; Treem & Leonardi, 2012). While management and information systems scholars have also embraced the concept of affordances, this chapter focuses on contributions by organizational communication researchers.

Evans and her team (2017) reviewed the literature to date on technology affordances, noting that researchers often identify affordances, but then fail to conceptually develop them. This is actually a strength in much organizational communication research because our scholars are now leading the effort to conceptualize and theorize around affordances of technologies. For example, one group of researchers has focused on the affordances of social media (Leonardi, 2014; Treem & Leonardi, 2012) and linked these concepts to expertise and knowledge-sharing (Ellison, Gibbs, & Weber, 2015; Gibbs et al., 2013). Stephens (2018) has elaborated the affordance of reachability and dimensionalized this affordance into the temporal variables *frequency* and *predictability*. In addition, Rice and colleagues have looked beyond the individual level to argue that there are organizational media affordances that exist beyond an individual ICT and which are associated with practices found in organizational life.

Enterprise social media. One area where organizational communication scholars have focused their work on affordances is in understanding enterprise social media. This type of social media is different from personal platforms, such as Facebook, because they are tools used only by organizational members (the enterprise.) Treem and Leonardi (2012) identified and elaborated four affordances that often exist in social media tools: visibility, persistence, editability, and association. These affordances are not necessarily unique to enterprise social media, but they reflect the relational perspective and the importance of human agency found in and around these forms of technology. Leonardi (2014) further developed the affordance of visibility into a grounded theory that reveals how organizational members experience the tensions of being open and sharing information while also managing their own impressions.

Table of Theories

This chapter has covered a host of theories so far. To facilitate understanding of this breadth of the field, Table 9.1 summarizes them before we move into our next section. Look back into the sections that describe these theories and see if you can find how they build on and diverge from earlier work.

ICT Diffusion Into Organizational Practices

It is not a given that ICTs designed and developed by technologists and software companies will become integrated into organizational life. Many ICTs are tried and rejected, and only some are adopted into organizational contexts. Furthermore, some ICTs become staples, while others are discontinued or replaced by newer ICTs. We now

Table 9.1 A timeline of ICT use theories situated in organizational life*

Social Presence Theory	Short, Williams, & Christie (1976)
Media Richness Theory	Daft & Lengel (1984) Trevino, Lengel, and Daft (1987)
Social Influence Model	Fulk (1993) Fulk, Schmitz, & Steinfield (1990)
Critical Mass	Markus (1990)
Adaptive Structuration Theory	DeSanctis & Poole (1994)
Channel Expansion Theory	Carlson & Zmud (1999)
ICT Succession Theory	Stephens (2007)
Multicommunicating	Reinsch, Turner, & Tinsley (2008)
Sociomateriality	Orlikowski (2007)
Materiality matters	Leonardi (2009)
Affordances of Enterprise Social Media	Treem & Leonardi (2012)

Please note that these do not include many of the group-communication, interpersonal, or information-systems theories that are related, but not discussed in this chapter.

turn the discussion to understanding how ICTs are adopted and diffused in modern organizational contexts.

When examining technology through the three lenses of organizational communication (as an organizing process, as an organizing structure, and as an entity), another branch of theoretical and empirical research on structures emerges. This area of research also has a long history, and it can be considered more macro-organizational because most of the scholarship has focused on how organizational entities acquire and deploy technology to enable communication and coordination.

Adoption and Diffusion

Adoption is defined as an individual organizational member's decision to accept, reject, and/or discontinue using a new technology, while diffusion refers to the systemic phenomenon of the spreading of a new technology as it integrates within organizational life (Kee, 2017a). The literature on adoption and diffusion is multidisciplinary, including research from sociology (Ryan & Gross, 1943), marketing (Feick & Price, 1987), public health (Valente & Pumpuang, 2007), and most importantly communication (Rogers, 1962, 2003). Everett Rogers, a pioneer in the field of communication, is the key figure who is most identified with diffusion and adoption research, including in organizational communication.

Originally trained in rural sociology, Everett Rogers spent most of his career as a Professor of Communication. Rogers published the first edition of his classic text, *Diffusion of Innovations* (1962), to describe a theory of how innovations are adopted and diffused, as he recognized a striking general pattern documented by researchers across diverse fields. Rogers explicitly defined *diffusion* as a communication process through which an innovation spreads in social systems via various communication channels over time. In the fifth and last edition of his classic text, Rogers (2003) described how the Internet was the fastest adopted and diffused innovation in human history.

Individual-level adoption. Diffusion research interested in understanding individual adoption of technologies focused on identifying innovation attributes, such as relative advantage, compatibility, complexity, trialability, and observability perceived by individual adopters (Rice, 2009; Rogers, 2003). Different types of adopters of technology have unique socio-psycho profiles: *innovators* (2.5 percent), *early adopters* (13.5 percent), *early majority* (34.0 percent), *late majority* (34.0 percent), and *laggards* (16.0 percent). This line of research helps researchers better understand why some organizational members tend to be the first to adopt and experiment with a new ICT, while some take longer to use it, and others never really get on board.

If one takes a deterministic perspective, the case of ICT adoption and diffusion in organizational contexts can be metaphorically described as *the ripple effect* or *the domino effect* (Kee, 2017a). However, organizational members have agency. An important concept in diffusion research is *reinvention*, which refers to the repurposing of a technology in creative ways unintended by the original designer. Rice and Rogers (1980) argued that reinvention is natural, showing ordinary users in their adaptation and modification of an innovation as they struggle to give meaning(s) to technology in the organizational contexts of their local problems and cultures. Furthermore, diffusion research also examines how individuals in social networks, especially opinion leaders with many *weak ties* (Granovetter, 1973, see also Chapter 9), naturally spread new technologies within social systems. This body of literature sheds light on how word-of-mouth and interpersonal communication are more powerful in persuading about the value of a new technology than official advertising messages from vendors and other sources.

Organization-level adoption. Organizational communication researchers also study organizational adoption of ICTs, in addition to individual adoption, because of *contingent adoption decisions* (Rice, 2009). Individuals only have access to an ICT after the organization has adopted it. Moreover, individuals do not always make adoption decisions by personal choice because they can be an organizational require-ment. Therefore, organizational adoption of ICTs is key to understanding the relation-ship between technology and organizational communication.

Organizational adoption of ICTs is usually driven by observations of practices in peer organizations and trends in the industries, such as in the case of early adoption of homepages by many organizations (Flanagin, 2000). More recently, drawing upon institutional theory, Zorn, Flanagin, and Shoham (2011) illustrated that organizational adoption of ICTs is driven by isomorphic pressure—conforming to industry norms. This pressure also stems from the perceived need for achieving organizational power derived from social and institutional legitimacy. Zorn and his team (2011) concluded that isomorphic pressures are most predictive of organiza-tional adoption of ICTs, stronger than other factors such as budget and company size.

When an innovation is adopted and integrated into organizational life, change often occurs. It is human nature to resist organizational change, although some people recognize the need to constantly innovate and adapt to new challenges. Laurie Lewis (2011, 2014) offers an alternative to treating organizational change as a reaction to new technologies. She argues that internal and environmental sensemaking usually occur simultaneously and are mutually influential. In other words, the change in the external environment often influences the change resulting from the adoption and diffusion of ICTs in organizational life, and vice versa. This insight reveals that sensemaking, communication, and interaction during ICT diffusion are complex rela-tionships, especially during reinvention (see also Chapter 21).

The Future of ICTs and Organizational Life

Big Data

Big data is a relatively new term that describes the immense amount of data (structured, semi-structured and unstructured) that now inundates organizations and outpaces the capabilities of traditional data management tools and practices. Big data is increasingly important for organizational communication. For example, a social network analysis of email exchanges can reveal the most central communicators in the organization (Kossinets & Watts, 2009). Big data is defined often by characteristics such as volume, variety, velocity (Laney, 2001), variability, veracity, and value (Gandomi & Haider, 2015). *Volume* refers to the size of data while *variety* denotes the diversity of data formats. *Velocity* describes data's production and processing speed, but *variability* expresses the fluctuating and erratic data flow rates. *Veracity* means despite imprecision and inexactitude, big data possess hidden insights. *Value* implies the significance of big data. Although the literature has discussed these six different characteristics, big data is generally defined in industry by what has become known as the "five Vs," omitting variability (Kee, 2017b).

Kee (2017b) recommends understanding the big data movement through a factory metaphor: data are being generated in a standardized, predictable, centralized, and efficient manner—akin to how goods were produced during the Industrial Revolution. Standardization and predictability can reduce the challenges of big data's variety and variability. Having centralized data repositories and efficient computing resources to process big data can support big data's volume and velocity. As noted in Chapter 5, classical management emerged during the Industrial Revolution due to the invention of steam engines and emergence of factories. A re-emergence of classical management principles and practices may inform how big data are integrated into organizational life in the third decade of the 21st century.

Many organizational processes continuously generate data, and in turn, use that data to guide decisions like changes to products, people, and processes. This is one reason we link information with communication when we have addressed technologies, or ICTs, in this chapter. ICTs are dynamic; software is continuously updated; and the latest smartphone today is old news tomorrow.

The future of communication technologies as a part of the fabric of organizational structures will likely be the integration of robots, artificial intelligence, and virtual reality. These technologies are studied in other fields (e.g., Stone, Neely, & Lengnick-Hall, 2018) and in areas of interpersonal communication, persuasion, and human–computer interaction (e.g., Lee & Liang, 2016; Liang & Lee, 2016). Imagine human paramedics and rescue robots working together as a team to save lives during a crisis or disaster. Customers enter an instant messenger chat with an artificial intelligence agent, or chatbot, for screening and pre-scripted answers before being escalated to a human agent. Dispersed workers use virtual reality to enable a robust collaboration as if they are co-located. It is important to consider how these technologies can enable, constrain, and assist humans in their organizational life, as they will be important areas of study for our field.

Communicating With and Through Technology in Organizing Processes

Many of the ICT use theories shared in the historical timeline can and likely do apply to organizing practices. Yet, there are important considerations of contemporary organizing, especially when groups are dispersed, loosely connected, and their communication and coordination practices are displayed visually through organizing software and platforms. When groups draw upon communicative affordances, like visibility found through social media (Leonardi, 2014; Treem & Leonardi, 2012), new connections can emerge and so can opportunities. In their book, *Collective Action in Organizations: Interaction and Engagement in an Era of Technological Change*, Bimber et al. (2012) illustrate the vital role that ICTs are playing in organizing and coordinating collective action in diverse organizations. While this growing body of research often is addressed separately from ICTs and organizational life, these ideas are becoming entwined, and that is why we put them in conversation with one another. Let us expand this idea and briefly discuss some core literature around networks, emergent groups, and ICT use.

Networks and Organizing

Networks connect people and provide opportunities for communication and organizing (see Chapter 9). Communication networks were rather invisible until ICTs, such as email and social media, became ubiquitous in organizations. Now connections and information flows are more easily seen and are linked often to the collection of and sensemaking around big data. Shumate and Contractor (2014) define communication networks as "relations among various types of actors that illustrate the ways in which messages are transmitted, exchanged, or interpreted" (p. 449). A unique contribution of this definition is the notion of "multidimensional networks"—networks consisting of different types of human and non-human nodes (e.g., individuals, organizations, and technologies) and different types of linkages (e.g., information transmission, collaborations) (Contractor, Monge, & Leonardi, 2011). Drawing from an earlier example in the MRT section of this chapter, instead of walking seven blocks to a person's office to ask for a copy of a report (i.e., a person–person link in the form of a communication request), you can download the report directly from the web (i.e., a person–technology link in the form of information retrieval). Both forms of networks are valid, and the latter is multidimensional.

Shumate and Contractor (2014) elaborate on the four types of communication networks in organizational contexts, as well as the three types of infrastructure networks that relate to how ICTs are discussed in this chapter. First, *flow* networks refer to message exchanges among organizational members, such as emails among coworkers. Second, *affinity* networks are the socially constructed (positive or negative) relationships among members, such as friendships. Third, *representational* networks suggest an association to an external audience. For example, when a person lists an organization on his/her LinkedIn profile, the hyperlink suggests an association between him/her and the listed organization. Finally, *semantic* networks mean shared meaning given to concepts or co-occurrence of words in text. For instance, the ways coworkers come to understand what diversity means and use common words to talk about it reveal the sematic networks in place.

Shumate and Contractor (2014) also describe three types of infrastructure networks that relate clearly to how ICTs are discussed in this chapter. First, *technological* networks support the message flow among technologies, such as telephone networks and Internet connections. Second, *physical* networks refer to how close or proximate organizational members are to each other in time and space. For instance, the locations and physical distance between offices demonstrates a physical network. Finally, *affiliation* networks imply the relation between members and their organizational entities. For example, organizations' memberships in the same consortium suggest a particular affiliation among them. These communication and infrastructure networks connect members and ICTs in a complex multidimensional web, and provide opportunities for communication and organizing.

Online and Emergent Groups

Groups that organize online, rather than in a physical space, are often called virtual groups, online groups, and digital groups. Organizational communication and crisis informatics scholars, as one relevant example, have studied how online groups emerge, organize, and coordinate their actions—often on a temporary basis—using ICTs during disasters and emergencies (e.g., Chewing, Lai, & Doerfel, 2013; Lai, 2017; Smith, Stephens, Robertson, Li, & Murthy, 2018; Starbird & Palen, 2011). Urgent situations are infused with uncertainty; official responses often vary, and community groups want to help (Smith et al., 2018). Starbird and Palen (2011) have coined the term "digital volunteers" to explain how dispersed volunteers self-organize through online platforms, like social media, to provide a collective response. In addition, ICTs often work hand-in-hand with organizing practices like information sharing, connecting people, and acquiring resources (Chewing et al., 2013). Furthermore, formal and informal groups use ICTs differently depending on the stage of a crisis and the recovery to that crisis (Chewing et al., 2013; Lai, 2017).

Research on online and emergent groups is highly interdisciplinary and extends well beyond organizational communication scholars. Group communication scholars, many of whom also study organizational communication, have focused some of their work in these areas. However, organizational scholars are in an ideal place to understand the role that structure—including ICTs—might play as online groups continue to self-organize and dissolve right before our digital eyes. ICTs play key roles in the global social justice movement, providing opportunities to connect people who are not co-located (Ganesh & Stohl, 2010). These findings have led scholars like Ganesh and Stohl (2014) to call for much more research in this area. They further explain that this is not only of interest to informal or emergent groups, but that as formal organizations become more embedded in a digital space, they could come to resemble the more informal online groups.

Culture and ICTs

Throughout this chapter, elements of culture have appeared. Whether in an understanding of how ICT adoption and diffusion is shaped by local culture, in models such as Fulk et al.'s (1990) social influence model or in DeSanctis and Poole's (1994) adaptive structuration theory, many aspects of culture are entwined with ICTs. In Chapter 1 of this book, a definition of culture is offered: "a negotiated set of shared symbolic systems that guide individuals' behaviors and incline them to function as a group" (Chen & Starosta, 1998, p. 26). When organizational communication scholars examine culture, we consider more than artifacts, belief, values, and norms; we examine how individuals perceive these cultures as well as they cultural roots of perceptual differences. Next, we address two additional ways notions of culture intersect with ICTs and organizational communication: work/life and occupational differences.

Work/Life

Culture considerations infuse the body of communication scholarship known as work/life, and ICTs have helped further complicate issues of agency and boundaries. In their handbook chapter on work/life, Kirby and Buzzanell (2014) highlight the myriad ways ICTs are entwined with work/life concerns and practices. For example, work practices like telework—meaning people who work either fully or partially out of their home—offer clear examples of the cultural complexity present when some employees are not physically present in the workplace. Leonardi, Treem, and Jackson (2010) studied these issues and found workers who used ICTs to work remotely experienced what they termed *the connectivity paradox*. The ICTs that appear to afford benefits of flexibility and working remotely are negated by the very ICTs that make the telework arrangement possible. In response, teleworkers use ICTs to create the impression they are working just like when they were co-located at a physical office.

Another intersection between ICTs, work–life, and culture concerns mobile communication. Through personal mobile devices, employees and coworkers are reachable regardless of whether it is during their work hours (Bittman, Brown, & Wajcman, 2009; Stephens, 2018). Further, most organizations have adopted some form of Bring Your Own Device to Work (BYOD) policy because some employees, and information technology departments, want people to provide and use their same communication tools for work and personal life (Stephens et al., 2017; Stephens, 2018). Coworkers and managers can pressure peers to be available when the team needs their help, and this expectation can develop into cultural norms (Stephens, 2018). When mobile communication devices enter organizational life, they enable and constrain both communication practices and organizational processes and structures.

Occupational Differences

Another culture-related consideration for ICTs and organizational life involves understanding that people in different occupations will often use ICTs in disparate ways. In their book *Technology Choices: Why Occupations Differ in Their Embrace of New Technology*, Bailey and Leonardi (2016) examine the question of technology choices among three different groups of engineers: structural engineers, hardware engineers, and automotive engineers. Although the three types of engineering work are equally complex, they approach their technology use differently. For example, structural engineers minimize the role of computers but prefer to depend on pen and paper, hardware engineers maximize their use of computers, and automotive engineers maintain a balance between relying on computer simulated crash tests versus physical crash tests for automotive design. Their study reveals that technologies are not universal, and workers vary in their embrace of technologies primarily based on their occupations and occupational cultures.

In her longitudinal study of people from 35 different occupations, Stephens (2018) found there were also differences in the policies and cultural practices surrounding ICT-use expectations depending on people's job roles. People in more powerful or knowledge worker positions had fewer restrictions than people in manual labor or customer service roles. However, in her book, *Negotiating Control: Organizations and Mobile Communication*, Stephens (2018) ultimately finds that regardless of occupation, most people have negotiated control over their communication with their friends and family, and some of those negotiations tie back to work–life issues.

Conclusion

Let us revisit the framework used in this chapter: *Organizational life is lived, and communication is shaped, through and around ICTs.* In this chapter, technology use and communication are constitutive components of organizational life, and we narrowed our discussions of ICTs to situate how organizational communication scholars have played an integral role in developing theories and understanding. ICT use is a practice and a process where organizational members use multiple ICTs concurrently and sequentially to achieve myriad goals, such as information, persuasion, or organizing.

Organization (O) is conceptualized and used by ICT scholars in myriad ways, and sometimes the same scholars use different approaches depending on the goals of their research. Early researchers—discussed in this chapter as those associated with the technological determinism wave—often viewed this as more of an entity (O_3); a place where technology was used (e.g., Daft & Lengel, 1984). This did not change substantially during the social construction wave, as scholars viewed ICT use as heavily shaped by people in and around organizations (O_3). During the third wave, when combinations of ICTs were studied, organization became viewed as a process (O_1); this was especially in the case in virtual organizations and as enterprise social media were included in the ICT mix.

Diffusion researchers, as well as many more contemporary scholars, view organization as an organizing process (O_1), sometimes considering how organizing occurs in, around, and through technologies over time (e.g., Smith et al., 2018). In that sense, diffusion is inherently organizational in nature, in that it can be understood as an organizing process (O_1) in the entity of an organization (O_3). For scholars who study big data, organizations and their members *are* the data sources for pattern recognition, detection, and/or prediction. Organizations are once again treated as an entity (O_3), but they also become the target to which conclusions are applied with the goal of improving organizing (O_1) and the structures associated with being organized (O_2). While in Chapter 1 O_3 is understood as the result of O_1 and O_2, here we see how O_3 can feed back to O_1 and O_2. Furthermore, many researchers discussed in this chapter consider organization as a structure (O_2) (DeSanctis & Poole, 1994; Ganesh & Stohl, 2010; Shumate & Contractor, 2014).

Finally, in keeping with the core questions considered in this book, this chapter acknowledged all three organization perspectives, but focused on how people have some choices in how they communicate, organize, and use ICTs. This chapter has both used and applied the C-O spiral introduced in Chapter 1 to illustrate the complexities of ICT use in organizational life, and to stress the mutual enabling and constraining relationship between communication and organization seen in ICTs. The examples and ideas shared here should illustrate the role that human agency plays as the communication and organization spiral incorporates ICTs into organizational life.

Recommended Supplementary Readings

Applied

Barley, S. R., Myers, D. E., & Grodal, S. (2011). E-mail as a source and symbol of stress. *Organization Science*, 22, 887–906.
A thought-provoking look at how we blame email for our stress.
Berkelaar, B. L. (2014). Cybervetting, online information, and personnel selection: New transparency expectations and the emergence of a digital social contract. *Management Communication Quarterly*, 28, 479–506.
Rich study examining the process of cybervetting—snooping online about employees.
Stephens, K. K., Waters, E. D., & Sinclair, C. (2014). Media management: The integration of HR, technology, and people. In M. E. Gordon, & V. D. Miller (Eds.), *Meeting the challenge of human resource management: A communication perspective* (pp. 215–226). New York: Routledge.
An accessible chapter that focuses on human resources and contemporary technology.

Historical Theory

Stephens, K. K., & Mandhana, D. M. (2017). Media choice/use in organizations. In C. R. Scott & L. K. Lewis (Eds.), *The international encyclopedia of organizational communication* (—online edition). Hoboken, NJ: Wiley-Blackwell.
This encyclopedia entry provides an accessible look at how the foundational theories have changed over time.

DeSanctis, G., & Fulk, J. L. (1994). *Shaping organization form: Communication, connection, and community*. Thousand Oaks, CA: SAGE.

Fulk, J. L., & Steinfeld, C. (1990). *Organizations and communication technology*. Thousand Oaks, CA: SAGE.

These books provide a grounding in organizational communication and technology.

Important Concepts: Define and Discuss

Adoption
Affordances
Big data
BYOD
Channels
Combinatorial ICT use
Cyberinfrastructure
Diffusion
Enterprise social media
Information and communication technologies (ICTs)
Materiality
Mobile devices
Multicommunicating
Networks
Online (social) movements
Social media
Technology
Also see Table 9.1 for a list of the core theories.

Discussion Questions

1. Skim the Internet for five minutes and identify the popular topics being discussed that are related to this chapter. Choose one topic and share how the research literature could help elevate and/or clarify this popular discourse.
2. Choose one theory in this chapter and apply it to your personal use of technology. If you can put it into an organizational context then that will help with the application.
3. Now it is time to debate agency and technology use. Write a 1–2-paragraph argument for how you have agency in your use of communication technologies in organizational life. Next, write a 1–2-paragraph argument discussing the limits and tensions you face concerning agency. You might want to refer to Chapter 1 and examine the communication and organization spiral that is driven by agency.
4. Look through the references in this chapter and notice the variety of publication outlets where organizational communication and technology scholars publish. Identify the top 3–4 outlets and look up those journals online. How do you think scholars decide where to submit their research considering that this is such a multidisciplinary field?
5. In contrast to early management research, summarize and briefly describe the unique contributions by organizational communication researchers to the understanding of technology and organizing.

6. Given the metaphor of 'factory' to describe the phenomenon of 'big data,' how can classical management or a modified version of classical management guide the organizing processes around data? Discuss the advantages and/or disadvantages of the classical approach.
7. If you were teaching an undergraduate course in organizational communication and technology, what are the top five topics you would cover in the class?
8. If you were covering a unit on technology in an undergraduate organizational communication class, what are the three topics you would include?

Practitioners' Corner

As a practitioner, you probably find yourself interfacing with ICTs on a regular basis. Here we share two scenarios useful for you to consider outside of a specific situation. By using the material in this chapter to think through these scenarios (often with your team), you can be better prepared to address organizational issues that arise. Finally, we share some take-aways that invite you to consider that not all people in your organization have access or use ICTs in the same ways.

Scenario 1: You have been asked to evaluate a new ICT—e.g., an enterprise social media system or a big data analytics software—for organization-wide adoption. Consider evaluating it with the five innovation attributes of relative advantage, compatibility, complexity, trialability, and observability. Discuss with your organizational decision-makers about the likelihood of the ICT being fully adopted, implemented, and optimized by majority, if not all, of the members. Explore possible ways for reinventions to better fit the ICT to local problems and/or organizational culture.

Scenario 2: Many organizations are complaining about being overloaded with email today. Use media richness theory's four factors of feedback timeliness, multiple cues available for interpretation, language variety, and personal focus to rate and rank the ICTs available in your organizational life. Evaluate when to use which ICT for a given communication situation. Remember the two factors to consider: Is the request meant to answer a question, otherwise known as reducing certainty? Is the request complex enough that emotions will be involved and you will need to interact to determine how to respond, known as an equivocal task? Work with your team to design a one-page guide of how you might establish rules to help you more effectively, and more meaningfully communicate through ICTs. Could these mutually agreed upon guidelines help you address email overload?

Take-away thoughts: When organizing a diverse group of collaborators (diverse in terms of occupations and job roles), design policies and encourage practices that strike a balance between being universal and being sensitive to cultural differences among occupational groups and/or individuals with different roles in the collective organizational life. Resist the desire to be overly universal at the detriment of becoming a barrier for some occupations and/or roles. Keep in mind that individuals, teams, occupations, and entire organizations vary in how they like to use ICTs to organize, collaborate, and share information. Finally, consider investigating the policies in your organization that encourage and discourage ICT use. Researchers are finding that these policies can marginalize some workers and that not only affects those individuals, but it can harm productivity as well (see Stephens & Ford, 2016 for an example).

References

Bailey, D. E., & Leonardi, P. M. (2016). *Technology choices: Why occupations differ in their embrace of new technology*. Cambridge, MA: MIT Press.

Barley, S. R. (1986). Technology as an occasion for structuring: Evidence from observations of CT scanners and the social order of radiology departments. *Administrative Science Quarterly, 31,* 78–108. doi:10.2307/2392767.

Barrett, A. K., & Stephens, K. K. (2017). The pivotal role of change appropriation in the implementation of healthcare technology. *Management Communication Quarterly, 31,* 163–193. doi:10.1177/0893318916682872.

Beniger, J. (1989). *The control revolution: Technological and economic origins of the information society*. Cambridge, MA: Harvard University Press.

Bimber, B., Flanagin, A., & Stohl, C. (2012). *Collective action in organizations: Interaction and engagement in an era of technological change*. Cambridge: Cambridge University Press.

Bittman, M., Brown, J. E., & Wajcman, J. (2009). The mobile phone, perpetual contact, and time pressure. *Work, Employment & Society, 23,* 673–691. doi:10.1177/0950017009344910.

Browning, L. D., Sætre, A. S., Stephens, K. K., & Sørnes, J. O. (2008). *Information & communication technologies in action: Linking theory and narratives of practice*. New York, NY: Routledge.

Carlson, J. R., & Zmud, R. W. (1999). Channel expansion theory and the experiential nature of media richness perceptions. *Academy of Management Journal, 42,* 153–170. doi:10.2307/257090.

Chewing, L. V., Lai, C-H., & Doerfel, M. L. (2013). Organizational resilience and using information and communication technologies to rebuild communication structures. *Management Communication Quarterly, 27,* 237–263. doi:10.1177/0893318912465815.

Contractor, N., Monge, P., & Leonardi, P. M. (2011). Multidimensional networks and the dynamics of sociomateriality: Bringing technology inside the network. *International Journal of Communication, 5,* 682–720. http://ijoc.org/index.php/ijoc/article/view/1131.

Daft, R. L., & Lengel, R. H. (1984). Information richness: A new approach to managerial behavior and organization design. In B. M. Staw & L. L. Cummings (Eds.), *Research in organizational behavior* (pp. 191–233). Greenwich, CT: JAI Press.

Daft, R. L., & Lengel, R. H. (1986). Organizational information requirements, media richness and structural design. *Management Science, 32,* 554–571. doi:10.1287/mnsc.32.5.554.

DeSanctis, G., & Fulk, J. (Eds.) (1999). *Shaping organization form: Communication, connection, and community*. Newbury Park, CA: SAGE.

DeSanctis, G., & Poole, M. S. (1994). Capturing the complexity in advanced technology use: Adaptive structuration theory. *Organization Science, 5,* 121–147. doi:10.1287/orsc.5.2.121.

D'Urso, S. C., & Rains, S. A. (2008). Examining the scope of channel expansion: A test of channel expansion theory with new and traditional communication media. *Management Communication Quarterly, 21,* 486–507. doi:10.1177/0893318907313712.

Ellison, N. B., Gibbs, J. L., & Weber, M. S. (2015). The use of enterprise social network sites for knowledge sharing in distributed organizations: The role of organizational affordances. *American Behavioral Scientist, 59,* 103–123. doi:10.1177/0002764214540510.

Evans, S. K., Pearce, K. E., Vitak, J., & Treem, J. W. (2017). Explicating affordances: A conceptual framework for understanding affordances in communication research. *Journal of Computer-Mediated Communication, 22,* 35–52. doi:10.1111/jcc4.12180.

Feick, L. F., & Price, L. L. (1987). The market maven: A diffuser of marketplace information. *Journal of Marketing, 51,* 83–97. doi:10.2307/1251146.

Flanagin, A. J. (2000). Social pressures on organizational website adoption. *Human Communication Research, 26,* 618–646. doi:10.1093/hcr/26.4.618.

Fulk, J. (1993). Social construction of communication technology. *The Academy of Management Journal, 36,* 921–950. doi:10.2307/256641.

Fulk, J., & Boyd, B. (1991). Emerging theories of communication in organizations. *Journal of Management, 17*, 407–446. doi:10.1177/014920639101700207.

Fulk, J., Schmitz, J., & Steinfield, C. W. (1990). A social influence model of technology use. In J. Fulk & C. Steinfield (Eds.), *Organizations and communication technology* (pp. 117–140). Newbury Park, CA: SAGE.

Fulk, J., & Steinfield, C. W. (Eds.) (1990). *Organizations and communication technology.* Newbury Park, CA: SAGE.

Gandomi, A., & Haider, M. (2015). Beyond the hype: Big data concepts, methods, and analytics. *International Journal of Information Management, 35*, 137–144. doi:10.1016/j.ijinfomgt.2014.10.007.

Ganesh, S., & Stohl, C. (2010). Qualifying engagement: A study of information and communication technology and the global social justice movement in Aotearoa/New Zealand. *Communication Monographs, 17*, 51–74. doi:10.1080/03637750903514284.

Ganesh, S., & Stohl, C. (2014). Collective action, community organizing and social movements. In D. K. Mumby & L. L. Putnam (Eds.), *The SAGE handbook of organizational communication: Advances in theory, research, and methods* (3rd ed., pp. 743–765). Newbury Park, CA: SAGE Publications.

Gibbs, J. L., Rozaidi, N. A., & Eisenberg, J. (2013). Overcoming the "ideology of openness": Probing the affordances of social media for organizational knowledge sharing. *Journal of Computer-Mediated Communication, 19*, 102-120. doi:10.1111/jcc4.12034.

Granovetter, M. S. (1973). The strength of weak ties. *American Journal of Sociology, 78*, 1360–1380. doi:10.1086/225469.

Kee, K. F. (2017a). Adoption and diffusion. In C. Scott, & L. Lewis (Eds.), *International encyclopedia of organizational communication* (—online edition). Hoboken, NJ: Wiley-Blackwell. doi:10.1002/9781118955567.wbieoc058.

Kee, K. F. (2017b). The 10 adoption drivers of open source software that enable e-research in data factories for open innovation. In S. Matei, N. Julien, & S. Goggins (Eds.), *Big data factories, computational sciences: Collaborative approaches* (pp. 51–65). New York: Springer. https://link.springer.com/chapter/10.1007/978-3-319-59186-5_5.

Kee, K. F., & Browning, L. D. (2010). The dialectical tensions in the funding infrastructure of cyberinfrastructure. *Computer Supported Cooperative Work, 19*, 283–308.

Kee, K. F., Cradduck, L., Blodgett, B., & Olwan, R. (2011). Cyberinfrastructure inside out: Definitions and influencing forces shaping its emergence, development, and implementation. In D. Araya, Y. Breindl & T. Houghton (Eds.), *Nexus: New intersections in Internet research* (pp. 157–189). New York: Peter Lang.

Kossinets, G., & Watts, D. J. (2009). Origins of homophily in an evolving social network. *American Journal of Sociology, 115*, 405–450. doi:10.1086/599247.

Kirby, E. L., & Buzzanell, P. M. (2014). Communicating work-life issues. In L. L. Putnam & D. K. Mumby (Eds.), *The SAGE handbook of organizational communication: Advances in theory, research, and methods* (3rd ed., pp. 351–373). Thousand Oaks, CA: SAGE

Lai, C-H. (2017). A study of emergent organizing and technology affordances after a natural disaster. *Online Information Review, 41*, 507–523. doi:10.1108/OIR-10-2015-0343.

Laney, D. (2001). 3D data management: Controlling data volume, velocity and variety. *META Group Research Note, 6*, 70. https://blogs.gartner.com/doug-laney/files/2012/01/ad949-3D-Data-Management-Controlling-Data-Volume-Velocity-and-Variety.pdf.

Lee, K. M. (2004). Presence, explicated. *Communication Theory, 14*, 27–50. doi:10.1111/j.1468-2885.2004.tb00302.x.

Lee, S. A., & Liang, Y. (2016). The role of reciprocity in verbally persuasive robots. *Cyberpsychology, Behavior, and Social Networking, 19*, 524–527. doi:10.1089/cyber.2016.0124.

Leonardi, P. M. (2009). Why do people reject new technologies and stymie organizational changes of which they are in favor? Exploring misalignments between social interactions and materiality. *Human Communication Research, 35*, 407–441. doi:10.1111/j.1468-2958.2009.01357.x.

Leonardi, P. M. (2013). When does technology use enable network change in organizations? A comparative study of feature use and shared affordances. *MIS Quarterly*, *37*, 749–775. doi:10.25300/MISQ/2013/37.3.04.

Leonardi, P. M. (2014). Social media, knowledge sharing, and innovation. Toward a theory of communication visibility. *Information Systems Research*, *25*, 796-816. doi:10.1287/isre.2014.0536.

Leonardi, P. M., & Barley, S. R. (2010). What's under construction here? Social action, materiality, and power in constructivist studies of technology and organizing. *The Academy of Management Annals*, *4*, 1–51. doi:10.1080/19416521003654160.

Leonardi, P. M., Nardi, B. A., & Kallinikos, J. (2012). *Materiality and organizing: Social interaction in a technological world*. Oxford: Oxford University Press.

Leonardi, P. M., Treem, J. W., & Jackson, M. H. (2010). The connectivity paradox: Using technology to both decrease and increase perceptions of distance in distributed work arrangements. *Journal of Applied Communication Research*, *21*, 82–105. doi:10.1080/00909880903483599.

Lewis, L. K. (2011). *Organizational change: Creating change through strategic communication*. Chichester: Wiley-Blackwell.

Lewis, L. K. (2014). Organizational change and innovation. In L. L. Putnam & D. K. Mumby (Eds.), *The SAGE handbook of organizational communication* (3rd ed. pp. 503–524). Thousand Oaks, CA: SAGE.

Liang, Y., & Lee, S. A. (2016). Advancing the strategic messages affecting robot trust effect: The dynamic of user- and robot-generated content on human-robot trust and interaction outcomes. *Cyberpsychology, Behavior, and Social Networking*, *19*, 538–544. doi:10.1089/cyber.2016.0199

Markus, M. L. (1990). Toward a "critical mass" theory of interactive media. In J. Fulk & C. Steinfield (Eds.), *Organizations and communication technology* (pp. 194–218). Newbury Park, CA: SAGE.

Orlikowski, W. J. (2007). Sociomaterial practices: Exploring technology at work. *Organizational Studies*, *28*, 1435–1448. doi:10.1177/0170840607081138.

Reinsch, N. L., Turner, J. W., & Tinsley, C. H. (2008). Multicommunicating: A practice whose time has come? *Academy of Management Review*, *33*, 391–403. doi:10.5465/amr.2008.31193450.

Rice, R. E. (1992). Task analyzability, use of new media, and effectiveness: A multi-site exploration of media richness. *Organization Science*, *3*, 475–500. doi:10.1287/orsc.3.4.475.

Rice, R. E. (1993). Media appropriateness: Using social presence theory to compare traditional and new organizational media. *Human Communication Research*, *19*, 451–484. doi:10.1111/j.1468-2958.1993.tb00309.x.

Rice, R. E. (2009). Diffusion of innovations: Theoretical extensions. In R. Nabi & M. B. Oliver (Eds.), *Handbook of media effects* (pp. 489–503). Thousand Oaks, CA: SAGE.

Rice, R. E., Evans, S. K., Pearce, K. E., Sivunene, A., Vitak, J., & Treem, J. W. (2017). Organizational media affordances: Operationalization and associations with media use. *Journal of Communication*, *67*, 106–130. doi:10.1111/jcom.12273.

Rice, R. E., Hiltz, S. R., & Spencer, D. (2004). Media mixes and learning networks. In S. R. Hiltz & R. Goldman (Eds.), *Learning together online: Research on asynchronous learning* (pp. 215–237). Mahwah, NJ: Erlbaum.

Rice, R. E., & Leonardi, P. M. (2014). Information and communication technology use in organizations. In L. L. Putnam & D. K. Mumby (Eds.), *The SAGE handbook of organizational communication* (3rd ed., pp. 425–448). Thousand Oaks, CA: SAGE.

Rice, R. E., & Rogers, E. M. (1980). Reinvention in the innovation process. *Science Communication*, *1*, 499–514. doi:10.1177/107554708000100402.

Rogers, E. M. (1962). *Diffusion of innovations*. New York, NY: Free Press.

Rogers, E. M. (2003). *Diffusion of innovations* (5th ed.). New York, NY: Free Press.

Ryan, B., & Gross, N. C. (1943). The diffusion of hybrid seed corn in two Iowa communities. *Rural Sociology*, *8*, 15–24.

Schrock, A. R. (2015). Communicative affordances of mobile media: Portability, availability, locatability, and multimediality. *International Journal of Communication*, *9*, 1229–1246. http://ijoc.org/index.php/ijoc/article/view/3288/1363.

Short, J. A., Williams, E., & Christie, B. (1976). *The social psychology of telecommunications*. New York, NY: John Wiley & Sons.

Shumate, M., & Contractor, N. S. (2014). Emergence of multidimensional social networks. In L. L. Putnam & D. K. Mumby (Eds.), *The SAGE handbook of organizational communication* (3rd ed., pp. 449–474). Thousand Oaks, CA: SAGE.

Smith, W. R., Stephens, K. K., Robertson, B. W., Li. J., & Murthy, D. (2018). Social media in citizen-led disaster response: Rescuer roles, coordination challenges, and untapped potential. In K. Boersma & B. Tomaszewski (Eds.), *Proceedings of the 15th International ISCRAM Conference*. Rochester, NY, May 2018.

Starbird, K., & Palen, L. (2011). Voluntweeters: Self-organizing by digital volunteers in times of crisis, *Proceedings of CHI 2011* (pp. 1071–1080), Vancouver, Canada.

Stephens, K. K. (2007). The successive use of information and communication technologies at work. *Communication Theory*, *17*, 486–509. doi:10.1111/j.1468-2885.2007.00308.x.

Stephens, K. K. (2018). *Negotiating control: Organizations and mobile communication*. Oxford: Oxford University Press.

Stephens, K. K., & Ford, J. L. (2016). Unintended consequences of a strategically ambiguous organizational policy selectively restricting mobile device use at work. *Mobile Media & Communication*, *4*, 186–204. doi:10.1177/2050157915619211.

Stephens, K. K., & Mandhana, D. M. (2017). Media choice/use in organizations. In C. R. Scott & L. K. Lewis (Eds.), *The international encyclopedia of organizational communication* (online edition). Hoboken, NJ: Wiley-Blackwell. doi:10.1002/9781118955567.wbieoc131.

Stephens, K. K., Sørnes, J. O., Rice, R. E., Browning, L. D., & Sætre, A. S. (2008). Discrete, sequential, and follow-up use of information and communication technology by managerial knowledge workers. *Management Communication Quarterly*, *22*, 197–231. doi:10.1177/0893318908323149.

Stephens, K. K., Zhu, Y., Harrison, M., Iyer, M., Hairston, T., & Luk, J. (2017). *Bring your own mobile device (BYOD) to the hospital: Layered boundary barriers and divergent boundary management strategies*. Proceedings of the Fiftieth Annual Hawaii International Conference on Social Systems, Computer Society Press, 2017.

Stone, C. B., Neely, A. R., & Lengnick-Hall, M. L. (2018). Human resource management in the digital age: Big data, HR analytics and artificial intelligence. In P. N. Melo & C. Machado (Eds.), *Management and technological challenges in the digital age* (pp. 13–42). Boca Raton, FL: CRC Press Taylor & Francis.

Treem, J. W., & Leonardi, P. M. (2012). Social media use in organizations: Exploring the affordances of visibility, editability, persistence, and association. In C. T. Salmon (Ed.), *Communication yearbook 36* (pp. 143–189). New York, NY: Routledge.

Trevino, L. K., Lengel, R. H., & Daft, R. L. (1987). Media symbolism, media richness, and media choice in organizations: A symbolic interactionist perspective. *Communication Research*, *14*, 553–574. doi:10.1177/009365087014005006.

Valente, T. W., & Pumpuang, P. (2007). Identifying opinion leaders to promote behavior change. *Health Education & Behavior*, *34*, 881–896. doi:10.1177/1090198106297855.

Weick, K. E. (1979). *The social psychology of organizing* (2nd ed.). Redding, MA: Addison-Wesley.

Zorn, T. E., Flanagin, A. J., & Shoham, M. D. (2011). Institutional and noninstitutional influences on information and communication technology adoption and use among nonprofit organizations. *Human Communication Research*, *37*, 1–33. doi:10.1111/j.1468-2958.2010.01387.x.

20 Globalization and Organizational Communication

Jennifer L. Gibbs and Shiv Ganesh

Globalization has been defined as the increasing interconnectedness of the world in terms of four dimensions: extensity (expanding scale), intensity (growing magnitude), velocity (speeding up), and impact (deepening consequences) of interregional flows and patterns of social interaction (Held & McGrew, 2003). It is a process of "intensification of worldwide social relations and interactions such that distant events acquire very localized impacts and vice versa" (Held & McGrew, 2007, p. 2). As such, globalization is fundamentally communicative and has important implications for organizational communication. Indeed, scholars of organizational communication have been studying global organizing processes for the past two decades, which have given rise to new global organizational forms such as global virtual teams, global social movements, and global network organizations. A unique feature of these new organizational forms is that they have no physical instantiation, such that they are entirely constituted through communication practices. Further, they allow for new forms of collective action and collaboration across time, space, and other boundaries.

Research on globalization spans a variety of disciplines including sociology, anthropology, political science, management, and communication. Organizational communication scholars draw on broader social traditions to study global patterns of interaction and new organizing forms in a variety of ways. Topics of study in organizational communication include global virtual team collaboration (Connaughton & Shuffler, 2007; Gibbs, 2009), global networks and network organizations (Fulk, Monge, & Hollingshead, 2005; Shumate & O'Connor, 2010), global social movements (Dempsey, Parker, & Krone, 2011; Ganesh & Stohl, 2010, 2013), corporate social responsibility (Stohl, Stohl, & Townsley, 2007; Zoller, 2004), use of communication technologies (Monge, 1998; Monge & Fulk, 1999), and globalization of organizational culture (Stohl, 2001; Wieland, 2011). Many studies of globalization have either explicitly or implicitly documented tensions that play out in various ways.

Dialectical Tensions in Globalization

Globalization involves inherent tensions between convergence and divergence (Held, McGrew, Goldblatt, & Perraton, 1999; Stohl, 2001). On the one hand, it involves processes of standardization that result in similar organizational structuring across nations; on the other, it involves processes of polarization as the centrifugal forces of cultural diversity and identity push back against the centripetal forces of convergence. It involves the interlacing of the global and the local, also known as "glocalization" (Robertson, 1992).

Precisely because globalization is a complex and multidimensional process consisting of economic, political, technological, cultural, and environmental dimensions and imperatives, it is also uneven, playing out differently in different spheres, with some countries or regions being more globalized than others and various dimensions of globalization interacting differently even in highly globalized regions. Thus, it involves restructuring of social relations and new patterns of global stratification and power relations at both supra-state and sub-state levels (Scholte, 2005). Key features of multidimensional globalization include: (1) Time-space distantiation, in which those in different locations can experience the same event through the compression of time and space; (2) the disembedding of events and institutions and new realignments and restructuring of social interaction across time and space, enabling collective action in new ways; and (3) an increase in global consciousness through processes of reflexivity as we establish our position in relation to the global system, heightening local politics and identity (Giddens, 1991; Monge, 1998).

Organizational communication scholars have begun to regard tensions and contradictions as normal, ubiquitous features of organizing (Putnam, Fairhurst, & Banghart, 2016; Trethewey & Ashcraft, 2004). A dialectical tension is defined as an opposition between two conflicting or competing poles, such that that both poles (goals, needs) are equally necessary and desired and it is not possible to make a simple either-or choice between one or the other. Productive strategies for managing dialectical tensions require the development of communicative practices that find a way to mutually attend to both poles in a way that acknowledges each one as well as overcoming or transforming the contradiction, through "both-and" approaches (Putnam & Boys, 2006).

The dialectical tensions inherent in globalization can be framed in terms of three broad types: ontological, epistemological, and axiological (see Chapter 4). Ontological refers to how globalization has been defined and what it is. Epistemological refers to how globalization has been studied. Axiological refers to how globalization is judged and evaluated. (Note that ontological, epistemological, and axiological commitments are not necessarily aligned. For instance, similar ontological commitments may produce very different epistemological or axiological assessments.) In the rest of the chapter, we will discuss each category of tensions both in terms of (1) how each pole of the tension has been studied in the literature, as well as (2) how framing the field through the lens of dialectical tensions can help us better conceptualize connections among interrelated phenomena that have previously been studied separately by communication scholars. In this way, we hope to help integrate and frame the field as well as provide a call to action for communication scholars to make more concerted efforts to place diverse and opposed views into dialogue with one another.

Ontological Tensions

Ontological tensions are evident both in terms of what globalization "is" and its impact, as well as how it has been defined. We examine two types of ontological tensions: transformationalist versus skeptical, and totalizing versus particularistic.

Transformationalist vs. skeptical. The first ontological tension concerns the degree to which globalization represents a novel phenomenon. Scholars often take one of two perspectives: *transformationalists* argue that globalization is fundamentally reshaping the world, while skeptics see it as a continuation of social, economic, or political processes that have been occurring for hundreds of years. Held and McGrew (2007) distinguish between the *globalists* and the *skeptics*. The globalists regard globalization as a process of growing convergence or interconnectedness, in which global markets, governance, and civil society are replacing nation states and national economies as dominant power structures. Scholars in this camp take both utopian and dystopian perspectives: Neoliberals celebrate world unification and seamless global markets ("global village") (McLuhan & Powers, 1989; Negroponte, 1995; Ohmae, 1995), while neo-Marxists critique global capitalism and corporations for creating growing inequalities and cultural imperialism ("global pillage") (Sklair, 1991; Wallerstein, 1974).

This debate has played out in public policy around the Washington Consensus, a neoliberal policy agenda consisting of ten policy points proposed by the economist John Williamson in 1989 (Williamson, 2002) and designed to help facilitate globalization in developing countries. Its points consist of financial and trade liberalization, deregulation, and privatization of state enterprises, among other things. Globalization has thus become largely synonymous with neoliberalism (or the view that free and open markets will provide for equality and social change), and while its impacts are hotly contested, it is generally regarded as a transformational process that is changing society in significant ways. Other scholars recognize that globalization is not a process of homogenization but may be an uneven process of transformation that is characterized by new patterns of global stratification that reinforce some power structures while reconfiguring others (Appadurai, 1990; Featherstone, 1990; Giddens, 2003; Tomlinson, 1999). Scholars in both of these camps agree on the fact that fundamental change is occurring due to globalization, however.

On the other hand, the *skeptical* view regards the world as less interdependent than in the 1890s (Held et al., 1999) and as characterized by divergence and fragmentation, discounting notions of global markets or global civil society (Johnson, 1991; McGee, 1990; Scott, 1997). In this view, some regionalization is occurring, but overall the nation-state is not dying and national economies and governments retain their power. Scholars taking a skeptical view argue that capitalism may have taken on new shape, but that a powerful class antagonism between employers and workers still exists (Cloud, 2001). Skeptics point to the increasing digital divide and marginalization of the South and developing countries (Hirst & Thompson, 1996), as well as the resurgence of nationalism and religious fundamentalism that has led to increasing conflicts among and within civilizations (Barber, 1995; Huntington, 1996; Kotkin, 1992). While the globalist/transformationalist view was the dominant one in the 1990s, post 9/11 the skeptical view has come to the forefront due to heightened ethnic, religious, and political polarization.

Totalizing vs. particularistic. Another difference in how globalization has been conceptualized has been in terms of either a totalizing process or a particularistic phenomenon. This relates to the tensions between convergence and divergence mentioned above (Stohl, 2001). Scholars who take a *totalizing* view tend to study globalization in terms of a universal set of processes or phenomena that transcends particular local contexts. For instance, Perlmutter's (1969) geocentric orientation describes a management style that is oriented to the world rather than to the company's home country (ethnocentric) or to the host country (polycentric). Multinational organizations taking a geocentric orientation attempt to find the best managers and workers to perform their work from across the globe, regardless of nationality. They also engage in collaboration between headquarters and subsidiaries to establish universal standards and policies, allowing for local variations as needed. Examples of organizational communication studies taking a totalizing approach include studies of global teams (Gibbs, 2009; Gibson & Gibbs, 2006), global network organizations (Fulk et al., 2005; Stohl & Stohl, 2005), and cross-cultural comparative studies that draw on established cultural taxonomies (Javidan, Dorfman, Sully de Luque, & House, 2006), as each type attempts to theorize globalization processes that transcend particular cultures or contexts.

Scholars who take a particularistic view, on the other hand, tend to focus on global phenomena as embedded in particular local contexts, with an attempt to trace the contextual features and provide deep understanding of a particular context or phenomenon rather than build to a grand narrative or theory. For instance, McAllum (2018) studied the important role of volunteers in long-term refugee resettlement, a particular aspect of the globalization process. Her qualitative study examines how volunteers' commitment was collectively structured by their relationships with other volunteer coordinators, their own significant others, and the refugees they were assisting in ways that led to organizational detachment or exit. While her study is not about globalization writ large, it helps to explain a particular aspect of national border crossing while also contributing theoretical understanding of an important organizational communication construct (organizational commitment). Another example of the particularistic strands of globalization is the theoretical and methodological parochialism discussed by Stohl (2001) that limits global research. She points out that many of our communication theories are Eurocentric yet positioned as universal; our methods are limited through different interpretations and translations of concepts and lack of equivalence in measures; and researchers are insulated in cultural and disciplinary silos, limiting international collaboration. These parochialisms result in more particularistic research perspectives (or totalizing views that are in fact less universal than claimed).

Research studies taking transformationalist versus skeptical or totalizing versus particularistic perspectives tend to remain largely separate in the literature. Positioning these as dialectical tensions requires scholars to put these seemingly competing views into constructive opposition with one another in order to place them in dialogue. Doing so will help to enrich larger ontological debates and conceptions of what globalization is. Each pole captures legitimate facets of contemporary globalization processes, which are multifaceted as well as changing over time in light of the current cultural and historical context. While the convergence (transformationalist, totalizing) view tended to dominate early globalization discourse in the 1990s during the Internet dot.com boom and celebration of open markets and the information superhighway (Sturken & Thomas, 2004), post-9/11 popular discourse about globalization in the 2000s and 2010s has shifted to emphasize divergence and polarization stemming from rising political populism and economic tribalism.

Prior to 9/11, globalization discourse often emphasized the harmonious "global village" notion of one unified, borderless world. Indeed, a survey of ethnically diverse residents of Los Angeles found that the majority of participants associated globalization with utopian visions of growing interconnectedness and inclusion as new technologies made the world smaller and brought people closer together (Gibbs, Ball-Rokeach, Jung, Kim, & Qiu, 2004). Such optimistic views seem rather naïve in a post-9/11 world that has become increasingly ruptured by ethnic and national conflicts and divisiveness. Indeed, the skeptical viewpoint has gained traction as increasingly scholars point to the war on terrorism and other conflicts as indicative of the end of globalization (Held & McGrew, 2007). This can also be seen in the shift in political discourse and policy from economic liberalization to protectionism and from building regional alliances such as NAFTA, the European Union, and ASEAN to the breakdown of these international unions through Brexit and the isolationist policies of current populist leaders. Putting totalizing and particularistic perspectives and discourses into tension with one another provides flexibility to allow for changes in how globalization has been regarded and experienced over time due to the changing political landscape while helping to integrate these diverse strands into a single (yet multifaceted) phenomenon. It also provides for a fuller understanding of the coexistence of contradictory and seemingly opposed processes and viewpoints.

Epistemological Tensions

A second set of tensions is evident in this research area around how globalization has been studied. We examine two types of epistemological tensions: micro versus macro, and foreground versus background.

Micro vs. macro. Scholars of organizational communication have studied globalization phenomena at a variety of levels of analysis, ranging from the individual and team levels to the organizational and societal levels. At the micro level, scholars have studied individual and team interactions, processes, and outcomes in globally distributed teams and organizations (e.g., Connaughton & Shuffler, 2007; Fulk et al., 2005; Gibson & Gibbs, 2006; Yuan & Gay, 2006). For example, Gibbs (2009) conducted an ethnography of a global software team involved in offshore outsourcing work and found that global team interaction was characterized by irresolvable tensions between autonomy versus connectedness, inclusion versus exclusion, and empowerment versus disempowerment. These tensions could be productive or detrimental, depending on the communicative responses to them. Those in higher-status positions, such as managers, were more likely to experience communicative tensions as empowering, whereas lower-level foreign assignees were more likely to be disenfranchised by them. At the macro-level, scholars have examined global discourses, networks, and social movements, taking into account the broader institutional logics represented in global organizing processes (e.g., Stohl & Stohl, 2005). For example, Ganesh & Stohl (2013) interviewed activists at the Occupy Wellington protest to capture the ubiquity of digital media and illustrate the various institutional logics operating in activist organizing practices.

Globalization crosses multiple levels of analysis and involves tensions between macro and micro phenomena. The same concepts may be studied at different levels. For example, questions of democracy and equality are at the heart of globalization. Globalization processes are fraught with power dynamics on a geopolitical scale as they exacerbate divides between developed and developing countries. Zoller (2004) examines transnational corporate power by studying discourse of the Transatlantic Business Dialogue (TABD), a formal agreement between business and governments of the European Union and the United States, finding that the discourse of dialogue can legitimate corporate hegemony and empower free markets in global trade. Power dynamics are also evident in more micro processes of global organizing such as in global team interaction and global collaboration processes. For instance, status differences have been found to arise in global work arrangements as members from the global headquarters site take on higher status than those at remote locations (Leonardi

& Rodriguez-Lluesma, 2013). Another study of a global organization found that the communication visibility afforded by enterprise social media brought to light knowledge disparities among status groups and thus reinforced status hierarchies (Kim, 2018).

However, once again the literature has primarily selected one level (either micro or macro) and focused on it without explicitly examining the connections across levels. Taking a dialectical tension-based approach would require considering the ways in which micro social interactions (at the individual or team level) scale up and both shape and are shaped by more macro phenomena such as institutional logics, discourses, and structures. For instance, studies could examine how larger institutional logics and discourses impact global team interaction and practices, or how the social networks of organizational members scale up to organizational networks among institutional actors.

Foreground vs. background. Early studies of organizational communication and globalization were prone to trying to understand what globalization itself was, attempting to *assess its impact in broad terms* on organizational communication processes, and in this sense, globalization was very much in the *foreground* of organizational communication studies. For instance, Stohl (1993) posits the emergence of three major types of international organizations— international governmental organizations (IGOS), international nongovernmental organizations (INGOs), and multinational corporations (MNCs)—as being a response to the increasing encounter with diversity and difference caused by the speed-up and intensification of transnational flows of information and capital. More locally, Stage (1999) assessed the impact of a global multinational corporate culture upon its subsidiary in Thailand, arguing that local employees had to explicitly negotiate the legitimacy global culture and values in the context of local expectations about such norms as participation and workload. Dempsey et al.'s (2011) work on Transnational Feminist Networks also looked at the impact that transnationalism had upon feminist forms of organizing, arguing that transnational feminist networks emerged in order to bridge scales of organizing and create intersectional forms of solidarity across borders and social categories.

In the late 1990s and early 2000s, researchers were more prone to trying to assess the impact and significance of *particular aspects of globalization*. For instance, the word "neoliberalism," which signifies the unfettered flow of private capital across markets over the world, epitomized in the slogan "free markets," came into organizational communication studies around the turn of the century. Ganesh (2003), for example, looks at how neoliberalism impacted the structure of a nongovernmental organization (NGO), arguing that the overall emphasis upon a market orientation to social change significantly truncated its ability to obtain its social change goals. Ganesh and Stohl (2013) looked at how networking logics produced in one location impact activist practice in another, focusing upon the Occupy Movement and its translation from Wall Street in New York to Wellington in Aotearoa New Zealand.

Even later, scholars started to look at aspects of organizational communication that were "post-global"; that is, were conceptualized and thought about after globalization became part of the conceptual vocabulary of organizational communication studies. In this sense, these studies treat globalization as part of the *background* of organizational communication studies, and regard it as ubiquitous, normal and unremarkable (Stohl & Ganesh, 2014). Concepts such as entrepreneurship that emphasize agency, initiative and freedom, as Rebecca Gill (2014) has argued, circulate as much as they do because they work to support neoliberal capitalism. Other scholars have studied similar post-global concepts such as outsourcing arrangements (Gibbs, 2009; Leonardi & Bailey, 2008), contingent labor (Townsley & Stohl, 2003), and cultural intelligence (Dutta & Dutta, 2013). We would argue that even the recent focus on cross-sectoral partnerships, exemplified well in work by Shumate and O'Connor (2010) on such notions as symbiotic sustainability between corporations and NGOs and in work by Mitra (2018) on natural resource management in the U.S. Arctic, is a product of a post-global sensibility in organizational communication studies.

While there has been a clear move from "foreground" to "background" thinking, we posit that a full consideration of globalization must involve holding foreground and background in dialectical tension, despite, and perhaps because of the increasing tendency to see it as a background concept. Doing so is useful because we observe that our use of the term "globalization" in organizational communication studies is increasingly casual, precisely because it is a background concept. Further, the lack of explicit emphasis on globalization as a concept does not mean that the phenomenon has disappeared; rather, it has become ubiquitous. We note for instance, that 63 entries in the 2017 *Encyclopedia of Organizational Communication* referenced the term on topics ranging from change to technology, gender, and collective action. The casualization of globalization vocabulary might encourage theoretical laziness about the term, and prevent us from understanding how globalization is itself changing and impacting organizational communication anew. For example, recent predictions and assessments about imminent contractions of the global economy (e.g., Sassen, 2014) upend our assumptions about the inexorable spread of globalization. What are the implications for global organizations?

Axiological Tensions

A third set of tensions deals with values, in terms of whether globalization is inherently positive or negative. We examine two types of axiological tensions. First, we examine whether globalization is understood broadly as a good or bad force, and second, we look specifically at plural versus imperial tensions in globalization.

Good vs. bad. Some scholars have understood globalization primarily as a force for social, cultural and political good, whereas others have considered it a corrosive or corrupt force. There are three dimensions along which scholars have tended to valorize globalization as either good or bad. First, scholars who have understood globalization in terms of cosmopolitanism have tended to see globalization as a positive force. This is particularly true of work that sees globalization in cultural terms. Taylor and Osland (2011), for example, posit that cosmopolitanism, which they understand as a cognitive and moral orientation towards the world outside the local, is a major factor in the development of cultural intelligence in organizations and promotes organizational learning. Sobre-Denton and Bardhan (2013) also developed the notion of "cosmopolitanism from below" in order to understand and explain communicative dynamics at play in an international youth hosteling chain, whose mission was to help young people gain a better appreciation and understanding of the world.

Others have valorized globalization along the lines of what one might call public and private dimensions. Some scholars understand globalization as a privatizing force, often taking an economic view of globalization in the process. Cheney and Cloud (2006), for instance, positioned globalization as a private system that privileges and promotes free markets, and consequently undermines worker rights in particular and workplace democracy more broadly. Conversely, other scholars who have understood globalization in more public and democratic terms have valorized it as a force for good. Stohl and Stohl (2005), for example, examined how global networks of nongovernmental organizations (NGOs) working on human rights issues have served to complement and strengthen not only an intergovernmental public regime that addresses human rights violations, but global governance at large.

A third, and perhaps more subtle way that scholarship in organizational communication studies has valorized globalization has been in its use of terms such as "global" or "local." Terms such as "local communities," for example, are often valorized as a force for good. Medved et al. (2001), for instance, studied how systemic exclusionary practices in healthcare could be overcome and ameliorated when providers engaged in comprehensive stakeholder dialogues with local communities. Scholars have on other occasions been aware of the need to critique and assess how local communities are valorized both in research and in practice. Dempsey (2010), for instance, used insights from transnational feminism to assess and evaluate campus–community partnerships in an American university, arguing that unreflexive understandings of local communities could perhaps undermine broader solidarities that could be formed across locations.

Plural vs. imperial. Another axiological tension in our treatment of globalization can be framed in terms of plural versus imperial. At first blush, it might appear that this tension is a subset of the large good–bad tension highlighted earlier; however, we observe that there are several instances when pluralist notions of globalization can be seen in negative terms, particularly when pluralism is understood as cultural relativism. Conversely, ostensibly imperial notions of globalization—such as global science—can actually be understood as a force for good. In organizational communication scholarship in particular, tension between pluralism on one hand and imperialism on the other has informed research in two senses.

First, researchers themselves have been committed to varying degrees as to whether they view globalization itself as a form of convergence or divergence (Stohl, 2001). That is, for some scholars, globalization is seen as a communicative encounter with difference, while for others it involves the imposition of a more specific set of communicative practices, discourses, and rationalities. For instance, scholarship that has explored issues of cultural diversity in organizations has often begun from the standpoint that globalization has created those conditions (e.g., Stage, 1999). Other scholars who have understood globalization as a particular set of economic rationalities (e.g., Ganesh, 2005; Ganesh, Zoller & Cheney, 2005) see it as being a powerful converging and transformative force.

In a second sense, scholars have argued that organizational communication research on globalization is itself imperial. Broadfoot and Munshi (2007, p. 249), for instance, argue that "much organizational communication scholarship conducted within the global context is performed and interpreted from the dominant Euro-American intellectual tradition, privileging those concepts as well as particular voices and traditions and often ignoring inequality and exploitation within the scholarly community." This view has been shared in varying degrees by other scholars. Stohl's (2001) work, which we have already mentioned, which identified a set of theoretical, methodological and pragmatic parochialisms associated with organizational communication scholarship, is a good example of this. However, scholars diverge in the extent to which they are willing to view organizational communication as an imperial force. Zoller's (2006) and Ashcraft's (2006) responses to a provocation by Prichard (2006), who argued that much organizational communication scholarship was a form of American imperialism, illustrate this tension vividly.

Our own view is that axiological tensions need to be understood in complex terms precisely because of the complexity and ambiguity associated with globalization. It is problematic to understand globalization as an unqualified good, but equally worrisome to treat it as a force for evil, especially at a time when, as we have discussed earlier, local and anti-democratic dynamics across the world appear to be eroding the democratic foundations of global civil society and the global commons. Whether we are studying ethics in virtual teams, the labor implications of outsourcing, the efficacy of transnational activist organizing, or the spread of NGO networks, it is critical to pay attention to both positive and negative dynamics of globalization, and to take broad synchronic (focusing on the current moment) as well as diachronic (examining changes over time) views of globalization. For instance, while the global HIV/AIDS pandemic was horrifying in its impact, historians have subsequently traced its pivotal role in the formation of LGBTQ activism in countries that had no overt track record of such mobilizations. In the final section, we will consider the different ways in which globalization research has treated communication, organization, and the C-O dynamic.

Treatment of Communication and Organization

Globalization scholars come from a variety of disciplines and adopt varying conceptualizations of communication. While scholars from disciplines such as sociology, management, and political science often treat communication as a simple process of *transmission of messages* and scholars in anthropology focus on *cultural meaning*, this chapter demonstrates that scholars in organizational communication tend to take *constitutive* approaches that regard global phenomena as communicatively constructed. For example, Gibbs (2009) examines discursive tensions in a global outsourcing organization and how they are experienced and managed by global team members. Another example is Kim's (2018) study of how social media use and status hierarchies are mutually constituted in global organizing processes. Indeed, the dialectical framework we draw on here is grounded in a constitutive approach (Putnam et al., 2016).

Scholarship in global organizational communication tends to vary in its treatment of organization, ranging from underlying assumptions of organization as process (O_1), structure (O_2), and entity (O_3). For instance, Dempsey et al.'s (2011) work on transnational feminist networks takes a process (O_1) approach by examining the ways in which transnationalism leads to the emergence of feminist forms of organizing. Other research on global network organizations takes a more structural (O_2) approach (Fulk et al., 2005; Monge & Fulk, 1999), as it takes as its object of inquiry the network structures that are enabled by new communication technologies. Still other scholars regard organizations as entitative beings (O_3). This line of scholarship is exemplified by Ganesh and Stohl's (2010) research on the social justice movement in Aotearoa New Zealand, which takes on the status of a coordinated or ordered entity through collective action of various stakeholders.

The C-O dynamic presented in Chapter 1 refers to the interrelationship between communication and organization. This dynamic is mirrored in globalization theory by the relationship between agency and structure. Approaches to globalization theory once again vary from views that emphasize structure including both utopian (Ohmae, 1995) and dystopian globalist views (Wallerstein, 1974) to views that highlight individual agency. For instance, Wallerstein's world-system theory regards core–periphery inequalities as determining forces and thus views global capitalism as systemic and totalizing rather than influenced by individual agency. On the other hand, anthropological and cultural approaches (e.g., Featherstone, 1990) situate globalization as a process of individual meaning making as individuals actively appropriate global forms to (re) negotiate local cultural identity within a globalizing context. Still other scholars such as Giddens (1991, 2003) conceptualize globalization as a structurational process in which individual agency and interactions both shape and are shaped by global forces and structural resources, such that the local and global are mutually constitutive. Organizational scholars vary in their treatment of the C-O dynamic, but it is fair to say that theory on global organizational communication has been heavily influenced by Giddens' recursive view of globalization (e.g., Monge, 1998; Stohl, 2001, 2005; Stohl et al., 2007). For example, Stohl et al. (2007) conceptualize the new generation of global corporate social responsibility (CSR) as incorporating four key features: (1) There is no longer a distinction between "out there" and "in here," such that all organizational stakeholders must establish themselves in relation to the global system rather than outside of it; (2) "glocalization" (Robertson, 1992) involving the restructuring of social interaction across time and space such that global structures and local interactions mutually shape one another; (3) complex communication networks among societies, cultures, institutions, and individuals; and (4) permeability of public and private boundaries. This conceptualization recognizes the dynamic interplay among local communication practices and stakeholders and global social, organizational, and institutional structures.

Conclusion

In this chapter, we have attempted to frame the literature on globalization and organizational communication through a theoretical framework of dialectical tensions. Our review has highlighted three overarching categories—ontological, epistemological, and axiological—that bring to light important differences in the ways that globalization has been studied by organizational communication scholars in terms of (1) its very nature and how it has been defined and conceptualized, (2) how it has been studied in terms of the phenomena and types of knowledge produced, and (3) the value judgments made about it and its ethical implications. We do not seek to resolve these debates, but rather to embrace them. Taken together, we hope that this framing will help to integrate the field of global organizational communication and provide conceptual tools to help advance scholarship in this area. Taking a tensional approach (Putnam et al., 2016) helps to articulate differences in approaches to scholarship in this area—for instance, totalizing vs. particularistic, micro vs. macro, and plural vs. imperial—and juxtapose them in order to find connections among seemingly disparate views. In addition, framing the field through a lens of dialectical tensions provides a call for communication scholars to better conceptualize intricate nuances among interrelated phenomena that have been studied separately in the literature by placing competing views into dialogue with one another. Given the multifaceted and historically changing nature of globalization, theorizing and studying its tensions is a way to provide for fuller understanding of its complexities and allow for the coexistence of contradictory processes and changing views, thus enriching the field and allowing it to continue to evolve.

Recommended Supplementary Readings

Ganesh, S., Zoller, H., & Cheney, G. (2005). Transforming resistance: Critical organizational communication meets globalization from below. *Communication Monographs*, *72*, 169–191.
Makes the case for organizational communication research to study global social movements.
Giddens, A. (2003). *Runaway world: How globalization is reshaping our lives.* New York: Routledge.
Primer on globalization theory from a transformationalist perspective.
Held, D., McGrew, A., Goldblatt, D., & Perraton, J. (1999). *Global transformations: Politics, economics, and culture.* Stanford, CA: Stanford University Press.
Provides a comprehensive overview of globalization theory and outlines the globalist, skeptic, and transformationalist views.
Held, D., & McGrew, A. (2007). *Globalization/anti-globalization: Beyond the great divide.* Malden, MA: Polity Press.
Provides a comparison of the globalist and skeptic views and challenges the skeptical view that globalization is over in a post-9/11 era.
Rooney, D., & Chavan, M. (2017). Globalization/internationalization. In C. Scott & L. Lewis (Eds.), *International encyclopedia of organizational communication* (online edition). Hoboken, NJ: Wiley-Blackwell.
Provides an overview of formal organizational dimensions of globalization.
Scholte, J. A. (2005). *Globalization: A critical introduction* (2nd ed.). New York: Palgrave Macmillan.
Provides a comprehensive overview of the dimensions of globalization, arguing that supraterritoriality is its most defining feature.
Stohl, C. (2001). Globalizing organizational communication. In F. M. Jablin & L. L. Putnam (Eds.), *The new handbook of organizational communication* (pp. 323–375). Thousand Oaks, CA: SAGE.
Provides the first comprehensive account of the state of research in globalization in organizational communication studies, drawing from a convergence/divergence dialectic.
Stohl, C., & Ganesh, S. (2014). Generating globalization. In L. L. Putnam & D. K. Mumby (Eds.), *The SAGE handbook of organizational communication* (3rd ed., pp. 717–741). Los Angeles: SAGE.
Categorizes research into three generations of globalization to show how conceptualizations and approaches have changed over time.

Important Concepts: Define and Discuss

Axiological
Eco-localism
Epistemological
Globalist
Globalization
Imperialism
Ontological
Particularistic
Pluralism
Skeptic
Totalizing
Transformationalist

Discussion Questions

1. What are the key ontological, epistemological, and axiological tensions in research on globalization?
2. How have conceptualizations of globalization and its impacts changed over time?
3. How has organizational communication research approached the study of globalization at both micro- and macro-levels of analysis?
4. What is the value of taking a tensional approach to study globalization, in particular, and in research more broadly?
5. Think of a pressing global problem (e.g., climate change, economic inequality, social injustice, terrorism). How might an organizational communication scholar go about addressing this problem? What communicative phenomena, types of interaction, and stakeholders would you study?

Practitioners' Corner: Eco-Local Design

Over the past 10–15 years, eco-local design has become a buzzword among practitioners in many fields, ranging from community planning and social movement organizers on one hand, to project managers and economic policy analysts on the other. The term "eco-localism" was coined to draw attention to the need for local communities to engage in cohesive communication and planning around potential global environmental and economic challenges such as climate change or global market collapse (Ganesh and Zoller, 2014). The impact of climate change, for example, is likely to be entirely local in how it manifests, and local governance mechanisms have to be developed to develop mitigating projects on a host of fronts, ranging from new stormwater drains and flood protections to robust forms of civil defense and disaster preparedness.

There are many examples of eco-local design. The Transition Initiatives project, which attempts to help communities be resilient in the face of environmental and economic collapse is a fairly high-profile one (see www.transitionus.org or www.transitionnetwork.org), but so are others like Ecolocal UK (www.ecolocal.org.uk), a social enterprise that creates products and services designed to help people and communities move to a more environmentally sustainable way of life. Have a look at these websites, and pay particular attention to how the various tensions listed in this chapter might help your understanding of eco-localism. For example, you will likely find both transformationalist and skeptical understandings of globalization coexisting in eco-localism—on one hand eco-localists believe that the global era is over, but on the other, they believe that a global localized approach is required to deal with global crises! Likewise, there are both foreground aspects to globalization as well as background aspects to globalization in eco-localism, inasmuch as eco-localists have to talk about globalization in some way to demonstrate the importance of their work, but at the same time, have to de-emphasize it in order to get people to think about and act upon these same issues in their everyday life.

Consider how the other tensions—totalizing versus particularistic, micro versus macro, good versus bad, and plural versus imperial—are evident in eco-localism. We have said in our chapter that all these tensions need to be held *together* rather than separately to enable good practice. Whether one is a community organizer, activist, policymaker, city planner or an elected official, designing appropriate forms of eco-local governance requires the ability to analyze the multiple and often contradictory dimensions of particular projects, and the template that we have presented here is helpful in this crucial analytical task that can enable appropriate eco-local design.

References

Appadurai, A. (1990). Disjuncture and difference in the global cultural economy. In M. Featherstone (Ed.), *Global culture: Nationalism, globalism and modernity* (pp. 295–310). London: SAGE.

Ashcraft, K. (2006). Falling from a humble perch? Rereading organizational communication studies with an attitude of alliance. *Management Communication Quarterly, 19,* 645–652. doi:10.1177/0893318905285389.

Barber, B. (1995). *Jihad vs. McWorld.* New York: Times Books.

Broadfoot, K. J., & Munshi, D. (2007). Diverse voices and alternative rationalities: Imaging forms of postcolonial organizational communication. *Management Communication Quarterly, 21,* 249–267. doi:10.1177/0893318907306037.

Cheney, G., & Cloud, D. (2006). Doing democracy, engaging the material: Employee participation and labor activity in an age of market globalization. *Management Communication Quarterly, 19,* 1–40. doi:10.1177/0893318905285485.

Cloud, D. (2001). Laboring under the sign of the new: Cultural studies, organizational communication, and the fallacy of the new economy. *Management Communication Quarterly 15,* 268–278. doi:10.1177/0893318901152006.

Connaughton, S. L., & Shuffler, M. (2007). Multinational multicultural distributed teams: A review and future agenda. *Small Group Research, 38,* 387–412. doi:10.1177/1046496407301970.

Dempsey, S. E. (2010). Critiquing community engagement. *Management Communication Quarterly, 24,* 359–390. doi:10.1177/0893318909352247.

Dempsey, S. E., Parker, P. S., & Krone, K. J. (2011). Navigating socio-spatial difference, constructing counter-space: Insights from transnational feminist praxis. *Journal of International and Intercultural Communication, 4,* 201–220. doi:10.1080/17513057.2011.569973.

Dutta, M. J., & Dutta, D. (2013). Multinational going cultural: A postcolonial deconstruction of cultural intelligence. *Journal of International and Intercultural Communication, 6,* 241–258. doi:10.1080/17513057.2013.790989.

Featherstone, M. (Ed.). (1990). *Global culture: Nationalism, globalism and modernity.* London: SAGE.

Fulk, J., Monge, P., & Hollingshead, A. B. (2005). Knowledge resource sharing in dispersed multinational teams: Three theoretical lenses. In D. L. Shapiro, M. A. Von Glinow, & J. L. C. Cheng (Eds.), *Managing multinational teams: Global perspectives* (pp. 155–188). San Diego, CA: Elsevier.

Ganesh, S. (2003). Organizational narcissism: Technology, legitimacy and identity in an Indian NGO. *Management Communication Quarterly, 16,* 558–594. doi:10.1177/0893318903252539.

Ganesh, S. (2005). The myth of the nongovernmental organization: Governmentality and transnationalism in an Indian NGO. In G. Cheney, & G. A. Barnett (Eds.), *International and multicultural organizational communication* (pp. 197–223). United States: Hampton Press.

Ganesh, S. & Stohl, C. (2010). Qualifying engagement: A study of information and communication technology and the global social justice movement in Aotearoa New Zealand. *Communication Monographs, 77,* 51–74. doi:10.1080/03637750903514284.

Ganesh, S., & Stohl, C. (2013). From Wall Street to Wellington: Protests in an era of digital ubiquity. *Communication Monographs, 80,* 425–451. doi:10.1080/03637751.2013.828156.

Ganesh, S. & Zoller, H. M. (2014) Organising transition: Principles and tensions in eco-localism. In M. Parker, G. Cheney, V. Fournier, & C. Land (Eds.), *The Routledge companion to alternative organisation.* Oxford: Routledge.

Ganesh, S., Zoller, H., & Cheney, G. (2005). Transforming resistance, broadening our boundaries: Critical organizational communication meets globalization from below. *Communication Monographs, 72,* 169–191. doi:10.1080/03637750500111872.

Gibbs, J. L. (2009). Dialectics in a global software team: Negotiating tensions across time, space, and culture. *Human Relations, 62*, 905–935. doi:10.1177/0018726709104547.

Gibbs, J. L., Ball-Rokeach, S. J., Jung, J., Kim, Y., & Qiu, J. (2004). The globalization of everyday life: Visions and reality. In M. Sturken, D. Thomas, & S. Ball-Rokeach (Eds.), *Technological visions: The hopes and fears that shape new technologies* (pp. 339–358). Philadelphia: Temple University Press.

Gibson, C. B., & Gibbs, J. L. (2006). Unpacking the concept of virtuality: The effects of geographic dispersion, electronic dependence, dynamic structure, and national diversity on team innovation. *Administrative Science Quarterly, 51*, 451–495. doi:10.2189/asqu.51.3.451.

Giddens, A. (1991). *Modernity and self-identity: Self and society in the late modern age.* Stanford, CA: Stanford University Press.

Giddens, A. (2003). *Runaway world: How globalization is reshaping our lives.* New York: Routledge.

Gill, R. (2014). "If you're struggling to survive day-to-day": Class optimism and contradiction in entrepreneurial discourse. *Organization, 21*, 50–67. doi:10.1177/1350508412464895.

Held, D., & McGrew, A. (2003). The great globalization debate: An introduction. In D. Held & A. McGrew (Eds.), *The global transformations reader* (pp. 1–50). Malden, MA: Blackwell Publishing Inc.

Held, D., & McGrew, A. (2007). *Globalization/anti-globalization: Beyond the great divide.* Malden, MA: Polity Press.

Held, D., McGrew, A., Goldblatt, D., & Perraton, J. (1999). *Global transformations: Politics, economics, and culture.* Stanford, CA: Stanford University Press.

Hirst, P., & Thompson, G. (1996). *Globalization in question: The international economy and the possibilities of governance.* Cambridge, MA: Polity Press.

Huntington, S. (1996). *The clash of civilizations and the remaking of world order.* New York: Simon & Schuster.

Javidan, M., Dorfman, P. W., Sully de Luque, M., & House, R. J. (2006). In the eye of the beholder: Cross cultural lessons in leadership from project GLOBE. *Academy of Management Perspectives, 20*, 67–90. doi:10.5465/amp.2006.19873410.

Johnson, H. J. (1991). *Dispelling the myth of globalization: The case for regionalization.* New York: Praeger Publishers.

Kim, H. (2018). The mutual constitution of social media use and status hierarchies in global organizing. *Management Communication Quarterly, 32*, 471–503. doi:10.1177/0893318918779135.

Kotkin, J. (1992). *Tribes.* New York: Random House.

Leonardi, P. M., & Bailey, D. E. (2008). Transformational technologies and the creation of new work practices: Making implicit knowledge explicit in task-based offshoring. *MIS Quarterly, 32*, 411–436. doi:10.2307/25148846.

Leonardi, P. M., & Rodriguez-Lluesma, C. (2013). Occupational stereotypes, perceived status differences, and intercultural communication in global organizations. *Communication Monographs, 80*, 478–502. doi:10.1080/03637751.2013.828155.

McAllum, K. (2018). Committing to refugee resettlement volunteering: Attaching, detaching, and displacing organizational ties. *Human Relations, 71*, 951–972. doi:10.1177/0018726717729209.

McGee, M. (1990). Text, context, and the fragmentation of contemporary culture. *Western Journal of Speech Communication*, 274–289. doi:10.1080/10570319009374343.

McLuhan, M., & Powers, B. R. (1989). *The global village: Transformations in world life and media in the 21st century.* New York: Oxford University Press.

Medved, C., Morrison, K., Dearing, J., Larson, S., Cline, G., & Brummans, B. (2001). Tensions in community health improvement initiatives: Communication and collaboration in a managed care environment. *Journal of Applied Communication Research, 29*, 137–152. doi:10.1080/00909880128107.

Mitra, R. (2018). Natural resource management in the U.S. Arctic: Sustainable organizing through communicative practices. *Management Communication Quarterly, 32*, 398–430. doi:10.1177/0893318918755971.

Monge, P. R. (1998). Communication structures and processes in globalization. *Journal of Communication, 48*, 142–153. doi:10.1093/joc/48.4.142.

Monge, P. R., & Fulk, J. (1999). Communication technology for global network organizations. In G. DeSanctis & J. Fulk (Eds.), *Shaping organization form* (pp. 71–100). Thousand Oaks, CA: SAGE. www.rcf.usc.edu/~monge/globenet.htm.

Negroponte, N. (1995). *Being digital.* New York: Knopf.

Ohmae, K. (1995). *The end of the nation state.* New York: Free Press.

Perlmutter, H. V. (1969). The tortuous evolution of the multinational corporation. *Columbia Journal of World Business*, 9–18. doi:10.4324/9781315199689-7.

Prichard, C. (2006). Global politics, academic dispositions, and the tilting of organizational communication: A provocation to a debate. *Management Communication Quarterly, 19*, 638–644. doi:10.1177/0893318905285388.

Putnam, L. L., & Boys, S. (2006). Revisiting metaphors of organizational communication. In S. Clegg, C. Hardy, & W. Nord (Eds.), *Handbook of organizational studies* (2nd ed., pp. 541–576). London: SAGE.

Putnam, L. L., Fairhurst, G. T., & Banghart, S. (2016). Contradictions, dialectics, and paradoxes in organizations: A constitutive approach. *The Academy of Management Annals, 10*(1), 65–171. doi:10.1080/19416520.2016.1162421.

Robertson, R. (1992). *Globalization: Social theory and global culture.* London: SAGE.

Sassen, S. (2014). *Expulsion: Brutality and complexity in the global economy.* Cambridge, MA: Harvard University Press.

Scholte, J. A. (2005). *Globalization: A critical introduction* (2nd ed.). New York: Palgrave Macmillan.

Scott, A. (Ed.). (1997). *The limits of globalization: Cases and arguments.* London: Routledge.

Shumate, M., & O'Connor, A. (2010). The symbiotic sustainability model: Conceptualizing NGO–corporate alliance communication. *Journal of Communication, 60*, 577–609. doi:10.1111/j.1460-2466.2010.01498.x.

Sklair, L. (1991). *Sociology of the global system: Social change in global perspective.* Baltimore: Johns Hopkins University Press.

Sobre-Denton, M., & Bardhan, N. (2013). *Cultivating cosmopolitanism for intercultural communication: Communicating as global citizens.* New York: Routledge.

Stage, C. W. (1999). Negotiating organizational communication cultures in American subsidiaries doing business in Thailand. *Management Communication Quarterly, 13*, 245–280. doi:10.1177/0893318999132003.

Stohl, C. (1993). International organizing and organizational communication. *Journal of Applied Communication Research, 21*, 377–384. doi:10.1080/00909889309365380.

Stohl, C. (2001). Globalizing organizational communication. In F. M. Jablin & L. L. Putnam (Eds.), *The new handbook of organizational communication* (pp. 323–375). Thousand Oaks, CA: SAGE.

Stohl, C. (2005). Globalization theory. In S. May & D. K. Mumby (Eds.), *Engaging organizational communication theory and research* (pp. 223–261). Thousand Oaks, CA: SAGE.

Stohl, C., & Ganesh, S. (2014). Generating globalization. In L. L. Putnam & D. K. Mumby (Eds.), *The SAGE handbook of organizational communication* (3rd ed., pp. 717–741). Los Angeles: SAGE.

Stohl, M., & Stohl, C. (2005). Human rights, nation states, and NGOs: Structural holes and the emergence of global regimes. *Communication Monographs, 72*, 442–467. doi:10.1080/03637750500322610.

Stohl, M., Stohl, C., & Townsley, N. (2007). A new generation of global corporate social responsibility. In S. May, G. Cheney, and J. Roper (Eds.), *The debate over* (pp. 30–44). Oxford: Oxford University Press.

Sturken, M., & Thomas, D. (Eds.). (2004). *Technological visions: The hopes and fears that shape new technologies*. Philadelphia: Temple University Press.

Taylor, S., & Osland, J. S. (2011). The impact of intercultural communication on global organizational learning. In M. Easterby-Smith & M. A. Lyles (Eds.), *Handbook of organizational learning and knowledge management* (pp. 581–604). Chichester: John Wiley & Sons.

Tomlinson, J. (1999). *Globalization and culture*. Chicago: University of Chicago Press.

Townsley, N., & Stohl, C. (2003). Contracting corporate social responsibility: Swedish expansions in global temporary agency work. *Management Communication Quarterly*, *16*, 599–605. doi:10.1177/0893318902250238.

Trethewey, A., & Ashcraft, K. L. (2004). Practicing disorganization: The development of applied perspectives on living with tension. *Journal of Applied Communication Research*, *32*(2), 81–88. doi:10.1080/0090988042000210007.

Wallerstein, I. (1974). *The modern world system*. New York: Academic Press.

Wieland, S. M. B. (2011). Struggling to manage work as a part of everyday life: Complicating control, rethinking resistance, and contextualizing work/life studies. *Communication Monographs*, *78*, 162–184. doi:10.1080/03637751.2011.564642.

Williamson, J. (2002). *Did the Washington Consensus fail?* Peterson Institute for International Economics. https://piie.com/commentary/speeches-papers/did-washington-consensus-fail.

Yuan, Y. C., & Gay, G. (2006). Homophily of network ties and bonding and bridging social capital in computer-mediated distributed teams. *Journal of Computer-Mediated Communication*, *11*, 1062–1084. doi:10.1111/j.1083-6101.2006.00308.x.

Zoller, H. M. (2004). Dialogue as global issue management: Legitimizing corporate influence in the transatlantic business dialogue. *Management Communication Quarterly*, *18*, 204–240. doi:10.1177/0893318904265126.

Zoller, H. M. (2006). Suitcases and swimsuits: On the future of organizational communication. *Management Communication Quarterly*, *19*, 661–666. doi:10.1177/0893318905285391.

21 Organizational Change

Laurie Lewis

The term *organizational change* refers to processes involved in introducing new ideas into practice. Oftentimes, in defining change, scholars will refer to a disrupted period or altered state and thereby imply that what precedes change is stability or continuity. However, in fact, organizing activity is made up of processes and thus is always in motion and always changing. As Poole (2004) argues, regarding the false separation of planned and unplanned modes of changing, "all planned change occurs in the context of the ambient change processes that occur naturally in organizations" (p. 4). Organizational life—made up of specific practices, objects, or ways of doing—can be experienced as more stable. At other times, organizational life can be punctuated by points of *change* where routine activities appear to be disrupted. At these times, we may experience our organizations as changing.

Change is a prominent process in organizational activity, whether it occurs in civic or religious organizations, governments, schools, or businesses. Engaging in change and attempts to bring change in organizations is often necessary in order to innovate, address injustices, remedy failing or poor practices, revitalize participant energy, maintain competitiveness, create variety, experiment, and adapt to environments. Scholars have examined changes of large scope including mergers, cultural transformation, reorganizations, as well as introduction of technologies, production methodologies, employee programs, process improvements, and policies requiring, proscribing, or forbidding behaviors, among many others.

Organizations would eventually fail to adapt to their environments, stakeholders, and participants if they are unable to change. It is likely that unchanging organizations would at some point become so mismatched with the demands made on them that they would become obsolete. Further, organizations are embedded in multiple streams of processes and thus are enmeshed in change. Organizations spend significant resources on selecting and launching change initiatives every year. Leaders of organizations are frequently expected to innovate at every level of organizational practice—bringing massive cultural changes, creating new programs, products, services, and/or rebranding old ones. Debates about how and what to change in organizations of every size, in every sector, every industry, and along a vast array of dimensions occupy a great deal of organizational discourse. Thus, both the nature of organizations and the discourse surrounding organizations tend to demand and reinforce cycles of change.

During periods of change there is likely to be disruption of routines, rewards, expertise, status, security, familiarity, relationships, and physical surroundings, and increased demands on cognitive, physical, and emotional capacities. Individuals who participate in change programs and/or are dependent on the operation of organization (i.e., stakeholders), feel these disruptions and are active in processing and engaging in sensemaking (see Chapter 2) about the change, its causes, its consequences, and the sponsors and detractors for it.

History of Organizational Change Scholarship

There has been a rich and multidisciplinary history of scholarship about organizational change. In 1979, Kotter and Schlesinger made an observation about the prevalence of organizational change in business environments of the day:

> Today, more and more managers must deal with new government regulations, new products, growth, increased competition, technological developments, and a changing workforce. In response, most companies ... find that they must undertake moderate organizational changes at least once a year and major changes every four or five.
>
> (Kotter & Schlesinger, 1979, p. 106)

Twenty years later, in 1999, Zorn, Christensen, and Cheney made the case that "change for change's sake" (p. 4) had become glorified to an extent that it could be considered managerial fashion for stakeholders to constantly demand change in their organizations. Zorn and colleagues also argue that the cultural and market pressures demanding constant change may lead to disastrous outcomes including faulty decisions about what to change, poor timing of change programs, dysfunctional internal dynamics of changing organizations, and exhaustion due to repetitive cycles of change. Further, change has also long been depicted and documented as difficult and prone to failure. Failure rates have been reported to be as high as 50–75 percent (Majchrzak, 1988). Human and organizational factors have been early and often blamed for failure and difficulties during change (Bikson & Gutek, 1984). Miller, Johnson, and Grau (1994) suggest that resistance (which they describe in terms of reduction of output, quarreling and hostility, work slowdowns, and pessimism regarding goals) plays a major role in change failure.

As organizational scholars in a variety of disciplines including management, education, social work, technology transfer, and communication (among many others) have tackled the subject of organizational change, a number of approaches and foci have developed over time. Some of this work—especially some earlier work—focused on the role communication played in promoting innovativeness and the spread of innovative ideas in organizations (see Albrecht & Ropp, 1984; Fairhurst & Wendt, 1993; Rice & Rogers, 1980; Rogers, 1995; Van de Ven, Angle, & Poole, 1989). Other scholarship has focused on the formation of attitudes regarding planned changes including resistant responses (see Ellis, 1992; Miller & Monge, 1986; Miller et al., 1994; Fairhurst, Green, & Courtright, 1995). More recent scholarship has increasingly focused on communication during the process of implementing change and how it influences stakeholders' perspectives, behaviors, as well as individual and organizational outcomes (Lewis, 2011).

Over time there have been a number of attempts to summarize and provide overviews of trends in the research (Lewis, 2014; Lewis & Sahay, 2017; Lewis & Seibold, 1998; Poole, 2004; Poole & Van de Ven, 2004). The following sections provide an overview of the historical developments in scholarship about organizational change and highlights some key turning points and foci.

Early and Classic Models and Approaches

Early models of organizational innovation and change tend to be presented in very linear terms with steps, stages, and phases. For example, Lewin's (1951) classic model of change suggested three phases of change: unfreezing, changing, and refreezing. In his model, organizations are depicted as existing as generally stable with broken discrete periods of change activity that temporarily disrupt routines before eventually resettling into new stable periods. In another model, Rogers (1995) included the critical concepts of agenda setting, matching, redefining and restructuring (reinvention), clarifying, and routinizing. This model explores initiating stages in the first two phases. In these phases new ideas are compared against perceived problems in organizations. In the last three stages implementation is examined. In these phases changes are brought into use and fit into existing practices.

Stages of stability–change–restabilization are a typical sequence in these early linear models; they imply that organizations follow a set pattern in which novel ideas are surfaced, embraced, introduced, and eventually rejected or routinized. We may critique these models in noting that they are overly linear and that they tend to assume perfectly rational consideration of benefits and disadvantages against a set of organizational needs or desires. These models often presume that needs and desires are known and agreed to at the outset of a change process and that novel ideas for change are considered in terms of their fit to solve problems or increase efforts at achieving known goals.

In the 1980s scholars of change developed descriptive models of change implementation. Implementation has been defined as

> the translation of any tool or technique, process, or method of doing, from knowledge to practice. It encompasses that range of activities which take place between "adoption" of a tool or technique ... and its stable incorporation into on-going organizational practice.
>
> (Tornatzky & Johnson, 1982, p. 193)

Thus, implementation involves a set of activities—many of them communication-related—which introduce, explain, describe, or encourage usage of a change. Implementation may involve persuasive efforts to convince individuals involved in the change of its benefits. Implementers often must counter negative perceptions and concerns related to the change or the process of changing. For some implementers this will entail reaching out to those who have less enthusiastic responses to the change to influence their opinions and behaviors. Even when change is welcomed, implementers will need to instruct employees, clients, and partners on how the change will work, how problems will be resolved, and how they should engage with it. In other activity, implementers will need to monitor the installation and functioning of change programs to understand if they are meeting goals. Implementers will assess and adjust change or the ways employees and others engage with it over the course of an implementation effort.

A number of scholars have attempted to develop models that describe the approach implementers take to their tasks of bringing change into operation. Bourgeois and Brodwin (1984) distinguished between the *commander* model and the *crescive* model. The commander model favors a highly centralized approach to implementation in which the implementer controls decision-making and adjustments during the process. However the *crescive* model, "draws on managers' natural inclinations to want to develop new opportunities as they see them in the course of their day-to-day management" (p. 242) and permits more localized control and responsiveness during implementation. These sorts of contrasting models of change implementation tended to focus on the tension between top-down control strategies and bottom-up autonomous adaption strategies (Lewis & Seibold, 1998). As early as the 1980s, scholars making these distinctions generally favored the more bottom-up autonomous approaches that involve more local control and lower-level influence. In general, evidence has found support for their relative success in completing implementation efforts and meeting intended goals (see Marcus, 1988; Baronas & Louis, 1988). That trend has become stronger over time.

Early multidisciplinary scholarship related to organizational change tended to focus on how managers and leaders can garner support for change and be successful in terms of managerial goals. This often boiled down to overcoming resistance to change. Some early models viewed resistance as a form of organizational politics. Frost and Egri (1989, p. 243) noted that implementation is the "most vulnerable time of the innovation process ... when the dysfunctional nature of organizational politics is most often highlighted." Some scholars concentrated on identifying the most effective counter-strategies to resistance. Schein (1985) argued that power bases including expertise, information control, political access, and group support needed to be skillfully wielded in order to defeat resistance. Assessment of strategies and tactics to defeat or forestall resistance was a frequent topic of scholarship during the 1980s and early 1990s. For example, Nutt (1986, 1987) developed four models of implementation strategies (intervention, participation, persuasion, and edict) and tested their relative success in gaining traction for change programs in organizations. These models varied in the degree to which they involved a variety of stakeholders in important decision-making.

Outcomes for non-managerial stakeholders was rarely a focus in early scholarship. When non-managerial stakeholders are considered, it tends to be in terms of the degree to which they respond favorably (or not) to change and how their reactions can be made to be more favorable. The strategic goals or stakes of employees, clients, customers, members, partner organizations, or communities, among other stakeholders, were not often a point of concern or theorizing in the models of organizational change offered in this earlier scholarship.

Modern Models of Change Process

In a more encompassing theoretical effort to explain various change processes, Van de Ven and Poole (1995) described four change motors: lifecycle, teleological, dialectical, and evolutionary. Poole (2004) argues that these four theories of change are distinguishable in terms of two key dimensions: The degree to which change is premised on the actions of a single or of multiple entities, and whether the change events are *a priori* or emerging as the change process unfolds. Each of these motors account for different generators of organizational change. Their *lifecycle* motor depicts change processes as progressing through a necessary sequence of phases proscribed through institutional, natural, or logical causes. The *teleological* model, closest to the notion of planned change, is accomplished through intentional goal formation, implementation, and modification of behaviors. The *dialectical* motor of change emerges through the development of conflicts between entities that espouse opposing theses. This motor conceptualizes a cycle of dialectical progression of confrontation and conflict between opposing entities that generates change. Finally, the *evolutionary* model of development and change consists of repetitive sequences of variation, selection, and retention events among entities. Van de Ven and Poole argue that evolutionary change is driven by competition for scarce resources.

In 1993, Lewis and Seibold developed a model of innovation modification during change processes. This initial model attempted to depict how an organizational change and the organization are both altered through a process of implementation. That model was further developed (Lewis, 2007) and elaborated (Lewis, 2011, 2019) by embracing stakeholder theory as a frame for accounting for dynamics of communication within organizational change processes. *Stakes* are those claims that individuals, groups, and organizations have in the operation of organizations and may be financial, material, social, and/or symbolic in nature. *Stakeholders* are those who have a stake in an organization's process or outputs. Figure 21.1 depicts the typical hub-and-spokes stakeholder perspective that highlights relationships between a focal organization and each of its various stakeholder groups.

In 2011 (and revised in 2019) Lewis' stakeholder model of change implementation communication focuses on change as a context within which organizational stakeholders assert stakes. The argument that Lewis makes in her 2011 (and revised 2019) book on organizational change depicts stakeholders in relationships with the focal

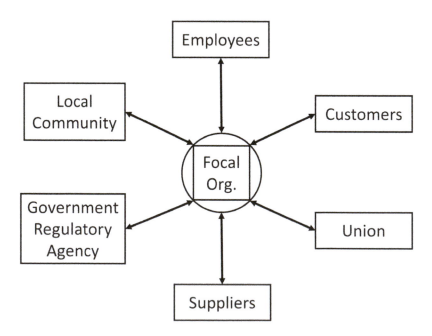

Figure 21.1 Hub and spokes model of stakeholder relationships

organization (in all of its parts and complexity) and in relationships with one another (see Figure 21.2). This model and the accompanying argument suggests that stakeholders likely spend as much or more time negotiating stakes with one another as with the organization.

According to Lewis (2011), stakeholders play multiple roles in organizations and throughout change processes. For example, individuals and groups of stakeholders may serve in roles as opinion leaders, as bridging connectors between groups of stakeholders, as supportive counselors, and as journalists sharing information and interpretations of events. This model and argument suggests that all stakeholders participate in strategic communication during change. That is, any stakeholder may have strategic goals (e.g., to defeat the change, to garner support for the change, to use the change as a context to gain resources) and will use communication in strategic ways (e.g., to spread rumors, highlight positives, upwardly distort information, feign ignorance, provide others with emotional support, build alliances with powerful stakeholders) to further those goals. The heart of this model concerns the communicative strategic dimensions and modes of interaction that drive the fulfillment, denial, and negotiation of stakes during change. The model depicts a fluid and complex process that occurs in the context of the organization's total environment.

Implementers' Communication

A significant portion of change communication scholarship has focused on the choices that implementers, leaders, and change agents make to introduce change, counter resistance, and increase cooperation with changed practices, policies, and technologies.

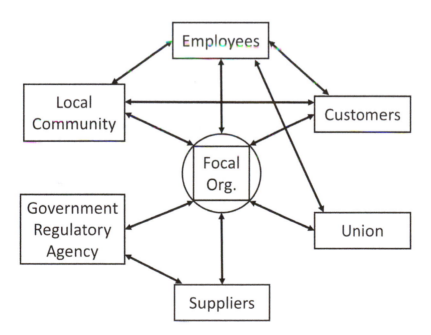

Figure 21.2 Complex stakeholder relationships

The term *change agent* and the characteristics of individuals filling this role in organizations has been a subject of significant exploration over time. Ottaway (1983) and Maidique (1980) provide historical reviews of this term and related terms (e.g., idea champion, innovator, sponsor). Kanter (1983) argues about change agents: "Any new strategy, no matter how brilliant or responsive, no matter how much agreement the formulators have about it, will stand a good chance of not being implemented fully —or sometimes, at all—without someone with power pushing it" (p. 296). Researchers devoted attention in the 1980s to detailing the characteristics of effective change agents including openness and responsiveness, comfort with ambiguity, comfort with oneself (Hamilton, 1988), technical qualifications, administrative ability, and leadership (Zaltman & Duncan, 1977), and risk-taking, innovativeness, and ability to articulate a compelling vision (Howell & Higgins, 1990).

Scholars' approaches to implementation communication have often tended to the central problem associated with planned organizational change: Uncertainty. Uncertainty is typically defined as a lack of information or confusion related to many available possible interpretations of events. Bordia, Hobman, Jones, Gallois, and Callan (2004) propose that uncertainty during organizational change involves three types: *Strategic uncertainty* (about the future of the organization and its situation in its environment); *structural uncertainty* (how the organization will operate and what its culture will be like); and *job-related uncertainty* (concerning an individual's rewards, job duties, and status). Organizations often assume that leaders' information sharing will reduce uncertainty. Scholars, leaders and consultants often focus on the best messaging and information strategies that implementers may use to reduce uncertainty. Also leaders often focus on discovering the inaccurate information about a change process and attempts to correct it.

Announcing change is one critical part of addressing uncertainty. Often the manner, timing, message, and spokesperson of change announcements can set a tone that may have implications for the entire implementation effort (Smeltzer, 1995). Schweiger and DeNisi (1991) undertook an extensive field study to determine the impact of realistic previews of complex change (i.e., merger) on the acceptance of the change. The researchers found that providing early previews of the details of the merger and its process significantly reduced uncertainty and increased job satisfaction, commitment, and perceived trustworthiness, among other positive outcomes.

In an another experimental study, Lewis, Laster, and Kulkarni (2013) examined the reactions of 218 working professionals to memos announcing change. Some respondents received messages highlighting negative aspects of the change and others received messages that were more positive in presenting the change. The study sought to understand whether downplaying or highlighting negative information about the change or change process had effect on perceptions of honesty and trustworthiness of implementers, as well as to judge the impact of negative previews on initial favorability towards the change. The study's results suggest that implementers' credibility was not enhanced by the use messages that previewed the "pain" of the upcoming change. The authors argued that complexity related to the context of the change, the expectations for implementers' communication, and the level of perceived riskiness of the change (e.g., more routine program change vs. major organizational shift) will likely drive reactions to introductory messages.

In other work related to information dissemination and announcement of change, some scholars (Leonard-Barton, 1987; Leonard-Barton and Kraus, 1985) have suggested that change implementation should be treated as an "internal marketing campaign" and that messages related to organizational change should be tailored to appeal to various audiences. However, Smeltzer's 1991 study of change announcements found that in only a few rare cases in their sample did management attempt to adapt their messages to multiple audiences. In 1992, Smeltzer and Zener found that organizations did not differentiate between internal and external audiences in the announcement of layoffs. The lack of attention to the unique needs, perspectives, and stakes of different audiences and stakeholders is likely to be ineffective and/or counterproductive.

Soliciting input is another communication approach to uncertainty reduction during change. Scholars have examined and promoted the idea of input solicitation under varied terms including participation, empowerment, positive climate, feedback, upward communication, and voice. Activities that constitute input solicitation include asking for opinions, seeking feedback, requesting opinions, and reactions to change. Such activities have long been encouraged by experts in order to manage feelings and concerns about change. Evidence suggests that soliciting input, especially in the context of a general philosophy of stakeholder participation in decision-making about change, can reap a number of benefits desired by implementers (see Bordia et al., 2004; Sagie & Koslowsky, 1994; Sagie, Elizur, & Koslowsky, 2001) including reduction of resistance, encouraging cooperativeness, and encouraging satisfaction of stakeholders during change. For example, management scholars argue that readiness to change can be created through early solicitation because that helps employees cope with resistance (Armenakis, Harris, & Mossholder, 1993). Such early conversations can promote openness, where stakeholders can discuss and understand the need for the change. According to Armenakis et al. (1993), stakeholders must believe that (a) change is necessary for the organization, (b) the particular proposed change is the correct one for them, (c) the organization is capable of implementing the change, and (d) opinion leaders are committed to the change. These beliefs can help increase the readiness or the commitment employees feel towards their organization and the change.

Research into the manner, method, and results of input solicitation during organizational change has increased over time. For example, Sahay and Lewis (2017, unpublished) have made the case that input solicitation may be designed in order to provide a full voice, limited voice, or what Sahay (2017) calls "faux voice." In the case of *full voice*, stakeholders are provided meaningful opportunities to engage in discussion and assessment about a change, while implementers and decision-makers use the input that is gathered in further decision-making. Sahay discusses *limited voice* as opportunities created primarily for the purpose of "checking the box" of collecting feedback by putting on a public show that input was solicited without seriously considering the perspectives that are offered. Implementers may cherry-pick issues and concerns if there is a sense that a minimal adjustment to the change could address them. Finally, *faux voice* involves providing channels for stakeholders to vent or deposit concerns and questions without having ability to influence the change initiative in any serious way.

Zorn, Page, and Cheney (2000) provide examples of limited or faux voice during change in their study of a New Zealand government organization's attempt to emulate Southwest Airline's change of culture. They reveal how employees were involved in ritual ways. These means of "involvement" of employees in the change effort were constructed in ways to ensure the predetermined outcome of acceptance of the CEO's vision. Their input was neither course-correcting nor empowering in the sense that it could alter original plans.

In an investigation of input solicitation practices of change implementers, Lewis and Russ (2012) collected interview data from implementers in 26 organizations, from a diverse set of industries, to discern both the specific methods used to solicit input as well as the criteria applied to received input to determine its value and credibility. The analyses of these data were used to construct five categories of approaches to input solicitation that refined the original Lewis (2011) categories.

- **Restricted** was the most common approach, which involved seeking input from a very select group of stakeholders and doing so in a manner that likely would confirm implementers' decisions. Input that could not easily be addressed, was very unique (not widely shared), was often discarded. Highly critical input was also often ignored and characterized as a product of general unhappiness in the organization.
- **Advisory** was the second most common approach observed in the data set. The major motivation for soliciting input was to seek affirming information or persuade providers to alter negative impressions of the change. Implementers using this approach tended to avoid "complainers." When negative input was encountered, it was typically used to identify the source of resistance.
- **Political** approach was used in only six of the 21. Specific "important" stakeholders were sought out for input. The "important" individuals tended to hold significant resources or other power bases.
- **Open** approach was extremely uncommon in these data (used in only three cases). In this approach, implementers solicited input from diverse groups of individuals and used a very open style of communicating. Implementers typically invited stakeholders to volunteer to offer input. If the input was viewed as "viable" it was included. If the input was considered to be "whining" or "complaining," it was discarded.
- **Widespread empowerment** approach was absent in these data. Lewis and Russ expected to find some evidence of implementers efforts to collect widespread input from diverse stakeholders and to make use of it through rigorous evaluation and consideration, but were surprised to find no examples of this model.

These categories varied in terms of commitment of implementers to maintain the change as was originally intended (fidelity) and the degree to which the implementer was genuinely interested in using collected input to direct the change (resource orientation).

In another example of a stakeholder approach to change, Barge, Lee, Maddux, Nabring, and Townsend (2008) conducted a case study on a planned organizational change in a multi-stakeholder initiative. A key finding of their study identified a key tension of inclusion–exclusion. This was a key challenge specific to participation. This study elaborated the conflict faced by implementers when including different stakeholders in different phases of the change because who got invited to the table and at which phase was critical for the organization. It raises the issue of how we resolve concerns about which stakeholders are able to voice their opinions, concerns, and viewpoints and which ones are not. Who controls those decisions, how opportunities for voice are created and the experiences of those who attempt to exercise their voice are paramount as we invite input in change initiatives.

Stakeholders' Communication During Change

Lewis (2011, 2019) argues that much consequential communication during organizational change occurs among stakeholders who are not in decision-making roles. Scholars have argued that uncertainty is not only reduced through formal information dissemination, but that stakeholders also share information with each other in order to cope with uncertainty. Several types of informal communication such as grapevine communication, informal discussions, peer mentoring, socially supportive communication, among other methods, can help stakeholders to resolve uncertainties regarding tasks, roles, and relationships. Kramer (1993), in his longitudinal study on socialization during job transfers, found that requests for information from peers increased as uncertainties regarding supervisors or task roles increased. In these situations, individuals relied on more informal sources of information instead of making information requests of supervisors directly. This highlights the importance of stakeholder information sharing among stakeholders. These non-supervisory employees turned to one another to answer their questions and make sense of the change in their organization.

Although much of the earlier communication research about organizational change focused on what messages that employees needed or wanted to receive, scant research has dealt with the strategic communication *among* stakeholders (including employees). For instance, stakeholders solicit input, just as implementers do. Nearly all the work on participation in implementation of change assumes that this is an activity designed by implementers who invite, to some extent or another, input from stakeholders. Those approaches ignore the important bids of stakeholders to solicit input from each other.

Ruben, Lewis, and Sandmeyer with Russ, Smulowitz, and Immordino (2008) explored this in their study of the higher education community's use of published outlets as a channel for a national conversation about the Spellings Report. The Spellings Report was a document examining the state of higher education that laid out the need for important and significant changes that needed to be made. In an effort to raise alarm and provoke strategic reactions to the Spellings Report, stakeholders wrote articles for *Inside Higher Education* and *Chronicle of Higher Education*. Other stakeholders wrote online responses to these publications. In a content analysis of those posts, there is evidence of stakeholders soliciting input from one another. In the end, the Spellings Report and the interactions that followed served as a wake-up call that stirred much reaction by various stakeholders encouraging sharing of perspectives and contrasts of opinion.

Other research has examined the ways in which stakeholders tell the stories of organizational change. Although much of the scholarship about managing meaning of change has highlighted the roles implementers play in actively shaping meaning and promoting their sense of what is going on or in manipulating others' sensemaking, there is a growing body of research exploring stakeholders' influence in framing change initiatives. For example, in a study of change in two Canadian banks, Cherim (2006) describes how managerial frames are appropriated by employees. She defines appropriation as acceptance of the frame and the identities the frame implies, including internalization of the values, goals, and means to achieving them. She illustrates employees' responses to managerial frames for change in terms of their willing appropriation, reluctant appropriation, and partial appropriation. As Fairhurst and Sarr note:

many individuals prefer to look to others to define what is real, what is fair, and what should count now and in the future. They are reluctant to manage meaning for themselves or others because there is risk involved when the stakes are high.

(Fairhurst & Sarr, 1996, p. 2)

Stakeholders' stories about change initiatives have consequences for the beliefs and concerns that are held concerning change. Both hearing stories and participating in their development and elaboration can shape perceptions, emotions, and expectations. As Whittle, Suhomlinova, and Mueller (2010) argue, "[stakeholders'] interests are not a fixed, essential entity that drives social action. Rather interests are negotiated and transformed in interaction" (p. 33). They argue that we should focus on how interests are *constructed in* discourse rather simply *expressed in* discourse. As Lewis notes, stakeholders' storytelling about change may call attention to key concerns about change.

Stakeholders' interactions have the ability to strategically or inadvertently give rise to these concerns for themselves and for others. The joint sensemaking about "what is really going" on during change will highlight certain aspects of the change experience and predict the future in ways that make some concerns more salient and important. Further, stakeholders may strategically highlight or de-emphasize concerns for other stakeholders with regards to key stakes those stakeholders value.

(Lewis, 2011, p. 248)

Paul Leonardi's (2009) study of the implementation of a new technology in an auto manufacturing plant was able to capture change sensemaking as it unfolded in real time. Leonardi argued that stakeholders develop interpretations of what a technology can do through both material interactions (actually using a new technology) and social interactions (talking with other stakeholders about the new technology and its use). In his study, the users of a new technology developed one interpretation of the change that so informed these stakeholders' expectations and interpretations of the change that it fundamentally shaped their material interactions with it. In this case, that shaping led to a negative assessment of what the technology could do. This study is an excellent example of empirical analysis of sensemaking as it unfolds over time and of the consequences of that sensemaking for the results of a change effort.

What Has Been the C-O Relationship in Organizational Change?

Throughout the body of scholarship about organizational change organizations are generally treated as entities within which change happens (O_3). Even scholars who adopt very process-oriented (O_1) views of organizational change itself, tend to treat the organization as a bounded place (physically and metaphorically). Organizations tend to be considered to be bounded by formal definitions (e.g., incorporation), membership (who is "in" and who is "out") and activities (those occurring "within" and those interactions between the organization and external actors).

Organizational change occurs in a flow of communicative and other activity and within a context of organizational structures (e.g., authority relations, decision-making rules, physical resources, budgetary constraints, production methodologies, governing policies). In the context of change (and other organizational activity) there is an interplay between that which organizational structures encourage, delimit, forestall, and/or compel and that which communicative engagement reinforces, challenges, and manifests. In short, the change *is* what the communication *makes it be* within the context of the organization's enacted structures.

The most obvious illustration of the interplay of structure and communicative agency (the C-O dynamic) in the context of organizational change concerns the very manner in which the change comes to have form in practice. As we consider a specific change—a new policy, a new production technique, a new method of service, a new procedure for decision-making—and then consider how that change looks in actual practice (e.g., the ways people really use/engage with the change), we can illustrate how what *it* is, is how it is perceived, used, and regarded in interaction. That is, a hammer isn't a hammer if the way it is used and regarded is more akin to a paintbrush. If the object is used to make artwork and it is regarded by users as a means to position paint on a canvas, then it is being installed in that setting as a means to create art. This same process occurs whenever any new program, policy, technology, process, practice, or other change is introduced into an organization. The members of that organization interpret the change, discuss what it is/what it means, influence how others incorporate it into the stream of other activity, and thus socially co-construct that change.

Just as communication can create the operational lived reality of an organizational change, the structures of an organization can give rise to, forestall, encourage, or shape communication about change. As the research noted earlier makes clear, implementers often take a stance on implementation-related communication that attempts to limit the amount of negative or resistant commentary. Organizational leaders and implementers often wish to limit the forums and opportunities for those most negative to change to speak. The creation of *faux voice* opportunities where complaints, concerns, and objections may be said but are not actually heard is a means of limiting what can be contributed by disempowered stakeholders in the installation of change. Organizations use authority, rules, and practices to limit how much influence some stakeholders may have in shaping change programs. Further, implementers may highlight and privilege speakers who promote an understanding of the change that is preferred. They may hold up their opinions and perspectives in ways that reinforce a version of the change that is in alignment with their own vision. Using their authority to highlight some communication over others further reinforces their own decision-making and choices.

In organizations where full voice is enabled, leaders and implementers use the structures of organizational expression—meetings, supervisory interactions, forums—in order to provide for the full elaboration of questions, expression of concerns, and perhaps articulation of arguments opposing change. Such decisions may give rise to changing the change through the interaction, debate, and discourse of stakeholders.

Recommended Supplementary Readings

Kramer, M., Dougherty, D. S., and Pierce, T. A. (2004) Managing uncertainty during a corporate acquisition: A longitudinal study of communication during an airline acquisition. *Human Communication Research*, 30(1), 71–101.

Excellent case study of a change.

Lewis, L. K., & Russ, T. (2012). Soliciting and using input during organizational change initiatives: What are practitioners doing? *Management Communication Quarterly*, 26(2), 267–294.
Details how organizations solicit input, use input, and defensively ignore or suppress input.
Scott, C. R., Lewis, L. K., & D'Urso, S. C. (2010). Getting on the "E" list: Email list use in a community of service provider organizations for people experiencing homelessness. In L. Shedletsky & J. E. Aitken (Eds.), *Cases on online discussion and interaction: Experiences and outcomes* (pp. 334–350). Hershey, PA: IGI-Global.
Case study for a network-wide organizational change.
Scott, C. R., Lewis, L. K., Davis, J. D., & D'Urso, S. C. (2009). Finding a home for communication technologies. In J. Keyton & P. Shockley-Zalabak (Eds.), *Case studies for organizational communication: Understanding communication processes* (2nd ed., pp. 83–88). New York: Oxford University Press.
Case study for network-wide organizational change.
Zorn, T. E., Christensen, L. T., & Cheney, G. (1999). *Do we really want constant change?* San Francisco, CA: Berrett-Koehler.
Excellent argument drawing attention to the costs of the "fashion" of constant organizational change.

Important Concepts: Define and Discuss

Faux voice
Implementation
Input solicitation
Managing meaning of change
Organizational change
Stakeholder
Uncertainty

Discussion Questions

1. Is it a healthy thing to frequently make change in organizations?
2. What are the significant costs to frequently changing organizations?
3. Which matters most during organizational change; the implementers' communication or that of other stakeholders?
4. How can stories about an organizational change make a difference in how the process unfolds and the outcomes that are achieved?

Practitioners' Corner

When faced with the task of implementing an organizational change, any manager will come to a point where s/he will need to decide how to go about announcing the change to employees and other audiences; introducing new expectations for activity, workflow, policy, and work practice; retiring previous processes, practices, policies, and procedures; addressing questions raised about how the new change will impact personnel evaluations and alterations in goals, plans, and priorities among myriad other possible topics; and evaluating the process and outcomes of the change.

In light of the challenges involved in change implementation, managers and leaders should be thorough and thoughtful in making plans for the introduction and roll-out of change. Leaders may feel that they know their own organizations, environments, and change projects well enough that they can be successful without devoting significant time to making a plan. Experienced leaders may be tempted to either "wing it" or to repeatedly use the same plan they've used before. Let's first examine each of these alternatives to engaging in specific planning for an upcoming change.

Winging It

"Winging it" involves saving time by skipping deep analysis and planning and instead approaching change through experience and gut instinct. In other words, make it up as you go along. Unfortunately, skipping the analysis and planning process in this manner can set up a scenario where the leader becomes reactionary and reliant on long-held assumptions rather than being data- or analysis-driven in their process. The "winging it" strategy can result in delay of proactive actions that might forestall problems in favor of focusing on catching problems before they become too toxic. Further, this approach may present an image to stakeholders that the implementation process as unplanned and reactionary.

Repeating an Old Plan

A second alternative to detailed analysis and planning relies on repeating what has worked in the past. Some leaders may wish to, but do so in a way that mimics past change rollouts without much reflection on needs or circumstances unique to the current change initiative. These leaders work from a framework for change that serves as default strategy. If something appeared to work before, the temptation to repeat it is very strong. The flaw in the "default template" method of implementation is missing that every change initiative is unique in terms of the ways that it fits the context, the organization, the stream of work, the initial and ongoing reactions of key stakeholders, and the degree to which resources for implementation support are available.

Qualities of Effective Planning Process

Effectiveness and efficiency in strategically preparing for implementation of change involves two stages: Analysis and planning. In the first phase, leaders must assemble knowledge and data about the context of the change, the change itself, the stakeholders who are relevant to the change process, and the resources and goals of the organization. In the second phase, leaders need to develop strategies and tactics to implement change in a context of existing priorities and goals for the change and the organization. Effective implementation planning should be data-driven, diversified, reflective, and recursive.

Data-driven. When planning change implementation, leaders need to be able to escape their own biases and expectations. One of the best ways to do this is to draw from credible sources of data that can help leaders to escape their own preferences for viewing their organizations, stakeholders, or history.

Diversified. In order to avoid groupthink and an unhealthy narrow analysis of how a change process may proceed, it is critical to have the input of participants who can represent different views and who have a good understanding of how different sets of goals, perspectives, values, experiences may come to influence the path of a change process.

Reflective. Being reflective requires leaders to consider challenging information and perspectives as plausible. Holding even problematic or questionable challenges to one's own view as plausible is the best check against dismissing a critical data point that might protect the interests of the organization.

Recursive. Fourth, one is never really done analyzing and planning. Leaders who are committed to a thoughtful and thorough planning process will continue to collect and analyze information—especially critical or disconfirming information—throughout an implementation process. Planning is not a "phase," it is an activity.

References

Albrecht, T. L., & Ropp, V. A. (1984). Communicating about innovation in networks of three U.S. organizations. *Journal of Communication, 4,* 78–91. doi:10.1037/0022-3514.72.4.775.

Armenakis, A. A., Harris, S. G., & Mossholder, K. W. (1993). Creating readiness for organizational change. *Human Relations, 46*(6), 681–703. doi:10.1177/001872679304600601.

Barge, J., Lee, M., Maddux, K., Nabring, R., & Townsend, B. (2008). Managing dualities in planned change initiatives. *Journal of Applied Communication Research, 36*(4), 364–390. doi:10.1080/00909880802129996.

Baronas, A. M. K., & Louis, M. R. (1988). Restoring a sense of control during implementation: How user involvement leads to system acceptance. *Management Information Systems Quarterly, 12,* 111–124. https://misq.org/restoring-a-sense-of-control-during-implementation-how-user-involvement-leads-to-system-acceptance.html

Bikson, T., & Gutek, B. (1984). *Implementation of office automation.* Santa Monica, CA: RAND Corporation.

Bordia, P., Hobman, E., Jones, E., Gallois, C., & Callan, V. (2004). Uncertainty during organizational change: Types, consequences, and management strategies. *Journal of Business and Psychology, 18*(4), 507–532. doi: 10.1023/B:JOBU.000.

Bourgeois, L. J., & Brodwin, D. R. (1984). Strategic implementation: Five approaches to an elusive phenomenon. *Strategic Management Journal, 5,* 241–264. doi:10.1002/smj.4250050305.

Cherim, S. (2006) Managerial frames and institutional discourses of change: Employee appropriation and resistance. *Organization Studies, 27*(9), 1261–1287. doi:10.1177/0170840606064106.

Ellis, B. H. (1992). The effects of uncertainty and source credibility on attitudes about organizational change. *Management Communication Quarterly, 6,* 34–57. doi:10.1177/0893318992006001002.

Fairhurst, G. T., Green, S., & Courtright, J. (1995). Inertial forces and the implementation of a socio-technical systems approach: A communication study. *Organization Science, 6,* 168–185. doi:10.1287/orsc.6.2.168.

Fairhurst, G. T., & Sarr, R. A. (1996). *The art of framing: Managing the language of leadership.* San Francisco: Jossey-Bass.

Fairhurst, G. T., & Wendt, R. F. (1993). The gap in total quality: A commentary. *Management Communication Quarterly, 6,* 441–451. doi:10.1177/0893318993006004005.

Frost, P. J., & Egri, C. P. (1989). The political process of innovation. In L. L. Cummings & B. M. Staw (Eds.), *Research in organizational behavior* (Vol. 13, pp. 229–295). Greenwich, CT: JAI.

Hamilton, E. E. (1988). The facilitation of organizational change: An empirical study of factors predicting change agents' effectiveness. *Journal of Applied Behavioral Science, 24,* 37–59. doi:10.1177/0021886388241006.

Howell, J. M., & Higgins, C. A. (1990). Champions of technological innovation. *Administrative Science Quarterly, 35*, 317–341. doi:10.2307/2393393.

Kanter, R. M. (1983). *The change masters.* New York: Simon & Schuster.

Kotter, J. P., & Schlesinger, L. A. (1979). Choosing strategies for change. *Harvard Business Review, 57*(2), 106–114. www.hbs.edu/faculty/Pages/item.aspx?num=45328

Kramer, M.W., 1993. Communication and uncertainty reduction during job transfers: Leaving and joining processes. *Communications Monographs, 60*(2), 178–198. doi:10.1080/03637759309376307.

Leonard-Barton, D. (1987). Implementing structured software methodologies: A case of innovation in process technology. *Interfaces, 17*, 6–17. doi:10.1287/inte.17.3.6.

Leonard-Barton, D., & Kraus, W. A. (1985). Implementing new technology. *Harvard Business Review, 63*(6), 102–110. https://hbr.org/1985/11/implementing-new-technology

Leonardi, P. (2009) Why do people reject new technologies and stymie organizational changes of which they are in favor? Exploring misalignments between social interactions and materiality. *Human Communication Research, 35*, 407–441. doi:10.1111/j.1468-2958.2009.01357.x.

Lewin, K. (1951). *Field theory in social science.* New York, NY: Harper.

Lewis, L. K. (2007). An organizational stakeholder model of change implementation communication. *Communication Theory, 17*(2), 176–204. doi:10.1111/j.1468-2885.2007.00291.x.

Lewis, L. K. (2011). *Organizational change: Creating change through strategic communication.* Chichester: Wiley-Blackwell.

Lewis, L. K. (2014). Organizational change and innovation. In L. L. Putnam, & D. K. Mumby (Eds.), *The new handbook of organizational communication* (pp. 503–524). Thousand Oaks, CA: SAGE.

Lewis, L. (2019). *Organizational change: Creating change through strategic communication* (2nd ed.). Chichester: Wiley-Blackwell.

Lewis, L. K., Laster, N., & Kulkarni, V. (2013). Telling 'em how it will be: Previewing pain of risky change in initial announcements. *Journal of Business Communication, 50*(3), 278–308. doi:10.1177/0021943613487072.

Lewis, L. K., & Russ, T. (2012). Soliciting and using input during organizational change initiatives: What are practitioners doing? *Management Communication Quarterly, 26*(2), 267–294. doi:10.1177/0893318911431804.

Lewis, L., & Sahay, S. (2017). Organizational change. In C. R. Scott & L. Lewis (Eds.) *International encyclopedia of organizational communication* (online edition). Hoboken, NJ: Wiley-Blackwell. doi:10.1002/9781118955567.wbieoc020.

Lewis, L., & Sahay, S. (2018). Strategic organizational change. In W. Johanssen & B. Heath (Eds.), *International encyclopedia of strategic communication*, Chichester: Wiley-Blackwell.

Lewis, L. K., & Seibold, D. R. (1993). Innovation modification during intra-organizational adoption. *Academy of Management Review, 18*, 322–354. doi:10.2307/258762.

Lewis, L. K., & Seibold, D. R. (1998). Reconceptualizing organizational change implementation as a communication problem: A review of literature and research agenda. In M. Roloff (Ed.), *Communication yearbook* (Vol. 21, pp. 93–151). Thousand Oaks, CA: SAGE.

Maidique, M. (1980). Entrepreneurs, champions, and technological innovation. *Sloan Management Review, 21*(2), 59–76.

Majchrzak, A. (1988). *The human side of factory automation.* San Francisco: Jossey-Bass.

Marcus, A. A. (1988). Implementing externally induced innovations: A comparison of rule-bound and autonomous approaches. *Academy of Management Journal, 31*, 235–256. doi:10.5465/256547.

Miller, K. I., & Monge, P. R. (1986). Participation, satisfaction, and productivity: A meta-analytic review. *Academy of Management Journal, 29*, 727–753. doi:10.5465/255942.

Miller, V. D., Johnson, J. R., & Grau, J. (1994). Antecedents to willingness to participate in a planned organizational change. *Journal of Applied Communication Research, 22,* 59–80. doi:10.1080/00909889409365387.

Nutt, P. C. (1986). Tactics of implementation. *Academy of Management Journal, 29,* 230–261. doi:10.2307/256187.

Nutt, P. C. (1987). Identifying and appraising how managers install strategy. *Strategic Management Journal, 8,* 1–14. doi:10.1002/smj.4250080102.

Ottaway, R. N. (1983). The change agent: A taxonomy in relation to the change process. *Human Relations, 36,* 361–392. doi:10.1177/001872678303600403.

Poole, M. S. (2004). Central issues in the study of change and innovation. In M. S. Poole & A. H. Van de Ven (Eds.), *Handbook of organizational change and innovation* (pp. 3–31). Oxford: Oxford University Press.

Poole, M. S., & Van de Ven, A. H. (2004). *Handbook of organizational change and innovation.* Oxford: Oxford University Press.

Rice, R. E., & Rogers, E. M. (1980). Re-invention in the innovation process. *Knowledge: Creation, Diffusion, Utilization, 1,* 499–514. doi:10.1177/107554708000100402.

Rogers, E. (1995). *Diffusion of innovations* (4th ed.). New York: Free Press.

Ruben, B. D., Lewis, L. K., & Sandmeyer, L. with Russ, T., Smulowitz, S., & Immordino, K. (2008). *Assessing the impact of the spellings commission: The message, the messenger, and the dynamics of change in higher education.* Washington, D.C.: National Association of College and University Business Officers.

Sagie, A., Elizur, D., & Koslowsky, M. (2001) Effect of participation in strategic and tactical decisions on acceptance of planned change. *Journal of Social Psychology, 130*(4), 459–465. doi:10.1080/00224545.1990.9924607.

Sagie, A., & Koslowsky, M. (1994) Organizational attitudes and behaviors as a function of participation in strategic and tactical change decisions: An application of path–goal theory. *Journal of Organizational Behavior, 15,* 37–47. doi:10.1002/job.4030150105.

Sahay, S. (2017). Communicative designs for input solicitation during organizational change: Implications for providers' communicative perceptions and decisions. Unpublished dissertation.

Sahay, S., & Lewis, L. (unpublished) *Perspectives on soliciting and providing input during organizational change: The provider, the executive, and the consultant.* Unpublished manuscript.

Schein, V. (1985). Organizational realities: The politics of change. In D. Warrick (Ed.), *Contemporary organizational development* (pp. 86–97). Glenview, IL: Scott Foresman.

Schweiger, D. M., & DeNisi, A. S. (1991). Communication with employees following a merger: A longitudinal field experiment. *Academy of Management Journal, 34*(1), 110–135. doi:10.2307/256304.

Smeltzer, L. R. (1991). An analysis of strategies for announcing organization-wide change. *Group and Organization Studies, 16,* 5–24. doi:10.1177/105960119101600102.

Smeltzer, L. R. (1995) Organization-wide change: Planning for an effective announcement. *Journal of General Management, 20,* 31–43. doi:10.1177/030630709502000303.

Smeltzer, L. R., & Zener, M. F. (1992). Development of a model for announcing major layoffs. *Group & Organization Management, 17*(4), 445–472. doi:10.1177/1059601192174009.

Tornatzky, L. G., & Johnson, E. C. (1982). Research on implementation: Implications for evaluation practice and evaluation policy. *Evaluation and Program Planning, 5,* 193–198. doi:10.1016/0149-7189(82)90069-6.

Van de Ven, A. H., Angle, H. L., & Poole, M. S. (1989). *Research on the management of innovations.* New York: Ballinger.

Van de Ven, A. H., & Poole. M.S. (1995). Explaining development and change in organizations. *Academy of Management Review, 20*(3), 510–540. doi:10.5465/amr.1995.9508080329.

Whittle, A., Suhomlinova, O., & Mueller, F. (2010). Funnel of interests: the discursive translation of organizational change. *Journal of Applied Behavioral Science, 46*(1), 16–37. doi:10.1177/0021886309357538.

Zaltman, G., & Duncan, R. (1977). *Strategies for planned change*. New York; John Wiley.

Zorn, T. E., Christensen, L. T., & Cheney, G. (1999). *Do we really want constant change?* San Francisco, CA: Berrett-Koehler.

Zorn, T. E., Page, D. J., & Cheney, G. (2000). Nuts about change: Multiple perspectives on change-oriented communication in a public sector organization. *Management Communication Quarterly, 13*(4), 515–566. doi:10.1177/0893318900134001.

Author's Index

Content Index

Lightning Source UK Ltd.
Milton Keynes UK
UKHW030837190722
406049UK00013B/173

9 781138 570313